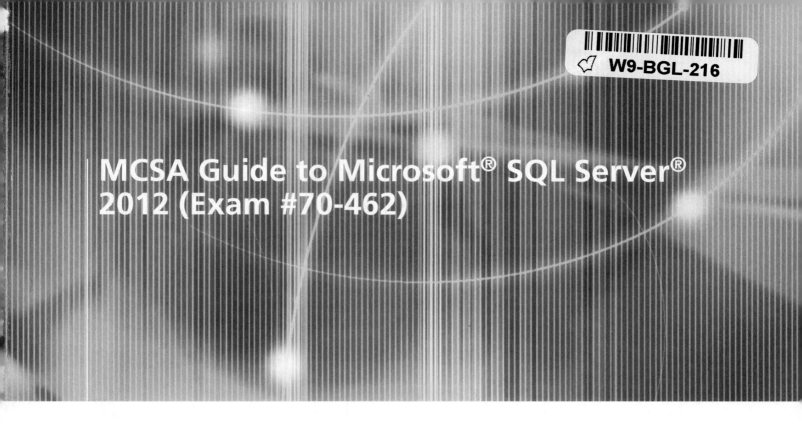

MCSA Guide to Microsoft® SQL Server® 2012 (Exam #70-462)

Faisal Akkawi

Kayed Akkawi

Gabriel Schofield

COURSE TECHNOLOGY
CENGAGE Learning·

Australia • Brazil • Japan • Korea • Mexico • Singapore • Spain • United Kingdom • United States

COURSE TECHNOLOGY
CENGAGE Learning·

MCSA Guide to Microsoft® SQL Server® 2012 (Exam #70-462)

Faisal Akkawi, Kayed Akkawi, and Gabriel Schofield

Vice President, Careers & Computing: Dave Garza

Acquisitions Editor: Nick Lombardi

Director, Development – Careers and Computing: Marah Bellegarde

Product Development Manager: Leigh Hefferon

Senior Product Manager: Natalie Pashoukos

Developmental Editor: Mary Pat Shaffer

Technical Editor: Nicole Spoto

Editorial Assistant: Torey Schantz

Vice President, Marketing: Jennifer Ann Baker

Marketing Director: Deborah Yarnell

Production Director: Wendy A. Troeger

Production Manager: Andrew Crouth

Content Project Manager: Allyson Bozeth

Art Director: GEX

Media Editor: William Overocker

Cover photo: ©Veerachai Viteeman/Shutterstock

> **For product information and technology assistance, contact us at**
> **Cengage Learning Customer & Sales Support, 1-800-354-9706**
>
> **For permission to use material from this text or product,**
> **submit all requests online at cengage.com/permissions**
> **Further permissions questions can be emailed to**
> **permissionrequest@cengage.com**

Microsoft® is a registered trademark of the Microsoft Corporation.

SQL Server® 2012 is a registered trademark of the Microsoft Corporation.

Library of Congress Control Number: 2013936880

ISBN-13: 978-1-133-13107-6

ISBN-10: 1-133-13107-7

Course Technology
20 Channel Center Street
Boston, MA 02210
USA

Cengage Learning is a leading provider of customized learning solutions with office locations around the globe, including Singapore, the United Kingdom, Australia, Mexico, Brazil, and Japan. Locate your local office at: **international. cengage.com/region**

Cengage Learning products are represented in Canada by Nelson Education, Ltd.

For your lifelong learning solutions, visit **www.cengage.com/ coursetechnology**

Purchase any of our products at your local college store or at our preferred online store **www.cengagebrain.com**

Visit our corporate website at **cengage.com.**

Microsoft and the Office logo are either registered trademarks or trademarks of Microsoft Corporation in the United States and/or other countries. Course Technology, a part of Cengage Learning, is an independent entity from the Microsoft Corporation, and not affiliated with Microsoft in any manner.

Course Technology, the Course Technology logo, and the Shelly Cashman Series® are registered trademarks used under license.

Course Technology, a part of Cengage Learning, reserves the right to revise this publication and make changes from time to time in its content without notice.

The programs in this book are for instructional purposes only. They have been tested with care, but are not guaranteed for any particular intent beyond educational purposes. The author and the publisher do not offer any warranties or representations, nor do they accept any liabilities with respect to the programs.

Printed in the United States of America
1 2 3 4 5 6 7 17 16 15 14 13

Brief Table of Contents

PREFACE ix

CHAPTER 1
Introduction to SQL Server 2012 **1**

CHAPTER 2
Deploying SQL Server 2012 **27**

CHAPTER 3
Architecture and Configuration **73**

CHAPTER 4
Creating SQL Server 2012 Databases **115**

CHAPTER 5
Transact-SQL Primer **151**

CHAPTER 6
SQL Server Security **197**

CHAPTER 7
Performance Monitoring and Optimization **237**

CHAPTER 8
Backup and Recovery **273**

CHAPTER 9
Data Integration **319**

CHAPTER 10
Monitoring SQL Server 2012 **361**

GLOSSARY 407

INDEX 419

Table of Contents

PREFACE ix

CHAPTER 1
Introduction to SQL Server 2012 — 1

SQL Server 2012 Editions, Capabilities, and Licensing — 2
  SQL Server 2012 Editions — 2
  Licensing Models — 4

Leveraging the Windows Server 2008 R2 Operating System — 8
  Introduction to the Windows Server 2008 R2 Operating System — 8
  Management Tools and Integrated Security — 8
  Building a Test Environment — 10

SQL Server Product Documentation and
Problem-Solving Strategies — 11
  Microsoft SQL Server 2012 Product Documentation — 12
  Problem-Solving Strategies — 12

Understanding the Minimum System Requirements and Preparing for Installation — 17

Chapter Summary — 22

Key Terms — 23

Review Questions — 25

Case Projects — 26

CHAPTER 2
Deploying SQL Server 2012 — 27

Planning a SQL Server 2012 Installation — 28
  Planning Steps — 28
  Selection of Components and Features — 28
  Hardware Design and Software Requirements — 30
  Security — 30

Installing SQL Server 2012 — 31
  Installation Options — 31

Repairing or Uninstalling an Existing SQL Server
2012 Installation — 59
  Repair — 59
  Uninstall — 59

Chapter Summary — 67

Key Terms — 67

Review Questions — 69

Case Projects — 70

Hands-On Projects — 71

CHAPTER 3
Architecture and Configuration — 73

SQL Server 2012 Database Architecture — 74
  Physical Database Files — 75
  Logical Database Objects — 76

SQL Server 2012 Configuration — 89
  Network Protocols — 89
  Linked Server — 98

Chapter Summary — 107

Key Terms — 108

Review Questions — 110

Case Projects — 112

Hands-On Projects — 112

CHAPTER 4
Creating SQL Server 2012 Databases   **115**

    Planning a New User Database   116
        Implementation Options   116
        Data and Log File Options   119
        Database Ownership and Permissions   120
        Data Types   122
        Object Naming Conventions   122

    Essential Database Administration Tasks   131
        Altering Database Configuration Settings   132
        Adding a Table with a Foreign Key Relationship   137

    Chapter Summary   145

    Key Terms   145

    Review Questions   146

    Case Projects   148

    Hands-On Projects   149

CHAPTER 5
Transact-SQL Primer   **151**

    Data Manipulation Language (DML)   152
        A Simple Query   153
        Renaming the Columns Returned in a Result Set   154
        Managing Duplicate Records in a Result Set   154
        Limiting the Number of Records Returned in a Result Set   154
        Adding Computed Columns to the Result Set   154
        Filtering the Records in a Result Set   155
        Sorting the Records in a Result Set   156
        Grouping and Summarizing Records in a Result Set   157
        Combining Data Using Joins   163
        Merging Data Using Unions   165
        Combining Data Using Subqueries   165
        Modifying Data Using INSERT, UPDATE, and DELETE Statements   169

    Data Definition Language (DDL)   172
        Creating a Table or View and Adding an Index   172
        Modifying a Table or View   173

    Data Control Language (DCL)   178
        Creating a SQL Server Login   178
        Creating a Database User   178
        Removing a Login or User   179
        Granting and Removing Permissions   179
        Managing Permissions Using Schemas and Roles   179

    Chapter Summary   187

    Key Terms   188

    Review Questions   190

    Case Projects   192

    Hands-On Projects   195

CHAPTER 6
SQL Server Security   **197**

    Establishing a Connection to SQL Server   198
        Authentication Modes   198
        SQL Server Logins   199
        Securing Client/Server Connections   208

    Database Object Access Control   211

    Database Encryption   221
        Symmetric vs. Asymmetric Keys   222
        Encryption Algorithms in SQL Server 2012   223

Encryption Architecture in SQL Server 2012 224
Transparent Data Encryption (TDE) 224
Encryption Key Management (EKM) 225

Chapter Summary 231

Key Terms 232

Review Questions 233

Case Projects 235

Hands-On Projects 235

CHAPTER 7
Performance Monitoring and Optimization **237**

High-Performance Design 238
Schema Design 239
Query Design 239
Index Design 240

Diagnosing Performance Problems and Optimizing Queries 240
Monitoring Performance of System Resources 240
Monitoring SQL Server Activity 246
Concurrency Control, Blocking Locks, and Deadlocks 249
Analyzing Execution Plans 255
Query Tuning 258

Maintenance of Indexes and Statistics 265
Index Fragmentation 265
Maintenance Plans 266

Chapter Summary 266

Key Terms 267

Review Questions 269

Case Projects 271

Hands-On Projects 272

CHAPTER 8
Backup and Recovery **273**

Defining Recovery Objectives 274
Evaluating the Risk of Data Loss 274
Evaluating the Business Requirements 275
Developing a Set of Recovery Objectives 276

Database Backup Types 277
Backup Sets 277
Full and Differential Database Backups 277
Transaction Log Backups 287

Implementing a Backup and Recovery Plan 292
Backup Plans 292
Restore Operations 294
Backup Plan Automation Using SQL Server Agent 303
Other Considerations 313

Chapter Summary 314

Key Terms 315

Review Questions 316

Case Projects 317

Hands-On Projects 318

CHAPTER 9
Data Integration **319**

SQL Server Data Integration Tools and Utilities 320

SQL Server Integration Services 320

Integration Services Packages   321
SQL Server Import and Export Wizard   322
SQL Server Data Tools   333
SQL Server Integration Services Package Execution   334

Bulk Copy Interface   347
bcp Utility   348
BULK INSERT Statement   352

Chapter Summary   355

Key Terms   356

Review Questions   357

Case Projects   359

Hands-On Projects   359

CHAPTER 10
Monitoring SQL Server 2012   **361**

Daily Monitoring Tasks and Configuring Automated Alerts   362
Essential SQL Server Monitoring Tasks   362
Automating Event Notification Using SQL Server Agent Alerts   369

Benchmarking and Real-Time Performance Monitoring   381
Benchmarking System Performance   381
SQL Server Activity Monitor   381
Dynamic Management Views and Functions   382

Capturing Performance Data   388

Database Audits   397

Chapter Summary   400

Key Terms   401

Review Questions   402

Case Projects   404

Hands-On Projects   405

GLOSSARY   **407**

INDEX   **419**

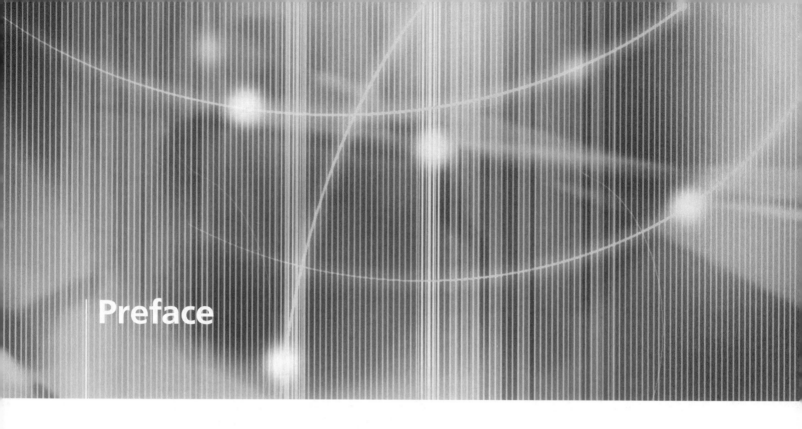

Preface

Relational database management systems serve a critical role—allowing organizations to organize, store, and manage large volumes of data. The database administrators who oversee these systems must be well versed in a broad range of topics, including database architecture and design, security, data integrity, performance optimization, backup and recovery, and system monitoring. Skilled database administrators are in high demand across every industry—a trend likely to continue as the volume of data grows. With a sizeable share of the market and tight integration with the Windows family of operating systems, Microsoft SQL Server provides an ideal learning environment and offers a path for the aspiring student to rewarding career opportunities. *MCSA Guide to Microsoft SQL Server 2012 (Exam #70-462)* is designed to teach the core skills and develop the confidence necessary to become an effective database administrator on Microsoft SQL Server 2012.

Purpose

The catalyst for embarking on this project was the growing need for a high-quality, academic textbook that covers the core database administration principles and practices for Microsoft SQL Server 2012. While there are a variety of books written about Microsoft SQL Server 2012, the majority are focused either on serving existing practitioners or exclusively on exam certification.

This book is written with the objective of providing a thorough introduction to database administration principles and practices necessary to perform Microsoft SQL Server administration in an enterprise environment and prepare for the Microsoft Certified Solutions Associate Exam 70-462.

Intended Audience

The intended audience ranges from students attending a taught database administration course—or embarking on self-study—to existing practitioners looking to transition their skills to Microsoft SQL Server. New students will appreciate the level of detail and supporting screenshots included for each activity. Although familiarity with the Windows operating system and a basic knowledge of database design are beneficial, the content makes no assumptions about the prior knowledge or skills of the reader. Experienced students will find the shortcuts, tips, and tricks helpful as they shift their existing skills to a new platform.

Organization and Chapter Descriptions

The chapters are sequenced in a manner intended to make this book accessible to a reader who has no prior experience working with Microsoft SQL Server. The book employs a lab-based approach, which helps the reader master the core knowledge and practical skills. The material in each chapter is organized to be easy to read, follow, and understand. Learning objectives are listed at the beginning of each chapter. Practical activities are interspersed throughout the chapters to reinforce the learning objectives and enable the reader to progressively build confidence. Each activity provides accurate and detailed steps that are complemented with a comprehensive set of screenshots. Each chapter concludes with a chapter summary, definitions of important terms, discussion questions, and case studies and projects to provide the reader with real-world context.

Chapter 1—Introduction to SQL Server 2012

Microsoft SQL Server is a powerful relational database management system with the primary function of storing data and providing access to client software applications. The opening chapter introduces the latest version of Microsoft SQL Server and outlines the capabilities and licensing options for the three main editions. This chapter describes the benefits of using a relational database management system that is tightly integrated with the Microsoft Windows operating system. Students will learn how to access online technical documentation, check recommended hardware and operating system requirements, and prepare for the installation of SQL Server 2012.

Chapter 2—Deploying SQL Server 2012

Planning is of paramount importance when undertaking a SQL Server 2012 installation. This chapter explains the steps necessary to plan a SQL Server 2012 installation and assesses the available installation options. Students will learn how to create an instance of the SQL Server 2012 Enterprise Edition using the SQL Server Installation Wizard or the command prompt. The chapter explores the system changes that take place during a SQL Server 2012 installation and how to perform a repair or uninstall of SQL Server 2012.

Chapter 3—Architecture and Configuration

The main editions of SQL Server 2012 come bundled with a suite of management applications and command-line utilities. This chapter begins by identifying the physical and logical components of the SQL Server 2012 architecture. Students will learn how to explore the objects within a database using Object Explorer in SQL Server Management Studio, configure server settings, create a linked server, and explain the advantages and disadvantages of using distributed queries. The chapter also explains how to configure and troubleshoot the supported network protocols used for remote client connectivity.

Chapter 4—Creating SQL Server 2012 Databases

Planning is an important, but often overlooked, aspect of implementing a new user database. This chapter discusses planning and implementing a new user database that supports the relevant business requirements. Students will learn how to construct a new database by using Object Explorer or by executing a SQL query using Query Editor. The chapter explains how to modify configuration settings for an existing database, how to rename a database, and how to delete a database. Lastly, students will learn how to create new tables, and apply a foreign key relationship between two tables.

Chapter 5—Transact-SQL Primer

Database administrators must attain a high level of proficiency in the SQL programming language because it is the de facto standard for managing and retrieving data from a relational database management system. This chapter explains how to use the Transact-SQL language to analyze and manipulate data, create and modify database objects, and create a simple but effective logical security model.

Chapter 6—SQL Server Security

Databases often contain sensitive or confidential information that must be protected both from accidental exposure to unauthorized users and from malicious attacks. This chapter describes how to choose an appropriate authentication mode and create secure client/server connections. Students will learn how to manage access controls on database and server securables using the permissions hierarchy, and how to evaluate the different options for encrypting sensitive or confidential data.

Chapter 7—Performance Monitoring and Optimization

The goal of performance optimization is to lower the overall duration of queries and to efficiently use the available system resources, including the processor, the physical disk, and memory. This chapter describes the different design factors that affect database performance. Students will learn how to manage database performance by using tools that help detect, analyze, and resolve performance issues. Finally, students will learn how to recognize index fragmentation and discuss the criteria that should be incorporated in the design of an index and statistics maintenance plan.

Chapter 8—Backup and Recovery

A comprehensive backup and recovery strategy is essential to safeguard against loss of data that may occur due to user error, hardware and software failure, or environmental changes. This chapter provides a framework for evaluating the risks of data loss in conjunction with the business requirements to define recovery objectives, and compares the main database backup types. Students will learn how to design a backup plan that is optimized against a set of recovery objectives, create database backups, and use SQL Server Agent to automate the backup tasks.

Chapter 9—Data Integration

The ability to integrate with other data sources is an important feature of a database management system. This chapter compares the different SQL Server management tools and utilities that can be used to integrate data from external sources. Students will learn how to design a SQL Server Integration Services package using both the SQL Server Import and Export Wizard and SQL Server Data Tools. The chapter explains how to construct commands that utilize the bulk copy interface to import and export data from a SQL Server database.

Chapter 10—Monitoring SQL Server 2012

To minimize the risk of unplanned service disruptions and ensure that agreed-upon service levels are met, a database administrator must monitor SQL Server 2012 on an ongoing basis. This chapter describes the daily monitoring tasks a database administrator should complete to evaluate the status of critical services and processes. It explains the importance of establishing a baseline set of values for use as a benchmark when monitoring system performance. Students will learn how to use SQL Server Agent to configure automated alerts in response to system events and performance conditions. Using SQL Server Activity Monitor and dynamic management views and functions, students will learn to assess the health of the system in real time. The chapter explains how to collect and analyze historical data using the data collector and the Management Data Warehouse repository. Finally, students will learn how to create and configure a SQL Server audit.

Features

- *Learning objectives*—Each chapter begins with a list of clearly defined objectives. This list provides students with a quick reference to the contents of that chapter and serves as a useful study aid.
- *Hands-on activities*—Interspersed throughout each chapter are hands-on activities—with accurate and detailed steps; these activities reinforce the learning objectives and enable the reader to progressively build confidence.
- *Screen captures and illustrations*—Screen captures are used extensively within the activities to provide supplementary guidance for students, and illustrations in each chapter help summarize important concepts.
- *Management tools*—Many of the core activities include information on a variety of management tools, which allow the reader to accomplish the tasks using either a graphical user interface or a command-based approach.
- *Planning, monitoring, and risk management frameworks*—Throughout the book, planning, monitoring, and risk management frameworks are used to provide students with a practical set of tools for day-to-day use.
- *Chapter summary*—Each chapter includes a summary of the key ideas presented in the chapter.
- *Definitions of key terms*—Important terms are highlighted with boldfaced text in the chapter and are included, along with their definitions, in a list of key terms at the end of each chapter.
- *Review questions*—Each chapter includes a set of review questions for assessing comprehension of chapter material.
- *Case projects and hands-on projects*—A wide variety of practical exercises are included at the end of each chapter to provide students with real-world context for applying their knowledge.

Text and Graphic Conventions

Wherever appropriate, additional information and exercises have been added to this book to help you better understand what is being discussed in the chapter. Icons throughout the text alert you to additional materials. The icons used in this textbook are as follows:

The Caution icon warns you about potential mistakes or problems and explains how to avoid them.

The Note icon is used to present additional helpful material related to the subject being described.

Activity icons precede each activity in the book, giving students real-world experience they will need on the job.

Case Project icons mark the case projects. These are more involved, scenario-based assignments. In this extensive case example, you are asked to implement independently what you have learned.

Tips offer extra information on resources, problem solving, and time-saving shortcuts.

Online Instructor Resources

The following supplemental materials are available when this book is used in a classroom setting. All the supplements available with this book are provided to the instructor on the Instructor Companion Site at *www.cengage.com*. Instructors can access these resources through one single sign-on experience. If you do not already have a Cengage SSO account, click on "Click HERE to register" in the Faculty single sign-on box to get started right away.

- *Electronic Instructor's Manual*—The Instructor's Manual that accompanies this book includes additional material to assist in class preparation, including suggestions for classroom activities, discussion topics, and additional activities.

- *Solutions*—The instructor resources include solutions to all end-of-chapter material, including review questions and case projects.

- *ExamView*®—ExamView®, the ultimate tool for objective-based testing needs, is a powerful test generator that enables instructors to create paper, LAN, or Web-based tests from test banks designed specifically for their Cengage Learning text. Instructors can utilize the ultraefficient Quick Test Wizard to create tests in less than five minutes by taking advantage of Cengage Learning's question banks, or customize their own exams from scratch.

- *PowerPoint*® *Presentations*—This book comes with Microsoft® PowerPoint® slides for each chapter. These are included as a teaching aid for classroom presentation, to make available to students on the network for chapter review, or to be printed for classroom distribution. Instructors, please feel free to add your own slides for additional topics you introduce to the class.

- *Figure files*—All figures and tables in the book are reproduced on the Instructor Companion Site. Similar to the PowerPoint presentations, they are included as a teaching aid for classroom presentation, to make available to students for review, or to be printed for classroom distribution.

About the Authors

Faisal Akkawi, Ph.D., is Executive Director of Information Systems Programs at Northwestern University School of Continuing Studies. He holds a doctorate in computer science and a master's degree in electrical engineering from Illinois Institute of Technology. Dr. Akkawi is an accomplished educator with experience in classroom instruction, curriculum development, faculty and course scheduling, faculty and student recruitment, and budgetary development. An active researcher, his work focuses on knowledge management, concurrent object-oriented software systems, aspect-oriented technology, and the evolution of technological education. Dr. Akkawi has been honored with two NASA Faculty Fellowships, completing projects within the Avionic Offices of both Johnson Space Center and the Ames Research Center. His fellowship work included designing and implementing a framework used in the Advanced Diagnostic and Advanced Caution and Warning System for the International Space Station (ISS), as well as the Integrated System Health Management (ISHM) Testbed project to develop next-generation technologies for the Crew Exploration Vehicle (CEV), lunar habitats and human missions to Mars.

Kayed Akkawi, Ph.D., is dean of the Morris Graduate School of Management at Robert Morris University. He holds a doctorate in computer science and a master's degree in electrical engineering from Illinois Institute of Technology (IIT). Dr. Akkawi has extensive teaching experience at the graduate level. His professional projects have included developing a natural language interface for information retrieval and a search engine for accessing large-scale databases, as well as designing a toolkit to measure retrieval accuracy for bilingual information. Dr. Akkawi serves as chair of the educational committee for the Chicago-Amman International Sister Cities Program.

Gabriel J. Schofield, MBA, CFA, is the Director of Application Development at Symphony Asset Management LLC. He holds an MBA from Durham University and is a CFA charterholder.

With over 15 years of experience as a financial services technology professional, he combines strong leadership skills with a passion for applying technology to solve complex business problems. Gabriel has led project teams that have delivered industry-leading solutions for a variety of front- and back-office financial applications. Gabriel is a proactive member of several industry groups that define and maintain financial messaging and data standards.

Acknowledgments

The authors would like to thank their families and friends for the tremendous level of support throughout this project. In particular, we would like to thank our wives, Brianna and Narges, and children, Chloe, Cameron, George, Nadine, and Sami, for their encouragement and unending patience, especially when the demands of the book encroached upon family time. We also would like to thank the following professors who provided useful feedback on the substantive content of earlier versions of the text: Basim Khartabil, Chris Nassar, Mohammed Abdul Salam, Dave Ross, and Rick Blazek.

Reviewers

We are extremely grateful to the contribution of the following individuals who provided invaluable chapter-by-chapter feedback:

Dave Braunschweig, MIS/M, MCT
Associate Professor
Harper College
Palatine, IL

Frank Chao, Ph.D.
Instructor of Database Management
Wake Technical Community College
Raleigh, NC

Joseph H. Hart PE, MBA, CNA, CNE
Network Management Instructor
Centura College
Richmond, Virginia

Special Thanks

We would like to thank the project team at Cengage Learning for their hard work, professionalism, and attention to detail:

Natalie Pashoukos, Senior Product Manager
Mary Pat Shaffer, Developmental Editor
Nicole Spoto, Technical Editor
Allyson Bozeth, Content Project Manager

Feedback

The authors encourage you to share your questions, comments, and suggestions. This feedback is an important input that will serve to shape future editions of this book. Please send all correspondence through Cengage Learning by contacting their customer and sales support team at 1-800-354-9706.

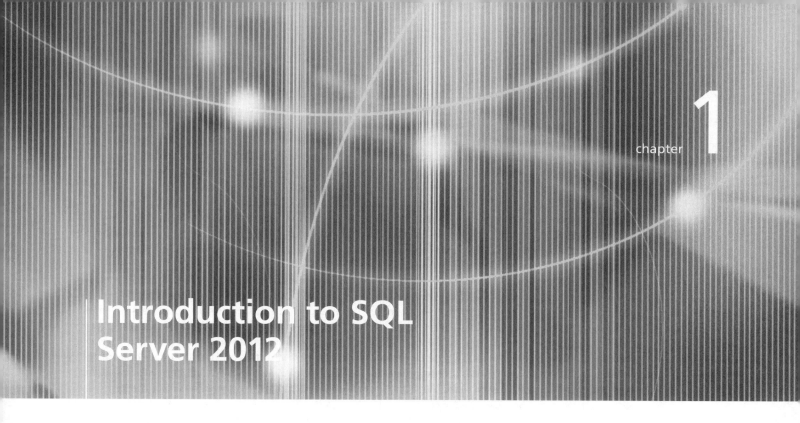

chapter 1

Introduction to SQL Server 2012

After reading this chapter and completing the exercises, you will be able to:

- Identify the capabilities and licensing options for the three main editions of SQL Server 2012

- Describe the benefits of using Windows Server 2008 R2 as the host operating system

- Access Microsoft's online technical documentation for SQL Server 2012, and utilize different problem-solving strategies when trying to resolve SQL Server 2012 performance issues

- Detail the recommended hardware and operating system requirements for running SQL Server 2012

- Prepare for the installation of SQL Server 2012 on a Windows 2008 R2 server

Structured Query Language (SQL) is a widely used database programming language. Microsoft SQL Server (SQL Server) is a powerful relational database management system (RDMBS), with the primary function of storing data and providing access to client software applications. According to Gartner Research, SQL Server has maintained 15 to 20 percent of market share in recent years based on total software revenue. SQL Server dominates deployments on the Microsoft Windows operating systems due to its tight integration with the Windows Server operating system.

The three most recent major versions of SQL Server are 10.0 (SQL Server 2008), 10.5 (SQL Server 2008 R2), and 11.0 (SQL Server 2012). SQL Server 2012 is designed to deliver high availability, scalability, and improved Business Intelligence capabilities that build upon the success of the previous version, SQL Server 2008 R2. **High availability (HA** is a term used to describe a system that must be online and available for user access at most times; unplanned downtime of a high-availability system is likely to cause serious business disruption.

Each version of SQL Server and Windows Server is offered in a number of main and specialized editions. SQL Server 2012 is offered in three main editions: Standard, Business Intelligence, and Enterprise. This book provides you with the knowledge and practical skills necessary to plan and implement a successful SQL Server 2012 Enterprise Edition deployment on a Windows Server 2008 R2 operating system and to perform routine database administration activities. In addition to the **database engine** (which is the core component within a database that controls data storage and access requests from client applications), SQL Server 2012 editions bundle features from **components** such as Master Data Services, Data Quality Services, Analysis Services, Integration Services, Reporting Services, and Replication. Although this book touches on several of these components, the primary focus is on the features provided by the core database engine and associated **management tools**—the suite of tools and utilities for managing the SQL Server database.

This introductory chapter introduces you to the different editions and licensing options for SQL Server 2012. It highlights the benefits of using the latest Windows Server 2008 R2 operating system and discusses the recommended hardware and software specifications for running SQL Server 2012. By completing the activities in this chapter, you will become familiar with Microsoft's product documentation. You will also download the media, mount the image, and undertake a series of preinstallation tasks.

SQL Server 2012 Editions, Capabilities, and Licensing

This section provides an overview of the key components and features of each SQL Server 2012 edition, and it explains the two licensing models offered by Microsoft. In the first activity of this chapter, you will access up-to-date online information on the SQL Server 2012 product family. When deciding on an edition of SQL Server for a particular deployment, you need to be aware of the range of options available in the various editions. And, even more important, you will need to build a thorough understanding of the relevant business requirements because these will ultimately determine which edition is most suited for a particular application.

SQL Server 2012 Editions

Microsoft has simplified its product lineup for the SQL Server 2012 family and offers three main editions: Standard, Business Intelligence, and Enterprise. In addition to the main editions, three specialized editions are also available: Developer, Express, and Web. All editions are available in both 32-bit and 64-bit versions. In addition to the core database engine and a common set of management tools, each edition is bundled with features from add-on components.

The three main editions form a tiered model. The Standard Edition includes the core database engine and basic Business Intelligence features. **Business Intelligence (BI)** is a term used to describe the range of activities involved in analyzing raw data that enables an organization to extract knowledge used for making key business decisions. The Business Intelligence Edition augments the capabilities of the Standard Edition with advanced Business Intelligence functionality. The Enterprise Edition is the most comprehensive offering and includes features specifically designed to support high availability, scalability, and data warehousing. The following is a summary of the three main SQL Server 2012 editions:

- *Standard Edition*—The Standard Edition includes the core database engine; basic features from the Analysis Services, Reporting Services, and Integration Services components; and a suite of management tools. Each installation of the Standard Edition is limited to 16 cores and 64 GB of memory. This edition is targeted at medium-sized deployments—for example, smaller organizations or departments that seek an easy-to-use, reliable, and cost-effective solution.

- *Business Intelligence Edition*—The Business Intelligence Edition inherits all the features and the same processor and memory limitations of the Standard Edition; in addition, it includes advanced features from the Master Data Services, Analysis Services, and Reporting Services components. These features make it ideally suited for organizations that need a robust database management system with an integrated set of advanced Business Intelligence capabilities.

- *Enterprise Edition*—The Enterprise Edition is designed for organizations that manage large **data warehouses**—databases designed for reporting and analytics—or run critical applications. The memory and processing power of SQL Server Enterprise Edition is limited only by the host operating system, and this edition is packaged with advanced features from all components currently available on the 2012 version of SQL Server. The features that distinguish the Enterprise Edition from the Business Intelligence Edition are support for all the high-availability, scalability, and security features in the database engine plus the advanced functionality within the Data Warehouse and Integration Services components. Figure 1-1 shows the major components and features of the main SQL Server 2012 editions. You'll learn more about these components in later chapters.

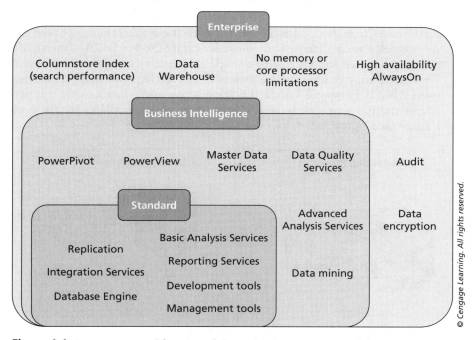

Figure 1-1 Components and features of the main SQL Server 2012 editions

Microsoft also offers three specialized editions of SQL Server 2012:

- *Developer Edition*—The Developer Edition includes all the features and functionality offered by the Enterprise Edition; however, use of the Developer Edition is strictly restricted to development and testing only. The Developer Edition is the only specialized edition that can be upgraded directly to an Enterprise license.

- *Express Edition*—The Express Edition is a free, entry-level database offering basic functionality; although memory is limited to 1 GB and database size is constrained to 10 GB, it is an economical choice for those seeking an introduction to SQL Server or those with limited needs for functionality and capacity.

- *Web Edition*—The Web Edition is targeted at hosted, Internet-facing deployments; this edition enables an organization to leverage the benefits of SQL Server 2012, exchanging the up-front hardware and software costs for ongoing variable costs. Amazon Web Services is an example of a service provider offering this option.

Licensing Models

Microsoft has two basic licensing options that cover the main editions of SQL Server 2012. The first, core-based licensing, is based on a measure of processing power, whereas the second, Server and Client Access License (CAL), focuses on the number of end users with access to the system:

- **Core-based licensing** measures the computing power of the host server by counting the number of processing cores. It replaces processor-based licensing in earlier versions of SQL Server. A **core** is a physical unit within a processor that reads and executes program instructions. Traditionally, a processor was based on a single core, although multicore processors are now commonplace. A **multicore processor** is a processor with more than one core processing unit; it is able to execute multiple instruction sets in parallel with a consequent improvement in performance. Given the widespread adoption of multicore processors, Microsoft considers the number of cores to be a more relevant metric to measure processing power for SQL Server 2012. The core-based licensing model is the only model available for the Enterprise Edition, and it might make sense for the Standard Edition when it is impractical to count the number of users. A license is based on a four-core minimum with one-core increments.

- **Server and Client Access License (CAL) licensing** is a user-centric licensing model. Under this model, a server license is required for each SQL Server 2012 installation and a CAL is required for each end user. With a single CAL, each user is able to access multiple servers. This model may be appropriate for organizations that can easily count the number of end users when deploying a Standard Edition server and when a single end user may need to access multiple database servers. It is the only option available for the Business Intelligence Edition. See Figure 1-2.

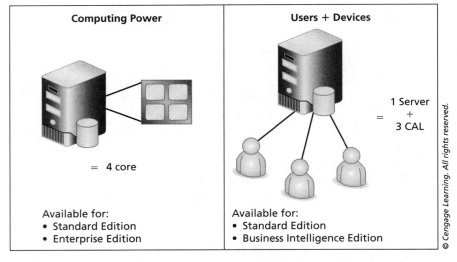

Figure 1-2 The differences between core-based and CAL-based licensing models

When selecting a licensing option, you should determine if you will require ongoing access to vendor support and upgrades. For example, evaluate the cost and benefits of enrolling in a Microsoft Enterprise Agreement, which is a volume-licensing program for large organizations that allows costs to be spread over several years and includes access to the latest software versions and support. **Microsoft Software Assurance** is a maintenance program that provides ongoing access to Microsoft support and product updates for an annual fee. Similar to the Microsoft Enterprise Agreement, the Microsoft Software Assurance program enables the cost of software to be spread over several years and should be considered—especially if you intend to keep current with the latest versions and require access to Microsoft support.

All the main editions of SQL Server 2012 can be installed for evaluation purposes with a 180-day evaluation edition license. The activities outlined later in this book are based on the SQL Server 2012 Enterprise Edition. At the end of this chapter, you will be guided through the download and preinstallation steps for SQL Server 2012 Enterprise Edition (64-bit).

Activity 1-1: Researching SQL Server 2012 Editions

Time Required: 30 minutes

Objective: Learn how to research SQL Server 2012 editions, components, and features by accessing Microsoft product documentation using a Web browser.

Description: In this activity, you will use a Web browser to explore SQL Server 2012 product information and find detailed information on editions, components, and features. The activity assumes you are using Microsoft Internet Explorer running on a Windows operating system.

1. If necessary, start your computer and log on.

2. Click the **Start** button, point to **All Programs**, and then click **Internet Explorer** to open your Web browser. See Figure 1-3.

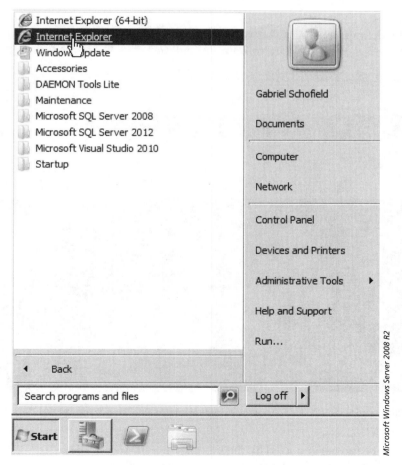

Figure 1-3 Launch Internet Explorer from the All Programs menu

3. Click in the **Address bar,** and type the following URL to explore SQL Server product information: **www.microsoft.com/sqlserver**. See Figure 1-4.

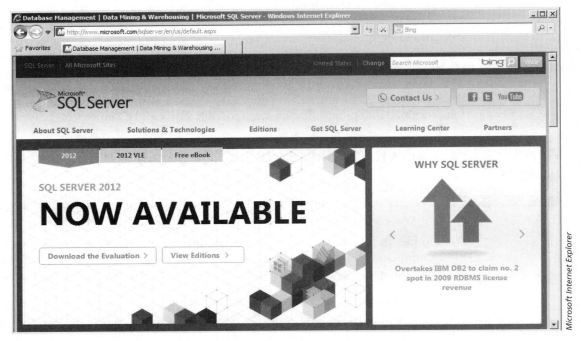

Figure 1-4 Microsoft SQL Server product home page

4. By default, this link takes you to information on the latest product version, currently SQL Server 2012. Point to **Editions** and then click **Compare Editions**. See Figure 1-5.

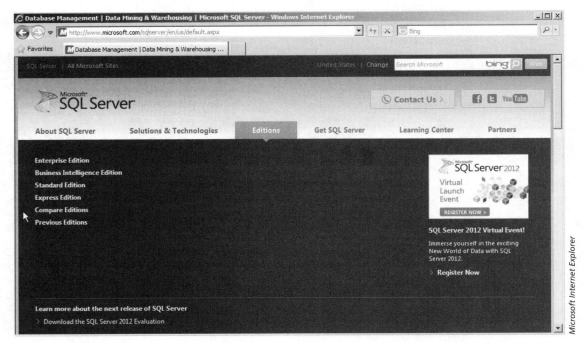

Figure 1-5 Click Compare Editions to view information on the various editions of SQL Server 2012

5. The Features Supported by the Editions of SQL Server 2012 page in the Books Online for SQL Server 2012 section of the Microsoft Developer Network (MSDN) Library opens. Scroll down the page to review the information and familiarize yourself

with the major differences in supported components and features between the main editions of SQL Server 2012. You can print a copy of the page by clicking the **printer** icon in the upper-right corner of the Web page. See Figure 1-6.

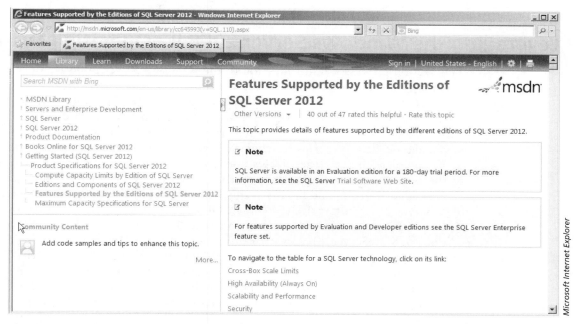

Figure 1-6　An explanation of the features supported by the different editions of SQL Server 2012

Microsoft Books Online is a comprehensive set of online technical product documentation that covers the features and tools for various Microsoft products; it includes how-to guides and a language reference.

6. In the menu on the left side of the page, click **Editions and Components of SQL Server 2012**. See Figure 1-7.

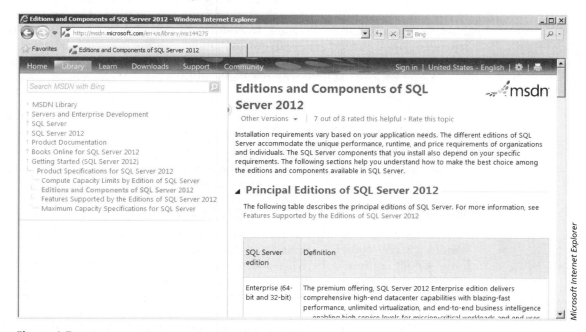

Figure 1-7　Editions and Components of SQL Server 2012

7. Scroll down the page and read the descriptions of the individual components in the Deciding Among SQL Server Components section.

8. When you are finished, leave your Web browser open for the next activity.

Leveraging the Windows Server 2008 R2 Operating System

This section provides an introduction to the Windows Server 2008 R2 operating system. The **operating system** is the platform that allows the hardware and software components to separately interface with multiple applications to perform requested functions and services. SQL Server 2012 differentiates itself from other commercial database systems due to its tight integration with the Microsoft Windows operating system. Although this model has a number of inherent advantages, it also constrains the choice of operating system to Microsoft Windows.

To complete the activities in this book, you must have an environment running a version of the Windows operating system that is compatible with the SQL Server 2012 Enterprise Edition. The activities and figures in this book are based on the Windows Server 2008 R2 and SQL Server 2012 Enterprise (64-bit) Editions. However, if you are using an older computer with a 32-bit processor, you can still complete the activities as Microsoft makes all the main editions of SQL Server 2012 available in a 32-bit version. If you are running an earlier version of Windows (such as Vista, Windows 7, or Windows Server 2008 with Service Pack 2 installed), the operating system menus may differ from those of SQL Server 2008 R2, but the SQL Server Installation Wizard and management tools should be the same. You will need to check your operating system and service pack level to ensure that you are running a compatible version of Windows.

Introduction to the Windows Server 2008 R2 Operating System

The Windows Server 2008 R2 operating system is available in three main editions: Standard, Enterprise, and Datacenter. Windows Server 2008 R2 is the first version of the Windows Server family that is only available as a 64-bit release. In addition to these editions, Microsoft produces a bare-bones version of the Windows Server 2008 operating system called **Server Core** that does not include the Windows Explorer Shell. The Server Core operating system is suited to mission-critical deployments as the smaller footprint reduces the number of potential security vulnerabilities and enables updates to be installed with less downtime.

The required feature set and the size of your network will determine which edition you select for a particular deployment. In addition, the hardware selection for the installation is dependent upon the system configuration along with the desired features and services of the end-user application. It is important to check the compatible operating systems and required service packs for the SQL Server 2012 edition that you intend to deploy. Keep the following guidelines in mind:

- The main editions of Windows Server 2008 R2 with the latest service pack will support all main editions of SQL Server 2012. To take full advantage of the features available in SQL Server 2012, use a 64-bit architecture.

- The SQL Server 2012 Standard Edition as well as the specialized editions will also run on the Windows 7 and Vista desktop versions of the Windows operating system.

Management Tools and Integrated Security

SQL Server 2012 is tightly integrated with many of the management features provided by the Windows Server 2008 R2 operating system. When Windows Server 2008 R2 is first installed, an Initial Configuration Tasks Wizard steps you through configuration of the server. This wizard continues to launch automatically upon each successful login until you check the Do not show me this console at logon check box. For routine administration, **Server Manager** provides a one-stop management interface—with quick access to tools for performing common tasks, such as querying the server status and changing roles and features. See Figure 1-8.

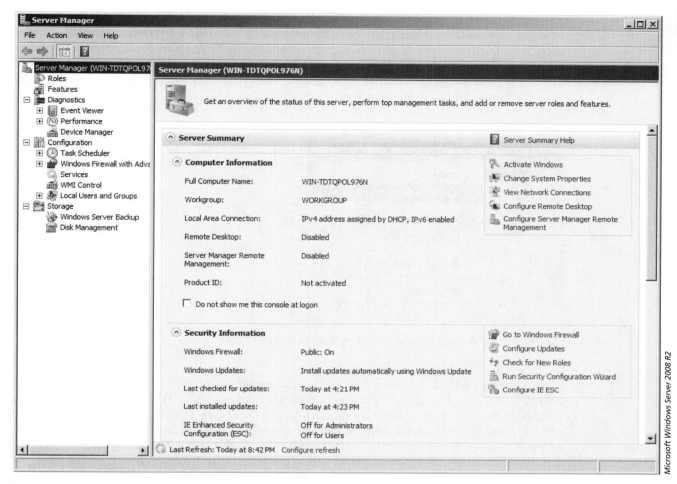

Figure 1-8 Server Manager

Server Manager is divided into the following categories:

- *Server Summary*—Displays computer information, such as domain name, wireless network connection, and product ID; from here, you can manage network connections, configure remote management, and manage security features, such as the Windows firewall and Windows Update policy.

- *Roles*—Lists the currently configured server roles along with a status of each; you can add and remove roles, or go to the selected role to make changes to the features.

- *Features*—Displays currently configured features; you can add and remove features.

- *Diagnostics*—Provides an event log viewer, hardware performance monitoring capabilities, and a device manager; this is one of the most useful features of Server Manager for day-to-day server management.

- *Configuration*—Displays options for server configuration; from here, you can manage local users and groups, create scheduled tasks, and start and stop services.

- *Storage*—Provides access to storage management and maintenance tasks; you can manage backup policies and perform routine disk maintenance.

Server Manager makes server administration more efficient by allowing administrators to perform routine tasks using a single tool. In prior versions of Windows Server, these functions were accomplished using multiple add-in components to the Microsoft Management Console (MMC).

User Account Control (UAC) is a Windows Server security feature that ensures that any administrative changes to the configuration of the server—such as software installation—require explicit authorization. When performing an administrative task on an application, you need to use a login that is a member of the local or domain Administrators role. Furthermore, you need to explicitly run the application as an administrator by right-clicking the application icon and selecting Run as administrator. See Figure 1-9.

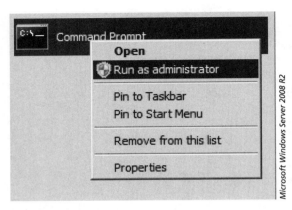

Figure 1-9 User Account Control (UAC) Run as administrator option

SQL Server 2012 is a directory-enabled application, and Active Directory Domain Services (AD DS) or Active Directory Lightweight Directory Service (AD LDS) can be used to provide a scalable and integrated security model. **Active Directory Domain Service (AD DS)** is a directory service that uses a **domain controller**—which is a server that is running a version of the Windows Server operating system, with Active Directory Domain Services (AD DS) installed—to store information about users, computers, and other devices on the network and to manage authentication. AD DS helps administrators securely manage this information and facilitates resource sharing and collaboration between users. AD DS is also required in order to install directory-enabled applications such as SQL Server 2012. **Active Directory Lightweight Directory Service (AD LDS)** is a lightweight implementation of AD DS that uses the same code base but does not require the creation of domains or domain controllers. Multiple instances of AD LDS may be run on a single server. An **instance** is an occurrence or copy of an object.

Both AD DS and AD LDS use the Lightweight Directory Access Protocol (LDAP) and Kerberos to provide authentication, role-based access to resources, and development of group policies for users and services. **Lightweight Directory Access Protocol (LDAP)** is a software protocol for enabling anyone to locate individuals and other resources, such as files and devices, on a network—whether on the Internet or on a private network. **Kerberos** is a widely used network authentication protocol. **Authentication** is the process of verifying the identity of a user, computer, process, or other entity by validating the credentials provided by the entity. Common forms of credentials are digital signatures, smart cards, biometric data, and a combination of usernames and passwords.

For security reasons, it is not recommended to install SQL Server 2012 on a host that is also a domain controller. Later in this book, we will discuss configuring SQL Server 2012 for use with AD DS via a domain controller on your network, or configuring AD LDS without a domain controller that provides dedicated directory services for your application.

Building a Test Environment

The activities in this book are based on the Enterprise (64-bit) Edition of the SQL Server 2012 database installed on a Windows Server 2008 R2 operating system running Service Pack 1 as a minimum. You will need to complete an installation of the Windows Server 2008 R2 operating system or use an existing Microsoft Windows operating system that is compatible with SQL Server 2012 before proceeding to the preinstallation steps and implementation of the SQL Server 2012.

As mentioned previously, if you are running an older computer with a 32-bit processor, you can still follow the activities in this book. Microsoft makes all the main editions of SQL Server 2012 available for a 32-bit installation. The menu options on your earlier Windows operating system may differ from those of Microsoft Windows Server 2008 R2, but the SQL Server Installation Wizard and management tools should be identical. At the time of writing, to install the 32-bit version of SQL Server 2012, you need Windows Vista, Windows 7, or Windows Server 2008 with Service Pack 2 installed. However, you should check the current requirements using the steps outlined in Activity 1-2.

A 180-day trial of the Windows Server 2008 R2 operating system with Service Pack 1 is available for download from Microsoft at the TechNet Evaluation Center: *http://technet.microsoft.com /en-us/evalcenter*.

We recommend that you set up a Windows Server 2008 R2 lab environment for your SQL Server 2012 implementation using **virtualization** software. This will enable you to install a version of Windows Server 2008 R2 as a **virtual machine** (an isolated guest operating system installed on top of a normal operating system) to test the SQL Server 2012 software without impacting the settings of your local operating system. A further advantage of using a virtual test environment is that virtualization software allows you to take snapshots as you proceed through the exercises, making it possible to revert to a previous point in time in the event that you cause an unrecoverable error. The following are two virtualization products that can be used to create a lab environment for your SQL Server 2012 implementation:

- VMware, Inc., offers a virtualization product called **VMware Workstation** that is suitable for building multiple virtual machines on top of a host Microsoft Windows operating system. VMware Workstation (*vmware.com/products/workstation*) is well suited for this purpose.

- Oracle provides a virtualization product called **Oracle VirtualBox** that provides the ability to build virtual machines on a Linux, Mac OS X, Solaris, or Windows host operating system. Oracle VirtualBox is available under a **GNU General Public License (GPL)**, a type of software license that is widely used for distributing free or open source software (*virtualbox.org/wiki/Downloads*).

Microsoft makes its software available for download as an ISO image file, and it is becoming increasingly rare to undertake an installation from physical media (e.g., a DVD). To run the installation program, you will first need to mount the downloaded image using a **virtual CD/ DVD drive emulator**, which is software that emulates a physical drive and enables a disk image to be mounted; it is often used for installing software distributed as an ISO file. You will need to download a third-party product to do this, as the Windows operating system does not include this functionality. There are several reputable vendors that provide a basic virtual drive emulator for free. A product called **DAEMON Tools Lite** (*daemon-tools.cc/eng/products/dtLite*) was used to mount the downloaded image file for the activities in Chapter 1.

SQL Server Product Documentation and Problem-Solving Strategies

This section introduces several important documentation and troubleshooting resources for SQL Server 2012. You'll begin by reviewing Microsoft's core technical documentation, and then you'll learn about different strategies for finding a solution to a specific technical problem after you have exhausted the documentation resources. Finally, you'll complete Activity 1-2 to become familiar with Microsoft's online technical documentation for SQL Server 2012.

Microsoft SQL Server 2012 Product Documentation

Microsoft publishes a comprehensive set of product documentation on two Internet sites: **TechNet** and **Microsoft Developer Network (MSDN)**. Both sites serve as portals hosting online product documentation, tutorials, and user forums. TechNet was originally intended for system administrators while MSDN was designed with the application development community in mind. Because SQL Server spans these two areas of specialization, both sites serve an almost identical set of SQL Server content, although with a slightly different look and feel. Microsoft no longer bundles a copy of its product documentation with the installation program, although it does provide a Help Viewer that can be configured to either access content online or download a local copy (Chapter 2 provides further details on this tool). Because Microsoft often updates its online product documentation, you should make a habit of accessing the content—either by using a Web browser or via the SQL Server 2012 Help Viewer. Microsoft splits its product documentation into four main areas:

- *Books Online for SQL Server 2012*—Presents a comprehensive set of technical product documentation that covers SQL Server 2012 features and tools; includes how-to guides and a database programming language reference. The documentation is organized by component and is supported by a glossary of terms; you have already reviewed two pages from Books Online for SQL Server 2012 as part of Activity 1-1, and this book makes frequent reference to this documentation.

- *Installation for SQL Server 2012*—Provides a detailed set of instructions that will enable you to plan, install, or upgrade to a SQL Server 2012 instance; we will review this documentation in detail during installation in Chapter 2.

- *Tutorials for SQL Server 2012*—Contains a series of lessons that teach you how to use a particular piece of functionality; the tutorials are intended to help you to get the most out of SQL Server 2012. Tutorials are included for readers at all levels, on topics ranging from introductions to basic concepts to getting started with the latest technology and features.

- *Developer Reference for SQL Server 2012*—Provides a resource intended for developers building client applications that access SQL Server 2012; this material is beyond the scope of this book.

In addition to product documentation, Microsoft publishes technical articles and white papers to the MSDN and TechNet sites. Microsoft also maintains several online forums that you'll explore later in this section.

Problem-Solving Strategies

Even as your skills as a database administrator develop, you will inevitably need to seek other resources from time to time to solve a problem. Often, the first step is to discuss the problem with a colleague, an instructor, or a friend. Describing the problem and getting another person's input can provide a fresh perspective. If this approach yields no success, alternative options include the following:

- Open a **support case** (a request for product support) with Microsoft Support—via email, by phone, or on the Microsoft Support site (*http://support.microsoft.com/ph/1044*). This option is appropriate for resolving a time-critical issue with a production database.

- Use crowd-sourcing to find a solution by tapping into the online community of SQL Server professionals through one of Microsoft's online forums, such as SQL Server Forums (*http://social.technet.microsoft.com/Forums/en-US/category/sqlserver*). **Crowd-sourcing** is general term for the outsourcing of tasks to a distributed, undefined group of people. Although this strategy can yield results, you will have most success if you have thoroughly researched the problem and provide a comprehensive description, including information such as version, configuration, relevant event log and error messages, and, if possible, an example that would enable a third party to replicate the problem. Remember that interactions on discussion boards or other online forums should always be professional and courteous.

Activity 1-2: Accessing Microsoft's Online Technical Documentation

Time Required: 30 minutes

Objective: Access Microsoft's online technical documentation for SQL Server 2012 using a Web browser.

Description: In this activity, you will use a Web browser to navigate to the TechNet and MSDN sites and explore Microsoft Books Online for SQL Server 2012.

1. Click in the **Address bar** of your Web browser, type **technet.microsoft.com**, and then press the **Enter** key to explore the Microsoft TechNet site. On the menu bar, click **Products**, and then click **SQL Server**. On the SQL Server TechCenter page, click **Library** to navigate to the TechNet Library. Then, in the left navigation pane, click **SQL Server 2012**, and then click **Product Documentation** to view the online product documentation available for SQL Server 2012. See Figure 1-10.

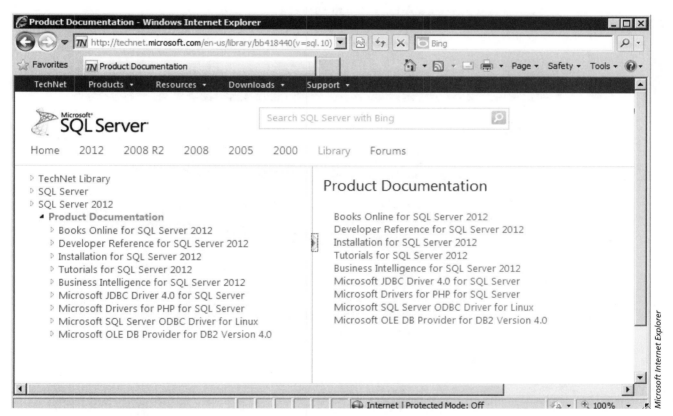

Figure 1-10 Microsoft TechNet online product documentation for SQL Server 2012

2. Notice how you can select different product versions in the toolbar below the Search SQL Server with Bing box. You can also toggle between the Library (the source of product documentation and technical articles) and Forums (the community discussion boards moderated by Microsoft). Bookmark this page by clicking the **Favorites** button, and then clicking **Add to Favorites**. See Figure 1-11.

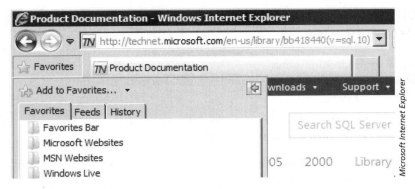

Figure 1-11 Add Microsoft TechNet site to Favorites

3. In the Add a Favorite dialog box, click in the **Name** box, provide a suitable name, and then click **Add**. See Figure 1-12.

Figure 1-12 Type a name that will appear in the Favorites list

4. Click the **Forums** menu option, and review the different types of discussion boards related to SQL Server. See Figure 1-13.

5. To explore the Microsoft MSDN site for SQL Server, click in the **Address bar** and type the following URL: **msdn.microsoft.com/en-us/sqlserver**. When the site opens, click **Library**, and then click **SQL Server 2012** from the left navigation menu. Next, click **Product Documentation** to view the MSDN product documentation for SQL Server 2012. Notice the similarities between the information provided on this site and the TechNet site. See Figure 1-14.

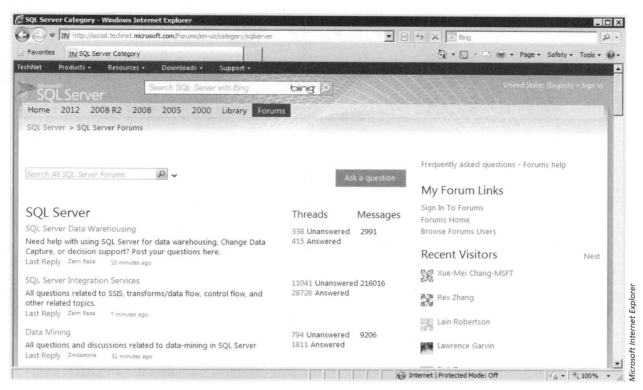

Figure 1-13 Microsoft MSDN SQL Server forums

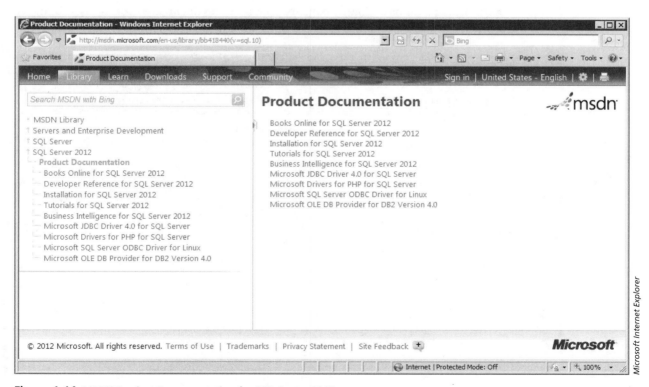

Figure 1-14 MSDN Product Documentation for SQL Server 2012

6. In the menu on the left side of the page, click **Books Online for SQL Server 2012** to open the Books Online for SQL Server 2012 welcome page. See Figure 1-15.

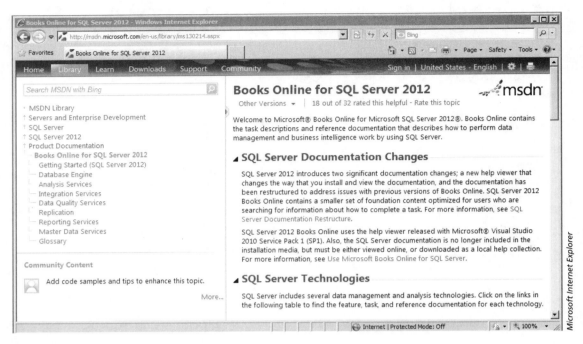

Figure 1-15 Books Online for SQL Server 2012

7. In the menu on the left side of the page, click **Database Engine** to open the SQL Server Database Engine page. Notice how the documentation is organized. See Figure 1-16.

Figure 1-16 Books Online for SQL Server 2012 "SQL Server Database Engine" topic

8. Click in the **Search MSDN with Bing** box in the upper-left corner of the page and type **SQL Server 2012 Hardware Software Requirements**. See Figure 1-17.

Figure 1-17 Search for topics on SQL Server 2012 hardware and software requirements

9. Click the **Search** button, and then click **Hardware and Software Requirements for Installing SQL Server 2012** in the list of search results. See Figure 1-18.

Figure 1-18 MSDN search results: SQL Server Hardware and Software Requirements for Installing SQL Server 2012

10. The Hardware and Software Requirements for Installing SQL Server 2012 page opens. Click the **printer** icon in the upper-right corner to print a copy of the page. You will refer to this information as you read the next section.

11. When you are finished, close your Web browser.

Understanding the Minimum System Requirements and Preparing for Installation

This section reviews the minimum set of hardware and software requirements that Microsoft has defined for running SQL Server 2012. In Step 10 of Activity 1-2, you printed a full set of these requirements, which you should review in detail. Always check the latest requirements during the planning phase of any implementation.

Although the minimum hardware requirements listed will be sufficient to undertake the activities described in this book, you might need to adjust these requirements depending on the intended usage of your SQL Server 2012 instance. For example, if you intend to build a lab environment, you need to ensure that you have sufficient memory and disk space available on your host operating system in addition to the resources required by the virtual machine you will be using to host SQL Server 2012. As a general rule of thumb, the more memory, physical disk space, and CPU you have at your disposal, the better. Table 1-1 summarizes the recommended requirements.

Table 1-1   Recommended minimum hardware and operating system specifications to run SQL Server 2012

Component	Recommended minimum specification
Hardware	• 2 GHz (x86-64 processor) • 1 GB memory • 6 GB available hard-disk space
Operating system	• Windows Server 2008 R2 SP1 64-bit
Other	• Physical DVD drive or virtual DVD drive emulator • Internet Explorer 7 or above • Internet connectivity

© Cengage Learning

Activity 1-3: Downloading SQL Server 2012 Installation Media and Running System Configuration Checker

Time Required: 90 minutes (depending on the speed of your Internet connection)
Objective: Download the installation media for SQL Server 2012 and run the SQL Server 2012 System Configuration Checker, ensuring that all prerequisites are met prior to undertaking an installation.

Description: In this activity, you will use a Web browser and Internet connection to navigate to the Microsoft SQL Server 2012 downloads page and download a trial version of the SQL Server 2012 installation software as an ISO image file. You should perform this task from the host running Windows Server 2008 R2 on which you will install SQL Server 2012. You will also need a virtual DVD drive emulator software package.

1. If necessary, start your computer and log on to your Microsoft Windows Server 2008 R2 host. For this activity, you will need to log on with an account that is a member of the Administrators role.

2. Open your Web browser.

3. Click in the **Address bar** and type the following URL **microsoft.com/sqlserver /en/us/get-sql-server/try-it.aspx** to open the SQL Server 2012 Trial page. See Figure 1-19.

4. Click the **Download SQL Server 2012** button to open the SQL Server 2012 page, where you can select a download option.

5. Under the Download DVD ISO Image option, select **United States (English)** from the Please select Language list box. Click the **Download ISO** button. See Figure 1-20.

6. If you are prompted to install an Active-X control, click to accept the terms of the agreement.

Figure 1-19 Microsoft SQL Server 2012 Trial Download home page

Figure 1-20 SQL Server 2012 download options

7. You will be prompted to save the SQLFULL_ENU ISO image. Be sure to choose a location with at least 4.2 GB of available disk space. See Figure 1-21.

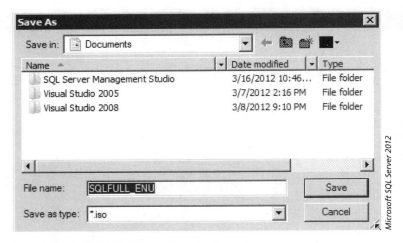

Figure 1-21 SQLFULL_ENU.iso Save As dialog box

8. Next, you will need to mount the ISO image as a local drive. To do so, you will need to install a virtual DVD drive emulator, such as DAEMON Tools Lite. If using Daemon Tools Lite, select **Add Images**, which prompts you to navigate to the download location of your **SQLFULL_ENU.iso** file. Right-click the ISO file, and select the **Mount Image** option from the drop-down menu. Then, click the **Start** button and click **Computer**. You should now see an additional drive listed under Devices with Removable Storage. See Figure 1-22.

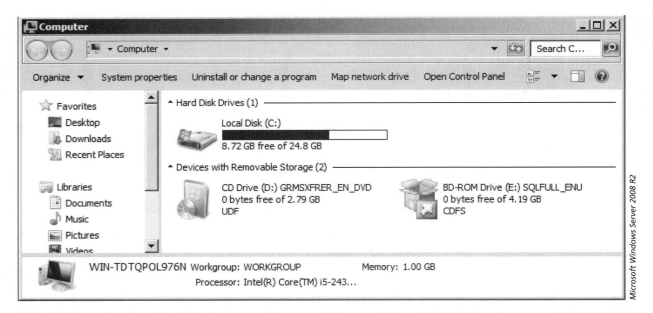

Figure 1-22 Windows Explorer displaying removable storage devices on local machine including the mounted SQLFULL_ENU image

9. Double-click the **virtual drive icon,** and click the **Yes** button when the User Account Control dialog box opens. See Figure 1-23.

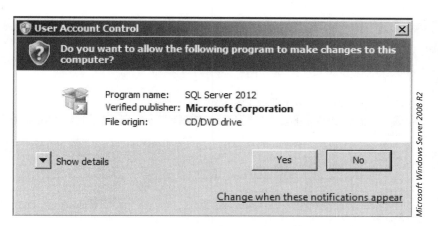

Figure 1-23 Microsoft Windows Server 2008 R2 User Account Control

10. In the SQL Server Installation Center window, click **Planning**, and then click **System Configuration Checker**. See Figure 1-24.

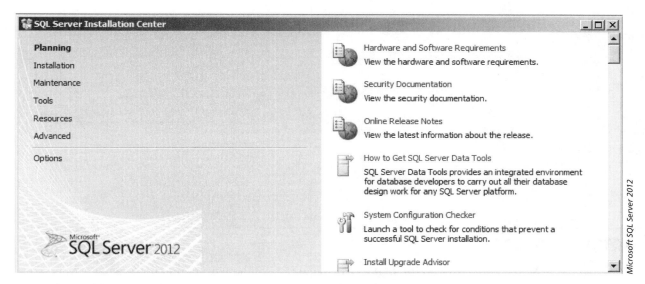

Figure 1-24 SQL Server Installation Center

11. SQL Server 2012 Setup Support Rules will run and check that your Windows Server 2008 R2 configuration meets the prerequisites for installing SQL Server Setup. See Figure 1-25.

12. If any of the rules fail, you will need to correct the issue by following the steps provided to you by the wizard.

 One common reason for failure is a Windows Server 2008 R2 installation that is not up to date with the latest recommended service pack or security updates installed.

13. After correcting any failures, you are ready to move on to Chapter 2 to perform an installation of SQL Server 2012.

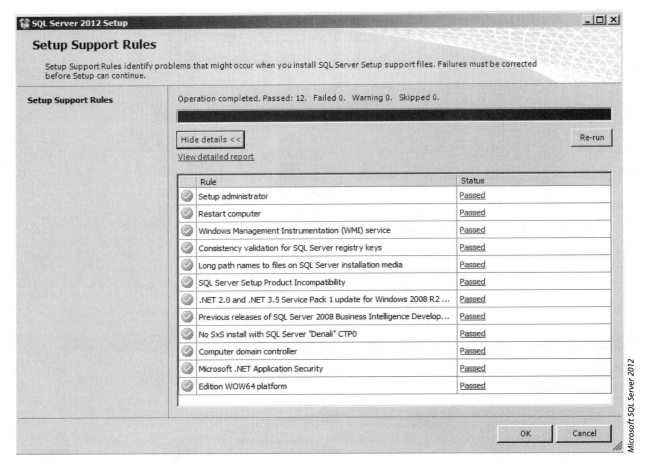

Figure 1-25 Setup Support Rules

Chapter Summary

- SQL stands for Structured Query Language, a database programming language. Microsoft SQL Server 2012 is a relational database server with the primary function of storing data and managing access requests from client applications.

- SQL Server 2012 is the latest release of SQL Server and is available in three main editions: Standard, Business Intelligence, and Enterprise. A number of specialized editions are also available.

- Each edition of SQL Server 2012 includes the core database engine and a suite of management tools, and is bundled with features from other components.

- SQL Server 2012 is offered via two licensing models: core-based licensing, which is based on processing power, and Server and Client Access License (CAL) licensing, which is based on the number of end users.

- SQL Server 2012 is tightly integrated with the Windows operating system and must be installed on a compatible version.

- Windows Server 2008 R2 is the latest version of the Windows Server operating system, and it includes features that improve security and manageability. It is available in three main editions: Standard, Enterprise, and Datacenter.

- Server Manager provides a one-stop management interface, introduced in Windows Server 2008, that provides quick access to tools for performing common tasks, such as querying server status, retrieving diagnostic information, starting or stopping services, and changing server roles and features.

- The use of Active Directory Domain Services (AD DS) or Active Directory Lightweight Directory Service (AD LDS) in Windows Server 2008 R2 provides an integrated security environment for authentication, mapping of network users and services to roles, and managing of permissions to schema objects.

- Building a test environment as a virtual machine is good practice when evaluating new software because it isolates the environment from your host operating system and enables rollback to a previous snapshot of the system if needed.

- Microsoft TechNet and MSDN Web sites are useful online resources for information pertaining to software downloads, partners, future direction of SQL, product information, edition descriptions, and support for SQL Server 2012.

- Books Online for SQL Server 2012 provides the latest recommended system requirements for a SQL Server 2012 installation.

- Running the System Configuration Checker prior to installation ensures that your host meets the necessary prerequisites and allows you to fix any issues prior to undertaking an installation.

Key Terms

Active Directory Domain Service (AD DS)   A directory service available in the Windows Server 2008 R2 operating system; uses a domain controller to store information about users, computers, and other devices on the network and to manage authentication. AD DS helps administrators securely manage this information and facilitates resource sharing and collaboration between users.

Active Directory Lightweight Directory Service (AD LDS)   A lightweight implementation of AD DS that uses the same code base but does not require the creation of domains or domain controllers. Multiple instances of AD LDS may be run on a single server.

authentication   The process of verifying the identity of a user, computer, process, or other entity by validating the credentials provided by the entity.

Business Intelligence (BI)   A range of activities involved in analyzing raw data that enables an organization to extract knowledge used for making key business decisions.

components   Core services bundled with a SQL Server edition, including the database engine, Master Data Services, Data Quality Services, Analysis Services, Integration Services, Reporting Services, and Replication.

core   A physical unit within a processor that reads and executes program instructions. Traditionally, a processor was based on a single core, although multicore processors are now commonplace. *See also* multicore processor.

core-based licensing   A SQL Server 2012 licensing option in which Microsoft measures the computing power of the host server by counting the number of processing cores; it replaces processor-based licensing in earlier versions of SQL Server.

crowd-sourcing   The outsourcing of tasks to a distributed, undefined group of people.

DAEMON Tools Lite   A third-party product that enables a disk image to be mounted as a virtual drive.

database engine   The core component within a database that controls data storage and access requests from client applications.

data warehouse   A database designed for reporting and analytics.

domain controller   A server running a version of the Windows Server operating system, with Active Directory Doman Services (AD DS) installed.

GNU General Public License (GPL)   A type of software license that is widely used for distributing free or open source software.

high availability (HA)   A term used to describe a system that must be online and available for user access at most times; unplanned downtime of a high-availability system is likely to cause serious business disruption.

instance   An occurrence or copy of an object.

Kerberos   A widely used network authentication protocol.

Lightweight Directory Access Protocol (LDAP)   A software protocol for enabling anyone to locate individuals, and other resources, such as files and devices, on a network—whether on the Internet or on a private network.

management tools   A suite of tools and utilities for managing the SQL Server database.

Microsoft Books Online   A comprehensive set of online technical product documentation that covers the features and tools for various Microsoft products; includes how-to guides and a language reference.

Microsoft Developer Network (MSDN)   A Microsoft portal hosting online product documentation and tutorials; MSDN was originally designed for application administrators.

Microsoft Software Assurance (SA)   An optional Microsoft maintenance program that provides ongoing access to Microsoft support and product updates for a fee.

multicore processor   A processor with more than one core processing unit; able to execute multiple instruction sets in parallel with a consequent improvement in performance.

operating system   A platform that allows a computer system's hardware and software components to interface separately with multiple applications to perform requested functions and services.

Oracle VirtualBox   A virtual machine software product from Oracle that allows you to install multiple virtual machines on a Linux, Mac OS X, Solaris, or Windows host operating system.

Server and Client Access License (CAL) licensing   A user-centric licensing model in which a server license is required for each SQL Server 2012 installation and a CAL is required for each end user. Each user is able to access multiple servers with a single CAL.

Server Core   A stripped-down version of the Windows Server 2008 operating system that does not include the Windows Explorer Shell and that reduces potential security vulnerabilities and improves uptime.

Server Manager   A one-stop management interface introduced in Windows Server 2008 that provides quick access to tools for performing routine tasks, such as querying the server status and changing roles and features.

Structured Query Language (SQL)   A database programming language.

support case   A request for Microsoft product support.

TechNet   A Microsoft portal hosting online product documentation, tutorials, and user forums; TechNet was originally designed for system administrators.

User Account Control (UAC)   A Windows Server security feature that ensures that any administrative changes to the configuration of the server—such as software installation—require explicit authorization.

virtual CD/DVD drive emulator   Software that emulates a physical drive and enables a disk image to be mounted; often used for installing software distributed as an ISO file. Windows does not provide native support for mounting disk images.

virtualization   The process of creating a virtual version of something—for example, a physical device, network resource, or operating system.

virtual machine   An isolated guest operating system installed on top of a normal operating system.

VMware Workstation   A virtual machine software product from VMware that enables multiple virtual machines to be installed on a host Windows operating system.

Review Questions

1. What is the primary function of SQL Server 2012?

   a. Business Intelligence

   b. Managing requests from client applications to access data

   c. Storing data

   d. Both options b and c

2. Service Pack 1 is a prerequisite if installing SQL Server 2012 Enterprise (64-bit) Edition on Windows Server 2008 R2. True or False?

3. Microsoft makes which of the following licensing models available for the main editions of SQL Server 2012?

   a. Core-based licensing

   b. GNU General Public License

   c. Server and Client Access License (CAL) licensing

   d. Both options a and c

4. Where does Microsoft publish its product documentation?

   a. TechNet

   b. w3schools

   c. MSDN

   d. Both options a and c

5. What were the major areas of focus in the SQL Server 2012 version release?

   a. Support for UNIX, Linux, Solaris, and Mac OS X operating systems

   b. High availability and Business Intelligence

   c. Discontinued support for the x86 32-bit processor

   d. All of the above

6. Why should you consider setting up a virtual test environment?

   a. It requires less system resources because it is virtualized.

   b. It segregates the test environment from the host operating system and allows you to roll back to an earlier snapshot in the event of an unrecoverable problem.

   c. Microsoft has a more cost-effective licensing model for virtualized systems.

   d. A virtual environment minimizes the attack surface area of the system and is therefore more secure.

7. Which of the following is *not* a function available through the Windows Server 2008 R2 Server Manager?

   a. Using the Event Viewer to analyze the application event log for errors

   b. Restarting a service

   c. Mounting an ISO image as a virtual drive in order to install new software

   d. Adding a new local user and assigning the local Administrators role

Case Projects

Case Project 1-1: Selecting a SQL Server 2012 Edition

Smith Medical Systems supplies hospitals throughout the Midwest. The chief marketing officer (CMO) has approved the purchase of a new customer relationship management system that will be used by the 20 members of the sales staff. The system requires a Microsoft SQL Server 2012 installation to host the application database. The CMO asks you to brief her on the differences between the main editions of SQL Server (as well as the different licensing options) and to provide a recommendation on both the edition and licensing option that you think is best suited to the company's needs. The CMO anticipates her sales force will grow by 25 percent per year, and she would like the option to develop a set of internal Business Intelligence tools in the future.

- Describe the key differences between the main editions of SQL Server 2012, and make a recommendation.
- Describe the licensing options available for the edition that you have recommended, and make a recommendation on the licensing option you think would work best for the company.
- How will the solution you have proposed be able to scale to meet the future needs of a growing user base and more advanced Business Intelligence capabilities?

Case Project 1-2: Troubleshooting SQL Server 2012

You work as a database administrator for TZW International Bank. A colleague who was recently hired to implement a Quality Assurance (QA) testing environment for the in-house application development team is experiencing some difficulties configuring the Windows Server 2008 R2 host and is unable to successfully test the SQL Server 2012 Setup Support Rules. He lacks experience with SQL Server 2012 and Windows Server 2008 R2 and has approached you for some guidance. Provide him with some suggestions for how to proceed that include the following:

- Information on accessing and searching online for Microsoft product documentation
- A basic strategy for diagnosing and resolving the problem

chapter 2

Deploying SQL Server 2012

After reading this chapter and completing the exercises, you will be able to:

- Describe the steps involved in planning a SQL Server 2012 installation

- Explain the different installation options for installing SQL Server 2012

- Create an instance of the SQL Server 2012 Enterprise Edition using the SQL Server Installation Wizard or the command prompt

- Analyze the system changes that take place during a SQL Server 2012 installation

- Manage an instance of SQL Server 2012 by performing repair and uninstall tasks

Planning is of paramount importance when undertaking a SQL Server 2012 installation. A single edition of SQL Server 2012 has a wide range of features that need to be tailored to each unique set of business requirements. It is important to understand the implications of each of these options on the software prerequisites, hardware and network design, and security model. To correctly implement the desired features, you must select the correct SQL Server parameters during the installation process. **SQL Server parameters** specify the type of setup (install, uninstall, or upgrade), features to install, and other configuration settings. To ensure a successful installation, you must also be familiar with the different tools at your disposal for installing, validating, and, if necessary, uninstalling or repairing a SQL Server 2012 deployment.

Chapter 1 provided an introduction to the main editions, licensing options, and minimum system requirements for a SQL Server 2012 installation. Chapter 2 builds on this foundation and provides you with the practical skills necessary to plan, deploy, validate, and troubleshoot a SQL Server 2012 installation. The first section of this chapter discusses the main steps involved in planning an installation. The second section covers the different installation tools and guides you through a SQL Server 2012 Enterprise Edition installation process using both the **installation wizard** (a Windows application that offers step-by-step installation guidance) and the command prompt. The **SQL Server Installation Center** provides a single point of access to the planning, installation, and maintenance wizards. The **command prompt** provides a means of installing SQL Server 2012 on the command line, or by referencing parameters in a text configuration file. Having validated these installations and analyzed the system changes that took place, you will then learn how to repair or uninstall an instance of SQL Server 2012 or one or more shared features.

Planning a SQL Server 2012 Installation

Understanding the relevant business requirements enables you to narrow down the choice of SQL Server 2012 editions and license models for a particular deployment. The option you select must not only satisfy current business needs, it must also have sufficient elasticity to scale to meet anticipated future demand. This section continues the planning and preparation process that started in Chapter 1, but at a more granular level.

Planning Steps

By gathering and analyzing the business requirements for a SQL Server deployment, you will attain the information that will form the foundation of the planning process. A project that delivers a solution that does not satisfy the business requirements has failed in its primary objective. The planning process often requires several iterations due to the interdependent nature of the different variables involved. Even after deployment of a SQL Server 2012 installation, there is always an element of fine-tuning; although you have the flexibility to adapt your SQL Server 2012 configuration postinstallation, you will save a lot of effort (and probably expense) later on if you make the up-front investment in undertaking a detailed planning exercise.

Having selected the SQL Server 2012 edition and license model, your next step is to break down the business requirements at a more detailed level. This enables you to identify which components and features within the selected edition are needed. Finally, hardware design and software requirements can be addressed that factor in system performance, availability, and recovery time objectives. Throughout this process, physical and logical security implications must be continually assessed. The SQL Server 2012 installation planning steps are illustrated in Figure 2-1.

Selection of Components and Features

Each instance of SQL Server 2012 must include the database engine at a minimum. This is the core service component in SQL Server 2012 that handles data storage, processing, and client access requests. The database engine hosts several **system databases**, created during the installation process, for storing system configuration information. The database engine also hosts one or more **user databases** that contain the data associated with a client application. In addition to the database engine, each edition of SQL Server 2012 has many optional components and features

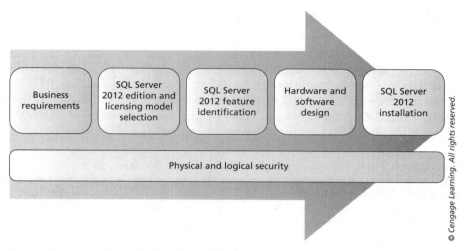

Figure 2-1 SQL Server 2012 installation planning steps

that you will need to choose from during the installation steps. These were reviewed in Activity 1-2 in Chapter 1, using the "Editions and Components of SQL Server 2012" product documentation from Books Online for SQL Server 2012.

It is good practice from a manageability, resource, and security standpoint to minimize the footprint of your SQL Server 2012 instance and only install the functionality you need. Your business requirements will help you understand which components to install; Analysis Services, Integration Services, and Reporting Services are all commonly selected options. **Analysis Services** provides a group of data mining and other analytical tools; **Integration Services** offers the capability to extract, transform, and load (ETL) data from external sources; and **Reporting Services** is a set of tools and services that enable you to create, deploy, and manage reports.

The practical activities in this book only address a stand-alone system, but if your production business application has a low tolerance for system downtime, you may need to select the AlwaysOn feature in SQL Server 2012. **AlwaysOn** is a high-availability and disaster recovery solution that significantly alters the design requirements of a deployment's physical infrastructure because it requires additional servers and storage devices that are connected over a network. AlwaysOn functionality consists of the Availability Groups (AG) and Failover Cluster Instance (FCI) and features. **Availability Groups (AG)** provide a failover environment consisting of a group of primary user databases with up to four replicas that will be used in the event the primary user database fails. **Failover Cluster Instance (FCI)** provides redundancy in the event of hardware or software failure on a SQL Server node. A failover cluster consists of redundant nodes that can be used to host the database instance should an error occur on the primary node.

Lastly, you also need to decide which management tools you need to install to perform database administration tasks. Each database instance includes a copy of the database engine (sqlservr.exe). Up to 50 instances of the database engine can run concurrently on a single SQL Server host. Each database server may have one default instance of SQL Server 2012 known as the **default instance**. If a client connects to the database server without specifying a named instance, it will be connected to the default instance. All other instances are known as **named instances**. Certain components, including Reporting Services and Analysis Services, are specific to each database instance and, if required, must be installed when installing an additional instance on a SQL Server host. Conversely, other components known as **shared features** are pooled between major versions of SQL Server and will only need to be installed once on a single server. Many management tools, such as Integration Services and Master Data Services, are shared features. **Master Data Services** provide a centralized means to manage and validate data. If you install multiple instances of SQL Server, you need to be aware of these dependencies and keep an accurate inventory. For further information, see the Microsoft Books Online for SQL Server 2012 topic "Work with Multiple Versions and Instances of SQL Server" (*http://msdn.microsoft.com/en-us/library/ms143694.aspx*).

Hardware Design and Software Requirements

Chapter 1 listed the minimum recommended hardware and software requirements for a new SQL Server 2012 installation. To provision appropriate hardware for the installation, you need to undertake a more detailed assessment, considering factors such as size and expected growth of the database, number of instances, usage, accessibility, and high-availability features that will determine hardware design criteria, such as disk arrangement and size, CPU, memory, network capacity, and the number of hosts. These factors are summarized in Table 2-1, with suggested questions that will help you determine the impact on your physical architecture.

Table 2-1 Factors determining hardware requirements for SQL Server 2012

Factor	Discovery question	Impact
Size and expected growth of the database	What are the anticipated sizes of the data and log files, and what is the expected rate of growth? What is the backup and recovery model (including retention periods)?	Disk space, off-site tape storage for backups
Number of database instances	Will the host support a single instance of SQL Server 2012, or will there be multiple instances running concurrently?	CPU, memory, disk space
Usage	Will the database be predominantly read-only or write intensive, or will it perform computationally intensive operations?	Disk speed and arrangement (e.g., dedicated disks), CPU, memory
Accessibility	How many users will the database support? How will the database be accessed?	Network capacity, protocol configuration
High-availability features	What are the design implications of the architecture selected for AlwaysOn high availability and disaster recovery?	Additional physical hosts, network capacity

© Cengage Learning

In addition to installing a new instance of SQL Server 2012, you can also upgrade from prior versions of SQL Server 2005, 2008, and 2008 R2 to SQL Server 2012. If you are upgrading an existing installation, you need to ensure that the upgrade path from the existing version to the chosen SQL Server 2012 edition is supported. This may involve installing additional service packs to the existing SQL Server instance or Windows operating system prior to the upgrade. It is also possible to perform an edition upgrade between different editions of SQL Server 2012. As part of the planning exercise in this chapter, you should check the latest information on supported upgrade paths by referring to the "Supported Version and Edition Upgrades" topic in the Books Online for SQL Server 2012 (*msdn.microsoft.com/en-us/library/ms143393.aspx*).

Security

Security considerations should be integrated throughout the planning process—beginning with establishing the business requirements; security is particularly important for a production installation. Start with an assessment of physical security; hardware should be maintained in a location with appropriate physical access controls. To satisfy disaster recovery needs, frequent backups should be created on media that is stored in a separate, secure physical location.

Logical security is the second dimension to consider. Microsoft recommends that SQL Server be installed on a dedicated server that is not shared with other Windows services such as a domain controller. With two critical applications running on a single server, it becomes difficult to isolate an administrative role to a single application and raises the likelihood that both services will be compromised in the event of a security breach. In earlier versions of SQL Server, the default account for running the individual Windows services associated with each component was the Network Service account. For SQL Server 2012, Microsoft recommends isolating the different SQL Server services by creating an individual account that is associated with each service with the minimum permission set for its designated role. Windows Server 2008 R2 improves the ease of managing multiple service accounts with the introduction of auto-managed local service accounts called **virtual accounts**. In Step 15 of Activity 2-1, you'll review the default virtual accounts that are created during the installation process and that are associated with each SQL Server service.

Installing SQL Server 2012

This section discusses SQL Server 2012's four installation options: the installation wizard, an attended or unattended installation from the command prompt, and SysPrep. Microsoft's SQL Server Installation Wizard allows you to install all required components in a single step rather than individually. It also provides the flexibility to modify an existing installation, for example to add new features to the installation. The activities in this chapter guide you through an attended installation using the installation wizard and then through a second installation using the command prompt. You will learn how to validate the installation by running a **SQL Server Features Discovery Report** in order to display the instances, tools, and features currently installed on the server. Note that sample databases are not included in the standard installation; you will be given installation instructions for these in a future chapter.

Installation Options

SQL Server 2012 can be installed in attended (interactive) or unattended (noninteractive) mode. An **attended installation** can be completed using either the installation wizard or the command prompt. An **unattended installation** of SQL Server 2012 can be completed either by using the command prompt combined with a configuration file and the quiet parameter (using the quiet parameter instructs the installer to complete the installation in quiet mode, which does not display any output in the user interface) or by using the SysPrep utility to create an image file for virtual deployments. The following list summarizes the different installation options:

- The SQL Server Installation Center provides an installation wizard to perform many of the necessary configuration functions, including installation and maintenance. The installation wizard is a Windows application that provides step-by-step guidance through the installation process.

- SQL Server 2012 can be installed from a command prompt by running setup.exe and specifying the SQL Server parameters and their settings as input parameters in attended mode. This approach may be more efficient for an experienced database administrator than the installation wizard, particularly when undertaking multiple installations that make use of a standardized template.

- The command prompt installation can be used with a quiet parameter and, optionally, a separate configuration file for completing unattended installations.

- SysPrep can be used to add a SQL Server installation as a template to the operating system build. SysPrep is a utility that allows the use of an operating system image as a template for rapid deployment of virtual systems; however, this topic is beyond the scope of this book.

Activity 2-1: Installing SQL Server 2012 Using the SQL Server Installation Wizard

Time Required: 120 minutes
Objective: Use the SQL Server Installation Wizard to install a new instance and the shared features of SQL Server 2012 on your test environment.

Description: In this activity, you will install an instance of SQL Server 2012 using the installation wizard, which you'll launch from within the SQL Server Installation Center. As a prerequisite to this activity, you need to have successfully completed the System Configuration Checker steps described in Activity 1-3 in Chapter 1. You need approximately 8 GB of free disk space on your local drive to complete this activity.

1. If necessary, start your computer and log on using an Administrator account. If you are using a virtual machine to host the installation, you should take a snapshot of the system.

2. Mount the installation image file as a virtual drive or insert the DVD into your DVD drive if using physical media. In Figure 2-2, SQLFULL_ENU is mounted on the E drive.

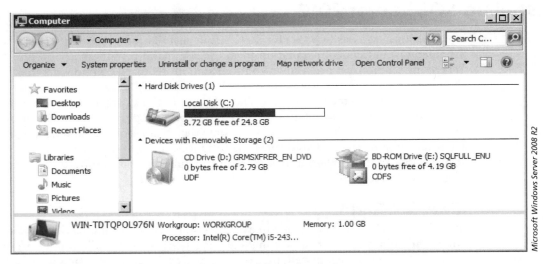

Figure 2-2 Windows Explorer displaying removable storage devices

3. Click the **Start** button, and then click **Computer**. Right-click the removable storage device that contains the installation media labeled SQLFULL_ENU, and then click **Open**. Launch the SQL Server Installation Center by double-clicking the **setup** application in the root folder. See Figure 2-3. Click the **Yes** button if prompted by the User Account Control dialog box.

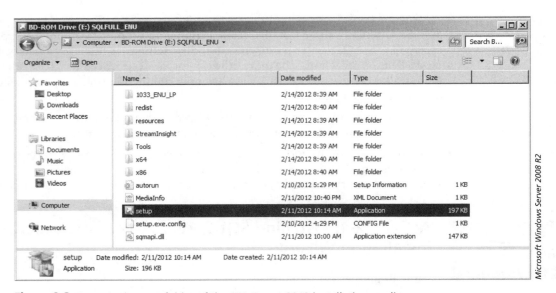

Figure 2-3 Setup in the root folder of the SQL Server 2012 installation media

4. In the SQL Server Installation Center window, click **Installation** in the left-hand navigation pane. Four submenus appear on the right side of the window; you can choose the type of installation you want to perform from the following options:

   • New SQL Server stand-alone installation or add features to an existing installation

   • New SQL Server failover cluster installation

- Add node to a SQL Server failover cluster
- Upgrade from SQL Server 2005, SQL Server 2008, or SQL Server 2008 R2

Click **New SQL Server stand-alone installation or add features to an existing installation**. See Figure 2-4.

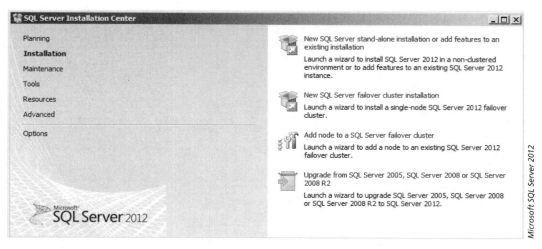

Figure 2-4 SQL Server Installation Center window

5. The SQL Server 2012 Setup Wizard for a new installation launches, and the Setup Support Rules window opens. Setup Support Rules runs a series of tests against the prerequisites for installing the SQL Server Setup support files. Click **Show Details** to view a detailed report and verify that all Setup Support Rules show a status of Passed. Review any warnings and follow the instructions given to correct any failures before proceeding to the next step. See Figure 2-5. Click **OK**.

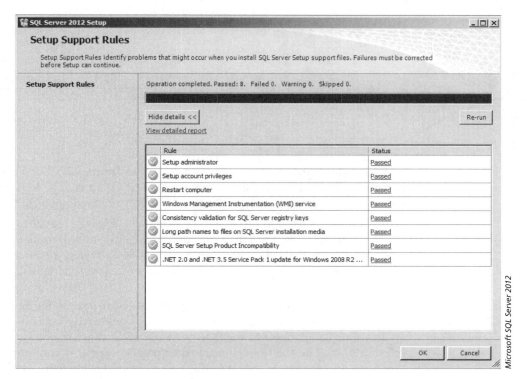

Figure 2-5 Setup Support Rules window

6. In the Product Key window, you need to either enter a product key for the relevant production edition of SQL Server 2012 or specify that you want to try a free edition such as Evaluation or Express. Select **Evaluation** from the Specify a free edition list box. See Figure 2-6. The SQL Server 2012 Evaluation license will be valid for 180 days. Click **Next**.

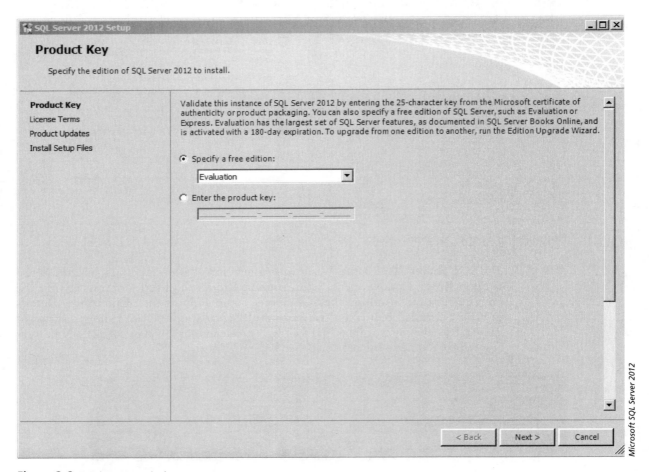

Figure 2-6 Product Key window

7. Read the Microsoft Evaluation Software License Terms. Click the **I accept the license terms** check box to select it. See Figure 2-7. Click **Next**. The SQL Server Installer checks and downloads any product updates before installing SQL Server 2012.

8. Setup Support Rules completes an additional check for potential problems that may occur when installing the setup support files. Click **Show Details** to view a detailed report and verify that all setup support rules passed. Review any warnings and follow the instructions given to correct any failures before proceeding to the next step. See Figure 2-8.

In Figure 2-8, a warning was generated by one of the Setup Support Rules because Windows Firewall was enabled. This is not necessarily a problem unless client applications will connect to the SQL Server 2012 instance remotely, in which case the relevant port(s) on the firewall need to be enabled to allow communication between the client and the server. Because this is a warning rather than a failure, it does not have to be corrected to move forward with the installation.

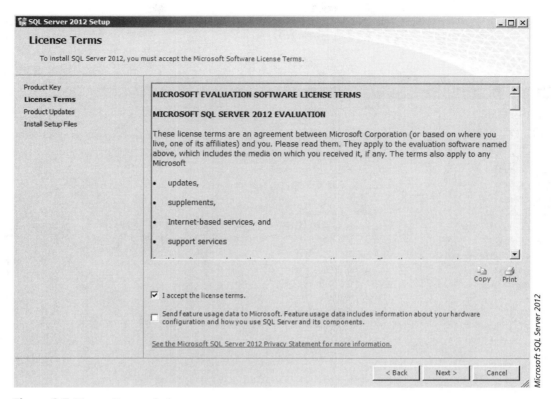

Figure 2-7 License Terms window

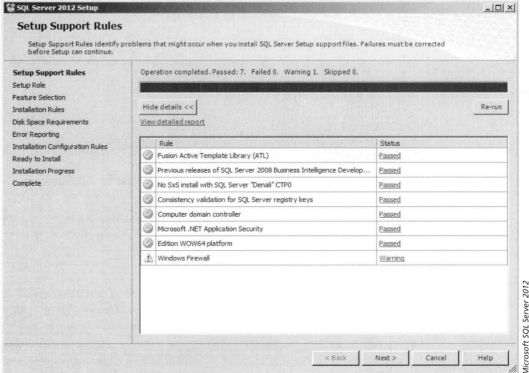

Figure 2-8 Setup Support Rules window

9. Click **Next**. In the Setup Role window, select the **SQL Server Feature Installation** option. See Figure 2-9.

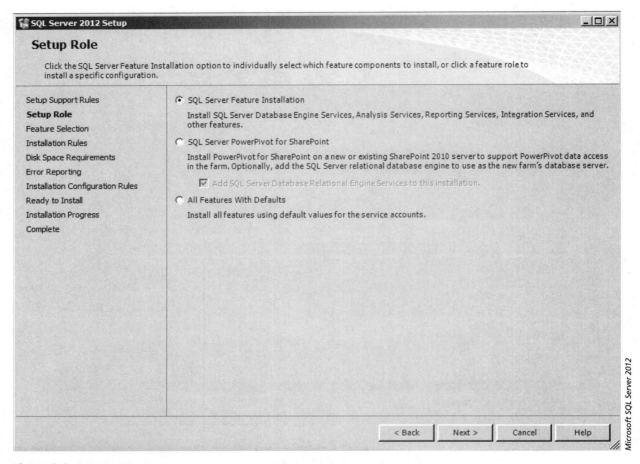

Figure 2-9 Setup Role window

10. Click **Next** to move to the window that allows you to select the individual features and components you want to install.

11. In the Feature Selection window, click the **Select All** button and keep the default Shared feature directory path. See Figure 2-10.

When an individual feature is highlighted in the Features pane, the two panes to the right of the window display a description of the feature along with installation prerequisites.

12. Click **Next**. The Installation Rules are a series of tests that check for any issues that may block the installation process. Click **Show Details**. Review all warnings and correct any failed rules before proceeding. See Figure 2-11.

13. Click **Next**. The Instance Configuration window allows you to choose either a Default instance or a Named instance. Each host can only support one default instance of SQL Server 2012. If a client establishes a remote connection specifying only the host address, it will be connected to the default instance. To connect to a named instance, the client must use both the host address and the instance name that it wants to

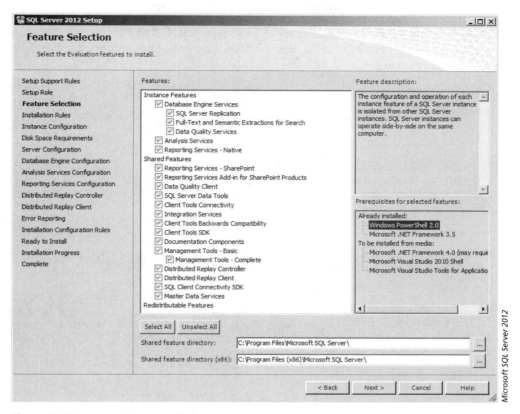

Figure 2-10 Feature Selection window

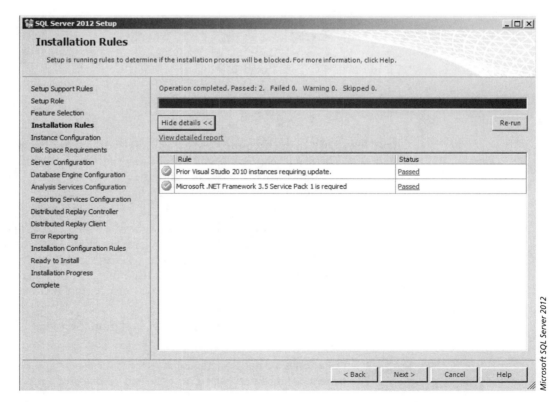

Figure 2-11 Installation Rules window

connect to in the connection string. Click the **Named instance** option, click in the **Named instance** text box, and type **SQLSERVERUA** as the named instance. Note that an instance name must be unique and must not conflict with a name already assigned. See Figure 2-12.

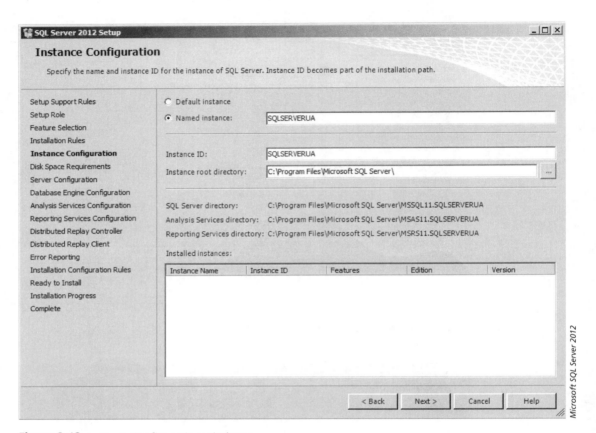

Figure 2-12 Instance Configuration window

14. Click **Next**. Disk Space Requirements check that you have sufficient disk space for installing the selected features. If you do not have sufficient disk space, you need to either allocate additional space by changing the path of the Shared feature directory to a different volume with more space or go back to the Feature Selection window and remove some features. See Figure 2-13.

15. Click **Next**. The Server Configuration window allows you to assign the accounts that will be used to run the individual services, set the service start-up behavior, and specify a default server collation. On the Service Accounts tab, keep the default service account settings. The virtual service accounts will be created automatically during the installation process. A separate service account will be created for each SQL Server service. See Figure 2-14.

16. On the Collation tab, keep the default Server Collation (SQL_Latin1_General_CP1_CI_AS). Click **Next**.

Collation is a database setting that specifies the character set, sort order behavior, and how characters are evaluated in comparison operations.

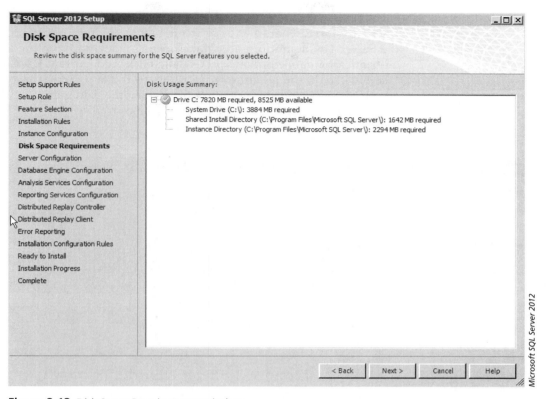

Figure 2-13 Disk Space Requirements window

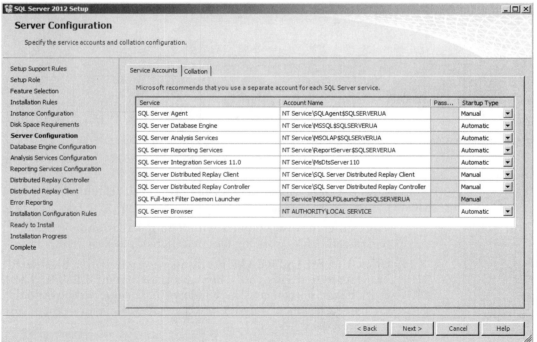

Figure 2-14 Server Configuration window

17. The database engine service handles data storage, processing, and access requests. There are three separate tabs in the database engine Configuration window. On the Server Configuration tab, which opens by default, keep the default **Windows authentication mode** option selected, and click **Add Current User**. This grants your Windows login the administrative rights to the SQL Server instance. Additional accounts can be added if necessary by clicking the **Add** button. In Figure 2-15, two accounts have been added as SQL Server administrators.

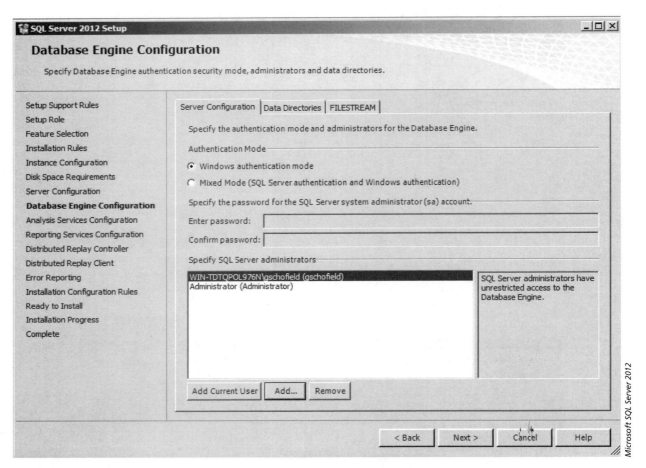

Figure 2-15 Server Configuration tab of the Database Engine Configuration window

18. Click the **Data Directories** tab, and review the default settings. See Figure 2-16.

    In a production environment, you might need to change these values if you will be using different disk volumes within an installation. For example, it is common to separate data files from log files on different physical disks.

19. Click the **FILESTREAM** tab, and then click the **Enable FILESTREAM for Transact-SQL access** check box and the **Enable FILESTREAM for file I/O** access check box to select them. The Windows share name text box should be populated with the named instance SQLSERVERUA that was added in the Instance Configuration step. See Figure 2-17.

20. Click **Next**. On the Server Configuration tab, keep the default **Server Mode** option selected. The server mode specifies the storage engine that Analysis Services uses to query data. Click the **Add Current User** button to add your user account to the

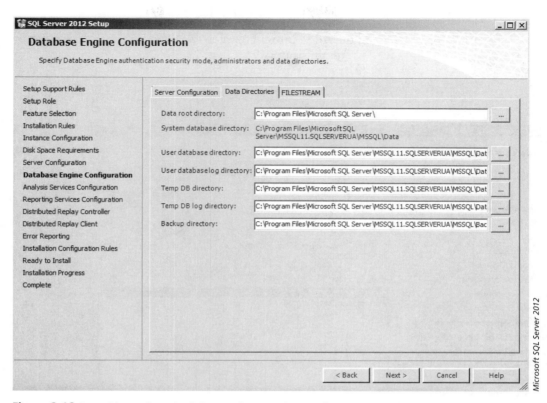

Figure 2-16 Data Directories tab of the Database Engine Configuration window

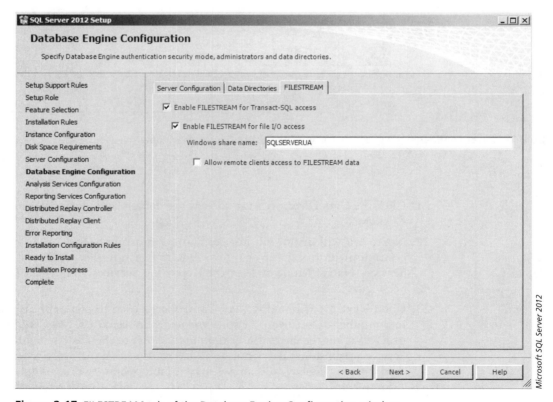

Figure 2-17 FILESTREAM tab of the Database Engine Configuration window

Administrators group. Additional users can be added to the Administrators group by clicking the **Add** button. Figure 2-18 shows an example where two users have been added as Administrators.

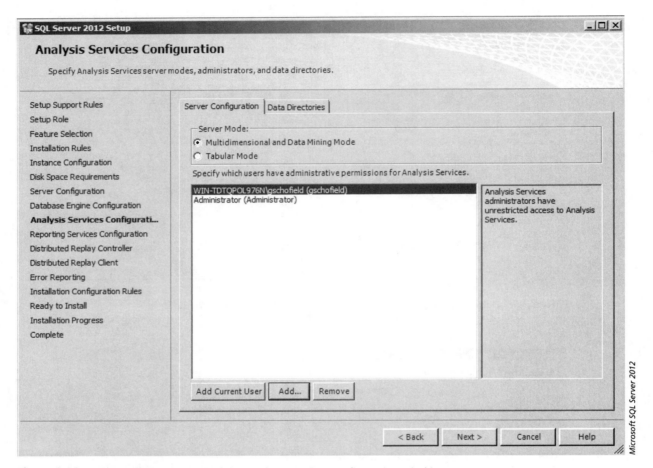

Figure 2-18 Server Configuration tab of the Analysis Services Configuration window

21. Click the **Data Directories** tab to view the default settings. Do not make any changes. Click **Next**.

22. Next, you will install but not configure Reporting Services; you will complete the configuration in a later chapter. Click the **Install only** options for the **Reporting Services Native Mode** and for the **Reporting Services SharePoint Integrated Mode**. See Figure 2-19.

23. Click **Next**. Distributed Replay Controller is used to test application compatibility in a number of hardware or software upgrade scenarios. Click **Add Current User** in order to grant the current user unlimited access to the Distributed Replay Controller Services. Additional users can be added to the Administrators group by clicking the **Add** button. Figure 2-20 shows an example where two users have been added as Administrators.

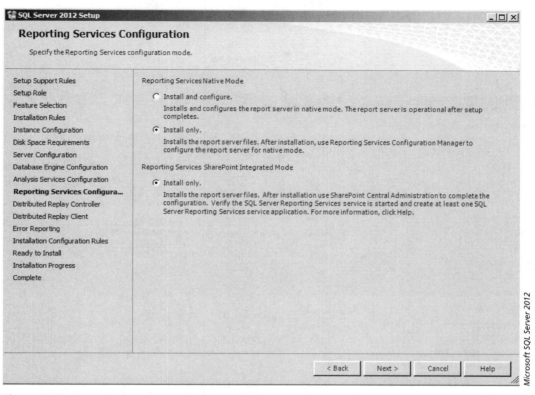

Figure 2-19 Reporting Services Configuration window

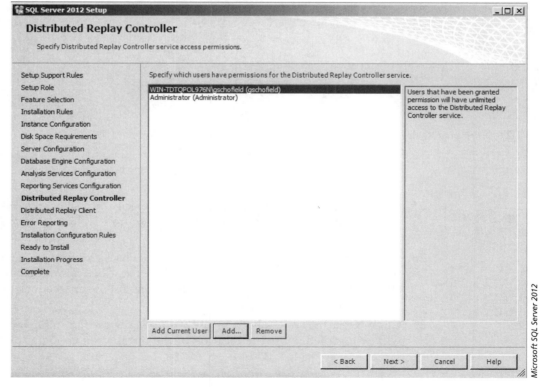

Figure 2-20 Distributed Replay Controller window

24. Click **Next**. In the Distributed Replay Client window, keep the default settings. See Figure 2-21.

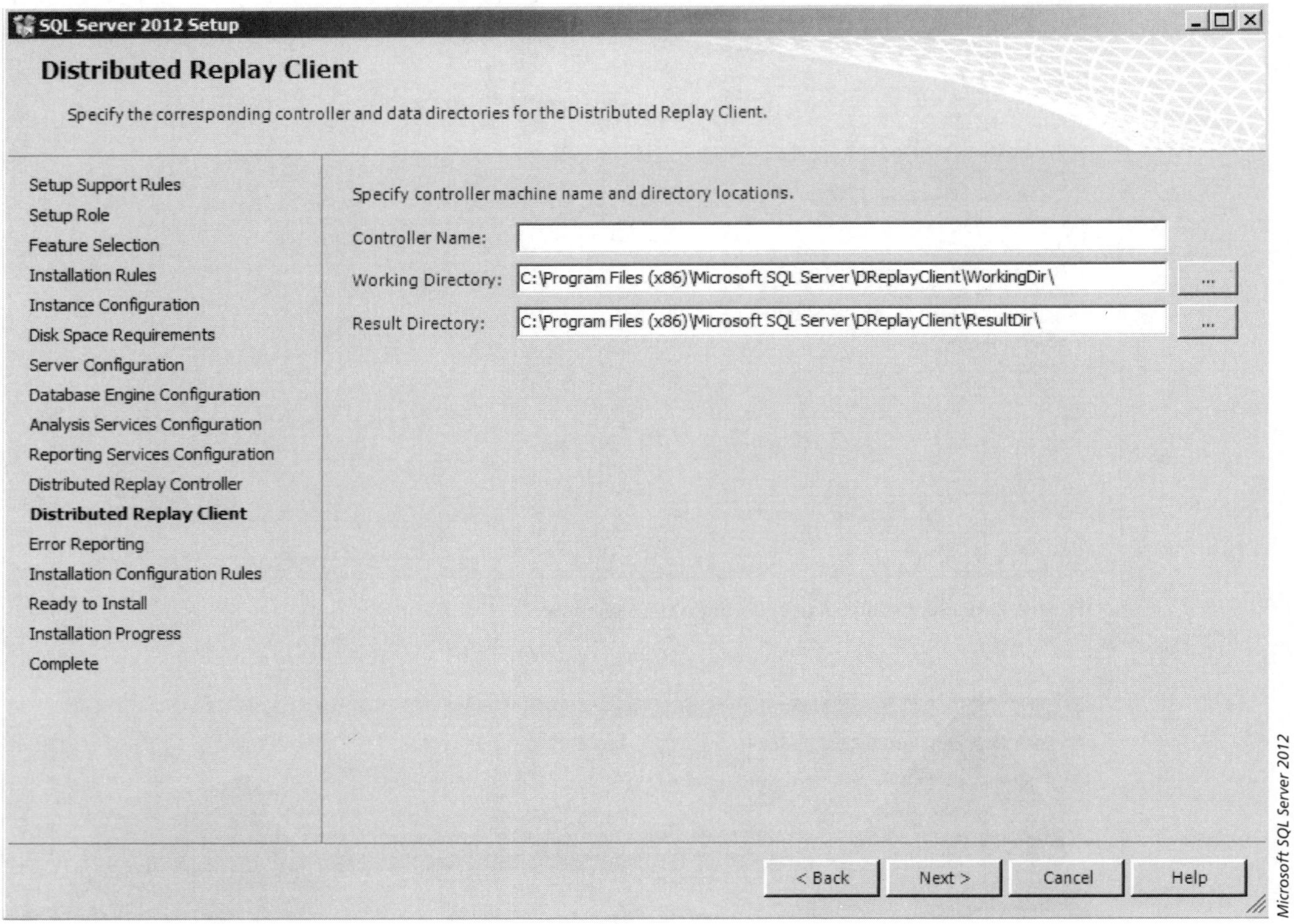

Figure 2-21 Distributed Replay Client window

25. Click **Next**. In the Error Reporting window, specify by clicking the check box whether you want to report errors securely to Microsoft to enable them to improve future releases of the product. See Figure 2-22.

26. Click **Next**. Installation Configuration Rules checks a set of prerequisites to ensure that the installation process will not be blocked. Click **Show Details** and verify that all rules have passed. Review any warnings and follow instructions to correct failures before proceeding. See Figure 2-23.

27. Click **Next**. In the Ready to Install window, review the summary of features that will be installed. Note the location of the installation configuration file for future

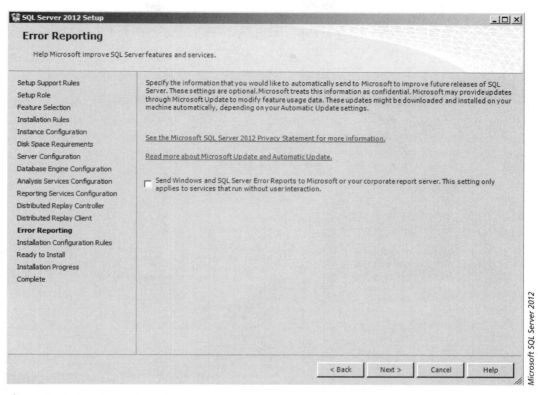

Figure 2-22 Error Reporting window

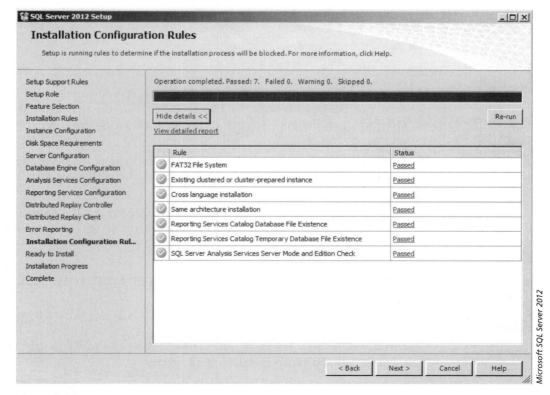

Figure 2-23 Installation Configuration Rules window

reference. See Figure 2-24. The ConfigurationFile.ini contains the individual parameter settings required for an unattended install using the command-line interface.

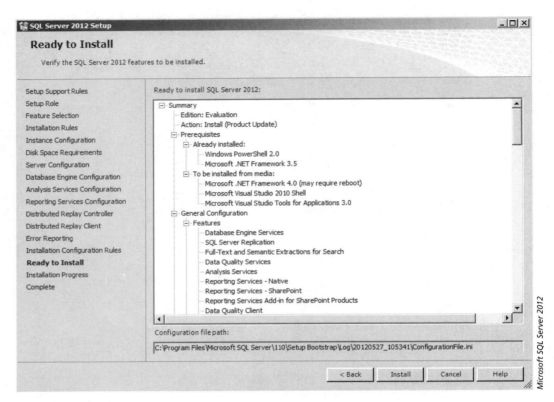

Figure 2-24 Ready to Install window

28. Click **Install**. During installation, a blue progress scroll bar provides you with the status of the installation. See Figure 2-25. Wait for the installation to complete. Depending on the performance of the host, the installation process could take over an hour to complete.

29. Once your installation successfully completes, review the installation status of each feature and the summary log file. If prompted, click **OK** to restart your computer. See Figure 2-26.

30. You have now successfully completed a SQL Server 2012 installation using the wizard. If you are using a virtual machine to host SQL Server, you should take a snapshot of your system.

Activity 2-2: Running the SQL Server Features Discovery Report

Time Required: 10 minutes
Objective: Use the SQL Server Features Discovery Report to display the SQL Server 2012 tools and features currently installed on the server.

Description: This activity shows you how to run the SQL Server Features Discovery Report from the Tools menu of the SQL Server Installation Center in order to display the tools and features currently installed on the local server.

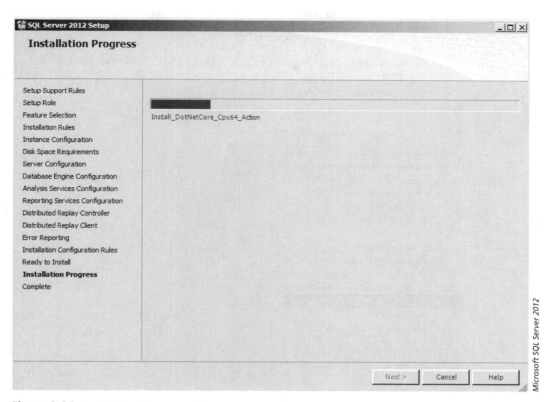

Figure 2-25 Installation Progress window

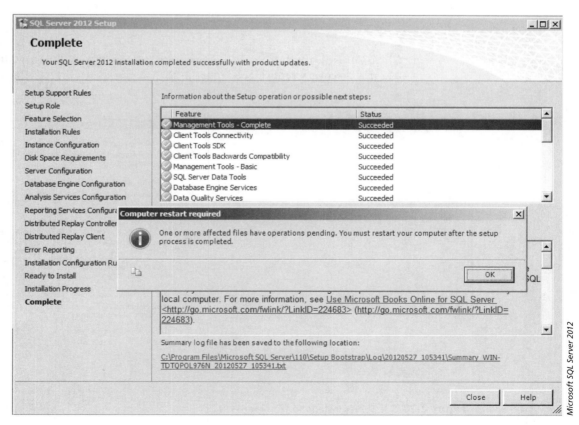

Figure 2-26 Installation complete

1. If necessary, start your computer and log on.

2. To launch the SQL Server Installation Center, click the **Start** button, point to **All Programs,** click **Microsoft SQL Server 2012,** click **Configuration Tools,** and then click **SQL Server Installation Center (64-bit).** See Figure 2-27. Click **Yes** if prompted by the User Account Control dialog box.

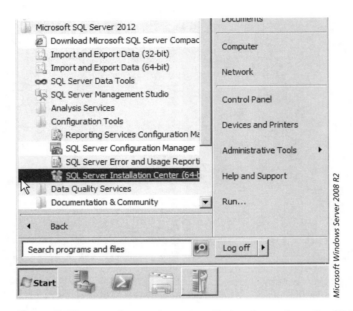

Figure 2-27 Open the SQL Server Installation Center from the All Programs menu

3. Click **Tools** in the left-hand navigation pane, and then click **Installed SQL Server features discovery report.** See Figure 2-28.

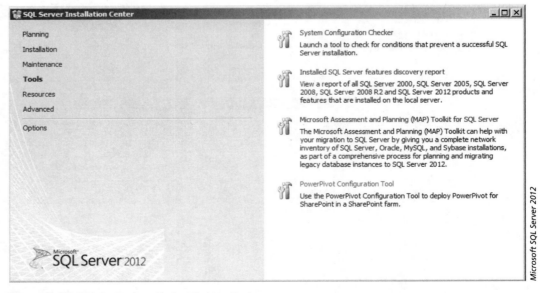

Figure 2-28 SQL Server Installation Center–Tools

4. After a few seconds, a Web browser launches displaying the Discovery Report. For shared features, the report displays the product, installed features, edition, language, clustered flag, and version. For features specific to an instance, the instance name and ID are also displayed. See Figure 2-29.

Microsoft SQL Server 2012 Setup Discovery Report

Product	Instance	Instance ID	Feature	Language	Edition	Version	Clustered
Microsoft SQL Server 2012	SQLSERVERUA	MSSQL11.SQLSERVERUA	Database Engine Services	1033	Enterprise Evaluation Edition	11.0.2100.60	No
Microsoft SQL Server 2012	SQLSERVERUA	MSSQL11.SQLSERVERUA	SQL Server Replication	1033	Enterprise Evaluation Edition	11.0.2100.60	No
Microsoft SQL Server 2012	SQLSERVERUA	MSSQL11.SQLSERVERUA	Full-Text and Semantic Extractions for Search	1033	Enterprise Evaluation Edition	11.0.2100.60	No
Microsoft SQL Server 2012	SQLSERVERUA	MSSQL11.SQLSERVERUA	Data Quality Services	1033	Enterprise Evaluation Edition	11.0.2100.60	No
Microsoft SQL Server 2012	SQLSERVERUA	MSAS11.SQLSERVERUA	Analysis Services	1033	Enterprise Evaluation Edition	11.0.2100.60	No
Microsoft SQL Server 2012	SQLSERVERUA	MSRS11.SQLSERVERUA	Reporting Services - Native	1033	Enterprise Evaluation Edition	11.0.2100.60	No
Microsoft SQL Server 2012			Management Tools - Basic	1033	Enterprise Evaluation Edition	11.0.2100.60	No
Microsoft SQL Server 2012			Management Tools - Complete	1033	Enterprise Evaluation Edition	11.0.2100.60	No
Microsoft SQL Server 2012			Client Tools Connectivity	1033	Enterprise Evaluation Edition	11.0.2100.60	No
Microsoft SQL Server 2012			Client Tools Backwards Compatibility	1033	Enterprise Evaluation Edition	11.0.2100.60	No
Microsoft SQL Server 2012			Client Tools SDK	1033	Enterprise Evaluation Edition	11.0.2100.60	No
Microsoft SQL Server 2012			Integration Services	1033	Enterprise Evaluation Edition	11.0.2100.60	No
Microsoft SQL Server 2012			Reporting Services - SharePoint			11.0.2100.60	No

Figure 2-29 Microsoft SQL Server 2012 Setup Discovery Report

Microsoft SQL Server 2012

5. When you are finished, close your Web browser, and close the SQL Server Installation Center by clicking the **X** icon in the upper-right corner of both windows.

Activity 2-3: Reviewing System Changes

Time Required: 30 minutes
Objective: Review system changes to network settings, services, and the Registry. Monitor the performance and resource utilization of the system.

Description: In this activity, you will learn how to review the system changes made during the SQL Server 2012 installation process. You'll use **SQL Server Configuration Manager** to review the server and client network configuration and obtain status of the SQL Server services. You will use the **Registry Editor**, a Windows management utility (regedit.exe), to review changes to the Registry. The Windows Registry stores configuration values, known as **Registry keys,** on behalf of installed software applications. Lastly, you will check resource utilization using Resource Monitor and Performance Monitor. **Resource Monitor** is a Windows management utility (resmon.exe) that was vastly improved in the Windows 7 and Windows Server 2008 R2 operating system release. It now enables you to monitor hardware resource utilization in real time using five individual tabs: Overview, CPU, Memory, Disk, and Network. **Performance Monitor** is a utility that enables you to view different performance attributes of the host server by viewing data in real time or by replaying data from a log.

1. If necessary, start your computer and log on.

2. To launch SQL Server Configuration Manager, click the **Start** button, point to **All Programs**, click **Microsoft SQL Server 2012**, click **Configuration Tools**, and then click **SQL Server Configuration Manager**. See Figure 2-30. Note that because you are only viewing rather than changing settings, you do not need to select Run as administrator when prompted by the User Access Control dialog box.

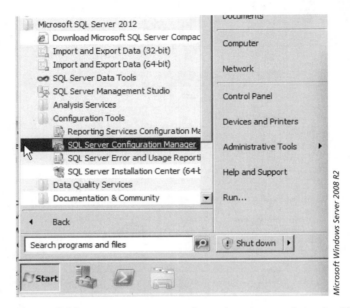

Figure 2-30 Open SQL Server Configuration Manager from the All Programs menu

3. In the SQL Server Configuration Manager window, click **SQL Server Services** in the left-hand navigation pane. Review the list of services in the right pane. The SQL Server service for the instance that you created in Activity 2-1 is the core service that runs the database engine. Verify that the state of this service is "Running" (also shown by a green triangular icon next to the service name).

You can right-click on any service name to view the current status, to stop or start the service, and to view the properties that are currently configured.

4. Expand SQL Server Network Configuration by clicking the **+** icon in the left-hand navigation pane. See Figure 2-31.

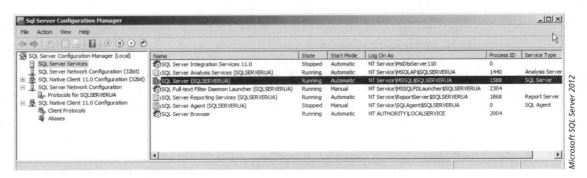

Figure 2-31 SQL Server Configuration Manager–SQL Server Services

5. View the enabled network protocols for the SQLSERVERUA instance by clicking **Protocols for SQLSERVERUA**. See Figure 2-32.

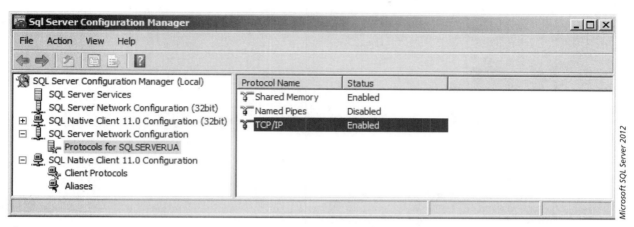

Figure 2-32 SQL Server Configuration Manager–SQL Server Network Configuration

6. Click **SQL Native Client 11.0 Configuration** in the left-hand navigation pane and double-click **Client Protocols**. View the enabled network protocols for client applications installed on the server. Right-click **TCP/IP**, and then click **Properties**. Note that the default port for client connections is 1433.

7. To launch the Registry Editor, click the **Start** button, click **Run**, click in the **Open** text box, and type **regedit**. See Figure 2-33. Click **OK** and click **Yes** if prompted by the User Account Control dialog box.

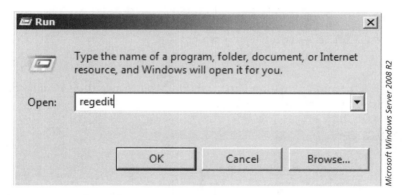

Figure 2-33 Launch the Registry Editor using the *regedit* command

8. Navigate through the tree view in the left-hand navigation pane to **Computer \HKEY_LOCAL_MACHINE\SYSTEM\CurrentControlSet\Services \SQLAgent$SQLSERVERUA**. See Figure 2-34.

9. SQL Server Agent is the service that enables jobs to be scheduled and monitors activity. Browse through the Registry settings that are associated with the SQL Server Agent. See Figure 2-35.

10. Click the **Start** button, click **Run**, click in the **Open** text box, and type **Perfmon** to open the Performance Monitor. Click **OK**.

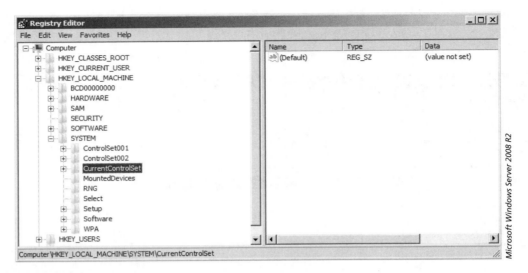

Figure 2-34 Navigate using the Registry Editor

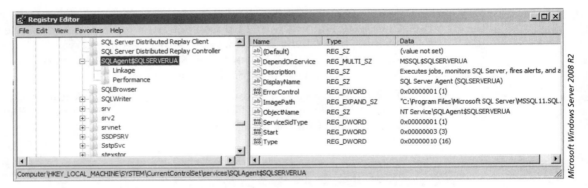

Figure 2-35 View the SQL Server Agent Registry settings

11. In the left-hand navigation pane, expand Monitoring Tools by clicking the **+** icon and then clicking **Performance Monitor**. See Figure 2-36.

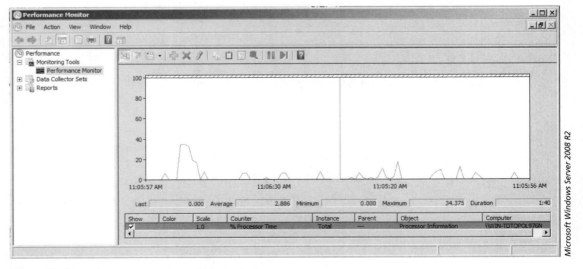

Figure 2-36 Performance Monitor window

By default, Performance Monitor displays CPU usage, although you can add counters by clicking the green **+** icon on the toolbar to add a new counter (e.g., Memory). To remove an existing counter, click the red **X** icon on the toolbar.

12. Launch Resource Monitor by clicking the **Start** button, clicking **Run**, clicking in the **Open** text box, and then typing **Resmon**. Click **OK**. See Figure 2-37.

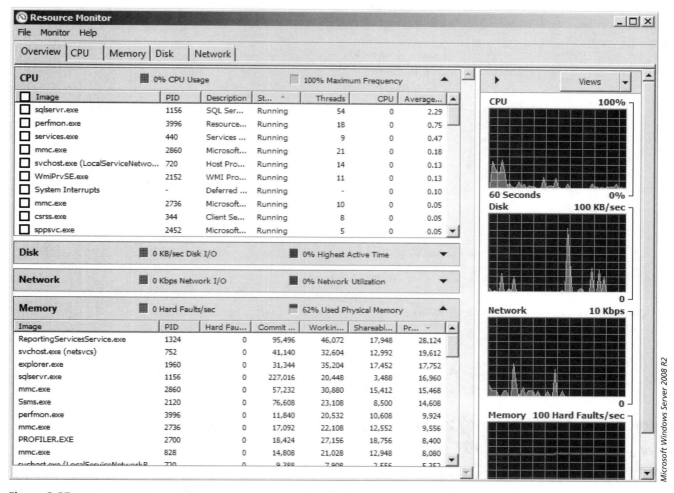

Figure 2-37 Resource Monitor window

13. In the upper CPU grid, sort the grid by clicking on the **Image** column. Scroll down and click the check box next to **sqlservr.exe**. You are now able to view the CPU, disk, network, and memory related to your SQL Server instance for anomalies.

14. Click the **Start** button, and then click **Computer** from the Start menu. Click in the **Navigation** text box, and then type **C:\Program Files\Microsoft SQL Server**. Here you can review the directory structure that was created when you installed SQL Server 2012. The folders 80, 90, 100, and 110 correspond to shared features and components associated with each major version of SQL Server. 110 is the version that corresponds to SQL Server 2012. At the same level, you will see a number of folders ending in an instance name. These correspond to the application data associated with each nonshared component that was installed for the instance. There were three non-shared components installed in the following example for a single instance: Database engine (MSSQL11.SQLSERVERUA), Reporting Services (MSRS11.SQLSERVERUA), and Analysis Services (MSAS11. SQLSERVERUA). See Figure 2-38.

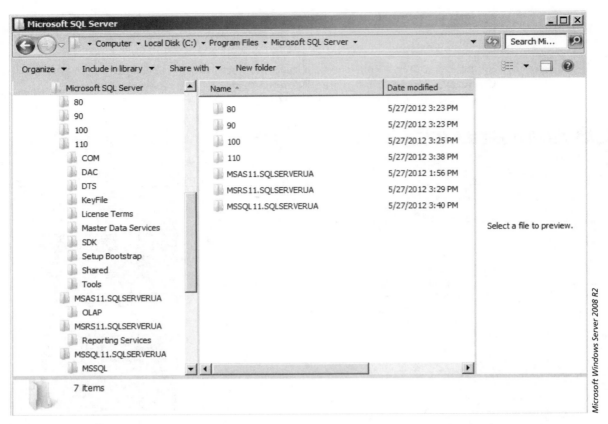

Figure 2-38 SQL Server physical folder structure

15. Close the windows that you opened during this activity by clicking the **X** in the upper-right corner of each window.

Activity 2-4: Installing SQL Server 2012 Using the Command Prompt

Time Required: 60 minutes
Objective: Undertake an installation of the SQL Server 2012 by running setup.exe from the command prompt.

Description: This activity guides you through the steps necessary to install a second named instance, SQLSERVERUA2, by running setup.exe from the command prompt. For simplicity, this instance will only include the database engine that represents the minimum feature set for completing a new SQL Server 2012 Enterprise Edition install. On completion of the activity, you should understand how to use the SQL Server parameters to tailor the features to meet your specific business requirements. The same set of features can be installed using the command prompt installation as with the SQL Server Installation Wizard. Because you will only be installing the database engine, and not any of the shared features, you will only need approximately 1 GB of free disk space on your local drive to complete this activity.

1. If necessary, start your computer and log on using an Administrator account.

2. To open a Web browser, click the **Start** button, point to **All Programs**, and then click **Internet Explorer**. See Figure 2-39.

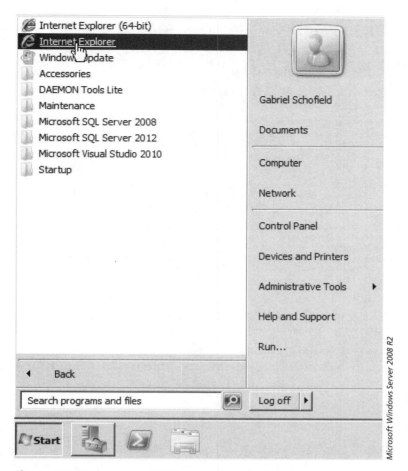

Microsoft Windows Server 2008 R2

Figure 2-39 Open Internet Explorer from the All Programs menu

3. Click in the **Address bar**, and type the following URL: **msdn.microsoft.com/library** to access the MSDN Library. In the Search MSDN with Bing box in the upper-left corner of the page, type **SQL Server 2012 Command Prompt** and click the **Search** icon. In the search results, click the top link, **Install SQL Server 2012 from the Command Prompt**, to open the Books Online for SQL Server 2012 "Install SQL Server 2012 from the Command Prompt" topic. See Figure 2-40.

   This page lists the SQL Server parameters that are supported when creating a command-line script. For each component, certain parameters are required—while others are optional. In the list of SQL Server components, focus in particular on the SQL Server Setup Control and SQL Server Database Engine components. These parameters can be entered as a list separated by spaces on the command prompt or by adding them to a configuration .ini file and referencing the location of this file from the command line.

4. Mount the installation image file as a virtual drive or insert the DVD into your DVD drive if using physical media. Click the **Start** button and then click **Computer** from the Start menu. Note the drive letter of the removable storage with the mounted installation media. In Figure 2-41, SQLFULL_ENU is mounted on the E drive.

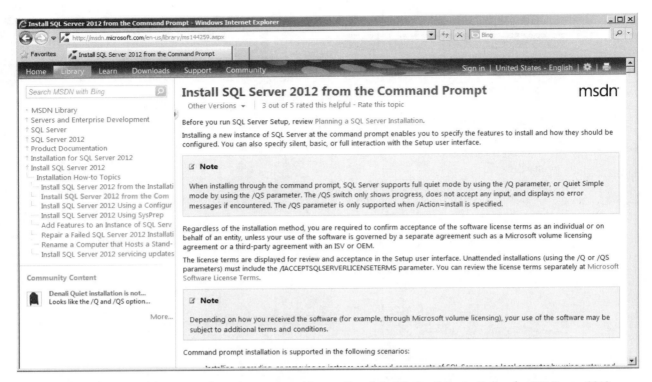

Figure 2-40 "Install SQL Server 2012 from the Command Prompt" topic in Microsoft Books Online for SQL Server 2012

Source: Microsoft Internet Explorer

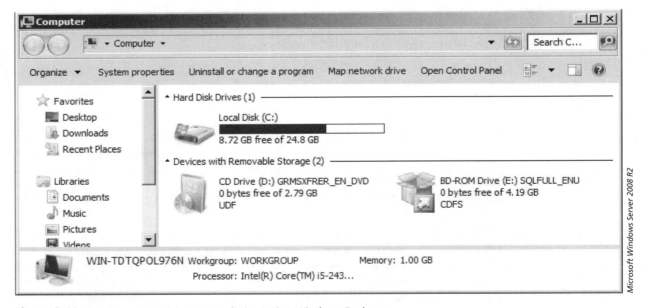

Figure 2-41 View the removable storage devices using Windows Explorer

5. Click the **Start** button, and from the Start menu click **Run**. In the Open text box, type **cmd**. See Figure 2-42.

6. Click **OK** to launch the command-line prompt (*C:\Windows\System32\cmd.exe*). At the command prompt, type the **drive letter** that you noted in Step 4 followed by **:** and then press the **Enter** key.

> **E:**

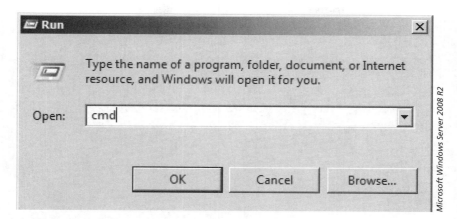

Figure 2-42 Open a Command Prompt window

7. Type **whoami** at the command prompt, and then press the **Enter** key to find the domain or computer name and username of the Windows Administrator account that you are using.

```
E:\> whoami
```

8. Type the SQL Server command-line application name **setup.exe** followed by the SQL Server Setup Control and SQL Server Database Engine **parameters** and then press **Enter.** Note that depending on your screen buffer width setting, the line may wrap onto additional lines in the Command Prompt window. You may find it easier to prepare this command using a text editor and then copy and paste it into your command prompt.

```
E:\> setup.exe /ACTION=INSTALL /Q /FEATURES=SQLEngine
/INSTANCENAME=SQLSERVERUA2 /SQLSYSADMINACCOUNTS=<Computer
Name>\<UserName> /IACCEPTSQLSERVERLICENSETERMS
```

The parameters instruct the SQL Server Installer application setup.exe to install a new named instance of the database engine called SQLSERVERUA2 in quiet mode. Quiet mode does not display any output in the user interface and is intended for unattended installations. Microsoft requires you to include the parameter /IACCEPT-SQLSERVERLICENSETERMS in order to accept license terms and conditions for quiet mode installations. You will need to replace <ComputerName>\<UserName> with the output of the whoami command. This account will be added to the SQL System Administrators group, which will enable you to manage the installation once setup is complete. In Figure 2-43, win-tdtqpo1976n is the computer name and gschofield is the username of the administrator's account.

Figure 2-43 Run the SQL Server Installer application setup.exe from the command prompt

9. Click **Yes** if prompted by the User Account Control dialog box.

10. A setup.exe console window appears while the installation program is running. See Figure 2-44.

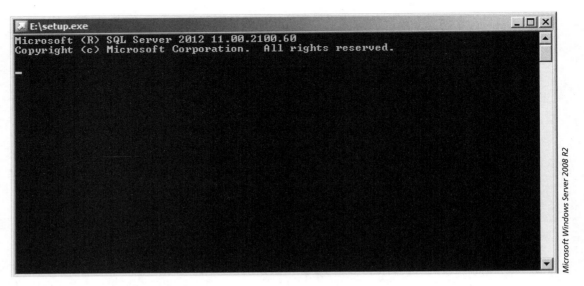

Figure 2-44 SQL Server Installer console

Once the installation process is complete, this window will automatically close. Because quiet mode was selected using the /Q parameter, no other dialog boxes will appear during setup. You can change this behavior to display progress by using either the /QS parameter, which will install in quiet simple mode and display progress messages, or the /INDICATEPROGRESS parameter, which will send the log output directly into the console.

11. Click the **Start** button and then click **Computer** from the Start menu. Click in the **Navigation** text box, type **C:\Program Files\Microsoft SQL Server\110\Setup Bootstrap\Log** and then press the **Enter** key. This opens the root folder location of the SQL Server Setup logs. Double-click the **Summary** document to view a summary of the installation that you performed. At the start of the file, you will see the Final result, which is either *Passed* or *Failed*. See Figure 2-45.

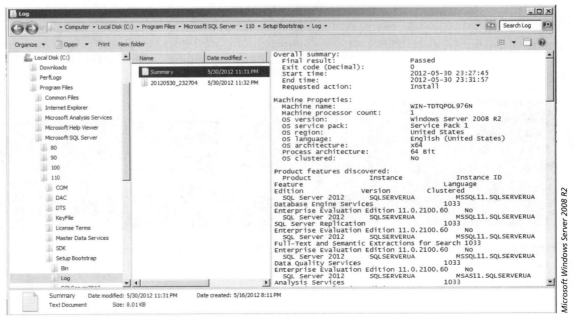

Figure 2-45 SQL Server Installer Log window

In the event that your installation failed, you will need to scroll to the bottom of the file and review the Rules with failures section and correct any errors before attempting the installation again. Common reasons for failure include incorrectly specified parameters or rules failing during the prerequisites checks. The subfolders contain detailed setup logs from the installation.

12. Having used the command-line prompt to complete a second installation of SQL Server 2012, you should now review the steps outlined in Activities 2-2 and 2-3 to validate your install and check the system changes.

Repairing or Uninstalling an Existing SQL Server 2012 Installation

This section explains how to repair or uninstall an instance or features of SQL Server 2012, and then you will undertake these two activities using a wizard.

Repair

Corrupt or missing application files and Registry settings, or bad configuration parameter values, may cause a SQL Server 2012 instance to fail to start. SQL Server 2012 stores the majority of configuration values within one of the system databases that was created automatically during installation. The Registry also contains a few important configuration values, such as the authentication mode, network settings, and paths to the application directories. You can repair a successfully installed instance or a failed upgrade of SQL Server 2012 from the Maintenance menu of the SQL Server 2012 Installation Center. The repair operation performs a number of steps, including the following:

- Missing or invalid configuration values are replaced with the system defaults
- Missing or corrupt application files are replaced
- Missing or corrupt Registry keys are replaced

Uninstall

Before uninstalling a SQL Server 2012 instance or making changes to installed features, make sure that you have taken a full backup of all production user databases. Under normal circumstances, you should always use functionality provided by the Uninstall or Change a Program feature that can be accessed from the Windows Server 2008 R2 Control Panel. Attempting to delete files, shortcuts, services, or Registry keys directly may result in undesirable system behavior or an unrecoverable error state. You can choose to uninstall an individual instance and associated features or the shared SQL Server features on the host. If you need to uninstall multiple instances, you will need to perform the operation multiple times for each instance that you want to remove. Be careful when uninstalling an instance that you do not inadvertently remove shared features on the server if they are still needed. Step 6 of Activity 2-6 addresses this issue in detail.

Activity 2-5: Repairing a SQL Server 2012 Installation

Time Required: 30 minutes
Objective: Use the SQL Server Installation Wizard to repair an instance or the shared features of a SQL Server 2012 installation.

Description: This activity guides you through the steps necessary to repair a SQL Server 2012 installation using the Maintenance function in the SQL Server Installation Wizard.

1. If necessary, start your computer and log on using an Administrator account. If you are using a virtual machine to host the installation, you should take a snapshot of the system.

2. Mount the installation image file as a virtual drive or insert the DVD into your DVD drive if using physical media.

3. Click the **Start** button, and from the Start menu click **Run.** In the Open text box, type **E:\setup.exe** and then click **OK** to open the SQL Server Installation Center. Note that you might need to change the drive letter to correspond with the drive letter of the removable device on which SQLFULL_ENU is mounted. Click the **Yes** button if the User Account Control dialog box opens.

4. In the SQL Server Installation Center, click **Maintenance**. See Figure 2-46.

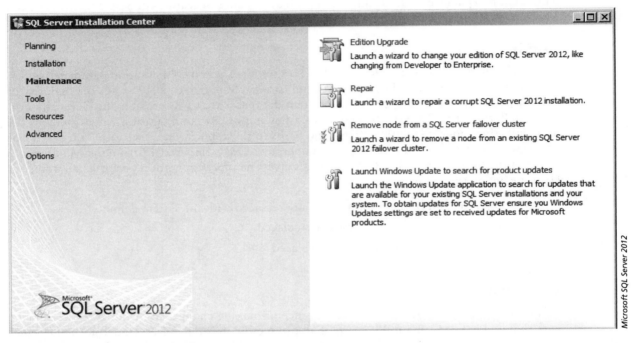

Figure 2-46 SQL Server Installation Center–Maintenance window

5. Click **Repair** in the right-hand pane.

6. In the Setup Support Rules window, verify that all tests have passed. Review any warnings, and follow the instructions given to correct any failures before proceeding to the next step. Click **OK.**

7. A second Setup Support Rules window appears. Verify that all tests have passed, and then click **Next.**

8. Select **SQLSERVERUA2** from the list box as the instance of SQL Server to repair. See Figure 2-47.

9. Click **Next.** In the Repair Rules window, verify that all tests have passed. Review any warnings, and follow the instructions given to correct any failures before proceeding to the next step. Click **Next.**

10. In the Ready to Repair window, review the set of features to be repaired. See Figure 2-48.

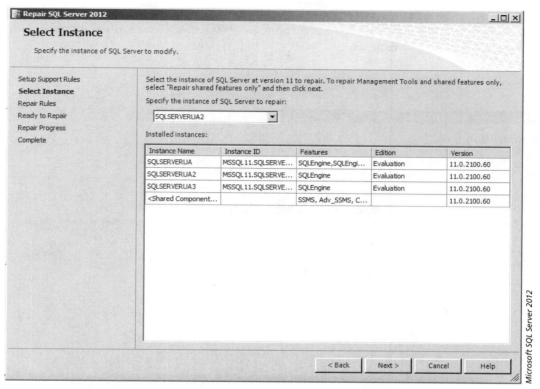

Figure 2-47 Repair SQL Server 2012–Select Instance window

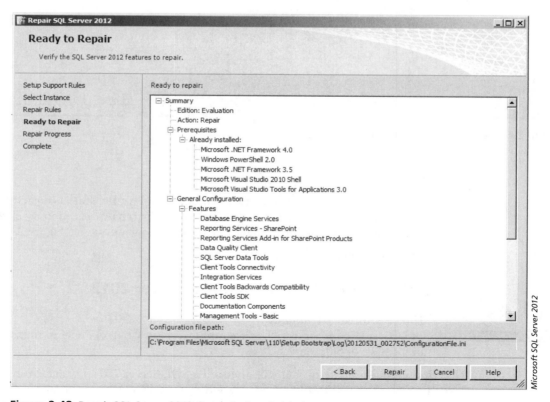

Figure 2-48 Repair SQL Server 2012–Ready to Repair window

11. Click **Repair**. During Repair, a blue progress scroll bar provides you with the status of the repair. See Figure 2-49. Wait for the repair to complete. This will take several minutes.

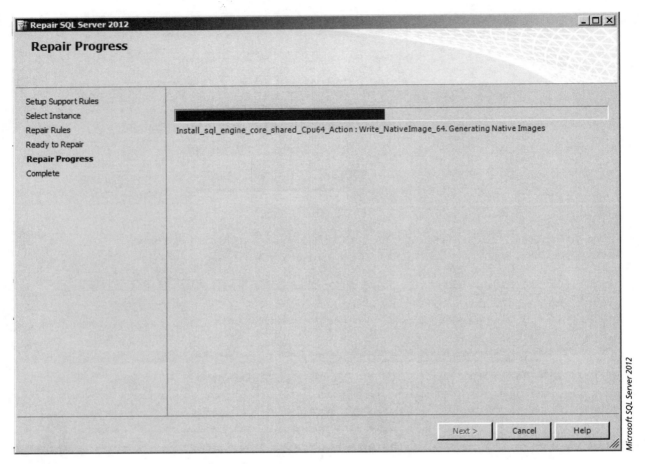

Figure 2-49 Repair SQL Server 2012–Repair Progress window

12. Once the repair is complete, a window displays the status of each feature that was repaired. You can review a detailed log of the repair operation by clicking the link to the **Summary log file** in the lower pane of the window. See Figure 2-50.

13. Click **Close**.

Activity 2-6: Uninstalling SQL Server 2012

Time Required: 30 minutes

Objective: Use the Uninstall a Program feature in Control Panel to uninstall features or an instance of SQL Server 2012.

Description: In this activity, you will uninstall a SQL Server 2012 instance using the Uninstall a Program feature in Control Panel. In a production environment, make sure that you have taken a full backup of all databases before performing any uninstall operation. Database backup is covered in Chapter 8.

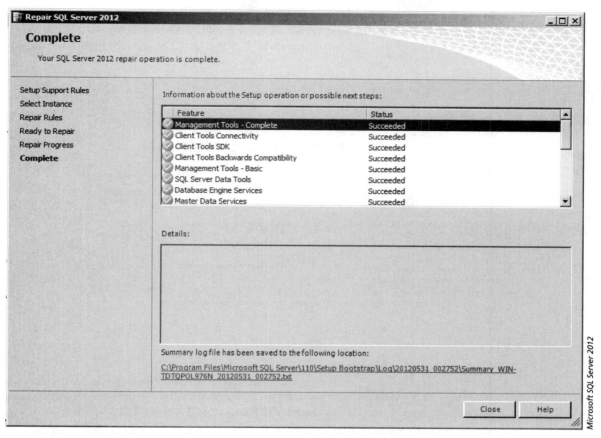

Figure 2-50 Repair SQL Server 2012–Complete window

1. If necessary, start your computer and log on using an Administrator account.
2. Click the **Start** button and from the Start menu click **Control Panel**. Click **Uninstall a program** from the Programs menu. See Figure 2-51.

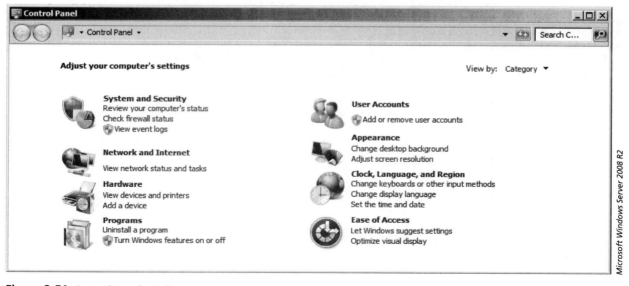

Figure 2-51 Control Panel window

3. In the Programs and Features window, scroll down the list of installed programs, and double-click **Microsoft SQL Server 2012 (64-bit)**. Click the **Remove** link from the SQL Server 2012 dialog box to launch SQL Server 2012 Setup. See Figure 2-52.

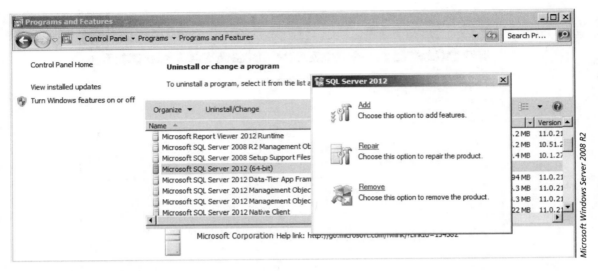

Figure 2-52 Uninstall or change a program window

4. In the Setup Support Rules window, verify that all tests have passed. Review any warnings and follow the instructions given to correct any failures before proceeding to the next step. Click **OK** to launch the Remove SQL Server 2012 Wizard.

5. Select **SQLSERVERUA2** from the list box as the instance of SQL Server to remove features from. See Figure 2-53.

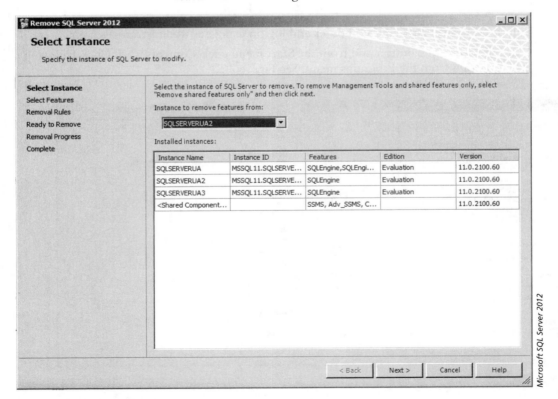

Figure 2-53 Remove SQL Server 2012–Select Instance window

6. Click **Next**. In the Select Features window, click **Database Engine Services** to select it, and then click **Next**. See Figure 2-54. Unless you are undertaking a complete uninstall, *do not select any Shared Features* because this will remove those features for all other instances of SQL Server 2012 on the server.

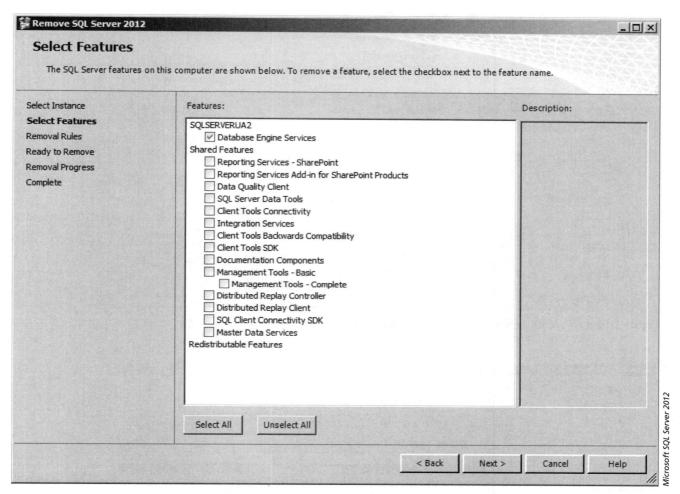

Figure 2-54 Remove SQL Server 2012–Select Features window

7. In the Removal Rules window, verify that all tests have passed. Review any warnings, and follow the instructions given to correct any failures before proceeding to the next step. Click **Next**.

8. In the Ready to Remove window, review the features to be uninstalled, and then click **Remove**. See Figure 2-55.

9. During uninstall, a blue progress scroll bar provides you with the status of the repair. Wait for the uninstall operation to complete. This will take less than a minute.

10. Once the uninstall operation is complete, a window displays the status. You can review a detailed log of the repair operation by clicking the link to the **Summary log file** in the lower pane of the window. Click **Close**. See Figure 2-56. You should now review the steps outlined in Activities 2-2 and 2-3 to validate your install and check the system changes.

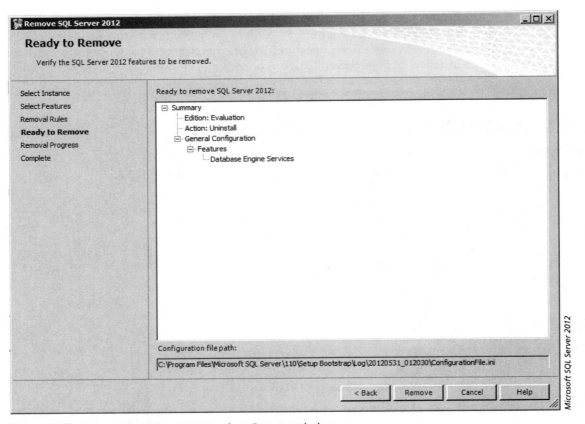

Figure 2-55 Remove SQL Server 2012–Ready to Remove window

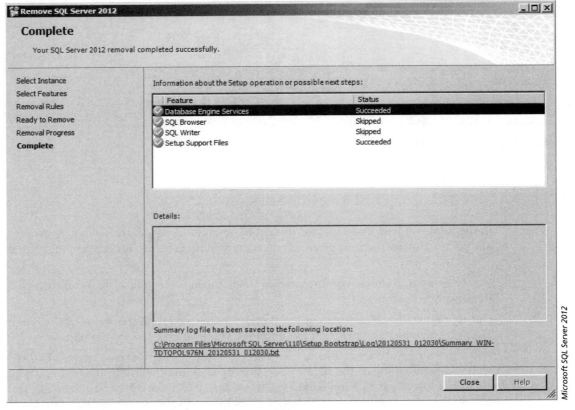

Figure 2-56 Remove SQL Server 2012–Complete window

Chapter Summary

- The planning stage of a SQL Server 2012 installation consists of a set of interdependent activities that include requirements analysis, selection of the edition and license model, feature selection, and hardware and software architecture design. All of these activities are driven by business requirements.

- Physical and logical security should be factored into each stage of the planning process. Physical security considerations should be addressed by placing hardware in a secure location with physical access controls. Logical security considerations should include minimizing the security footprint of the installation, isolating the services using individual service accounts, and installing SQL Server on a dedicated server.

- Up to 50 instances of SQL Server 2012 can be installed and run concurrently on the same host. Each instance has a set of features that is unique to that instance (e.g., Database Engine, Analysis Services, Integration Services, and Reporting Services), while other features are shared (e.g., management tools).

- The SQL Server Features Discovery Report can be run to list the installed instances, features, and shared features on the server.

- SQL Server 2012 can be installed using the installation wizard or the command prompt in attended mode. The command prompt and SysPrep can also be used for installing an instance or features in unattended mode.

- Changes to the server should be validated after an installation using Windows management tools such as the Registry Editor, Performance Monitor, Resource Monitor, and SQL Server Configuration Manager.

- Corrupt or missing application files and Registry settings, or bad configuration parameter values, may cause a SQL Server 2012 instance to fail to start. A repair operation can be run from the SQL Server Installation Center to replace corrupt or missing files and bad settings with their defaults.

- An uninstall operation should always use the functionality provided by the Uninstall or Change a Program feature that can be accessed from the Windows Server 2008 R2 Control Panel.

- Always take a full backup of all databases before making any changes in a production environment—for example, when adding or removing features.

Key Terms

AlwaysOn　A high-availability and disaster recovery solution offered in the Enterprise Edition of SQL Server 2012; requires additional servers and storage devices that are connected over a network.

Analysis Services　A data mining and analytical component of SQL Server 2012.

attended installation　An interactive installation of SQL Server 2012 completed using either the installation wizard or the command prompt.

Availability Groups (AG)　A compononent of AlwaysOn functionality; consists of a group of primary user databases with up to four replicas that will be used in the event the primary user database fails.

collation　A database setting that specifies the character set, sort order behavior, and how characters are evaluated in comparison operations.

command prompt　A command-line interpreter that provides a means of installing SQL Server 2012—by running setup.exe—and specifying SQL Server parameters on the command line, or by referencing a Configuration File (ConfigurationFile.ini).

default instance　The instance of SQL Server 2012 to which a client who connects to the database will connect to if they don't specify a named instance; each database server may have one default instance of SQL Server 2012.

Failover Cluster Instance (FCI)   A set of redundant nodes that can be used to host the database instance should an error occur on the primary node; provides redundancy in the event of hardware or software failure on a SQL Server node.

installation wizard   A Windows application that provides step-by-step guidance though the installation process; launched through the SQL Server Installation Center.

Integration Services   A SQL Server 2012 component that provides extract, transform, and load (ETL) capabilities.

Master Data Services   A SQL Server 2012 component that provides a centralized means to manage and validate data.

named instance   A database instance on a server other than the default instance; each server can support up to 50 instances of SQL Server 2012.

Performance Monitor   A Windows management utility (perfmon.exe) that provides a view of different performance attributes on the host server by viewing data in real time or by replaying data from a log.

Registry Editor   A Windows management utility (regedit.exe) that allows you to view, alter, or delete Registry keys.

Registry key   A configuration value associated with a particular Windows software application.

Reporting Services   A set of tools and services in SQL Server 2012 that enable you to create, deploy, and manage reports.

Resource Monitor   A Windows management utility (resmon.exe) for monitoring hardware resource utilization in real time using five individual tabs: Overview, CPU, Memory, Disk, and Network.

shared features   A set of SQL Server features that are shared between multiple instances of SQL Server 2012 on a single host; includes many of the management tools, Integration Services, and Master Data Services.

SQL Server Configuration Manager   A tool for configuring SQL Server 2012 network protocols and managing component services.

SQL Server Features Discovery Report   A report that displays the SQL Server 2012 instances, tools, and features currently installed on the server.

SQL Server Installation Center   A user interface that provides a single point of access to the various planning, installation, and maintenance wizards.

SQL Server parameters   Settings entered during the SQL Server 2012 installation process; used to specify the type of setup (install, uninstall, or upgrade), features to install, and other configuration settings. SQL Server parameters are specified manually for a command-line install or are generated automatically by the installation wizard to a ConfigurationFile.ini file.

system database   A database created during the SQL Server installation process for storing system configuration information.

unattended installation   A noninteractive installation of SQL Server 2012 completed either by using the command prompt combined with a configuration file and the quiet parameter or by using the SysPrep utility to create an image file for virtual deployments.

user database   A database that contains the data associated with a client application; each SQL Server instance may have one or more user databases.

virtual account   An auto-managed local service account, introduced in Windows 7 and Windows Server 2008 R2 to improve security and ease of management.

Review Questions

1. What is the primary objective of the planning process?

    a.   Ensure that the SQL Server 2012 deployment meets business requirements.

    b.   Obtain the lowest quote for the required hardware.

    c.   Address physical and logical security issues.

    d.   Define the configuration parameter values for the SQL Server installation.

2. How many default instances of a SQL Server 2012 can a single server host?

    a.   Fifty

    b.   One

    c.   Depends on the SQL Server 2012 edition

    d.   Unlimited

3. What application(s) could be used to identify both the currently installed instances and features of SQL Server?

    a.   Resource Monitor

    b.   SQL Server Configuration Manager

    c.   SQL Server Features Discovery Report

    d.   Both options b and c

4. How would you uninstall a SQL Server 2012 instance?

    a.   Delete the instance directory in C:\Program Files\Microsoft SQL Server\.

    b.   Open the SQL Server Installation Center from the installation media and select Uninstall from the navigation menu in the left pane.

    c.   Use the Uninstall or Change a Program feature that can be accessed from the Windows Server 2008 R2 Control Panel.

    d.   Use the Uninstall menu in the SQL Server Configuration Manager.

5. What does the Repair SQL Server 2012 operation do?

    a.   Replaces missing or corrupt files

    b.   Replaces missing or bad configuration parameters with the default settings

    c.   Replaces missing or corrupt Registry keys

    d.   All of the above

6. Which of the following are valid options to install SQL Server 2012?

    a.   Use the command prompt

    b.   Use Windows Deployment Services

    c.   Launch the SQL Server Installation Wizard from the SQL Server Installation Center

    d.   Both options a and c

7. It is possible to upgrade previous versions of SQL Server to SQL Server 2012. True or False?

8. Which of the following components must be installed for every SQL Server 2012 instance?

    a.   SQL Server Integration Services

    b.   Database engine

    c.   SQL Server Reporting Services

    d.   All of the above

9. Which of the following features are shared between SQL Server instances?

   a. SQL Server Integration Services

   b. SQL Server Reporting Services

   c. Master Data Services

   d. Both options a and c

10. Which of the following types of installation would be best suited for rapid deployment of multiple instances of SQL Server that use a standard configuration?

    a. An attended installation using the installation wizard

    b. An attended installation using the command prompt

    c. An unattended installation using the command prompt or the SysPrep utility

    d. Both options b and c

11. Which of the following statements is incorrect?

    a. SQL Server should be installed on a dedicated server.

    b. A domain controller should be installed on the same host as SQL Server.

    c. You should only install the features necessary to meet the business requirements.

    d. Up to 50 instances of SQL Server 2012 may be installed and run concurrently on a single host.

12. What would happen if you attempted to connect to a SQL Server host without specifying a named instance in the connection string?

    a. The connection would fail.

    b. You would be connected to the default instance.

    c. You would connect to the first available named instance.

    d. It depends upon the network protocol that is used.

Case Projects

CASE PROJECTS

Case Project 2-1: Planning a SQL Server 2012 Installation

You work as a database administrator for a software company, Human Scale LLC, which markets hosted software applications that support human resource management. The application database resides on a SQL Server 2012 instance, and for security reasons the company has chosen to install a separate instance of SQL Server for each client. When you joined the company, you noticed that they used the installation wizard for all new installations. This was sustainable for a while but now the company is taking on many new clients each week. Additionally, you have noticed several differences in the configuration parameters between instances, even though each instance should be based on standardized configuration settings. You have decided to raise your concerns to the chief technology officer (CTO). Complete the following:

- Explain why you believe an unattended installation using the command prompt and a configuration file will improve the installation process efficiency and consistency when deploying new instances of SQL Server 2012.
- The CTO is concerned that there may be other inconsistencies between the different instances of SQL Server 2012. Based on the knowledge that you have gained from Chapter 2, describe how you could check the configuration parameter values that were used for any given installation.

Hands-On Projects

Hands-On Project 2-1: Installing a SQL Server Instance

In this hands-on project, you will install a new SQL Server named instance called *SQLSERVERHOA*. You may complete the installation using either the installation wizard or the command prompt.

1. Your installation should only include the database engine and Integration Services components. Add your local user account to the SQL System Administrators group for the SQLSERVERHOA named instance so you can administer it after the installation is complete. Keep all other default settings during the installation process. Once you have successfully completed the installation, save a copy of the *summary.txt* file located in C:\Program Files\Microsoft SQL Server\110\Setup Bootstrap\Log\.

2. Verify that the Windows services for the database engine and Integration Services have been successfully installed using SQL Server Configuration Manager. Take a screen shot of this step.

3. Analyze the other system changes that resulted from this installation. Briefly list the steps that you took to review these changes.

After you have completed this hands-on project, submit the *summary.txt* file, a screen shot of the SQL Server Configuration Manager, and a list of the steps taken to analyze the systems changes to your instructor. Do not make any other changes to the SQLSERVERHOA instance, as you will use this for hands-on projects in upcoming chapters.

chapter 3

Architecture and Configuration

After reading this chapter and completing the exercises, you will be able to:

- Identify the physical and logical components of the SQL Server 2012 architecture

- Explore the objects within a database using Object Explorer in SQL Server Management Studio

- Configure a linked server, and explain the advantages and disadvantages of using distributed queries

- Apply your knowledge of network protocols that are supported by SQL Server 2012 to manage and troubleshoot remote client connectivity

- Explain how to configure SQL Server 2012 settings

The main editions of SQL Server 2012 come bundled with a suite of management applications and command-line utilities. To use these tools to effectively administer a SQL Server instance, you need to understand the physical and logical components of the SQL Server database architecture. You must also be familiar with the options available to connect to the server remotely from a client application and how to access data that is external to the SQL Server instance.

This chapter begins with an introduction to the physical and logical architecture of SQL Server 2012. Your understanding will be reinforced by completing Activity 3-2 where you will use Object Explorer to navigate through the logical objects that constitute the sample database. Because the SQL Server 2012 installation does not include any user databases, you will install a sample user database on your computer. This book uses the sample Adventure Works 2012 database to provide a realistic set of test data for use in the activities.

Client applications, which include the SQL Server management tools, frequently need to connect to the SQL Server instance remotely. In the second section of the chapter, you will learn about the different network protocols that are supported by the SQL Server database engine, and you'll complete an activity to configure a TCP/IP listener on a static TCP port for your named instance of SQL Server. You will discover how to test and troubleshoot the network connection by using a loopback address on your computer that enables you to simulate a physical network.

The final section in this chapter provides an introduction to the linked server object. Linked servers allow you to run a query against remote data sources; however, before using linked servers, you should be aware of the associated network cost and security implications. Activity 3-4 demonstrates how to configure a connection to an external data source from within SQL Server using the linked server object. Activity 3-5 teaches you how to use the sp_configure procedure, the SQL Server Configuration Manager, and Object Explorer to view or change basic and advanced configuration settings.

SQL Server 2012 Database Architecture

The primary purpose of a database is to organize and store data in a secure manner while providing a flexible set of access methods for data retrieval and manipulation by client applications. Each SQL Server 2012 instance contains several system databases and one or more user databases. See Figure 3-1.

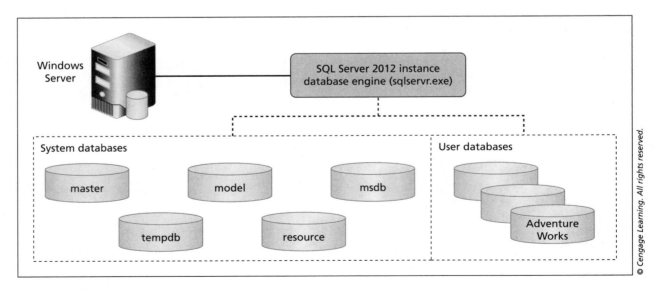

Figure 3-1 Each instance of SQL Server 2012 hosts multiple system and user databases

There are five system databases: master, tempdb, model, msdb, and resource; each database has a specific purpose, as summarized in Table 3-1.

Table 3-1 Primary functions of the system databases

System database	Function
master	Stores information on the structure of other databases and their components; maintains configuration settings, including security
tempdb	Stores temporary data that is generated when the database engine executes processes
model	Stores a database template that is used as a blueprint when creating a new user database
resource	Stores the system objects in a read-only database; these logically appear in each database in the sys schema
msdb	Stores information related to jobs, schedules, and database backups

© Cengage Learning

The **master database** is a system database that stores the configuration settings that describe the structure and security of all the other databases. Care should be taken when viewing the master database, as a SQL Server instance may fail to start up if the master database becomes corrupt or contains bad configuration values. The **model database** is a system database that is used as a template when creating a new user database and can be customized to suit your organization.

SQL Server encodes the data into a **binary format** in which data is represented as a series of zeros and ones, and it uses the file system on the local Windows operating system for physical storage. Each database is organized using a logical structure of database objects that overlay the physical storage. A **logical structure** is a way of organizing data, with defined rules for storing, manipulating, and retrieving the data; client applications interact with these logical objects within a database rather than the physical files.

Physical Database Files

Each database that is mounted on a SQL Server instance has two main physical file types, as shown in Figure 3-2.

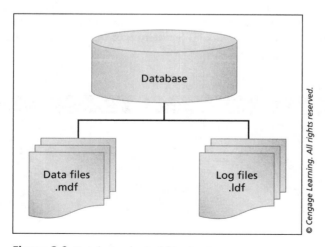

Figure 3-2 Database physical file structure

Data files store the database objects and their underlying data. These files are given a .mdf file extension. Data files are subdivided into physical units of storage called **pages**, which are grouped together for space management into **extents**, which are collections of eight pages. **Log files** record the series of changes that occur to a database over time, and they enable a database to be restored to a specific point in time. These files are given an .ldf file extension. Log files are covered in more detail during the discussion of backup and recovery topics in Chapter 8.

Although the physical file structure is generally transparent to an end user, it is important for a database administrator to understand the main file types and their implementation for a number of reasons, including the following:

- *Physical resources*—The size of the physical files needs to be factored into planning and must be closely monitored to ensure that ample disk space is available for the server.

- *Backup and recovery operations*—Ongoing backup and recovery operations make extensive use of the data and log files and necessitate that these files are periodically backed up to an archive location.

- *Security*—Database security is managed through the logical object model; it is therefore important to ensure that the underlying physical files are secured and can only be accessed by the SQL Server database engine or a system administrator.

Logical Database Objects

The basic building blocks of a database are tables and indexes. A **table** is a collection of data stored in a database. In a relational database, tables are typically designed to model real-world objects and the relationships that exist between them. A table is organized as a two-dimensional structure consisting of rows and columns (see Table 3-2).

Table 3-2 Data in a sample table "Employees"

EmployeeID	HireDate	FirstName	LastName	IsActive
1	05/11/2009	Sanjay	Barve	True
2	08/31/2010	Petros	Aretos	False
3	04/12/2011	Kristina	Bauer	True
4	07/14/2012	Kashif	Khan	True

© Cengage Learning

A **row** is a logical instance, commonly called a *record*, of the object that the table is modeling (e.g., an employee or an appointment), and it may contain several attributes that are defined as **columns** (e.g., first name, last name, or Social Security number). Columns are defined with a unique column name and data type (see Table 3-3).

Table 3-3 Column design view of sample table "Employees"

Column name	Data type
EmployeeID	int
HireDate	date
LastName	nvarchar(20)
FirstName	nvarchar(20)
IsActive	bit

© Cengage Learning

The **data type** is a column attribute that defines what type of data it can store. It acts as a constraint because it imposes a limitation on the type of values that can be stored in a column. The main data types include unique identifiers, numbers of varying precision, dates and times, and text strings. Columns may also have additional **constraints**, or conditions, attached to them—such as being a mandatory field or having a referential dependency upon the values in another table.

Tables have a procedural mechanism called a **trigger** that can be configured to automatically fire an event when a row is inserted, modified, or deleted. This is a useful feature that is easily implemented and often used to satisfy compliance aspects of the business requirements, such as the following:

- *Time stamps*—Triggers are frequently used to automatically update columns that contain metadata about the row. For example, if a row changes, the business may require that the database automatically records the user making the change with a corresponding time stamp.

- *Audit*—Triggers may be used to cascade details of a change into related tables. For example, if a row is deleted, the business may require that a copy of the record be maintained in an audit table. A delete trigger can be used to insert a copy of the record into another table before committing the transaction.

A **database index** is a logical database structure used to improve the speed and efficiency of data access. It serves a purpose similar to that of the index at the back of this book, which enables you, based on a particular keyword, to quickly locate a page number that references a particular entry in the book. A database index is constructed based on a unique key, and it contains pointers to the underlying rows within the table that match the key. Each table should have a default index, which is typically based upon a **primary key**—the column or combination of columns that uniquely identify each record. It is possible to define additional indexes that are usually based upon the criteria that will be used to search for a given record. If no index is defined, a query will require the database engine to undertake a full **table scan** on every record within the table in order to find matches. For large tables, this has a serious impact on performance. However, there is also a cost associated with maintaining too many indexes on a table in terms of both disk space and performance. It is somewhat intuitive that indexes must occupy additional disk space, which can be substantial. The performance implication might be less obvious, but consider that each time a record is inserted, deleted, or changed, the operation must update any dependent indexes with an associated processing overhead. Indexes are reviewed in detail during the discussion of database performance and optimization in Chapter 7.

Figure 3-3 illustrates the logical objects that have been discussed in this section along with a few others. **Views** are a type of saved query, and **procedures** are precompiled blocks of code that

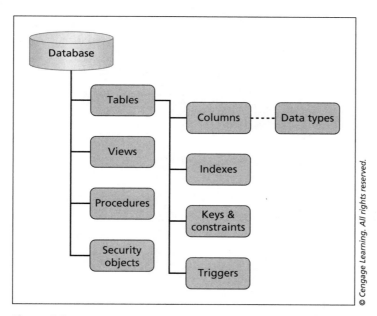

Figure 3-3 Main logical components within a SQL Server database

enable frequently performed tasks for querying and/or manipulating data to be stored as objects within the database. SQL Server also uses logical objects to manage security—including users, roles, and permissions.

SQL Server Management Studio is a management tool used to configure, manage, and administer the Database Engine Services, Analysis Services, Integration Services, and Reporting

Services. Object Explorer in SQL Server Management Studio provides a tree view of the different database schema objects organized as a series of folders that can be used to manage the SQL Server instance. **Query Editor**, another important component of SQL Server Management Studio, allows you to create SQL queries to be executed against a database.

Activity 3-1: Installing the Online Transaction Processing (OLTP) Adventure Works 2012 Sample Database

Time Required: 45 minutes
Objective: Download and install the Adventure Works 2012 sample database.

Description: In this activity, you will download and install the Online Transaction Processing (OLTP) variant of the Adventure Works 2012 sample database from the Microsoft CodePlex site. **CodePlex** is Microsoft's open source project hosting site where you can find useful sample code for a wide range of Microsoft products. **Online Transaction Processing (OLTP)** is a method of processing data that is geared toward transaction-oriented applications that have a substantial write component in their interaction with the database. An OLTP database is a database defined by a high volume of individual read and write transactions. This sample database will be used in several of the activities later in this chapter and in the remaining chapters of the book.

1. If necessary, start your computer and log on using an Administrator account.

2. Click the **Start** button, point to **All Programs**, and then click **Internet Explorer**.

3. Click in the **Address bar** and type the following URL: **msftdbprodsamples.codeplex.com** to access the SQL Server Database Product Samples at CodePlex page. Click the **SQL Server 2012 OLTP** icon to open the Adventure Works for SQL Server 2012 page. See Figure 3-4.

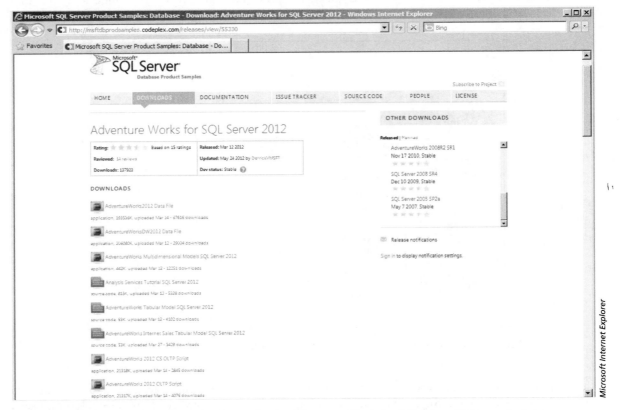

Figure 3-4 Microsoft CodePlex download page for the Adventure Works for SQL Server 2012 sample database

4. Scroll down the page, and click the **AdventureWorks 2012 OLTP Script** link. Depending upon your settings, the following warning message may appear in the Internet Explorer Information bar: "To help protect your security, Internet Explorer blocked this site from downloading files to your computer. Click here for more options." Click the **Internet Explorer Information bar,** and then click **Download File.**

5. In the Save As dialog box, keep the default location **C:\Downloads\ AdventureWorks_2012_OLTP_Script.zip,** and click the **Save** button. See Figure 3-5.

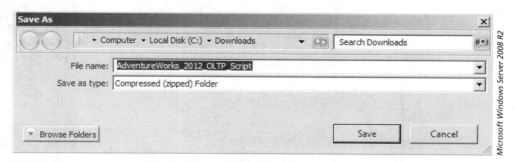

Figure 3-5 Save As dialog box for the Adventure Works 2012 sample database

6. To launch SQL Server Management Studio, click the **Start** button, point to **All Programs,** click **Microsoft SQL Server 2012,** and then click **SQL Server Management Studio.** See Figure 3-6.

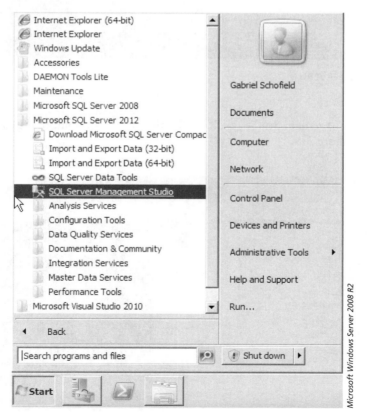

Figure 3-6 Launch SQL Server Management Studio

7. In the Connect to Server dialog box, keep the default values for the Server type and Authentication modes. In the Server name text box, type your computer name and instance name in the format **<ComputerName>\<InstanceName>**. Click **Connect**. See Figure 3-7.

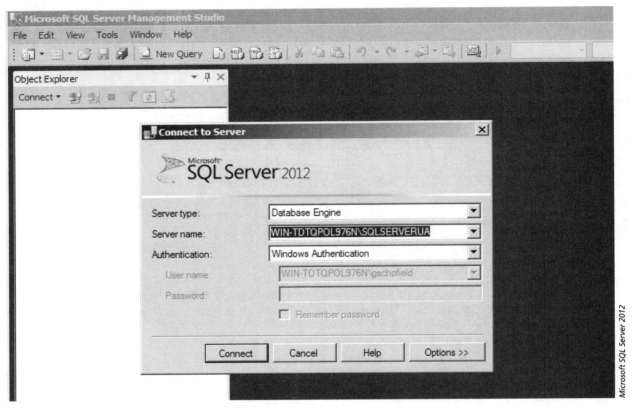

Figure 3-7 Connect to named instance SQLSERVERUA

8. In SQL Management Studio, click **File** on the menu bar, point to **Open,** and then click **File.** See Figure 3-8.

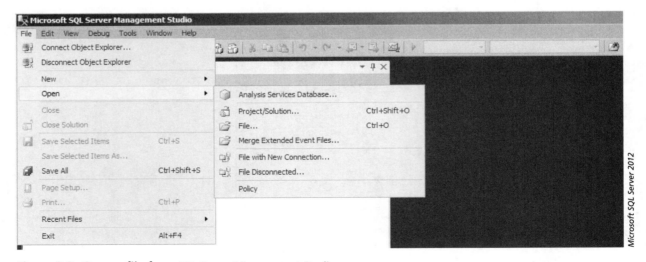

Figure 3-8 Open a file from SQL Server Management Studio

9. In the Open File dialog box, navigate to the folder location of the downloaded ZIP file containing the Adventure Works sample database **C:\Downloads**. Double-click the ZIP file **AdventureWorks_2012_OLTP_Script.zip**. Click the **Extract All files** button on the menu bar to extract the files in the zipped folder. Use the default location **C:\Downloads\AdventureWorks_2012_OLTP_Script** and click **Extract**. Open the subfolder **AdventureWorks 2012 OLTP Script** that contains the extracted files. You will see a number of CSV files that contain the data and a SQL script called instawdb.sql. Double-click **instawdb.sql** to open the script in SQL Server Management Studio.

10. You need to run the script in SQLCMD mode. In SQL Server Management Studio, click **Query** on the menu bar, and then click **SQLCMD Mode**. See Figure 3-9.

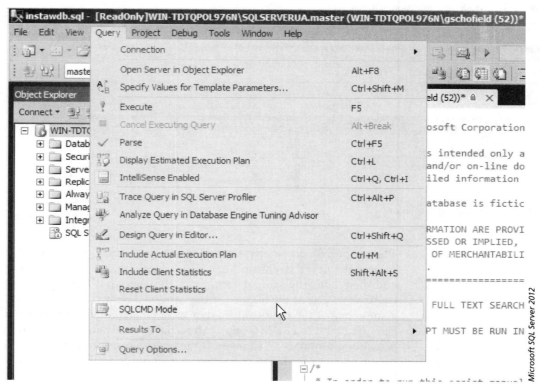

Figure 3-9 Switch to SQLCMD mode

11. The instawdb.sql script will create the database objects on your SQL Server and use a procedure called BULK INSERT to load data into the various tables from the individual CSV files. Read the comments at the start of the script, and note that during the installation process of SQLSERVERUA we specified that the full text search feature should be switched on. Before executing the script, you must change the variables that store the location of the source data files and the path to the database that will be created. Change the variable SqlSamplesDatabasePath to match the location of the data files of your instance: **C:\Program Files\Microsoft SQL Server \MSSQL11.SQLSERVERUA\MSSQL\Data**. Next, change the variable SqlSamplesSourceDataPath to match your unzipped download location: **C:\Downloads\AdventureWorks_2012_OLTP_Script\AdventureWorks 2012 OLTP Script**. Figure 3-10 shows the script with the corrected variables.

12. Run the script by clicking the **Execute** button on the menu bar or by pressing the shortcut key **F5**. See Figure 3-11.

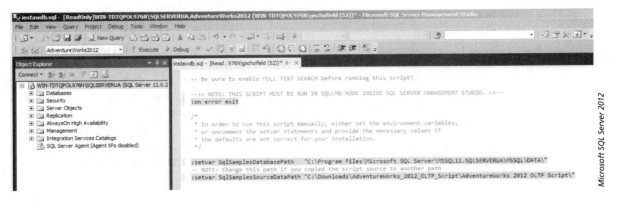

Figure 3-10 Modify variables in SQL script

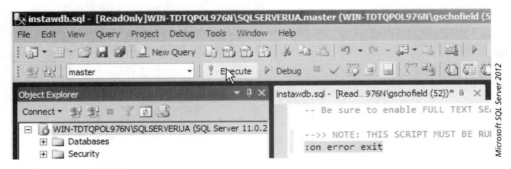

Figure 3-11 Execute SQL query

The script first drops any existing databases named AdventureWorks2012. Next, it creates the new AdventureWorks2012 database, adds the database schema objects, and then loads the sample data. Once the query has finished running, you will see a success message at the bottom of the window below the results grid. This grid contains a summary of the physical files that were created during installation of the database. See Figure 3-12. The Messages tab in the output pane at the bottom of the window provides a summary of changes. If the query fails, you will need to diagnose the cause that is likely to be due to an incorrect entry when setting the variable in Step 11.

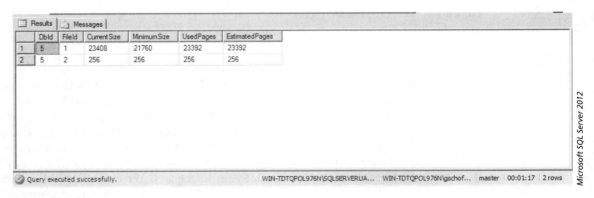

Figure 3-12 SQL query results grid

13. Click the **Refresh** icon in Object Explorer, and expand the folders by clicking the **+** symbol to the left of the Databases folder. You should see an AdventureWorks2012 user database with the various schema object types listed beneath. See Figure 3-13.

Figure 3-13 View the AdventureWorks2012 database in Object Explorer

14. Close the SQL Server Management Studio. If prompted, do not save changes.

Activity 3-2: Navigating SQL Server Management Studio Using Object Explorer

Time Required: 45 minutes

Objective: Navigate the AdventureWorks2012 database using Object Explorer.

Description: The SQL Server Management Studio is a management tool used to configure, manage, and administer the Database Engine Services, Analysis Services, Integration Services, and Reporting Services. In this activity, you will learn how to use Object Explorer to navigate and manage the database schema objects in the AdventureWorks2012 sample user database. As you work through the activity, remember that pressing the F1 shortcut key at any time will provide context-sensitive topics from Books Online for SQL Server 2012.

1. If necessary, start your computer and log on using an Administrator account.

2. Click the **Start** button, point to **All Programs**, click **Microsoft SQL Server 2012**, and then click **SQL Server Management Studio**. In the Connect to Server dialog box, click **Database Engine** as the server type, type **LOCALHOST\SQLSERVERUA** in the Server name text box, and then click **Windows Authentication** from the Authentication list box. See Figure 3-14.

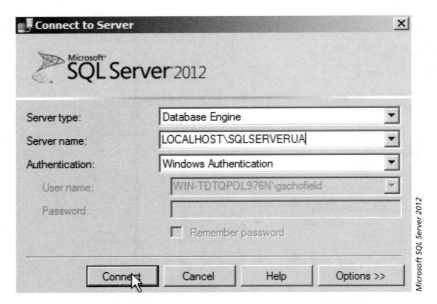

Figure 3-14 Connect to named instance SQLSERVERUA on the local host

3. Click **Connect**. Object Explorer opens in the left navigation pane. Object Explorer provides a tree view of the different database schema objects organized as a series of folders. Click the **+** symbol to drill down to the next level of detail. Click the **−** symbol to collapse a set of folders. Click the **+** symbol next to the **Databases** folder to expand it. Then, expand the **AdventureWorks2012** database folder that you installed in Activity 3-1. See Figure 3-15.

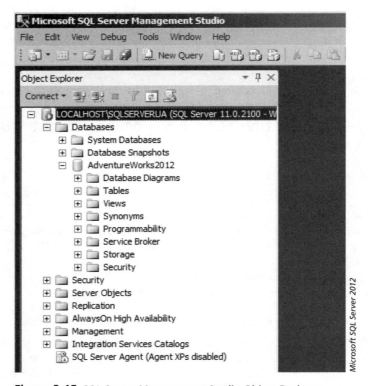

Figure 3-15 SQL Server Management Studio Object Explorer

Should you accidentally close Object Explorer, you can reopen it at any time either by clicking View on the menu bar and then clicking Object Explorer or by pressing the F8 shortcut key from within SQL Server Management Studio.

4. Click the **+** symbol next to the **Tables** folder to expand it. Tables are the logical, two-dimensional structures that contain data.

5. Right-click **dbo.DatabaseLog** to view the shortcut menu. See Figure 3-16.

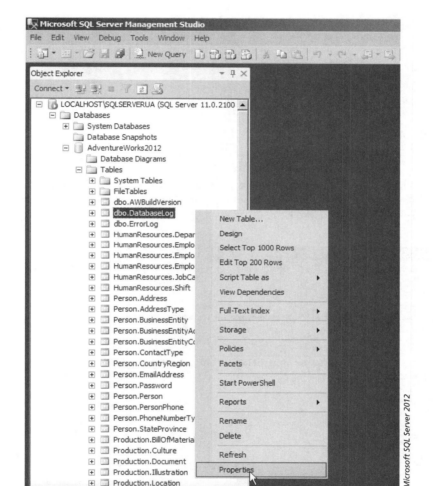

Figure 3-16 Object Explorer shortcut menu

Every object in Object Explorer has a shortcut menu that is dependent upon the object type. From here, you can view or modify properties of the object, such as viewing the physical storage space requirements or changing permissions to the object. You can also make changes to the schema or view the underlying data.

6. Click the **Design** option from the menu. See Figure 3-17. A tabular view of the dbo.DatabaseLog table schema displays in the right pane. Each row represents a column in the table, and the Data Type attribute corresponds to the type of data that can be stored in the column. The Allow Nulls attribute specifies whether a value for a field must be present for every record. The yellow key to the left of DatabaseLogID indicates that the field is the primary key (i.e., it is a unique pointer to a given record).

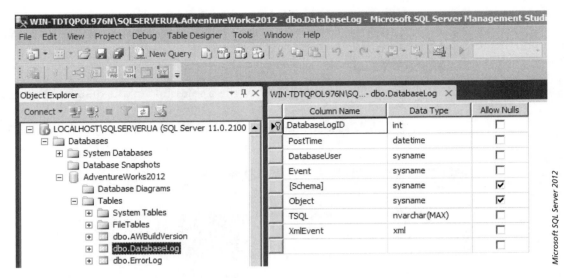

Figure 3-17 Object Explorer table design

7. The table attributes can also be viewed directly in Object Explorer. Click the + symbol next to the table dbo.DatabaseLog, and then click the + symbol next to the Columns folder. See Figure 3-18.

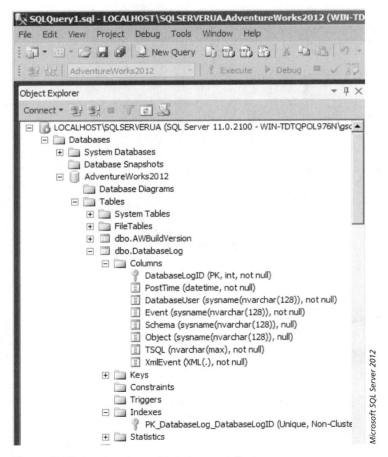

Figure 3-18 DatabaseLog table column attributes

8. Object Explorer is tightly integrated with Query Editor and can be used to automatically generate SQL queries for the schema objects. Right-click **dbo.DatabaseLog**, point to **Script Table as**, point to **SELECT To**, and then click **New Query Editor Window**. See Figure 3-19.

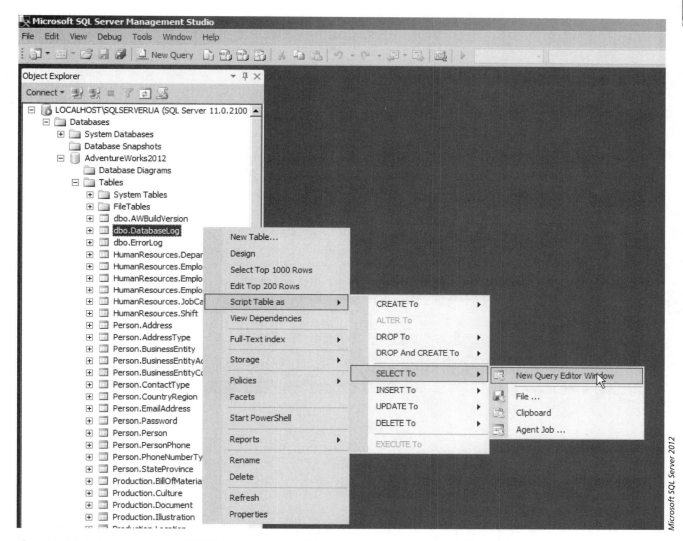

Figure 3-19 Auto-generating a SELECT statement for a table using the script as functionality in Object Explorer

 SQL as a database programming language is discussed in detail in Chapter 4.

9. SQL Server automatically generates a SQL SELECT statement into a Query Editor window in the right pane. The SQL script in Query Editor indicates which database to use for the query, the table to return data from, and the actual field names that are needed. Click the **Execute** button in the toolbar, or press the **F5** key, to execute the script. See Figure 3-20.

At the bottom of Query Editor is a Results and Messages tab. The Messages tab displays any system-generated or user-defined messages as output from the query.

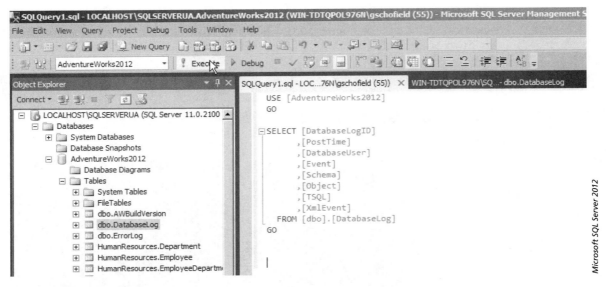

Figure 3-20 SELECT To script in Query Editor

This normally includes the number of records returned by the query, but it may include warning or error messages if the query fails. The data set returned on the Results tab is a tabular two-dimensional results grid where each row represents a record from the table and each column a field. See Figure 3-21.

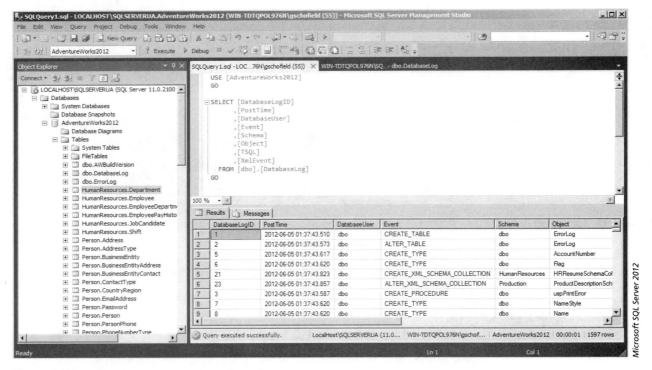

Figure 3-21 Executed SQL query with results and messages

10. Close Microsoft SQL Server Management Studio by clicking the **X** in the upper-right corner of the window.

SQL Server 2012 Configuration

Frequently, client applications (including the management tools) need to establish a remote connection to SQL Server. In this section, you will learn about the network protocols that are directly supported by the SQL Server database engine. In Activity 3-3, you will configure a listener for your named instance using the SQL Server Configuration Manager. A **listener** is a service that enables a client to connect to the SQL Server instance over a network. You will then test these network connections from the **SQLCMD** command prompt that enables you to connect to the database and execute SQL commands and scripts using a **loopback address**, which is an IP address that sends outbound packets of data directly back to the host computer to simulate a physical network. You will use the NETSTAT utility, Activity Monitor, and SQL Profiler to troubleshoot the client/server connections.

Next, you will learn about the linked server object, which is a useful feature when running a query against a distributed set of data. (However, you should be aware of the network cost and possible security implications of this approach.) During Activity 3-4, you will configure a connection to an external data source from within SQL Server using the linked server object. Finally, in Activity 3-5, you will use the sp_configure procedure, the SQL Server Configuration Manager, and Object Explorer to manage the basic and advanced configuration settings of SQL Server.

Network Protocols

SQL Server 2012 uses messages called **Tabular Data Stream (TDS) packets** for communication. When a remote client is connected to a SQL Server instance, these TDS packets must be encapsulated within a standard network protocol packet to enable the data to be sent over the network between the client and server. The handoff between SQL Server and the operating system occurs at an endpoint on the **SQL Server Network Interface layer** within the database engine. An endpoint is defined for each network protocol that has been enabled. As a prerequisite, the network protocol must also be installed and supported on both the client and server operating system to function correctly. The following network protocols are supported by SQL Server 2012:

- **Shared memory** is a local procedure call, and it requires the client application to be running on the same host as the SQL Server instance. No configuration options are available with a shared memory connection.

- **Named Pipes** is an older interprocess communication mechanism that enables a client application to connect to a server process on the same or different hosts. Each SQL Server instance is able to listen on one named pipe.

- **TCP/IP** is the most common protocol used for remote connectivity. The default instance of SQL Server is configured to listen on TCP port 1433; other TCP ports are assigned for a named instance dynamically when the database engine service starts. This can cause a problem if there is a firewall in place between the server host and client that is blocking the port. To avoid this problem, it is recommended that you follow the steps outlined in Activity 3-3 to configure a fixed port for each SQL Server instance and open the relevant port on the firewall to allow network traffic to reach the server.

Each of the network protocols listed supports Kerberos, which is a widely used and highly secure network authentication mechanism.

Because a single Windows server can host several SQL Server instances concurrently, Microsoft introduced a service called **SQL Server Browser** that uses **SQL Server Resolution Protocol (SSRP)** to simplify communication. The SQL Server Browser service is able to perform an instance lookup and name resolution, similar to the function that a DNS server would perform on behalf of a network. The SQL Server Browser service listens by default on port 1434 to incoming requests and provides information about named instances of SQL Server running on the host. For example, if you attempt to connect via a client, specifying only the host and named instance, SQL Server Browser will respond with the correct TCP port or Named Pipes, which that named instance has been configured to listen on.

Figure 3-22 provides an overview of the supported network protocols for remote connections to SQL Server 2012.

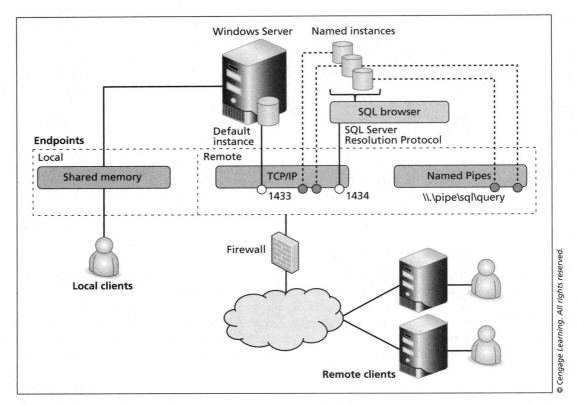

Figure 3-22 Network protocols for remote connections to SQL Server

Activity 3-3: Configuring SQL Server Network Protocols

Time Required: 60 minutes
Objective: Configure SQL Server network protocols to access a named SQL Server instance from a client application.

Description: In this activity, you will configure the TCP/IP network protocol for the named instance SQLSERVERUA using a static TCP port for the listener. You will use SQL Configuration Manager to configure these settings. SQLCMD will be used in conjunction with the loopback adapter to establish a connection using both the TCP/IP protocol and shared memory. You will monitor the connection using the NETSTAT utility—the Activity Monitor in SQL Management Studio—and then run a trace using SQL Profiler.

1. If necessary, start your computer and log on using an Administrator account.

2. Click the **Start** button, point to **All Programs**, and then click **Microsoft SQL Server 2012.** Click **Configuration Tools,** and then click **SQL Server Configuration Manager.** Click **Continue** if prompted by the User Account Control dialog box. See Figure 3-23.

3. In SQL Server Configuration Manager, click **SQL Server Services** in the left navigation pane. In the details pane, check that the SQL Server database engine service named SQL Server (SQLSERVERUA) is running. If the state shown is *Stopped*, then right-click **SQL Server (SQLSERVERUA)**, and click **Start.** See Figure 3-24.

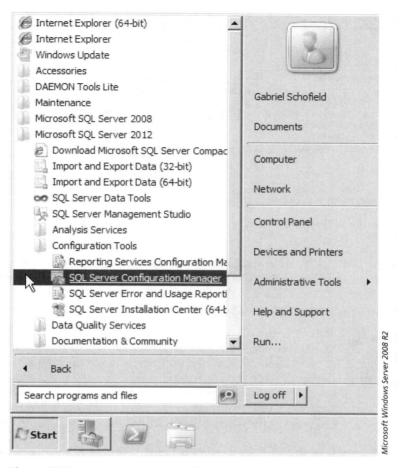

Figure 3-23 Launch SQL Server Configuration Manager

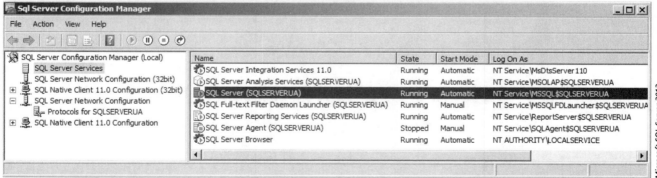

Figure 3-24 View the services in SQL Server Configuration Manager

4. If necessary, expand SQL Server Network Configuration by clicking the **+** symbol in the left navigation pane. Click **Protocols for SQLSERVERUA** to list the network protocols that are configured on the SQL Server instance for client connectivity. Right-click the **TCP/IP** protocol name, and then click **Properties**. See Figure 3-25.

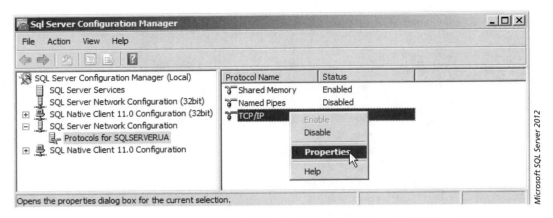

Figure 3-25 View the network protocols configured for named instance SQLSERVERUA

5. In the TCP/IP Properties window, click the **IP Addresses** tab. This tab lists all the Internet Protocol version 4 and 6 (IP4 and IP6) network addresses that are currently configured on the server. Scroll down to the IP address 127.0.0.1, which is the default address for the loopback adapter. Set the enabled field to **Yes** in order to enable the address.

Rather than use TCP dynamic ports, we will specify a static (or fixed) TCP port to use. This is important for client/server connections that involve a firewall to minimize the number of ports that need to be open. To avoid potential conflict with TCP ports used by other applications installed on the host, we will choose one from the list provided by the Internet Assigned Numbers Authority (IANA) that is currently marked as unassigned *(www.iana.org/ assignments/service-names-port-numbers/service-names-port-numbers.txt).*

6. Delete the **0** in the TCP Dynamic Ports field. Type **4409** in the TCP Port field. See Figure 3-26.

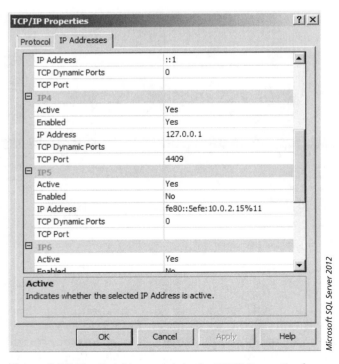

Figure 3-26 The IP Addresses tab in the TCP/IP Properties for named instance SQLSERVERUA

7. Scroll down to the bottom section labeled IPAll, and delete any values in the **TCP Dynamic Ports** and **TCP Ports** fields.

8. Click the **Protocol** tab. Check that the Enabled field is set to **Yes**. Because we only want the server to listen on the loopback adapter address, set the Listen All field to **No**. Click **Apply**. See Figure 3-27.

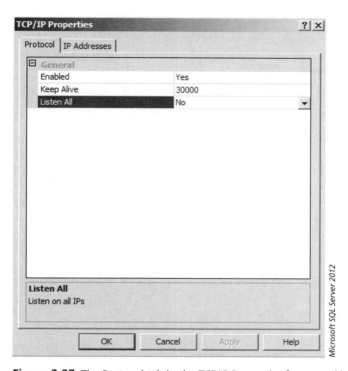

Figure 3-27 The Protocol tab in the TCP/IP Properties for named instance SQLSERVERUA

9. Click **OK** to the warning prompt advising, "Any changes made will be saved; however, they will not take effect until the service is stopped and restarted." Click **OK** again. The SQL Server instance SQLSERVERUA is now configured to listen for client connections to IP address 127.0.0.1 on TCP port 4409.

10. For the changes to take effect, you will need to restart the database engine service for the SQL Server instance SQLSERVERUA using SQL Server Configuration Manager. Click **SQL Server Services** in the left navigation pane. In the details pane, right-click **SQL Server (SQLSERVERUA)**, and then click **Restart**. See Figure 3-28.

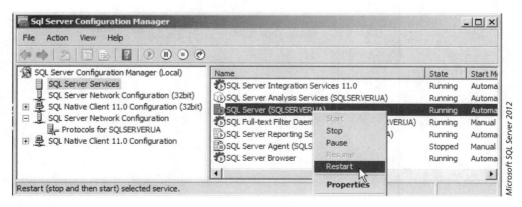

Figure 3-28 Restart the SQL Server database engine service

A dialog box opens, showing the status of the stop service command. Once the service has been successfully stopped, a second dialog box opens, showing the status of the start service command.

11 Next, you will use the SQLCMD.exe utility as a client to test connectivity to the SQLSERVERUA database instance. To open a Command Prompt window, click the **Start** button, click **Run**, type **cmd** in the text box, and then click **OK**. The SQLCMD.exe utility allows you to connect to the database from a command-line interface to execute SQL commands and scripts.

12. Type the following commands at the command prompt, and press the **Enter** key after each command to test different methods of connecting to the SQLSERVERUA database instance:

```
C:\> SQLCMD -S LPC:LOCALHOST\SQLSERVERUA -Q "SELECT GETDATE();"

C:\> SQLCMD -S LOCALHOST\SQLSERVERUA -Q "SELECT GETDATE();"

C:\> SQLCMD -S 127.0.0.1\SQLSERVERUA -Q "SELECT GETDATE();"
```

The previous three commands each use shared memory (a local procedure call) to connect to the SQLSERVERUA named instance and execute a simple SQL query. The command in double quotation marks, SELECT GETDATE(), returns the current date and time.

13. Next, you enter a command that will use a TCP/IP connection to connect to the named instance using the listener on TCP port 4409 that was created in Steps 5 and 6:

```
C:\> SQLCMD -S TCP:127.0.0.1\SQLSERVERUA,4409 -Q "SELECT GETDATE();"
```

14. Finally, you create a TCP/IP connection that will be left open for the remaining steps in the activity:

```
C:\> SQLCMD -S TCP:127.0.0.1\SQLSERVERUA,4409
```

Figure 3-29 shows all of the commands that you have entered in Steps 12 through 14.

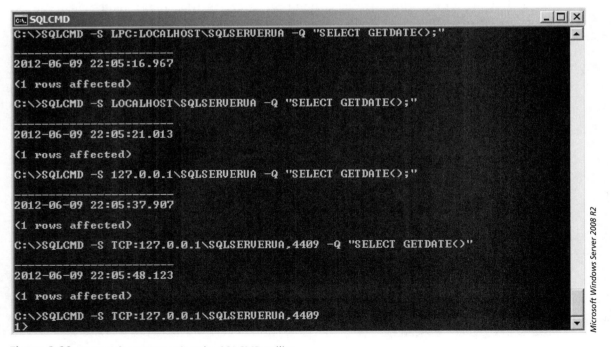

Figure 3-29 Output from tests using the SQLCMD utility

15. Open a second Command Prompt window by clicking the **Start** button, clicking **Run**, typing **cmd** in the text box, and then clicking **OK**. At the command prompt, type **NETSTAT** and press the **Enter** key. As shown in Figure 3-30, you will see the active network connection that was left open at the end of Step 9. Figure 3-30 shows a server connection on TCP port 4409 and a dynamically assigned client connection on TCP port 49292. See Figure 3-30.

Figure 3-30 Active network connections viewed using the NETSTAT command-line utility

 Note that the shared memory connections at the start of Step 9 will not appear under network interfaces because shared memory does not use a configured network protocol on the operating system.

16. Click the **Start** button, point to **All Programs**, click **Microsoft SQL Server 2012**, and then click **SQL Server Management Studio**. In the Connect to Server dialog box, enter **LOCALHOST\SQLSERVERUA**, and then click **Windows Authentication** from the Authentication list box.

 LOCALHOST will resolve to the name of your computer that is hosting SQL Server. However, if connecting from a remote client, you will need to specify a server name or IP address of the remote host.

17. Click the **Options** button in the lower-right corner of the Connect to Server dialog box, and then click the **Connection Properties** tab. By modifying the settings on the Connection Properties and Additional Connection Parameters tabs, you can override the server defaults—such as specifying a particular network protocol to use when connecting to the server. In this case, you'll keep the default settings. Click **Connect**. See Figure 3-31.

18. On the right side of SQL Server Management Studio toolbar, click the **Activity Monitor** icon, or press the shortcut keys **Ctrl+Alt+A**, to launch Activity Monitor. See Figure 3-32.

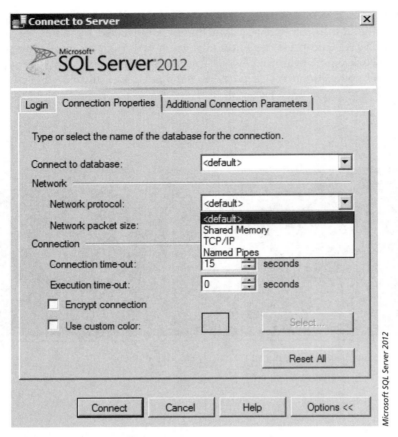

Figure 3-31 SQL Server Management Studio advanced connection properties

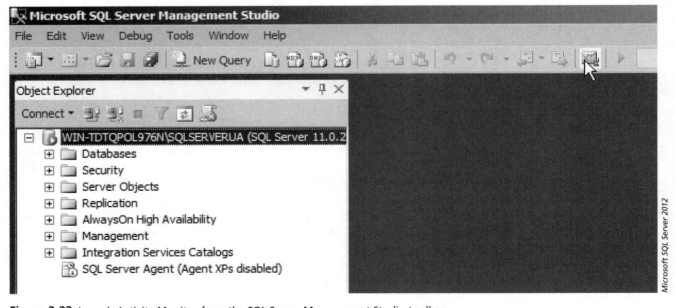

Figure 3-32 Launch Activity Monitor from the SQL Server Management Studio toolbar

19. In Activity Monitor, click **Processes**, and confirm that you can locate the open SQLCMD session running from the command prompt. Right-click the **session row**, and then click **Trace Process in SQL Server Profiler**. See Figure 3-33.

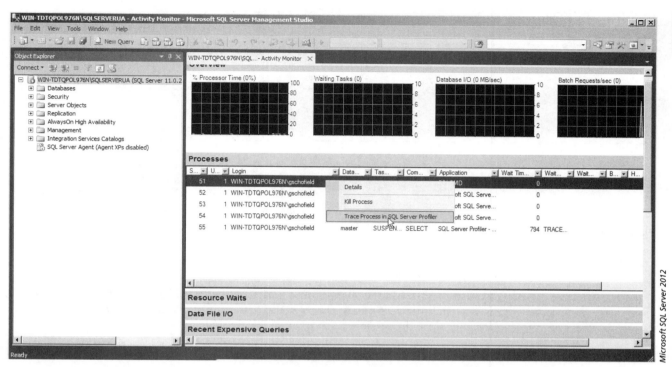

Figure 3-33 Right-click on the process to start a trace in Activity Monitor

Clicking the Trace Process in SQL Server Profiler menu option opens SQL Server Profiler and starts a trace for the SQLCMD session. A **trace** is a log of events on the database management system that are captured using the SQL Server Profiler and commonly used for troubleshooting SQL Server performance issues.

20. At the command prompt for your existing SQLCMD session, type the following and press the **Enter** key at the end of each line:

```
1> SELECT GETDATE();

2> GO
```

See Figure 3-34.

Figure 3-34 Opening a TCP/IP session to the named instance using the SQLCMD command prompt

21. Go back to SQL Profiler and review the entries in the trace, which should reflect the commands you just executed. Stop the trace by clicking the red **Stop** icon on the toolbar. See Figure 3-35.

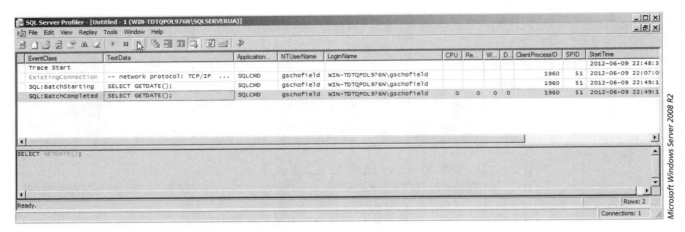

Figure 3-35 View the trace in SQL Profiler

22. Close SQL Profiler.

23. Return to SQL Management Studio and view the Processes pane of Activity Monitor. Right-click the **session row** with SQLCMD running, and then click **Kill Process** to forcibly close the session.

24. At the command prompt with the open SQLCMD session, type the following:

```
1> SELECT GETDATE();

2> GO
```

25. You should receive a communication link failure message. See Figure 3-36.

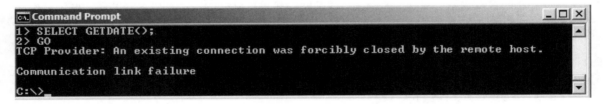

Figure 3-36 Attempt to execute another SQL query from the SQLCMD command prompt
Microsoft Windows Server 2008 R2

26. Close all the **Command Prompt** windows, but leave SQL Server Management Studio open for Activity 3-4.

Linked Server

A **linked server** provides the capability to execute queries against a remote data source and can be invaluable for combining information across a number of different data sources known as a distributed query. A linked server uses shared software components from the dynamic-link library (DLL) on the server. These components, called data providers, manage the interface between SQL Server and the external data source. There are a wide variety of data providers available that not only support connections to other databases but also support nondatabase file formats. Many of the providers are specific to a particular data source (e.g., the Oracle provider) while others, such as the Open Database Connectivity (ODBC) provider, enable a connection to be established to virtually any database or file, irrespective of the operating system in use. See Figure 3-37.

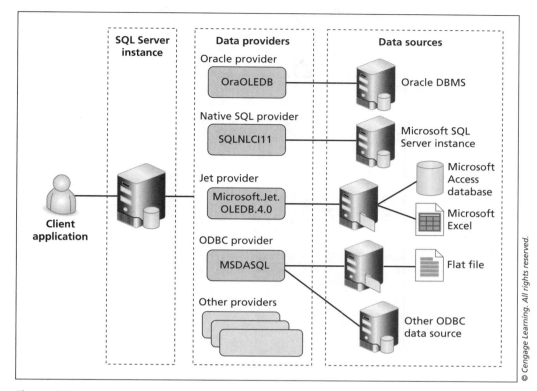

Figure 3-37 Common data providers and data sources that can be configured using the linked server object

In Activity 3-4, you will create a linked server data source provider using the wizard in Object Explorer. Common to managing other SQL Server configuration settings, linked servers can also be created, modified, or dropped by executing a system procedure using a SQL query. The primary disadvantages of using a linked server are the implicit network cost and potential security issues. When defining a linked server, it is possible to override the integrated authentication with a stored username and password in order to impersonate that user on the remote system.

Activity 3-4: Adding a Linked Server

Time Required: 30 minutes

Objective: Configure a linked server object using Object Explorer in SQL Server Management Studio.

Description: The linked server object allows a query to be distributed across multiple data sources. A data source may be another SQL Server instance, another database hosted on a database management system from another provider, or a file containing data. In this activity, you will configure and test a linked server object. Because only a single database instance is configured in the test environment, you will create a linked server object that establishes a connection back to SQLSERVERUA using Object Explorer in SQL Server Management Studio. This is known as a loopback linked server and would normally only be used for testing.

1. In Object Explorer navigation pane in SQL Server Management Studio, expand **Server Objects**, right-click **Linked Servers**, and then click **New Linked Server**. See Figure 3-38.

2. On the General tab of the New Linked Server Wizard, click in the **Linked server** text box and type **127.0.0.1\SQLSERVERUA**. Click the **SQL Server** option button under Server type to select the native SQL Server provider SQLNLCI11. See Figure 3-39.

Figure 3-38 Select New Linked Server from the Linked Servers shortcut menu in Object Explorer

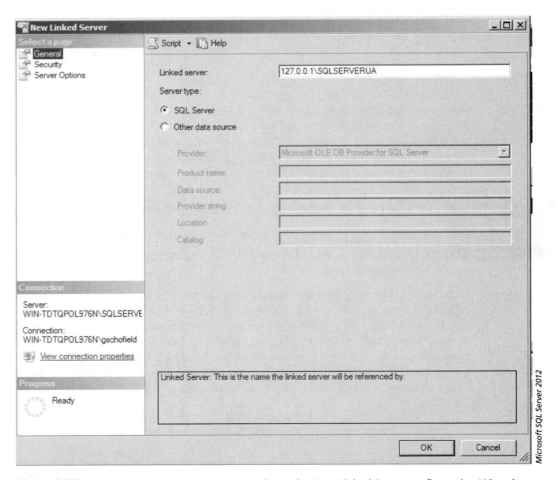

Figure 3-39 Configure the name and data provider in the New Linked Server configuration Wizard

3. Click **Security** in the left navigation pane of the New Linked Server Wizard, and then click the **Be made using the login's current security context** option button. See Figure 3-40.

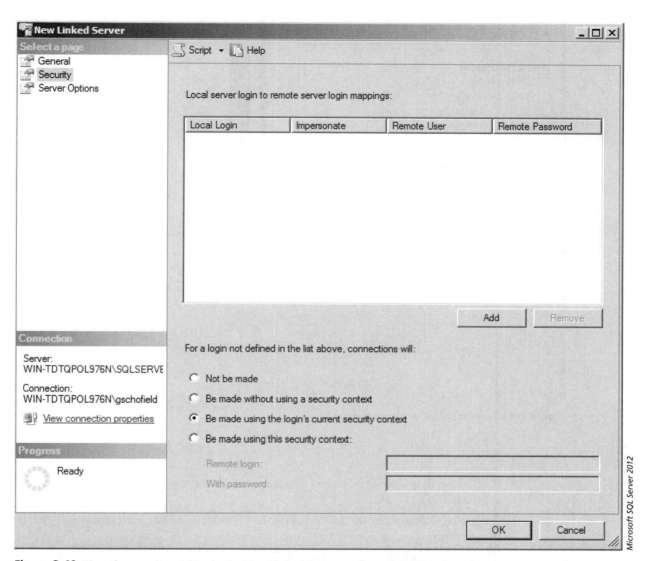

Figure 3-40 View the security settings in the New Linked Server configuration Wizard

4. Click **Server Options** in the left navigation pane and review the settings. For the purposes of this activity, we will retain the default settings. Click **OK**.

Serious security implications could arise when using impersonation or a different security context in the Security properties of the linked server object.

5. In the Object Explorer pane, if necessary, expand the Linked Servers folder by clicking the **+** icon to the right of the folder name. Right-click the newly created linked server **127.0.0.1\SQLSERVERUA**, and then click **Test Connection**. See Figure 3-41.

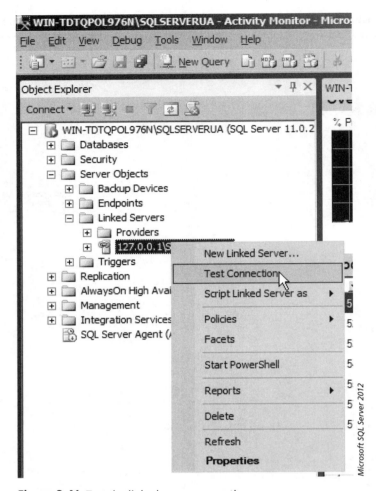

Figure 3-41 Test the linked server connection

6. A window should appear with the message "The test connection to the linked server succeeded." Click **OK**.

7. Expand **Catalogs** beneath **127.0.0.1\SQLSERVERUA** to browse the schema objects that the linked server allows you to access. See Figure 3-42.

8. Close all open windows by clicking the **X** in the upper-right corner of each application.

Activity 3-5: Viewing and Modifying Global Configuration Settings

Time Required: 30 minutes
Objective: Use the sp_configure system procedure to view or modify global configuration settings for the SQL Server instance.

Description: The **sp_configure** procedure can be used to view and alter global configuration settings. In this activity, you will go through the steps necessary to view existing settings and make changes.

Note that changing configuration settings can lead to undesired consequences, so it is always a good practice to take a full backup of production systems and test the impact of the change in a segregated test environment before deploying to production.

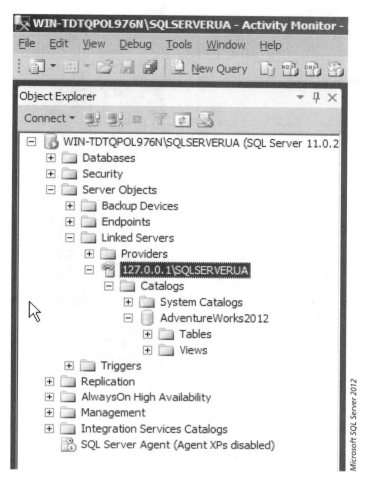

Figure 3-42 View the database objects available
through the linked server

1. Click the **Start** button, point to **All Programs**, click **Microsoft SQL Server 2012**, and
   then click **SQL Server Management Studio**. In the Connect to Server dialog box,
   enter **LOCALHOST\SQLSERVERUA**, select **Windows Authentication** from the
   Authentication list box, and then click **Connect**.

2. In Object Explorer navigation pane in SQL Server Management Studio, expand
   Databases, expand **System Databases**, right-click the **master** database, and then click
   New Query. See Figure 3-43.

 We started the new query in the master database because that is where
the system procedure sp_configure is stored.

3. A new query session window opens as a tab in the right pane. Click in the Query window,
   type the SQL command **EXEC sp_configure;**, and then click the **Execute** button in the
   toolbar, or press the shortcut key **F5**, to run the procedure. In the Results pane below the
   query tab, a list of the basic SQL Server instance configuration settings will be displayed
   along with their currently configured values. The config_value is the value persisted in the
   database table; the run_value is the value in memory for the running instance. The query
   also shows the allowable range of values for each setting in the minimum and maximum
   columns. It is also possible to view and modify the advanced settings by changing the
   configured value for show advanced options from 0 to 1. See Figure 3-44.

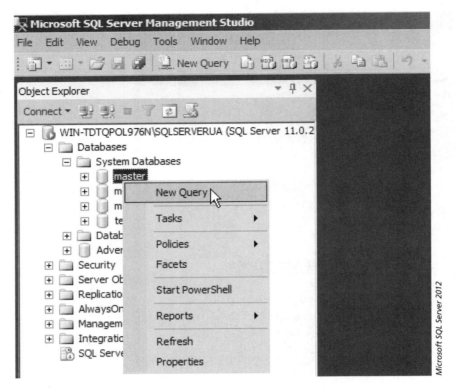

Figure 3-43 Create a new query using the master system database

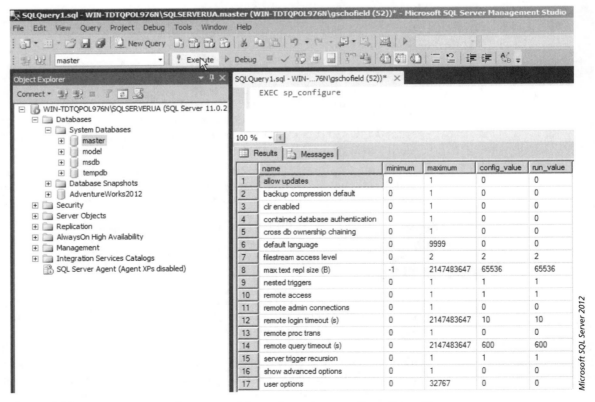

Figure 3-44 Execute the sp_configure procedure to view current configuration settings

4. You will change the remote query timeout setting's configured value from 600 seconds to 300 seconds. Click in the Query window, and type the following command to pass the setting name and new value as parameters into the sp_configure procedure:

```
EXEC sp_configure @configname='remote query timeout (s)', @
configvalue=300
```

Press **F5** to execute the query. See Figure 3-45.

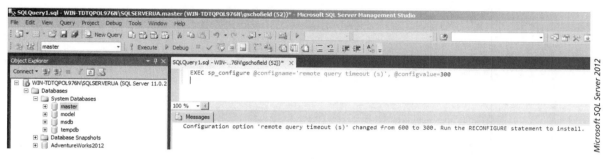

Figure 3-45 Use sp_configure to change the value of the remote query timeout setting

5. To change the run_value, run the RECONFIGURE command by typing the following:

```
RECONFIGURE;
```

Press the **Enter** key and type the following:

```
EXEC sp_configure;
```

Press **F5** to execute. Check to see that the run_value has been updated. See Figure 3-46.

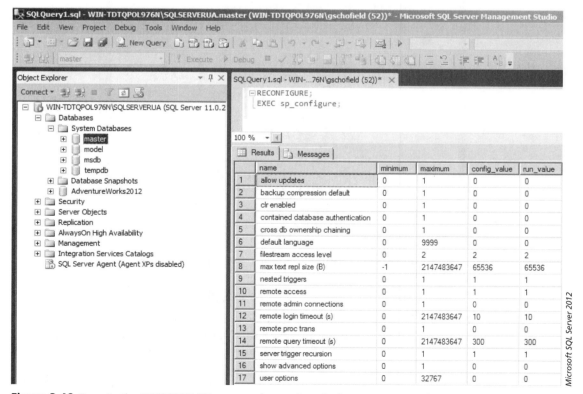

Figure 3-46 Execute the RECONFIGURE command to update the in-memory run value

6. Configuration settings can also be modified by opening the Properties form of the SQL Server instance. Right-click the **SQL Server instance name** in Object Explorer navigation pane, and then click **Properties**. See Figure 3-47.

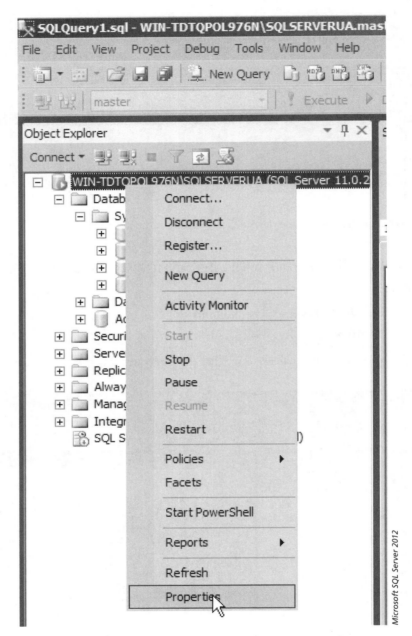

Figure 3-47 Open the SQL Server named instance Properties window using Object Explorer

7. In the Server Properties window, click **Connections** in the left navigation pane. Verify that the **Remote query timeout** setting matches the value that was set using the sp_configure procedure. You can switch between viewing Configured and Running values by toggling the option buttons at the bottom of the window. See Figure 3-48. It is important to note that advanced configuration settings can only be modified using the sp_configure procedure.

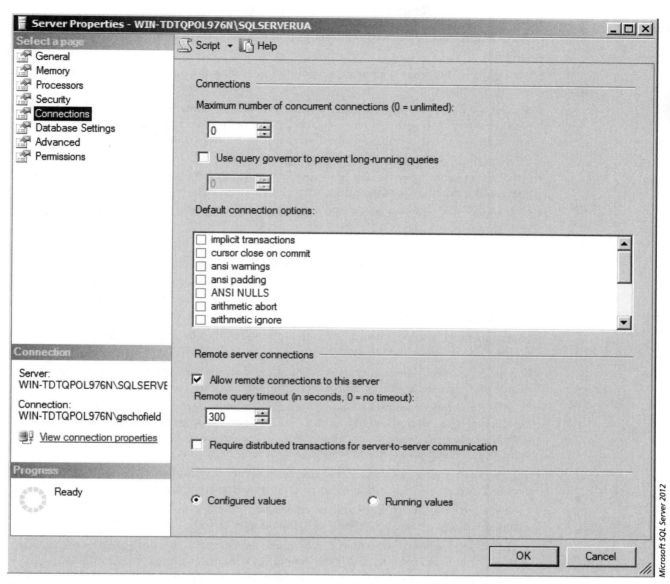

Microsoft SQL Server 2012

Figure 3-48 Validate the new Remote query timeout settings using Object Explorer

8. You have now completed Activity 3-5. Close all open windows by clicking the **X** in the upper-right corner of each application.

Chapter Summary

- The primary purpose of a database is to organize and securely store data while providing a flexible set of access methods for data retrieval and manipulation by client applications.

- Each SQL Server instance consists of five system databases (master, tempdb, model, resource, and msdb) used by the database management system to store configuration information and perform other functions.

- The basic building blocks of a database are tables and indexes.

- A row is a logical instance, commonly called a record, within a table of the real-world object that is being modeled, and it may contain several attributes that are defined as columns.
- Data types define what type of data a column can store; the main data types include unique identifiers, numbers of varying precision, dates and times, and text strings.
- A database index is a logical database structure used to improve the speed and efficiency of data access by storing a pointer to each record based upon a key. Each table should have a default index that is typically based upon a primary key—the column or combination of columns that uniquely identify each record.
- Other logical components include views (a type of saved query), procedures (scripts that query and manipulate data), and security objects such as users and roles.
- SQL Server 2012 uses messages called Tabular Data Stream (TDS) packets to communicate with client applications.
- When a remote client is conmmunicating with a SQL Server instance, TDS packets are encapsulated within a network protocol packet to enable transmission over a network.
- SQL Server provides direct support for three network protocols: shared memory, Named Pipes, and TCP/IP. Each protocol supports Kerberos, which is a widely used and highly secure network authentication mechanism.
- Shared memory is a local procedure call and requires the client application to be running on the same host as the SQL Server instance.
- Named Pipes is an older interprocess communication mechanism that enables a client application to connect to a server process on the same or different hosts.
- TCP/IP is the most common protocol used for remote connectivity. The default instance of SQL Server 2012 is configured to listen on TCP port 1433; ports for other named instances are either assigned dynamically when the database engine service starts or configured as static ports. Fixed ports should be used whenever a firewall is present.
- SQL Server Browser is a service that uses SQL Server Resolution Protocol (SSRP) to perform lookup and resolution of network protocol settings for named instances.
- Linked server objects use components called data providers to establish an interface with external sources of data and enable distributed queries to be run.
- SQL Server configuration settings can be managed using the sp_configure procedure, SQL Server Configuration Manager, or the Properties window in Object Explorer. Advanced settings can only be modified using the sp_configure procedure.

Key Terms

binary format A data format in which data is represented as a series of zeros and ones.

CodePlex Microsoft's open source project hosting site where you can find useful sample code for a wide range of Microsoft products.

column A representation of an attribute of the object being modeled by a table; defined with a unique column name and data type.

constraint A condition that imposes a limitation on a value or action; a column constraint specifies the allowable range of values that a column may contain, such as specific data types.

database index A logical database structure used to improve the speed and efficiency of data access. A database index is constructed based on a unique key, and it contains pointers to the underlying rows within the table.

data file A file that stores database objects and their underlying data; these files are given a .mdf file extension. Data files are subdivided into physical units of storage called pages that are grouped together into extents for space management.

data type A column attribute that defines the type of data a column can store; acts as a constraint because it limits the type of values that can be stored. The main data types include unique identifiers, numbers of varying precision, dates and times, and text strings.

extent A physical storage unit that is a collection of eight pages, grouped together for space management.

linked server A server that provides the capability to execute queries against a remote data source for running distributed queries. A linked server uses shared software components (called data providers) from the dynamic-link library (DLL) on the server to manage the interface between SQL Server and the external data source.

listener A service that enables a client to connect to the SQL Server instance over a network.

log file A file that records the series of changes that occur to a database over time, and they enable a database to be restored to a specific point in time.

logical structure A way of organizing data, with defined rules for storing, manipulating, and retrieving the data; client applications interact with logical objects within a database rather than the physical files.

loopback address An IP address that sends outbound packets of data directly back to the host computer to simulate a physical network.

master database A system database that stores the configuration settings that describe the structure and security of all the other databases.

model database A system database that is used as a template when creating a new user database.

Named Pipes An older interprocess communication mechanism that enables a client application to connect to a server process on the same or different hosts. Each SQL Server instance is able to listen on one named pipe.

Object Explorer A component of SQL Server Management Studio that provides a tree view of the different database schema objects organized as a series of folders.

Online Transaction Processing (OLTP) A method of data processing that is geared toward transaction-oriented applications that have a substantial write component in their interaction with the database; an OLTP database is defined by a high volume of individual read and write transactions.

page A physical storage unit in a data file.

primary key The column or combination of columns that uniquely identify each record within a table.

procedure A precompiled block of code that enables frequently performed tasks for querying and/or manipulating data to be stored as objects within the database.

Query Editor A component of SQL Server Management Studio that enables you to create SQL queries to be executed against a database.

row A logical instance of an object, commonly called a *record*, that is modeled by a table (e.g., an Employee); may contain several attributes that are defined as columns (e.g., first name, last name, Social Security number).

shared memory A local procedure call that requires the client application to be running on the same host as the SQL Server instance. No configuration options are available with a shared memory connection.

sp_configure A procedure that can be used to view and alter global configuration settings.

SQLCMD A utility that enables you to connect to the database from a command prompt and execute SQL commands and scripts.

SQL Server Browser A service that performs instance lookup and name resolution for remote clients.

SQL Server Management Studio A management tool used to configure, manage, and administer the Database Engine Services, Analysis Services, Integration Services, and Reporting Services.

SQL Server Network Interface layer The network protocol layer that manages the handoff of TDS packets between the SQL Server and the operating system–supported network protocol at an endpoint.

SQL Server Resolution Protocol (SSRP)   A protocol used by SQL Server Browser for performing instance lookup and name resolution for remote clients.

table   A collection of data stored in a database. In a relational database, tables are typically designed to model real-world objects and the relationships that exist between them. Tables are organized as a two-dimensional structure consisting of rows and columns.

table scan   A scan of every record within a table, undertaken by a database engine in the absence of a suitable index for a query.

Tabular Data Stream (TDS) packet   A message used by SQL Server for communication; when SQL Server is connected to a remote client, TDS packets must be encapsulated within a standard network protocol packet to enable the data to be sent over the network between the client and server.

TCP/IP   The most common protocol used for client/server connectivity.

trace   A log of events on the database management system that are captured using the SQL Server Profiler and commonly used for troubleshooting SQL Server performance issues.

trigger   A procedural mechanism that can be configured to automatically fire an event when a row is inserted, modified, or deleted; often used to satisfy compliance aspects of the business requirements by cascading details of a change into a related table or autopopulating metadata within a record.

view   A type of saved query.

Review Questions

1. Which of the following are objects within a database?

   a. Triggers

   b. Indexes

   c. Tables

   d. All of the above

2. What additional step must be taken to propagate changes made to the supported network protocols in SQL Server Configuration Manager into production?

   a. Execute the RECONFIGURE command in Query Editor.

   b. Restart IIS.

   c. Restart the SQL Server service from SQL Server Configuration Manager.

   d. Flush the DNS cache using the IPCONFIG utility.

3. Which shortcut key should be used to access context-sensitive help within Microsoft SQL Server Management Studio?

   a. F5

   b. F1

   c. F12

   d. F8

4. Which utilities could you use to activate a database trace?

   a. Activity Monitor

   b. NETSTAT

   c. SQL Profiler

   d. Both options a and c

5. For what purpose might a linked server be most useful?

    a. Limiting dependency upon a single data center

    b. Reducing the security footprint and associated management overhead

    c. Optimizing query performance over the network

    d. Integrating distributed data sources within a single query

6. SQL Server advanced configuration settings can be modified using _____.

    a. the sp_configure procedure

    b. SQL Server Configuration Manager

    c. Object Explorer within SQL Server Management Studio

    d. All of the above

7. Which of the following protocols is *not* directly supported by the SQL Server database engine for client connectivity?

    a. Shared Memory

    b. HTTP

    c. Named Pipes

    d. TCP/IP

8. Which shortcut key should be used to execute a SQL query from a Query Editor window?

    a. F5

    b. F1

    c. F12

    d. F8

9. What is the name of the authentication protocol that is supported by the different network protocols used by SQL Server?

    a. RADIUS

    b. Host Identity Protocol

    c. Kerberos

    d. All of the above

10. What is the most likely impact of a corrupt data file for the master system database?

    a. The SQL Server instance may fail to start.

    b. Processes may fail as they will be unable to store temporary data.

    c. Scheduled jobs will be unable to run.

    d. The template used to create new databases will be lost.

11. Why should you consider using an index?

    a. To improve speed and efficiency of data access

    b. To prevent full table scans

    c. To improve performance of data updates

    d. Both options a and b

12. Which of the following applications could you use to execute a SQL query?

    a. SQLCMD.exe

    b. SQL Configuration Manager

    c. Query Editor in SQL Server Management Studio

    d. Both options a and c

Case Projects

Case Project 3-1: The Rogue Developer

Alabama Life and Casualty Insurance Corporation specializes in underwriting commercial farm policies throughout the southern United States. The company's chief information officer has become increasingly concerned that one of the company's recent hires, a tech-savvy actuary, is directly accessing several production SQL Server databases using unapproved tools and access methods. Before approaching the employee's supervisor, he has asked you, as the database administrator, to gather some additional information on the client application, network protocol, and queries that he believes the actuary is using on a routine basis. Your SQL Server 2012 instance is configured for Windows Authentication only and you manage role security using Active Directory. The database server is only accessible from within the local area network (LAN), and no firewalls are present between the server and client applications. Complete the following:

- Devise and document a plan that includes the database and/or network utilities that you would use to gather the information that has been requested.
- Describe the potential pitfalls you envisage in trying to execute this plan.
- Explain which data elements you think will be most challenging to capture, and why.

Case Project 3-2: Configuration Options

An application developer has proposed using the xp_cmdshell procedure to move some files to a staging directory on a network drive. She has attempted to call this procedure from within her development environment but is receiving the following error message when executing the SQL query:

```
Msg 15123, Level 16, State 1, Procedure sp_configure, Line 51

The configuration option 'xp_cmdshell' does not exist, or it may be
an advanced option.
```

A junior database administrator looked into the issue, but he was unable to find the configuration option for this procedure within Object Explorer of SQL Server Management Studio. The issue has now been escalated to you. Both the developer and her project manager are anxious to resolve the problem due to a looming client deadline. Complete the following:

- Using Books Online for SQL Server 2012 and other online resources, research the xp_cmdshell procedure and the error message described previously.
- Describe the steps that you would take to configure the xp_cmdshell procedure.
- Based upon your research, do you have any concern about enabling this option?
- Write a brief summary of your research, focusing in particular on any security or resource considerations.

Hands-On Projects

Hands-On Project 3-1: Client/Server Connectivity

For this hands-on project, you will use the SQL Server named instance SQLSERVERHOA that you created in Hands-On Project 2-1. The objective of this project is to configure and test client/server connectivity using a variety of network protocols that are supported by SQL Server. Document your work by taking a screen shot at the end of each step.

1. Begin by ensuring that the Shared Memory and TCP/IP protocols are enabled for your instance using SQL Server Configuration Manager. Configure the TCP/IP server listener to use the static TCP port 4459.

2. Use SQLCMD to test connecting to the SQLSERVERHOA named instance using Shared Memory.

3. Use SQLCMD to test connecting to the SQLSERVERHOA TCP/IP listener on TCP port 4459. Use the 127.0.0.1 loopback address to simulate the network.

4. Troubleshoot any failures in Steps 2 and 3. For each failure, document the steps (using a bulleted list) that were taken to diagnose and resolve each issue.

chapter 4

Creating SQL Server 2012 Databases

After reading this chapter and completing the exercises, you will be able to:

- Plan a new user database that supports the relevant business requirements

- Explain the benefits of tailoring the model system database settings for your organization

- Construct a new database from Object Explorer or by executing a SQL query using Query Editor

- Modify the configuration settings of an existing database, rename a database, and delete a database

- Create new tables, and apply a foreign key relationship between two tables

Planning is an important, but often overlooked, aspect of implementing a new user database. Neglecting the planning phase prior to creating a new database is likely to result in a legacy of time-consuming support issues, user frustration, and unnecessary management overhead.

This chapter builds upon your knowledge of the SQL Server physical and logical architecture you acquired in Chapter 3. You will learn the practical skills needed to plan and implement a new user database that addresses current business needs, scales to meet future growth, and minimizes ongoing maintenance and support. You will also learn how to set up data and log files, manage physical file growth, adopt consistent object naming conventions, and understand the flexibility of the logical security model. SQL Server 2012 offers several options for creating a database; in the practical activities included with this chapter, you will walk through the necessary steps to create a database using Object Explorer in SQL Server Management Studio and by executing a SQL command in Query Editor. In Chapter 3, you were introduced to the functions of the four system databases. In this chapter, you will explore the model database and default configuration options in more detail.

A production database requires ongoing maintenance and support for a number of reasons. Business users change over time, and the security model of the database must be adjusted accordingly. The database is likely to grow, which means you must actively manage the database size and physical resources. Lastly, business needs change, and you may be required to rename or delete a database, as well as extend the database by adding new objects such as tables. In Activity 4-4, you will complete the steps necessary to create new tables and apply the relationships that exist between them by adding a foreign key.

Planning a New User Database

You can create a new user database in a matter of seconds, but in order to satisfy the business requirements and ensure that the database is maintainable in the context of your organization, you must tailor certain configuration options. Because a database may remain in existence long after you have departed an organization, you should create the database in a manner that makes it easy for other database administrators to understand and manage it.

 Although it is possible to change the configuration of a database after it is created, doing so can be more challenging because you must ensure that any changes you make do not adversely impact client applications that have become dependent upon the existing logical object model.

This section discusses the steps and considerations involved in planning a new user database, and it introduces the different tools available for creating a new database in SQL Server 2012. You will learn how the model database is used as a template for new user databases, and you will gain an understanding of the benefits of tailoring these defaults to suit the needs of your organization. In the activities in this chapter, you will learn two different methods of creating a database using the graphical tools in Object Explorer of SQL Server Management Studio and by using the SQL programming language. Although there are many settings that can be tuned for individual situations, the following important elements are discussed in this section:

- A physical file architecture that addresses high performance and recovery
- A simple yet robust security model
- Intuitive and consistent naming conventions for the logical objects in the database
- Selection of appropriate data types for the database objects

Implementation Options

Each database contains a number of **configuration options**, which are settings that determine the behavior of the database. Before creating a new database, you should always make a full backup of the master system database, which stores the configuration settings. There are two main approaches to creating a new user database using SQL Server Management Studio—via a graphical interface accessed through Object Explorer and by running a SQL query in Query Editor. You have worked with both Object Explorer and Query Editor in previous chapters.

SQL Server Management Studio provides a graphical interface for creating a new database that can be launched from within Object Explorer. This tool provides a good introduction to the available configuration options and does not require extensive experience with the SQL programming language.

User databases can also be created by executing the CREATE database syntax and supplying a set of configuration parameters using the SQL programming language. The **CREATE** statement is a SQL instruction to create an object. This option is sometimes preferred by experienced database administrators because it allows them to create standardized scripts, rather than having to manually change each configuration parameter in a Windows form. You used a script in Chapter 3 to create the Adventure Works 2012 database. SQL scripts can be executed through a variety of tools that include the Query Editor window in SQL Server Management Studio and the SQLCMD command prompt. Object Explorer can also be used to automatically generate a SQL script that will re-create, alter, or delete any existing object. The resulting script can either be saved as a file for later use or executed from a Query Editor window.

Unless you explicitly choose to override a configuration option, the database will be created using default settings. In fact, the only required setting that must be supplied when creating a database is a unique database name. Recall from Chapter 3 that the model system database is used as the template when creating a new user database. The majority of the settings in the model system database can be changed, and any subsequent new databases that are created on the SQL Server instance will inherit these settings. By customizing the model database template to the standard settings you have chosen for your organization, you can greatly improve the efficiency and consistency of creating new databases. The steps to modify the model database settings are identical to those of a user database and are described later in this chapter.

Activity 4-1: Exploring the Configuration Options for Creating a Database

Time Required: 30 minutes
Objective: Find out more information about the default database configuration settings using Books Online for SQL Server 2012.

Description: Using Microsoft Books Online for SQL Server 2012, you will learn more about database configuration settings and the default settings of the model database.

1. If necessary, start your computer and log on using an Administrator account.

2. Click the **Start** button, point to **All Programs**, and click **Internet Explorer** to launch your Web browser. In the Address bar, type **msdn.microsoft.com** and then press the **Enter** key to load the Microsoft Developer Network site. See Figure 4-1.

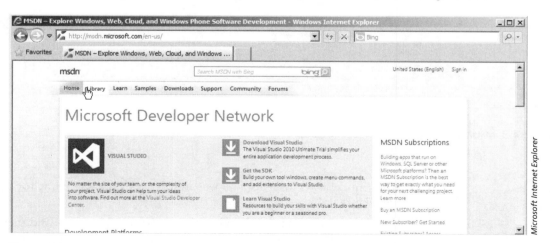

Figure 4-1 Microsoft Developer Network site

3. Click **Library** to open the MSDN Library. In the search box in the upper-left corner of the window, type **model Database** and then click the **Search** icon. See Figure 4-2.

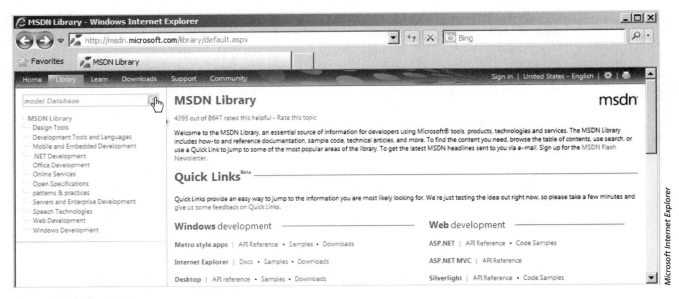

Figure 4-2 MSDN Library

4. Click the **model Database** link, which should be the top result in the search pane. See Figure 4-3.

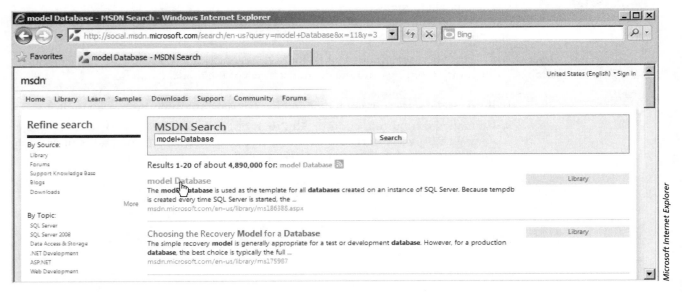

Figure 4-3 MSDN search results for model Database

5. The "model Database" topic opens in Microsoft Books Online for SQL Server 2012. See Figure 4-4.

6. Scroll down the page, and review the configurable settings and their defaults in the Database Options section. Next, review the Restrictions section for settings that may not be altered in the model database.

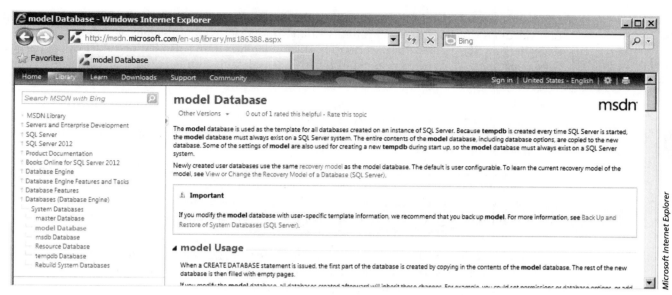

Figure 4-4 "Model Database" topic in Microsoft Books Online for SQL Server 2012

7. Click in the search box in the upper-left corner of the window, type **create database** and click the **Search** icon. Click the **CREATE DATABASE (Transact-SQL)** link at the top of the search results to open the topic.

8. Scroll down to the Arguments section, and read the descriptions of the arguments, which include the database configuration settings. Scroll further down to the Examples section, and read example A "Creating a database without specifying files" and example B "Creating a database that specifies the data and transaction log file."

9. Close your Web browser.

Data and Log File Options

The logical object model in SQL Server 2012 overlays a physical file structure, which you were introduced to in the architecture section of Chapter 3. There are two main types of physical files: data files and log files. A SQL Server database must have at least one of each file type.

Data files store the data that is organized in tables and indexes as well as the schemas to the various objects that represent the logical structure of the database. A **schema** is a logical container that groups together collections of objects within a database and allows them to be managed as a group. Data files are placed into **filegroups** for storage management. Each database must have a primary filegroup with at least one data file. However, a database may have more than one data file in a filegroup; the database is able to use all the data files concurrently, which can improve performance. If using more than one data file within a filegroup, the data files should all be the same size as the database attempts to fill them equally. Secondary user-defined filegroups can be created for a specific purpose, for example to store the data from a specific object or database partition to improve **I/O performance**, a term used to describe the number of read and write operations that can be processed by the physical disk in a given time frame. To properly configure multiple data files and filegroups for best performance, you must know how the physical drive is configured.

Log files record the database transaction activity. A **database transaction** is a logical unit of work reading or writing from a database. Database transactions are important for maintaining the integrity and consistency of the database. A database transaction is designed to roll back should the transaction fail. The rollback capability relies on writing the transaction to the log file prior to committing the transaction to the data file. The log of database transactions is also necessary when recovering a database from a backup—which is done by replaying the transaction activity from the log to ensure no loss of data. It is possible to have more than one log file for a single database; however, because the database only uses one log file at a time, the only advantage of this approach is to distribute storage across multiple physical disks.

By default, SQL Server 2012 stores the data and log files in the installation folder of your SQL Server instance. In a production environment, these default settings should be changed so that the data and log files are stored on different physical disks due to the following:

- If the physical disk that stores the data files becomes damaged, you will need the log files to recover the database and avoid data loss. If the log is sitting on the same physical disk as a corrupt or damaged data file, there is a high probability that the log files will also be lost.

- Storing data and log files on the same physical disk increases the likelihood of contention. **Contention** is the term used to describe a situation in which two processes compete for the same resource, in this case the physical disk. The result is an increase in the workload the disk must perform, which in turn increases the odds that a process will have to wait for another process to finish before it can write to the disk.

Lastly, we will consider the database settings—Initial Size, Autogrowth, and Maxsize—that govern the initial file sizes and define how the database engine manages growth of these files. These settings typically need to be changed from their defaults.

The **Initial Size** setting defines the initial size of the data and log files; the default sizes are 4 MB and 1 MB, respectively. Increasing the file size after a database has been created consumes significant resources and will lead to degraded performance. Other than the space that the files occupy on a physical disk, there is no harm in setting a file size that is much larger than the space that the data occupies.

The **Autogrowth** and **Maxsize** settings define the actions that the database management system will take when it fills up either the log or data file. The Maxsize allows you to specify a limit on the size of the database. Best practice is not to use the Maxsize setting (which is done by setting Maxsize to unlimited, which is the default setting) because the consequences of the database reaching the size limit can be disastrous. However, without a limit on the growth of the database, you must proactively monitor the physical disk space, database file size, and perform routine maintenance tasks to ensure that sufficient space is made available. The Autogrowth setting specifies how much the database will increase the size of the physical files once the space that was initially allocated to them becomes full; the Autogrowth setting can be stated in absolute or relative terms. The defaults are 1 MB for the data file and 10 percent for the log file. Due to the performance impact of increasing the size of the files, you should make these settings sufficiently large to make file growth a very infrequent event. As you will see in Activity 4-3, it is also possible to manually expand the log or data file size.

Database Ownership and Permissions

A key step in planning a database involves ensuring that the users have an appropriate set of permissions to perform their specific job function, while at the same time restricting wider permissions that may compromise the security of the data. You also should design this aspect of the database in a way that minimizes the amount of support required when a permission change is needed, for example when a user leaves or joins the firm. Fortunately, SQL Server 2012 has a very flexible logical security model that can help you to achieve all of these goals if implemented properly. See Figure 4-5.

Chapter 6 is dedicated to the logical security model. However, because it is important to include security considerations when planning a database, a summary has been included here to help you become familiar with the topic.

SQL Server 2012 supports two types of authentication for connecting to the database server: Windows authentication and SQL Server authentication. The logins associated with authentication on a SQL Server instance are distinct from the security principals known as database users that are defined for each database. Each login may be mapped to one or more database user. For database objects, permissions are granted to a database user and not to the login that is used for authentication. A **permission** is a right to be able to perform an action against a database object.

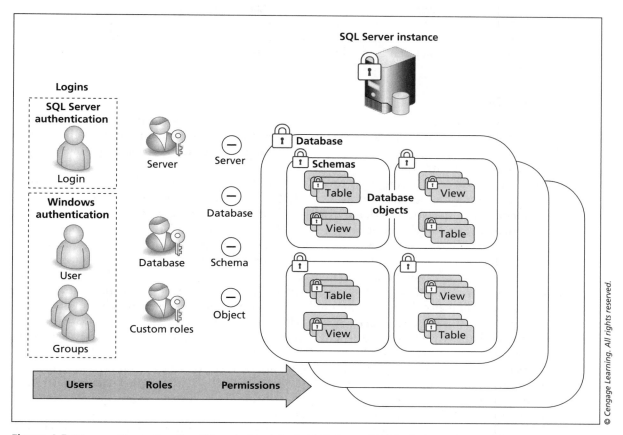

Figure 4-5 Diagram illustrating the different objects in the SQL Server 2012 logical security model

Connecting to a database, reading data from a table, and modifying a view are all examples of actions that require a certain permission. Permissions can be granted to database users at different levels within the hierarchy of objects on a database server. The widest reaching are server-level permissions that allow a user to perform a set of actions on any database hosted by the server. Server-level permissions should be used with extreme discretion. At the next level down, database permissions apply to all objects in a database. For example, granting the EXECUTE permission to a user on a database allows the user to execute any procedure within that database. At a more granular level, permissions can be applied to an individual object within a database, for example to a particular table.

Granting or revoking permissions for each individual user at the level of the objects within a database that has several hundred different users will rapidly become unsustainable and will make it difficult to decipher who has access to what resources. SQL Server 2012 has two additional objects that can be used to simplify management of permissions while maintaining a similar level of control for each object:

- A **role** groups together permissions on different database objects. A role can be granted to an individual user, known as a member in the context of the role, and that user will inherit the permissions granted to the role. Roles should be used whenever possible to manage permissions for groups of database users with similar access needs. SQL Server 2012 has several predefined roles at both the server and database level. An example of a server role is the sysadmin role, which can perform any function on the database server. An example of a database role is the db_owner role, which can perform any function for an individual database. Roles can also be used to model a business function to differentiate different access levels that groups of users need at a granular level.

- As explained earlier, schemas group together collections of objects within a database and allow them to be managed as a group. Because permissions can be granted on a schema to a user or role, they can be used to simplify management of a particular segment of the database.

Data Types

A data type is a predefined form of data that specifies the data values that a logical database object can store. A data type attribute must be defined for each column and variable in a database. The main categories of data type are character and Unicode string types, binary types, numeric types, and date types.

SQL Server offers a number of predefined system data types and also allows custom user-defined types to be configured. User-defined data types are typically used to ensure consistency at an application level. For example, if a database administrator needs to store a value in a particular format that can be reused across the system (e.g., a ZIP + 4 postal code), then a user-defined data type may be warranted. When assigning a data type attribute to a database object, a database administrator must weigh the storage implications against the required level of precision, scale, and length. **Precision** refers to the number of places after the decimal point in a numeric data type or the accuracy in the case of a date data type. **Scale** is the maximum number of digits that a numeric data type can hold, and **length** is the maximum number of characters that a string can store. A character data type with a length of 250 characters that is used to store a text string that will never exceed 50 characters in length results in wasted storage because the system preallocates storage based on the defined data type regardless of the actual size of the value being stored. Conversely, an integer should not be used for a price field because an integer stores whole numbers only and the decimal precision would be lost. Assigned data types must be used consistently across a database to avoid unnecessary data type conversions when combining or comparing data. For example, storing a date as a character string in one table but as a date in another table would necessitate a data type conversion in a query if the dates needed to be compared against each other. This results in needless system overhead when performing the data type conversion. A list of common data types that you will encounter throughout this book are shown in Table 4-1.

Object Naming Conventions

The names of database objects serve as a communication system that enables users and administrators to easily interact with a database. Because there are few restrictions enforced by the database management system when selecting object names, a variety of different naming conventions exist and are a topic of continuous debate within the database community. Whatever naming convention you decide to use, it should be intuitive, unambiguous, and applied consistently across the database.

Object names, also known as identifiers, must be unique within each database. Column names must be unique within a table. The Adventure Works 2012 sample database provides a good reference model that we recommend you adopt. Keep the following guidelines in mind when creating an object-naming model:

- **Camel case** is a naming convention that concatenates (links together) words using uppercase for the first character of each word. Examples of this style are FirstName, LastName, and AdventureWorks2012. Camel case is easier to read than linking words together using underscores or other characters and should form the basic syntax for naming objects.

- Tables are the only type of object that should be named without a character prefix. For all other objects, a standard character prefix should be used for each object type to delineate between the different object types. For example *v* for view, *usp* for user-defined stored procedures, and *ufn* for user-defined functions.

- There are rules that govern the format of an identifier and certain characters and words should not be used. For example, object names should not include certain special characters such as a space. The use of **reserved keywords**, which are words that also belong

Table 4-1   Commonly used system data types

Data type	Description	Example
char(n)	A char(n) is a fixed-length character string data type that can store a maximum of 8000 characters; the number in parentheses to the right of the data type specifies the maximum length of the string.	char(25)
varchar(n)	A varchar(n) is a variable-length character string data type that can store a maximum of 8000 characters; a varchar uses only the number of bytes needed to store the actual column value but will result in an additional system cost to allocate storage space when a value is inserted or modified relative to a char whose storage is preallocated.	varchar(50)
nchar(n)	An nchar(n) is a fixed-length Unicode string data type that can store a maximum of 4000 characters.	nchar(50)
nvarchar(n)	An nvarchar(n) is a variable-length Unicode string data type that can store a maximum of 4000 characters.	nchar(50)
bit	A bit is an integer data type that may only store the values 0 or 1.	bit
int	An int is an integer data type that may store whole numbers that range from negative 2,147,483,648 to positive 2,147,483,647.	int
decimal (precision, scale)	The decimal data type stores numeric data with fixed precision and scale. The precision determines the number of decimals that are stored after the decimal point; the scale determines the total number of digits that can be used.	decimal (8, 18)
float	The float data type stores numeric data with floating decimal precision.	float
money	The money data type stores monetary data with four decimal places of precision.	money
date	The date data type stores the date only with values that may range from 0001-01-01 to 9999-12-31.	date
datetime	A datetime data type stores a date and time with 3.33 milliseconds of precision; it may hold values ranging from 1753-01-01 to 9999-12-31.	datetime

© Cengage Learning

to the SQL programming language, is restricted because their use may lead to ambiguity. Although not recommended, reserved keywords and special characters may still be used in object names, but they must be enclosed in delimiters: double quotation marks or square brackets. For example, naming a table column *First Name* creates two problems. First, the name contains a space and second, Name is a reserved keyword. Referencing this column would require the use of delimiters, such as [First Name] or "First Name." FirstName would avoid these issues.

- Abbreviated terms (e.g., Qty) should be used sparingly and only when the term has a common, unambiguous interpretation.

Activity 4-2: Creating a New Database

Time Required: 60 minutes

Objective: Create a new user database in Microsoft SQL Server Management Studio.

Description: Changing business needs typically dictate when a new database needs to be created. In this activity, you will learn the steps involved in creating a new user database by launching the New Database dialog box from Object Explorer in SQL Server Management Studio. You will then use Object Explorer to automatically generate a SQL script to create a second user database that clones the configuration settings of the first database. Finally, you will write a simple SQL query in a Query Editor window using the CREATE database syntax to create a third database that uses all of the default settings from the model system database. You will use Windows Explorer to view the physical data and log files that will be created on the local operating system.

1. If necessary, start your computer and log on using an Administrator account.

2. Click the **Start** button, point to **All Programs**, click **Microsoft SQL Server 2012**, and then click **SQL Server Management Studio**. In the Connect to Server dialog box, select **Database Engine** as the server type, type **LOCALHOST\SQLSERVERUA** in the Server name text box, and select **Windows Authentication** from the Authentication list box. Click **Connect**.

3. In the Object Explorer navigation pane on the left of the SQL Server Management Studio window, expand the SQLSERVERUA folder by clicking the **+** symbol. Right-click the **Databases** folder, and in the shortcut menu, click **New Database** (see Figure 4-6) to launch the New Database dialog box.

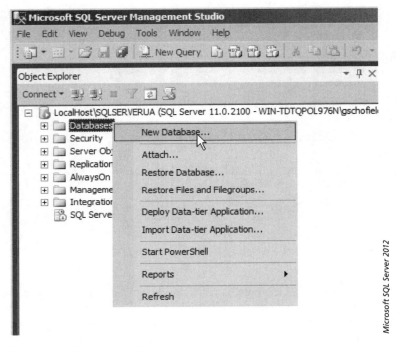

Figure 4-6 Databases folder shortcut menu

4. In the New Database dialog box, click in the **Database name** text box and type **TestOne** (using camel case) as your database name. Click in the **Initial Size (MB)** text box, and type **50** for the data file (first row) and type **20** for the log file (second row). Click the **...** icon in the Autogrowth/Maxsize column for the data file. In the Change Autogrowth for TestOne dialog box, click the **Enable Autogrowth** check box, and then type **10** in the File Growth In Megabytes text box. Keep the default maximum file size set to unlimited. Click **OK**. Now Click the **...** icon in the Autogrowth/Maxsize column for the log file. In the Change Autogrowth for TestOne_log dialog box, click the **Enable Autogrowth** check box, and then type **5** in the File Growth In Megabytes text box. Keep the default maximum file size set to unlimited. Click **OK** to return to the New Database dialog box. Note that this window gives you the ability to add additional data or log files by clicking the Add button. It also allows you to change the owner of the database and the path to the physical files. See Figure 4-7.

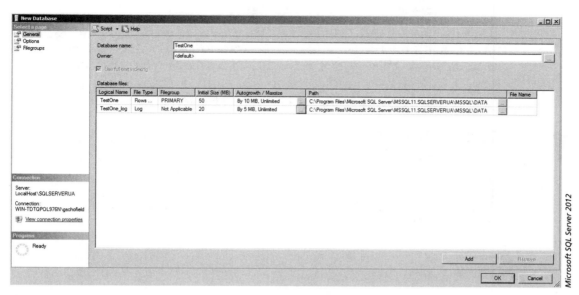

Figure 4-7 New Database dialog box—General page

5. In the left navigation pane, click **Options** to open the Options page of database properties in the New Database dialog box. See Figure 4-8.

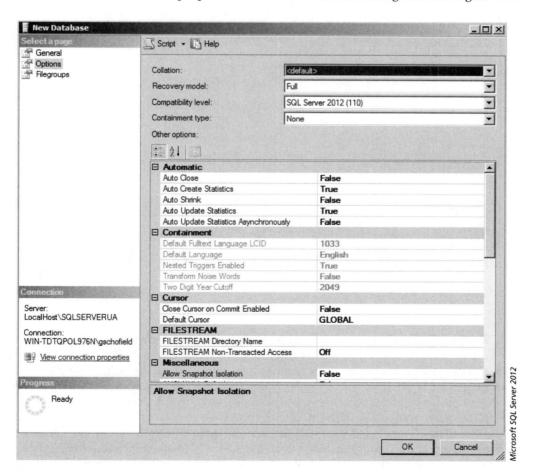

Figure 4-8 New Database dialog box—Options page

This page allows you to view or modify the configuration options for the new database. Many of these options should be familiar to you because you read about them in Activity 4-1 when you accessed the "CREATE DATABASE (Transact-SQL)" topic on Books Online for SQL Server 2012. Keep the default configuration options.

6. In the left navigation pane, click **Filegroups** to open the Filegroups page of database properties in the New Database dialog box. See Figure 4-9.

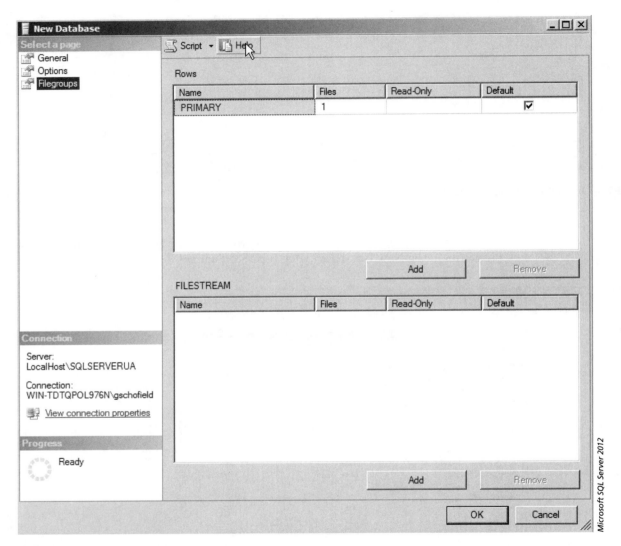

Figure 4-9 New Database dialog box—Filegroups page

7. This page allows you to view or modify the filegroups or filestreams for the database. Every database must have a primary filegroup, which the database will use as its default data storage location. A filegroup contains one or more data files, which the database management system will fill in roughly equal proportions. Additional user-defined filegroups can be added to improve performance. For example, a nonprimary filegroup may be designated as the data storage location for a particular table. Filestreams are only needed if you intend to store unstructured data within the database. Click the **Help** button at the top of the dialog box to open the "Database Properties (Filegroups Page)" topic on Books Online for SQL Server 2012 in your Web browser. When you are finished reviewing the information, close your Web browser.

8. In the New Database dialog box, click **OK** to create the database. The New Database dialog box closes, and you are returned to Object Explorer.

The left navigation page of Object Explorer does not automatically refresh after a change is made to a schema object. You must manually refresh the user interface to see the changes.

9. Click the **Databases** folder in Object Explorer, and then click the **Refresh** button on the toolbar. If the Databases folder is not already expanded, click the + symbol to the left of the folder to expand. You should see your new database named TestOne listed beneath AdventureWorks2012. See Figure 4-10.

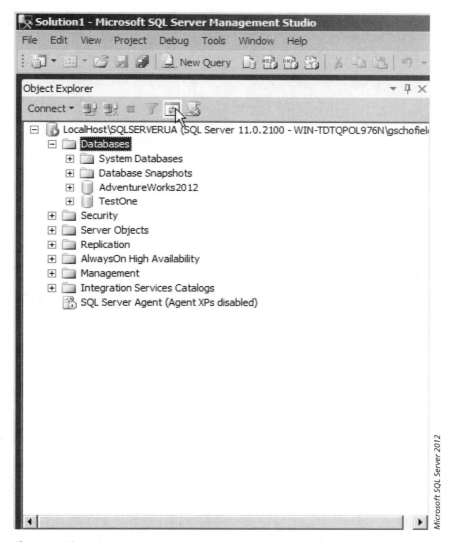

Figure 4-10 TestOne database is visible in the Databases folder of Object Explorer

10. In Object Explorer, right-click the **TestOne** database, and then click **Properties** to open the Database Properties dialog box and view the configuration settings of the database that you created in Step 8. See Figure 4-11. Close the Database Properties dialog box by clicking the **X** in the upper-right corner of the window.

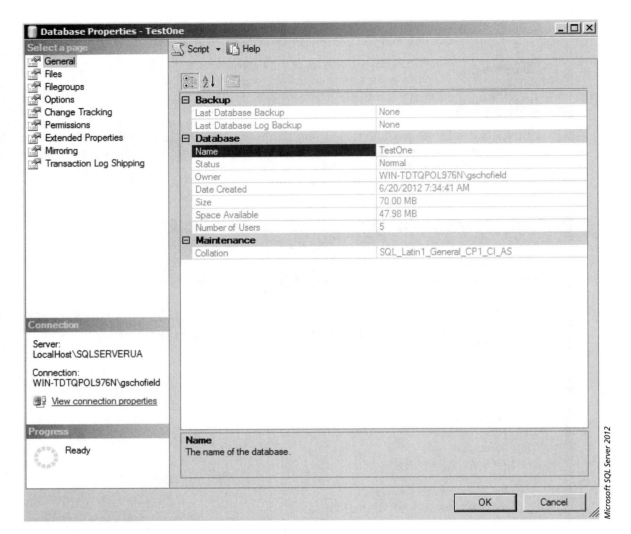

Figure 4-11 Database Properties dialog box for the TestOne database.

11. Using Object Explorer, you will now instruct the database to generate a SQL CREATE DATABASE script that will open in a Query Editor window using the TestOne database as your template for the configuration. Right-click the **TestOne** database, point to **Script Database as**, point to **CREATE To**, and then click **New Query Editor Window**. See Figure 4-12.

12. The CREATE DATABASE script appears in a Query Editor window on your right. You are making a clone of the TestOne database, but you must use a different name because a database name is unique. On the menu bar of SQL Server Management Studio, click **Edit**, point to **Find and Replace**, and then click **Quick Replace**. See Figure 4-13.

13. In the Find and Replace dialog box, type **TestOne** in the Find what text box, and type **TestTwo** in the Replace with text box. Click **Replace All**. A dialog box opens informing you that you have replaced 38 occurrences of *TestOne* with *TestTwo* in the current document. Click **OK**, and then close the Find and Replace dialog box.

14. Review the SQL database CREATE script in the Query Editor window. Note that some of the occurrences of TestTwo are underlined in red. This is because the database management system does not yet recognize TestTwo as a valid database object (you are about to create it). Click the **Execute** button on the toolbar or press the **F5**

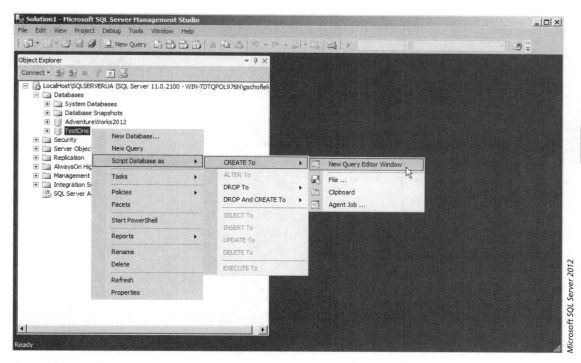

Figure 4-12 Menu options to automatically generate a CREATE DATABASE script in SQL

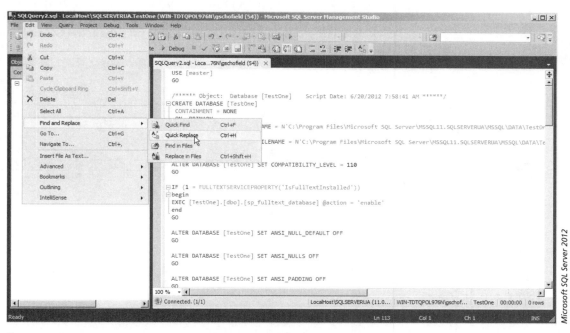

Figure 4-13 Use Quick Replace to replace TestOne with TestTwo

shortcut key to execute the query and create the TestTwo database. See Figure 4-14. The message "Command(s) completed successfully" should appear in a pane at the bottom of Query Editor.

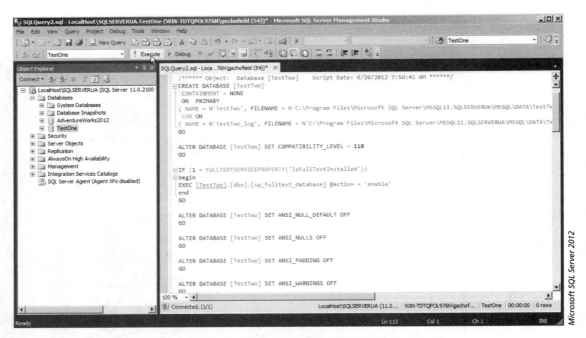

Figure 4-14 CREATE DATABASE script for the TestTwo database prior to execution

15. In Object Explorer, click **Databases**, and then click the **Refresh** button on the toolbar. Expand the Databases folder, right-click the **TestTwo** database, and then click **Properties** to open the Database Properties dialog box. Click **Files** in the left navigation menu. Scroll to the right, and make a note of the file path and filename for the data and log file in the Database files section. Copy the file path into your Clipboard by clicking the top cell in the Path column and pressing **Ctrl+C**. See Figure 4-15.

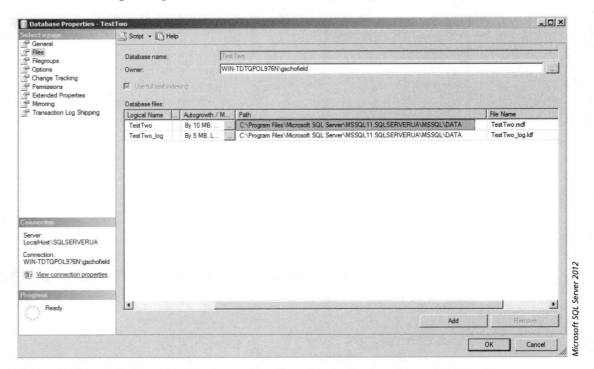

Figure 4-15 Find the file path of the data and log files using the Database Properties dialog box

16. Click **Cancel** to close the Database Properties dialog box. Click the **Start** button, and then click **Computer** to launch Windows Explorer. Navigate to the file path location you wrote down in Step 15, either by clicking through the folder structure in the left navigation pane, or by clicking in the **Address bar**, entering the file path, and then pressing the **Enter** key. See Figure 4-16.

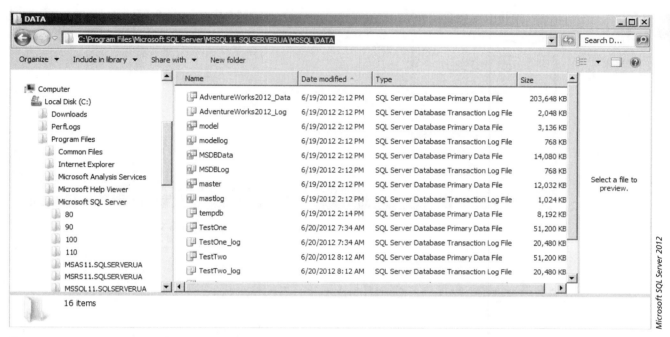

Figure 4-16 Navigate to the Data folder of the SQL server instance SQLSERVERUA

17. Note that this folder contains a data and log file for each of the system databases and the user database that you have created. For a production database server, it is not recommended that you use the same physical disk for both file types. Close Windows Explorer.

18. Return to SQL Server Management Studio and click the **New Query** button on the toolbar to launch an empty Query Editor window. Type the following SQL query in the Query Editor window: **CREATE DATABASE TestThree**. Press the **F5** shortcut key to execute your SQL query. See Figure 4-17.

19. You have now created a new database called TestThree using the SQL programming language using the defaults from the model system database. You can view this in Object Explorer by clicking the **Databases** folder, clicking the **Refresh** button on the toolbar, and then expanding the Databases folder.

Essential Database Administration Tasks

A database will require changes to its configuration settings as business needs evolve with time. This section provides an introduction to several important administration tasks that a database administrator must know how to perform. These tasks include deleting and renaming databases, managing the physical data and log file size, and adding and modifying database objects such as tables and keys. Changing logical security and managing backup and recovery options are also core day-to-day tasks; each of these tasks is covered in its own chapter later in the book.

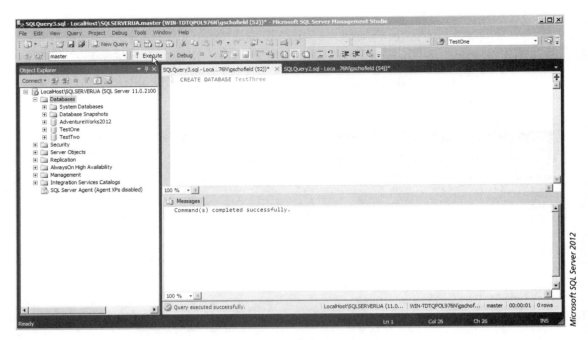

Figure 4-17 Create a database based on the model database defaults using a SQL query

Altering Database Configuration Settings

The database configuration settings can be modified using the Database Properties dialog box from Object Explorer in SQL Server Management Studio or by executing a SQL query. Before making changes in a production environment, you should take a full backup of the master system database and the user database. You should also assess all dependencies, for example renaming the database may impact client applications that attach to the database; therefore, the change will require coordination with the owner of the application. If possible, planned changes to database configuration settings should always be undertaken during a maintenance window when the database is not in use by client applications. In the SQL language, the CREATE statement is used to add a new object, the **ALTER** statement is an instruction to change an existing object, and the **DROP** statement is used to delete an object. Chapter 5 covers the SQL language in more depth.

Activity 4-3: Altering Database Configuration Settings

Time Required: 30 minutes
Objective: Use Object Explorer and Query Editor to make changes to the database configuration settings and to delete and rename a database.

Description: In this activity, you will learn the steps to alter configuration settings by using options available in the Database Properties window and by using the ALTER statement in Query Editor. You will also use the menu options in Object Explorer to automatically create a script to DROP a database. Finally, you will rename a database in Object Explorer and use the Delete Object dialog box to delete a database.

1. If necessary, start your computer and log on using an Administrator account.

2. Click the **Start** button, point to **All Programs**, click **Microsoft SQL Server 2012**, and then click **SQL Server Management Studio**. In the Connect to Server dialog box, select **Database Engine** as the server type, type **LOCALHOST\SQLSERVERUA** in the Server name text box, and select **Windows Authentication** from the Authentication list box. Click **Connect**.

3. In the Object Explorer navigation pane on the left of the SQL Server Management Studio window, expand the SQLSERVERUA folder and the Databases folder by clicking the **+** symbol. Right-click the **TestTwo** database, and then click **Properties**. In the Database Properties dialog box, click **Options** in the left navigation menu. Select **Simple** from the Recovery model drop-down list. See Figure 4-18.

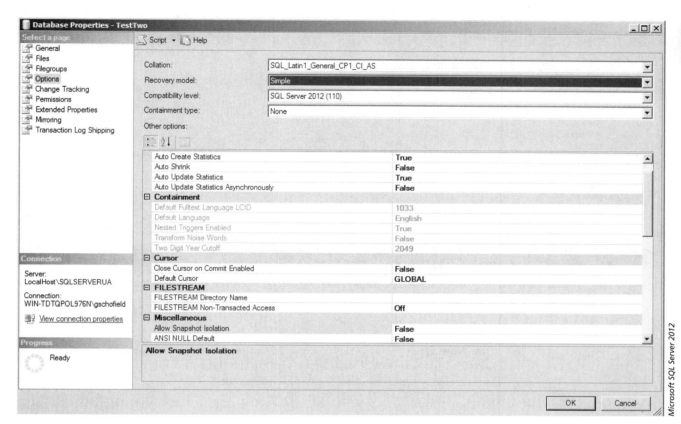

Figure 4-18 Changing the recovery model for the TestTwo database using the Database Properties dialog box

 The recovery model is a configuration setting that specifies which type of database transactions should be recorded in the transaction log. The simple recovery model does not record any database transactions in the transaction log. Chapter 8 covers SQL Server recovery models in detail.

Next, you'll change the recovery model of the TestOne database by using the ALTER statement in Query Editor. The full recovery model records all database transactions in the transaction log.

4. Click **OK**, and then click **New Query** on the SQL Server Management Studio toolbar to launch a new Query Editor window. Type the following SQL commands:

```
USE MASTER

GO

ALTER DATABASE TestOne

SET RECOVERY FULL

GO
```

5. Click the **Execute** button on the toolbar or press the **F5** shortcut to run the query and change the recovery model for TestOne to Full. See Figure 4-19.

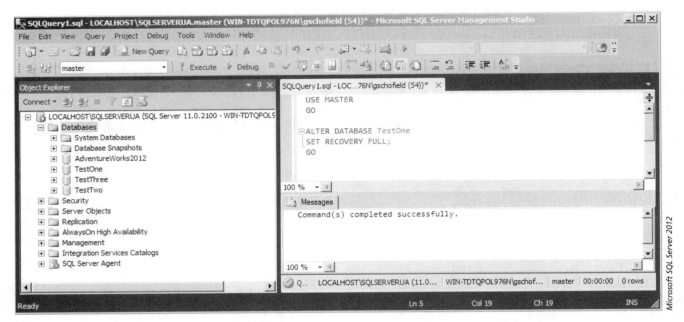

Figure 4-19 Changing the recovery model for the TestOne database by running a SQL command from Query Editor

6. Click **New Query** in the SQL Server Management Studio toolbar to launch a new Query Editor window. Expand the size of the data and log files for the TestThree database by typing the following SQL command:

```
USE MASTER

GO

ALTER DATABASE TestThree

MODIFY FILE (NAME = TestThree, SIZE = 25)

ALTER DATABASE TestThree

MODIFY FILE (NAME = TestThree_Log, SIZE = 10)

GO
```

7. Click the **Execute** button on the toolbar or press the **F5** shortcut to run the query. See Figure 4-20. Note that the filename refers to the logical name of the file.

   Next, using Object Explorer, you will instruct the database to delete the TestThree database by generating a SQL DROP DATABASE script into a Query Editor window.

8. Right-click the **TestThree** database, and then click **Script Database as**, point to **DROP To** and click **New Query Editor Window**. Click the **Execute** button on the toolbar or press the **F5** shortcut to run the query. See Figure 4-21.

9. Return to Object Explorer and click the **Databases** folder, click the **Refresh** button on the toolbar, and then expand the Databases folder. The TestThree database should no longer appear as you have deleted it. Next, you will rename the TestOne database using Object Explorer.

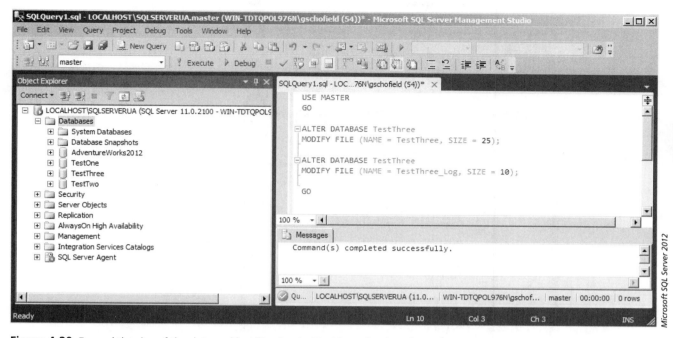

Figure 4-20 Expand the size of the data and log files for the TestThree database by running a SQL command from Query Editor

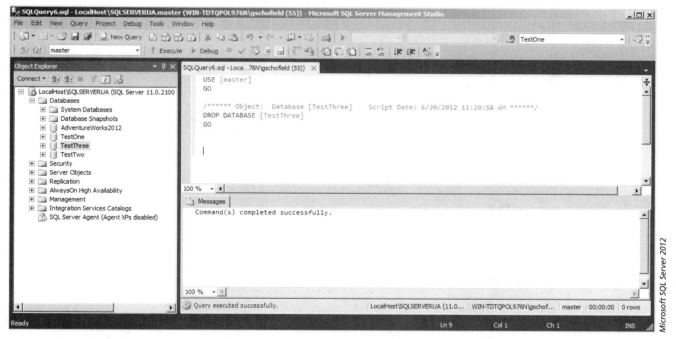

Figure 4-21 Script database as DROP to new Query Editor window

10. Right-click the **TestOne** database folder and click **Rename**. In the database name field, highlight **One**. See Figure 4-22.

11. Press the **Delete** key, and then click anywhere outside of the name field to save the change. You have just renamed the TestOne database to Test.

Figure 4-22 Rename a database in Object Explorer

It is important to be aware that this operation only changes the database name and not the logical and physical names for the data and log files.

Finally, you will delete the TestTwo database using Object Explorer.

12. Right-click the **TestTwo** database folder, and then click **Delete**. In the Delete Object dialog box, keep the default options, and then click **OK**. See Figure 4-23.

13. Click the **Databases** folder, click the **Refresh** button on the toolbar, and then expand the Databases folder. The TestTwo database should no longer appear as you have deleted it.

14. Close SQL Server Management Studio.

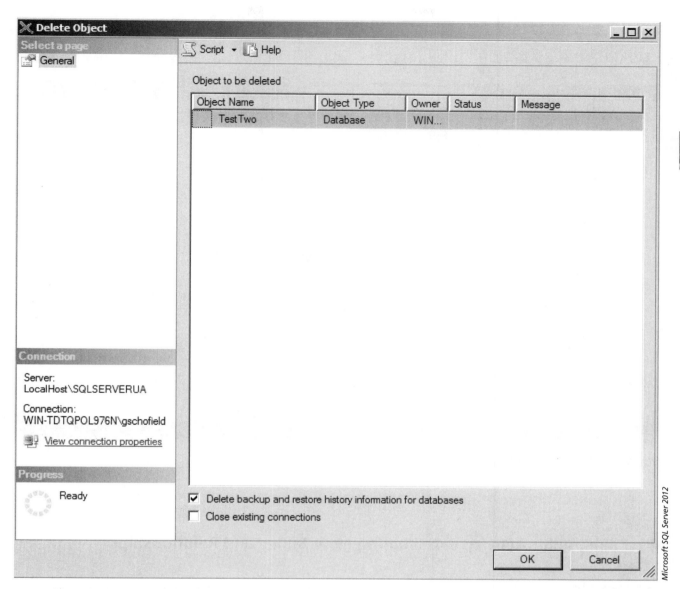

Figure 4-23 Use the Delete Object dialog box to delete a database

Adding a Table with a Foreign Key Relationship

Tables and indexes are the main building blocks of a database and you should become familiar with the different methods for creating new tables, adding a primary key, and implementing **foreign key relationships**, which are constraints that model the relationship that exists between two tables. For illustrative purposes only, Figure 4-24 shows two tables and a foreign key relationship that you will implement during Activity 4-4. In this example, the Account table (that models Accounts) is connected to the Contact table (that models Contacts) in a one-to-many relationship by posting the primary key of Account into the Contact table as a foreign key.

A new table can be created either by using the CREATE table SQL syntax or by using the graphical Table Designer that is accessible from Object Explorer in SQL Server Management Studio.

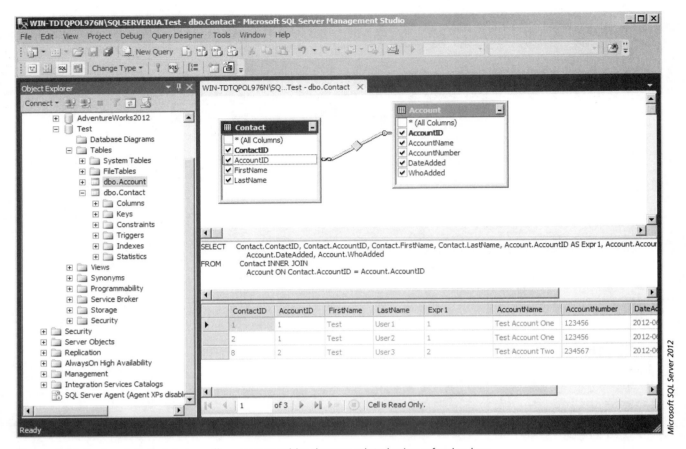

Figure 4-24 During Activity 4-4 you will create two tables that are related using a foreign key

Activity 4-4: Creating New Tables and Relationships

Time Required: 45 minutes

Objective: Create new tables, add primary keys, and establish relationships between two tables using a foreign key.

Description: In this activity, you will learn the steps to create a new table. You will use Object Explorer and Query Editor to create new tables, add primary keys, and establish relationships between two tables by adding a foreign key.

1. If necessary, start your computer and log on using an Administrator account.

2. Click the **Start** button, point to **All Programs**, click **Microsoft SQL Server 2012**, and then click **SQL Server Management Studio**. In the Connect to Server dialog box, select **Database Engine** as the server type, type **LOCALHOST\SQLSERVERUA** in the Server name text box, and then select **Windows Authentication** from the Authentication list box. Click **Connect**.

3. In the Object Explorer navigation pane on the left of the SQL Server Management Studio window, expand the SQLSERVERUA folder and the Databases folder by clicking the + symbol next to each folder. Click the + symbol next to the Test database folder to expand it. Right-click **Tables**, and then click **New Table** to launch the Table Designer as a tab in the right pane of the SQL Server Management Studio window.

4. In the Table Designer, click in the Column Name column of the first row and type AccountID. Click into the Data Type column of the first row and type int. Click out of the row, and then repeat this step until you have added all of the column names and associated data types shown below.

Column name	Data type
AccountID	int
AccountName	nvarchar(50)
AccountNumber	nvarchar(12)
DateAdded	date
WhoAdded	nvarchar(50)

5. Uncheck the **Allow Nulls** attribute for each column.

6. Right-click the **AccountID** row, and then click **Set Primary Key**. See Figure 4-25.

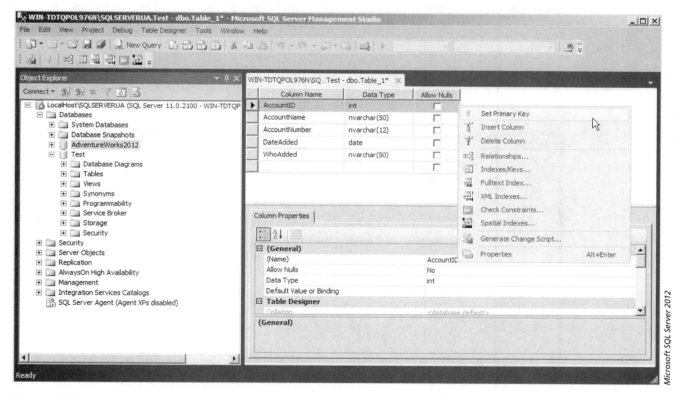

Figure 4-25 Set the primary key on the new table

A yellow key icon should now appear to the left of the AccountID.

7. Click the **AccountID** row. On the Column Properties tab, scroll down to the Identity Specification section and set the (Is Identity) property to **Yes**. This setting causes the AccountID field to automatically increment by 1 each time a record is added to the table. See Figure 4-26.

8. Click the **Save** button on the SQL Server Management Studio toolbar, and type **Account** in the Choose Name dialog box. See Figure 4-27. Click **OK** to save changes.

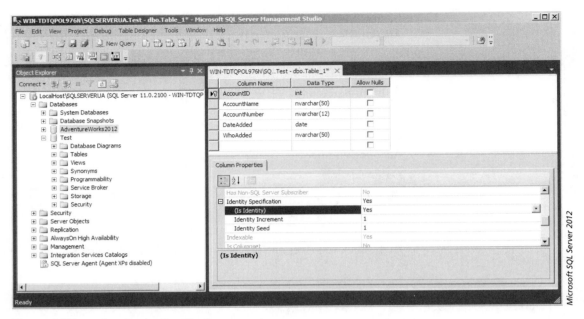

Figure 4-26 Set the Identity Specification property

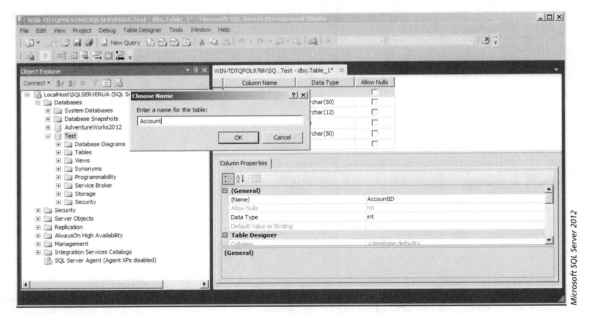

Figure 4-27 The save table action launches the Choose Name prompt dialog box

9. Using SQL command syntax in a Query Editor window, you will now create another new table named Contact. Click the **New Query** button on the toolbar. If prompted by a Connect to Server dialog box, enter the same details as you did in Step 2, and then click **Connect**. Type the following SQL into the Query Editor window.

```
USE Test

GO

CREATE TABLE Contact (
```

```
    ContactID int IDENTITY (1,1) NOT NULL PRIMARY KEY,

AccountID int NOT NULL,

FirstName nvarchar(50) NOT NULL,

LastName nvarchar(50) NOT NULL)

GO
```

10. This SQL query instructs the database management system to create a new table inside the Test database called Contact. The Contact table has four columns: ContactID (which will automatically increment and is the primary key), AccountID, FirstName, and LastName. All of the fields must contain values for each record. Click the **Execute** button or press the **F5** shortcut key to run the query. The message "Command(s) completed successfully" should appear on the Messages tab at the bottom of the window. Click the **Tables** subfolder beneath the Test database in Object Explorer, and then click the **Refresh** button on the toolbar. See Figure 4-28.

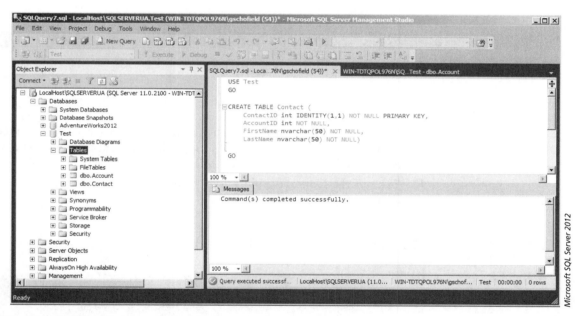

Figure 4-28 Create a new table using a SQL query

11. Right-click the **Account** table, and then click **Edit Top 200 Rows**. Enter three rows of data as shown below. Enter the data one row at a time, and press the **Enter** key at the end of each row. See Figure 4-29. Note that you do not need to enter a value for AccountID because these will autopopulate.

AccountName	AccountNumber	DateAdded	WhoAdded
Test Account One	123456	1/1/2013	Test
Test Account Two	234567	1/1/2013	Test
Test Account Three	345678	1/1/2013	Test

The red circles with a white exclamation point in the center appear next to any attributes of records that have not been committed to the database. The AccountID field will autopopulate after committing each record.

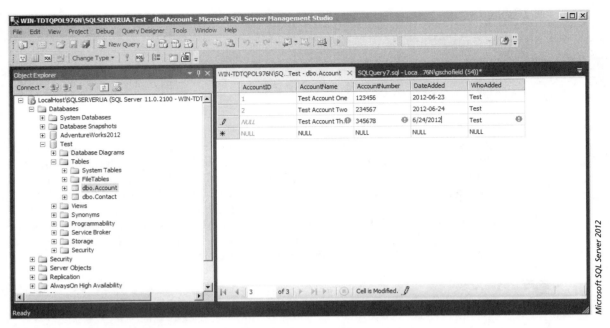

Figure 4-29 Enter test data one row at a time into the Account table

Next, you will add a foreign key relationship between the Contact table and the Account table using the AccountID as the key in the relationship. The AccountID in the Account table is the primary key; the AccountID in the Contact table is the foreign key.

12. Expand the **Contact** table folder, right-click the **Keys** folder, and then click **New Foreign Key**. See Figure 4-30.

Figure 4-30 New Foreign Key menu option

13. In the Foreign Key Relationships dialog box, click the **...** button to the right of the Tables And Columns Specifications. See Figure 4-31.

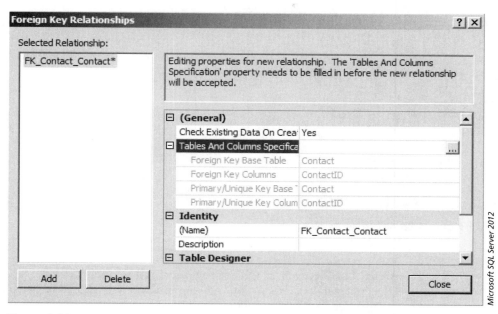

Figure 4-31 Foreign Key Relationships dialog box

14. In the Tables and Columns dialog box, click **Account** from the Primary key table drop-down list, and then in the first column of the top row, click **AccountID** from the drop-down list. Then, in the second column of the top row, click **AccountID** from the drop-down list. See Figure 4-32. Keep the default relationship name as FK_Contact_Account, and click **OK**.

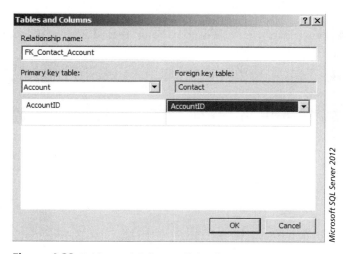

Figure 4-32 Tables and Columns dialog box

15. Click the **Save** button on the SQL Server Management Studio toolbar to save the changes to the Account and Contact tables. In the Save dialog box, click **Yes**. See Figure 4-33.

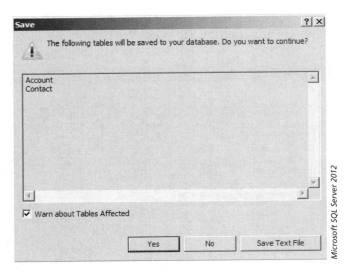

Figure 4-33 Save changes dialog box

16. Right-click **Account** in Object Explorer, and then click **View Dependencies**. In the Object Dependencies – Account dialog box, Contact should be listed as an object that is dependent on Account. Close the dialog box.

17. Right-click **Contact** in Object Explorer, and then click **Edit Top 200 Rows**. Enter the information shown below (ContactID is set to autopopulate).

ContactID	AccountID	FirstName	LastName
<autopopulated>	1	Test	User1
<autopopulated>	1	Test	User2
<autopopulated>	4	Test	User3

Notice what happens when you attempt to commit the third record by clicking out of the row. A warning message appears indicating that the data in row 3 was not committed because the INSERT statement conflicted with a foreign key constraint. See Figure 4-34. This is because there is no Account record with an AccountID value of 4.

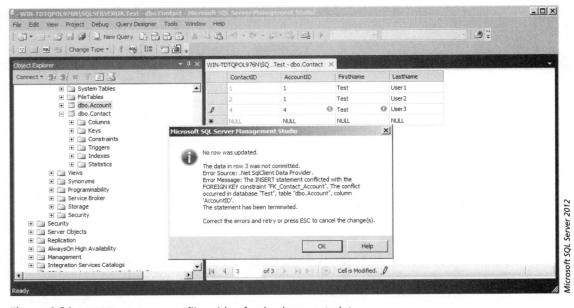

Figure 4-34 INSERT statement conflict with a foreign key constraint

18. Click **OK**. Change the value of the AccountID in row 3 to **2**. The record will now save.

19. You have now completed Activity 4-4. Close SQL Server Management Studio.

Chapter Summary

- Neglecting the planning phase prior to creating a database is likely to result in a legacy of support issues, user frustration, and unnecessary management overhead.

- Each database has a variety of configuration options that determine the behavior of the database; these options must be tailored to satisfy the relevant business requirements and ensure that the database is maintainable.

- The model system database is used as the template when creating a new user database. The settings in the model system database can be tailored to the standard settings you have chosen for your organization to improve the efficiency and consistency of creating new databases.

- To create and manage objects and configuration options, Microsoft provides a set of graphical interfaces that are accessed through SQL Server Management Studio; options to perform the same tasks are also available using the SQL programming language in Query Editor.

- In a production environment, data and log files should be stored on different physical disks. Storing data and log files on the same physical disk increases the likelihood of data loss and of contention, a situation in which two processes compete for the same resource. If the data files become damaged, you will need the log files to recover the database and avoid data loss.

- The Initial Size setting defines the initial size of the data and log files. The Autogrowth and Maxsize settings define the actions that the database management system will take when it fills up either the log or data file.

- SQL Server 2012 has a very flexible logical security model. Roles and schemas should be used to apply permissions in a granular manner, while also minimizing the amount of on-going maintainance and support required.

- The names of database objects serve as a communication system that enables users and administrators to easily interact with a database. Database object names must be unique, and the naming convention used should be intuitive, unambiguous, and applied consistently across the database.

- Camel case concatenates (links together) words using uppercase for the first character of each word. Camel case is easier to read than linking words together using underscores or other characters, and it should form the basic naming syntax for naming objects.

- Tables are the only type of object that should be named without a character prefix. For all other objects, a standard character prefix should be used for each object type to delineate between the different object types.

Key Terms

ALTER A SQL statement used to change an existing object.

Autogrowth A setting that specifies how much the database will increase the file size once it reaches a limit; can be stated in absolute or relative terms. The defaults are 1 MB for the data file and 10 percent for the log file. These settings should be sufficiently large to make file growth an infrequent event.

camel case A naming convention that concatenates (links together) words using uppercase for the first character of each word. Examples of this style are FirstName, LastName, and AdventureWorks2012. Camel case is easier to read than linking words together using underscores or other characters and should form the basic syntax for naming objects.

configuration options   Settings that determine the behavior of a database. Before creating a new database, you should always take a full backup of the master system database, which stores the configuration settings.

contention   A term used to describe a situation in which two processes compete for the same resource.

CREATE   A SQL statement used to create an object.

database transaction   A logical unit of work reading or writing from a database. Database transactions are important to maintain the integrity and consistency of the database. A logical unit of work reading or writing from a database; designed to roll back should the transaction fail.

DROP   A SQL statement used to delete an object.

filegroup   A group of data files used for storage management. Each database must have a primary filegroup with at least one data file.

foreign key relationship   A constraint that models the relationship that exists between two tables.

Initial Size   A setting that defines the initial size of the data and log files; the defaults are 4 MB and 1 MB, respectively.

I/O performance   A term used to describe the number of read and write operations that can be processed by the physical disk in a given time frame.

length   The maximum number of characters that a string data type can store.

Maxsize   A setting that allows you to specify a limit on the size of the database.

permission   A right to perform an action against a database object.

precision   The number of places after the decimal point in a numeric data type or the accuracy in the case of a date data type.

reserved keyword   A word that also belongs to the SQL programming language and is restricted because its use may lead to ambiguity. If used as an object name, a reserved keyword must be surrounded by square bracket or double-quoted delimiters.

role   A database object that groups together permissions on different database objects.

scale   The maximum number of digits that a numeric data type can hold.

schema   A logical container that groups together collections of objects within a database and allows them to be managed as a group.

Review Questions

1. Which of the four system databases does the database management system use as a template for creating new user databases?

   a. msdb

   b. tempdb

   c. model

   d. master

2. In a production environment, why should the data and log files be stored on a different physical disk than the data files?

   a. Log files are required to recover the database if the data files are damaged. If both sets of files are stored on the same physical disk, there is a higher probability of losing them both.

   b. SQL Server's logical object model negates any advantage of using different physical disks.

c.   Storing data and log files on different physical disks reduces the likelihood of contention.

   d.   Both options a and c

3. When configuring the initial size settings for the data and log file size, what value should be used?

   a.   It varies depending upon the situation, but you should always be conservative and allocate more space than you would reasonably expect to need.

   b.   The model database default settings

   c.   The initial size of the data and log files, plus 10 percent room for growth

   d.   10 GB for the data and 1 GB for the log; then shrink the data and log files if you overestimate the initial size

4. Which of the following guidelines should form part of your naming convention?

   a.   Use camel case.

   b.   Always abbreviate terms to reduce the length of names.

   c.   Use a character prefix to delineate between the different object types.

   d.   Both options a and c

5. What actions should be taken prior to making a configuration change in a production environment?

   a.   Back up the master database.

   b.   Schedule the changes during a maintenance window when the system will be offline.

   c.   Assess dependencies and coordinate the change with client application owners.

   d.   All of the above

6. Which objects in the logical security model can be used to grant a granular set of permissions to each user but with minimal overhead?

   a.   Users and logins

   b.   Logins and permissions

   c.   Roles and schemas

   d.   Owners and roles

7. What are the implications of setting the Maxsize database configuration setting to unlimited?

   a.   It eliminates the need to monitor physical disk storage and reduces management overhead required to monitor physical disk storage.

   b.   It allows unconstrained growth of the database and therefore requires proactive monitoring of the physical disk space and data file size.

   c.   It removes the possibility that a database may stop functioning properly when it reaches a predetermined size.

   d.   Both options b and c

8. Which of the following data types should you use to store a character string that will always be between 30 and 45 characters in length within a table that is frequently changed?

   a.   char(50)

   b.   varchar(50)

   c.   char(30)

   d.   Either a or b

9. Which of the following data types should you use to store a whole number that will always be between 0 and 1,000,000?

   a. decimal(8,0)

   b. int

   c. float

   d. Either a or b

10. Which of the following actions is likely to result in improved I/O performance?

    a. Storing the log and data files on different physical disks

    b. Creating additional user-defined filegroups for a database partition

    c. Creating additional log files that are stored on different physical disks

    d. Both options a and b

11. Which of the following data types should you use to store a time stamp for the last modified date of a record in a table?

    a. date

    b. char(20)

    c. datetime

    d. None of the above

12. What are some of the main considerations when selecting an appropriate data type for a database object?

    a. Physical storage

    b. Precision, scale, and length

    c. Consistency and reducing potential data type conversions

    d. All of the above

Case Projects

Case Project 4-1: Improving Database Maintainability

You work for Resultant Data Corporation, a large and well-respected database consulting firm. One of your clients, an international pharmaceutical firm, has requested some assistance in creating a new database. The database will be used for tracking and managing the firm's $8 billion research and development budget. Your client's internal project team is under enormous pressure to deliver a substantial component of the project by year-end. They have chosen to pursue an agile approach to managing the project with four-week delivery cycles. The technical lead on the project is aware that this will require a series of incremental changes to the SQL Server 2012 database in order to support the application and is concerned that the database may quickly become unmanageable. Write a response that explains how you might incorporate one or more of the following elements to address his concerns:

- Role and schema objects
- Naming conventions
- Data types

Case Project 4-2: Green Alpha LLC

You work for an investment company that specializes in managing investment portfolios for high net worth individuals—with a focus on renewable energy projects. The application team at your firm has recently developed a new analytics tool that will be used to evaluate potential investments. They are about to deploy this into a production environment and have asked you to create a production database. As part of this deployment, you need to consider the optimal database configuration settings and physical file architecture to ensure high performance and redundancy. Complete the following:

- Discuss the performance and redundancy options that you might consider for the physical file architecture in a production environment.
- List the key database configuration settings, and explain the criteria you would use to choose an appropriate setting for the Initial Size, Maxsize, and Autogrowth.

Hands-On Projects

Hands-On Project 4-1: Creating Databases and Tables

For this hands-on project, you will use the SQL Server named instance SQLSERVERHOA that you created at the end of Chapter 2. The objective of this activity is to configure two new user databases and to create new tables and a foreign key relationship.

1. Use SQL Server Management Studio to connect to the SQLSERVERHOA instance. Create a new user database with the name HandsOnOne using the New Database dialog box from Object Explorer. Use the default database settings with the following exceptions:

   a. Data file initial size: 30 MB

   b. Log file initial size: 10 MB

   c. Autogrowth enabled with 10 MB in file growth

   d. Unlimited maximum file size

2. Use Object Explorer to generate a CREATE DATABASE script from the HandsOnOne database in a new Query Editor window. Change the name of the database in the SQL script to HandsOnTwo, and modify the data file initial size to 25 MB. Execute the SQL script to create the database named HandsOnTwo. Document this step by saving a copy of the SQL script, and after executing the command, take a screen shot of the Query Editor window, showing that the query completed successfully.

3. Using either Object Explorer or Query Editor, set the recovery mode for the HandsOnOne database to full. Set the recovery mode for the HandsOnTwo database to simple. Document this step by taking a screen shot of the options page of the database properties window for each database.

4. Using Object Explorer—or by running a SQL command in the Query Editor window—rename the HandsOnTwo database to HandsOnTwo_Delete.

5. Execute a SQL command to DROP the HandsOnTwo_Delete database. After executing the SQL command, document this step by taking a screen shot of the Query Editor window to show that it completed successfully.

6. Using Object Explorer, create a new table named Customer with the following column names, associated data types, and constraints:

Column name	Data type	Constraint
CustomerID	Int	Primary key
CustomerName	nvarchar(50)	Not null
CustomerAddressID	Int	Not null

Take a screen shot of the Table Designer window to document this step.

7. Using Query Editor, construct and execute a SQL command to create a new table named Address with the following column names, associated data types, and constraints:

Column name	Data type	Constraint
AddressID	Int	Primary key
Street	nvarchar(50)	Not null
City	nvarchar(50)	Not null
State	char(2)	Not null
ZipCode	nvarchar(10)	Not null

After executing the SQL command, document this step by taking a screen shot of the Query Editor window to show that the query completed successfully.

8. Using Object Explorer, create a foreign key relationship between the Customer and Address tables. The AddressID of the Address table is the primary key, and the CustomerAddressID of the Customer table is the foreign key. After creating the key, view the dependencies of the Address table in Object Explorer, and take a screen shot to document this step.

chapter 5

Transact-SQL Primer

After reading this chapter and completing the exercises, you will be able to:

- Analyze and manipulate data stored in a SQL Server 2012 database using the Transact-SQL language

- Create and modify database objects on a SQL Server 2012 instance using the Transact-SQL language

- Construct a simple but effective logical security model for a SQL Server 2012 database using the Transact-SQL language

Database administrators must attain a high level of proficiency in the SQL programming language because it is the de facto standard for managing and retrieving data from a relational database management system. SQL (pronounced S-Q-L or sequel) stands for Structured Query Language, which was first developed by IBM in the 1970s to manipulate or retrieve sets of data from a relational database management system. SQL has been formalized as a standard by the American National Standards Institute (ANSI) and ratified under the International Organization for Standardization (ISO) standard ISO/IEC 9075. SQL is widely supported by the majority of commercial database management systems, but several variants have emerged as DBMS vendors have extended the language to support functionality that was unavailable in the SQL standard. One such variant is **Transact-SQL**, which has been developed jointly by Microsoft and Sybase; you will use Transact-SQL throughout this book.

Unless otherwise noted, references to SQL in this book refer to the Transact-SQL variant of the language.

SQL is a **declarative language,** which means that it uses a set of logical statements to specify what it is trying to accomplish, rather than specifying how to accomplish the results. The SQL Server **query optimizer** is the component within the database engine that builds a physical execution plan from the logical steps defined in a SQL query. Separating the logical specification of a query from actual implementation yields several benefits. A complex query can be written in a very concise manner because the user can leave the implementation details to the query optimizer. Because the language is written using logical expressions, it can be kept simple and very intuitive, making it easy for nonprogrammers to use. The query optimizer that manages physical implementation is highly efficient and ensures consistency, both in terms of physical implementation and query performance.

This chapter breaks down the practical aspects of programming the SQL language into three functionally based sections. In the first section, you'll learn how to use Transact-SQL as a data manipulation language (DML). **Data manipulation language (DML)** provides the means to query and manipulate data, and it is the most widely used component of the SQL language. The second and third sections of the chapter introduce the components of the SQL language that enable you to manage and administer the database. These two components are data definition language and data control language. **Data definition language (DDL)** provides the means to create and manage the schema of the logical objects in a database. **Data control language (DCL)** allows you to configure the logical security in the database, such as by creating users and roles and by granting permissions to the various database objects.

Data Manipulation Language (DML)

This section discusses how to retrieve and manipulate data stored in a database using the DML components of the SQL language. You will learn how to create a query that harnesses the flexibility of SQL to turn the raw data stored in the database into a powerful information source. You will learn how to construct a SQL query to insert, update, or delete data in a database.

The examples and activities in this section use Query Editor in SQL Server Management Studio in conjunction with the AdventureWorks2012 sample database that you installed during Chapter 3. Query Editor has a number of features that will help to accelerate your progression in learning to read and write SQL code. For example, Query Editor distinguishes between the different elements in the SQL syntax through color coding the text as follows:

- Blue: keywords
- Black: data values
- Red: text strings
- Teal: database objects
- Green: comments
- Gray: operators

Query Editor also has **IntelliSense,** a text AutoComplete feature that helps with navigating the object hierarchy and SQL language. For example, if you type *SELECT * FROM A*, IntelliSense prompts you with a set of matches based on the *A* character that forms the start of a new word. The top match is *AdventureWorks2012*, which has a database icon to the left of the name. If you press the Tab key, IntelliSense automatically fills in *AdventureWorks2012* in the text. Type a period after *AdventureWorks2012*, and IntelliSense supplies you with a list of available child objects in the AdventureWorks2012 database. A **child object** is an object that is contained within a parent object, for example a table is a child object of a database.

Before getting started, note that the SQL language is not case sensitive; however, the normal convention is to write all keywords (e.g., SELECT) in uppercase. Consistent use of naming conventions makes your SQL query easier to read and follow, especially once you start writing more complex queries. The **statement terminator** is a semicolon placed to mark the end of a SQL statement. It is not currently required for all statements, but it is good practice to use a semicolon to future-proof your queries as the SQL standards evolve.

A Simple Query

The **SELECT** statement is used to retrieve data from a database, and it is the most commonly used statement in the SQL language. Data retrieved by a SELECT query is returned as a two-dimensional **result set.** When writing a SELECT statement, you follow the SELECT keyword with a list of the column names that you want to be included in the result set. The column names can either be specified by using a comma-separated list, or by using an asterisk (*), which provides a quick way of selecting all columns in a table. After specifying the column names, you follow the **FROM** keyword with a list of the table and view names that will be used to retrieve data. The basic syntax for a SELECT statement is as follows:

```
SELECT [Column Name]

FROM [Table Name];
```

Tables or views in the FROM clause must be specified in a manner that will not lead to ambiguity. (A **view** is a virtual table that uses the result set of a saved query.) When you establish a session with SQL Server, you also connect to an individual database known as the **database context** (the default database unless otherwise specified). If you do not specify in your query which database an object belongs to, the database engine attempts to resolve the object name using the current database context. This leads to a resolution error if your database context is different from the database that contains the object. A **USE** statement can be executed to change the database context:

```
USE [Database Name];
```

Alternatively, you must identify the object using a qualified name. A **qualified name** is a combination of identifiers that uniquely defines the location of a database object. A qualified name is constructed by using up to four identifiers that represent the logical structure and hierarchy of the SQL Server instance, the database name, the database schema, and the database object. When written in code, each identifier must be separated by periods. An object that is referenced with a four-part identifier is known as a **fully qualified name** and uses the following syntax:

```
SELECT *

FROM [SQL Server Instance].[Database Name].[Schema Name].[Database
     Object];
```

Depending upon the context of the session, it might not be necessary to use a fully qualified name. For example, a two- or three-part name might be adequate for the database engine to uniquely resolve an object when connected to a specific instance of a SQL Server and querying a database residing on that same instance. This is because the database engine assumes the current SQL Server instance name specified in the connection and the current database context in order to resolve the object.

Renaming the Columns Returned in a Result Set

The **AS** keyword can be used to create a column alias for an individual column, renaming the column that is returned in the result set. This is necessary when naming a computed column or to remove ambiguity when merging data from different tables with similar or the same column names:

```
SELECT [Column Name] AS [Column Alias]

FROM [Table Name];
```

Managing Duplicate Records in a Result Set

By default, the SELECT statement implicitly returns all rows from the table or view, which may include duplicate records. The **ALL** keyword can be used as an explicit instruction to return all rows in the result set using the following syntax:

```
SELECT ALL [Column Name]

FROM [Table Name];
```

The use of the keyword **DISTINCT** removes duplicates from the result set so that only unique records are returned:

```
SELECT DISTINCT [Column Name]

FROM [Table Name];
```

Limiting the Number of Records Returned in a Result Set

The use of the keyword **TOP** limits the result set to the number of rows defined by the expression that follows in parentheses. The expression can be either an absolute number or a percentage of the row count. The TOP keyword is often used in conjunction with an ordered query:

```
SELECT TOP (expression) [Column Name]

FROM [Table Name];
```

Adding Computed Columns to the Result Set

The result set returned by a query may also include **computed columns** that are calculated using arithmetic or string concatenation operators applied to values in existing columns. Computed columns are typically used in conjunction with the AS keyword to assign an alias to the column; without the AS keyword, the computed column will not have a name. Table 5-1 lists the arithmetic operators.

Table 5-1 Arithmetic operators

Arithmetic operator	Description
+	Addition
-	Subtraction
*	Multiplication
/	Division
%	Modulo (finds the remainder of a division)

© Cengage Learning

Arithmetic operators can be used to perform operations on columns that contain numeric data. The syntax to select a computed column using an arithmetic operator is as follows:

```
SELECT [Column Name1] * [Column Name2] as [Column Alias]

FROM [Table Name];
```

Columns containing character strings may be combined using the **string concatenation operator**. The following syntax to perform a string concatenation assumes that both columns contain a character string data type:

```
SELECT [Column Name1] + [Column Name2] as [Column Alias]

FROM [Table Name];
```

Because the string concatenation operator uses the same + character as the addition arithmetic operator, the operation performed and the resulting value will depend upon the data types of the columns.

When using operators to combine or compute new values based on existing columns, you must watch out for null values. A **null value** is a column value that does not exist. An arithmetic or string concatenation operation evaluates to null if one of the input columns is null. For example, the expression 10 multiplied by null equals null. In addition, combining a text string with a null value results in a null value. If a statement returns null values, you may need to change the column properties to not allow nulls by using the NOT NULL constraint, or you can place code within your query to handle this issue, for example, by testing for null values using the IS NULL operator.

When using operators to perform operations on multiple columns, you must also make sure that the column data types are compatible. For example, it is not possible to use the string concatenation operator to combine a number and a text string, without first converting the number into a text string. You can use the keywords CAST or CONVERT to perform an explicit conversion between data types:

```
SELECT CAST([Column Name] AS [Data Type])

FROM [Table Name];
```

Refer to the "Data Types (Transact-SQL)" and "Data Type Conversion (Database Engine)" topics in Books Online for SQL Server 2012 for more information on data types and the keywords CAST and CONVERT.

Filtering the Records in a Result Set

The **WHERE** keyword is used to filter the result set from a SELECT statement. Comparison and logical operators are used in the WHERE clause to specify the filter criteria:

```
SELECT [Column Name]

FROM [Table Name]

WHERE [Criteria];
```

Comparison operators are used to compare two values, and when used, return a result of TRUE, FALSE, or UNKNOWN. A SELECT query only returns records that evaluate to TRUE. Single quotes should be placed around any text strings in the SQL query so the database engine interprets them as a string data type. Table 5-2 shows some commonly used comparison operators.

Table 5-2 Comparison operators

Comparison operator	Description
=	Equal to
<	Less than
>	Greater than
<=	Less than or equal to
>=	Greater than or equal to
<>	Not equal to

Logical operators can be used in conjunction with—or in place of—comparison operators to test column values. By using the AND and OR logical operators, you can create **compound conditions** by combining multiple conditions in the WHERE clause. The NOT logical operator can be used in conjunction with another logical operator or comparison operator to reverse the truth of the original condition. The IN, IS NULL, and LIKE logical operators can be used to test a column value. The following is a list of commonly used logical operators:

- *AND*—All conditions must be true.

```
WHERE [Condition 1] AND [Condition 2]
```

- *OR*—Any condition must be true.

```
WHERE [Condition 1] OR [Condition 2]
```

- *NOT*—Reverses the truth of the original condition.

```
WHERE NOT [Condition 1]
```

- *IS NULL*—Evaluates a column for the presence of a null value.

```
WHERE [Column Name] IS NULL
```

- *LIKE*—Matches a string based on a pattern; **wildcards** are used to match unknown characters within a string. The % wildcard is used to match a variable-length unknown string. The _ wildcard can be used to substitute individual unknown characters within a string. The following statement would return any rows in which the column characters 2-4 are *EST*:

```
WHERE [Column Name] LIKE '_EST%'
```

- *IN*—Used to compare a value of a column against multiple values.

```
WHERE [Column Name] IN ([Value1], [Value2], [Value3])
```

 The IN keyword can be a more succinct way of specifying the criteria rather than using a comparison operator, which would be written as follows:

```
WHERE [Column Name] = [Value1]

OR [Column Name] = [Value2]

OR [Column Name] = [Value3]
```

- *EXISTS*—Used to compare a value of a column against the results of a subquery:

```
WHERE [Column Name] EXISTS (SELECT * FROM [Table Name2]
```

Sorting the Records in a Result Set

The **ORDER BY** clause is used to sort the result set and should be added after the WHERE clause of the SELECT statement:

```
SELECT [Column Name]

FROM [Table Name]

WHERE [Criteria];

ORDER BY [Column Name] [ASC | DESC];
```

A comma-separated list of column names must be provided after the ORDER BY keyword. The default behavior is to sort columns in ascending order. The **ASC** and **DESC** keywords can be specified after each sort column name to indicate the sort direction. Because ascending is the default sort direction, the ASC keyword is rarely used.

Grouping and Summarizing Records in a Result Set

The **GROUP BY** clause can be used in a SELECT statement to collect data across multiple records and group the results by one or more columns. Grouping creates groups of rows that share common characteristics. You can group data on a particular column and then calculate statistics. The **HAVING** clause is used instead of the WHERE clause to filter grouped data. The WHERE clause limits rows whereas the HAVING clause limits groups. Both clauses may be used together if the condition involves both rows and groups:

```
SELECT [Column Name],

FROM [Table Name]

GROUP BY [Column Name];

HAVING [Criteria];
```

Aggregate functions are used to summarize data in a grouped column or for all records in a table. Aggregate functions differ from the other types of operator that have been discussed because their syntax allows them to accept one or more arguments that are required to return a result. The arguments are specified in parentheses following the function name:

```
SELECT [Aggregate Function](Arg1, Arg2, …)

FROM [Table Name];
```

Table 5-3 lists some of the commonly used aggregate functions. The expression to be evaluated should be placed in parentheses after the function.

Table 5-3   Aggregate functions

Aggregate function	Description
COUNT	Counts the number of rows in a table or a group.
AVG	Returns the average of a set of column values in a group or a table; each value must be a numeric data type. Null values are ignored.
MAX	Returns the largest column value within a group or a table.
MIN	Returns the smallest column value within a group or a table.
SUM	Calculates the sum of values in a column in a table or group; each value must be a numeric data type. Null values are ignored.

© Cengage Learning

Activity 5-1: Querying Data in a Single Table

Time Required: 60 minutes
Objective: Construct a SQL query to analyze data in a single view or table.

Description: In this activity, you will construct a simple SELECT…FROM query, filter using the WHERE clause, sort using the ORDER BY clause, group using the GROUP BY clause, and filter the grouped set of data using the HAVING clause. When creating these queries, you will gain experience using commonly used SQL functions and operators.

1. If necessary, start your computer and log on using an Administrator account.
2. Click the **Start** button, point to **All Programs**, click **Microsoft SQL Server 2012**, and then click **SQL Server Management Studio**. In the Connect to Server dialog box, select **Database Engine** as the server type, type **LOCALHOST\SQLSERVERUA** in the Server name text box, and then click **Windows Authentication** in the Authentication list box. Click **Connect**.

3. Click **New Query** on the SQL Server Management Studio toolbar to launch a new Query Editor window, and then enter the following text in the Query Editor window:

```
SELECT ProductCategoryID, Name

FROM AdventureWorks2012.Production.ProductCategory;
```

This statement retrieves an unsorted list of the names and IDs of all product categories. Note that the ProductCategory table is identified using the database name and schema name to which it belongs.

4. Click the **Execute** button on the toolbar or press the **F5** key to run the query. See Figure 5-1.

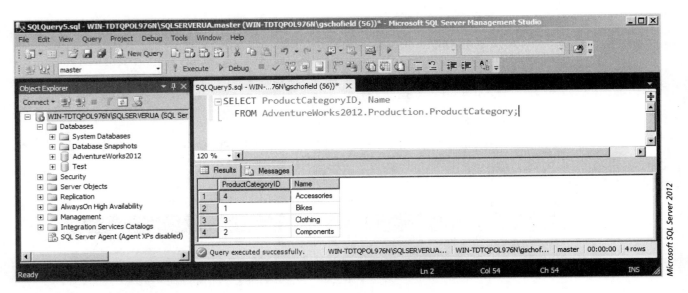

Figure 5-1 Creating a simple query

5. Delete the text in the Query Editor window, and then type the following text in the Query Editor window:

```
USE AdventureWorks2012;

SELECT ProductCategoryID, Name

FROM Production.ProductCategory;
```

6. Click the **Execute** button on the toolbar or press the **F5** key to run the query. This statement retrieves the same result set as the statement in Step 3. However, you changed the database context in the USE statement at the start of the query; therefore, you did not need to specify the database name for the ProductCategory table in the FROM clause. See Figure 5-2.

7. Delete the text in the Query Editor window, and then type the following text:

```
USE AdventureWorks2012;

SELECT *

FROM Production.Product

WHERE Color = 'Black' AND StandardCost = 0;
```

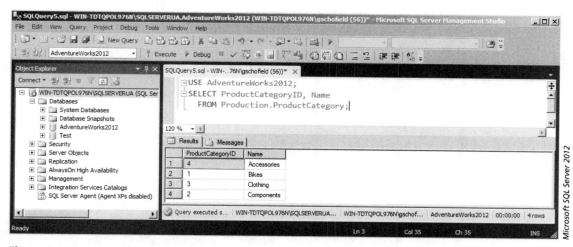

Figure 5-2 Changing the database context

This query instructs the database engine to retrieve all columns from the Product table, and it uses the WHERE clause to filter only on rows where the color is black and the standard cost of the product is zero.

8. Click the **Execute** button on the toolbar or press the **F5** key to run the query. See Figure 5-3.

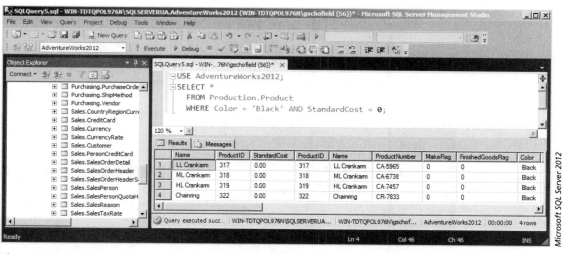

Figure 5-3 Adding the WHERE clause to filter the results

9. Delete the text in the Query Editor window, and then type the following:

```
USE AdventureWorks2012;

SELECT DISTINCT FirstName

FROM Person.Person

ORDER BY FirstName ASC;
```

10. This query returns a unique list of first names from the Person table, ordered in ascending alphabetical order. Click the **Execute** button on the toolbar or press the **F5** key to run the query. See Figure 5-4.

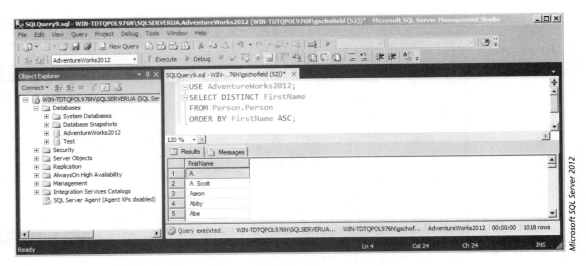

Figure 5-4 Return DISTINCT values only in a sorted list

11. Delete the text in the Query Editor window, and then type the following:

```
USE AdventureWorks2012;

SELECT FirstName + ' ' + LastName as FullName

FROM Person.Person

ORDER BY FirstName, LastName ASC;
```

> This query uses the string concatenation operator to combine the values in the First-Name and LastName columns with a space in between, and it uses the AS keyword to give the computed column an alias name of FullName. The result set is sorted by first name followed by last name in ascending order.

12. Click the **Execute** button on the toolbar or press the **F5** key to run the query. See Figure 5-5.

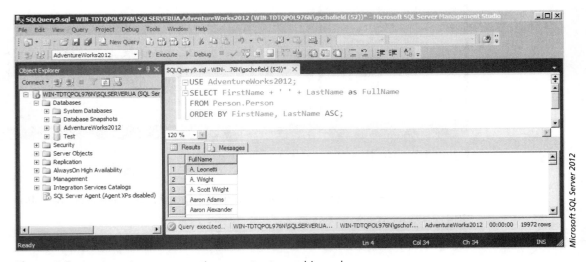

Figure 5-5 Use the string concatenation operator to combine values

13. Delete the text in the Query Editor window, and then type the following:

```
USE AdventureWorks2012;

SELECT AVG(SubTotal) AS AverageOrderSubTotal

FROM Sales.SalesOrderHeader;
```

This query uses the AVG aggregate function to compute the average value of the SubTotal column in the SalesOrderHeader table. It uses the AS keyword to give the computed column a suitable column alias.

14. Click the **Execute** button on the toolbar or press the **F5** key to run the query. See Figure 5-6.

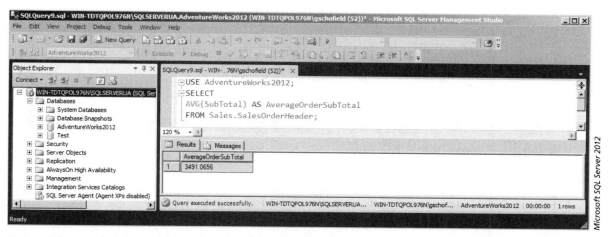

Figure 5-6 Use an aggregate function to summarize data in a table

15. Delete the text in the Query Editor window, and then type the following text:

```
USE AdventureWorks2012;

SELECT FirstName, LastName, JobTitle, PhoneNumber

FROM Sales.vSalesPerson

WHERE JobTitle LIKE '%Manager%'

AND PostalCode IN ('98052', '98011')

AND PhoneNumber IS NOT NULL;
```

This query uses a series of logical operators to build a compound condition. The result set will include any records for which the job title contains the word Manager, the postal code is either 98052 or 98011, and the phone number column contains a not null value.

16. Click the **Execute** button on the toolbar or press the **F5** key to run the query. See Figure 5-7.

17. Delete the text in the Query Editor window. Type the following text in the Query Editor window:

```
USE AdventureWorks2012;

SELECT TOP 5

SalesOrderNumber,

SubTotal,

CAST(ShipDate - OrderDate AS int) AS DaysToShip

FROM Sales.SalesOrderHeader

WHERE OrderDate < '8/1/2005' AND OrderDate >= '7/1/2005'

ORDER BY SubTotal DESC;
```

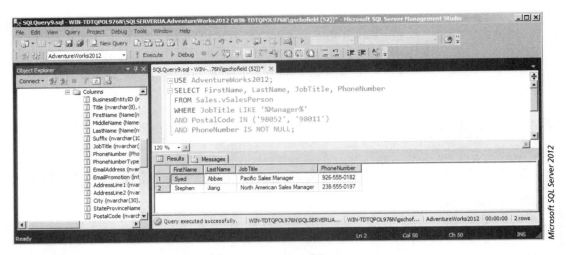

Figure 5-7 Use logical operators to build a compound condition

This query retrieves the five largest sales orders from July 2005 by sorting the records in descending order by subtotal and then using the TOP keyword to return the top five results. The query also calculates the number of days that the order took to ship. Note the use of the CAST operator to convert the results of the date difference from a date into a whole number.

18. Click the **Execute** button on the toolbar or press the **F5** key to run the query. See Figure 5-8.

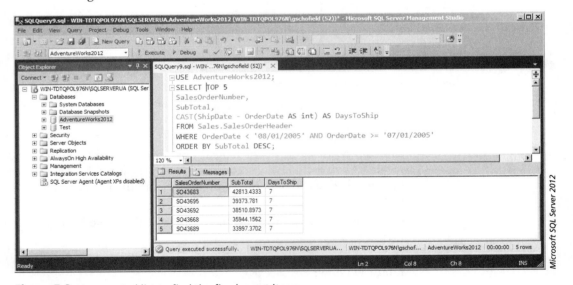

Figure 5-8 Use a sorted list to find the five largest items

19. Delete the text in the Query Editor window, and then the following text:

```
USE AdventureWorks2012;

SELECT TOP 5

CustomerID

SUM(SubTotal) as TotalOrders,

FROM Sales.SalesOrderHeader

WHERE OrderDate < '1/1/2006' AND OrderDate >= '1/1/2005'

GROUP BY CustomerID
```

```
HAVING SUM(SubTotal) > 100000

ORDER BY SUM(SubTotal) DESC;
```

This query groups the sales orders from 2005 by customer—where the order total for the year for a given customer is more than $100,000. By sorting the total in descending order, it can then retrieve the top five largest customers by sales for the year.

20. Click the **Execute** button on the toolbar or press the **F5** key to run the query. See Figure 5-9.

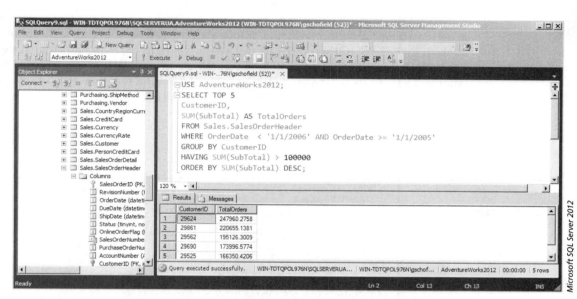

Figure 5-9 Grouping data in a table

21. Delete the text in the Query Editor window, but leave SQL Server Management Studio and the Query Editor window open for the next activity.

Combining Data Using Joins

A **join** is a database operation that can be used to merge and retrieve data that is stored in more than one table or view. Inner and outer joins use **join conditions**—using the ON clause—that specify which columns from each table should be used as the matching key. Each join condition uses a comparison operator (typically =) to compare the values of columns in each table. The AND operator can be used to create a compound join condition. The syntax of a join is as follows:

```
SELECT t1.[Column Name], t2.[Column Name]

FROM [Table Name 1] t1

INNER JOIN [Table Name 2] t2

ON t1.[Column Name] = t2.[Column Name];
```

NOTE Because column names are only unique to an individual table, when combining columns from two tables there is a chance that your SELECT statement will end up with ambiguous column names (i.e., the same column name exists in both tables). To avoid this problem, which will cause an error if you attempt to run your query, you must prefix each reference to a column name with the table name so it is clear to the database engine which column you are referring to, for example, [Table Name].[Column Name].

To avoid having to repetitively write out each table name, give each table a short alias in the FROM statement that can be referenced in the other clauses. The syntax for a table alias is to leave a space between the table name and table alias. This is slightly different from a column alias, which is defined with the AS keyword.

An **INNER JOIN** returns all columns from both tables, but it only returns rows that satisfy the join condition. Inner joins are the most commonly used join in a SQL query. A **FULL OUTER JOIN** returns all columns from both tables, and it returns rows that satisfy the join condition; where there is no matching row in one table, null values are returned for the columns in the other table. A **LEFT OUTER JOIN** returns all rows from the table to the left of the join statement and any matching rows from the table to the right of the join statement; where there is no matching right table row, null values are returned for all right table columns. Conversely, a **RIGHT OUTER JOIN** returns all rows from the right table and any matching rows from the left table. Where there is no matching left table row, null values are returned for all left table columns. See Figure 5-10. A **self join** is a special case of a join in which a table joins onto itself.

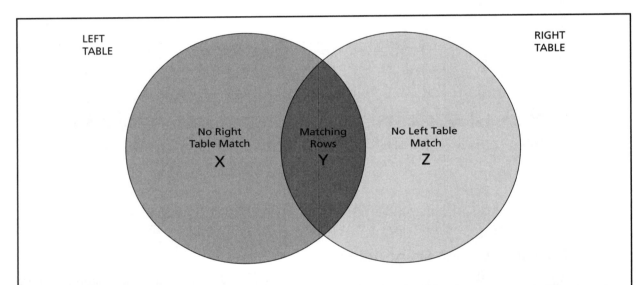

JOIN TYPE	RESULT SET	DESCRIPTION
INNER	Y	Returns all columns from both tables; only returns rows where the join column values are equal.
LEFT OUTER	X + Y	Returns all columns from both tables; returns all rows from the left table and any matching rows from the right table. Where there is no matching right table row, null values are returned for all right table columns.
RIGHT OUTER	Z + Y	Returns all columns from both tables; returns all rows from the right table and any matching rows from the left table. Where there is no matching left table row, null values are returned for all left table columns.
FULL OUTER	X + Y + Z	Returns all columns from both tables; for rows which do not have a matching row in the other table null values are returned for that table's columns.

Figure 5-10 INNER and OUTER Joins

Merging Data Using Unions

The UNION, INTERSECT, and EXCEPT operators allow the results of multiple SQL statements to be merged together. For these operators to function correctly, each result set must have the same set of columns, in the same order, and with similar data types. The operator describes how the rows should be combined into a single result set.

The **UNION** operator combines the rows from multiple SQL statements into a single result set:

```
SELECT [Column Name]

FROM [Table Name 1]

UNION

SELECT [Column Name]

FROM [Table Name 2];
```

By default, UNION filters out any duplicated rows. This behavior can be changed by adding ALL after the UNION operator, which causes all rows to be retained.

The **INTERSECT** operator only combines rows that exist in both result sets:

```
SELECT [Column Name]

FROM [Table Name 1]

INTERSECT

SELECT [Column Name]

FROM [Table Name 2];
```

Lastly, the **EXCEPT** operator returns rows from the first query that do not exist in the second query:

```
SELECT [Column Name]

FROM [Table Name 1]

EXCEPT

SELECT [Column Name]

FROM [Table Name 2];
```

Combining Data Using Subqueries

Data can also be combined using a **subquery**, which is a SQL query embedded within another SQL query. In the following example, a subquery is nested in the SELECT clause, and a second subquery is nested in the WHERE clause:

```
SELECT

(SELECT [Column Name1] FROM [Table Name1]) as [Column Alias],

[Column Name],

FROM [Table Name2]

WHERE

[Column Name] IN

(SELECT DISTINCT [Column Name] FROM [Table Name3]);
```

When a subquery is used in a SELECT clause, the values that are returned for an individual column are retrieved from the subquery rather than from the set of available columns in the main SQL statement. When a subquery is used in the WHERE clause, the values returned by the subquery are used to filter the result set.

Activity 5-2: Using Joins, Unions, and Subqueries to Combine and Merge Data

Time Required: 45 minutes

Objective: Learn to construct queries using joins, unions, and subqueries to integrate data from multiple database objects.

Description: In this activity, you will learn how to construct a SQL query that combines records from multiple database objects using the JOIN operations, merge data using UNION operations, and use subqueries to integrate other sources of data within the record set or for filtering.

1. Using the same Query Editor session that you established in Activity 5-1, type the following text in the Query Editor window:

```
USE AdventureWorks2012;

SELECT P.FirstName, P.LastName, E.JobTitle, E.VacationHours FROM
HumanResources.Employee E

INNER JOIN Person.Person P

ON E.BusinessEntityID = P.BusinessEntityID

WHERE E.VacationHours > 80

ORDER BY E.VacationHours DESC;
```

2. Click the **Execute** button on the toolbar or press the **F5** key to run the query. This query retrieves the names and titles of employees with more than 80 vacation hours. Because titles and vacation hours are stored in the Employee table and names are stored in the Person table, a join must be established between the two tables to return all columns in a single query. See Figure 5-11.

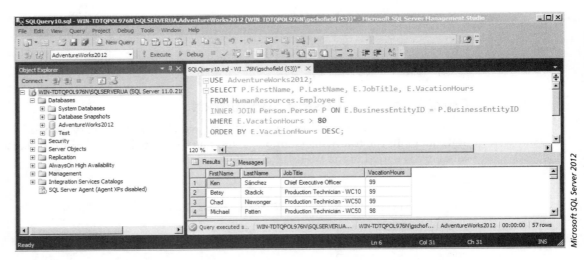

Figure 5-11 Combine multiple tables using an INNER JOIN

3. Delete the text in the Query Editor window, and then type the following text in the Query Editor window:

```
USE AdventureWorks2012;

SELECT p.ProductID, p.Name, p.ProductNumber
```

```
FROM Production.Product p

LEFT OUTER JOIN Sales.SalesOrderDetail s

ON s.ProductID = p.ProductID

WHERE s.ProductID IS NULL;
```

4. Click the **Execute** button on the toolbar or press the **F5** key to run the query. This query locates all products that do not have any associated sales orders. See Figure 5-12.

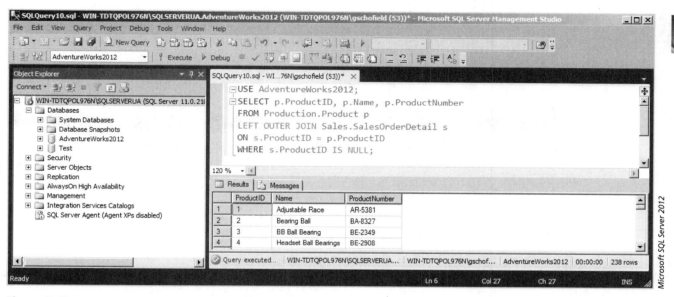

Figure 5-12 Use a LEFT OUTER JOIN to locate missing records

5. Delete the text in the Query Editor window, and then type the following text:

```
USE AdventureWorks2012;

SELECT p.ProductID, p.Name, p.ProductNumber

FROM Production.Product p

WHERE p.ProductID NOT IN

(SELECT DISTINCT ProductID FROM Sales.SalesOrderDetail);
```

6. Click the **Execute** button on the toolbar or press the **F5** key to run the query. This query uses a subquery in the WHERE statement to arrive at the same result as the query you entered in Step 3 (i.e., all products that have no recorded sales). See Figure 5-13.

7. Delete the text in the Query Editor window, and then type the following text:

```
USE AdventureWorks2012;

SELECT p.ProductID, p.Name, p.ProductNumber

FROM Production.Product p

LEFT OUTER JOIN Sales.SalesOrderDetail s

ON s.ProductID = p.ProductID

WHERE s.ProductID IS NULL
```

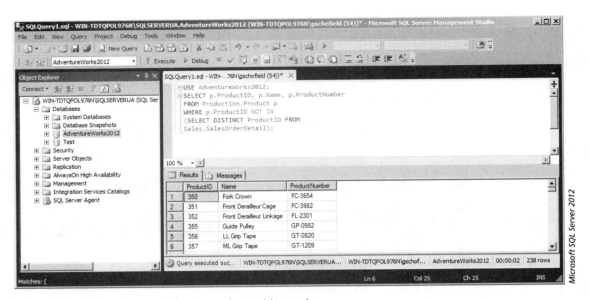

Figure 5-13 Use a subquery to locate products with no sales

```
EXCEPT

SELECT p.ProductID, p.Name, p.ProductNumber

FROM Production.Product p

WHERE p.ProductID NOT IN

(SELECT DISTINCT ProductID FROM Sales.SalesOrderDetail);
```

Notice that this query is a combination of the queries in Step 3 and Step 5, and it uses the EXCEPT operator to combine the results. Because the result sets from the queries in Step 3 and Step 5 are identical, this query returns no rows in the result set.

8. Click the **Execute** button on the toolbar or press the **F5** key to run the query. See Figure 5-14.

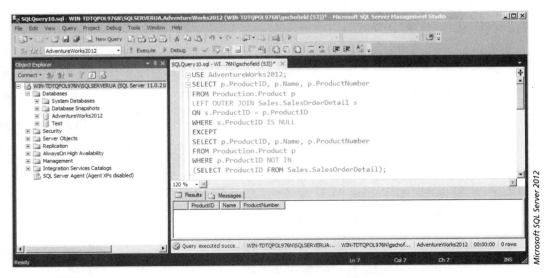

Figure 5-14 Use the EXCEPT operator to combine the output of multiple queries

9. Delete the text in the Query Editor window, but leave SQL Server Management Studio and the Query Editor window open for the next activity.

Modifying Data Using INSERT, UPDATE, and DELETE Statements

A typical database has a ratio of 80 percent read transactions to 20 percent write transactions; substantially more time is spent writing queries to retrieve and analyze data than modifying data. Data modification also tends to be undertaken in a more controlled manner—through a client application—rather than through ad hoc queries. It is important though to understand the mechanics of modifying data, and this section discusses how to use three DML statements: INSERT, UPDATE, and DELETE. Fortunately, the syntax for each is very similar to a SELECT statement.

A **DELETE** statement is used to delete rows from a table, and it uses the following syntax:

```
DELETE

FROM [Table Name]

WHERE [Criteria];
```

Because the scope of a DELETE statement is at the row level, no columns need to be specified in the DELETE clause. The filter criteria syntax is identical to the SELECT statement, and it is used to instruct the database engine which records to delete.

Be extremely careful when executing the DELETE statement without a WHERE clause because this will result in all the rows from the referenced table being deleted. It is a good idea before running a DELETE statement to first execute the equivalent SELECT statement with an asterisk to validate the filter criteria and then replace the SELECT command with the DELETE keyword. An alternative option is to nest the statement inside BEGIN TRANSACTION and ROLLBACK TRANSACTION statements that will execute the transaction without committing any changes to the database. Once the query has been thoroughly tested, the ROLLBACK TRANSACTION can be replaced with a COMMIT TRANSACTION to write the changes to the database.

An **INSERT** statement is used to insert a new row into a table. To insert a single row into a table, use the VALUES clause and type the individual column values into a comma-separated list as follows:

```
INSERT INTO [Table Name] (Column1, Column2, Column3)

VALUES (Value1, Value2, Value3)
```

A SELECT statement can be used in place of the VALUES clause to insert multiple rows into a table at once:

```
INSERT INTO [Table Name] (Column1, Column2, Column3)

SELECT Value1, Value2, Value3

FROM [Table Name2]

WHERE [Criteria];
```

Keep in mind the following key requirements when creating an INSERT statement:

- The column values in the VALUES or SELECT clause must match the order and data types of the columns specified in the INSERT clause.

- The column values in the VALUES or SELECT clause must respect any constraints present in the table, for example foreign keys or NOT NULL constraints.

- The columns do not have to be individually listed in the INSERT statement. If they are not listed, they are assumed to follow the default column order in the table and a value must be provided for each column.

An **UPDATE** statement is used to modify column values of an existing row in a table, and it uses the following syntax:

```
UPDATE [Table Name]

SET Column1 = Value1, Column2 = Value2

WHERE [Criteria];
```

The **SET** parameter is used in conjunction with an UPDATE statement to specify the name of the column to update in conjunction with a new column value. As with a SELECT statement, you can nest subqueries as a replacement to any expression in the SET or WHERE clauses. A more complex example involves updating one table with values from another table by joining the two tables together:

```
UPDATE [Table Name]

SET [Column Name] = t1.[Column Name]

FROM [Table Name] t

INNER JOIN [Table Name1] t1

ON t1.[Column Name] = t.[Column Name]

WHERE [Criteria];
```

Activity 5-3: Using a SQL Query to Modify Data

Time Required: 45 minutes

Objective: Use the DELETE, INSERT, and UPDATE statements to modify data in a table.

Description: In this activity, you will use the DELETE statement to delete records from a table, the INSERT statement to add new records to a table, and the UPDATE statement to modify the column values of existing records within a table.

1. Using the same Query Editor session that you left open in Activity 5-2, type the following text in the Query Editor window:

```
USE AdventureWorks2012;

DELETE

FROM Person.PersonPhone

WHERE PhoneNumberTypeID = 1

AND BusinessEntityID = 234;
```

2. Click the **Execute** button on the toolbar or press the **F5** key to run the query. This query deletes the cell phone number for the employee with business entity ID of 234. See Figure 5-15.

3. Delete the text in the Query Editor window, and then type the following:

```
USE AdventureWorks2012;

INSERT Person.PersonPhone

(BusinessEntityID, PhoneNumber, PhoneNumberTypeID, ModifiedDate)

VALUES (234, '555-621-8769', 1, GETDATE());
```

4. Click the **Execute** button on the toolbar or press the **F5** key to run the query. This query inserts a new cell phone number for the employee with business entity ID of 234. See Figure 5-16.

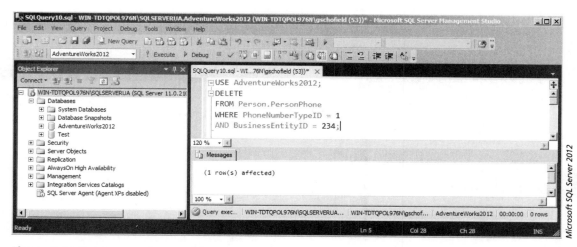

Figure 5-15 Delete a row from a table

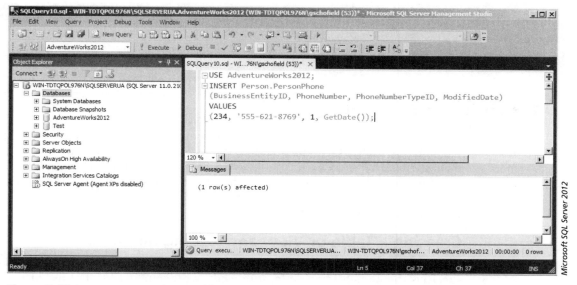

Figure 5-16 Insert a new row into a table

5. Delete the text in the Query Editor window, and then type the following text:

```
USE AdventureWorks2012;

UPDATE Person.PersonPhone

SET PhoneNumber = '555-621-8770',

ModifiedDate = GETDATE()

WHERE BusinessEntityID = 234

AND PhoneNumberTypeID = 1;
```

6. Click the **Execute** button on the toolbar or press the **F5** key to run the query. This query updates the cell phone number and the modified date time stamp for the employee with business entity ID of 234. See Figure 5-17.

7. Delete the text in the Query Editor window, but leave SQL Server Management Studio and the Query Editor window open for the next activity.

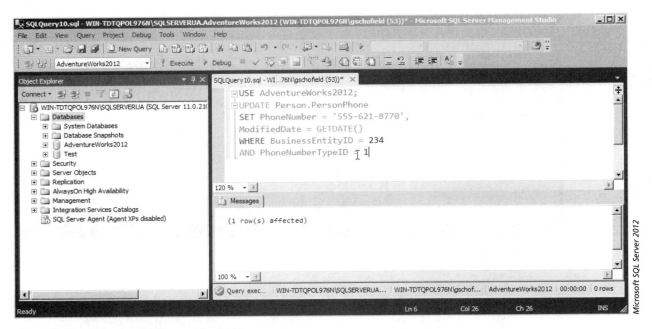

Figure 5-17 Update an existing row in a table

Data Definition Language (DDL)

The DDL components in the SQL programming language are used to define the database schema. The DDL SQL syntax can be used to create, modify, or delete database objects and their attributes. Experienced database administrators often prefer using DDL statements to the Windows form-based tools to make schema changes because they can be used more efficiently and allow more flexibility. For example, a DDL script can be saved for future use or used to generate many clones of the same object.

Creating a Table or View and Adding an Index

The CREATE TABLE statement is used to create new tables in a database. The basic syntax specifies the name of the table, followed by a comma-separated list of column names and associated data types enclosed in parentheses:

```
CREATE TABLE [Table Name]

([Column Name] [Data Type]);
```

Data types describe the type of data values that a column can store. The main data type categories are numerics, dates and times, and strings.

Refer to the "Data Types (Transact-SQL)" topic in Books Online for SQL Server 2012 for more information about the supported data types in SQL Server 2012.

Typically, tables need constraints, beyond data types, to control the data that can be added. The common constraints are listed below, accompanied by the syntax to add the constraint in line with the column specification:

- *NOT NULL*—A column-level constraint; added after the data type in the column definition, specifying that the column may not accept a null value:

```
[Column Name] [Data Type] NOT NULL
```

- *PRIMARY KEY*—A table-level constraint that uniquely identifies each record in the table; as such, it must be unique and may not hold null values:

```
[Column Name] [Data Type] PRIMARY KEY
```

- *FOREIGN KEY*—A column-level constraint that references a field in another table:

```
[Column Name] [Data Type] FOREIGN KEY REFERENCES [Table Name]
([Column Name])
```

- *UNIQUE*—A column-level constraint that enforces a unique value in the column:

```
[Column Name] [Data Type] UNIQUE
```

- *DEFAULT*—A constraint that causes the value of a field to be autopopulated on insertion of a record if the value is not specified:

```
[Column Name] [Data Type] DEFAULT [expression]
```

- *CHECK*—A constraint that can be used to limit values of a column before a change is committed to the database—for example, a modified date may not be prior to the current date:

```
[Column Name] [Data Type] CHECK [Criteria]
```

Constraints can also be added after the column specification in a comma-separated list using the syntax:

```
CONSTRAINT [Constraint Name] [Constraint Type] [Criteria]
```

As noted earlier in the chapter, a view is a virtual table that uses the result set of a saved query. A view can be created using the CREATE VIEW statement:

```
CREATE VIEW [View Name] AS

SELECT...FROM;
```

Indexes can greatly improve performance of queries on a table and can be added to the database using the CREATE INDEX statement. For an index on multiple columns, the column names can be specified in a comma-separated list inside the parentheses:

```
CREATE INDEX [Index Name]

ON [Table Name] ([Column Name]);
```

Modifying a Table or View

The **DROP** statement is used to delete objects in a database using the following syntax:

```
DROP [Object Name];
```

The ALTER statement is used to modify or rename existing views and tables; it is followed by an ADD, DROP, or ALTER for each column or constraint in the object that needs to be changed. Only columns can be altered; in order to alter a constraint, the constraint must be dropped and then re-created.

To drop a column or constraint, use the following syntax:

```
ALTER [Table Name]

DROP COLUMN [Column Name] | CONSTRAINT [Constraint Name];
```

To alter a column and change the data type, use the following syntax:

```
ALTER [Table Name]

ALTER COLUMN [Column Name] [Data Type];
```

To add a column or constraint, use the following syntax:

```
ALTER [Table Name]

ADD [Column Name] [Data Type];

ALTER [Table Name]

ADD CONSTRAINT [Name] [ConstraintType] [Criteria];
```

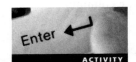

Activity 5-4: Creating and Managing Database Objects

Time Required: 60 minutes
Objective: Learn to create and manage database objects using the SQL programming language.

Description: In this activity, you will create tables, views, and indexes using the DDL components of the SQL programming language. You will then learn to manage these objects by adding additional constraints or altering column data types. Finally, you will drop these objects from the database.

1. Using the same Query Editor session that you left open from Activity 5-3, type the following text in the Query Editor window to create a new table called Bikes in the AdventureWorks2012 database:

```
USE AdventureWorks2012;

CREATE TABLE Production.Bikes (

BikeID int NOT NULL PRIMARY KEY,

Name nvarchar(100) NOT NULL,

Color nvarchar(15) NULL,

ListPrice money NOT NULL,

Size nvarchar(5) NULL,

ModifiedDate datetime NOT NULL);
```

2. Click the **Execute** button on the toolbar or press the **F5** key to run the query. See Figure 5-18.

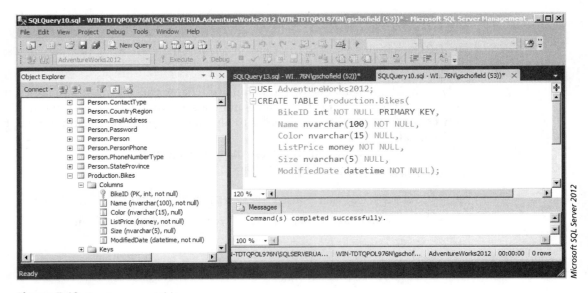

Figure 5-18 Create a new table

3. Delete the text in the Query Editor window, and then type the following text in the Query Editor window to add a new column with a foreign key constraint:

```
USE AdventureWorks2012;

ALTER TABLE Production.Bikes

ADD ProductSubcategoryID INT

FOREIGN KEY REFERENCES

Production.ProductSubCategory (ProductSubCategoryID);
```

4. Click the **Execute** button on the toolbar or press the **F5** key to run the query. See Figure 5-19.

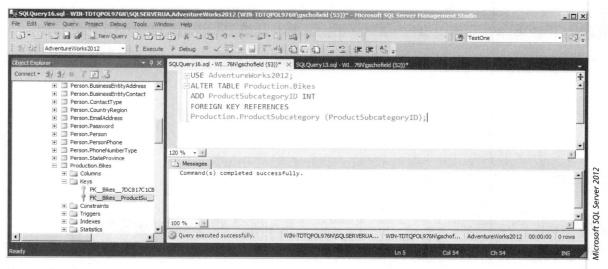

Figure 5-19 Alter a table adding a new column with a foreign key constraint

5. Delete the text in the Query Editor window, and then type the following text to add two new constraints. The first is for the ModifiedDate column to default to the current datetime; the second is to check that the list price on all bikes is greater than 100:

```
USE AdventureWorks2012;

ALTER TABLE Production.Bikes

ADD CONSTRAINT DF_Modified DEFAULT (GetDate()) FOR ModifiedDate;

ALTER TABLE Production.Bikes

ADD CONSTRAINT CK_ListPrice

CHECK (ListPrice > 100)
```

6. Click the **Execute** button on the toolbar or press the **F5** key to run the query. See Figure 5-20.

7. Delete the text in the Query Editor window, and then type the following text to create a new index:

```
USE AdventureWorks2012;

CREATE INDEX AK_Bike_Name ON Production.Bikes

(Name ASC);
```

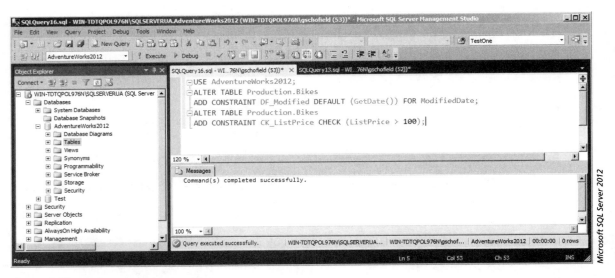

Figure 5-20 Add constraints to a table

8. Click the **Execute** button on the toolbar or press the **F5** key to run the query. See Figure 5-21.

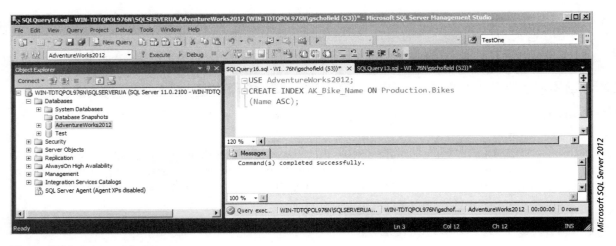

Figure 5-21 Create an index

9. Delete the text in the Query Editor window, and then type the following text to create a new view that shows a subset of columns in the Bikes table, renames several columns, and filters for bikes over $2000:

```
CREATE VIEW Production.vExpensiveBikes

AS

SELECT DISTINCT BikeID, Name, ListPrice as Price, Color

FROM AdventureWorks2012.Production.Bikes

WHERE ListPrice > 2000;
```

10. Click the **Execute** button on the toolbar or press the **F5** key to run the query. See Figure 5-22.

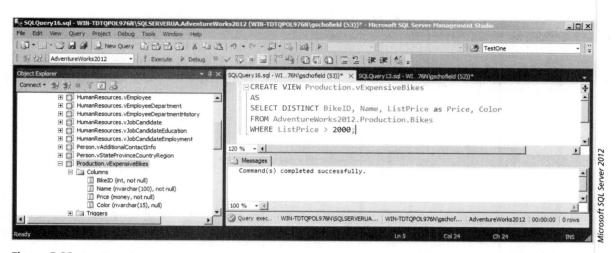

Figure 5-22 Create a view

11. Delete the text in the Query Editor window, and then type the following text to change the data type length of the Color column from 15 to 50:

```
USE AdventureWorks2012;

ALTER TABLE Production.Bikes

ALTER COLUMN Color nvarchar(50);
```

12. Click the **Execute** button on the toolbar or press the **F5** key to run the query. See Figure 5-23.

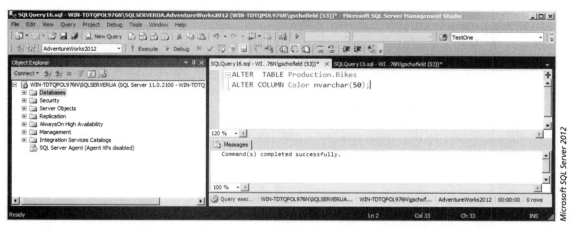

Figure 5-23 Change a column data type

13. Delete the text in the Query Editor window, and then type the following text to delete the view and table that were created during this activity:

```
USE AdventureWorks2012;

DROP VIEW Production.vExpensiveBikes

DROP TABLE Production.Bikes;
```

14. Click the **Execute** button on the toolbar or press the **F5** key to run the query. See Figure 5-24. Leave your SQL Server Management Studio open for the final activity in this chapter.

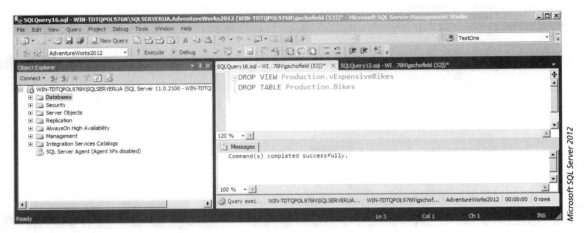

Figure 5-24 Drop a view or table

Data Control Language (DCL)

Chapter 4 provided you with an overview of the logical security model in the context of planning a new database. This section furthers your understanding of granting and revoking permissions to database users and using schemas and roles to manage permissions efficiently—using the DCL component of the SQL programming language.

Creating a SQL Server Login

SQL DCL statements can be used to create logical security objects and to grant or revoke permissions. To connect to a database, a user must be able to authenticate using either a Windows or SQL Server **login**. SQL Server can be configured to use either Windows authentication (which leverages the host operating system), a local SQL Server login using SQL Server authentication, or both SQL Server and Windows authentication. The authentication mode is set during the SQL Server installation, and it can be changed using the properties of the SQL Server instance in Microsoft SQL Server Management Studio. The database engine and agent service must be restarted before the change will take effect.

A new login can be added using the CREATE LOGIN statement, but the syntax is slightly different depending on the authentication mode. For Windows, the syntax is as follows:

```
CREATE LOGIN [DomainName\Login] FROM WINDOWS;
```

To create a new login that uses SQL Server authentication, a password also needs to be created:

```
CREATE LOGIN [Login Name]

WITH PASSWORD = [Password];
```

Creating a Database User

A permission is a right granted to a database user or role that enables it to perform an action against an object in a database. Permissions cannot be granted directly to a login. Instead, a database user must be created and then linked to a login using the CREATE USER statement:

```
CREATE USER [User Name]

FROM LOGIN [Login Name];
```

Removing a Login or User

Logins and users can be removed using the DROP LOGIN and DROP USER statement:

```
DROP USER [User Name];

DROP LOGIN [Login Name];
```

Granting and Removing Permissions

Permissions can be assigned directly to a database user using the **GRANT** statement:

```
GRANT [Permission Name]

ON [Object Name]

TO [User Name];
```

The WITH GRANT OPTION can be optionally added to the GRANT statement to enable the user to grant the permission to other database users:

```
GRANT [Permission Name] WITH GRANT OPTION

ON [Object Name]

TO [User Name];
```

Permissions can be removed from a database user using the **REVOKE** statement:

```
REVOKE [Permission Name]

ON [Object Name]

TO [User Name];
```

Table 5-4 lists several permissions that you should be familiar with.

Table 5-4   Database permission types

Permission	Description
SELECT	Retrieve data from the object
INSERT	Add new records to the table
UPDATE	Modify existing records in the table
DELETE	Delete records from the table
ALTER	Change the schema of the object
EXECUTE	Execute a command string or stored procedure

© Cengage Learning

Managing Permissions Using Schemas and Roles

To improve the ease of managing permissions across different objects, a database schema can be created to manage groups of objects. Database schemas can be created using the CREATE SCHEMA statement. The database user specified in the AUTHORIZATION clause is the owner of the schema:

```
CREATE SCHEMA [Schema Name] AUTHORIZATION [Database User];
```

Objects can be added to the schema during the CREATE OBJECT statement:

```
CREATE TABLE [Database Name].[Schema Name].[Table Name]

([Column Name] [Data Type]);
```

A **database role** is an object that can be used to manage permissions on behalf of several database users without having to grant or revoke individual permissions for each user. Users can belong to multiple database roles as members; members inherit the permissions of the role. SQL Server 2012 has several preconfigured database roles; for example, the db_datareader role allows members read-only (i.e., SELECT) access to all the objects in the database. Custom database roles can be created to fine-tune the sets of permissions that are relevant to your organization, using the CREATE ROLE statement:

```
CREATE ROLE [Role Name];
```

A database role's permissions can be granted or revoked using the same syntax as for a database user:

```
GRANT [Permission Name] ON [Object Name] TO [Role Name];

REVOKE [Permission Name] ON [Object Name] TO [Role Name];
```

A database role can also be granted a permission on a database schema. The syntax is slightly different than for an individual object:

```
GRANT SELECT ON SCHEMA :: [Schema Name] TO [Role Name];
```

Using the same syntax as other database objects, a database role or schema can be deleted using the DROP statement or renamed using the ALTER statement:

```
ALTER ROLE [Role Name]

WITH NAME = [New Role Name]
```

The ALTER statement can be used to add or remove members from a database role:

```
ALTER ROLE [Role Name]

ADD MEMBER [Database User];

ALTER ROLE [Role Name]

DROP MEMBER [Database User];
```

Activity 5-5: Managing Database Permissions

Time Required: 60 minutes
Objective: Manage database permissions using a variety of security objects using the SQL programming language.

Description: In this activity, you will use the DCL components of the SQL language to create new database logins and users, grant and revoke permissions to users and roles, and manage database schemas and role membership.

1. To begin this activity, you need to ensure that the authentication mode in the database server properties is set to SQL Server and Windows Authentication mode. In SQL Server Management Studio, right-click **SQLSERVERUA** in the left navigation pane of Object Explorer, and then click **Properties**. In the Server Properties window, click **Security** in the left navigation pane. Click the **SQL Server and Windows Authentication mode** option button, and then click **OK** twice. See Figure 5-25.

2. For the changes to take effect, you must restart the SQL Server database engine and agent services. Click the **Start** button, point to **All Programs**, and then click **Microsoft SQL Server 2012**. Click **Configuration Tools**, and then click **SQL Server Configuration Manager**. Click **Yes** if prompted by the User Account Control dialog box. In the SQL Server Configuration Manager, click **SQL Server Services** in the left navigation pane. In the details pane, right-click **SQL Server (SQLSERVERUA)**, and then click **Restart**. See Figure 5-26.

3. Perform the same action on the row labeled **SQL Server Agent (SQLSERVERUA)**. Close SQL Server Configuration Manager.

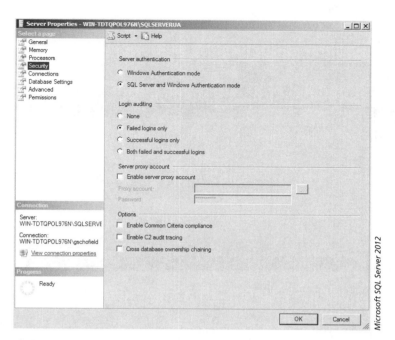

Figure 5-25 Change the authentication settings using the Server Properties window

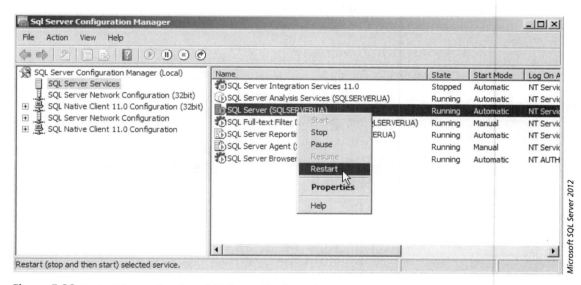

Figure 5-26 Restart the services from SQL Server Configuration Manager

4. Return to SQL Server Management Studio. Click the **New Query** button on the toolbar. If prompted by the Connect to Server dialog box, enter **LOCALHOST\ SQLSERVERUA**, select **Windows Authentication** from the authentication options, and then click **Connect**.

5. You will now create a new login that uses SQL Server authentication, and you'll create a database user that is linked to this login. Type the following commands in the Query Editor window:

```
CREATE LOGIN TestLogin WITH PASSWORD = 'Pa$$w0rd';

CREATE USER TestUser FOR LOGIN TestLogin;
```

6. Click the **Execute** button on the toolbar or press the **F5** key to run the query. See Figure 5-27.

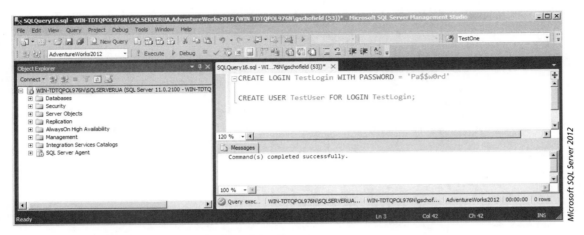

Figure 5-27 Create a new SQL Server login and database user

7. In this step, you will set the database context to the AdventureWorks2012 database, and you'll create a new schema named TestSchema that will be owned by TestUser. Delete the text in the Query Editor window, and then type the following text in the Query Editor window:

```
CREATE SCHEMA TestSchema

AUTHORIZATION TestUser;
```

8. Click the **Execute** button on the toolbar or press the **F5** key to run the query. See Figure 5-28.

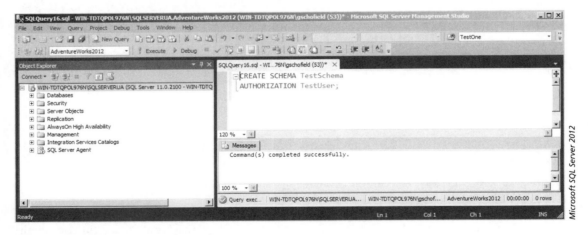

Figure 5-28 Create a new database schema

9. You will now create a new table named TestTable in the schema that you created in the previous step. Delete the text in the Query Editor window, and then type the following text:

```
USE AdventureWorks2012;

CREATE TABLE TestSchema.TestTable

(TestID INT);
```

10. Click the **Execute** button on the toolbar or press the **F5** key to run the query. See Figure 5-29.

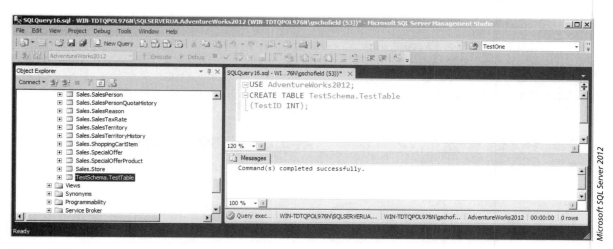

Figure 5-29 Create a table in the new schema

11. Delete the text in the Query Editor window, and then type the following text to create a new database role named TestRole:

```
USE AdventureWorks2012;

CREATE ROLE TestRole;
```

12. Click the **Execute** button on the toolbar or press the **F5** key to run the query. See Figure 5-30.

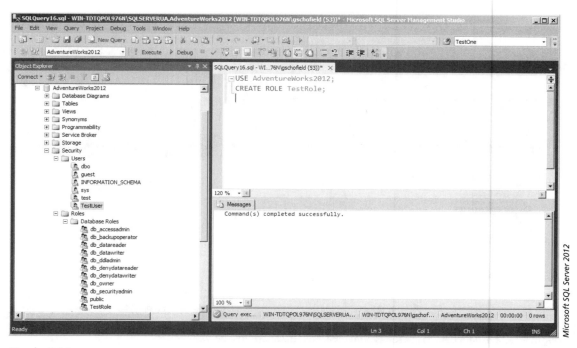

Figure 5-30 Create a new database role

13. Delete the text in the Query Editor window, and then type the following text to add the SELECT permission on the TestSchema to the TestRole:

```
USE AdventureWorks2012;

GRANT SELECT ON SCHEMA :: TestSchema TO TestRole;
```

14. Click the **Execute** button on the toolbar or press the **F5** key to run the query. See Figure 5-31.

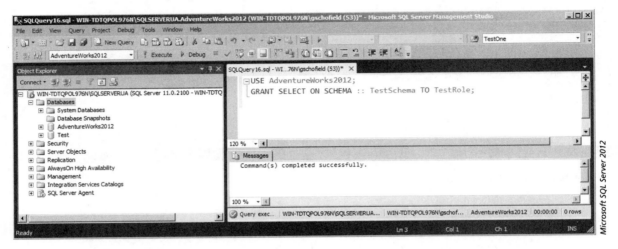

Figure 5-31 Grant a permission on a schema to a role

15. Delete the text in the Query Editor window, and then type the following text to add the TestUser as a member of the TestRole:

```
USE AdventureWorks2012;

ALTER ROLE TestRole

ADD MEMBER TestUser;
```

16. Click the **Execute** button on the toolbar or press the **F5** key to run the query. See Figure 5-32.

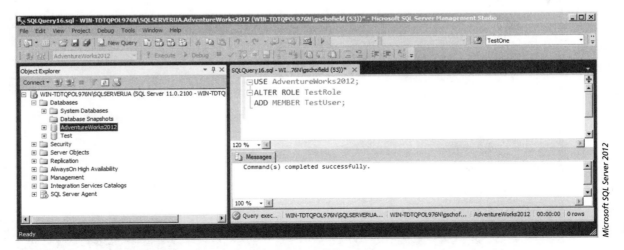

Figure 5-32 Add a database user as a member to a database role

17. Delete the text in the Query Editor window, and then type the following text to change the name of the role:

```
USE AdventureWorks2012;

ALTER ROLE TestRole WITH NAME = NewTestRole;
```

18. Click the **Execute** button on the toolbar or press the **F5** key to run the query. See Figure 5-33.

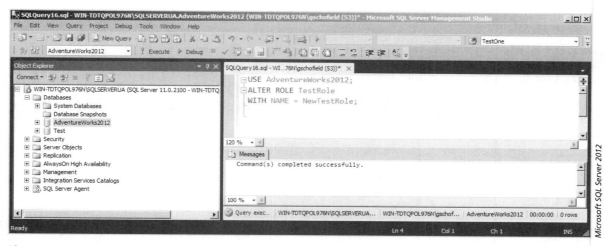

Figure 5-33 Rename a database role

19. Delete the text in the Query Editor window, and then type the following text to remove TestUser from the role:

```
USE AdventureWorks2012;

ALTER ROLE NewTestRole

DROP MEMBER TestUser;
```

20. Click the **Execute** button on the toolbar or press the **F5** key to run the query. See Figure 5-34.

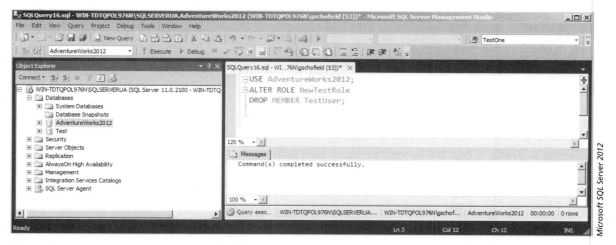

Figure 5-34 Remove a member from a database role

21. Delete the text in the Query Editor window, and then type the following text to revoke SELECT permissions from TestUser on the TestTable:

```
USE AdventureWorks2012;

REVOKE SELECT ON TestSchema.TestTable TO TestUser;
```

22. Click the **Execute** button on the toolbar or press the **F5** key to run the query. See Figure 5-35. Notice that this cannot be completed because the TestUser is the owner of the TestSchema schema in which the table resides.

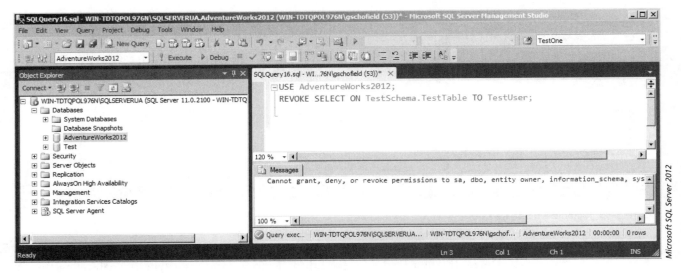

Figure 5-35 Revoke a permission

23. Delete the text in the Query Editor window, and then type the following text to delete the TestUser, TestLogin, TestTable, TestSchema, and TestRole:

```
USE AdventureWorks2012;

DROP ROLE NewTestRole;

GO

DROP TABLE TestTable;

GO

DROP SCHEMA TestSchema;

GO

DROP USER TestUser;

GO

DROP LOGIN TestLogin;

GO
```

These queries need to be executed separately with the GO keyword because several of the objects reference each other.

24. Click the **Execute** button on the toolbar or press the **F5** key to run the query. See Figure 5-36.

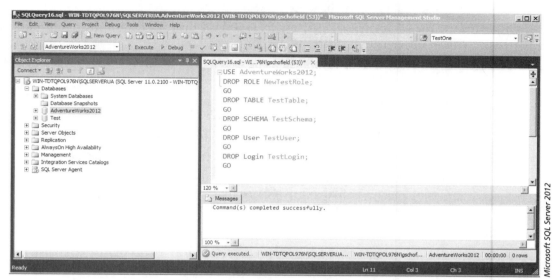

Figure 5-36 Drop multiple objects

Chapter Summary

- SQL is the standard programming language for managing and retrieving data from a relational database management system. Transact-SQL is a variant of SQL that was developed by Microsoft and Sybase and is used in SQL Server 2012.

- SQL is a declarative language that uses a set of logical expressions to specify what it is trying to accomplish, rather than specifying how to accomplish the results. The language is simple and intuitive, making it easy for nonprogrammers to use in a productive manner.

- The query optimizer in SQL Server's database engine builds a physical execution plan from the logical steps that are defined by a SQL query, and it ensures consistent implementation and query performance.

- Data manipulation language (DML) provides the means to query and manipulate data, and it is the most widely used component of the SQL language.

- Data definition language (DDL) provides the means to create and manage the schema of the logical objects in a database.

- Data control language (DCL) allows you to configure the logical security in the database, such as creating users, roles, and granting permissions to the various database objects.

- The SELECT statement is used to retrieve data from a database, and it is the most commonly used statement in the SQL language. Data retrieved by the SELECT query is returned as a two-dimensional result set.

- The WHERE clause is used to filter a result set. Comparison and logical operators are used in the WHERE clause to specify the filter criteria by testing column values.

- A null value is a column value that does not exist. An arithmetic operation or string concatenation will evaluate to null if one of the input columns is null.

- The ORDER BY clause is used to sort the result set.

- The GROUP BY clause can be used in a SELECT statement to collect data across multiple records and group the results by one or more columns. The HAVING clause is used instead of the WHERE clause to filter grouped data.

- Joins can be used to merge and retrieve data that is stored in more than one table or view. Inner and outer joins use join conditions in the ON clause that specify which columns from each table should be used as the matching key.

- The UNION, EXCEPT, and INTERSECT operators allow the results of multiple SQL statements to be merged together.

- Data can also be combined using a subquery, which is a SQL query embedded within another SQL query.

- Rows in a table can be modified using the INSERT, UPDATE, and DELETE statements, which have a similar syntax to the SELECT statement.

- The CREATE TABLE statement is used to create new tables in a database.

- Database objects can be changed or deleted using the ALTER and DROP statements.

- A permission is a right granted to a database user or role that enables it to perform an action against an object in a database. A permission can be assigned or removed using the GRANT and REVOKE statements.

Key Terms

aggregate function   A function used when grouping data to summarize data in a grouped column.

ALL   A SQL keyword used to return all rows from a table or view.

AND   A logical operator that specifies that all conditions must be true.

AS   A SQL keyword that can be used to create a column alias for an individual column, renaming the column returned in the result set.

ASC   A SQL keyword used after a sort column name to indicate an ascending sort direction.

CHECK   A constraint used to limit values of a column before a change is committed to the database—for example, a modified date may not be prior to the current date.

child object   An object that is contained within a parent object, for example a table is a child object of a database.

comparison operator   A word in a SQL statement that is used to compare two values; returns a result of TRUE, FALSE, or UNKNOWN.

compound conditions   A combination of conditions; can be created by combining multiple conditions in a WHERE or HAVING clause.

computed column   A column computed using arithmetic operators or string concatenation operators applied to values in existing columns.

database context   The database that is used by the database engine to resolve object names; unless otherwise specified, the database context is the default database.

database role   An object used to manage permissions on behalf of several database users without having to grant or revoke individual permissions for each user.

data control language (DCL)   The component of the SQL language that allows you to configure the logical security in the database, such as by creating users and roles and by granting permissions to the various database objects.

data definition language (DDL)   The component of the SQL language that provides the means to create and manage the schema of the logical objects in a database.

data manipulation language (DML)   The most widely used component of the SQL language; provides the means to query and manipulate data.

declarative language   A programming language that uses a set of logical expressions to specify what to accomplish, rather than how to accomplish the results.

DEFAULT   A constraint that causes the value of a field to be autopopulated on insertion of a record if the value is not specified.

DELETE   A SQL statement used to delete rows from a table.

DESC   A SQL keyword used after a sort column name to indicate a descending sort direction.

DISTINCT   A SQL keyword used to remove duplicates from the result set and only return unique records.

DROP   A SQL statement is used to delete objects in a database.

EXCEPT   An operator that returns rows from the first query that do not exist in the second query.

EXISTS   An operator used to compare a value of a column against the results of a subquery.

FROM   A SQL keyword used to specify a list of the names of tables or views that a query will use to retrieve data.

FULL OUTER JOIN   A type of join that returns all columns from both tables as well as rows that satisfy the join condition; where there is no matching row in one table, null values are returned for the columns in the other table.

fully qualified name   An object that is referenced using all four identifiers.

GRANT   A SQL statement used to assign permissions directly to a database user or via a role.

GROUP BY   A SQL keyword used in a SELECT statement to collect data across multiple records and then group the results by one or more columns. Grouping creates groups of rows that share common characteristics.

HAVING   A SQL keyword used instead of the WHERE keyword to filter grouped data.

IN   A logical operator used to compare a value of a column against multiple values.

INNER JOIN   A type of join that returns all columns from both tables but only those rows that satisfy the join condition.

INSERT   A SQL statement used to insert a new row into a table.

IntelliSense   A text AutoComplete feature that helps with navigating the object hierarchy and SQL language.

INTERSECT   An operator that only combines rows that exist in both result sets.

IS NULL   A logical operator used to evaluate a column for the presence of a null value.

join   A database operation used for merging and retrieving data that is stored in more than one table or view.

join conditions   A condition, included in the ON clause of a join statement, that specifies which columns from each table should be used as the matching key.

LEFT OUTER JOIN   A type of join that returns all rows from the left table and any matching rows from the right table; where there is no matching right table row, null values are returned for all right table columns.

LIKE   A logical operator used to match a string based on a pattern.

logical operator   A word in a SQL statement that is used in conjunction with, or in place of, comparison operators to test column values.

login   An authentication mechanism used to validate the identity of a user on a database server.

NOT   A logical operator that reverses the truth of the original condition.

NOT NULL   A column-level constraint, added after the data type in the column definition, that specifies that the column may not accept a null value.

null value   A column value that does not exist.

OR   A logical operator that specifies that any condition must be true.

ORDER BY   A SQL keyword used to sort a result set; should be added after the WHERE clause of the SELECT statement.

qualified name   A combination of identifiers that uniquely defines the location of a database object.

query optimizer   The component within the SQL Server database engine that builds a physical execution plan from the logical steps defined in a SQL query.

result set   The data returned by a SQL query.

REVOKE   A SQL statement used to remove permissions directly from a database user or from a role.

RIGHT OUTER JOIN   A type of join that returns all rows from the right table and any matching rows from the left table. Where there is no matching left table row, null values are returned for all left table columns.

SELECT   A statement used to retrieve data from a database object.

self join A special case of a join in which a table joins onto itself.

SET A parameter used in an UPDATE statement that specifies the name of the column to update along with the new column value.

statement terminator A semicolon placed to mark the end of a SQL statement.

string concatenation operator An operator that may be used to combine columns containing character strings.

subquery A SQL query embedded within another SQL query.

TOP A SQL keyword used to limit the result set to the number of rows defined by an expression in parentheses, which follows the keyword.

Transact-SQL A variant of the SQL language, developed by Microsoft and Sybase.

UNION An operator that combines the rows from multiple SQL statements into a single result set.

UNIQUE A column-level constraint that enforces a unique value in the column.

UPDATE A SQL statement used to modify column values of an existing row in a table.

USE A SQL statement that changes the database context to a specified database.

view A virtual table that uses the result set of a saved query.

WHERE A SQL keyword used to filter the SELECT...FROM result set; operators are used within the WHERE clause to specify the filter criteria.

wildcard A character used in a SQL statement to match unknown characters within a string.

Review Questions

1. Transact-SQL _____.
   a. is a variant of the SQL programming language that extends the features of the SQL ISO standard
   b. has been formalized as a standard by ANSI
   c. is a declarative language
   d. Both options a and c

2. Which of the following cannot be used to combine data from different tables or views in a SQL query?
   a. UNION
   b. INNER JOIN
   c. MERGE
   d. Subquery

3. Which of the following keywords should be used in conjunction with the GROUP clause to filter results from the group?
   a. WHERE
   b. HAVING
   c. WITH
   d. None of the above

4. SQL is a declarative language that _____.
   a. separates logical specification from physical implementation
   b. uses logical expressions to specify what to accomplish, rather than how to accomplish a set of results
   c. is simple and easy to use
   d. All of the above

5. Which of the following is the most commonly used statement in the SQL language?

   a.   SELECT statement to query tables or views in a database

   b.   DELETE statement to delete rows from a table

   c.   UPDATE statement to modify rows in a table

   d.   CREATE statement to add new objects to the database

6. Which of the following will constrain the values that can be stored in a table?

   a.   NOT NULL constraint

   b.   Primary Key constraint

   c.   Data type associated with a column

   d.   All of the above

7. Which of the following objects can be granted a permission?

   a.   Database role

   b.   Database schema

   c.   Database user

   d.   Both options a and c

8. Which of the following objects can be used to improve manageability of security in a database?

   a.   Database role

   b.   Database schema

   c.   Database user

   d.   Both options a and b

9. Which of the following permissions should be granted to enable a database user or role to execute a command string or stored procedure?

   a.   EXECUTE

   b.   RUN

   c.   SELECT

   d.   UPDATE

10. How does an aggregate function differ from other types of SQL operators?

   a.   They are always used to evaluate conditions in the WHERE clause.

   b.   They are always used in conjunction with a GROUP BY clause.

   c.   The syntax allows them to accept one or more arguments that are required to return a result.

   d.   None of the above

11. Which of the following qualified names would not be sufficient to remove ambiguity in order for the database engine to correctly resolve a name?

   a.   A three-part name when querying a table outside the current database context but that resides on the same SQL Server instance that the current session is connected to

   b.   A three-part name when querying a table that is located on a different SQL Server instance

   c.   A two-part name when querying a table in the current database context

   d.   A fully qualified name

12. Which of the following components of the SQL lanaguage can be used to modify database schema objects?

    a.   Data control language (DCL)

    b.   Data manipulation language (DML)

    c.   Data definition language (DDL)

    d.   Transaction control language (TCL)

Case Projects

CASE PROJECTS

Case Project 5-1: Implementing a New Database

You have been asked to implement a database that will track products, product categories, suppliers, and current product inventory for a cookware supply store. You have been given a database specification that includes table requirements and sample data for the test environment. The design calls for four tables to be created: Inventory, Product, ProductCategory, and Supplier. Tables 5-5 through 5-10 contain the column names, data types, constraints, and keys that must be implemented for each table. Tables 5-11 through 5-14 contain the sample data that you will need to insert into each table for testing.

Table 5-5   Column definitions for the Inventory table

Key	Name	Data type	Allow nulls	Default
PK	InventoryID	int	N	
FK	ProductID	int	N	
	UnitsOnHand	int	N	
	ModifiedOn	datetime	N	(getdate())

© Cengage Learning

Table 5-6   Foreign key definitions for the Inventory table

Name	Columns
FK_Inventory_Product	ProductID->dbo.Product.ProductID

© Cengage Learning

Table 5-7   Column definitions for the Product table

Key	Name	Data type	Allow nulls	Default
PK	ProductID	int	N	
FK	ProductCategoryID	int	N	
FK	SupplierID	int	N	
	Description	nvarchar(50)	N	
	Color	nvarchar(20)	N	
	UnitPrice	money	N	
	ModifiedOn	datetime	N	(getdate())

© Cengage Learning

Table 5-8   Foreign key definitions for the Product table

Name	Columns
FK_Product_ProductCategory	ProductCategoryID->dbo.ProductCategory.ProductCategoryID
FK_Product_Supplier	SupplierID->dbo.Supplier.SupplierID

© Cengage Learning

Table 5-9   Column definitions for the ProductCategory table

Key	Name	Data type	Allow nulls	Default
PK	ProductCategoryID	int	N	
	Description	nvarchar(50)	N	
	ModifiedOn	datetime	N	(getdate())

© Cengage Learning

Table 5-10   Column definitions for the Supplier table

Key	Name	Data type	Allow nulls	Default
PK	SupplierID	int	N	
	SupplierName	nvarchar(50)	N	
	City	nvarchar(50)	N	
	Country	nvarchar(50)	N	
	ContactPhone	nvarchar(20)	N	
	ModifiedOn	datetime	N	(getdate())

© Cengage Learning

Table 5-11   Sample data for the Inventory table

InventoryID	ProductID	UnitsOnHand	ModifiedOn
1	1	40	7/3/12 8:56
2	2	24	7/3/12 8:57
3	4	5	7/3/12 8:57
4	5	2	7/3/12 8:57
5	6	7	7/3/12 8:57
6	7	16	7/3/12 8:57
7	8	12	7/3/12 8:57
8	10	27	7/3/12 8:58

© Cengage Learning

Table 5-12   Sample data for the Product table

ProductID	ProductCategoryID	SupplierID	Description	Color	UnitPrice	ModifiedOn
1	2	3	Stainless steel flatware	Silver	30.99	7/3/12 8:49
2	2	4	Serving spoons	Nickel	18.5	7/3/12 8:50
3	5	1	Chef's knife	Silver	25	7/3/12 8:50
4	5	1	Cutting board	Black	15.77	7/3/12 8:50
5	5	2	Sharpening steel	Carbon	12.24	7/3/12 8:51
6	3	2	Napkin set	Red	9.31	7/3/12 8:52
7	3	2	Table cloth	Various	21.89	7/3/12 8:52
8	1	3	Large frying pan	Black	13.5	7/3/12 8:53
9	1	3	Small frying pan	Black	7.25	7/3/12 8:53
10	1	3	Nonstick saucepan	Silver	16	7/3/12 8:54

© Cengage Learning

Table 5-13 Sample data for the ProductCategory table

ProductCategoryID	Description	ModifiedOn
1	Cookware	7/3/12 8:37
2	Cutlery	7/3/12 8:38
3	Linens	7/3/12 8:38
4	Tableware	7/3/12 8:38
5	Cooks Tools	7/3/12 8:38

© Cengage Learning

Table 5-14 Sample data for the Supplier table

SupplierID	SupplierName	City	Country	ContactPhone	ModifiedOn
1	Sanzone	Oakland	USA	(510) 555-7200	7/3/12 8:44
2	Itex	Frankfurt	Germany	+49 (0) 8731-9140	7/3/12 8:45
3	Newnix	New York	USA	(212) 555-8100	7/3/12 8:46
4	Zenice	Chicago	USA	(707) 555-1400	7/3/12 8:47
5	Waredom	Paris	France	+33 (0) 123-4496	7/3/12 8:47

© Cengage Learning

Complete the following:

1. Using the CREATE DATABASE command, create a new test database on your SQLSERVERUA instance that uses the default schema. The database should be named ProductInformation.

2. Create and execute a SQL query to create the four individual tables Product, ProductCategory, Supplier, and Inventory with the null and default constraints.

3. Using the ALTER TABLE syntax, add a primary key and a foreign key constraint to each table.

4. Use the INSERT statement to add the sample rows to the tables. Use the column default for the ModifiedOn column.

5. Use an UPDATE statement to change the SupplierName of SupplierID 2 to Cuisinex.

6. Using a DELETE statement that contains a subquery in the WHERE clause, delete the inventory record(s) for the Product Description Nonstick saucepan.

7. Using a LEFT OUTER JOIN, retrieve all Product Descriptions that have no associated inventory.

8. Create a SELECT query that lists the Product Descriptions and the total inventory on hand (expressed as UnitPrice * UnitsOnHand). Use a column alias to assign any calculated columns a meaningful name in the result set.

9. Create a SELECT statement that returns the top two products with the most inventory units on hand.

10. Create a SELECT statement that lists the total inventory on hand (expressed as UnitPrice * UnitsOnHand) for each ProductCategory. Only return records where the total inventory on hand for a product category is greater than $150. Order the output by total inventory on hand in descending order. Use a column alias to assign any calculated columns a meaningful name in the result set.

11. Create a view vTotalInventoryByProductCategory that lists the ProductCategory description and the total inventory on hand.

12. Add an index to the Product table on the Description column.

Hands-On Projects

Hands-On Project 5-1: Creating Databases and Tables

For this hands-on project, you will use the SQL Server named instance SQLSERVERHOA and the HandsOnOne database and tables that you created at the end of Chapters 2 and 4, respectively. The objective of this activity is to hone your skills at manipulating data using SQL DML statements. Use Query Editor throughout this exercise, and document each step by taking a screen shot of the Query Editor window after executing the SQL command to show that it completed successfully.

1. Construct and execute INSERT statements to add the sample data in Tables 5-15 and 5-16 to the Customer and Address tables in the HandsOnOne database.

Table 5-15 Sample data for the Customer table

CustomerID	CustomerName	CustomerAddressID
1	Western Supply Company	1
2	Nick Harper	3
3	Alice Harper	3
4	Abacus Consulting	4

© Cengage Learning

Table 5-16 Sample data for the Address table

AddressID	Street	City	State	ZipCode
1	2400 Broadway	Missoula	MT	59802
2	320 21st Street	Billings	MT	59101
3	439 Skyline Blvd	Denver	CO	80002
4	56 Park Avenue	New York	NY	10001

© Cengage Learning

2. Construct and execute a query to list all customers with their corresponding city and state. The list should be sorted in ascending numerical order by ZIP code followed by customer name alphabetically.

3. Construct and execute a SQL query to list the Street, City, State, and ZipCode of all addresses that do not have a customer associated with them.

4. Construct and execute a SQL query to count the number of customers in each state. The list should be ordered by the number of customers in descending order, then by state code in ascending order.

5. Construct and execute a SQL query to delete all customers who live in ZIP code 10001.

6. Construct and execute a SQL query to change Alice Harper's address to 320 21st Street, Billings, MT 59101.

7. Construct and execute a SQL query to list the state and ZIP codes in a single column. The list should not contain any duplicate records and should be sorted in descending alphabetical order.

8. Construct and execute a SQL query to list the full name of all customers who have Harper in their name.

chapter 6

SQL Server Security

After reading this chapter and completing the exercises, you will be able to:

- Choose an appropriate authentication mode

- Create secure client/server connections

- Manage access controls on database and server securables using the permissions hierarchy

- Evaluate the different options for encrypting sensitive or confidential data

Databases often contain sensitive or confidential information that must be protected both from accidental exposure to unauthorized users and from malicious attacks. The news media frequently provides salient reminders on the devastating, long-term consequences that a security breach can have on an organization and its customer base. The implications of a compromised database range from the immediate costs of repairing the problem and compensating customers to long-term damage to the firm's reputation, increased regulatory scrutiny, and even civil or criminal charges. The best approach to securing a database is to use a **layered security** model (also known as defense-in-depth) that involves combining multiple security controls to prevent unauthorized access; even if a vulnerability can be exploited in one of the layers, an attacker must still overcome several other security controls before gaining access to the data.

Earlier chapters in this book introduced several aspects of security that you should consider when planning a SQL Server implementation or a new database—including implementing physical access controls to the building and server room that contains the hardware and securing any backup media that is stored off-site. Direct access to the physical data and log files on disk should be restricted, and, for Internet-facing deployments, a network security appliance or firewall should be configured to control access to the network. The potential number of security vulnerabilities, sometimes referred to as **surface area,** can be significantly reduced by enabling only the SQL Server functionality that is needed to satisfy business requirements. The database planning discussion in Chapter 4 introduced the importance of logical access controls to secure objects within a database, and you gained some practical experience creating these access controls using the SQL programming language in Chapter 5.

Chapter 6 focuses on three additional important aspects of security: authentication, server and database access controls, and encryption. The first section discusses security controls when connecting to a SQL Server instance. You will examine the different methods of authenticating with the SQL server, and you'll learn how to secure client/server connections. The second section in the chapter examines database and server **securables,** which are the various objects in a database and on a SQL Server instance that can be secured. Permissions, rights to perform a particular action against a securable, are granted to **security principals,** entities that can request access to resources or securables. You will explore the hierarchical nature of this security model and the flexibility that it affords. After completing the activities in this chapter, you should understand how to design and implement access controls using Object Explorer and SQL commands. The final section in this chapter covers the options available for encrypting data stored in the database. **Encryption** is a reversible process involving the use of a key or passcode and an algorithm to convert data into an unreadable form. Encryption provides a last line of defense if an attacker breaches the access controls; data is useless to an attacker if he or she is unable to understand what the data means.

Establishing a Connection to SQL Server

Authentication is performed during logon when a user requests access to a system. The user provides credentials and the host system authenticates the identity of the user against an authentication database. A user in this context is also known as a security principal, someone who can request access to a resource. Security principals can be organized as single users or as groups. This section discusses the following three types of security principal that may request access to a SQL Server instance:

- Windows account
- Windows group
- SQL Server Login (using SQL Server authentication)

Windows accounts and groups may be created on the local operating system of the Windows server, or configured on a domain controller using Active Directory.

Authentication Modes

A user who wants to connect to a SQL Server instance must have an associated SQL Server login that specifies the type of authentication used by that login. SQL Server 2012 supports the following types of authentication mode:

- Windows authentication mode (default mode)
- Mixed authentication mode (both Windows and SQL Server authentication)

Both options include Windows integrated authentication, which cannot be disabled. When a user requests access to SQL Server using Windows authentication, the SQL server does not need to authenticate the identity of the user because this step has already been performed by the Windows operating system. Instead, SQL Server validates the user using an **access token** containing a user identifier from the Windows operating system that was created when the user initially logged on. Windows authenticated connections are also known as **trusted connections**.

By contrast, SQL Server authentication uses logins that are distinct from the Windows operating system. Each time a user requests access to SQL Server, the user must enter credentials for the SQL server to authenticate his or her identity. The credentials for these logins are stored in the master system database. SQL Server authentication has three optional password policies: change password on next login, enforce password expiration, and enforce password policy of the local operating system.

Windows authentication is generally considered to be the most secure method of authenticating with SQL Server for the following reasons:

- The Windows operating system allows for a greater range of policies, such as password complexity, lockout support, and password expiration.

- Windows authentication also uses the Kerberos protocol, which provides a robust and secure means to authenticate a user's identity.

- With Windows authentication, a user does not need to keep track of and enter multiple usernames and passwords.

Despite the clear advantages offered by Windows authentication, an organization may still choose, for a variety of reasons, to enable SQL Server authentication. For example, Windows authentication cannot be used on networks with mixed operating system environments, Web applications, or for clients that reside in unknown or untrusted domains.

SQL Server Logins

SQL Server logins operate at the level of the SQL Server instance and are, therefore, server-level security principals. Permissions on server-level securables may be granted to a SQL Server login using the SQL programming language or Object Explorer in SQL Server Management Studio. For example, the ALTER ANY DATABASE permission enables a login to modify any database on the server. Each SQL Server instance has a number of predefined fixed roles; beginning with SQL Server 2012, it is also possible to create user-defined server roles. Most of the individual server-level permissions and fixed roles are associated with performing administrative functions on the server, for example:

- *sysadmin* may perform any task on the server.
- *security admin* may modify any login.
- *dbcreator* may create or alter any database.

Server-level permissions and roles should be granted with caution due to their broad scope. The majority of functions that server-level roles allow a login to perform can also be assigned using database-level roles. The default role assigned to every login is the public role, which should be assigned minimal permissions beyond being able to connect to the server. A login can be added or removed from membership of a role either through the login properties in Object Explorer or by using the ALTER ROLE SQL syntax.

When SQL Server authentication is enabled using mixed mode, there is a default system Administrator account called **sa**. If SQL Server authentication is enabled during installation, the system prompts you to enter a password for the sa account, and the account will be enabled. If you decide not to enable SQL Server authentication at installation, the sa account will remain disabled until you enable it and set a password.

Because the sa account is widely known and belongs to the sysadmin role, it is often the target of hackers looking to gain unauthorized access to a system. For this reason, it is recommended that you disable the sa account and assign the sysadmin role to a login associated with a Windows account or group.

Activity 6-1: Managing SQL Server Logins

Time Required: 45 minutes

Objective: Create and manage SQL Server logins that use Windows authentication and SQL Server authentication.

Description: In this activity, you will change the different password policies for a Windows account and a SQL Server login. You will create new Windows accounts and groups on the local operating system of your computer, and you will map these to SQL Server logins. Using SQL Server Management Studio, you will also discover how to enable mixed mode authentication and set up a SQL Server login that uses SQL Server authentication.

1. If necessary, start your computer and log on.

2. Click the **Start** button and click **Run**. In the Run dialog box, type **secpol.msc** in the Open text box, and then click **OK** to launch the Microsoft Management Console (MMC) Local Security Policy window. See Figure 6-1.

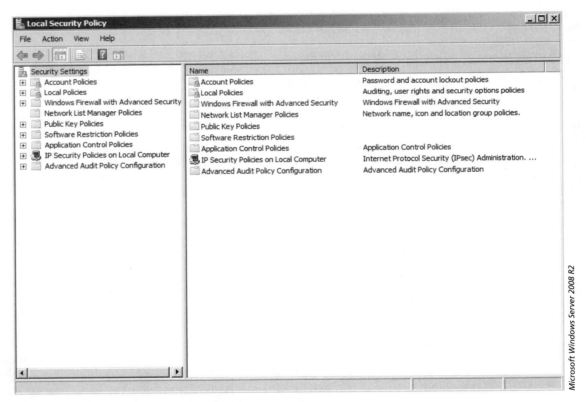

Figure 6-1 Local Security Policy window – Security Settings

3. In the left navigation pane of the Local Security Policy window, click the **+** symbol to expand the Account Policies folder. Then, click the **Password Policy** folder to view the current password policies and associated security settings in the right pane. See Figure 6-2. These policies control the settings for Local Users that are configured on the server. The same policies can also be applied for domain users on a domain controller.

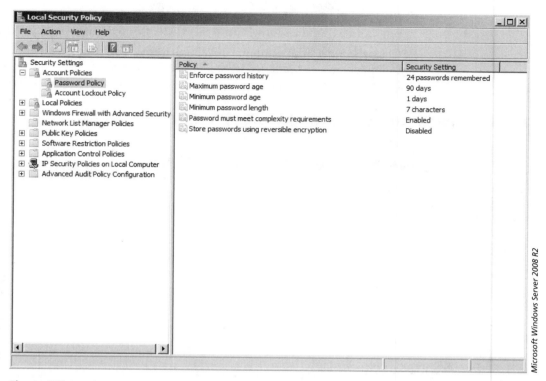

Microsoft Windows Server 2008 R2

Figure 6-2 Local Security Policy window – Password Policy

4. In the right pane, right-click **Password must meet complexity requirements,** and then click **Properties.** On the Local Security Setting tab of the Password must meet complexity requirements Properties window, click **Enabled.** See Figure 6-3.

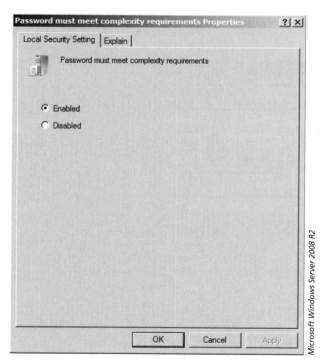

Microsoft Windows Server 2008 R2

Figure 6-3 Password must meet complexity requirements Properties: Local Security Setting tab

5. Click the **Explain** tab, and read the description of the policy. Click **OK** to save the settings and exit the window. Close the MMC Local Security Policy window.

6. Click the **Start** button, point to **Administrative Tools**, and then click **Server Manager** to launch Server Manager. In the left navigation pane, click the **+** symbol to expand Configuration, expand Local Users and Groups, and then click **Users**. See Figure 6-4.

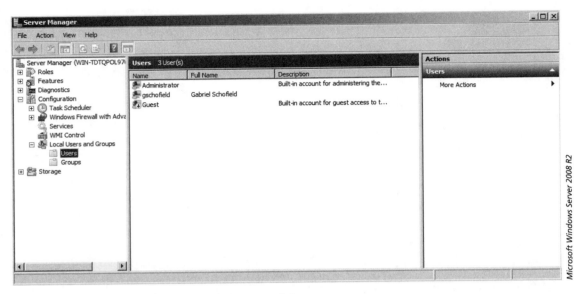

Figure 6-4 Server Manager window – Local Users and Groups

7. On the menu bar, click **Action,** and then click **New User.** In the New User dialog box, type **wintest1** in the User name text box, and then type **Windows Test One** in the Full name text box. Type **Compl3$xity** in the Password and Confirm password text boxes. Uncheck the **User must change password at next logon** check box because you will only be using this account for testing. See Figure 6-5.

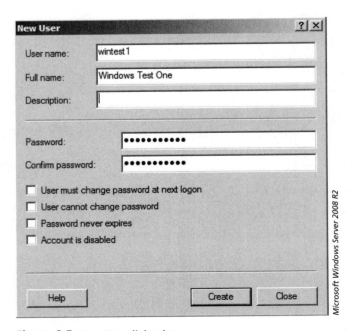

Figure 6-5 New User dialog box

8. Click **Create** to create the new Windows user. A blank New User dialog box opens. Following the same steps and settings as for the wintest1 user, create a second test user called **wintest2**. Set the full name to **Windows Test Two**, and use **Comple3$xity** for the password. Click **Close** after creating the second user.

9. In the left navigation of Server Manager, click **Groups** below Local Users and Groups. On the menu bar, click **Action**, and then click **New Group**. In the New Group dialog box, type **WinTestGroup** in the Group name text box, and then click the **Add** button. Type **wintest2** in the Select Users dialog box, and then click **Check names**. The name should resolve automatically to <Computer Name>\wintest2. Click **OK** to return to the New Group dialog box. See Figure 6-6.

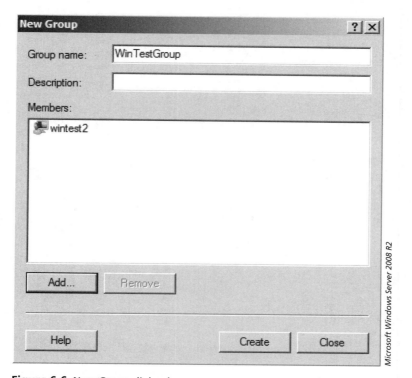

Figure 6-6 New Group dialog box

10. In the New Group dialog box, click **Create** to create the new WinTestGroup group with member wintest2. Click **Close** to exit the New Group dialog box, and then close Server Manager.

11. Click the **Start** button, point to **All Programs**, click **Microsoft SQL Server 2012**, and then click **SQL Server Management Studio**. In the Connect to Server dialog box, select **Database Engine** as the server type, type **LOCALHOST\SQLSERVERUA** in the Server name text box, and then select **Windows Authentication** from the Authentication list box. Click **Connect**.

12. In SQL Server Management Studio, right-click **SQLSERVERUA** in the left navigation pane of Object Explorer, and then click **Properties**. Click **Security** in the left navigation menu of the Server Properties window. Review the Server authentication settings, which you set in Activity 5-5 to SQL Server and Windows Authentication mode. See Figure 6-7. Click **Cancel** to close the Server Properties window.

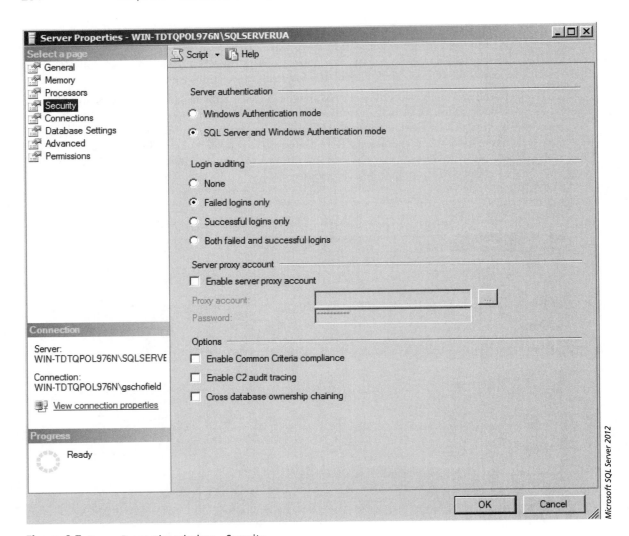

Figure 6-7 Server Properties window – Security

Changing any settings requires a restart of the Database Engine Service for the settings to take effect.

13. In SQL Server Management Studio, click the **+** symbol to expand the SQLSERVERUA instance in the Object Explorer left navigation pane. Click the **+** symbol to expand the Security folder, and then expand the Logins folder. Right-click the **Logins** folder, and click **New Login**. See Figure 6-8.

14. On the General page of the Login – New window, keep the default Windows authentication option checked, and click the **Search** button to the right of the Login name text box. In the Select User or Group dialog box, type **wintest1** in the Enter the object name to select text box, and then click **Check Names** to resolve this name. Click **OK**. See Figure 6-9.

15. In the left navigation pane of the Login – New window, click **Server Roles**. This page allows you to assign server-level roles. Check that only the public role is checked for the wintest1 login. In the left navigation pane, click **Securables**. This page allows you to view the individual server-level permissions of the login.

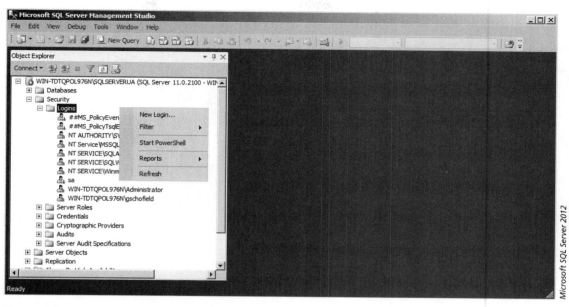

Figure 6-8 SQL Server Management Studio – Server Logins

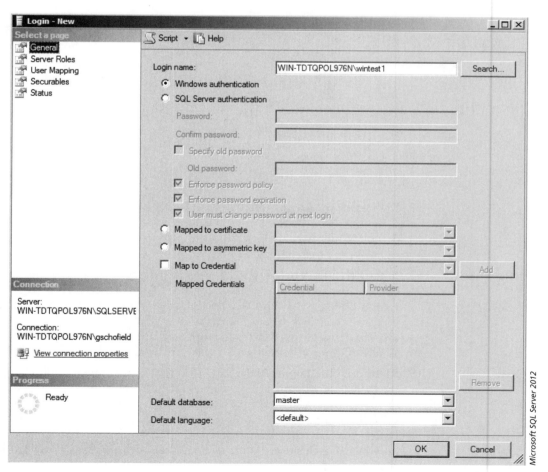

Figure 6-9 Login – New window – General

16. In the left navigation pane, click **Status**. Check that Permission to connect to the database engine is set to Grant and the Login status is Enabled. See Figure 6-10. Click **OK** to create a login for the Windows account wintest1.

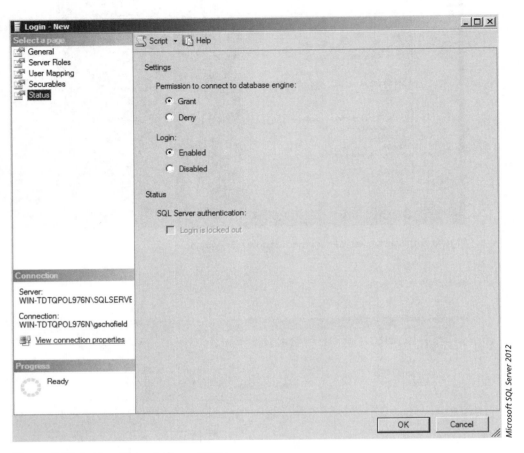

Figure 6-10 Login – New window – Status

17. Right-click the **Logins** folder in SQL Server Management Studio Object Explorer, and then click **New Login**. On the General page of the Login – New window, keep the default Windows authentication option checked, and click the **Search** button to the right of the Login name text box.

18. In the Select User or Group dialog box, click the **Object Types** button, and then check **Groups** in the Object types dialog box. Click **OK** to return to the Select User or Group dialog box. Type **WinTestGroup** in the Enter the object name to select text box, and then click **Check Names** to resolve this name. Click **OK** to create a login for the Windows group WinTestGroup. Any Windows account that is a member of the WinTestGroup Windows group will now be able to log in to the SQL Server instance.

19. Right-click the **Logins** folder in SQL Server Management Studio Object Explorer and then click **New Login**. On the General page of the Login – New window, type **sqltest1** in the Login name text box. Click the **SQL Server authentication** option button to select it, and then type **Comple3$xity** in the Password and Confirm password text boxes. Uncheck the **User must change password at next login** check box as you will only be using this user ID for testing. Keep the other two password policies enabled. Note the difference between the available password policies for a SQL Server login versus Windows. See Figure 6-11.

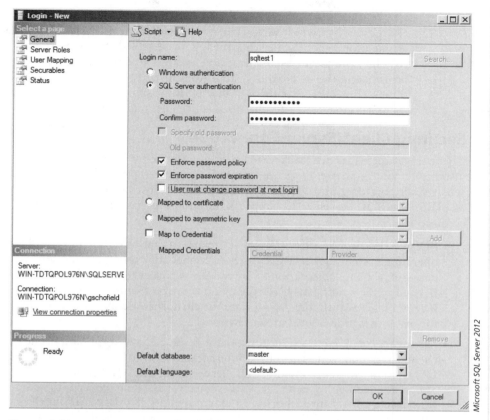

Figure 6-11 Create a new SQL Server login

20. Click **OK** to create the SQL Server login sqltest1. You should now see the new logins that you created appear in the Logins folder of Object Explorer. Note that the icon for the group login that you created in Step 18, WinTestGroup, is different from the user logins. Notice also that the sa login has a small red downward pointing arrow on its icon, indicating that it is disabled. See Figure 6-12.

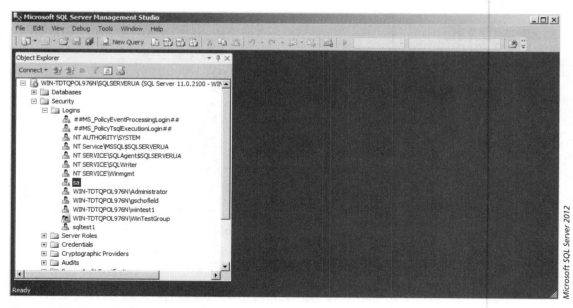

Figure 6-12 Object Explorer Logins folder

21. Right-click the user **sa**, and then click **Properties**. On the General tab of the Login Properties – sa window, you can add a new password. Click the **Status** page in the left navigation menu. Notice that the login is disabled. To enable a login, you would need to click the Login Enabled option button. Due to the security concerns associated with using the sa default system Administrator account, you will leave it disabled. Click **Cancel** to exit the window without saving any changes. You can leave SQL Server Management Studio open for the next activity.

Securing Client/Server Connections

Client/server messages are transported over a network for clients who connect to a SQL Server instance remotely and are, therefore, susceptible to interception. For communication that involves sensitive or confidential data, the message content must be encrypted rather than transmitted as plain text. SQL Server 2012 supports the following two methods for securing client/server connections:

- *Internet Protocol Security (IPSec)*—A protocol that has been integrated with the Windows operating system to secure client/server connections on an Internet Protocol (IP)–based network; the implementation of IPSec is transparent to an application such as SQL Server. Beyond implementing an IPSec policy on the server and client computers, no configuration is required. IPSec is most appropriate for client/server connections on the same network, for instance within a local area network (LAN).

- *Secure Sockets Layer (SSL)*—A protocol designed to encrypt data inside messages to secure client/server connections over the Internet and is suited for communications beyond the LAN; SSL is configured within SQL Server using the SQL Server Configuration Manager. SQL Server can either generate a self-signed certificate to encrypt the data or use a certificate from a **certificate authority**, an external entity that issues and verifies digital certificates, that has been registered on the local computer. Self-signed certificates offer much weaker security than certificates issued by a certificate authority.

The only disadvantage of securing the client/server connection using either of the approaches listed above is that they add a small processing overhead as message contents must be encrypted prior to transmission and decrypted upon receipt.

Activity 6-2: Securing Connections Using SSL

Time Required: 30 minutes
Objective: Configure a SQL Server instance to use SSL encryption for all client/server connections.

Description: In this activity, you will use SQL Server Configuration Manager to configure the SQLSERVERUA instance to use SSL encryption for all connections using a self-signed certificate. Using Query Editor in SQL Server Management Studio, you will then run a test to check the encryption status of your connected session.

1. If necessary, start your computer and log on.

2. Click the **Start** button, point to **All Programs**, and then click **Microsoft SQL Server 2012**. Click **Configuration Tools**, and then click **SQL Server Configuration Manager**. Click **Yes** if prompted by the User Account Control dialog box. In SQL Server Configuration Manager, expand SQL Server Network Configuration in the left navigation pane, right-click **Protocols for SQLSERVERUA**, and then click **Properties**. See Figure 6-13.

3. In the Protocols for SQLSERVERUA Properties dialog box, click the **Certificate** tab, and view the settings options. If you were using a certificate issued by a certificate authority that is installed in the Certificate Store of your Windows operating system, you would select it from the Certificate drop-down list box. See Figure 6-14.

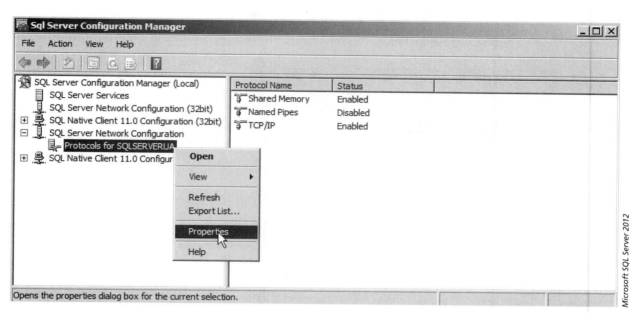

Figure 6-13 SQL Server Configuration Manager

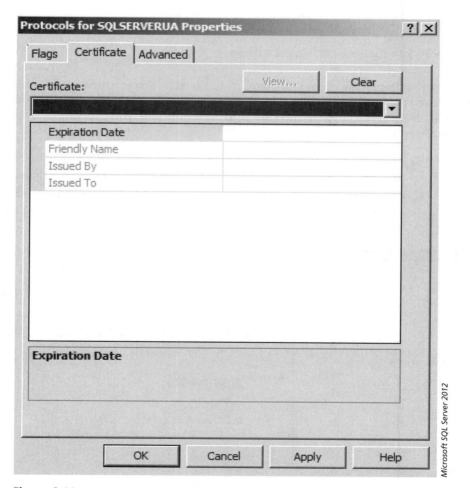

Figure 6-14 Protocols for SQLSERVERUA Properties: Certificate tab

4. Click the **Flags** tab, and then select **Yes** from the Force Encryption drop-down list box. See Figure 6-15.

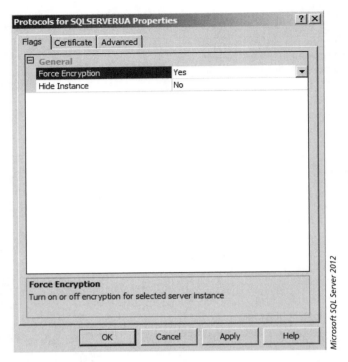

Figure 6-15 Protocols for SQLSERVERUA Properties: Flags tab

This setting forces any client that connects to the SQL Server instance to use SSL. If the client is unable to support SSL, it will not be able to connect. If a certificate has not been selected from the Certificate Store (Step 3), then the SQL Server instance will generate its own self-signed certificate at start-up.

5. Click **Apply**, and then click **OK** in the Warning dialog box. Click **OK** to save your changes and exit the Protocols for SQLSERVERUA Properties dialog box.

6. In SQL Server Configuration Manager, click **SQL Server Services** in the left navigation pane. In the right pane, right-click **SQL Server (SQLSERVERUA)** and click **Restart**. See Figure 6-16.

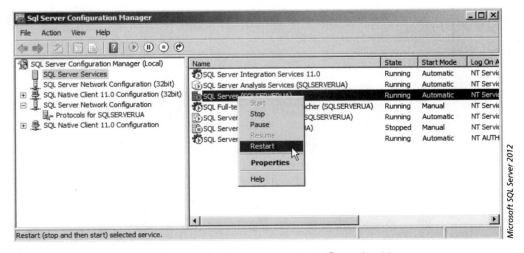

Figure 6-16 Restart the database engine from SQL Server Configuration Manager

7. Return to SQL Server Management Studio, which you left open at the end of Activity 6-1. Click **New Query** on the toolbar. Type **sp_who2;** in the Query Editor window, and then press the **F5** key or click the **Execute** button to run the query.

8. Scroll down to find your current session and make a note of the **Server Process ID (SPID)**, which identifies the individual connections or sessions on the SQL server. Delete the text in the Query Editor window and type the following SQL query replacing <SPID> with your SPID:

```
SELECT encrypt_option

FROM sys.dm_exec_connections

WHERE session_id = <SPID>;
```

9. Run the query by pressing the **F5** key or by clicking the **Execute** button. The encrypt_option value returned should be TRUE if you configured SSL using a self-signed certificate correctly in the previous steps. See Figure 6-17. Close the Query Editor window but leave SQL Server Management Studio open for the next activity.

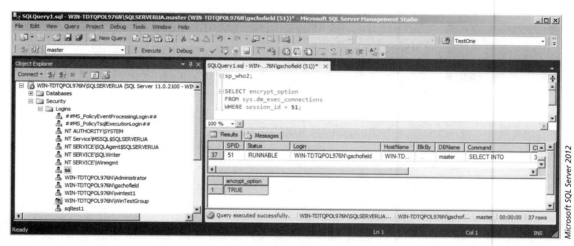

Figure 6-17 Check that new connections to the server are encrypted

Microsoft SQL Server 2012

Database Object Access Control

Other than members of the sysadmin fixed server role, a SQL Server login may not access a database directly or be granted permissions to any of the underlying database objects because a SQL Server login is a server-level principal. To access a database, the SQL Server login must first be mapped to a **database user**, which is a database-level security principal. This mapping includes the name of the database user (the default is to create database users with the same name as the server login) and a default schema to use when connected to the database. Each SQL Server login is also assigned a default database to attach to when a new session is established.

Recall that a permission is a right to perform a particular action against a database object. Connecting to a database, reading data from a table, and modifying a view are all examples of actions that require a permission. Permissions are applied in a hierarchical manner to objects within the database. Database-level permissions apply to all objects in a database. For example, if the EXECUTE permission is granted to a user on a database, the user will be able to execute any procedure within that database. At a more granular level, permissions can be applied to an individual object within a database—for example, to a particular table. Schemas are securables that group together a collection of objects within a database and allow them to be managed as a group. Because permissions can be granted on a schema to a user or role, they can be used to simplify management of a particular segment of the database.

Granting or revoking permissions for each individual user at the level of the objects within a database that has several hundred different users would rapidly become unsustainable and would make it very difficult to understand who has access to what resources. Roles and schemas can be used to simplify management of permissions, and they enable you to maintain a similar level of control for each object. A role groups together several database users (similar to a Windows group). Permissions on different database objects can be granted to the role. A role can be granted to an individual user, known as a member in the context of the role, and that user will inherit the permissions granted to the role. Whenever possible, roles should be used to manage permissions for groups of database users with similar access needs.

SQL Server 2012 has several fixed (predefined) roles at the database level that are documented in the Books Online for SQL Server topic "Database-Level Roles." Flexible (user-defined roles) roles can also be created that are tailored to the business needs. For example, a role may model a business function to differentiate between access levels that groups of users need at a granular level. Roles are database-wide in their scope. An example of a database role is the db_owner role, which can perform any function for an individual database. Be careful of assigning permissions to the public database role. In the absence of specific permissions on a database object, a database user will inherit the permissions defined in the public role.

Activity 6-3: Managing Server and Database Permissions Using Object Explorer

Time Required: 45 minutes
Objective: Manage database permissions using a variety of security objects using Object Explorer in SQL Server Management Studio.

Description: In this activity, you will use Object Explorer in SQL Server Management Studio to manage database logins; create and map new database users; create new roles and manage role membership; and grant permissions to logins, users, and roles.

1. On the SQL Server Management Studio Object Explorer toolbar, click the **Connect** drop-down list box, and then click **Database engine**. In the Connect to Server dialog box, keep the default Server name (<LocalHost>\SQLSERVERUA), but change the Authentication to **SQL Server Authentication**. In the Login text box, type **sqltest1** and type **Compl3$xity** in the Password text box. See Figure 6-18.

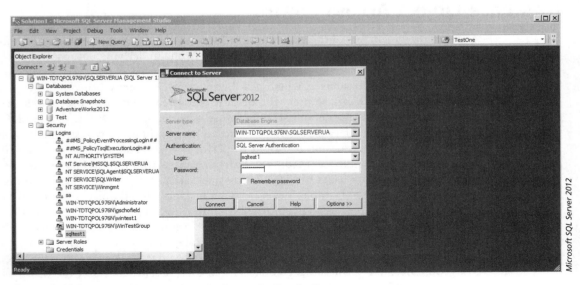

Figure 6-18 Connect to Server using SQL Server Authentication

2. Click **Connect**. A new connection to the SQLSERVERUA instance appears below the existing connection in Object Explorer. In Object Explorer, the root folder of each connection is named <SQL Server Host>\<SQL Server Instance> (SQL Server <Version Number> - <SQL Server Login >). In this example, the root folder is named WIN-TDTQPOL976N\SQLSERVERUA (SQL Server 11.0.2100 – sqltest1). In the steps that follow, you might need to expand the width of the Object Explorer pane in order to see the SQL Server login name as you switch between different connections.

3. In Object Explorer, click the **SQLSERVERUA** root folder of the new connection. Click **New Query**. In the Query Editor window, type the following SQL query, and then press the **F5** key or click the **Execute** button:

```
CREATE DATABASE PermissionTest;
```

You should receive the error message "CREATE DATABASE permission denied in database 'master'." See Figure 6-19. This is to be expected as sqltest1 has been granted no permissions other than the fixed server public role.

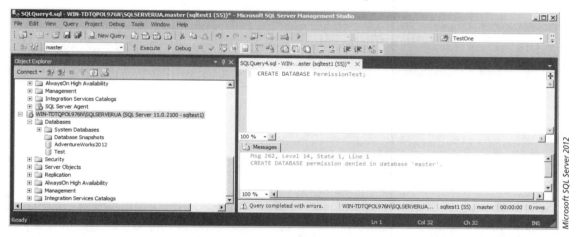

Figure 6-19 Permission to create a new database denied

4. In Object Explorer, scroll back up to the connection established during Activity 6-1 under the login that is a member of the sysadmin group. Click the **+** symbol to expand the Security folder below the SQLSERVERUA instance, and then expand the Logins folder. See Figure 6-20.

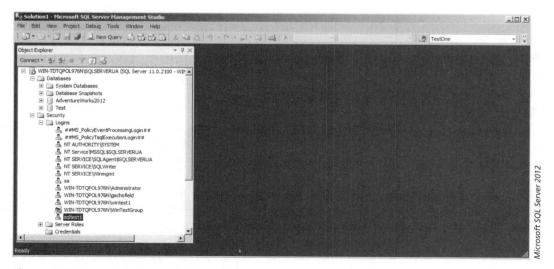

Figure 6-20 Expand the Logins folder in Object Explorer

5. Right-click the **sqltest1** login, and then click **Properties**. In the Login Properties – sqltest1 window, click **Securables** in the left navigation pane. On the Explicit tab at the bottom of the window, scroll down, and check the **Grant** check box for the Create any database permission. See Figure 6-21.

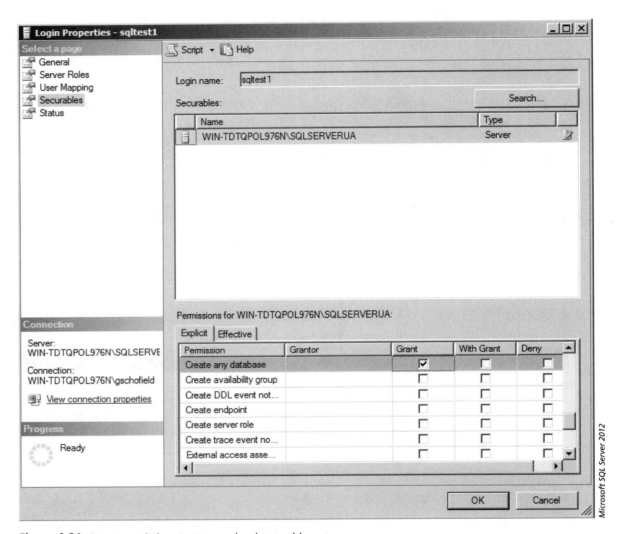

Figure 6-21 Grant permissions to a server-level securable

6. Click **OK** to save the changes and close the Login Properties – sqltest1 window. Return to the Query Editor screen on the right and press the **F5** key, or click the **Execute** button to run the same query as Step 3. The query should now complete successfully. See Figure 6-22.

7. In Object Explorer, scroll back down to the connection established using the sqltest1 login. Click the **+** symbol to expand the Databases folder, and then expand the AdventureWorks2012 folder. You should receive the following error message: "The database AdventureWorks2012 is not accessible. (Object Explorer)." See Figure 6-23. This error occurred because the sqltest1 login has no database user associated with it. Click **OK**.

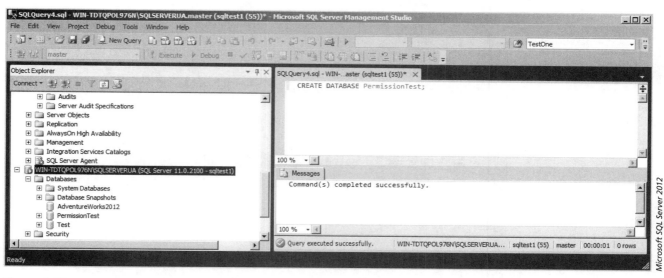

Figure 6-22 Create database command completed successfully

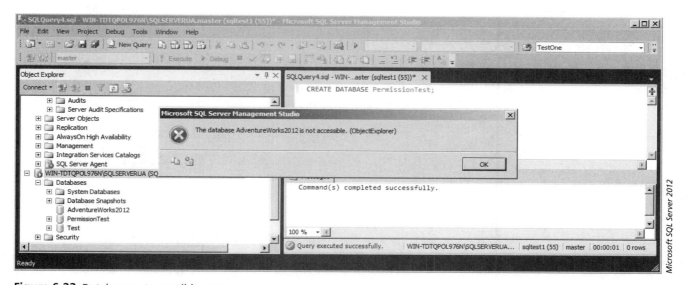

Figure 6-23 Database not accessible error

8. Return to the connection established under the login that is a member of the sysadmin group. Right-click the **sqltest1** login, and then click **Properties**. In the Login Properties – sqltest1 window, click **User Mapping** in the left navigation pane to display the mapping of database users to this login. Note that the only database with a mapped database user is the PermissionTest database that you just created. In the Users mapped to this login section, click the row with the database name **PermissionTest**. In the Database role membership for: Permission-Test section, notice that you are mapped to the dbo user and are a member of the db_owner role. This occurred because you created a database using the default settings. See Figure 6-24.

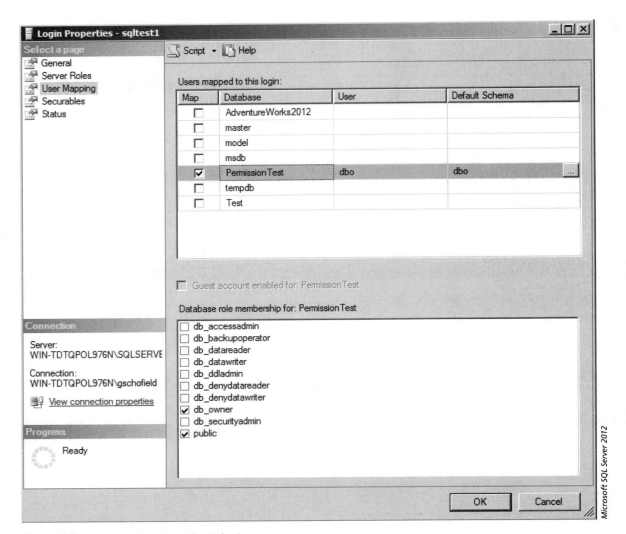

Figure 6-24 User mappings to sqltest1 login

9. In the Users mapped to this login section, click the AdventureWorks2012 database row to select it. Click the **Map** check box to enable the row. Notice that a default database user that matches the name of the login now appears in the user column. In the Default Schema field, type **HumanResources**. In the Database role membership for: AdventureWorks2012 section, click the **db_datareader** role check box to add the sqltest1 database user as a member. This is a fixed database role that allows members to query any table or view in the database. See Figure 6-25.

10. Click **OK** to save the changes and close the Login Properties window. Return to the Query Editor screen that is connected using the sqltest1 login. Delete the existing text in Query Editor. Type the following SQL query, and then press the **F5** key or click the **Execute** button:

```
USE AdventureWorks2012;

SELECT TOP 100 *

FROM HumanResources.Employee;
```

This query should execute successfully as the database user sqltest1 that you just created is a member of the db_datareader role. See Figure 6-26.

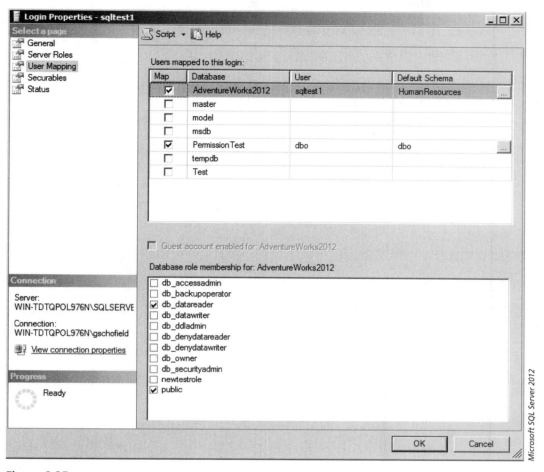

Figure 6-25 Adding a user mapping for the AdventureWorks2012 database

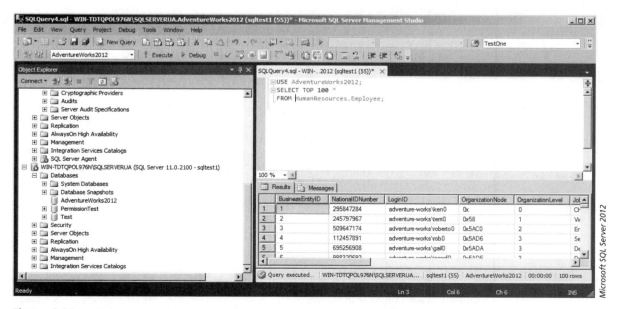

Figure 6-26 Testing permissions to query a table in the AdventureWorks2012 database

11. Delete the existing text in Query Editor. Type the following SQL query, and then press the **F5** key or click the **Execute** button:

```
USE AdventureWorks2012;

UPDATE HumanResources.Employee

SET NationalIDNumber = 111111111

WHERE BusinessEntityID = 1;
```

You should receive the following error message: "The UPDATE permission was denied on the object 'Employee,' database AdvertureWorks2012." This is to be expected because the database user sqltest1 has been given no permissions to update tables in the database. See Figure 6-27.

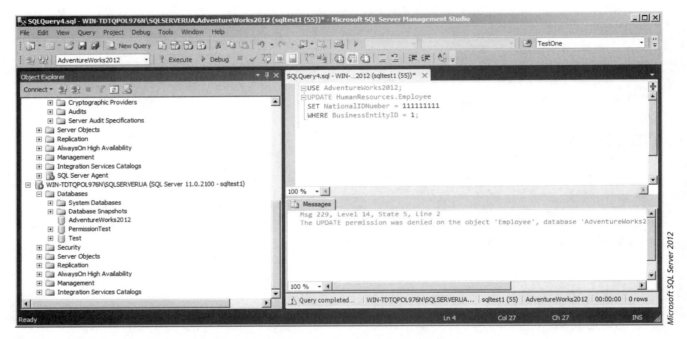

Figure 6-27 Testing permissions to update a table in the AdventureWorks2012 database

12. Return to the connection established under the login that is a member of the sysadmin group. Click the **+** symbol to expand the Databases folder, and then expand the AdventureWorks2012 folder, the Security folder, and the Roles folder. Then, right-click **Database Roles** and click **New Database Role**. On the General page of the Database Role – New window, type **TestDatabaseRole** in the Role name text box, and then type **dbo** in the Owner text box. Under Role Members, click **Add**. In the Select Database User or Role dialog box, click **Browse**. Click the **sqltest1** check box. Click **OK**, and then click **OK** again. See Figure 6-28.

13. Click **Securables** in the left navigation pane of the Database Role – New window, and then click the **Search** button below the Database role name text box. In the Add Objects dialog box, click the **All Objects Belonging to the Schema** option button. Select the schema **Human Resources** from the Schema name list box, and then click **OK** to return to the Database Role – New window.

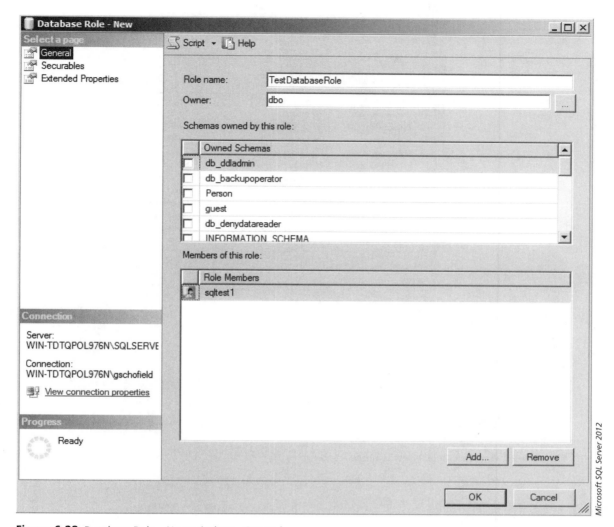

Figure 6-28 Database Role – New window – General

14. In the Securables matrix of the Database Role – New window, click the row for the **Employee** table. In the Explicit matrix at the bottom of the window, check the Grant check box for the Insert, Select, and Update permissions. Check the Deny check box for the Delete permission. See Figure 6-29.

15. Click **OK** to save the changes and exit the Database Role – New window. Return to the Query Editor screen on the right that is connected using the sqltest1 login. Press the **F5** key or click the **Execute** button to run the same query as in Step 11. The query should now complete successfully because sqltest1 inherited the Update permission from the new TestDatabaseRole that you created. See Figure 6-30.

16. Delete the existing text in the Query Editor window. Type the following text, and then press the **F5** key or click the **Execute** button:

```
USE AdventureWorks2012;

DELETE

FROM HumanResources.Employee

WHERE BusinessEntityID = 1;
```

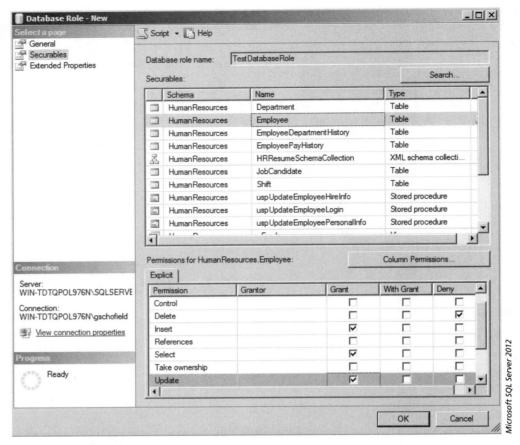

Figure 6-29 Database Role – New window – Securables

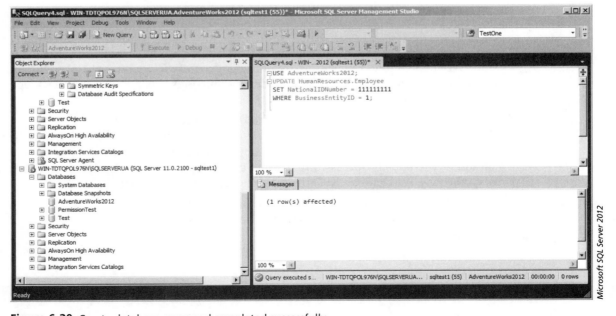

Figure 6-30 Create database command completed successfully

You should receive the following error message: "The DELETE permission was denied on the object 'Employee'." In Step 12, you explicitly denied the Delete permission on the HumanResources.Employee object so this error validates that the permission is working.

17. Delete the text in Query Editor. Type the following query, and then press the **F5** key or click the **Execute** button:

```
USE AdventureWorks2012;

SELECT * FROM fn_my_permissions (NULL, 'SERVER');

SELECT * FROM fn_my_permissions (NULL, 'DATABASE');

SELECT * FROM fn_my_permissions

('HumanResources.Employee', 'OBJECT');
```

The query returns three result sets showing the effective permissions granted to sqltest1 on the server, on the AdventureWorks2012 database, and for the HumanResources.Employee table. Effective permissions are the combination of direct permissions granted and permissions inherited through role membership. See Figure 6-31.

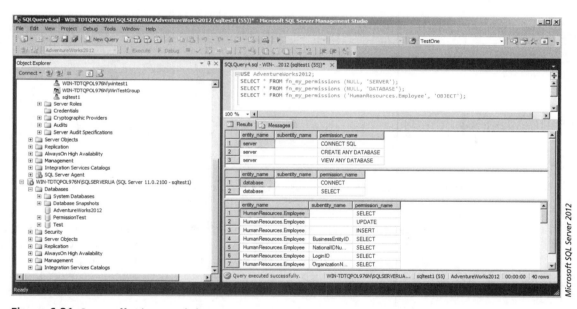

Figure 6-31 Query effective permissions

18. Recall that in Activity 5-5 you used the SQL programming language to manage permissions. Go back to that activity now to review those steps in light of what you have learned in this activity. Once you have finished, close SQL Server Management Studio.

Database Encryption

The previous sections of this chapter focused on controlling who has access to data on a SQL Server instance. If these controls fail and an unauthorized user gains access to the data, encryption can provide additional protection by making the data unintelligible. It is important to note that unauthorized access does not need to be malicious but can occur inadvertently if access controls have been incorrectly configured. Encryption does not prevent data loss, but it can limit the ramifications of data loss.

Symmetric vs. Asymmetric Keys

A **key** is a parameter used in conjunction with a cryptographic algorithm, known as a **cipher**, to encrypt data. There are two types of encryption keys:

- **Symmetric keys** (also known as secret keys) use the same key to encrypt and decrypt the data. Anyone with the key can decode the data. This may be a problem when transferring data over the Internet or other networks because both the key and the encrypted data are being transferred. It is, however, the most commonly used form of encryption for protecting or storing data as it offers much better performance than asymmetric encryption. See Figure 6-32.

Figure 6-32 Symmetric key encryption steps

- **Asymmetric keys** (also known as public keys) use a public key to encrypt and a different, private key to decrypt data. Anyone can use the public key to encrypt a message, but only the holder of the private key can decrypt that message. Although more secure than a symmetric key, an asymmetric key requires more processing power. With asymmetric encryption, the sender requests a public key from the recipient. Then the sender's data is encrypted with the key and sent to the recipient where it is decrypted using a private key. See Figure 6-33. The only items being transferred in this scenario are the public key and the encrypted data. Even if someone intercepts both of these, they are still unable to decode the sensitive data.

Asymmetric algorithms generally offer stronger encryption than symmetric algorithms with the same length key, but their performance is slower. For this reason, they are typically used only when data is transmitted over a network and is, therefore, at risk of being intercepted. Keys can also be encrypted in the same way that data is encrypted, thereby adding an additional layer of security. For example, when securing a large amount of data—and in situations in which performance is a factor—it may be a good idea to encrypt the data with a symmetric key and then encrypt the symmetric key with an asymmetric key. Secure Internet transactions typically use this mechanism, and in a secure Internet transaction, initial key exchange is performed that allows a symmetric key to be used for encrypting data in the session. The session key is then protected using asymmetric public/private key encryption that allows the performance benefits of symmetric encryption to be realized while retaining the security features inherent to asymmetric encryption. Certificates are used in conjunction with keys as a way to assure the identity of the user who is sending the public key matches the user who issued the public key. Third-party certificate authorities—such as VeriSign—issue certificates used for this purpose.

Figure 6-33 Asymmetric key encryption steps

Encryption Algorithms in SQL Server 2012

When encrypting data, you must choose an encryption algorithm. The trade-off is primarily performance versus security. As we have already discussed, asymmetric encryption is more secure than symmetric encryption, but it has an additional performance overhead. For this reason, this section only covers symmetric algorithms for encrypting data.

 To improve performance, data should be compressed before encryption. Encrypted data cannot be compressed but compressed data can be encrypted.

There are many different symmetric algorithms to choose from in SQL Server 2012. Understanding all the options and choosing the best algorithm for a particular deployment can be a challenging process. There is no single solution that will perfectly satisfy all situations. The 3-key Triple Data Encryption Standard (DES) algorithm and the more recent Advanced Encryption Standard (AES) algorithm are generally considered to have the best balance of security and performance and are described below:

- **3-key Triple DES** applies the DES cipher three times to the data using three different 64-bit keys. This is a very common standard, but it is more resource intensive because the cipher has to be applied three times.

- **AES** is the successor to the DES algorithm. It is a **block cipher** that translates fixed-size blocks of unencrypted data into corresponding fixed-sized blocks of encrypted data. It uses a 128-bit block cipher in conjunction with varying key sizes (128-bit, 192-bit, and 256-bit).

A larger key size generally equates to stronger security but slower performance.

For the activities in this book, the AES cipher is used because Triple DES is steadily being phased out.

Encryption Architecture in SQL Server 2012

SQL Server uses a hierarchical approach to encryption—each layer of encryption protects the layer directly beneath it. There are several layers of encryption, starting with the key management system within the Windows operating system and then followed by application-specific layers:

- **Windows Data Protection API (DPAPI)** is the key management system within the Windows operating system. SQL Server uses the DPAPI to encrypt the service master key.

- **Service master key (SMK)** is created the first time a SQL Server instance is started; it is used to encrypt linked server credentials, login credentials, and the database master keys. In SQL Server 2012, the SMK uses the AES 256-bit algorithm.

- **Database master key (DMK)** is a symmetric key used to protect asymmetric private keys and certificates that are stored in the database. In SQL Server 2012, the DMK uses the AES 256-bit algorithm.

Within a database, data can be encrypted at a column level using SQL functions that enable individual data items to be encrypted as the records are inserted or updated. The following two types of symmetric encryption are available:

- **EncryptByPassphrase()**—A SQL function that uses a passphrase to generate a key and uses the Triple DES algorithm to encrypt the data; this approach does not require a key to be registered in advance with the database

- **EncryptByKey()**—A SQL function that encrypts data using a key that has been registered with the database; this provides the flexibility to choose the encryption algorithm that will be used.

Similar functions are available that enable encryption using asymmetric keys and certificates. However, due to the performance implications, these are less widely used for encrypting data.

Even after encrypting data, there are still ways for a hacker to attack encrypted column-level data because encrypted values can be moved between records. For example, a hacker could retrieve the encrypted hexadecimal values for one record and insert them into another record. By making some assumptions based on data in unencrypted columns (e.g., employee position), it would be possible to update data in an encrypted column (e.g., salary). These types of attacks can be foiled using an authenticator when encrypting and decrypting data. An **authenticator**, also known as a salt value in cryptography, is another column value that is unique to the row and used in conjunction with the key to secure the data being encrypted. This prevents a hacker from moving an encrypted value between rows. The authenticator selected should be one that is not likely to change; if it does, the ability to decrypt the data is lost.

Transparent Data Encryption (TDE)

Transparent Data Encryption (TDE) uses a symmetric key called the **database encryption key (DEK)** to encrypt the individual pages within the physical data and log files. TDE is designed to render data in the physical data and log files unusable should someone gain unauthorized access to these files. Once TDE is enabled, it is managed as a background process by the database engine, and it is transparent to an end user. The DEK is stored in the database and is protected by an asymmetric key that is stored at the SQL Server instance level in the master system database. To recover a database that has been protected using TDE, both the asymmetric and symmetric keys must be available. Enabling TDE for the first time consumes a lot of resources because every page in the database must be encrypted; therefore, it is best to do this during a maintenance window.

Encryption Key Management (EKM)

Encryption key management (EKM) is a feature that enables third-party key management solutions to be used in conjunction with SQL Server. Use of a third-party product can improve the key management function that encompasses generation, storage, distribution, and retrieval of keys. When EKM is used, keys can be stored independently from the encrypted data and additional authorization checks can be configured for key retrieval. EKM enables increased efficiency of key management activities through centralization, while enabling these activities to be segregated from other SQL administrative tasks.

Activity 6-4: Implementing Column-Level and Database Encryption

Time Required: 60 minutes
Objective: Encrypt column-level data, enable Transparent Database Encryption (TDE) for database-level encryption, and back up keys and certificates.

Description: In this activity, you will learn how to create the necessary certificates and keys to encrypt and decrypt column-level data in a table and to enable Transparent Database Encryption (TDE). You will learn how to take backups of keys and certificates that are critical for recovering an encrypted database.

1. If necessary, start your computer and log on.

2. Click the **Start** button, point to **All Programs**, click **Microsoft SQL Server 2012**, and then click **SQL Server Management Studio**. In the Connect to Server dialog box, select **Database Engine** as the server type, type **LOCALHOST\SQLSERVERUA** in the Server name text box, and select **Windows Authentication** from the Authentication list box. Click **Connect**.

   By default, there is no database master key (DMK) when a database is created, so you will create one to encrypt and decrypt any asymmetric keys or certificates that are added to the database. You will also create a certificate, which is protected by the DMK, in order to encrypt the symmetric key. Finally, you will create the symmetric key, protected by the certificate, that will be used for encrypting and decrypting column-level data.

3. In SQL Server Management Studio, click **New Query** to open a Query Editor window. Type the following SQL code, and then press the F5 key or click the **Execute** button to run the query (see Figure 6-34):

```
USE AdventureWorks2012;

GO

CREATE MASTER KEY ENCRYPTION BY

PASSWORD = 'AdventureWorks2012Password';

GO

CREATE CERTIFICATE EncryptKeyForSocialSecurity

WITH SUBJECT = 'Certificate for encrypting symmetric key used to
  encrypt Social Security Numbers';

GO

CREATE SYMMETRIC KEY SocialSecurityEncryptionKey

WITH ALGORITHM = AES_256

ENCRYPTION BY CERTIFICATE EncryptKeyForSocialSecurity

GO
```

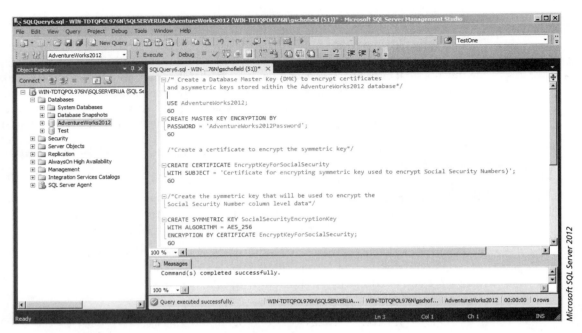

Figure 6-34 Create a database master key, certificate, and a symmetric key to use for column-level encryption

The Query Editor window shown in Figure 6-34 contains comments between each section of code. Comments are useful for communicating the purpose of a section of code. Single-line comments can be added by placing -- before the comment text. For comments spanning multiple lines, as illustrated in Figure 6-34, the comment text should be enclosed using the following syntax: /*<comment text>*/

4. In this step, you will alter the HumanResources.Employees table and add a new column that will hold encrypted values of the NationalIDNumber. You will then open the symmetric key (using the certificate to decrypt it) and update the new column with the encrypted values. Delete the text from the previous query in Query Editor. Type the following query, and then press the **F5** key or click the **Execute** button (see Figure 6-35):

```
USE AdventureWorks2012;

GO

ALTER TABLE HumanResources.Employee

ADD EncryptedNationalIDNumber varbinary(128);

GO

OPEN SYMMETRIC KEY SocialSecurityEncryptionKey

DECRYPTION BY CERTIFICATE EncryptKeyForSocialSecurity;

UPDATE HumanResources.Employee

SET EncryptedNationalIDNumber =

EncryptByKey
(key_GUID('SocialSecurityEncryptionKey'),NationalIDNumber);

CLOSE SYMMETRIC KEY SocialSecurityEncryptionKey;

GO
```

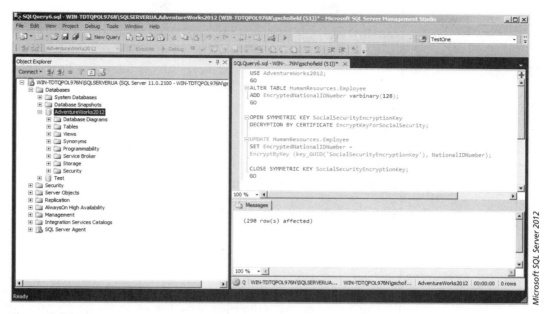

Figure 6-35 Add a new column and update with encrypted data

5. Next, you'll verify that the EncryptedNationalIDNumber column that you updated in Step 4 contains encrypted values by querying the data in the column. Delete the text from the previous query in Query Editor. Type the following query, and press the **F5** key or click the **Execute** button:

```
USE AdventureWorks2012;

GO

SELECT EncryptedNationalIDNumber

FROM HumanResources.Employee;

GO
```

Figure 6-36 shows the result set of the query containing the encrypted values of the employee national ID number.

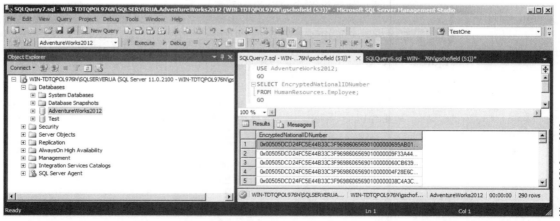

Figure 6-36 Query the encrypted records

6. Delete the text from the previous query in Query Editor. Type the following query, and then press the **F5** key or click the **Execute** button:

```
USE AdventureWorks2012;

GO

OPEN SYMMETRIC KEY SocialSecurityEncryptionKey

DECRYPTION BY CERTIFICATE EncryptKeyForSocialSecurity;

SELECT

CONVERT (nvarchar, DecryptByKey(EncryptedNationalIDNumber))

AS DecryptedNationalIDNumber

FROM HumanResources.Employee;

CLOSE SYMMETRIC KEY SocialSecurityEncryptionKey;

GO
```

This query decrypts the symmetric key using the certificate, and then it uses the symmetric key to decrypt the encrypted NationalIDNumber values. The values must be converted from their hexadecimal value into a string in order for them to be legible. See Figure 6-37.

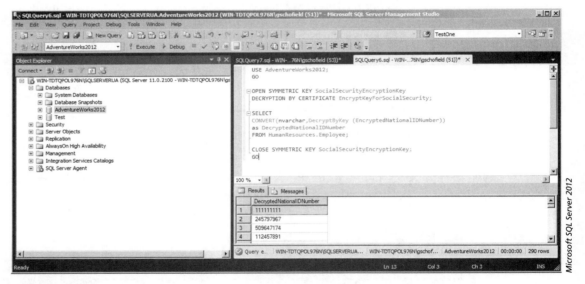

Figure 6-37 Decrypt the encrypted records

7. Next, you will enable Transparent Data Encryption (TDE) on the AdventureWorks2012 database. There are several configuration steps involved with enabling TDE: creating a master key and certificate for the server instance, creating a database encryption key that will be protected by the certificate, and finally, switching the encryption on. Delete the text from the previous query in Query Editor. Type the following query, and then press the **F5** key or click the **Execute** button:

```
USE master;

GO

CREATE MASTER KEY
```

```
ENCRYPTION BY PASSWORD = 'Instance$Password';

GO

CREATE CERTIFICATE SQLSERVERUACert

WITH SUBJECT = 'DEK Certificate';

GO

USE AdventureWorks2012;

GO

CREATE DATABASE ENCRYPTION KEY

WITH ALGORITHM = AES_256

ENCRYPTION BY SERVER CERTIFICATE SQLSERVERUACert;

GO

ALTER DATABASE AdventureWorks2012

SET ENCRYPTION ON;

GO
```

Note that when executing these queries you will receive a warning message advising you to immediately back up the certificate and associated private key because these will be needed in the event that you need to recover the database. See Figure 6-38.

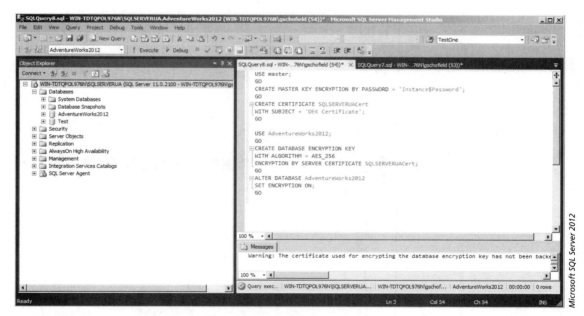

Figure 6-38 Enabling Transparent Data Encryption (TDE)

8. You will now back up the master service key, the master key, and the certificate and private key used for encrypting the database encryption key. Delete the text from the previous query in Query Editor. Type the following query, and then press the **F5** key or click the **Execute** button (see Figure 6-39):

```
USE master;

BACKUP SERVICE MASTER KEY

TO FILE = 'C:\Program Files\Microsoft SQL Server\MSSQL11.SQLSERVERUA\
  MSSQL\Backup\SMK_20120708.bak'

ENCRYPTION BY PASSWORD = 'Service$MasterKey';

GO

BACKUP MASTER KEY

TO FILE = 'C:\Program Files\Microsoft SQL Server\MSSQL11.SQLSERVERUA\
  MSSQL\Backup\MK_20120708.bak'

ENCRYPTION BY PASSWORD = '$MasterKey';

GO

BACKUP CERTIFICATE SQLSERVERUACert

TO FILE = 'C:\Program Files\Microsoft SQL Server\MSSQL11.SQLSERVERUA\
  MSSQL\Backup\SQLSERVERUACert_20120708.bak'

WITH PRIVATE KEY

(FILE = 'C:\Program Files\Microsoft SQL Server\MSSQL11.SQLSERVERUA\
  MSSQL\Backup\SQLSERVERKey.bkey',

ENCRYPTION BY PASSWORD = 'DEK$Certificate');
```

 These keys and certificates should be stored in an extremely secure place as they will be needed in the event of a database recovery. For a production database, you should use very strong passwords to encrypt the backups.

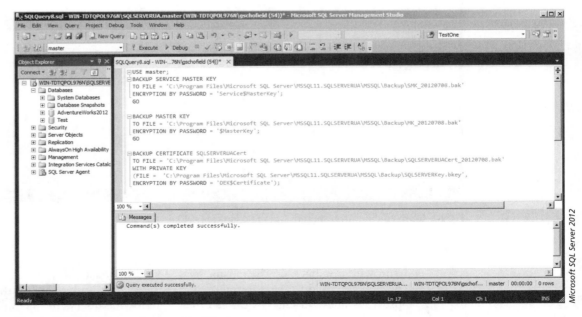

Figure 6-39 Backing up keys and certificates

9. Click the **Start** button, click **Computer**, and navigate to the following directory:

`C:\Program Files\Microsoft SQL Server\MSSQL11.SQLSERVERUA\MSSQL\`
`Backup\`

If the backups that you took in Step 8 were successful, you should see the four backup files in this folder. See Figure 6-40. Note that backups of keys and certificates should be stored permanently in a location other than your normal backup folder (i.e., they should be kept separate from your data and log backups).

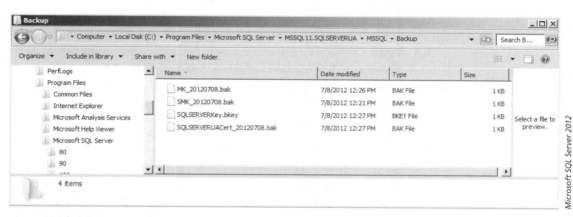

Figure 6-40 Viewing key backups

10. You have now completed this activity. Close any open applications on your computer.

Chapter Summary

- Databases often contain sensitive or confidential information that must be protected both from accidental exposure to unauthorized users and from malicious attacks.

- Securables are the objects in a database and on a SQL Server instance that can be secured. Permissions are rights granted to a security principal that allow it to perform a particular action on a securable. A security principal is an entity that can request access to a securable.

- SQL Server logins operate at the level of the SQL Server instance and are server-level security principals. Permissions on server-level securables may be granted to a SQL Server login using the SQL programming language or Object Explorer in SQL Server Management Studio.

- A user connecting to SQL server must have an associated SQL Server login that specifies the type of authentication used by that login.

- Authentication is performed during logon when a user requests access to a system. Windows authentication is the default authentication mechanism and cannot be disabled. SQL Server authentication is also supported but less secure.

- Client/server messages are susceptible to interception. For communication that involves sensitive or confidential data, the message content should be encrypted using the SSL or IPSec protocols.

- A SQL Server login may not access a database directly because it is a server-level principal. To access a database, the SQL Server login must first be mapped to a database user, which is a database-level security principal.

- Roles and schemas can be used to simplify management of permissions. A role is a principal that groups together several database users. Schemas are securables that group together a collection of objects within a database and allow them to be managed as a group for the purposes of granting permissions.

- Encryption does not prevent data loss but can limit the ramifications of data loss by making the data unintelligible. It offers a last line of defense in the event that access controls fail.
- A key is used in conjunction with a cryptographic algorithm known as a cipher to encrypt data. Selecting an appropriate encryption technology is primarily a trade-off between security and performance. There are two types of encryption keys: symmetric and asymmetric.
- Symmetric keys use the same key to encrypt and decrypt the data. This is the most commonly used form of encryption when protecting or storing data because it offers much better performance over asymmetric encryption.
- Asymmetric keys use a public key to encrypt and a different, private key to decrypt data. Anyone can use the public key to encrypt a message, but only the holder of the private key can decrypt that message. Although more secure, this requires more processing power. This type of encryption is commonly used when transferring data over a network or to encrypt other symmetric keys.
- SQL Server uses a hierarchical approach to encryption—each layer protects the layer directly beneath it. Windows Data Protection API (DPAPI) is the key management system within the Windows operating system. SQL Server uses the DPAPI to encrypt the service master key. The service master key (SMK) encrypts linked server credentials, login credentials, and the database master keys. The database master key (DMK) is a symmetric key used to protect asymmetric private keys and certificates stored in the database. Both these keys use the AES 256-bit algorithm.
- Transparent Data Encryption (TDE) uses a symmetric key called the database encryption key (DEK) to encrypt the individual pages within the physical data and log files. TDE is designed to render data in the physical data and log files unusable should someone gain unauthorized access to these files.
- Encryption key management (EKM) is a feature that enables third-party key management solutions to be used in conjunction with SQL Server.

Key Terms

3-key Triple DES   A widely used symmetric encryption algorithm that applies the DES cipher three times to the data using three different 64-bit keys.

access token   A user identifier from the Windows operating system that is created when the user initially logs on; applications that use Windows integrated authentication use access tokens to validate the user.

AES   The successor to the DES algorithm; uses a 128-bit block cipher in conjunction with varying key sizes (128-bit, 192-bit, and 256-bit).

asymmetric keys   A type of encryption key that uses a public key to encrypt data and a different, private key to decrypt data; also known as a public key. Anyone can use the public key to encrypt a message, but only the holder of the private key can decrypt that message.

authentication   A process performed during logon when a user or application requests access to a system; the user provides credentials and the host system authenticates the identity of the user against an authentication database.

authenticator   A column value that is unique to the row and is used in conjunction with the key to secure the data being encrypted; also known as a salt value.

block cipher   A class of encryption algorithms that translates fixed-size blocks of unencrypted data into corresponding fixed-sized blocks of encrypted data.

certificate authority   An external entity that issues and verifies digital certificates used for encrypting data.

cipher   A cryptographic algorithm used in conjunction with a key to encrypt data.

database encryption key (DEK)   A key used to encrypt the individual pages within the physical data and log files for Transparent Data Encryption.

database master key (DMK)   A symmetric key used to protect asymmetric private keys and certificates that are stored in the database. In SQL Server 2012, the DMK uses the AES 256-bit algorithm.

database user   A database-level security principal; SQL Server logins are mapped to database users to access objects on an individual database.

EncryptByKey   A SQL function that encrypts data using a key that has been registered with the database; provides the flexibility to choose an encryption algorithm.

EncryptByPassphrase   A SQL function that uses a passphrase to generate a key and uses the Triple DES algorithm to encrypt the data; does not require a key to be registered in advance with the database.

encryption   A reversible process involving the use of a key or passcode and an algorithm to convert data into an unreadable form.

encryption key management (EKM)   A feature that enables third-party key management solutions to be used in conjunction with SQL Server.

Internet Protocol Security (IPSec)   A protocol that has been integrated with the Windows operating system to enable secure client/server connections on an Internet Protocol (IP)–based network.

key   A parameter used in conjunction with a cryptographic algorithm to encrypt data.

layered security   A database security model (also known as defense-in-depth) that involves combining multiple security controls to prevent unauthorized access.

sa   The default system Administrator login when using SQL Server authentication.

securables   The various objects in a database and a SQL Server instance that can be secured.

Secure Sockets Layer (SSL)   A protocol designed to encrypt data inside messages to secure client/server connections over the Internet.

security principal   An entity that can request access to a resource or securable; can be organized as single users or as groups.

Server Process ID (SPID)   An identifier that is assigned to each connection or session on the SQL Server.

service master key (SMK)   A key that is created the first time a SQL Server instance is started; used to encrypt linked server credentials, login credentials, and the database master keys. The SMK uses the AES 256-bit algorithm.

SQL Server login   A login that operates at the level of the SQL Server instance and is a server-level security principal; may be granted permissions on server-level securables.

surface area   The number of potential security vulnerabilities that are exposed on an application due to the functionality that has been enabled.

symmetric keys   A type of key that uses the same key to encrypt and decrypt data; also known as a secret key.

Transparent Data Encryption (TDE)   A type of encryption that uses a symmetric key called the database encryption key (DEK) to encrypt the individual pages within the physical data and log files.

trusted connection   A connection established using Windows authentication.

Windows Data Protection API (DPAPI)   The key management system within the Windows operating system; SQL Server uses the DPAPI to encrypt the service master key.

Review Questions

1. Which of the following is *not* an advantage of Windows authentication?

    a.   It offers a comprehensive set of password policies.

    b.   It allows users to connect from untrusted domains.

    c.   It prevents users having to remember multiple credentials.

    d.   It uses the Kerberos protocol.

2. Which of the following logins would be able to connect to a database?

    a.   An enabled SQL login that is mapped to a database user

    b.   An enabled SQL login that is a member of the fixed server sysadmin role

    c.   An enabled SQL login that is a member of the fixed server public role

    d.   Both options a and b

3.   In the context of SQL Server, which protocol would you choose for securing connections beyond the LAN?

    a.   IPSec

    b.   SFTP

    c.   SSL

    d.   SSH

4.   Which of the following are security principals on SQL Server?

    a.   Database and server roles

    b.   Database users

    c.   SQL Server logins

    d.   All of the above

5.   Which of the following are securables?

    a.   Database

    b.   Schema

    c.   Database table

    d.   All of the above

6.   Why is encryption an important security control on a SQL Server database?

    a.   It prevents an unauthorized user from being able to understand the data.

    b.   It prevents an unauthorized user from gaining access to the data.

    c.   It can prevent data loss.

    d.   None of the above

7.   Which of the following statements is *not* true?

    a.   A symmetric key typically offers less security but higher performance than the equivalent asymmetric key.

    b.   Asymmetric keys should be used when transmitting data over a network.

    c.   Symmetric keys should be used to encrypt asymmetric keys to provide an additional layer of security.

    d.   Symmetric keys should be used when encrypting large quantities of data.

8.   How can you combine the performance benefits of symmetric encryption with the security of asymmetric encryption within a single process?

    a.   Use a symmetric key to encrypt the data and an asymmetric key to decrypt the data.

    b.   Use symmetric encryption for encrypting/decrypting the data and asymmetric encryption for encrypting/decrypting the symmetric key.

    c.   Use asymmetric encryption for encrypting/decrypting the data and symmetric encryption for encrypting/decrypting the asymmetric key.

    d.   It is not possible to combine asymmetric and symmetric encryption within a single process. You must select the encryption technique based on whether performance or security is the greater concern.

9.   Which of the following is *not* a supported SQL Server authentication mode?

    a.   Windows authentication

    b.   Mixed authentication

    c.   SQL Server authentication

    d.   None of the above

10.   Which of the following should be used to protect a symmetric key used for encrypting column-level data in a database?

    a.   Database master key

    b.   Service master key

    c.   Certificate

    d.   Database encryption key

11.   Transparent Data Encryption (TDE) is used to do which of the following?

    a.   Encrypt column-level data in a database table

    b.   Enable encryption key management

    c.   Encrypt the database encryption key (DEK)

    d.   Encrypt the physical data and log files of a database

12.   In order to connect to a SQL Server instance, a user must have which of the following?

    a.   A SQL Server login that uses Windows integrated authentication or SQL Server authentication

    b.   A database user mapped to the SQL Server login

    c.   A Windows account

    d.   All of the above

Case Projects

Case Project 6-1: Online Payments Company

You have been employed as a database administrator by a start-up company in Menlo Park, California. The company is developing a new payments system that is attracting a lot of attention from venture capitalists. Customers will be able to process credit card transactions remotely and transmit payment information over the Internet to your data center. During the latest round of negotiations for funding, one of the potential backers announced that he or she would be conducting a due diligence assessment to ensure that you have adequate security controls. This potential backer is particularly concerned about customer privacy issues as this is a hot topic in California, and elsewhere. Your manager, the chief technology officer (CTO) of the firm, has asked you to make recommendations on several aspects of SQL Server database security. Write a one-page brief summarizing how you propose to do the following, and include information on any other measures you may take to increase security:

- Secure the client/server connections over the Internet
- Authenticate users
- Encrypt sensitive information

Hands-On Projects

Hands-On Project 6-1: Managing Users and Permissions

For this hands-on project, you will use the SQL Server named instance SQLSERVERHOA and the HandsOnOne database and tables that you created in previous chapters. The objective of this project is to practice creating a new SQL Server login, granting and testing server-level and database-level permissions, and enabling or disabling the login.

1. Create a new Windows user account called WinHoa1.

2. Create a new SQL Server login that uses Windows authentication and is mapped to the Windows user WinHoa1. Ensure that the SQL Server login is enabled and granted permission to connect to the SQLSERVERHOA instances.

3. Map the new SQL Server login to a new database user on the HandsOnOne database. Grant the database user the db_datareader role.

4. Test the new SQL Server login by logging on to your computer using the new Windows user account, WinHoa1 that you created in Step 1, and use SQL Server Management Studio to connect to the SQLSERVERHOA instance using Windows integrated authentication. In Object Explorer, confirm that you are able to browse the folders within the HandsOnOne database but not the AdventureWorks2012 database.

5. You will now test that the database user has read access to all tables in the HandsOnOne database. In SQL Server Management Studio logged on as the WinHoa1 user, open a new Query Editor window. Write a SELECT statement to query all rows in the Customer and Address tables. Document this step by taking a screen shot of the Query Editor window after successfully executing the query.

6. You will now test that the database user does not have INSERT permission to add records to the tables in the HandsOnOne database. Write a SELECT statement to INSERT a new record in the Address table. Document this step by taking a screen shot of the Query Editor window after attempting to execute the query.

7. You will now test that the database user does not have permission to delete records from the tables in the HandsOnOne database. Write a DELETE statement to delete a record from the Customer table. Document this step by taking a screen shot of the Query Editor window after attempting to execute the query.

8. Close SQL Server Management Studio and log off of your computer. Log back on using your usual administrator account and disable the WinHoa1 SQL Server login and the associated WinHoa1 Windows account.

Hands-On Project 6-2: Encrypting and Decrypting Data

For this hands-on project, you will use the SQL Server named instance SQLSERVERHOA and the HandsOnOne database and tables that you created in previous chapters. The objective of this activity is to practice generating keys and encrypting/decrypting data. Document each step by taking a screen shot of the Query Editor window after successfully executing each SQL query.

1. In SQL Server Management Studio, open a new Query Editor window, which you will use for completing all steps in this activity.

2. Create a SQL query to generate a new database master key and certificate for the HandsOnOne database.

3. Construct a SQL query to generate a new symmetric key for encrypting data. The symmetric key should use the AES algorithm with a 256-bit key size, and it should be protected by the certificate that you created in Step 2.

4. Construct a SQL query to alter the Customer table and add a new column named CustomerNameEncrypted with data type varbinary(128). This column will be used to store the encrypted values of the CustomerName column.

5. Using the symmetric key that you created in Step 2, write a SQL UPDATE query that encrypts the values in the CustomerName column and adds the encrypted values to the CustomerNameEncrypted column.

6. Construct a SQL SELECT query to view the encrypted values of the CustomerNameEncrypted column in the Customer table.

7. Construct a SELECT SQL query that uses the symmetric key to decrypt the values in the CustomerNameEncrypted column. Note that you will need to convert the hexidecimal values into a character string in order to read the decrypted values.

8. Close SQL Server Management Studio.

chapter 7

Performance Monitoring and Optimization

After reading this chapter and completing the exercises, you will be able to:

- Describe the different design factors that affect database performance

- Manage database performance by using tools that help detect, analyze, and resolve performance issues

- Recognize index fragmentation and discuss the criteria that should be incorporated in the design of an index and statistics maintenance plan

The goal of performance optimization is to lower the overall duration of queries and to efficiently use the available system resources, including the processor, the physical disk, and memory. This chapter focuses on performance issues that arise from the design of the database schema and queries rather than hardware selection. Hardware is an important element of a well-functioning database management system, and it should be sized appropriately from the outset—for example, by ensuring that the system has sufficient RAM to fit all indexes into memory. On the other hand, queries and database schemas tend to evolve as business needs change; poor design may result in a client application that becomes unstable or unusable as the volume of data or usage increases. At that point, upgrading the hardware may temporarily reduce the symptoms, but it is unlikely to provide a long-term solution to the underlying problem.

The first section of the chapter discusses important design principles relating to schema, query, and index design; following these principles will help you to create a high-performing database system that will scale to meet future business needs. There is no substitute for investing time in the planning and design phase; this is particularly important for the database schema, which includes tables, their relationships, and constraints. Well-formed queries are the second element of good design because the SQL programming language has the flexibility to achieve an end result in numerous ways—each of which has its own performance characteristics. Lastly, construction of indexes and **indexed views** (database objects that physically store a copy of the data and perform as a virtual table) are crucial to query performance because they reduce the amount of overhead required to locate a particular record in a database. However, indexes must be maintained and updated whenever data in the underlying table changes, which can lead to a trade-off between write versus read performance. For this reason, indexes should be implemented based on actual needs.

Troubleshooting database performance issues can be challenging. The second section of this chapter introduces the core Windows utilities and SQL Server management tools you can use to monitor the performance of a SQL Server instance, detect and analyze problems, and optimize queries. A production SQL Server instance needs to be monitored frequently because the performance characteristics will change over time as the databases grow in size, database objects change, and new queries are developed and executed. You will learn to spot potential performance issues by analyzing the physical resources and correlating any abnormalities with events on the SQL Server database engine. Having identified the underlying cause, you will learn how to use **query tuning**, which is an optimization process to lower the duration of a query and overall costs by improving the design of the SQL code (a process known as **refactoring**), or by adding indexes.

Over time, changes to data in a database will gradually degrade performance; records may be stored out of order, which reduces the efficiency of indexes and causes the statistics used by the database management system to create an optimal query execution plan (e.g., a count of the number of records in a particular table) to become outdated. The final section of this chapter explains how to recognize index fragmentation and understand the criteria that should be incorporated into design of a maintenance plan to ensure optimal indexes and accurate database statistics.

High-Performance Design

Design of the database schema and queries are major factors that influence the speed and efficiency with which information is retrieved or modified in a database management system. Many databases grow in a haphazard manner as tables are added incrementally without much attention paid to the overall design. This can lead to unanticipated performance problems. In addition, making changes once a database is in production is likely to impact many dependent processes, resulting in significant expense. Poorly designed queries do not make efficient use of the resources available. As you'll learn in the final section, indexes can significantly improve performance in a number of situations.

Schema Design

Database design is a multistage process that involves creating a logical model of different real-world entities and the relationships that exist between them. A physical model—in the form of a set of relations—is then derived from the logical model. The physical model is often subjected to **normalization**, a process that systematically splits relations that contain duplicate data in order to eliminate data redundancy and ensure data integrity. The physical model is used as a blueprint to implement the tables, primary keys, foreign key relationships, and other constraints in the database. To maximize database performance, keep in mind the following important considerations when implementing the physical design:

- Normalization improves the integrity of the database and reduces storage needs, but it also has the effect of splitting data across multiple tables. When querying this data, these tables must be joined back together, causing a degradation in performance. For optimal performance on heavily queried data sets, it may be appropriate to normalize data for storage and integrity but use denormalized (flattened) views of the data for querying (i.e., reversing the normalization process to improve performance). This can be achieved by creating an indexed view of the relevant data set that is persisted in the database.

- All relationships (e.g., foreign keys) and constraints (e.g., unique values) should be explicitly defined in the database. Constraints and relationships provide the query optimizer with valuable information about the expected results of a query.

- Data types must be carefully selected as discussed in Chapter 4. In general, the data type that requires the least allocation of storage space while preserving the accuracy of the value should be chosen for each attribute. You should also be aware of how the data will be queried when selecting data types for implementing tables. Avoid choosing a data type that will cause a data type mismatch in a comparison operator or one that will require an implicit or explicit data type conversion that adds processing overhead. For example, comparing a set of dates stored as a date in one column against a set of dates stored as an INT in another column leads to this type of problem.

Query Design

Query design has a significant impact on database performance. The following simple and intuitive query design guidelines can help you greatly reduce demands on the physical resources with a corresponding improvement in performance:

- Avoid operators, such as LIKE, that add significant overhead to the query. Useful in certain circumstances, the LIKE operator will result in a full table scan that causes the database to evaluate every row in a table to produce a result set.

- In the SELECT statement, specify only data that is actually needed in the result set. Avoid using * as a substitute for column names.

- Sorting is a memory-intensive operation and should only be performed if absolutely necessary. Often, it may be beneficial to return an unsorted result set and let the client application perform the sort operation, thereby moving the system overhead away from the SQL server.

- Use fully qualified names when referring to database objects in a query (i.e., the schema name followed by the object name). This saves the overhead of the database engine having to resolve the logical name each time the query is run.

- Include all columns that are part of a foreign key in a JOIN clause.

- Avoid placing implicit or explicit functions in the WHERE clause; for example, subqueries will significantly degrade performance.

Index Design

Indexes improve query performance by providing the database engine with a quick way of locating a particular record based on the value of a column or columns. This prevents the database engine from having to scan every record in the database, which is extremely inefficient. Although an index can significantly improve the performance of a read operation, indexes must be maintained and updated during a write operation, which adds processing overhead to these transactions. Therefore, indexes should be selectively added or removed based on usage and their impact on query performance. An index is always created for the primary key on a table, and one should also be created for each foreign key because these are both used as join criteria. As a general rule of thumb, indexes should also be created on columns in the WHERE, ORDER BY, GROUP BY, and DISTINCT clauses. Indexes perform most efficiently when they are based on a small number of columns. For **composite indexes**, which are indexes on multiple columns, the most selective column should be placed first because it reduces the amount of data that must be read from the disk.

Covering indexes or indexed views can be created for the most frequently run and performance-sensitive queries. A **covering index** is a database object that physically stores all columns that are needed to query a single table; unlike a normal index, a covering index is able to return the required data directly to the query, thus eliminating the additional step of retrieving data from the underlying tables. An indexed view is similar to a covering index, but it can be used to join and store data across several tables. Both techniques have the benefit of moving data retrieval operations—and the potential for contention and bottlenecks—away from the primary table. Covering indexes and indexed views should be used sparingly because they must be updated whenever any of the data in the underlying tables changes.

Diagnosing Performance Problems and Optimizing Queries

In this section, you will learn about the core Windows utilities and SQL Server management tools that can be used to monitor system resources and database activity to detect and analyze performance issues. A database management system must be able to support access by multiple users at the same time, and you must understand how resource access controls used by the database engine to maintain data consistency may impact a database query. You will also learn how to analyze a query execution plan and use the Database Engine Tuning Advisor to improve the performance of queries by refactoring the SQL code and adding indexes.

Note that several of the activities in this section use Windows utilities in addition to SQL Server management tools. These utilities may differ slightly depending on the Windows operating system that you are using to host your SQL Server instance. The steps and figures reflect the use of Microsoft Windows Server 2008 R2.

Monitoring Performance of System Resources

Requests to use a particular system resource such as the physical disk, memory, or processor are serviced sequentially by the Windows operating system. If a resource is busy, then the request will be added to a queue and serviced once the backlog of requests ahead of it is cleared. There are two types of system performance metrics that are useful for troubleshooting SQL Server performance issues. The first are basic measures of resource utilization (e.g., processor utilization, available memory, and average disk throughput). These metrics (for example, sustained activity or spikes in activity relative to the baseline performance) help you understand how busy a resource is and whether the level of activity is abnormal. The second type of metric enables further diagnosis of a problem by analyzing the number of backlogged requests that are waiting for the resource to become available. The underlying processes being generated by SQL Server should be investigated if a physical resource is unusually busy and there are a number of backlogged requests.

Windows Task Manager, introduced in Chapter 2, is a monitoring tool that can assist in basic troubleshooting. For more detailed analysis, another Windows utility, Windows Performance

Monitor, can be used to monitor activity of the physical resources that are managed by the operating system. Windows Performance Monitor uses metrics called **performance counters** to collect time series data on particular performance characteristics of the operating system. **Data collector sets** are collections of performance counters that are configured and scheduled to record time series data on a particular group of performance counters. The recorded data can then be analyzed further and correlated with the activity that was occurring on the SQL server during that time period. Windows Performance Monitor has a wide range of performance counters to choose from. For the purposes of troubleshooting SQL Server performance issues, the performance counters that capture resource utilization and bottlenecks for CPU, disk I/O, and memory are most relevant. The following performance counters represent a good starting point:

- *Processor Information: % Processor Time*—Measures how busy the processor is (i.e., the level of CPU utilization); high values are not always a sign of an abnormality. For example, it is often normal for a new process to raise CPU utilization for a short time. Sustained values over 70 percent during normal activity should be investigated further by analyzing the Processor Queue Length counter.

- *System: Processor Queue Length*—Displays a count of the number of processes that are waiting for the processor to finish processing the active request; a sustained or frequent queue length greater than two backlogged processes is indicative of a CPU bottleneck, particularly when correlated with high CPU utilization.

- *Memory: Available Bytes*—Measures the amount of physical memory that is available for allocation; low levels of available memory (10 percent or less as a percentage of total memory) may result in a memory bottleneck and degraded performance.

- *Memory: Pages/sec*—Measures the activity transferring data between the physical disk and memory; if data that is required by the SQL Server process is not available in memory, or if there is insufficient memory to retain data in memory, pages will be requested from or written to the physical disk. A high rate of paging memory to disk (or vice versa) is indicative of insufficient memory and may cause bottlenecks.

- *Logical Disk: Avg. Disk sec/Read*—Measures disk throughput; a high number indicates that the disk is operating efficiently in servicing requests to read data.

- *Logical Disk: Avg. Disk sec/Write*—Measures disk throughput for processes writing data to the disk; this counter is the counterpart to Avg. Disk sec/Read. Significant variations from the average in conjunction with a high disk queue length may indicate a disk I/O bottleneck.

- *Logical Disk: Avg. Disk Queue Length*—Provides a count of the number of requests waiting to read or write data from the physical disk.

Activity 7-1: Configuring a Data Collector Set

Time Required: 45 minutes
Objective: Configure the settings for capturing a data collector set using the Windows Performance Monitor utility.

Description: In this activity, you will configure a data collector set using the Windows Performance Monitor utility, which will enable you to capture activity in a log that includes performance counters for the main physical resources used by SQL Server.

1. If necessary, start your computer and log on using an Administrator account.

2. Click the **Start** button, point to **All Programs**, click **Microsoft SQL Server 2012**, click the **Performance Tools** folder, and then click **SQL Server Profiler** to launch SQL Server Profiler. In SQL Server Profiler, click **Tools** on the menu bar, and then click **Performance Monitor** to launch the Windows Performance Monitor utility. See Figure 7-1.

Figure 7-1 Launch Windows Performance Monitor from SQL Server Profiler

 You can also start the Windows Performance Monitor by typing
`perfmon.exe` from a command prompt.

3. In the left pane of Windows Performance Monitor, expand the **Data Collector Sets** folder, and then click the **User Defined** folder. On the menu bar, click **Action**, point to **New**, and then click **Data Collector Set**. In the Create new Data Collector Set Wizard, type **SQLSERVERUA** in the Name text box. Click the **Create Manually (Advanced)** option button. See Figure 7-2.

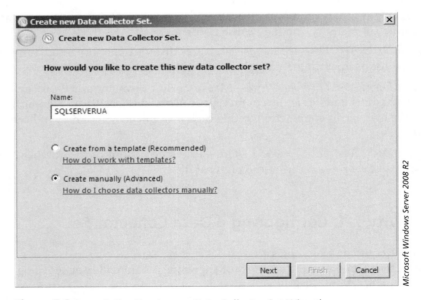

Figure 7-2 Launch the Create new Data Collector Set Wizard

4. Click the **Next** button. In the Create new Data Collector Set Wizard, click the **Performance counter** check box. Click the **Next** button. See Figure 7-3.

5. In the Create new Data Collector Set Wizard, click the **Add** button. In the upper-left pane of the window, click the **+** icon to the right of Processor, scroll down the list of counters, and then click **% Processor Time**. See Figure 7-4. Click the **Add** button to launch the Add Counters window.

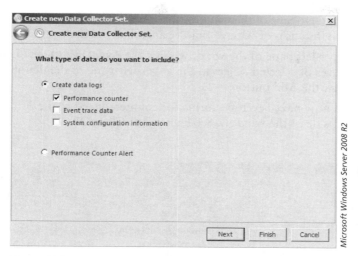

Figure 7-3 Data Collector Set Wizard – specify data types to include

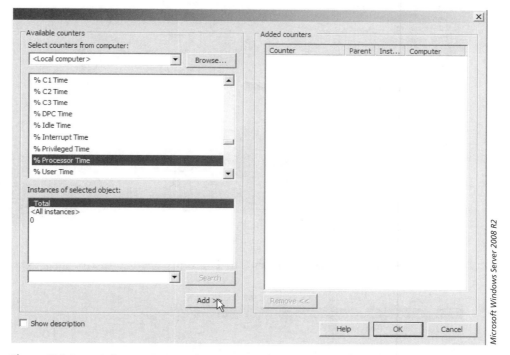

Figure 7-4 Data Collector Set Wizard – add counters

6. You will now repeat Step 5 for the six other counters discussed earlier in this section:
   - In the upper-left pane of the window, click the + icon to the right of System, scroll down, and then click **Processor Queue Length**. Click the **Add** button.
   - In the upper-left pane of the window, click the + icon to the right of Memory, scroll down, and then click **Available Bytes**. Click the **Add** button.
   - In the upper-left pane of the window, click the **Pages/sec** counter in the Memory section. Click the **Add** button.
   - In the upper-left pane of the window, click the + icon to the right of LogicalDisk, scroll down, and then click **Avg. Disk sec/Read**. In the Instances of selected object pane, click the **C:** drive. Click the **Add** button.

- In the upper-left pane of the window, click **Avg. Disk sec/Write** in the LogicalDisk section. In the Instances of selected object pane, click the **C:** drive. Click the **Add** button.

- In the upper-left pane of the window, click the **Avg. Disk Queue Length** counter. In the Instances of selected object in the lower-left pane of the dialog box, click the **C:** drive. Click the **Add** button.

7. You should now have seven performance counters listed in the Added counters pane on the right side of the window. See Figure 7-5. Click **OK**.

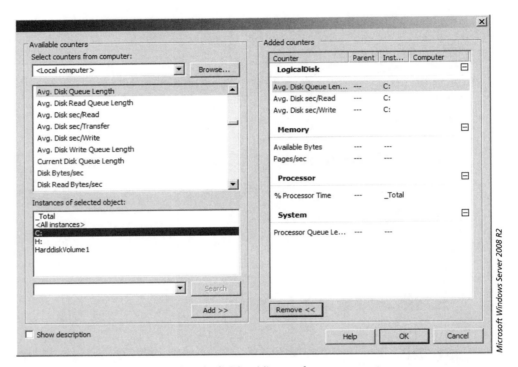

Figure 7-5 Data Collector Set Wizard – finish adding performance counters

8. Change the Sample interval to **2 seconds**. See Figure 7-6. Click **Next**.

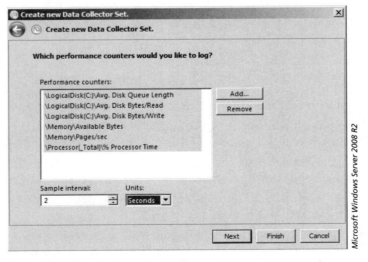

Figure 7-6 Data Collector Set Wizard – set the sample interval

9. In the next window, make a note of the Root directory. The default Root directory should be listed as %systemdrive%\PerfLogs\Admin\SQLSERVERUA. See Figure 7-7. Click the **Next** button.

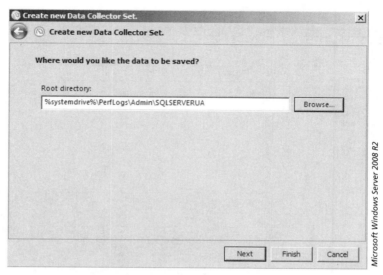

Figure 7-7 Data Collector Set Wizard – specify a location to save the data

10. In the next window, keep the default settings, and click the **Finish** button to create the new data collector set. See Figure 7-8. Do not start the data collector set at this point.

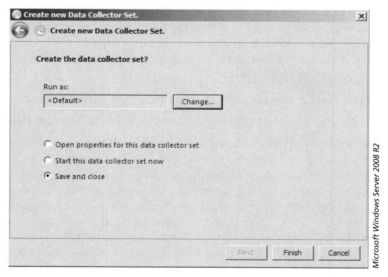

Figure 7-8 Create the new Data Collector Set

11. In Performance Monitor, you should now see the new SQLSERVURA data collector set appear below the User Defined folder in the left navigation pane. The data collector set will save the data collected on the chosen performance counters to a log file. Keep the Performance Monitor and SQL Query Profiler applications open for the subsequent activities in this chapter.

You can also add counters to a real-time display by clicking Performance Monitor below Monitoring Tools in the left navigation pane of the Performance Monitor window, and then clicking the green **+** icon to launch the same Add Counters dialog box that you used in Step 5. See Figure 7-9.

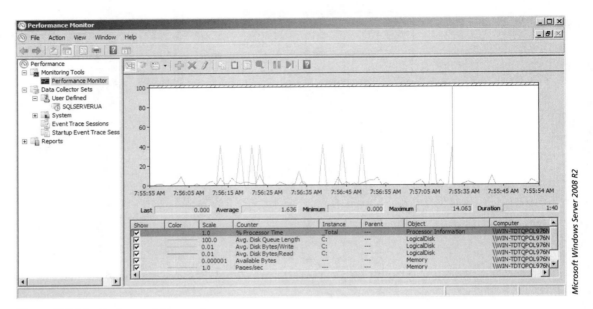

Figure 7-9 Monitoring real-time performance

Monitoring SQL Server Activity

- The **SQL Server Profiler** management tool is a graphical interface that enables a database administrator to capture events for the purposes of optimizing query performance, identifying and troubleshooting problematic queries, and monitoring workload. An **event** is any activity executed by the SQL Server database engine, such as the following:
- Execution of DML, DDL, or DCL statements
- Errors being written to the log file of the SQL Server instance
- Login connections and disconnections to the SQL Server instance

The result set of database events captured by SQL Server Profiler is known as a **trace**. A trace can be configured to capture all events for a given time period or to only record certain events by using filters—for example, capturing events that are related to a specific database or session. To identify problematic queries, a trace can be filtered on *duration* and *count* to highlight long-running and frequently run queries, respectively. Trace results are displayed as a two-dimensional matrix in SQL Server Profiler and can also be saved as a database trace file. A **database trace file** enables the events to be replayed at a later point in time for analysis. SQL Server Profiler is able to correlate time series events saved in a trace file with a data collection set from Performance Monitor to identify the underlying event(s) that resulted in the abnormal resource activity.

Activity 7-2: Configuring a Trace Using SQL Server Profiler

Time Required: 45 minutes

Objective: Configure a trace using SQL Server Profiler to capture SQL Server events.

Description: In this activity, you will configure a trace using SQL Server Profiler. The trace will capture SQL Server events and save them to a database trace file.

1. Return to the SQL Server Profiler window. Click **File** on the menu bar, and then click **New Trace**. In the Connect to Server dialog box, select **Database Engine** as the server type, type **LOCALHOST\SQLSERVERUA** in the Server name text box, and then select **Windows Authentication** from the Authentication list box. Click **Connect**.

2. On the General tab of the Trace Properties window, type **SQLSERVERUA -1** in the Trace name text box. Click **Standard (default)** from the Use the template drop-down list box. Click the **Save to File** check box to launch the Save As dialog box.

3. In the Save As dialog box, click **Local Disk (C:)** in the left navigation display.

 Depending on your local computer settings, you may need to drill down to locate the C: drive.

4. Click the **New Folder** button on the toolbar to add a folder called New Folder. Delete the text **New Folder** in the folder text box and type **Trace** to rename the folder. Click anywhere on the screen outside the folder text box to save the change to the folder name. In either the main folder pane or the left navigation pane, double-click the folder that you just renamed **Trace**. Keep the default filename as SQLSERVERUA -1 and the file type as SQL Server Profiler trace files (*.trc). Click the **Save** button to return to the Trace Properties window. See Figure 7-10.

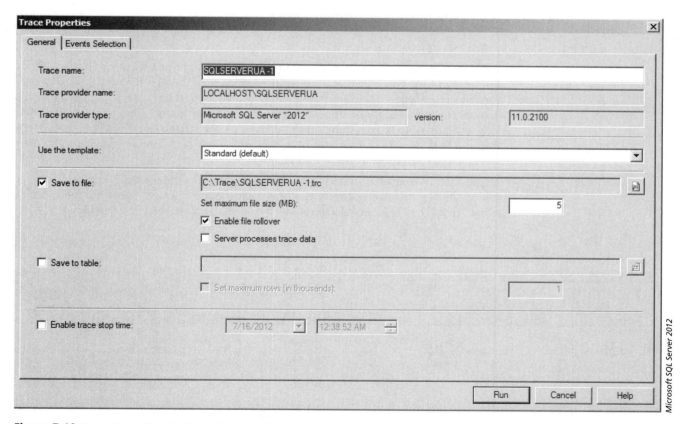

Figure 7-10 Trace Properties window – General tab

5. In the Trace Properties window, click the **Events Selection** tab. See Figure 7-11. This tab specifies which SQL Server events will be captured by the trace. The event types and columns can be changed using the Show all events and Show all columns check boxes.

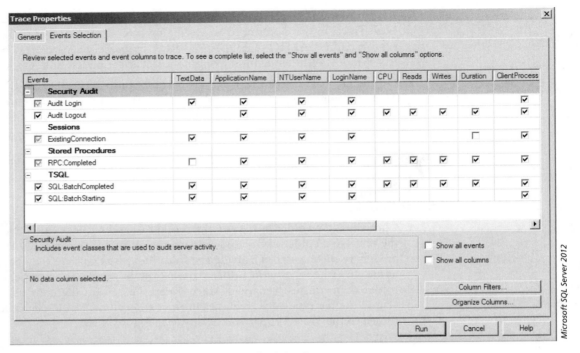

Figure 7-11 Trace Properties window – Events Selection tab

6. Click the **Column Filters** button to launch the Column Filters window. In the Column Filters window, you can place a filter on any of the columns that have been chosen for your trace; you can also opt to exclude events from the trace if the filter condition is met. For the purpose of this activity, you will not use any filters because there will be very little activity occurring on the database other than the events you generate by running SQL queries. Close the Column Filters window by clicking the **Cancel** button to return to the Trace Properties window.

7. In the Trace Properties window, click **Run** to begin running the trace and return to the main SQL Server Profiler window. Notice that the trace is now capturing the specified events from the SQL Server instance as a two-dimensional matrix. See Figure 7-12.

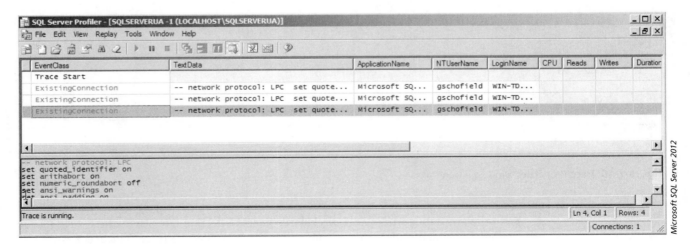

Figure 7-12 Viewing captured events in the trace window of SQL Server Profiler

Each row represents an event on the SQL Server instance. You can view more details of an event in the lower pane by clicking a row. The trace is simultaneously writing the output to the database trace file that you specified in Step 2.

8. In the SQL Server Profiler window, click the **stop selected trace** icon (the red square) on the toolbar, and then erase the trace data by clicking the white **clear trace window** icon. See Figure 7-13.

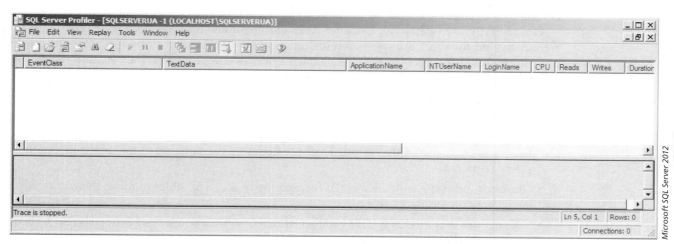

Figure 7-13 Trace cleared in the SQL Server Profiler window

9. Keep the SQL Server Profiler window open as you will need this for Activity 7-5.

Concurrency Control, Blocking Locks, and Deadlocks

Concurrency control is an important feature of a multiuser relational database management system that protects the integrity of data. At any given time, there may be multiple users or client applications querying or modifying data; therefore, controls are necessary to ensure data consistency. Allowing uncontrolled access to the database may result in a number of problems, including the following:

- **Dirty read** problems can occur when a transaction that is updating the database fails and the updated values are rolled back to their original state. If a concurrent process is reading the data, it may retrieve the values that were not ultimately committed to the database.

- **Lost update** problems can occur if two processes attempt to update the same record concurrently and the updates of one process are overwritten by the second process.

- **Incorrect summary** problems can occur if a transaction attempts to read and summarize column values while the data is in an inconsistent state due to a concurrent update process. The summary may not tie back to either the initial or end state of the values in the table due to the timing of the read.

To prevent these issues, **lock-based concurrency control** is used by the SQL Server database engine as a mechanism to ensure that transactions that access the same logical database resources are executed in a nonconflicting manner. When a process executes a transaction against a database, a lock is created against the logical database object(s) that will be used by the transaction. SQL Server 2012 supports different **lock modes**, which govern when another process is eligible to gain concurrent access to a particular resource with a lock. The strictest lock mode is an exclusive lock, which prevents any other process from accessing the resource until the lock is released. Locks can be taken out against a row, a table, or a page. If another process attempts to access a resource with a lock and the database engine determines that the transaction is ineligible for concurrent access, the transaction will be placed in a queue until the active transaction releases the lock on the object. In this situation, known as a **blocking lock,** a process must wait for locks to be released by other active processes before it can proceed. Because a process that is waiting to execute takes out locks on resources as they become available, a deadlock situation can arise. A **deadlock** is a situation in which two transactions each have a lock on a resource that the other transaction needs in order to complete. After a period of time has elapsed, SQL Server deals with this situation by picking one of the deadlocked transactions as the **deadlock victim,** and it cancels that transaction. The transaction of the deadlock victim is not automatically resubmitted for processing by the database engine, so the client application or user must resubmit, if necessary.

On a heavily used database, blocking locks are unavoidable. Typically they happen only infrequently and for short durations. Recurring and long duration blocking locks and deadlocks must be analyzed and avoided through changes to the design of queries, indexes, and tables. The following guidelines can help you avoid blocking locks and deadlocks:

- Transactions should be kept as short as possible. Queries that take out and then release multiple locks as a single transaction should be avoided.
- Ensure that multiple-table updates are always performed in the same order. Deadlocks are liable to occur when different processes are updating the same set of tables but in the opposite sequence.
- Clustered indexes should be created for frequently accessed tables to move the workload away from the primary table.
- SQL queries that modify a large number of rows within a single transaction should be broken into smaller transactions.

SQL Server has two useful procedures that can be used to identify locking. The *sp_who2* procedure lists all sessions connected to the SQL Server instance and identifies the process(es) causing any blocking locks in real time. The *sp_lock* procedure can be used to display all locks that are currently taken out on the SQL Server instance.

Activity 7-3: Detecting Locks

Time Required: 45 minutes
Objective: Detect locks from the Query Editor in SQL Server Management Studio.

Description: In this activity, you will execute the system stored procedures *sp_who2* and *sp_lock* in a Query Editor window within SQL Server Management Studio to detect a blocking lock or deadlocked process.

1. Click the **Start** button, point to **All Programs,** click **Microsoft SQL Server 2012,** and then click **SQL Server Management Studio.** In the Connect to Server dialog box, select **Database Engine** as the server type, type **LOCALHOST\SQLSERVERUA** in the Server name text box, and then select **Windows Authentication** from the Authentication list box. Click **Connect.**

2. In this step, you will update a table with an exclusive lock, but you'll leave the transaction uncommitted in the database—for testing purposes only. Note that you would not normally execute a query that leaves an uncommitted transaction in the database indefinitely. In SQL Server Management Studio, click the **New Query** button on the toolbar, and then type the following in the Query Editor window:

```
SET IMPLICIT_TRANSACTIONS ON

BEGIN TRANSACTION

UPDATE AdventureWorks2012.HumanResources.Employee WITH (XLOCK, TABLOCK)

SET NationalIDNumber = 222222223

WHERE BusinessEntityID = 1;
```

3. Click the **Execute** button on the toolbar or press the **F5** key to run the query. You should see the following message in the Messages pane at the bottom of the Query Editor window: (1 Row(s) affected). See Figure 7-14.

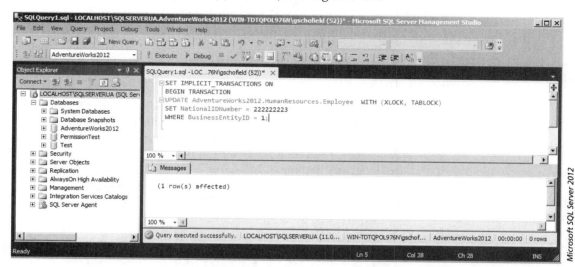

Figure 7-14 Update a row that takes an exclusive lock on a table without committing the transaction

In the query, IMPLICIT_TRANSACTIONS is set to ON in order to prevent the database engine from auto-committing the update. The table hints XLOCK and TABLOCK in the WITH clause instruct the database that the process requires an exclusive lock on the table. Because a COMMIT TRANSACTION statement was not issued at the end of the query, this has the effect of leaving an uncommitted update in the table and an exclusive lock in place.

4. You will now create a SQL query that attempts to read from the same table that you used in Step 3. In SQL Server Management Studio, click the **New Query** button on the toolbar to open another Query Editor window, and then type the following command in the Query Editor window:

```
SELECT * FROM AdventureWorks2012.HumanResources.Employee;
```

5. Click the **Execute** button on the toolbar or press the **F5** key to run the query. See Figure 7-15. Note that this transaction does not complete and the status bar at the

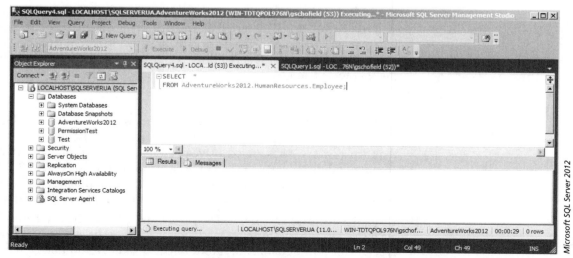

Figure 7-15 The query continues to execute while it waits for the lock on the table to be released

bottom of the window shows the transaction status as Executing query. The query will continue to execute while it waits for the lock on the table that you caused during Step 3 to be released.

6. Having caused a blocking lock, you will now troubleshoot the problem using the *sp_who2* procedure. In SQL Server Management Studio, click the **New Query** button on the toolbar to open a third Query Editor window, and then type the following command in the Query Editor window:

```
EXECUTE sp_who2;
```

7. Click the **Execute** button on the toolbar or press the **F5** key to run the query. Scroll through the result set until you see a value in the column named BlkBy. Make a note of the process ID in the SPID column. This process, the SELECT query that you executed in Step 5, is being blocked by the uncommitted update process that you executed in Step 3. In Figure 7-16, notice that process ID (SPID) 52 has created one or more blocking locks that are causing process ID 53 to be suspended pending release of the lock(s) by process ID 52.

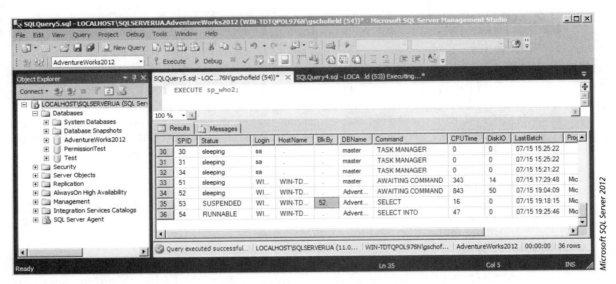

Figure 7-16 Execute the sp_who2 procedure to locate the blocking process

8. You have now identified the process ID of the problematic query that is causing the blocking lock. However, you do not know which lock(s) are causing the process to be blocked. In the current Query Editor window, delete the previous command, and type the following command:

```
EXECUTE sp_lock;
```

9. Click the **Execute** button on the toolbar or press the **F5** key to run the query. This procedure lists all locks on logical resources on the database instance. Figure 7-17 shows that process ID 52 has an exclusive table lock (denoted by the TAB entry in the type column and the X entry in the mode column) on the object ID 1237579447 in database ID 5. You should make a note of the object and database IDs of the exclusive table lock in your query results as the IDs may differ from the example.

10. Using the database and object IDs, you can now locate the database and table with the exclusive lock. In the current Query Editor window, delete the previous command, and type the following command, substituting the values for object_id and database_id that you noted in Step 9:

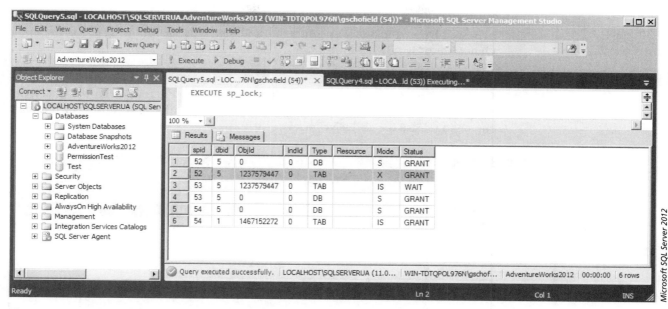

Figure 7-17 Execute the sp_lock procedure to identify current locks

```
SELECT name, type_desc FROM sys.objects

WHERE object_id = 1237579447;

SELECT name FROM sys.databases

WHERE database_id = 5;
```

11. Click the **Execute** button on the toolbar or press the **F5** key to run the query. The
    returned result sets should list the AdventureWorks2012 database and the Employees
    USER_TABLE as the table with the exclusive lock. See Figure 7-18.

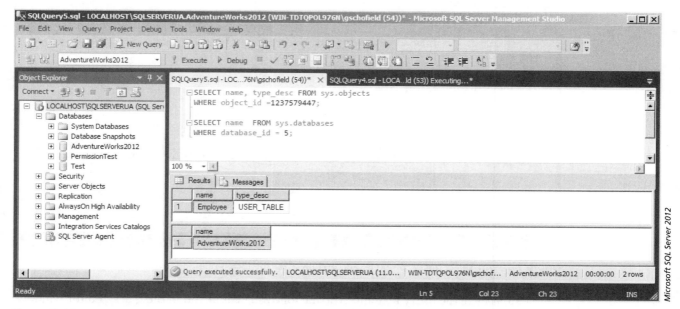

Figure 7-18 Look up the database and the table name with the exclusive table lock

12. Click the tab of the Query Editor window that you used to create the exclusive lock in Step 2. Delete the previous command, and then type the following command in the Query Editor window:

```
COMMIT TRANSACTION;
```

13. Click the **Execute** button on the toolbar or press the **F5** key to run the query. See Figure 7-19. Committing the transaction updates the table and causes the database engine to release the exclusive lock.

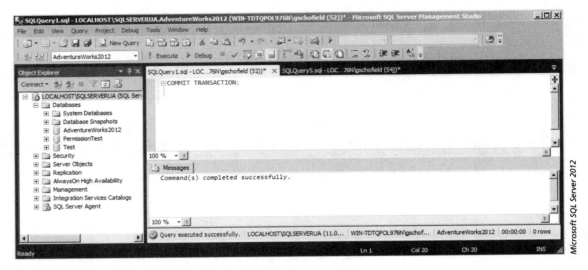

Figure 7-19 Commit the original update transaction

14. Click the tab of the Query Editor window that you used to create the SELECT query in Step 4. You should now see that this query has successfully completed and that it includes the updated NationalIDNumber in the result set. See Figure 7-20.

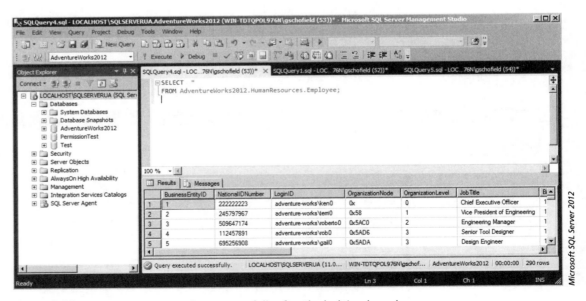

Figure 7-20 The select query completes successfully after the lock is released

15. Delete the query text and type the following command in the Query Editor window:

```
EXECUTE sp_who2;
```

16. Click the **Execute** button on the toolbar or press the **F5** key to run the query. Scan the BlkBy column and verify that there are no longer any blocking processes. Close the open Query Editor tabs by clicking the X icon at the top of each tab. Keep SQL Server Management Studio open for the next activity.

Analyzing Execution Plans

The SQL Server database engine has a query optimizer that builds a physical execution plan from a SQL query. The query optimizer uses a **cost-based algorithm** to select the best execution plan—by estimating the costs (e.g., number of I/O operations) for each alternative. To estimate costs, the algorithm uses **statistics** about the distribution of values for a particular table or index (e.g., the number of rows or the size of the key).

Query Editor in SQL Server Management Studio allows you to display a visual representation of the physical execution steps—and their relative cost—for a query. The **Display Estimated Execution Plan** option displays the execution steps based on the costs that the optimizer has estimated using the statistics. The **Include Actual Execution Plan** option can be set prior to running the query to display the actual execution plan steps and costs once the query has completed. Additional commands to generate execution statistics as part of the result set can be included in the SQL query. For example, the SET STATISTICS IO command can be added to show the physical and logical reads and the scan count for a query.

To read an execution plan for a single statement, you need to work through the steps beginning at the right side of the pane and moving left. If the query has multiple statements, they will be listed from top to bottom in the order that they will be executed. At the top of each statement is a summary of the cost of the statement relative to the whole execution plan. Each step has a graphical icon that represents the type of operation being performed, a description of the step, and the cost relative to the statement.

The execution plan is a powerful tool for optimizing a query as it can help you quickly locate the most costly steps in a query. The query can then be refactored or indexes added to optimize the performance using the following guidelines:

- Focus on the highest cost steps or statements.

- Look for any full table scans. A full table scan is an expensive operation as the database engine must search each row in the table to find the data required. Full table scans are usually an indicator that an index is necessary.

- Sort operations are performed in memory and should be avoided if possible.

Activity 7-4: Analyzing an Execution Plan

Time Required: 30 minutes

Objective: Analyze an execution plan from Query Editor in SQL Server Management Studio.

Description: In this activity, you will learn how to display both an actual and an estimated execution plan, and you'll analyze the plan steps from Query Editor in SQL Server Management Studio. You will see the impact of removing an index that is used by the execution plan.

1. In SQL Server Management Studio, click the **New Query** button on the toolbar, and then type the following command in the Query Editor window:

```
SELECT e.NationalIDNumber, p.FirstName, p.LastName

FROM AdventureWorks2012.HumanResources.Employee e

INNER JOIN AdventureWorks2012.Person.Person p

ON e.BusinessEntityID = p.BusinessEntityID;
```

2. On the menu bar, click **Query**, and then click **Display Estimated Execution Plan**. See Figure 7-21. This query produces a fairly simple execution plan. You should analyze the steps beginning on the right side of the execution plan. Notice that the plan has found useful indexes to locate the required data from each table. This plan is well optimized because it is able to locate the relevant records by leveraging an alternate key index in the Employee table and the primary key index on the Person table. The plan then completes an inner join on the retrieved records to return the result set. If you click an individual step, you can view more details about the selected step.

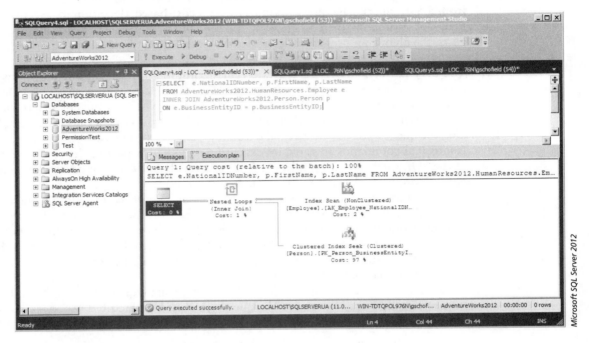

Figure 7-21 Display the estimated execution plan

3. On the menu bar, click **Query**, and then click **Include Actual Execution Plan**. Click the **Execute** button on the toolbar or press the **F5** key to run the query. Click the **Execution Plan** tab in the lower pane of the Query Editor window to view the actual execution plan that was returned in addition to the result set and messages. See Figure 7-22. Notice that the actual execution plan is almost identical to the estimated execution plan. This is a good indication that the statistics used by the query optimizer for estimating the best execution plan are accurate.

4. Now, you will remove the foreign key and alternative key index in the Employee table to see the effect that this has on the execution plan. In SQL Server Management Studio, click the **New Query** button on the toolbar to open another Query Editor window, and then type the following command in the Query Editor window:

```
USE AdventureWorks2012

GO

DROP INDEX AK_Employee_NationalIDNumber

ON HumanResources.Employee;

GO

ALTER TABLE HumanResources.Employee

DROP CONSTRAINT FK_Employee_Person_BusinessEntityID;

GO
```

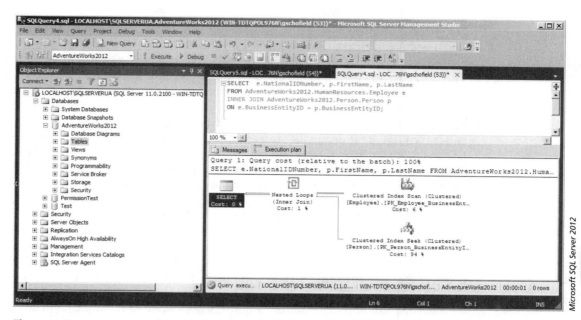

Figure 7-22 Include the actual execution plan with the query results

5. Click the **Execute** button on the toolbar or press the **F5** key to run the query. See Figure 7-23.

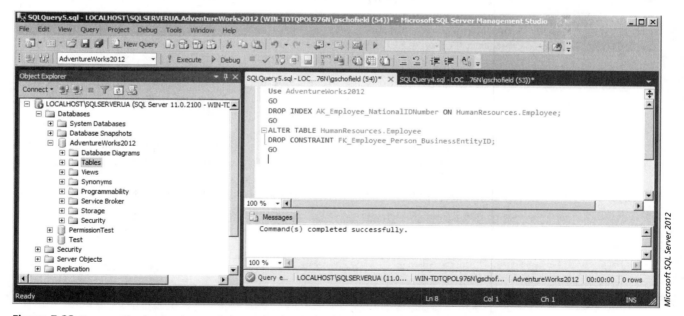

Figure 7-23 Remove the foreign key and alternative key index from the Employees table

6. Return to the previous Query Editor window, click **Query** on the menu bar, and then click **Display Estimated Execution Plan**. Note that the steps have subtly changed. Instead of using the alternative index, the query now uses the primary key index on the Employees table that causes a slight increase in cost to locate the employee records. Leave this query open as you will use it in the next activity.

Query Tuning

The objective of query tuning is to lower the duration of a query and overall costs, which are defined by the number of read and write operations, memory consumption, and CPU utilization. The **Database Engine Tuning Advisor** is a query-tuning wizard that uses the same optimization information as the query optimizer to provide a set of recommendations that may include the use of additional indexes, indexed views, and partitions to improve query performance. The Database Engine Tuning Advisor quantifies the expected performance gain for each recommendation, and it includes the functionality to automatically add the changes to the database or to generate DDL SQL scripts for manual implementation. To generate the recommendations, the Database Engine Tuning Advisor requires a workload to analyze. A **workload** may either be a stand-alone query or a previously saved trace file that was generated using SQL Server Profiler. The Database Engine Tuning Advisor also allows you to adjust the row counts for each table—which can be useful for scenario analysis if you expect the table size to grow significantly over time.

Tuning a query is typically an iterative process. It is advisable to implement the recommendations that constitute the most significant performance gains first and then rerun the analysis again to look for further improvements. The Database Engine Tuning Advisor assesses the workload in isolation from other processes that update the underlying tables and that bear the overhead of maintaining the new indexes. Consequently, you must carefully consider the full impact of adding a new index relative to the increased maintenance overhead and disk space that will be required. Any recommendations that account for performance gains of less than 5 percent should normally be discounted. The Database Engine Tuning Advisor is a useful tool as it does not require the database administrator to have detailed knowledge of the underlying query structure or database schema. For best results, however, you should use the Database Engine Tuning Advisor in conjunction with analysis of the execution plan.

Activity 7-5: Troubleshooting and Tuning Query Performance

Time Required: 60 minutes

Objective: Correlate SQL Server events with system performance counters and improve the performance of poor-performing queries.

Description: In this activity, you will correlate SQL Server events captured in a trace file with the output from a data collector set. You will then use the Database Engine Tuning Advisor to create recommendations that will improve the performance of queries.

1. Return to the Performance Monitor window that you left open at the end of Activity 7-1. In the left navigation page, right-click the **SQLSERVERUA** data collector set in the User Defined Data Collector Sets folder, and then click **Start** to begin capturing performance counters for the data collector set. See Figure 7-24.

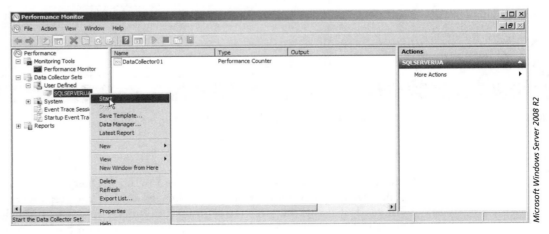

Figure 7-24 Start the SQLSERVERUA data collector set

2. Return to the SQL Server Profiler window that you left open at the end of Activity 7-2. Click the **Start Selected Trace** button with the green triangle icon on the toolbar. See Figure 7-25.

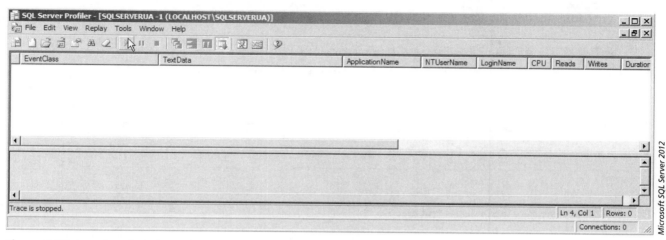

Figure 7-25 Start the selected trace in SQL Server Profiler

3. In the SQL Server Profile warning dialog box, click **No**. Check the **Save to File** check box in the Trace Properties window. In the Save As dialog box, keep the default location that you entered in Activity 7-2, and then click **Save**. In the Confirm Save As dialog box, click **Yes** to replace the original trace file, and in the Trace Properties window, click **Run** to start the Trace.

4. Return to the SQL Server Management Studio window that you left open at the end of the last activity. Select the Query Editor window with the SELECT query that you entered in Step 1 of Activity 7-4. On the menu bar, click **Query**, and then click **Include Actual Execution Plan** to turn this feature off. Click the **Execute** button on the toolbar or press the **F5** key to run the query. See Figure 7-26.

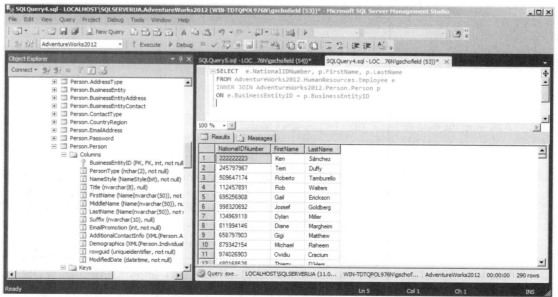

Figure 7-26 Run the SELECT query in Query Editor

5. Return to the SQL Server Profiler window, and click the red **Stop Selected Trace** button on the toolbar to stop the trace. See Figure 7-27.

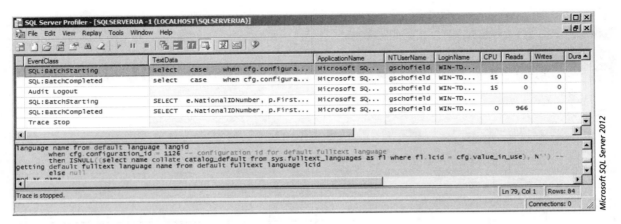

Figure 7-27 Stop the trace in SQL Server Profiler

6. Return to the Performance Monitor window. In the left navigation page, right-click the SQLSERVERUA data collector set in the User Defined Data Collector Sets folder, and then click **Stop** to stop the data collector set from capturing further activity. Make a note of the location of the output file location listed in the right pane. See Figure 7-28.

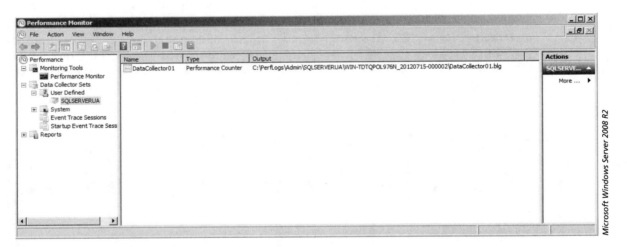

Figure 7-28 Stop the data collector set in Performance Monitor

7. Close SQL Server Profiler by clicking the X icon in the upper-right corner. Click the **Start** button, point to **All Programs**, click **Microsoft SQL Server 2012**, click the **Performance Tools** folder, and then click **SQL Server Profiler**. In the SQL Server Profiler window, click **File** on the menu bar, click **Open**, and then click **Trace File**.

8. In the Address bar at the top of the Open File window, type **C:\Trace**. Click the **SQLSERVERUA -1.trc** file in the Trace folder, and then click **Open**. In the SQL Server Profiler window, click **File**, and then click **Import Performance Data**. Using the left navigation menu or the Address bar, navigate to the Data Collector Set folder location that you noted in Step 6. Click the **DataCollector01** file (see Figure 7-29) and click **Open**.

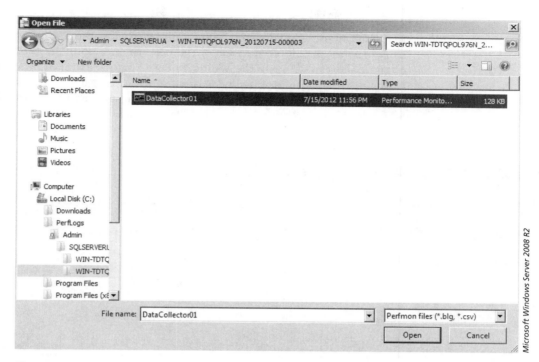

Figure 7-29 Open the data collector file

9. In the Performance Counters Limit Dialog box, click the check box to the left of your **server name** to import all counters in the data collector set. See Figure 7-30. Click **OK**.

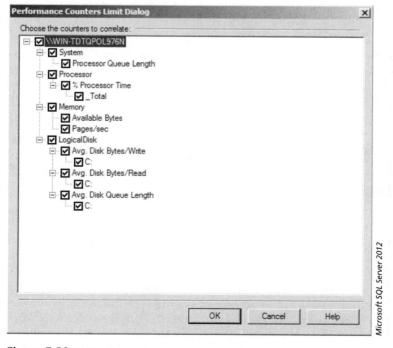

Figure 7-30 Select the performance counters to import

10. The top pane of SQL Server Profiler contains the output of the database trace file that you ran using SQL Server Profiler. Directly below the trace output is a line graph showing the variation over time of the performance counters that you captured as a data collector set using the Windows Performance Monitor. A legend is included below the graph that also includes some statistics on each performance counter. The bottom pane includes the event details from the selected row in the database trace. Scroll down, and click the **SQL: BatchStarting** row for the query that you executed in Step 4. See Figure 7-31.

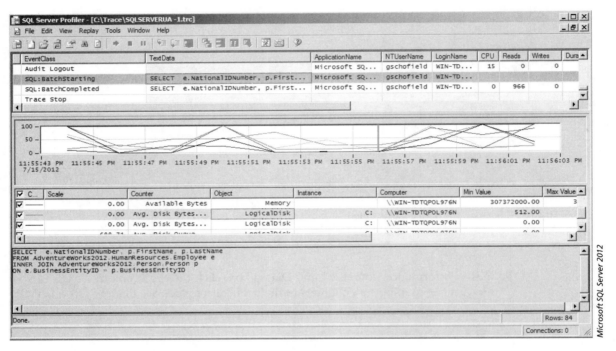

Figure 7-31 Correlate the SQL events with the performance counters using SQL Server Profiler

Notice how the red vertical line on the performance counter pane automatically moves to the time that this event occurred. This allows you to directly correlate the events that occurred on SQL Server with the performance of physical resources at that time. In this particular scenario, the SQL query had a negligible impact on system performance and would not normally require further investigation.

 When recording events using SQL Server Performance Monitor for a production system, you should narrow down the selection of events by filtering the trace for high duration or frequently occurring SQL events.

11. Return to the open instance of SQL Server Management Studio. Select the Query Editor window with the SELECT query you entered in Step 1 of Activity 7-4. On the menu bar, click **Query**, and then click **Analyze Query in Database Engine Tuning Advisor**. SQL Server Management Studio automatically passes the contents of the Query Editor window as workload to the Database Engine Tuning Advisor. You can also open the Database Engine Tuning Advisor from the Performance Tools folder in the SQL Server 2012 Programs menu, and then manually load a database trace file or SQL query as the workload. If unchecked, click the **AdventureWorks2012** check box in the Select databases and tables to tune section, and then click the **Start Analysis** button on the toolbar. See Figure 7-32.

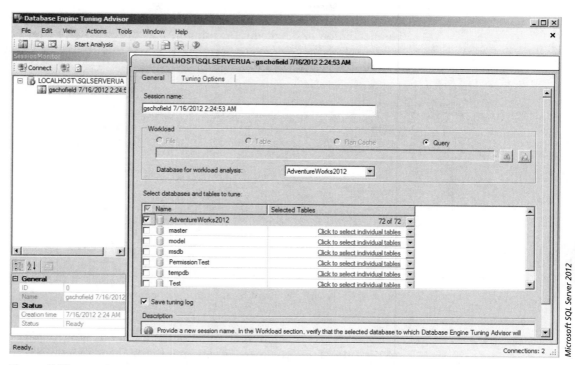

Figure 7-32 Start the workload analysis in Database Engine Tuning Advisor

12. A Progress tab opens, displaying the current progress of each step in the tuning process. Wait for the Database Engine Tuning Advisor to successfully complete the analysis. A Recommendations tab opens, listing recommended changes to the database object that will improve the performance of your query. In this case, the Database Engine Tuning Advisor has recommended that you create two new indexes on two different tables in the database. Based on the same cost-optimization algorithm used by the query optimizer, the Database Engine Tuning Advisor estimates that you will achieve a 70 percent improvement in performance by implementing the recommendations. See Figure 7-33.

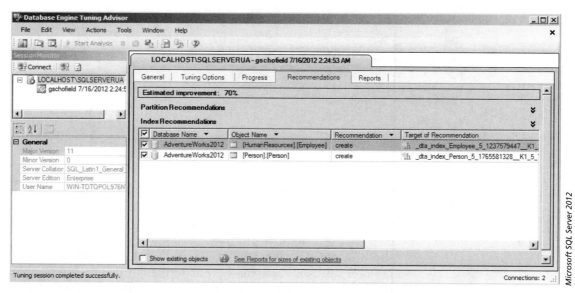

Figure 7-33 View the Database Engine Tuning Advisor recommendations

13. Scroll to the right of the recommendations, and click the **hyperlink** for the first recommendation in the definition column. This opens a SQL Script Preview dialog box that displays the SQL DDL statement that will implement the recommendation. See Figure 7-34. Click the **Close** button.

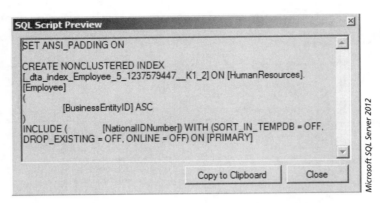

Figure 7-34 View the SQL DDL statement for the recommendation

14. You can choose which recommendations you want to apply by selecting the check box to the left of the recommendation in the Recommendations tab. The Database Engine Tuning Advisor enables you to apply recommendations directly to the database or save the SQL DDL statements as scripts that you can manually apply later. This second option may be appropriate if you want to make changes such as making the naming convention consistent with the other objects in your database. In this activity, you will automatically apply the recommendations. On the menu bar, click **Actions**, and then click **Apply Recommendations**. In the Apply Recommendations dialog box, click the **Apply Now** option button, and then click **OK**. An Applying Recommendations dialog box displays the status of the changes being applied. See Figure 7-35. Click **Close**.

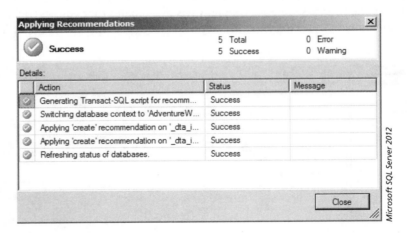

Figure 7-35 Applying Recommendations dialog box in Database Engine Tuning Advisor

15. Return to SQL Server Management Studio, and open the Databases folder by clicking the **+** icon in the left navigation pane of Object Explorer. Click the **AdventureWorks2012** database, and then click the **Refresh** button on the Object Explorer toolbar. Click the **+** icons in the left navigation pane of Object Explorer to expand the AdventureWorks2012 database folder, the Tables folder, the HumanResources.Employee table, and, finally, the Indexes folder.

16. Right-click the new index with a name beginning with **_dta_index_employee,** click **Script Index as,** click **CREATE to,** and then click **New Query Editor Window.** The SQL DDL query in the Query Editor window should be identical to the SQL DDL statement that you viewed in Step 13. See Figure 7-36.

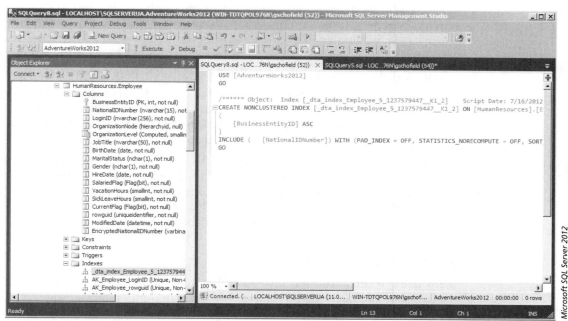

Figure 7-36 View the new index in SQL Server Management Studio

17. You have now successfully completed Activity 7-5. Close all open application windows.

Maintenance of Indexes and Statistics

Over time, changes to data in the database degrade index performance and cause the statistics used by the cost-based query optimizer to become stale. In this section, you will learn how to recognize index fragmentation, and you'll learn the criteria that should be incorporated into design of a maintenance plan to ensure optimal indexes and accurate database statistics.

Index Fragmentation

For an optimal index, records are stored on the disk **contiguously,** meaning next to each other and in sequence. As data is modified, deleted, or added to the underlying tables, the corresponding indexes must also be updated to reflect these changes. These changes can lead to **fragmentation,** a situation in which database records are stored out of order, which causes a degradation in index performance. There are two main types of fragmentation, as described in the following list:

- **Internal fragmentation** occurs due to an accumulation of free space between records stored in the index page files, the basic logical storage unit used by SQL Server. Internal fragmentation results in growth of the index, and the unequal distribution of records causes increased I/O and reduced performance. Furthermore, if a page has insufficient space to store new data in sequential order (e.g., due to inserted records), page files can become split. This is known as **logical fragmentation,** and it causes additional system overhead.

- **External fragmentation** occurs when the logical storage of data in pages and extents does not match the physical storage on disk, causing increased workload that the physical disk has to perform in order to retrieve the data.

Internal and logical fragmentation are the main problems that a database administrator must contend with. SQL Server 2012 has a dynamic management function in the master system database, *sys.dm_db_index_physical_stats*, that can be queried to return the size of the index and level of fragmentation. The function can also be supplied with parameters to return data for an individual database, table, or index. The level of logical fragmentation is returned in the *avg_fragmentation_in_percent* column. This metric should be used to decide whether the index requires maintenance in conjunction with the number of records in the index. Index maintenance has only a limited performance impact for indexes with a low record count (i.e., less than 10,000). The following two types of corrective action can be taken to defragment an index:

- **Reorganizing** an index using the ALTER INDEX REORGANIZE statement should be undertaken for any indexes for which the logical fragmentation is above 5 percent. Reorganization occurs when the database is online, and it requires minimal system overhead. Reorganization compacts the data in the page files to eliminate unused space, and it corrects the logical order of the pages that occurred due to page splits.

- **Rebuilding** the index using the ALTER INDEX REBUILD statement drops and re-creates the index from scratch and should be considered for indexes where the logical fragmentation is above 30 percent. Rebuilding indexes can be done with the database online or offline. However, due to the system overhead involved, it is recommended that you undertake this activity during a maintenance window when the database is offline.

Maintenance Plans

Index defragmentation is a routine task that must be performed to ensure the optimal health of the database and query performance. If an index becomes too fragmented, the statistics used by the query optimizer will become stale over time, resulting in suboptimal query execution plans. Statistics can be updated using the UPDATE STATISTICS statement. Statistics are automatically updated when reorganizing or rebuilding an index.

Defragmenting indexes and updating statistics is a task that should be automated. **SQL Server Agent** is a service that allows routine management jobs to be created and scheduled for a SQL Server instance. SQL Server has a Maintenance Plan Wizard that allows you to schedule routine maintenance tasks by leveraging the SQL Server Agent. An activity in Chapter 8 guides you through creation of a SQL Server maintenance plan using the wizard, which also allows you to schedule backups and complete database integrity checks. An alternative database maintenance option is to build a stored procedure that queries and then executes a SQL maintenance statement that is determined by the current fragmentation levels. The suggested thresholds are as follows:

- Update statistics if the logical fragmentation is less than 5 percent.

- Reorganize index if the logical fragmentation is between 5 percent and 30 percent.

- Rebuild index if the logical fragmentation is greater than 30 percent.

There are a number of SQL-based third-party solutions that will simplify setting up these maintenance tasks. For example, Ola Hallengren (*ola.hallengren.com*) has a maintenance solution that includes stored procedures for backup, integrity checks, and index and statistics maintenance. These procedures enable you to set custom thresholds as parameters for the type of action that should be performed.

Chapter Summary

- The goal of performance optimization is to make the most efficient use of available system resources (including the number of read and write operations, memory consumption, and CPU utilization) and to lower the overall duration of queries.

- Design of the database schema and queries are major factors that influence the performance of retrieving or modifying information in a database management system.

- Normalization improves the integrity of the database and reduces storage needs, but it also has the effect of splitting data across multiple tables. When querying this data, these tables must be joined back together, causing a performance overhead.

- All relationships and constraints should be explicitly defined in a database. Constraints and relationships provide the query optimizer with valuable information about the expected results of a query.

- Query design has a significant impact on database peformance.

- Indexes improve query performance by providing the database engine with a quick way of locating a particular record based on the value of a column or columns. This prevents the database engine from having to scan every record in the database, which is extremely inefficient.

- Covering indexes and indexed views physically store a copy of the data as a virtual table and move I/O and the potential for contention and bottlenecks away from the primary table.

- Two types of system resource performance metrics are relevant to troubleshooting SQL Server performance issues: resource utilization measures and the number of backlogged requests waiting for a resource to become available.

- Windows Performance Monitor is a Windows utility you can use to monitor activity of the physical resources that are managed by the operating system.

- The SQL Server Profiler management tool is a graphical interface that enables a database administrator to capture events for the purpose of optimizing query performance, identifying and troubleshooting problematic queries, and monitoring workload.

- Lock-based concurrency control is used by the SQL Server database engine as a mechanism to ensure that transactions that access the same resources are executed in a serial manner.

- The query optimizer uses a cost-based algorithm to select the best execution plan—by estimating the costs (e.g., the number of data retrieval operations) for each alternative.

- The execution plan functionality in Query Editor provides a visual representation of the physical execution steps and their relative cost for a query.

- The Database Engine Tuning Advisor is a query-tuning wizard that uses the same optimization information as the query optimizer to provide a set of recommendations that may include the use of additional indexes, indexed views, and partitions to improve query performance.

- Changes to data can lead to fragmentation, a situation in which database records are stored out of order, causing a degradation in index performance. Internal and logical fragmentation are the main problems that a database administrator must contend with.

- Statistics used by the query optimizer will become stale over time, resulting in suboptimal query execution plans.

- Defragmenting indexes and updating statistics is a task that should be automated using a SQL Server Agent scheduled job.

Key Terms

blocking lock A situation that is caused when a process must wait for locks to be released by other active processes before it is able to proceed.

composite index An index on multiple columns; the most restrictive column should be placed first in a composite index because only the first column is used for building statistics.

concurrency control An important feature of a multiuser relational database management system that protects the integrity of data by controlling access to logical resources.

contiguous   A term used to describe records that are stored next to each other in sequence.

cost-based algorithm   A query optimization approach used to select the best execution plan by estimating the costs (e.g., number of I/O operations) for each alternative.

covering index   A database object that physically stores all columns that are needed to query a single table; unlike a normal index, a covering index is able to return the required data directly to the query, thus eliminating the additional step of retrieving data from the underlying tables.

Database Engine Tuning Advisor   A query-tuning wizard that uses the same optimization information as the query optimizer to provide a set of recommendations that may include additional indexes, indexed views, and partitions to improve query performance.

database trace file   A saved trace that can be replayed at a later point in time for analysis.

data collector set   A collection of performance counters that is configured and scheduled on Performance Monitor to record time series data on a particular group of performance counters.

deadlock   A situation in which two transactions each have a lock on a resource that the other transaction needs in order to complete.

deadlock victim   The transaction that SQL Server chooses to cancel in order to deal with a deadlock situation.

dirty read   A database integrity problem that can occur when a transaction updating the database fails and the updated values are rolled back to their original state. If a concurrent process is reading the data at the same time, it may retrieve the values that were not ultimately committed to the database.

Display Estimated Execution Plan   A Query Editor option that displays the execution steps of a query based on the costs that the optimizer has estimated using database statistics.

event   Any activity executed by the SQL Server database engine.

external fragmentation   A type of fragmentation that occurs when the logical storage of data in pages and extents does not match the physical storage on disk, causing increased workload that the physical disk has to perform in order to retrieve the data.

fragmentation   A situation in which database records are stored out of order, causing a degradation in index performance.

Include Actual Execution Plan   A Query Editor option that can be set prior to running a query in order to display the actual execution plan steps and costs once the query has completed.

incorrect summary   A database integrity problem that occurs if a transaction attempts to read and summarize values while the data is in an inconsistent state due to a concurrent update process.

indexed view   A database object that physically stores a copy of the data and performs as a virtual table. An indexed view is similar to a covering index but can be used to join and store data across several tables.

internal fragmentation   A type of fragmentation that occurs due to an accumulation of free space between records stored in the index page files, the fundamental logical storage unit used by SQL Server. Internal fragmentation results in growth of the index, and the unequal distribution of records leads to increased I/O and reduced performance.

lock-based concurrency control   A mechanism used by the SQL Server database engine to ensure that transactions that access the same resources are executed in a serial manner.

lock modes   A type of database locking mechanism that governs when a process is eligible to gain concurrent access to a particular resource. The strictest form of lock mode, which does not allow concurrent access under any circumstances, is an exclusive lock.

logical fragmentation   A type of fragmentation that occurs if a page has insufficient space to store new data in sequential order (e.g., due to inserted records), and as a result, the page files become split.

lost update A database integrity problem that can occur if two processes attempt to update the same record concurrently and the updates of one process are overwritten by the second process.

normalization A step in the design process of physical relations that systematically splits relations that contain duplicate data in order to eliminate data redundancy and ensure data integrity.

performance counter A metric used by Performance Monitor to collect time series data on a particular performance characteristic of the operating system.

query tuning An optimization process to lower the duration of a query and overall costs by improving the design of the SQL code or by adding indexes.

rebuilding An approach to defragmentation in which the index drops and re-creates the index from scratch and should be considered for indexes where the logical fragmentation is high.

refactoring The process of improving the design of code.

reorganizing An approach to defragmentation in which data is compacted in the page files to eliminate unused space and the logical order of the pages that occurred due to page splits is corrected.

SQL Server Agent A service that allows routine management jobs to be created and scheduled for a SQL Server instance.

SQL Server Profiler A management tool that enables a database administrator to capture events for the purpose of optimizing query performance, identifying and troubleshooting problematic queries, and monitoring workload.

statistics Information about the distribution of values for a particular table or index (e.g., the number of rows or the size of the key) and used by the cost-based query optimizer.

trace The result set of database events captured by SQL Server Profiler.

workload A stand-alone query or a previously saved trace file that was generated using SQL Server Profiler; used for analysis by the Database Engine Tuning Advisor.

Review Questions

1. Normalization improves the integrity of the database and reduces duplicative data. A side effect of normalization is that it increases the number of joins necessary to return a denormalized result set. What is the best course of action to improve query performance?

   a. Store all frequently accessed data in a denormalized form.

   b. Add more memory.

   c. Create an indexed view.

   d. Upgrade the CPU.

2. The database engine uses a cost-based optimizer to create a physical execution plan from a SQL query. Which of the following factors does the optimizer consider (indirectly or directly)?

   a. Statistics

   b. Performance counters

   c. Foreign keys and constraints

   d. Both options a and c

3. Which of the following operations may add significant overhead to a query?

   a. The LIKE operator

   b. Using * in the SELECT statement

   c. Sorting the data

   d. All of the above

4. Why is it important to monitor performance of a production SQL Server 2012 instance on an ongoing basis?

    a. The performance characteristics of the database will change over time as the underlying data changes and the database schema is modified.

    b. Indexes will become fragmented.

    c. Statistics that are used by the query optimizer will become stale.

    d. All of the above

5. Which of the following performance counters is *not* relevant for troubleshooting a SQL Server database?

    a. Processor Information: % Processor Time

    b. TCP: Connections Established

    c. Memory: Available Bytes

    d. Logical Disk: Avg. Disk Queue Length

6. Which of the following is *not* an event that can be captured by SQL Server Profiler?

    a. DML SQL query

    b. Login connections and disconnections to the SQL Server instance

    c. Login connections and disconnections to the Windows operating system

    d. Errors written to the SQL Server instance log file

7. Why is concurrency control important for a multiuser relational database management system?

    a. It prevents dirty reads, lost updates, and incorrect summary problems.

    b. It allows uncontrolled access to the database.

    c. It enables auto-resubmission of processes that are chosen as deadlock victims.

    d. All of the above

8. Which of the following actions can be taken to reduce the impact of blocking locks?

    a. Keep transactions as short as possible.

    b. Keep the scope of data changed by transactions as small as possible.

    c. Keep transactions as short as possible and the scope of data changed by each transaction as small as possible.

    d. Modify data in a single transaction to reduce the number of transactions that may potentially cause blocking locks.

9. You are analyzing an estimated execution plan for a query. Which of the following steps would you *not* investigate further?

    a. A step that displays *Index Seek* with an estimated cost of 4%

    b. A step that displays *Cost: 63%*

    c. A step that displays *Table Scan* above the estimated cost

    d. A step that displays *Sort*

10. You have been asked to set up a weekly index and statistics maintenance plan using SQL Server Agent. In which of the following scenarios would you update statistics?

    a. An index that will be rebuilt

    b. An index that will be reorganized

    c. Indexes that will be rebuilt or reorganized

    d. All indexes other than those that are rebuilt or reorganized

11. Which type(s) of fragmentation is (are) most likely to cause performance problems?

    a.   External fragmentation

    b.   Internal and logical fragmentation

    c.   Internal fragmentation

    d.   External and internal fragmentation

12. Which of the following is *not* a problem that would result from uncontrolled access to a database?

    a.   Incorrect read

    b.   Incorrect summary

    c.   Lost update

    d.   Dirty read

Case Projects

Case Project 7-1: Health Insurance Company Acquisition

You work as a junior database administrator for a nationwide health insurance company, Universal Health, which is aggressively expanding its market share by acquiring smaller firms. Universal Health believes that it can achieve significant economies of scale by consolidating the IT systems of its acquisitions onto a single platform. This is a major undertaking and will not be complete for another 18 months. In the interim, you have been asked to take over support for one of the acquired company's databases, which handles insurance claims. The systems administrator who manages the virtualized Windows Server infrastructure has recently noticed some abnormal behavior on one of the servers that hosts a SQL Server instance. She is noticing a spike in CPU utilization and available memory declining below 5 percent at around 9:00 p.m. each evening, and she has asked you to investigate the possible cause of the problem. Complete the following:

- What additional performance metrics from the Windows operating system would be helpful in analyzing the problem? Justify your response.
- Outline your strategy for troubleshooting the issue. Include the steps that you would take in sequence along with the SQL Server management tools that you would use.

Case Project 7-2: X-Tex

In your role as the database administrator for X-Tex, a small but successful company that designs and manufactures high-tech fabrics, you have been asked to help optimize a query that will provide a dynamic view of your supply chain. You are to work with a developer who is tasked with integrating the data into a Web portal that is used by the manufacturing operations team. The developer explains that he has not had much experience working with SQL, but he seems keen to learn. Complete the following:

- Provide the developer with a practical summary of design considerations that will help to ensure that the query performs well.
- The developer has specified that he needs the result set to be sorted. Explain the possible performance ramifications of sorting the result set, and suggest an alternative.
- Explain how you can test a prototype query to fine-tune its performance characteristics.

Case Project 7-3: HomeSense, LLC

You recently joined a real estate firm, HomeSense, LLC, as a database administrator. HomeSense had to lay off a number of staff during the economic downturn, and the previous database administrator numbered among them. The remaining IT staff, who have only a basic knowledge of database administration, have managed to maintain the SQL Server databases since his departure, but no significant changes have been made in the interlude. Several realtors have complained that the performance of their applications has steadily decreased, and they have asked you to investigate. After a cursory analysis, you have concluded that the database was well designed; however, no routine maintenance is being undertaken against the database. Complete the following:

- Discuss the possible causes of the poor performance, and list the indicators you would use to support your hypothesis.
- Describe the steps that you would take to resolve the performance issues. Your plan should include construction of a maintenance plan, if you deem it necessary, given the facts presented.

Hands-On Projects

Hands-On Project 7-1: Monitoring and Analyzing Performance

For this hands-on project, you will use the SQL Server named instance SQLSERVERHOA and the HandsOnOne database and tables that you created in previous chapters. The objective of this project is to practice using Windows utilities and SQL Server management tools to monitor performance and diagnose query performance.

1. Using the Windows Performance Monitor utility, add a set of counters to the real-time performance monitor display that you consider most relevant to the performance of your SQL Server instance. Document this step by taking a screen shot of the real-time display.

2. In SQL Server Management Studio, construct a SQL query that uses a SELECT statement and a JOIN clause to query data from both the Customer and Address tables. Analyze the estimated execution plan.

   a. Identify the most costly plan steps.

   b. Are any of the steps that you identified in Step 2(a) a cause for concern? Explain.

   c. Describe how the performance of the query could be improved, or explain why the query is already optimal.

3. Implement any changes identified in 2(c) and execute the query using the option Include Actual Execution Plan. Document this step by taking a screen shot of the actual execution plan.

4. Use SQL Server Profiler to capture a trace and execute the query again. Analyze the trace and determine how many milliseconds the query took to execute. Take a screen shot of the trace that shows the execution of your query to document this step.

5. Launch the Database Engine Tuning Advisor from Query Editor to analyze your query. Did the analysis generate any recommendations? Explain why or why not.

6. Run the *sp_who2* procedure to determine the current sessions that are connected to the SQLSERVERHOA instance.

chapter 8

Backup and Recovery

After reading this chapter and completing the exercises, you will be able to:

- Evaluate the risks of data loss in conjunction with the business requirements to define recovery objectives

- Compare the main database backup types

- Design a backup plan that is optimized against a set of recovery objectives, and create database backups

- Use SQL Server Agent to automate the backup tasks

A comprehensive backup and recovery strategy is essential to safeguard against loss of data that may occur due to user error, hardware and software failure, or environmental changes. Although the probability of an individual risk materializing may be low, loss of data can have a significant and in some cases crippling impact on the ability of an organization to function. Data is increasingly treated as a strategic asset of an organization and any risk that may result in data loss must be treated seriously. Partnership with the business teams and a strong emphasis on risk management are the keys to designing a cost-effective backup and recovery strategy.

The first section of this chapter evaluates the four main categories of risk with which a database administrator must contend. A typical database administrator does not have the luxury of an unconstrained budget and resources; therefore, when defining a set of recovery objectives, the costs associated with mitigating these risks must be carefully balanced against the business requirements.

Backup and restore functionality is available on all editions of SQL Server 2012 and is a time-proven means to limit data loss. A **backup** is the process of taking a copy of a database file, which can later be used to restore the database in the event of a data loss. The second section of the chapter discusses the different types of backup and storage media options. The final section of the chapter considers how to schedule and combine the different backup types within a backup plan to achieve different recovery objectives. SQL Server Agent is presented as a utility that can be used to automate routine backup operations. You will learn how to recover a database by restoring the backups, and you'll learn why it is necessary to frequently test this aspect of a backup and recovery strategy.

Defining Recovery Objectives

A backup and recovery strategy must satisfy a set of business requirements under a variety of different data loss scenarios while factoring in operational constraints. Neglecting to invest time in this important planning step may result in a backup and recovery strategy that fails to adequately meet the needs of the organization or that squanders valuable resources due to poorly defined recovery objectives.

Evaluating the Risk of Data Loss

A **risk assessment** should be undertaken to identify and objectively quantify all potential data loss scenarios. The output of a risk assessment is used to prioritize the allocation of resources in the most effective manner possible, given the business requirements and operational constraints. Several different methodologies of varying degrees of complexity can be used to assess and manage risk. Many organizations adopt a single, standardized risk management framework across their enterprise to ensure consistency. If you lack experience in risk management, you should pick a framework that is straightforward to implement and understand. This section presents one such framework.

For each risk identified, the assessment should consider three primary factors: the probability of occurrence, the magnitude of the impact, and the difficulty of timely detection. These factors can be combined to determine the overall threat level that a particular risk represents. Table 8-1 provides a simple example of this approach, which can be tailored for use in your organization.

Table 8-1   Risk assessment matrix

Risk	Probability of occurrence	Magnitude of impact	Difficulty of timely detection	Overall threat
Sample scenario	Low	Medium	High	Medium

© Cengage Learning

The probability of occurrence identifies the likelihood of the risk materializing. For some risks, this probability may be extremely low. However, if a risk is likely to have a significant impact on the business (e.g., loss of a data center) and could occur with little warning, it is important that it is factored into the backup and recovery strategy. Organizations often make sizable investments preparing for risks that will likely never materialize—for example by maintaining redundant facilities and infrastructure—because the magnitude of the impact would be high.

The following four broad categories of risk may lead to data loss (sample scenarios are listed for each category in Table 8-2):

Table 8-2 Sample scenarios in the major risk categories

Risk category	Sample scenario
User error	• Accidental deletion or modification of data by an authorized user • Bug in client application, which causes incorrect modification of data • Incorrect shutdown of SQL Server database management system • Deletion of data by an unauthorized person
Hardware failure	• Physical disk failure • Other component failure
System software failure	• Bug introduced by latest SQL Server service pack • SQL Server version incompatibility with Windows operating system
Environmental events	• Temporary power outage (< one hour) • Major power outage (> one hour) • Loss of data center due to fire

© Cengage Learning

- *User errors*—Data loss caused by user error has the highest probability of occurrence, although its impact is typically limited to a single database or application. User errors may result from accidental modification or deletion of data by an authorized user, or they may be the outcome of malicious, unauthorized access. Database administrators represent a particularly high-risk category of authorized user due to the broad set of permissions necessary to perform database management functions. Client applications that lack adequate testing and contain bugs, which cause systematic errors, are also a type of user error.

- *Hardware failure*—System hardware has a limited life span and may fail unexpectedly. Failure of certain components, such as the RAM, may result in system downtime while a spare part is obtained and installed. On the other hand, damage or corruption to a physical storage device may result in the loss of data in addition to system downtime. A database administrator must have a solid contingency plan for any type of physical storage failure.

- *System software failures*—A software failure may lead to data loss or unplanned downtime. A software bug in the Windows operating system or the database management system, or a compatibility issue between the operating system and the database server, are common causes of this type of failure. This type of risk has a medium likelihood of occurrence but generally a low impact, assuming that system updates are thoroughly tested prior to production deployment.

- *Environmental events*—An environmental event can have a catastrophic effect on the infrastructure of an organization even though its probability of occurring may be very low. This type of risk is highly dependent upon the location of the data center and its susceptibility to natural events, such as flooding, fire, seismic events, or tornadoes. Environmental events may disrupt a facility due to power failure or loss of Internet connectivity. Lastly, some organizations operate in countries that are prone to political turmoil or conflict. Because natural or human-caused environmental events tend to impact an entire data center, the key risk mitigation strategy should be planning for site redundancy and secure storage of the backup media off-site.

Evaluating the Business Requirements

A significant cost is associated with implementing a backup and recovery strategy that fully addresses all potential risks of data loss. The preventive costs tend to follow an exponential growth pattern as the business tolerance to data loss and downtime decreases. Analyzing the business requirements of a particular deployment will help you determine the right level of investment to mitigate the risks of data loss and system downtime. These requirements should be reevaluated periodically in conjunction with the risk assessment because their scope of the business requirements will change over time. For each production user and system database, the evaluation should consider the following factors:

- *Availability*—Understanding when the business requires the database to be available is important as it enables a database administrator to determine the optimal time to schedule backups. For example, if a database is only required to be available Monday through Friday during normal business hours, the database administrator has a significant window each night and during the weekend for undertaking maintenance activities. Conversely, a mission-critical system (e.g., an air traffic control system) may need the database to be available continuously and have zero tolerance to downtime. In such a case, backups have to be taken concurrently with business operations.

- *Value*—In many organizations, data has become a strategic asset and may represent a sizable portion of the organization's value. Quantifying the value of the data and the implications of data loss to the business will help you determine how much should be invested to safeguard the data. For example, a retail bank would not be viable as a business without customer transaction records and should, therefore, be prepared to make a significant investment to protect these assets.

- *Size*—Large databases present a particular challenge to the database administrator because regular backup and restore operations may reach physical resource limitations (i.e., there are simply not enough hours in the day to complete a backup with the available hardware). The database administrator may need to develop alternative strategies, such as splitting backups into smaller units.

- *Performance*—Database backups performed while a user database is online consume physical resources, such as disk throughput, memory, and processor time. This means fewer resources are available to other users, which may cause resource bottlenecks and degraded performance. It is, therefore, necessary to analyze the level of user activity over time and understand peak load periods to ensure that the backup and restore strategy does not adversely affect business operations.

- *Change*—The rate at which a database changes will determine the frequency with which backups must occur in order to minimize data loss. A read-only database such as a data warehouse will require infrequent backups. Conversely, an online transaction processing database (OLTP) with constantly changing data will need frequent backups to minimize the potential for data loss.

- *Interdependencies*—Although the focus of risk analysis is predominantly at the level of the individual database, the assessment of business requirements should identify any interdependencies between different databases. For example, a client application may require both a user database and the organization's email database to function properly.

Developing a Set of Recovery Objectives

By undertaking an assessment of the risk factors and business requirements, you can build a set of objectives for each production database under different risk scenarios that define the following:

- **Recovery time objective (RTO)**—The amount of downtime that should be expected by the business before the system is restored; for a single database, this may vary depending on the type of risk.

- **Recovery point objective (RPO)**—The maximum amount of data that may be lost; this is expressed as a time frame (e.g., loss of up to one hour of changes to the database) rather than as a quantity of data.

Recovery objectives are typically tailored for each individual database for a given scenario. For example, the RTO that addresses recovery from the failure of a single disk that impacts only a single database may be two hours. However, in the event of the loss of the entire data center, the RTO for the same database may be 24 hours. For data loss scenarios that impact multiple databases simultaneously, an organization will have to prioritize recovery operations to make the best use of finite IT management resources and other operational constraints. These constraints will inevitably lead to increased downtime for certain systems.

Defining a set of recovery objectives that are feasible given budget and resource constraints but that also satisfy the business requirements is an iterative process and must be undertaken with close cooperation with the business teams. Many organizations formally document recovery objectives within their business continuity and disaster recovery plans. This helps the business teams and customers understand what to expect under different data loss scenarios. It also demonstrates to other stakeholders—such as shareholders and regulators—that the organization is sufficiently prepared to deal with major business disruptions.

Database Backup Types

In SQL Server 2012, backups can be performed using the SQL language or the BackUp Database dialog box, which is accessed from Object Explorer within SQL Server Management Studio. Backups may be performed while a database is online or offline, although there are performance ramifications when performing an online operation. A database administrator can perform three main types of backup to achieve different recovery objectives: full database backups, differential database backups, and transaction log backups.

Backup Sets

With SQL Server 2012, you can back up database files and transaction logs to two types of media: tape and physical disk (which also includes removable media such as DVD). The result of each backup operation is the creation of a file (known as a **backup set**) that is stored on the physical media. Backup sets can be assigned an **expiration date**, which helps to ensure that existing backups on the media will not be overwritten until a specified time in the future. When performing a backup operation, the physical backup location can be specified directly, or a backup device can be used. A **backup device** is a logical storage device that references a physical location where the backup sets will be stored.

For reasons that should be self-evident, production database backups must never be stored on the same physical disk as the database log or data files. Backing up to a physical disk is usually preferable from a performance perspective for both backup and restore operations. The backups can then be transferred to DVD or tape for long-term storage off-site. Physical security of backup sets should be considered carefully, and controls must be implemented that prevent backups from being deleted, removed, or copied. You can achieve this goal by restricting and monitoring logical and physical access to the backup location and by encrypting the backup.

Full and Differential Database Backups

A **full database backup** makes a copy of all nonempty pages in a data file, and it also creates a duplicate of the section of the transaction log for transactions that occurred during the backup. Full database backups are the foundation of any backup and recovery strategy because a normal database restore operation requires a full backup of the database at minimum. Full database backups take time and significant physical resources to perform and they are, therefore, undertaken periodically, normally during a maintenance window or a period of low activity. The basic SQL syntax for performing a full database backup is as follows:

```
BACKUP DATABASE <DatabaseName>

TO <BackupDevice>;
```

A **differential database backup** only copies pages that have changed since the last full database backup and is, therefore, less resource intensive. A differential database backup must be used in conjunction with the most recent full database backup during a restore operation. The basic SQL syntax for performing a differential database backup is as follows:

```
BACKUP DATABASE <DatabaseName>

TO <BackupDevice>

WITH DIFFERENTIAL;
```

By default, a full or differential database backup is performed at the level of an individual database. A database backup can also be performed as a **file** or **filegroup backup**, which may be used if a database administrator needs to break a database backup into smaller units for performance reasons. Finally, with a **partial backup**, only data in the primary filegroup and read-write filegroups are backed up by default.

Database backups should be performed with a checksum stored for each page. A **checksum** is a unique variable that is computed based on the data contained in a page and used to verify the integrity of the data. When a restore operation later reads the page from storage, it also computes a checksum and checks that this matches the stored value. A match indicates that the integrity of the data has likely been retained.

Activity 8-1: Performing Full Database Backup Operations

Time Required: 60 minutes
Objective: Create a new backup device and perform a full database backup operation.

Description: In this activity, you will create a logical backup device for storing backup sets, and you'll perform a full database backup using the BackUp Database dialog box in SQL Server Management Studio.

1. If necessary, start your computer and log on.

2. Click the **Start** button, point to **All Programs**, click **Microsoft SQL Server 2012**, and then click **SQL Server Management Studio**. In the Connect to Server dialog box, select **Database Engine** as the server type, type **LOCALHOST\SQLSERVERUA** in the Server name text box, and then select **Windows Authentication** from the Authentication list box. Click **Connect**.

3. In Object Explorer, click the **SQLSERVERUA** root folder of the new connection. Click **New Query**. In the Query Editor window, type the following SQL query to create a new database with a single table that you will use for testing backup and restore operations throughout this chapter:

```
CREATE DATABASE BackupRestoreTest

GO

CREATE TABLE BackupRestoreTest.dbo.TestTable

(TestID int NOT NULL,

TestDescription nvarchar(50) NOT NULL);

GO
```

Press the **F5** key or click the **Execute** button to run the query. See Figure 8-1.

4. Next, you'll create a new physical folder on the file system to store your backup sets and grant permissions to the service account that is running the Database Engine Service for the SQLSERVERUA instance. Launch Windows File Explorer by clicking the **Start** button, and then clicking **Computer**. Click the **C:** drive in the left navigation pane of Windows File

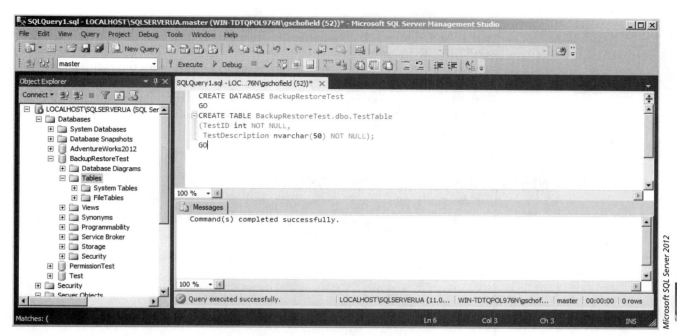

Figure 8-1 Create a new database and table for testing backup and recovery operations

Explorer, and then click the **New Folder** button on the toolbar. Rename the folder by typing **Backup** as the folder name. Right-click the **Backup** folder and then click **Properties**.

5. In the Backup Properties dialog box, click the **Security** tab. Click the **Edit** button to modify the folder permissions. In the Permissions for Backup dialog box, click the **Add** button. In the Select Users or Groups dialog box, enter **NT Service\ MSSQL$SQLSERVERUA** as the object name to select, and then click the **Check Names** button to resolve the name. Click **OK** to exit the Select Users or Groups dialog box and return to the Permissions for Backup dialog box. Click **MSSQL$SQLSERVERUA** in the Group or user names list, and then check the **Allow** check box for Full control in the lower permissions list to grant full permissions to the Database Engine Service account. See Figure 8-2. Click **OK** to grant the permissions.

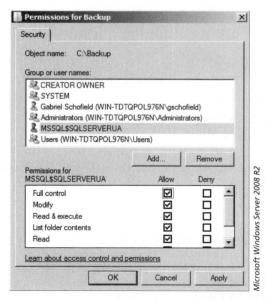

Figure 8-2 Grant folder permissions to the Database Engine Service account

6. You will now define a new logical backup device that will be used for storing the backup sets that you'll create later in the activity. In Object Explorer, expand the **SQLSERVERUA** root folder, expand the **Server Objects** folder, and then right-click the **Backup Devices** folder. Select **New Backup Device** from the menu to open the Backup Device dialog box. In the Device name text box, type **BackupRestoreTest_1**. In the Destination section, click the **File** option button, and then type **C:\Backup \BackupRestoreTest_1.bak** as the filename. See Figure 8-3. Click **OK** to create the new backup device.

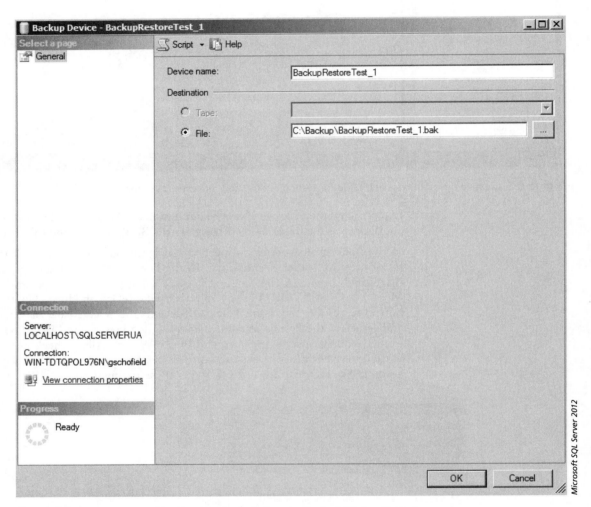

Figure 8-3 Create a new logical backup device using the Backup Device dialog box

For a production database, you should always create a backup device on different physical media than where either the production data or log files reside.

7. In Object Explorer, expand the **SQLSERVERUA** folder, and then expand the **Databases** folder. You should see the Backup Restore Test database that you created in Step 3 listed as a user database. If it does not appear, click the **Refresh** button on the toolbar of Object Explorer. Right-click the **Backup Restore Test** user database, point to **Tasks,** and then click **Back Up** to display the Back Up Database dialog box.

8. On the General page of the Back Up Database dialog box, select **Full** from the Backup type list box, and then select **Database** as the Backup component. In the Destination section, click the default backup destination, and then click the **Remove** button to remove the default backup device. In the Destination section, click **Add.** In the Select Backup Destination dialog box, click the **Backup device** option button, and then select the backup device **BackupRestoreTest_1** that you created in Step 6. Click **OK** to return to the Back Up Database dialog box. Keep the rest of the defaults on the page. See Figure 8-4.

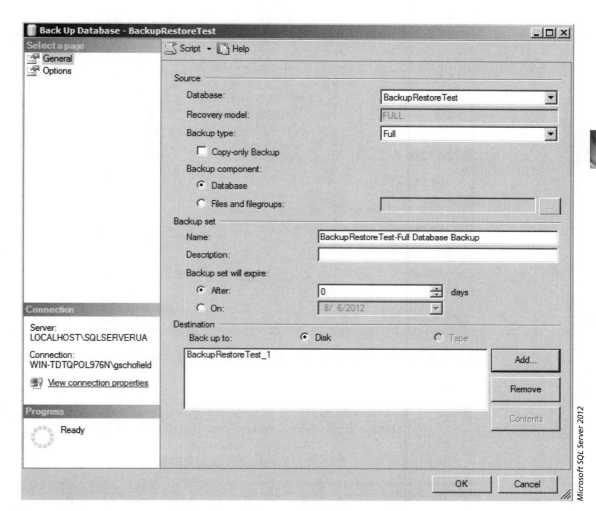

Figure 8-4 Create a full database backup using the Back Up Database dialog box – General page

The default backup set expiration of 0 days specifies that the backup will never expire. This can optionally be changed if you want to overwrite older files on your backup device after a certain period.

9. In the Back Up Database dialog box, click **Options** in the left navigation pane. In the Overwrite media section, keep the default options **Back up to the existing media set** and **Append to the existing backup set**. In the Reliability section, click the **Verify backup when finished** and **Perform checksum before writing to media** check boxes to select them. See Figure 8-5. Click **OK** to perform the full database backup operation.

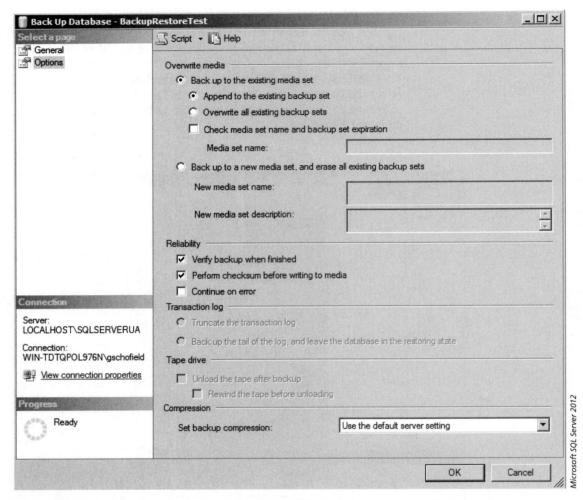

Figure 8-5 Create a full database backup using the Back Up Database dialog box – Options page

10. You should receive an informational message box with the message: The backup of database 'Backup Restore Test' completed successfully. See Figure 8-6. Click **OK**.

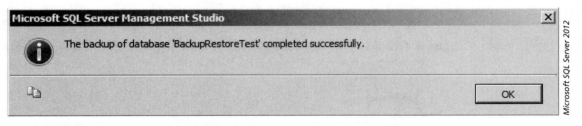

Figure 8-6 Backup completed successfully message box

11. Return to Windows File Explorer, and double-click the **Backup** folder. You should see a new file named BackupRestoreTest_1.bak, which contains the full database backup that you performed in Step 9. See Figure 8-7.

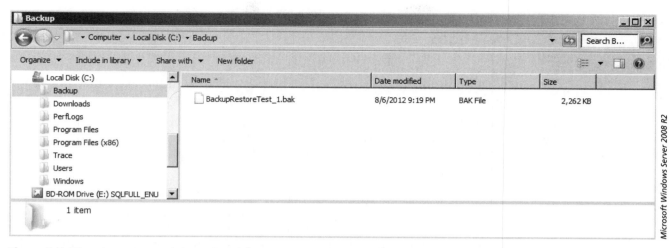

Figure 8-7 View the contents of the Backup folder using Windows Explorer

12. Return to SQL Server Management Studio, and delete the text in the open Query Editor window. Type the following SQL command to insert a record into the test table that you created in Step 5:

```
INSERT INTO BackupRestoreTest.dbo.TestTable

(TestID, TestDescription)

VALUES

(1, 'Test1');
```

Press the **F5** key or click the **Execute** button to run the query. See Figure 8-8.

Figure 8-8 Insert a record into the test table

Activity 8-2: Performing Differential Database Backup Operations

Time Required: 30 minutes
Objective: Perform differential database backup operations using an existing backup device.

Description: In this activity, you will perform differential database backups using the Back Up Database dialog box in SQL Server Management Studio. You will also learn how to execute a SQL command from Query Editor to perform a full backup to a physical disk.

1. You will now perform a differential database backup and append it to the existing backup set. This will create a copy of any pages that have changed since the full backup that you performed in Step 9 of Activity 8-1. Return to Object Explorer that you left open at the end of Activity 8-1. Right-click the **Backup Restore Test**, click **Tasks**, and then click **Back Up** to display the Back Up Database dialog box. On the General page, select **Differential** from the Backup type list box, and then select **Database** as the Backup component. In the Destination section, click **BackupRestoreTest_1** to select the backup device that you created in Step 6 of Activity 8-1. Keep the rest of the defaults. See Figure 8-9.

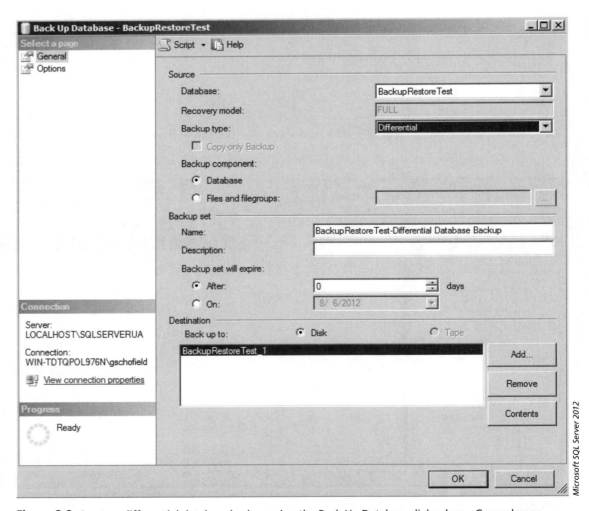

Figure 8-9 Create a differential database backup using the Back Up Database dialog box – General page

2. In the Back Up Database dialog box, click **Options** in the left navigation pane. In the Overwrite media section, keep the default options **Back up to the existing media set** and **Append to the existing backup set**. In the Reliability section, click the **Verify backup when finished** and **Perform checksum before writing to media** check boxes to select them. See Figure 8-10. Click **OK** to perform the differential database backup operation. Click **OK** when the successful completion message box appears.

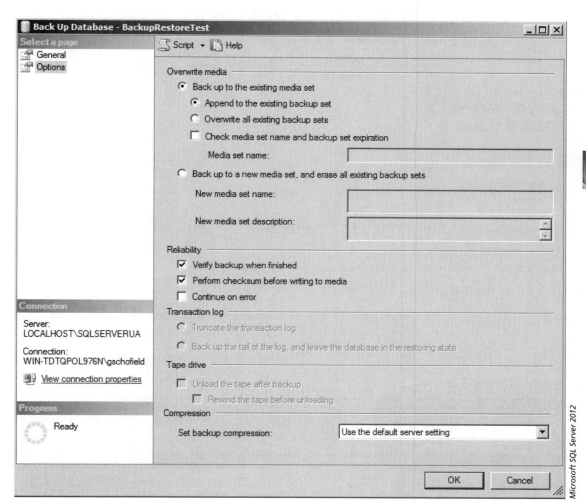

Figure 8-10 Create a differential database backup using the Back Up Database dialog box – Options page

3. In Object Explorer, expand the **Server Objects** folder and the Backup Devices subfolder. Right-click the **BackupRestoreTest_1** device, and then click **Properties**. Click **Media Contents** in the left navigation pane. See Figure 8-11. Review the two backup sets listed that you created earlier in the activity. Click **Cancel** to exit.

4. Occasionally, it is necessary to perform a one-off backup to disk. You will now perform a full database backup to a user-defined file location using a SQL command. Return to SQL Server Management Studio, and delete the text in the open Query Editor window. Type the following SQL command to perform a full database backup:

```
BACKUP DATABASE BackupRestoreTest

TO DISK = 'C:\Backup\BackupRestoreTest_OneTime.bak';
```

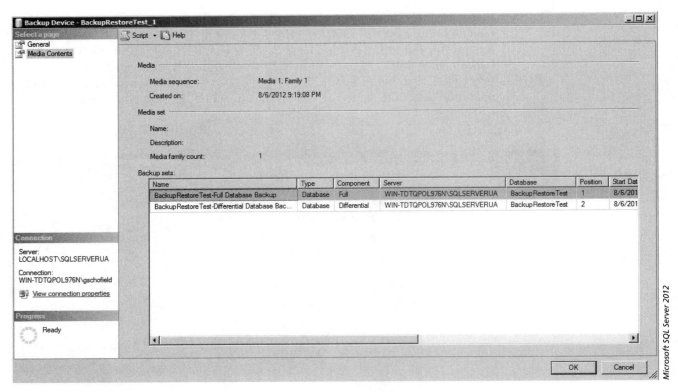

Figure 8-11 View the media contents and backup sets on the Backup Device

Press the **F5** key, or click the **Execute** button to run the query. The Messages pane of Query Editor displays statistics about the backup, including the number of pages processed. See Figure 8-12.

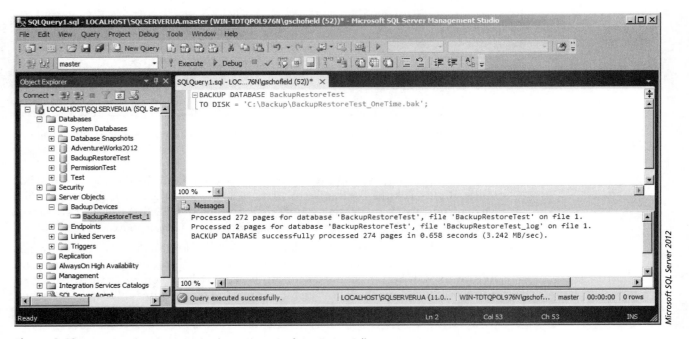

Figure 8-12 Execute a full database backup using SQL from Query Editor

5. Return to Windows File Explorer, and click the **Refresh** button to the right of the Address bar. A new file named Backup Restore Test_One Time.bak, which contains the full database backup that you performed in Step 4 appears in the Backup folder. See Figure 8-13.

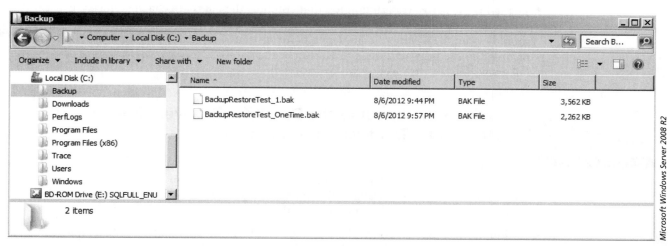

Figure 8-13 View the contents of the Backup folder using Windows Explorer

6. You have now completed this activity. Delete the SQL command text in the open Query Editor window, but leave SQL Server Management Studio and Windows File Explorer open for the next activity.

Transaction Log Backups

Transaction logs record changes that occur to the data in a database over time. To recover lost data within a database that occurred after the last full or differential backup, one or more sequential transaction logs must be available to apply the most recent activity to the database and restore transactional integrity. Transaction logs are also required in the event that a database needs to be restored back to a specific point in time. For example, if a large set of data is erroneously deleted due to user error, the business may decide that the best course of action is to restore the database to the last known good state.

Each database has a **recovery model** configuration setting that specifies which type of database transactions should be recorded in the transaction log. The transaction logging setting is important because it determines what recovery operations are possible. Databases that use the **simple recovery model** do not record any events in a transaction log. This simplifies maintenance and ensures minimal database growth, but it does not allow point-in-time restores or recovery of data since the last database backup. A simple recovery model would normally only be used for nonproduction databases, system databases, and read-only databases where the underlying data does not change.

The **full recovery model** causes all changes to the database to be written to the transaction log. Because a full history of changes is available in the transaction log, the database administrator is able to complete point-in-time restores and recover the database to its current state. The full recovery model should be used for most production databases where the business has a low tolerance for data loss and where the underlying data changes frequently.

The **bulk logged recovery model** sits between the full and simple recovery models and selectively logs changes to the database. In particular, it does not record database changes as individual transactions that occurred due to **bulk transactions** such as large inserts of data in a bulk copy operation. The bulk logged recovery model does not support point-in-time restores and only allows recovery of data since the last database backup provided that no bulk transaction activity has occurred during that time frame. The bulk logged recovery model requires less processing overhead and disk space.

Transaction logs must be frequently backed up for two primary reasons:

- Each time it is backed up, the transaction log is **truncated,** which causes space to be made available in the active transaction log for recording new activity. This has the effect of limiting the growth of the database. Left unattended, a transaction log will grow indefinitely until it runs out of physical disk space or reaches the maximum file size defined in the database configuration settings.

- The **tail** is the active transaction log that contains the database changes since the last transaction log backup. The active transaction log could become corrupted or deleted. If this should occur, the ability to complete a point-in-time restore for the time frame of events recorded in the transaction log or to restore the database to the current state is lost. As the tail grows in size, the level of this exposure increases.

Activity 8-3: Changing the Database Recovery Model and Performing a Transaction Log Backup

Time Required: 30 minutes
Objective: Change the database recovery model and perform a transaction log backup by using the BackUp Database dialog box in SQL Server Management Studio and by executing a SQL command in query analyzer.

Description: In this activity, you will change the database recovery model from simple to full, and you'll perform a transaction log backup by using the BackUp Database dialog box in SQL Server Management Studio and by executing a SQL command in query analyzer.

1. For the database to record all activity in the transaction log, the database recovery model must be set to Full. Return to the SQL Server Management Studio, which you left open from the previous activity. In Object Explorer, right-click the **Backup Restore Test** database, and then click **Properties** to open the Database Properties dialog box. In the left navigation pane, click **Options**. Select **Full** from the Recovery model drop-down list box (see Figure 8-14) and then click **OK** to save the changes and return to the Object Explorer window.

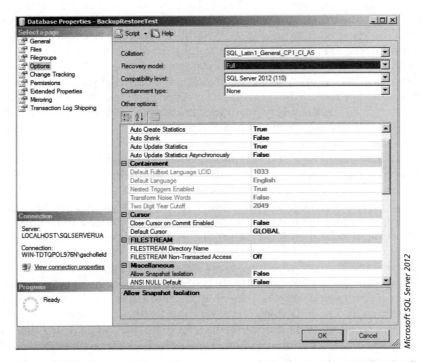

Figure 8-14 View and change the recovery model in the Database Properties dialog box

You can also perform the same operation in Query Editor by executing the following SQL command:

```
ALTER DATABASE BackupRestoreTest

SET RECOVERY FULL;
```

2. To insert two more records into the test table, type the following SQL command in the Query Editor window:

```
INSERT INTO BackupRestoreTest.dbo.TestTable

(TestID, TestDescription)

VALUES

(2, 'Test2');

INSERT INTO BackupRestoreTest.dbo.TestTable

(TestID, TestDescription)

VALUES

(3, 'Test3');
```

Press the **F5** key or click the **Execute** button to run the query.

3. You will now perform a transaction log backup using a SQL command. This creates a copy of all changes captured in the active transaction log and then truncates the log. In SQL Server Management Studio, delete the text in the open Query Editor window. Type the following SQL command to perform a transaction log backup:

```
BACKUP LOG BackupRestoreTest

TO BackupRestoreTest_1;
```

Press the **F5** key or click the **Execute** button to run the query. The Messages pane of Query Editor displays some statistics about the backup that was performed, including the number of pages processed. See Figure 8-15.

In this query, you specified the logical name of the backup device. Alternatively, you can specify a physical location by using the TO DISK or TO TAPE clause (see Step 4 of Activity 8-2).

4. You will now perform a transaction log backup using the Back Up Database dialog box. In Object Explorer, right-click the **Backup Restore Test**, point to **Tasks**, and then click **Back Up** to display the Back Up Database dialog box. On the General page, select **Transaction Log** from the Backup type list box. In the Destination section, click **Backup Restore Test_1** to select the backup device that you created in the previous activity. Keep the rest of the default settings. See Figure 8-16.

5. In the Back Up Database dialog box, click **Options** in the left navigation pane. In the Overwrite media section, keep the default options **Back up to the existing media set** and **Append to the existing backup set**. In the Reliability section, click the **Verify backup when finished** and **Perform checksum before writing to media**

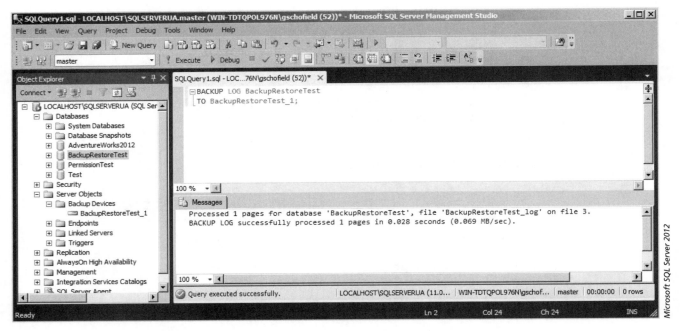

Figure 8-15 Back up the transaction log by executing a SQL statement in the Query Editor window

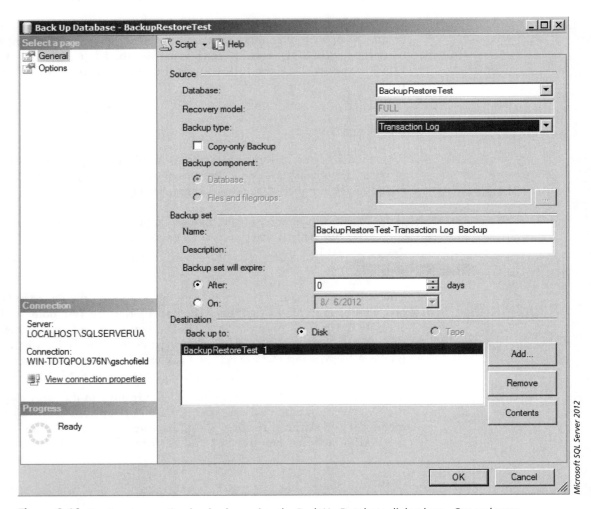

Figure 8-16 Create a transaction log backup using the Back Up Database dialog box – General page

check boxes to select them. In the Transaction log section, click the **Truncate the transaction log** option button. See Figure 8-17. Click **OK** to perform the transaction log backup operation. Click **OK** when the successful completion message box appears.

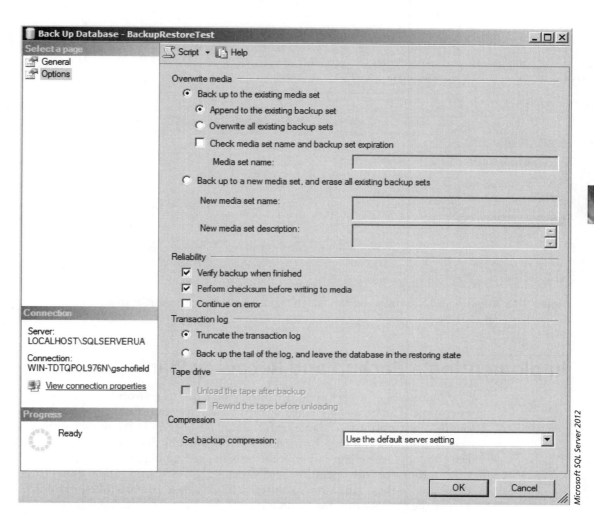

Figure 8-17 Create a transaction log backup using the Back Up Database dialog box – Options page

6. In Object Explorer, expand the **Server Objects** folder and the Backup Devices subfolder. Right-click the **BackupRestoreTest_1** device, and then click **Properties**. Click **Media Contents** in the left navigation pane. See Figure 8-18. You should now see four items listed in the backup sets grid: a full database backup, a differential database backup, and the two transaction log backups. Close the Backup Device properties window by clicking **Cancel**.

7. You have now completed this activity. Close the Query Editor window but leave SQL Server Management Studio and Windows File Explorer open for the next activity.

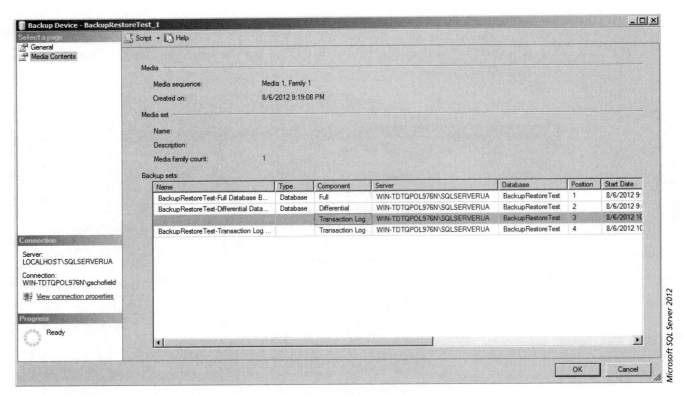

Microsoft SQL Server 2012

Figure 8-18 View the media contents and backup sets in the Backup Device properties window

Implementing a Backup and Recovery Plan

The objectives of a backup and recovery plan are to recover lost data and to minimize system downtime. The type and frequency of the database and transaction log backups will determine the recovery options available. A full database backup is essential for any recovery operation; transaction logs can then be used to recover updates that were made to the database since the last backup. Overreliance upon frequently backed-up log files can create excessive system downtime during a restore operation because each log file must be applied sequentially to the restored database. In these situations, a differential database backup taken periodically can be used to reduce the number of transaction log backups that need to be applied.

Backup Plans

A backup plan should be developed for each database that will satisfy the recovery objectives that have been defined. There are four commonly used types of backup plan:

- *Full database backup, simple recovery model (transaction log not used)*—This plan involves periodically taking a full database backup. In the event of data loss, the database can be restored from the last full backup. Any data that has changed since the last backup will be lost and a point-in-time restore is not possible, as illustrated in Figure 8-19. Although this plan requires minimal overhead to manage, it should be reserved for nonproduction databases, system databases, and read-only user databases.

- *Single transaction log backup plus full database backup*—With this plan, the full recovery model is used and the transaction log is backed up immediately prior to each full database backup. Because both the transaction log and full backup are retained, a point-in-time restore is possible. Assuming that the tail of the transaction log since the last backup has not been damaged, there will be no data lost during recovery, as illustrated in Figure 8-20.

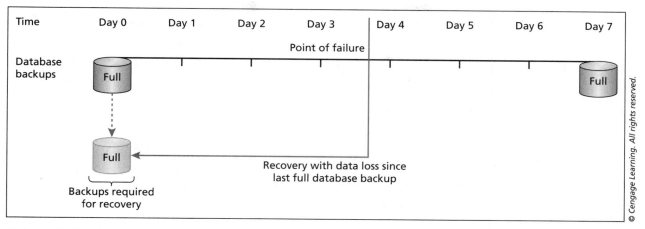

Figure 8-19 Full database backup with simple recovery model

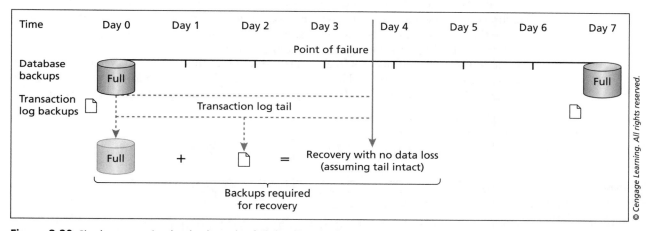

Figure 8-20 Single transaction log backup plus full database backup

- *Full database backup plus multiple transaction log backups*—With this plan, the full recovery model is used, and the transaction log is backed up on a regular basis. This improves upon the previous plan by reducing the risk of losing the tail of the transaction log. If recovery of the database is necessary, the database will be restored using the last full database backup and then the individual transaction log backups will be restored sequentially to recover the database up to the point of failure. The disadvantage of this plan is that it can take a long time to apply the individual log backups resulting in significant downtime. For example, assume the transaction log files on a particular database are backed up every 15 minutes. If the last full database backup occurred at midday on Sunday and the database fails at midday on the following Friday, the database administrator would have to restore 480 individual transaction logs to prevent any data from being lost. Figure 8-21 illustrates this plan in detail.

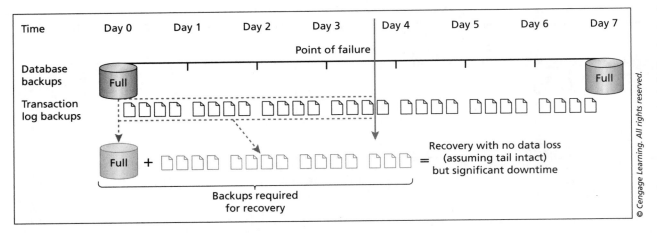

Figure 8-21 Full database backup plus multiple transaction log backups

- *Full database backup plus differential database backup plus multiple transaction log backups*—With this plan, the full recovery model is used and the transaction log is backed up on a frequent basis. It improves on the previous plan by taking regular differential database backups that will reduce the number of files involved in a restore operation. See Figure 8-22. Using the previous example—and assuming that a differential backup is performed at midnight each day—the same failure on Friday at midday would require the database administrator to restore the last full database backup, the differential database backup that took place at midnight on Thursday, and then 48 individual transaction logs. This translates to a sizable reduction in the amount of system downtime necessary to perform a restore. However, this backup plan creates additional IT management and physical resource overhead to perform and monitor the additional backups.

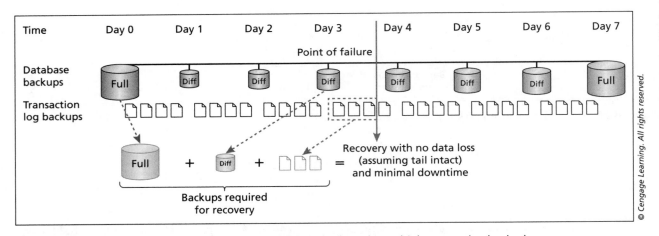

Figure 8-22 Full database backup plus differential database backup plus multiple transaction log backups

In addition to the database files, the host operating system should be backed up periodically—particularly when making significant changes to the system (e.g., prior to software installations).

Restore Operations

To recover a database using backups, the database administrator must first perform a sequence of restore operations. These can be performed by executing SQL commands or by using the Restore Database dialog box that is accessible from Object Explorer in SQL Server Management Studio. Before performing a restore operation, the tail of the transaction log should always be backed up to prevent any further data loss.

Restore operations must be performed sequentially, beginning with the most recent full database backup, followed by the most recent differential backup, and then the transaction log files in order, with no gaps. Finally, the database can be recovered. Once the recovery is complete, the logical and physical integrity of the database should be checked. While the restore operations are being performed, the database should be left in a nonoperational state to prevent uncommitted transactions from being rolled back and the database entering an inconsistent state. Figure 8-23 illustrates the sequence of events during a database recovery.

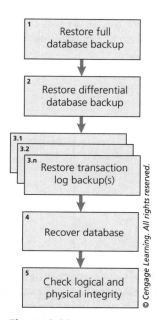

Figure 8-23 Sequence of events to recover a database

The SQL syntax for recovering a database is listed below. First, the database is restored from the full database backup:

```
RESTORE DATABASE <DatabaseName>

FROM <BackupDevice>

WITH NORECOVERY;
```

Next, the database is restored from the differential database backup:

```
RESTORE DATABASE <DatabaseName>

FROM <BackupDevice>

WITH NORECOVERY;
```

The logs are then applied in sequence, beginning with the oldest. The WITH FILE clause specifies the position of the file within a backup set:

```
RESTORE LOG <LogFileName>

FROM <BackupDevice>

WITH FILE = n

WITH NORECOVERY;
```

After all backups have been restored, the database is recovered. The WITH RECOVERY option applies the log file to either the point-in-time of the restore or the end of the log; then it rolls back any uncommitted transactions:

```
RESTORE DATABASE <DatabaseName>

WITH RECOVERY;
```

Finally the logical and physical integrity of the database should be checked for consistency errors by running the DBCC CHECKDB command:

```
DBCC CHECKDB ('<DatabaseName>')
```

If a point-in-time restore is desired rather than recovery to the present time, a STOPAT command can be issued with each of the transaction log restores that specifies a date and a time to restore to. For example:

```
RESTORE DATABASE <DatabaseName>

FROM <BackupDevice>

WITH NORECOVERY;

RESTORE LOG <LogFileName>

FROM <BackupDevice>

WITH NORECOVERY, STOPAT = 'Jul 4, 2010 10:42 AM';

RESTORE DATABASE <DatabaseName>

WITH RECOVERY;
```

Fortunately, database recovery tends to be a relatively rare event, but for this reason, it is important for a database administrator to frequently test the backup and recovery strategy. This ensures that in the event of a real disaster, the database administrator is sufficiently prepared to perform multiple restore operations in a situation that is likely to be chaotic and stressful.

Activity 8-4: Recovering a Database

Time Required: 45 minutes
Objective: Recover the database by restoring a full backup, differential backup, and transaction log backup.

Description: In this activity, you will recover the database. First, you'll delete the primary data file of the Backup Restore Test database to simulate a data loss scenario. You'll then recover the database by backing up the tail of the transaction log. Next, you'll restore a full backup, a differential backup, and a transaction log backup using the Restore Database dialog box in Object Explorer. After recovering the database, you will check the physical and logical integrity of the database.

1. To delete the primary data file of the Backup Restore Test database, you must take the database offline. In Object Explorer, right-click the **Backup Restore Test**, point to **Tasks**, and then click **Take Offline**. A Take Database Offline status dialog box opens. After it indicates that the action has successfully completed, click **Close**. You will now be able to delete the primary data file for the Backup Restore Test database.

You may experience delays in taking the database offline if you have open connections to the database.

2. Return to Windows File Explorer, which you left open at the end of the last activity. Navigate to the following folder location either by clicking through the folder hierarchy in the left navigation pane or by typing the file path in the Address bar:

C:\Program Files\Microsoft SQL Server\MSSQL11.SQLSERVERUA\MSSQL\DATA

Right-click the **BackupRestoreTest** MDF file, and then click **Delete**. The BackupRestoreTest MDF file should no longer appear in the Data folder. See Figure 8-24.

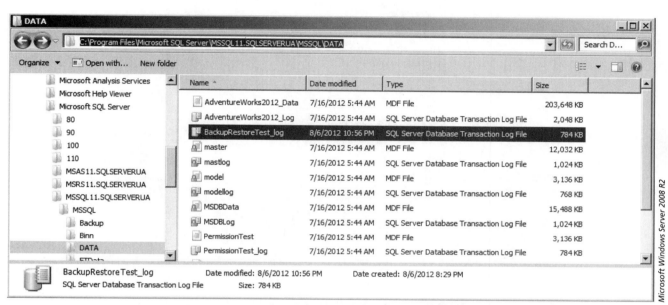

Figure 8-24 View the DATA folder using Windows Explorer

3. Return to Object Explorer in SQL Server Management Studio, right-click the **Backup Restore Test**, point to **Tasks**, and then click **Bring Online**. A Bring Database Online status dialog box opens and indicates that the operation has completed with errors. The cause of the error is the deletion of the primary data file that you performed in Step 2. Click **Close** to return to Object Explorer.

4. Before restoring the database, you will back up the tail of the transaction log to ensure that no changes are lost. In Object Explorer, expand the **Server Objects** folder, expand the **Backup Devices** folder, right-click the **Backup Restore Test_1** backup device, and then click **Back Up a Database** to launch the Back Up Database dialog box. On the General page, select **Backup Restore Test**from the Database drop-down list box, and then select **Transaction Log** from the Backup type drop-down list box. In the Destination section, click **Backup Restore Test_1** to select the backup device that you created in Activity 8-1. Keep the rest of the defaults. See Figure 8-25.

5. In the Back Up Database dialog box, click **Options** in the left navigation pane. In the Overwrite media section, keep the default options **Back up to the existing media set** and **Append to the existing backup set** selected. In the Reliability section, click the **Verify backup when finished** and **Perform checksum before writing to media** check boxes to select them. In the Transaction log section, click the **Back up the tail of the log, and leave the database in the restoring state** option button. See Figure 8-26.

Click **OK** to back up the tail of the transaction log. Click **OK** when the successful completion message box appears. Notice that the BackupRestoreTest database now displays "Restoring" in parentheses after the database name in Object Explorer.

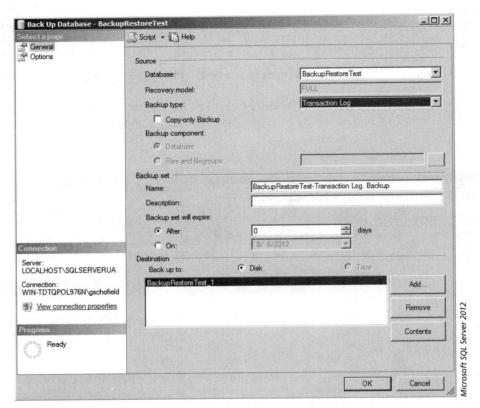

Figure 8-25 Back up the tail of the transaction log using the Back Up Database dialog box – General page

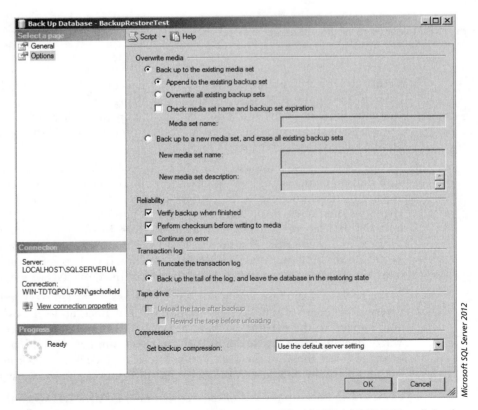

Figure 8-26 Back up the tail of the transaction log using the Back Up Database dialog box – Options page

6. You will now launch the Restore Database dialog box from Object Explorer. In Object Explorer, right-click the **BackupRestoreTest**, point to **Tasks**, click **Restore**, and then click **Database** to open the Restore Database dialog box. See Figure 8-27.

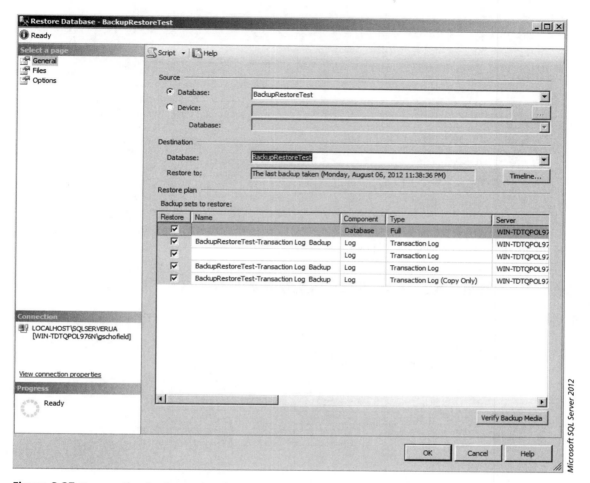

Figure 8-27 Recover the database using the Restore Database dialog box – General page

The General page of the Restore Database dialog box displays the name of the source database to restore and the destination for the backup. In this case, they are both the same. In some situations, such as a point-in-time recovery, you might want to recover the database to a different database. In the Backup sets to restore pane at the bottom of the window, you should see the backups that you performed in the last two activities as well as the transaction log tail backup that you performed in Step 4; all of these are available to use for the recovery.

7. On the General page of the Restore Database dialog box, click the **Timeline** button to open the Backup Timeline dialog box. See Figure 8-28.

This dialog box provides several options for specifying the point-in-time to which you want to recover the database. The default setting, which you will use for this activity, is Last backup taken. The Backup Timeline dialog box can also be used to specify a specific date and time for a point-in-time restore. You can also use the horizontal scrolling feature of the Timeline Interval to see the timing of the available backups. Click **OK**.

8. On the General page of the Restore Database dialog box, click the **Verify Backup Media** button to check the integrity of the backup sets. In the left navigation pane, click **Files**. See Figure 8-29. This page allows you to choose a different physical location to restore the database and log files to. Keep the default settings.

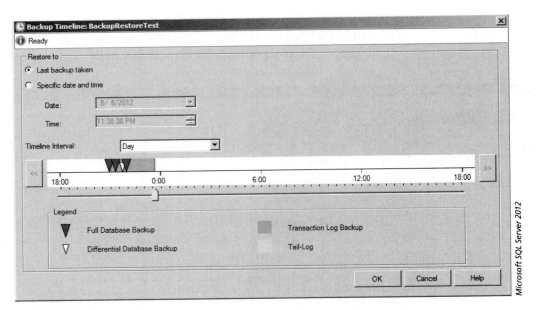

Figure 8-28 Backup Timeline dialog box

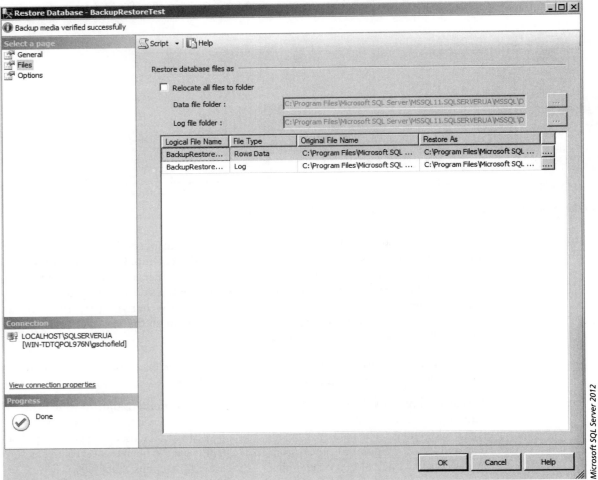

Figure 8-29 Restore the database using the Restore Database dialog box – Files page

9. In the left navigation pane of the Restore Database dialog box, click **Options**. In the Restore options section, click the **Overwrite the existing database (WITH REPLACE)** check box to select it. Click **RESTORE WITH RECOVERY** from the Recovery state drop-down list box. This option leaves the database ready to use once the recovery is complete. The Tail-log backup and Server connections sections are deactivated because you already took the database offline and backed up the tail of the transaction log earlier in this activity. See Figure 8-30.

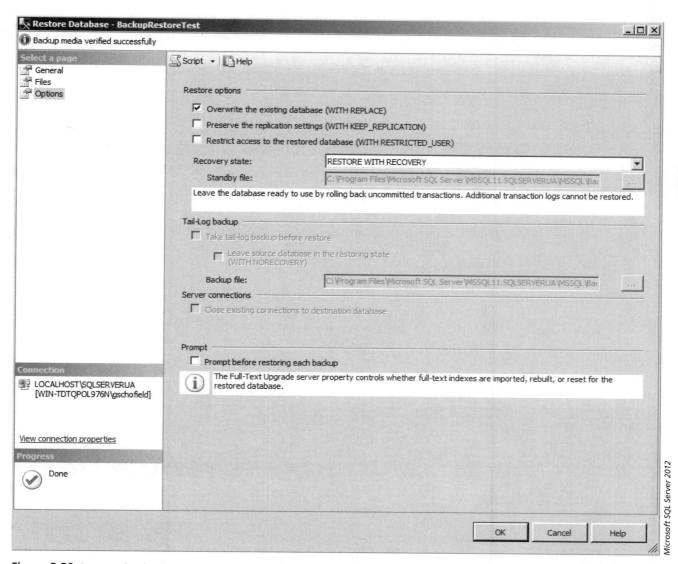

Figure 8-30 Restore the database using the Restore Database dialog box – Options page

10. On the toolbar of the Restore Database dialog box Options page, click the drop-down arrow on the right side of the **Script** button. Click **New Query Editor Window** from the Script options menu. Return to SQL Server Management Studio, and you will see the series of SQL commands that the Restore Database dialog box will execute in order to recover the database. See Figure 8-31.

11. Return to the Restore Database dialog box, and click **OK** to begin the restore operations. The information bar at the top of the dialog box displays the progress of the restore operations. Upon successful completion, a message box informs you that the database BackupRestoreTest restored successfully. Click **OK**.

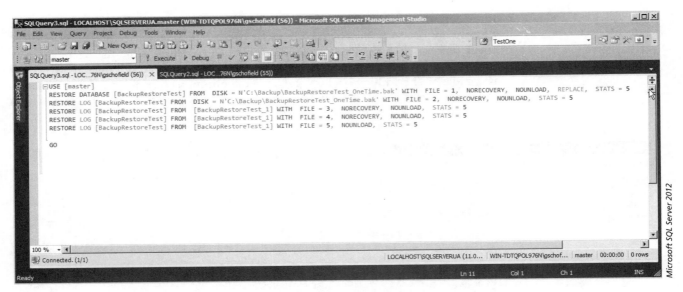

Figure 8-31 View the SQL code to restore the backups and recover the database

12. In SQL Server Management Studio, click **New Query**. In the Query Editor window, type the following SQL command to perform a consistency check on the recovered database.

```
DBCC CHECKDB (BackupRestoreTest);
```

Press the **F5** key, or click the **Execute** button to run the query. Review the output of the query in the Messages pane, and check that there are no allocation or consistency errors at the bottom of the Messages pane. See Figure 8-32.

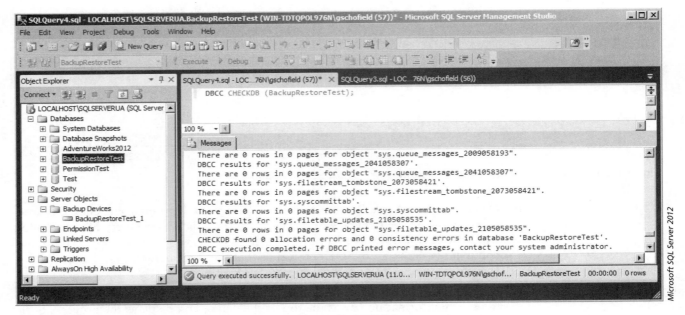

Figure 8-32 Check the database consistency by running the DBCC CHECKDB command

13. In the Query Editor window, delete the existing text and type the following SQL command to check the content of the test table:

```
SELECT *

FROM BackupRestoreTest.dbo.TestTable;
```

Press the F5 key or click the **Execute** button to run the query. Review the output of the query in the Messages pane, and check that there are no allocation or consistency errors at the bottom of the Messages pane. See Figure 8-33.

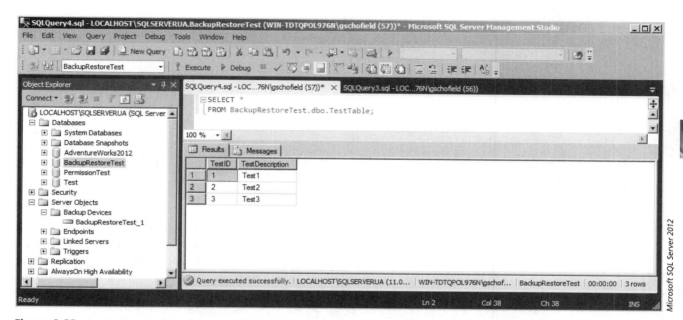

Figure 8-33 Check the records in the test table have been successfully recovered

14. You have now successfully completed this activity. Close any open Query Editor windows, but leave SQL Server Management Studio open for the next activity.

Backup Plan Automation Using SQL Server Agent

SQL Server Agent can be used to automate backup jobs along with other routine database maintenance functions. SQL Server provides a Maintenance Plan designer and wizard for creating routine database management tasks that include taking backups. The maintenance plan can be created to run on an ad hoc basis, or it can be added to a SQL Server Agent job schedule.

Activity 8-5: Automating Backup Tasks

Time Required: 60 minutes

Objective: Automate backup tasks using the Maintenance Plan Wizard and SQL Server Agent.

Description: In this activity, you will automate backup tasks using the Maintenance Plan Wizard and SQL Server Agent.

1. Return to SQL Server Management Studio, which you left open from the previous activity. In Object Explorer, expand the **Management** folder, right-click the **Maintenance Plans** folder, and then right-click **Maintenance Plan Wizard** to launch the SQL Server Maintenance Plan Wizard. See Figure 8-34. Click **Next**.

Figure 8-34 SQL Server Maintenance Plan Wizard starting page

2. In the Select Plan Properties window of the Maintenance Plan Wizard, type **Maintenance Plan - BackupRestoreTest** in the Name text box. Click the **Separate schedules for each task** option button, as you'll need to set up different schedules for each backup type. See Figure 8-35. Click **Next**.

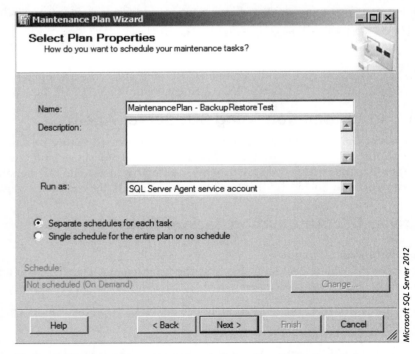

Figure 8-35 Maintenance Plan Wizard – Select Plan Properties window

3. In the Select Maintenance Tasks window of the Maintenance Plan Wizard, check the **Back Up Database (Full)**, **Back Up Database (Differential)**, and **Back Up Database (Transaction Log)** task check boxes to select them. See Figure 8-36. Click **Next**.

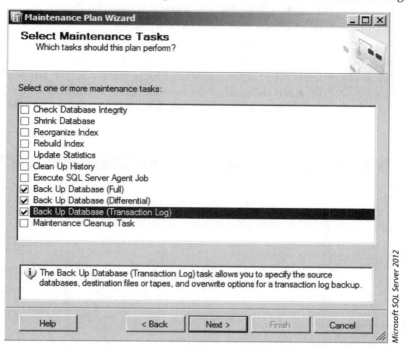

Figure 8-36 Maintenance Plan Wizard – Select Maintenance Tasks window

4. The Select Maintenance Task Order window of the Maintenance Plan Wizard is used to specify the order that tasks will run within a single schedule. See Figure 8-37. Because you will set up a separate schedule for each task, you do not need to specify the task order. Click **Next**.

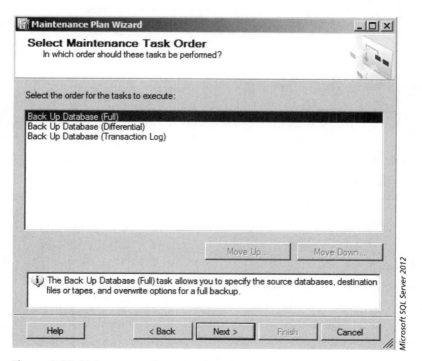

Figure 8-37 Maintenance Plan Wizard – Select Maintenance Task Order window

5. The Define Back Up Database (Full) Task window of the Maintenance Plan Wizard is used to configure the full database backup task. Click the Database(s) drop-down list arrow, click the **these databases** option button, click the **BackupRestoreTest** database check box, and then click **OK**. Click the **Back up databases across one or more files** option button, and then click the **Add** button.

6. In the Select Backup Destination dialog box, click the **Backup device** option button, and then select the **BackupRestoreTest_1** backup device from the drop-down list box. Click **OK** to return to the Maintenance Plan Wizard. Click the **Verify backup integrity** check box. Keep the system defaults for all other settings. See Figure 8-38. Click the **Change** button next to the Schedule section at the bottom of the window.

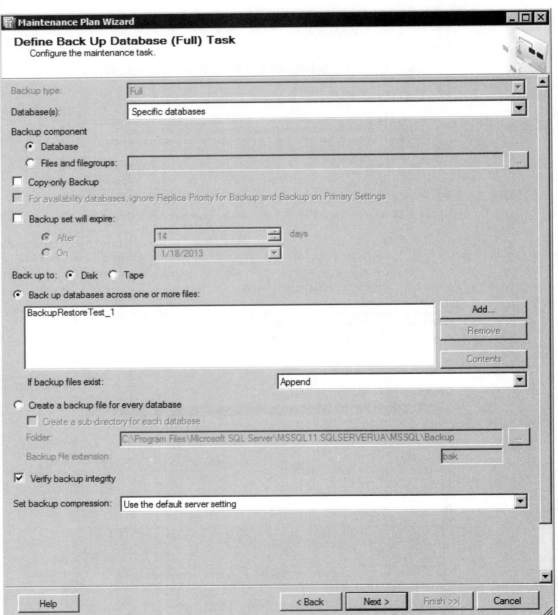

Figure 8-38 Maintenance Plan Wizard – Define Back Up Database (Full) Task window

7. In the New Job Schedule dialog box, keep the default settings. This creates a weekly schedule that will trigger the full database backup at 12:00 a.m. each Sunday. See Figure 8-39. Click **OK** to return to the Define Back Up Database (Full) Task window. Click **Next**.

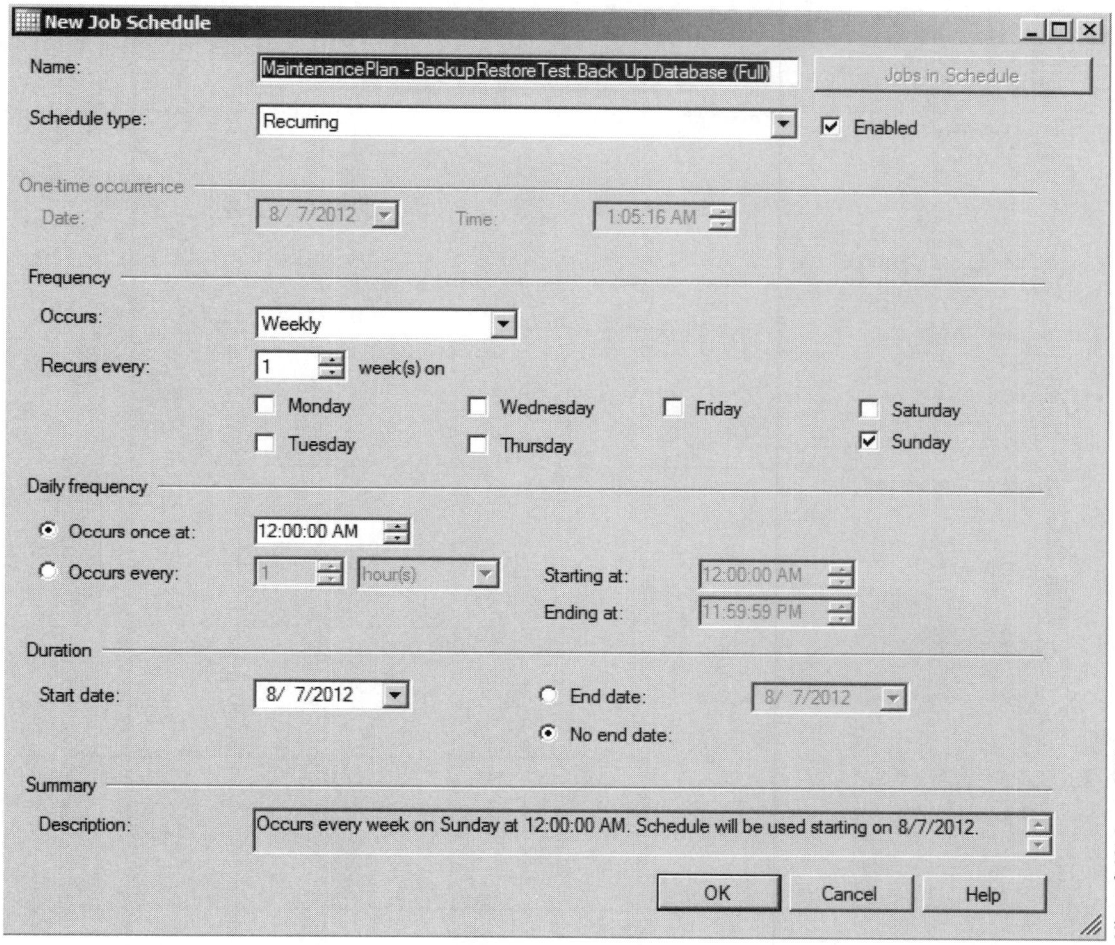

Figure 8-39 Maintenance Plan Wizard – New Job Schedule window

8. The Define Back Up Database (Differential) Task window of the Maintenance Plan Wizard is used to configure the differential database backup task. Click the Database(s) drop-down list arrow, click the **these databases** option button, click the **BackupRestoreTest** database check box, and then click **OK**. Click the **Back up databases across one or more files** option button, and then click the **Add** button.

9. In the Select Backup Destination dialog box, click the **Backup device** option button, and then select the **BackupRestoreTest_1** backup device from the drop-down list box. Click **OK** to return to the Maintenance Plan Wizard. Click the **Verify backup integrity** check box. Keep the system defaults for all other settings. See Figure 8-40. Click the **Change** button next to the Schedule section at the bottom of the window.

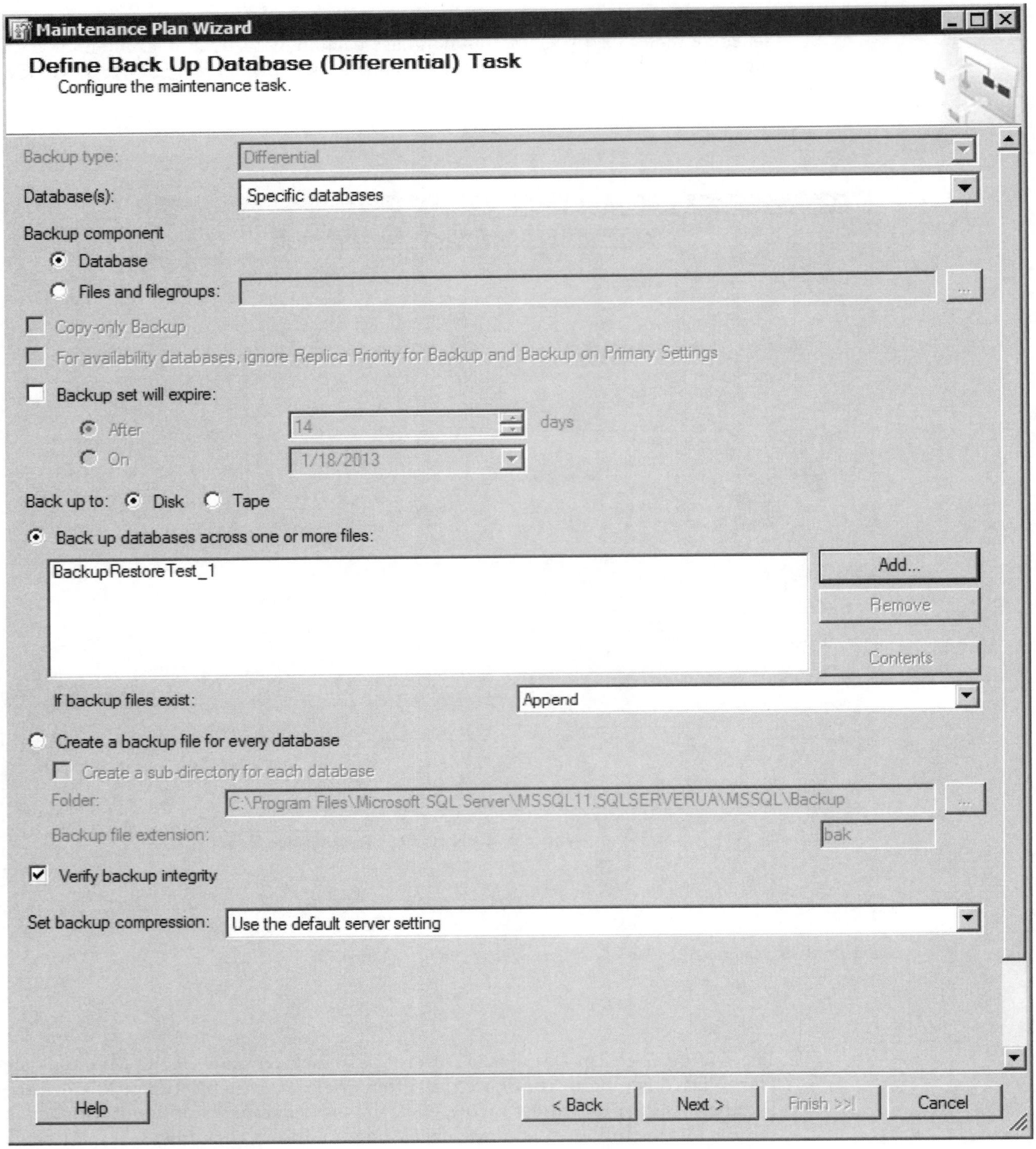

Microsoft SQL Server 2012

Figure 8-40 Maintenance Plan Wizard – Define Back Up Database (Differential) Task window

10. In the New Job Schedule dialog box, keep the default settings but change the recurrence by clicking the **Tuesday**, **Wednesday**, **Thursday**, **Friday**, and **Saturday** check boxes. This creates a weekly schedule that will trigger the differential database backup at 12:00 a.m. to back up the prior weekday's data. See Figure 8-41. Click **OK** to return to the Define Back Up Database (Differential) Task window. Click **Next**.

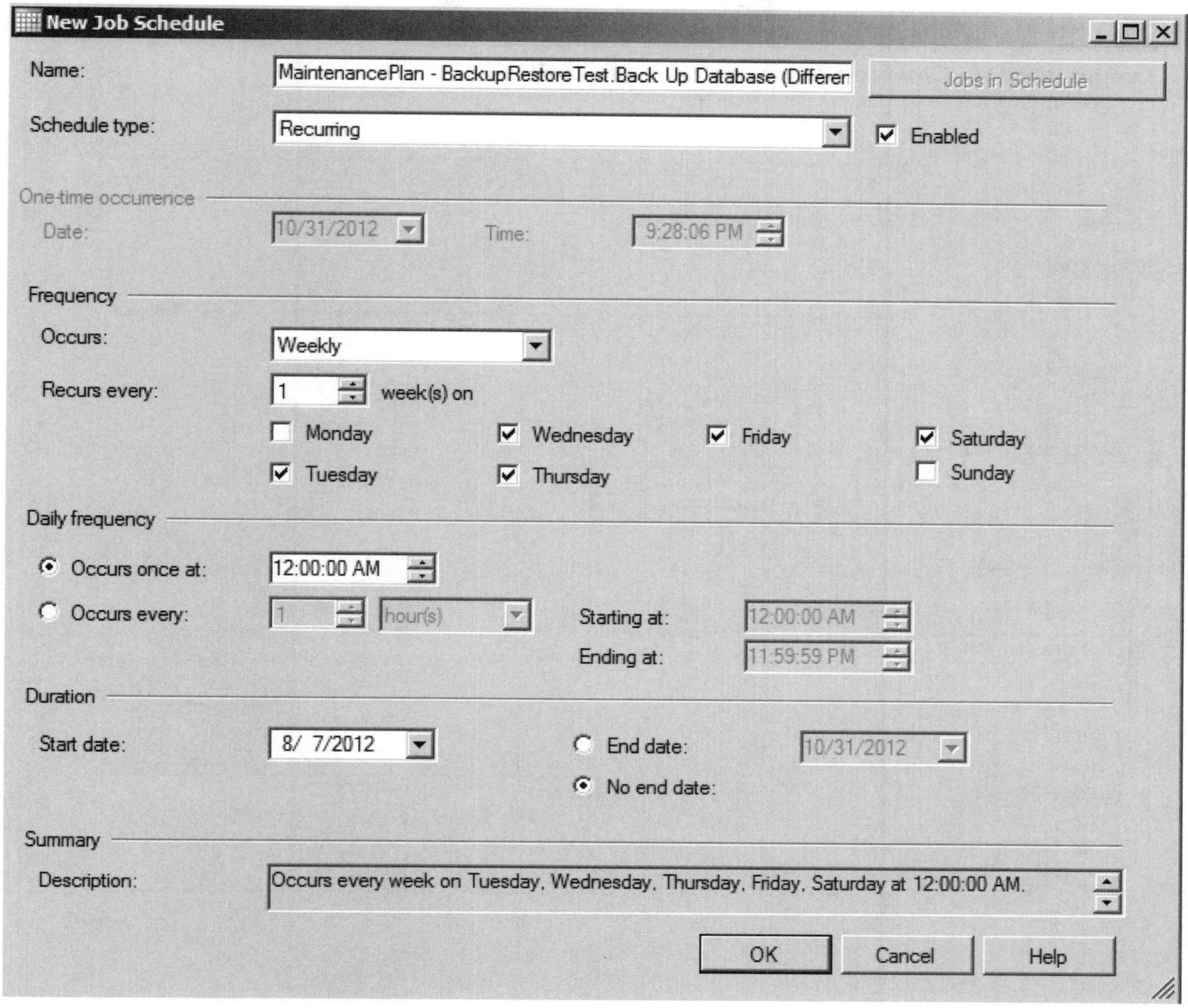

Figure 8-41 Maintenance Plan Wizard – schedule the differential database backup task

11. The Define Back Up Database (Transaction Log) Task window of the Maintenance Plan Wizard is used to configure the transaction log backup tasks. Click the Database(s) drop-down list arrow, click the **these databases** option button, click the **BackupRestoreTest** database check box, and then click **OK**. Click the **Back up databases across one or more files** option button, and then click the **Add** button.

12. In the Select Backup Destination dialog box, click the **Backup device** option button and select the **BackupRestoreTest_1** backup device from the drop-down list box. Click **OK** to return to the Maintenance Plan Wizard. Click the **Verify backup integrity** check box. Keep the system defaults for all other settings. See Figure 8-42. Click the **Change** button next to the Schedule section at the bottom of the window.

13. In the New Job Schedule dialog box, change the frequency to **Daily**, and set the recurrence to Occurs every **4 hour(s)**. Keep the rest of the default settings. See Figure 8-43. Click **OK** to return to the Define Back Up Database (Transaction Log) Task window. Click **Next**.

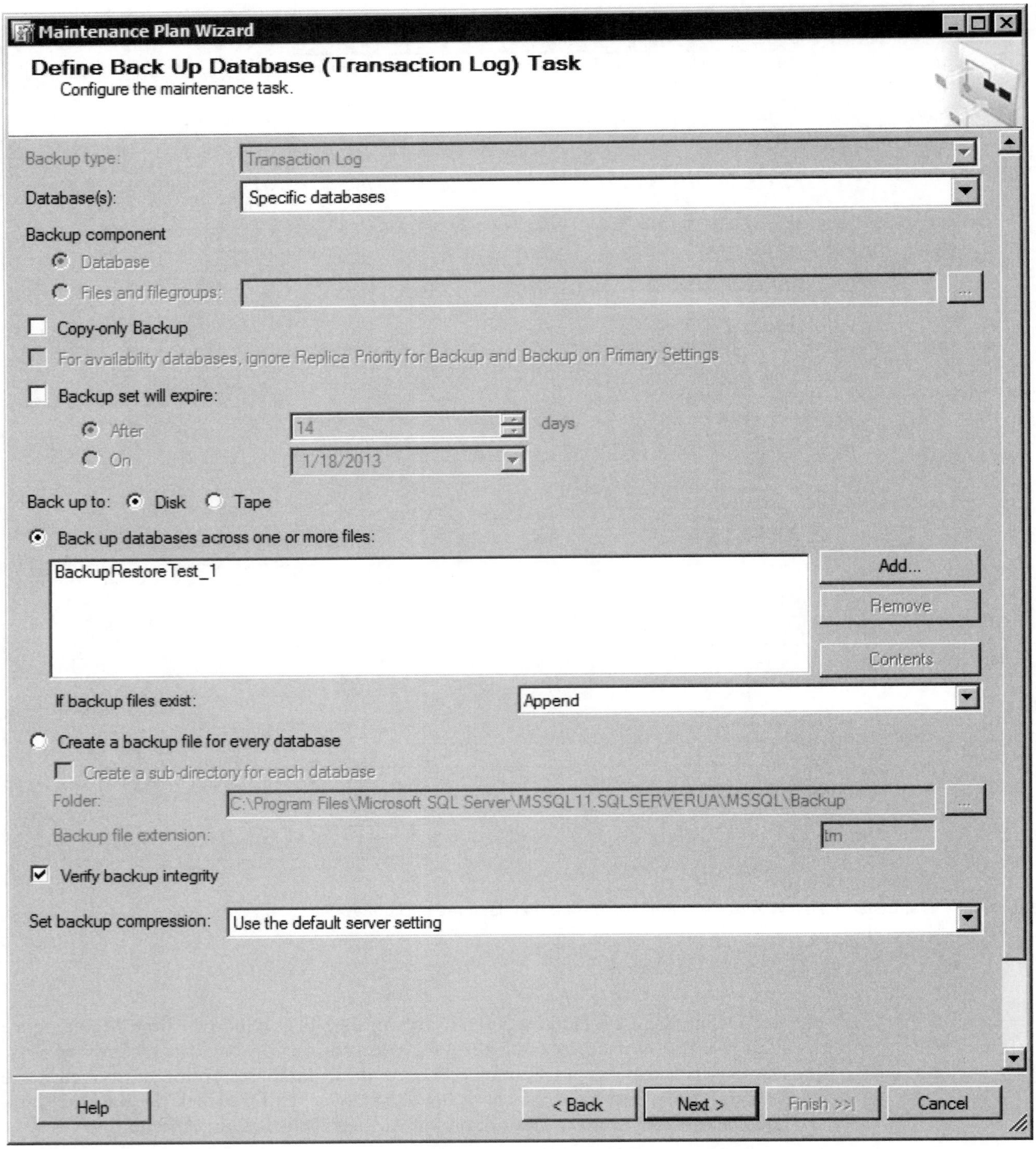

Maintenance Plan Wizard

Define Back Up Database (Transaction Log) Task
Configure the maintenance task.

Backup type:	Transaction Log
Database(s):	Specific databases

Backup component

○ Database

○ Files and filegroups: [   ] [...]

☐ Copy-only Backup

☐ For availability databases, ignore Replica Priority for Backup and Backup on Primary Settings

☐ Backup set will expire:

    ○ After [14] ⬍ days

    ○ On [1/18/2013 ▾]

Back up to: ● Disk ○ Tape

● Back up databases across one or more files:

BackupRestoreTest_1	Add...
	Remove
	Contents

If backup files exist: [Append ▾]

○ Create a backup file for every database

    ☐ Create a sub-directory for each database

    Folder: C:\Program Files\Microsoft SQL Server\MSSQL11.SQLSERVERUA\MSSQL\Backup [...]

    Backup file extension: [trn]

☑ Verify backup integrity

Set backup compression: [Use the default server setting ▾]

| Help | | < Back | Next > | Finish >>| | Cancel |

Microsoft SQL Server 2012

Figure 8-42 Maintenance Plan Wizard – Define Back Up Database (Transaction Log) Task window

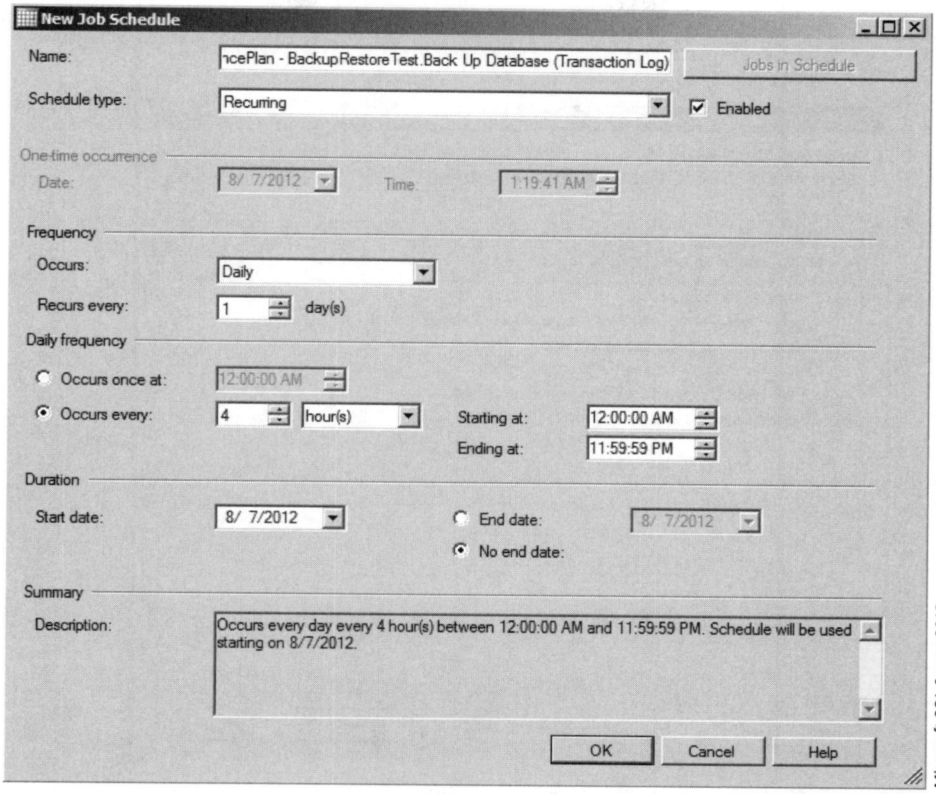

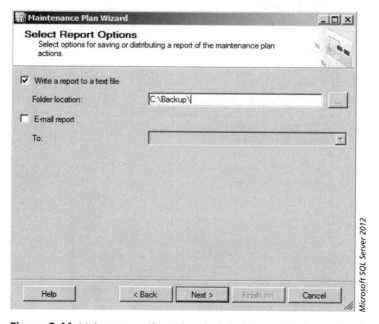

Figure 8-43 Maintenance Plan Wizard – New Job Schedule window

14. In the Select Report Options window of the Maintenance Plan Wizard, click the **Write a report to a text file** check box to select it, and then type **C:\Backup** in the Folder location text box. See Figure 8-44. Click **Next**.

Figure 8-44 Maintenance Plan Wizard – Select Report Options window

15. In the Complete the Wizard window of the Maintenance Plan Wizard, click **Finish**. See Figure 8-45.

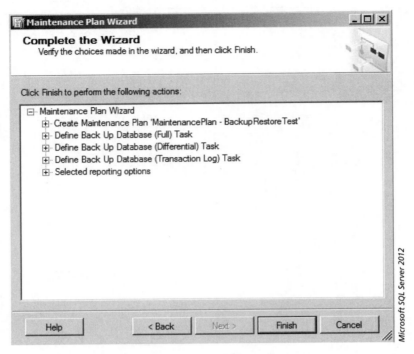

Figure 8-45 Maintenance Plan Wizard – Complete the Wizard window

16. A Maintenance Plan Wizard Progress window opens and provides a status of each step. See Figure 8-46. Once the wizard completes successfully, click **Close**. In Object Explorer of SQL Server Management Studio, click the **Refresh** button on the toolbar.

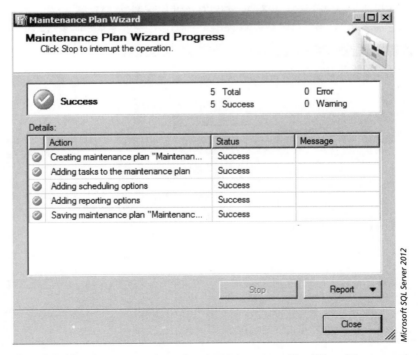

Figure 8-46 Maintenance Plan Wizard – Maintenance Plan Wizard Progress window

17. In Object Explorer, expand the **Management** folder, followed by the Maintenance Plans subfolder. Double-click **Maintenance Plan – BackupRestoreTest** to view details of the plan and subplans that you created. See Figure 8-47. Once it completes successfully, click **Close**. In Object Explorer of SQL Server Management Studio, click the **Refresh** button on the toolbar.

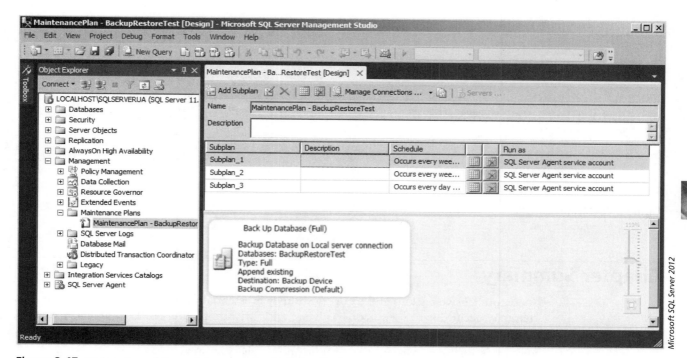

Figure 8-47 Design view of the maintenance plan in Object Explorer

18. In Object Explorer, right-click **SQL Server Agent**, and then click **Start**. Click **Yes** if prompted by the User Account Control dialog box. Click **Yes** when prompted by the "Are you sure you want to start the SQLAGENT$SQLSERVERUA service on <LocalHost>?"dialog box. After SQL Server Agent has successfully started, click the **+** icon next to it to expand the folder, and then expand the **Jobs** folder. You should see the three subplans, which you just created using the Maintenance Plan Wizard.

19. Right-click **Maintenance Plan – BackupRestoreTest.Subplan_1**, and then click **Start Job at Step**. Click **Close** once the Start Jobs dialog box displays a success status. Return to Windows File Explorer, and navigate to **C:\Backup**. Double-click the file that begins with **Maintenance Plan – BackupRestoreTest_Subplan**. This is the log from the SQL Server Agent job that you ran. See Figure 8-48. After you have reviewed the log and validated that the job has completed successfully with no error or warning messages, you can close SQL Server Management Studio and Windows File Explorer.

Other Considerations

This chapter has covered the basic backup and recovery features that are available within SQL Server 2012. The AlwaysOn capabilities in SQL Server 2012 offer several additional features that can be used to provide high availability and advanced disaster recovery capabilities such as mirroring, replication, and failover. These features augment but should not replace the time-proven approach of taking regular backups that can be used to restore the database in the event of data loss.

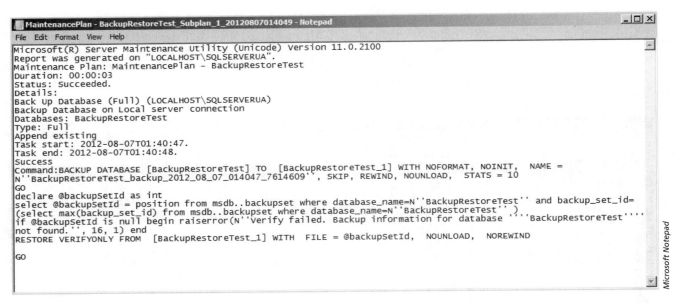

Figure 8-48 Maintenance Plan log from SQL Server Agent job

Chapter Summary

- A comprehensive backup and recovery strategy is essential to safeguard against loss of data that may occur due to user error, hardware and software failure, or environmental changes.

- Partnership with the business teams and a strong emphasis on risk management are the keys to designing a cost-effective backup and recovery strategy.

- Backup and restore functionality is available on all editions of SQL Server 2012 and can be used to limit data loss.

- A backup is the process of taking a copy of a database file, which can later be used to restore the database in the event of a data loss.

- Risk assessment should be undertaken to identify and objectively quantify all potential data loss scenarios within four broad categories of risk: user error, hardware failure, software failure, and environmental events.

- Evaluation of business requirements should consider database availability, data value, size of the data, performance requirements, the rate of change, and interdependencies.

- Each production database should have a set of recovery objectives that define the acceptable level of data loss and the amount of downtime before resumption of normal operations.

- A backup consists of making a copy of the data files that will be used to restore data in the event of a loss. There are two types of database backup: full and differential.

- A full database backup makes a copy of all nonempty pages in a data file, and it also creates a duplicate of the section of the transaction log for transactions that occurred during the backup. Full database backups are the foundation of any backup and recovery strategy because a normal database restore operation requires a full backup of the database. Full database backups are resource intensive and normally only performed periodically during maintenance windows or periods of low activity.

- Differential backups only copy pages that have changed since the last full database backup and are, therefore, less resource intensive.

- The recovery model configuration setting specifies which database transactions should be recorded in the transaction log.

- Transaction logs record changes that occur to the data in a database over time. To recover lost data within a database that occurred after the last full or differential backup, one or more sequential transaction logs must be available from backup to apply the most recent activity to the database.

- Restore operations should be performed sequentially, beginning with the most recent full database backup, followed by the most recent differential backup, and then the transaction log files in order, with no gaps. Finally, the database can be recovered.

- Once a database recovery is complete, the logical and physical integrity of the database should be checked for consistency errors.

- SQL Server provides a Maintenance Plan designer and wizard for creating routine database management tasks that are automated using SQL Server Agent.

Key Terms

backup   The process of taking a copy of a database file that can later be used to restore the database should a loss of data occur.

backup device   A logical storage device that references a physical location where backup sets will be stored.

backup set   The file that is the result of a backup operation.

bulk logged recovery model   A recovery model setting that selectively logs changes to the database; in particular, it excludes logging data related to bulk transactions.

bulk transaction   A large update to data, such as the insertion of data in a bulk copy operation.

checksum   A unique variable that is computed based on the data contained in a page and used to verify the integrity of that data.

differential database backup   A type of database backup in which copies are made only of pages that have changed since the last full database backup; less resource intensive than a full database backup.

expiration date   A date assigned to a backup set; helps to ensure that existing backups on the media will not be overwritten until a specified time in the future.

file (or filegroup) backup   A type of database backup in which a database backup is broken into smaller units (files or filegroups) for performance reasons.

full database backup   A type of database backup in which a copy of all nonempty pages in a data file is made; in a full database backup, the section of the transaction log for transactions that occurred during the backup is also copied.

full recovery model   A recovery model setting that causes all changes to the database to be written to the transaction log.

partial backup   A type of database backup in which only data in the primary filegroup and read-write filegroups are backed up by default.

recovery model   A type of configuration setting that specifies which type of database transactions should be recorded in the transaction log.

recovery point objective (RPO)   The maximum amount of data that may be lost, expressed as a time frame.

recovery time objective (RTO)   The amount of downtime that should be expected by the business before the system can be restored.

risk assessment   A process undertaken to identify and objectively quantify all potential data loss scenarios.

simple recovery model   A recovery model setting that causes the database engine not to record any events in the transaction log.

tail   The active transaction log that contains the database changes since the last transaction log backup.

transaction logs A database log that records changes that occur to the data in a database over time.

truncation A process that occurs each time a database is backed up; causes space to be made available in the active transaction log for recording new activity.

Review Questions

1. What are the main categories of risk that may result in data loss?

   a. Operational

   b. Legal and reputational

   c. Financial

   d. User error, hardware and software failure, and environmental change

2. What are the main recovery objectives?

   a. Point-in-time recovery

   b. Minimizing data loss and system downtime

   c. High availability

   d. None of the above

3. How much should an organization invest in backup and recovery?

   a. An amount that is commensurate with the value of the data being protected

   b. As a rule of thumb, between 20 and 30 percent of the IT budget

   c. The minimum necessary to meet regulatory requirements

   d. The amount necessary to fully protect the business against any data loss scenario

4. Differential database backups are useful because they_____.

   a. are less resource intensive than a full database backup

   b. simplify recovery operations by reducing the number of transaction log files that must be restored

   c. reduce the number of backups that must be performed

   d. Both options a and b

5. Which of the following is *not* a valid recovery model?

   a. Bulk logged

   b. Transactional

   c. Full

   d. Simple

6. Which of the following are *not* suitable candidates for using the simple recovery model?

   a. Online transactional databases with a high rate of change

   b. Read-only databases

   c. System databases

   d. Nonproduction databases

7. What is the maximum amount of data that can be lost when taking a single transaction log backup just prior to a full database backup?

   a. No data loss, assuming that the active transaction log is available

   b. All changes since the last full backup, if the active transaction log is unrecoverable

   c. None of the above

   d. Both options a and b

8. What action should be taken to reduce the amount of downtime associated with restoring multiple transaction logs?

    a. Perform periodic differential database backups

    b. Decrease the frequency of taking backups

    c. Change the recovery model to simple mode

    d. Both options a and c

9. In what order should you restore backups to recover a database?

    a. Full, differential, and transaction logs applied sequentially, starting with the oldest, and without gaps in the history

    b. Order is not important if the database is nonoperational

    c. Transaction logs applied sequentially, differential, and full

    d. None of the above

Case Projects

CASE PROJECTS

Case Project 8-1: Defining Recovery Objectives

Choose an organization you are familiar with, for example your place of work, the college or university that you attend, or a local community organization. Complete the following:

- Complete an evaluation of the data loss risks that the organization faces.
- Conduct a short interview with a member of the organization to capture the data requirements.
- Define a set of recovery objectives based on the risk assessment and analysis of the business requirements.
- Document your findings at each step.

Case Project 8-2: Dave Bench Consulting LLC

Dave Bench Consulting LLC specializes in change management. Its major client, a publicly listed company, has recently made a new acquisition of a small privately held company, which needs to be integrated into the client's Sarbanes-Oxley audit process. Dave Bench, the principal, has accepted a consulting engagement to assist the client with this transition, but he has limited technical knowledge of database recovery planning. Dave is concerned about the absence of a well-documented business continuity plan, and he has contacted you informally to learn more about database backup and recovery. Complete the following:

- Explain the main objectives of a backup and recovery strategy.
- Outline the main types of backup plans and how they can be used to meet different recovery objectives.

Case Project 8-3: Gourmet Importers LLC

You work as a database administrator for Gourmet Importers LLC a wholesale merchant that specializes in importing gourmet foods from Europe for sale in the North American market. You are in the final stages of deploying a new stock inventory system and you recently met with the vice president of operations to discuss her business requirements. Based on your discussion—and after a thorough analysis of the data loss risks—you have agreed upon a recovery time objective of four hours and a recovery point objective of 30 minutes, except in the event of the loss of the on-premises data center. There is a daily maintenance window between midnight and 2:00 a.m. and a weekly maintenance window for 12 hours each Sunday. During these periods, the database may be taken offline. Complete the following:

- Design a backup plan that will meet the agreed-upon recovery objectives, and state any assumptions that you made when designing your plan.

- Several months later, Gourmet Importers has decided to create an online distribution platform that will be integrated with the inventory system. This platform will need to be available to customers on a 24/7 basis. Outline the impact that this change in scope may have on your existing plan.

Hands-On Projects

Hands-On Project 8-1: Recovering from Accidental Deletion of Data

For this hands-on project, you will use the SQL Server named instance SQLSERVERHOA and the HandsOnOne database and tables that you created in previous chapters. The objective of this project is to practice recovering data that was accidentally deleted by a user. Document each step by taking screen shots of the configuration settings and/or query execution results.

1. In SQL Server Management Studio, create a new backup device named HandsOnOne in the destination folder C:\Backup\.
2. Perform a full backup of the HandsOnOne database to the HandsOnOne backup device.
3. Use Query Editor to create and execute a SQL statement that returns all records from the customer table.
4. In this step, you will simulate the accidental deletion of all records from the customer table. Use a second Query Editor window to create and execute a SQL statement that deletes all records from the customer table in the HandsOnOne database.
5. Back up the tail of the HandsOnOne database transaction log, appending it to the existing backup set.
6. Restore the HandsOnOne database to the point in time prior to the deletion of customer records.
7. Use a new Query Editor window to write and execute a SQL statement that returns all records from the customer table in order to validate that the customer records deleted in Step 3 have been successfully recovered.

Hands-On Project 8-2: Creating a Scheduled Backup Plan

For this hands-on project, you will use the SQL Server named instance SQLSERVERHOA, the HandsOnOne database and tables that you created in previous chapters, and the HandsOnOne backup device created in the previous activity. The objective of this activity is to create a scheduled backup plan for the HandsOnOne database given certain business constraints.

1. In SQL Server Management Studio, use the Maintenance Plan Wizard to create a backup plan for the HandsOnOne database given the following constraints:
   a. The HandsOnOne database is actively used by the business six days per week (Monday to Saturday).
   b. You are permitted to perform system maintenance at any time each Sunday.
   c. There is minimal user activity on the database between 9:00 p.m. and midnight each day.
   d. The business has specified that it can risk losing no more than one hour of data. Document this step by taking screen shots of the configuration settings.
2. Manually trigger each job in the plan and review the log file to verify that it has completed successfully. Document this step by saving a copy of each log file.

chapter 9

Data Integration

After reading this chapter and completing the exercises, you will be able to:

- Compare the different SQL Server management tools and utilities that can be used to integrate data from external sources

- Design a SQL Server Integration Services package using both the SQL Server Import and Export Wizard and SQL Server Data Tools

- Construct commands that utilize the bulk copy interface to import and export data from a SQL Server database

The ability to integrate with other data sources is an important feature of a database management system. A database administrator might need to integrate other data sources with a SQL Server database to accomplish a variety of goals. In some cases, a one-time load of data might be sufficient. In other cases, a database administrator might need to set up a batch process that moves data on a regular schedule. For example, a recurring data integration batch process might be required to incorporate supplier or customer data into an online transactional database or to take a regular snapshot of data that will be stored in a data warehouse for reporting and analytical use.

SQL Server Data Integration Tools and Utilities

The process of data integration involves extracting, transforming, and loading (ETL) data. Data transformations include data type conversions, calculated field updates, and information summarization. SQL Server offers several different management tools that can help facilitate the data integration process. When selecting the appropriate data integration tool for a given situation, a database administrator should consider a variety of factors, including performance, data source type, source file schema, and any logic that must be applied to transform the data as it is moved between the external source and the SQL Server database.

In Chapter 3, you learned that one approach to integrating an external data source is to configure a linked server, which enables a data source to be queried directly from within SQL Server. This technique works well for static data sources but it has limitations when dealing with dynamic sources of data. For example, if a vendor sends over a daily file that has a time stamp appended to the filename, the linked server object would have to be reconfigured with the new filename each day to be able to successfully connect to the file.

Two data integration frameworks supported by SQL Server provide greater flexibility in dealing with situations that involve variable filenames, data transformation, and workflow: SQL Server Integration Services (SSIS) and the bulk copy interface.

SQL Server Integration Services (SSIS) is a component of SQL Server that can be used to integrate many different types of external data sources, while applying complex business rules and workflow logic during the integration process. The first section of this chapter focuses on SQL Server Integration Services, including the following two tools, which can be used to design an Integration Services solution:

- The **SQL Server Import and Export Wizard** provides step-by-step instructions for designing a solution that meets basic data integration needs.

- **SQL Server Data Tools** is a comprehensive development environment that can be used to create a solution that caters to more complex data integration situations.

The **bulk copy interface** enables a client application to efficiently perform bulk copy operations between a view or table on a SQL Server database and an external data file. The second section of the chapter covers the following two methods of moving data that leverage the bulk copy interface:

- The **bcp utility** is a stand-alone application that is run from a command prompt and that can be used for bidirectional data transfers.

- The **BULK INSERT** SQL statement can be executed to insert records from an external data file source into a SQL Server table.

SQL Server Integration Services

SQL Server Integration Services, sometimes referred to simply as SSIS or Integration Services, is a component of SQL Server 2012 that offers powerful and flexible data integration, transformation, and workflow capabilities. You installed Integration Services when you installed SQL Server 2012 as part of the activities in Chapter 2. Integration Services was introduced with SQL Server 2005

(Version 9.0), and it replaced **Data Transformation Services (DTS)**, a legacy data integration tool with a graphical designer that had a limited range of functionality. Integration Services offers several different design tools that enable a database administrator to develop solutions that move data between locations and inject complex business logic into the process to selectively modify data. In addition to data integration capabilities, Integration Services also supports integration of workflow into the process that includes tasks, event handlers, constraints, and variables. This section introduces two main Integration Services designer tools that can be used to create and debug packages: the SQL Server Import and Export Wizard and SQL Server Data Tools within Visual Studio 2010 and Visual Studio 2012.

Integration Services Packages

An **SSIS package** groups together a set of one or more tasks—as a series of logical steps—into a single object that can be executed using the SQL Server Integration Services service. A package is stored with a .dtsx file extension irrespective of the method used to create it. The basic building blocks within an SSIS package are known as **tasks**, each of which performs a specific activity or function. There are many different types of tasks that can be added to an SSIS package. These are categorized broadly by the function they perform and include the following:

- **Data flow tasks** move data between a source and a destination, and they may include transformations that manipulate the data as it is moved. For example, if the data types differ between the source and destination, a transformation component may be used to convert the source data type to the destination data type. Transformations may also be used to filter or summarize data.

- **Data preparation tasks** perform file or directory operations. Examples of data preparation tasks include downloading a data file from an FTP site or creating, renaming, deleting, or moving a data file or directory on the Windows file system.

- **Workflow tasks** permit the package to interact with other applications. Examples of workflow tasks include executing another SSIS package, sending email alerts, or launching a batch process.

- **Scripting tasks** allow custom code to be executed to extend the functionality of the basic set of tasks. For example, a script may be used to dynamically populate a variable with a formatted date that can then be used to append a time stamp to a data file.

- **SQL Server tasks** perform operations on schema objects and data on a SQL server. A SQL Server task can be used to execute a SQL query.

- **Analysis Service tasks** enable an SSIS package to interact with SQL Server Analysis Services to process data or perform a data mining operation.

- **Maintenance tasks** perform essential database maintenance functions, including rebuilding an index or completing database backups. During Chapter 8, you used the Maintenance Wizard to create an SSIS package to back up the database on a regular schedule.

The order in which each task is executed in an SSIS package is known as the **control flow**. Precedence constraints can be added between tasks in the control flow to determine under what conditions the subsequent tasks in the control flow should run, and, therefore, the overall sequence. The constraints that can be set are: on success, on error, and on completion. **Event handlers** are software routines that specify what should happen if a certain event occurs during package execution; for example, an event handler could be used to specify that an email alert should be sent if an error occurs. **User variables** can be configured to store values within a package; they are set either with a static value or at run time.

In this chapter, we are primarily interested in the data flow task, which is used to move data between a source and a destination. Integration Services supports a wide range of data sources for use within the data flow task. Data sources are defined using a **connection manager**, an object that stores the configuration information necessary to connect to the data source. A data flow task consists of one or more **data flow components**, which are a series of connected steps within a data flow. A data flow task may include one or more data flows, but, unlike the sequence in a control flow, which is determined by the precedence constraints, the order of execution within a data flow task is determined by the data flow engine within Integration Services. **Transformation components** that manipulate data during the data flow can be added as the data moves between the source and the destination.

Figure 9-1 illustrates a typical control flow within an Integration Services package, which includes data flow components in a data flow task.

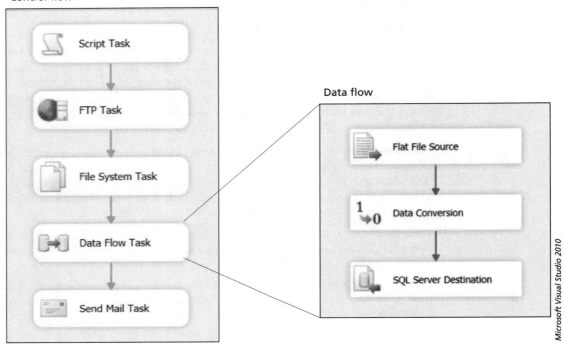

Figure 9-1 An illustration of the control flow within a typical Integration Services package, which includes data flow components in a data flow task

A hypothetical scenario that follows the flow shown in Figure 9-1 could start with a script task that is executed to dynamically calculate and set user-defined variables, such as the current date. Next, an FTP task downloads a flat file with the current date appended to the filename. A **flat file** is a text file that contains data. Each row in a flat file represents a record, and individual fields within a record either occupy a fixed number of characters or are separated by a special character known as a delimiter. Common delimiters include commas and semicolons. A file system task is then used to rename the downloaded file. The data flow task moves data from the downloaded file to a SQL Server table and performs a data type conversion for several fields within the data flow using the data conversion component. Finally, after the data load has successfully completed, the send mail task will send an email to a notification list.

SQL Server Import and Export Wizard

As explained earlier, the SQL Server Import and Export Wizard provides step-by-step instructions for designing a solution that meets basic data integration needs. The wizard moves data between a source and a destination, albeit with a limited range of data transformation capabilities. The SQL Server Import and Export Wizard enables a database administrator to quickly define a source connection, a destination connection, and the data mappings between the source and the destination. Although its functionality is limited, the wizard is an excellent introduction to Integration Services, and it is useful for quickly setting up an ad hoc process to move data.

Activity 9-1: Importing and Exporting Data Using the SQL Server Import and Export Wizard

Time Required: 45 minutes

Objective: Move data between SQL Server and a data file using the SQL Server Import and Export Wizard.

Description: In this activity, you will move data between a flat file and a SQL Server table using the SQL Server Import and Export Wizard to create a SQL Server Integration Services package.

1. If necessary, start your computer and log on.

2. For the activities in this chapter, you will use a flat file containing a list of country codes and names. Click the **Start** button, point to **All Programs,** and then click **Internet Explorer.** Type the following text in the Address bar: **www.iso.org/iso /country_names_and_code_elements_txt.** Press the **Enter** key. See Figure 9-2.

Figure 9-2 A delimited list of country names and code elements is available on the Web site of the International Organization for Standardization (ISO)

3. Click **File,** and then click **Save As.** In the left navigation pane of the Save Webpage dialog box, click **Computer,** and then double-click **Local Disk (C:)** to navigate to the C:\Downloads folder. Double-click **Downloads.** Note that if the Downloads folder does not exist, you should create it by navigating to the C:\ drive in the Save Webpage dialog box and clicking the **New Folder** button on the toolbar. In the File name text box, type **country_codes,** click **Text File (*.txt)** from the Save as type drop-down list box, and then click **Unicode UTF-8** in the Encoding drop-down list box. See Figure 9-3. Click the **Save** button.

4. Click the **Start** button, point to **All Programs,** click **Accessories,** and then click **Note-pad.** Click **File** on the menu bar, and then click **Open.** In the left navigation pane of the Open dialog box, click **Computer,** and then double-click **Local Disk (C:)** to navigate to the C:\Downloads folder. Double-click **Downloads.** In the folder view, click the **country_codes** file, and then click **Open.**

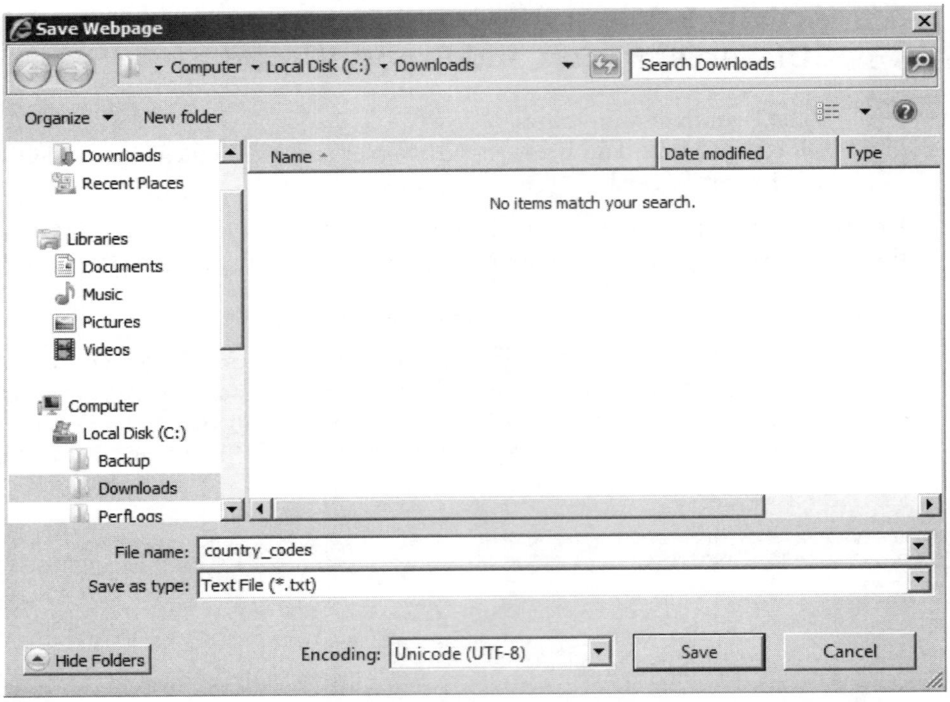

Microsoft Windows Server 2008 R2

Figure 9-3 The Save Webpage dialog box can be used to save the ISO country names and code elements to a text file

5. Familiarize yourself with the content of the country_codes.txt file, which contains country name and country code fields separated by a semicolon. The file has a header row at the top that contains column names. Scroll down to the bottom of the file, and delete any blank lines. Figure 9-4 shows a file with two blank lines at the end of the file that should be deleted.

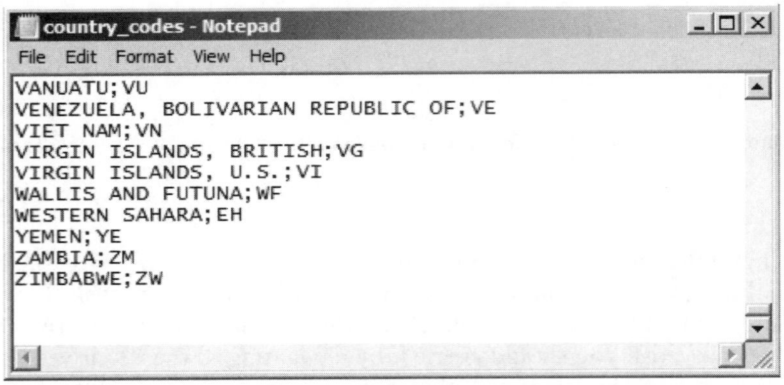

Microsoft Windows Server 2008 R2

Figure 9-4 The country list and code elements text file may contain empty records at the end of the file that should be removed

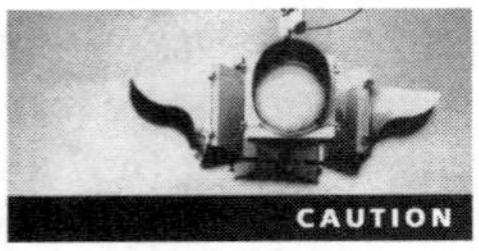

For an import operation to be successful, the syntax of every line in the file should be consistent. An empty line will cause an error.

6. Click the **Start** button, point to **All Programs**, click **Microsoft SQL Server 2012**, and then click **SQL Server Management Studio**. In the Connect to Server dialog box, select **Database Engine** as the server type, type **LOCALHOST\SQLSERVERUA** in the Server name text box, and then select **Windows Authentication** from the Authentication list box. Click **Connect**.

7. In Object Explorer, click the **SQLSERVERUA** root folder of the new connection. Click **New Query**. In Query Editor, type the following SQL query to create a new database with a single table, which you will use for testing backup and restore operations throughout this chapter:

```
CREATE DATABASE ImportExportTest;

GO

CREATE TABLE ImportExportTest.dbo.Country

(CountryName varchar(100) NOT NULL,

IsoCode char(2) NOT NULL);

GO
```

Press the **F5** key, or click the **Execute** button to run the query. See Figure 9-5.

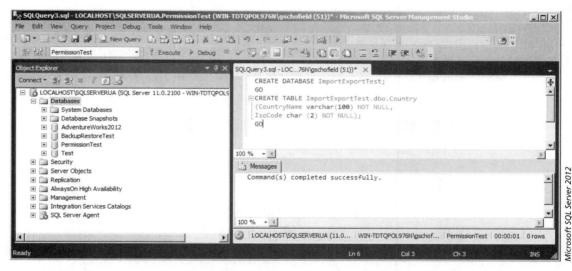

Figure 9-5 Execute a SQL command using Query Editor to create a new database with a single table for testing backup and restore operations

8. Click the **Start** button, point to **All Programs**, and then click **Microsoft SQL Server 2012**. If you are running a 64-bit Windows operating system, you will see two Import and Export data options: a 64-bit and a 32-bit version. If you are running a 32-bit Windows operating system, you will only see a single version. For the purpose of this activity, it does not matter which option you use. Click **Import and Export data (64-bit)** to launch the SQL Server Import and Export Wizard. See Figure 9-6.

9. In the SQL Server Import and Export Wizard, click **Next**. In the Choose a Data Source window of the wizard, select **Flat File Source** from the Data source drop-down list box. Click the **Browse** button. In the left navigation pane of the Open dialog box, click **Computer**, and then double-click **Local Disk (C:)**. Double-click **Downloads**. In the folder view, click the **country_codes** file and then click **Open** to exit the dialog box and return to the wizard. Leave the default values for all other fields. See Figure 9-7.

Figure 9-6 The launch page of the SQL Server Import and Export Wizard

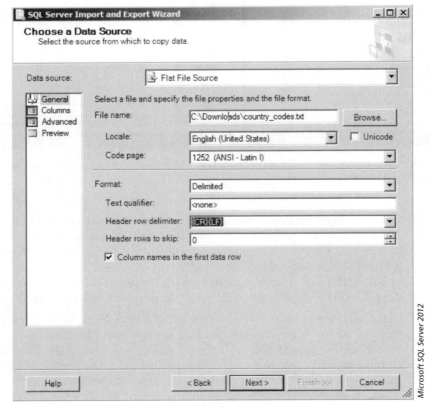

Figure 9-7 Choose a Data Source window in the SQL Server Import and Export Wizard

10. In the left pane of the Choose a Data Source window, click **Columns**. On this page, you'll define the characters that delimit the columns and rows. Note that the wizard has already preselected these delimiters and displays a preview of the data. See Figure 9-8.

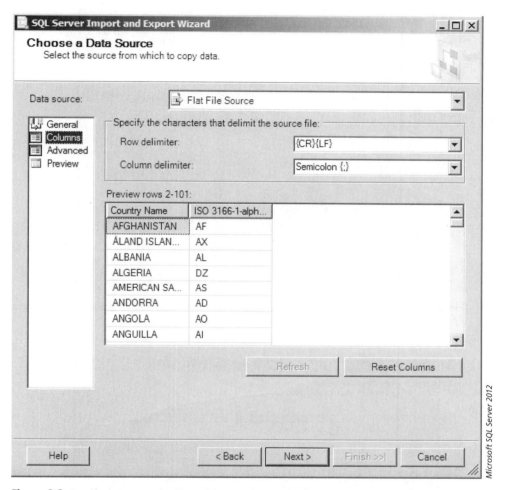

Figure 9-8 Specify the row and column delimiters for the flat file source in the SQL Server Import and Export Wizard

11. In the left pane of the Choose a Data Source window, click **Advanced**. On this page, you'll configure the output properties for each column to match the data type of the columns in the table that you created in Step 7. The Country Name column should be selected in the middle pane. In the right pane, type **100** in the OutputColumnWidth field. Next, click **ISO 3166-1-alpha-2 code** in the middle column, and then type **2** in the OutputColumnWidth field. See Figure 9-9.

12. In the left pane of the Choose a Data Source window, click **Preview**. This page displays a preview of the first 100 rows in the file. On this page, you can also specify the number of data rows, if any, you want to skip at the start of the file when the package executes. Leave the Data rows to skip field set to 0. See Figure 9-10. Click **Next**.

13. In the Choose a Destination window of the SQL Server Import and Export Wizard, keep the default destination SQL Server Native Client 11.0. The server name

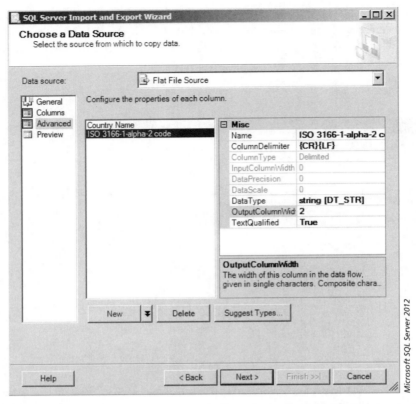

Figure 9-9 Configure the output properties for each column of the flat file using the SQL Server Import and Export Wizard

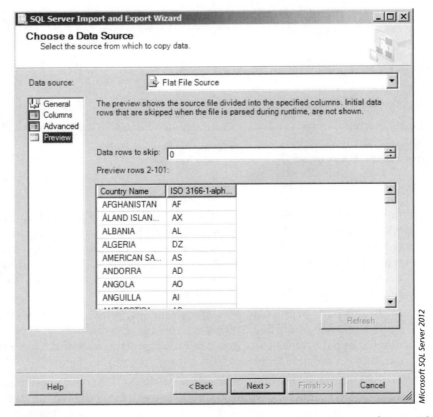

Figure 9-10 Preview the flat file data source using the SQL Server Import and Export Wizard

should default to <ComputerName>\SQLSERVERUA. Keep the default Windows Authentication mode, and then select **ImportExportTest** in the Database drop-down list box. See Figure 9-11. Click **Next**.

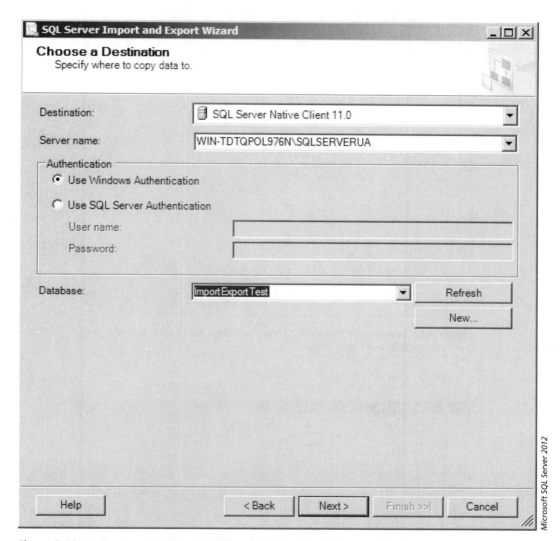

Figure 9-11 Configure a destination SQL Server database using the SQL Server Import and Export Wizard

14. In the Select Source Tables and Views window, select **[dbo].[Country]** from the Destination drop-down list box. See Figure 9-12.

15. Click the **Edit Mappings** button. The Column Mappings dialog box allows you to change the mappings between source and destination columns and to specify the operation that you want to perform on the destination table. Keep the existing column mappings and the action to append rows to the destination table. See Figure 9-13. Click **OK**.

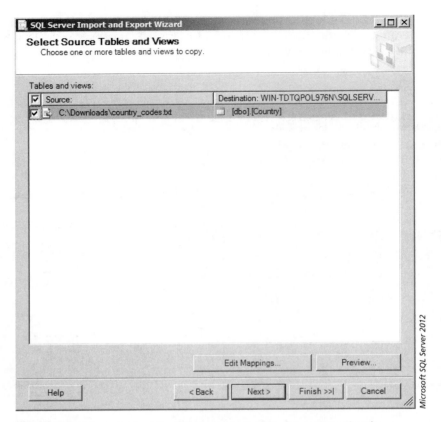

Figure 9-12 Select a table as the SQL Server destination data source using the
SQL Server Import and Export Wizard

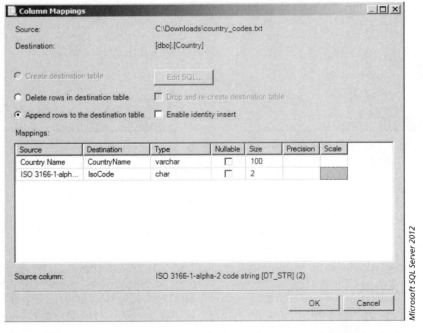

Figure 9-13 Review the column mappings between the source and destination in the
SQL Server Import and Export Wizard

16. The Save and Run Package window allows you either to run the package immediately or to save it to a file destination or to SQL Server. Click the **Run immediately** and the **Save SSIS Package** check boxes, and then click the **File system** option button. Select **Do not save sensitive data** from the Package protection level drop-down list box. See Figure 9-14. Click **Next**.

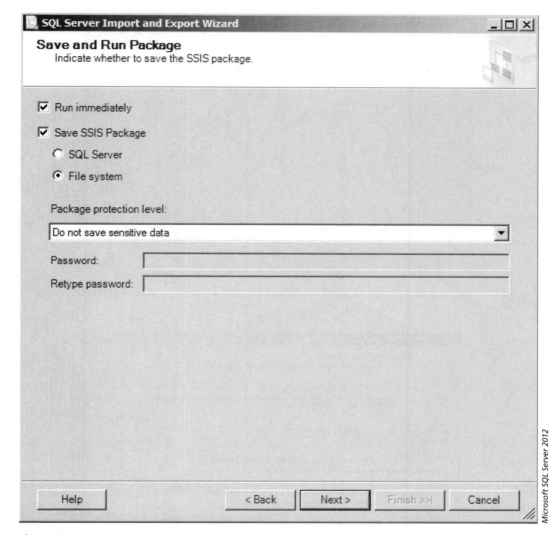

Figure 9-14 Save and run the SSIS package using the SQL Server Import and Export Wizard

17. In the Save SSIS Package window, type **ImportCountry** in the Name text box, and then type **C:\Downloads\ImportCountry.dtsx** in the File name text box. See Figure 9-15. Click **Next**.

18. Review the actions that the wizard will perform. See Figure 9-16. Click **Finish**.

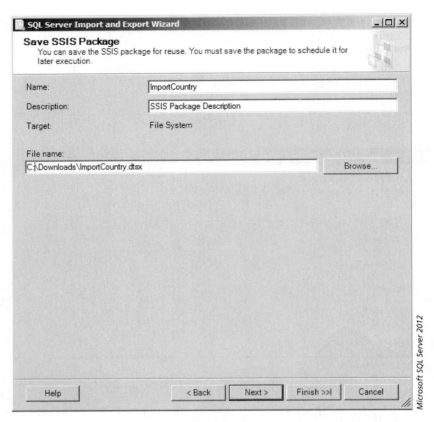

Figure 9-15 Save SSIS Package window in the SQL Server Import and Export Wizard

Figure 9-16 Complete the SQL Server Import and Export Wizard

19. After clicking Finish in the previous step, a status window displays the results of the package execution. See Figure 9-17. After reviewing the results, click **Close** to exit the wizard.

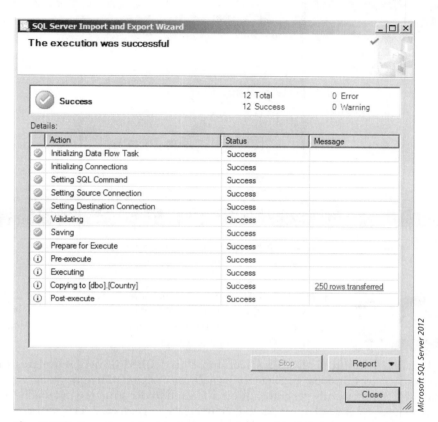

Figure 9-17 Execution status window on completion of the SQL Server Import and Export Wizard

20. Return to SQL Server Management Studio. Delete the text in the open Query Editor window, and then type the following SQL command:

```
SELECT * FROM ImportExportTest.dbo.Country;
```

Press the **F5** key, or click the **Execute** button to run the query. You should see that the records (excluding the header row) from the flat file have been imported into the Country table. See Figure 9-18.

21. You have now completed this activity. Leave your Web browser and SQL Server Management Studio open for the next activity in this chapter.

SQL Server Data Tools

An **integrated development environment (IDE)** is an application that provides a developer with a comprehensive set of development tools to design, compile, and debug software within a single user interface. **Visual Studio**—Microsoft's IDE—includes a graphical designer, a code editor, and a debugger. SQL Server Data Tools, which are part of the SQL Server 2012 installation, use Visual Studio as the IDE for developing database-oriented solutions for Analysis Services, Reporting Services, and Integration Services. This section and the accompanying activity describe how to create an Integration Services package by creating an Integration Services Business Intelligence project in Visual Studio 2010.

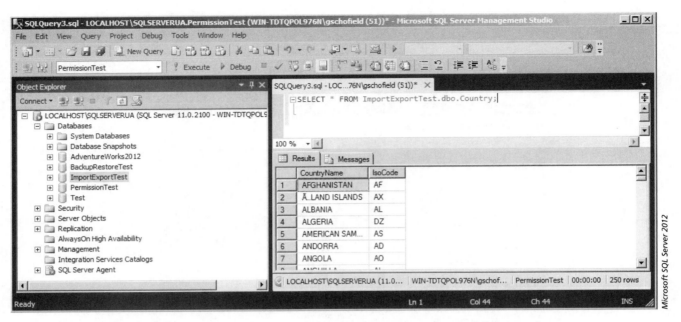

Figure 9-18 Query the destination table using Query Editor to verify that the records were successfully imported

NOTE Visual Studio 2010 is the IDE that was bundled with the SQL Server installation used by this text. SQL Server Data Tools are also compatible with a more recent version of Visual Studio 2012, which can be downloaded as a stand-alone installation.

SQL Server Data Tools have a selection of predefined project templates that include the Integration Services Business Intelligence project for designing Integration Services packages. This template will automatically generate a project file and folder structure that includes a folder named "SSIS packages," with a default package named Package.dtsx. A project may contain multiple Integration Services packages. Within Visual Studio, Solution Explorer displays the project name as well as the physical folders and files within the project. The package designer pane in the middle of the user interface displays the different elements of the package as a series of tabs: Control Flow, Data Flow, Parameters, Event Handlers, and Package Explorer. On the left side of the window is an SSIS Toolbox, which contains the different tasks that you can drag and drop onto the Control Flow and Data Flow tabs of your package.

SQL Server Integration Services Package Execution

Integration Services has a runtime component that is installed as a Windows service—along with the Database Engine—to enable a package to be executed. An Integration Services package can be executed using a variety of methods, including the following:

- Using SQL Server Data Tools and the Debug menu in Visual Studio
- Running the dtexec.exe utility from a command prompt, with or without a configuration file
- Running the dtexecui.exe utility from a command prompt to launch a Windows application in which you can set package property values
- Creating a SQL Server Agent job that can also be used to execute the package on a regular schedule

It is often necessary to configure a package to run in different environments. For example, you will likely need to use different data connections in your production and development environments. A **package configuration file**, with a .dtsconfig file extension, can be generated from within SQL Server Data Tools for each environment and used in conjunction with the package to allow properties in the package to be overridden with the values in the configuration file. Logging can also be implemented to output the execution status of runtime events into a file or table to assist with troubleshooting the package should it fail.

Activity 9-2: Importing and Exporting Data Using the SQL Server Data Tools

Time Required: 45 minutes

Objective: Move data between SQL Server and a data file by creating a package using the SQL Server Data Tools.

Description: In this activity, you will move data between a flat file and a SQL Server table by creating an Integration Services Business Intelligence project using Visual Studio 2010.

1. Click the **Start** button, point to **All Programs**, click the **Microsoft Visual Studio 2010** folder, and then click the **Microsoft Visual Studio 2010** application. In the Choose Default Environment Settings dialog box, select **Business Intelligence Settings** from the list of settings. See Figure 9-19. Click the **Start Visual Studio** button to launch the Microsoft Visual Studio 2010 integrated development environment.

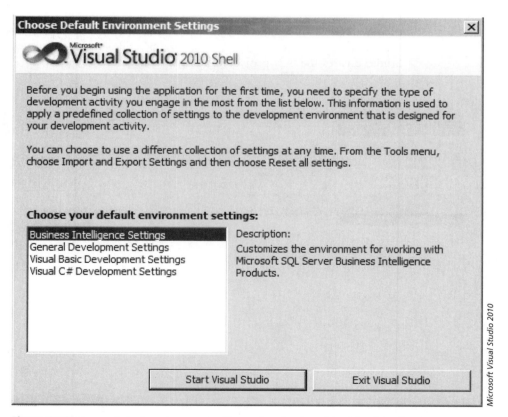

Figure 9-19 Choose default environment settings when first launching Visual Studio 2010

2. On the Microsoft Visual Studio Start Page, click **New Project**. See Figure 9-20.

3. In the New Project dialog box, select **Integration Services Project** from the list of Business Intelligence project templates. In the lower section of the dialog box, type

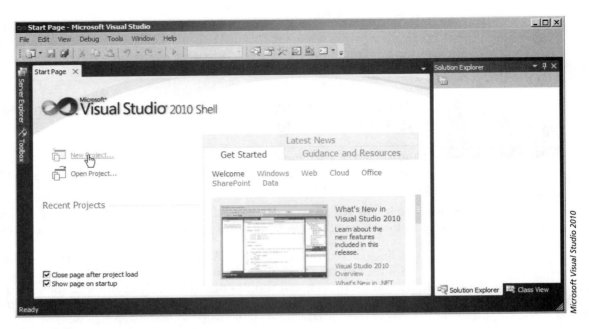

Figure 9-20 Visual Studio 2010 Start Page

CountryTest in the Name and Solution name text boxes. Type **C:\Downloads** in the Location text box. See Figure 9-21. Click **OK** and wait for a few seconds while Visual Studio creates the new project and folder structure.

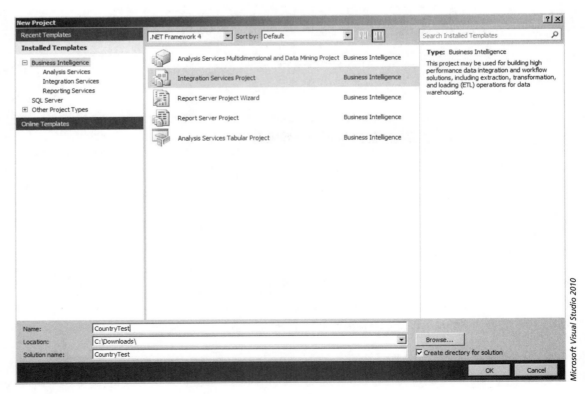

Figure 9-21 Add a new Integration Services project

4. Spend some time familiarizing yourself with the layout of the user interface. On the right, Solution Explorer displays the project name as well as the physical folders and files within the project. The package designer pane in the middle of the user interface displays the different elements of the package in a series of tabs. Click each **tab** in turn. On the left, the SSIS Toolbox contains the different tasks that you can drag and drop onto the Control Flow and Data Flow tabs of your package. See Figure 9-22.

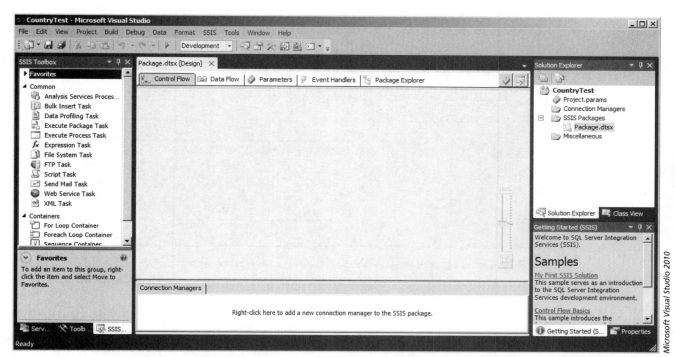

Figure 9-22 SSIS Package Design view in Visual Studio 2010

5. In this step, you'll add the package that you created during Activity 9-1 so you can review the connections, control flow, and data flow. In Solution Explorer, right-click the **SSIS Packages** folder, and then click **Add Existing Package**. In the Add Copy of Existing Package dialog box, click the . . . button next to the Package path text box.

6. In the left navigation pane of the Load Package dialog box, click **Computer**, and then click **Local Disk (C:)** to navigate to the C:\Downloads folder. Double-click **Downloads**. In the folder view, click the **ImportCountry** file, and then click **Open**. See Figure 9-23. Click **OK** to add the package.

7. In Solution Explorer, double-click the **ImportCountry.dtsx** file to open the package in Design view. On the Control Flow tab, notice that the package contains a single data flow task. In the lower pane, the two data connections that were created appear. See Figure 9-24.

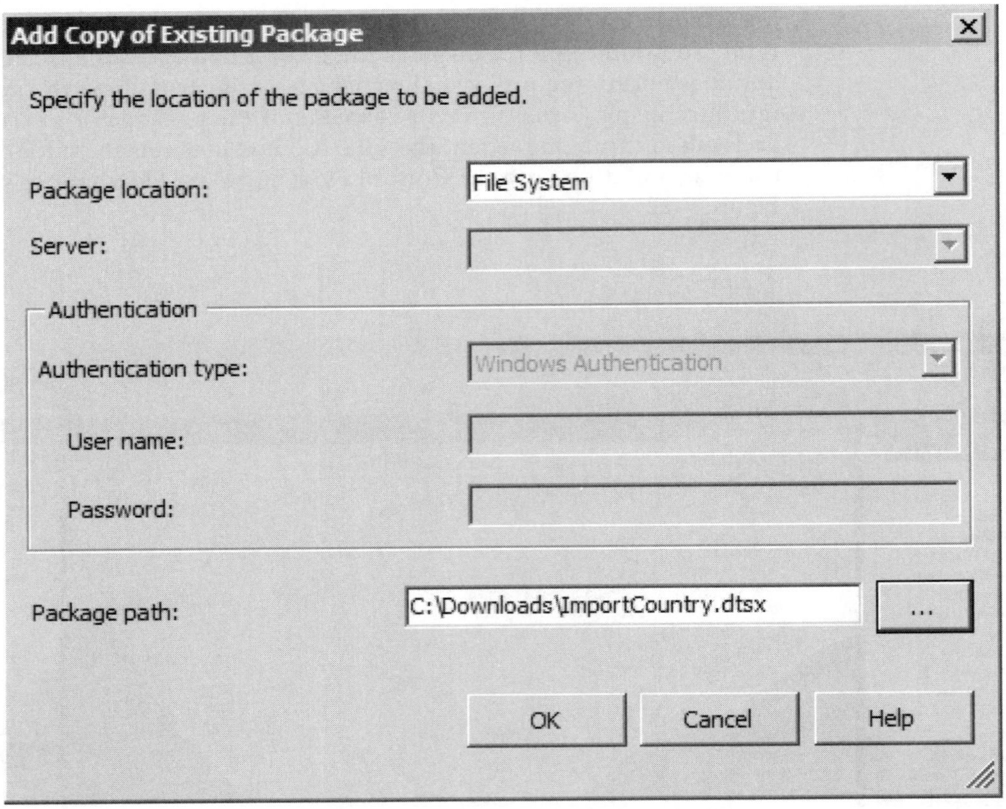

Add Copy of Existing Package

Specify the location of the package to be added.

Package location: | File System

Server:

Authentication

Authentication type: | Windows Authentication

User name:

Password:

Package path: | C:\Downloads\ImportCountry.dtsx | ...

OK | Cancel | Help

Microsoft Visual Studio 2010

Figure 9-23 Adding a copy of an existing SSIS package to the Integration Services project

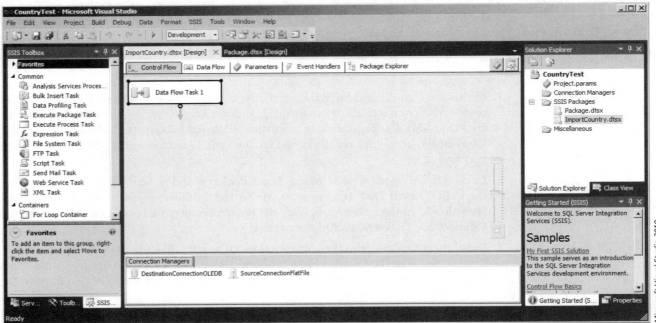

Figure 9-24 Review the control flow of the ImportCountry SSIS package

8. On the Control Flow tab, double-click **Data Flow Task 1** to open it in the Data Flow tab. See Figure 9-25. Data Flow Task 1 contains the data flow between the flat file source (country_codes.txt) and the destination table in the database (Country). To recap, this task was created to import data from the flat file source into the SQL Server database table.

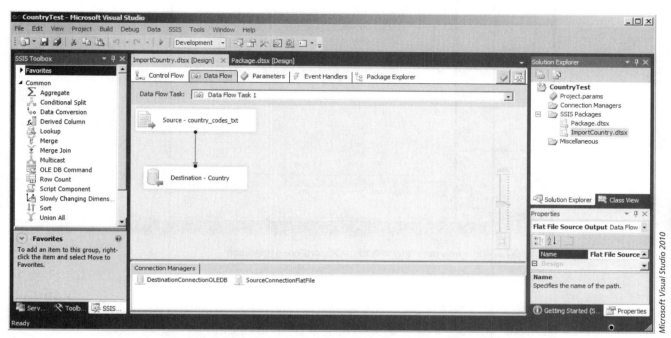

Figure 9-25 Review the data flow of the ImportCountry SSIS package

9. You will now add a second data flow task, which you'll later configure to export data from SQL Server. Click the **Control Flow** tab in the ImportCountry.dtsx package designer. In the SSIS Toolbox, click **Favorites,** and then click and drag **Data Flow Task** onto the Control Flow tab of the package designer. On the Control Flow tab, click the task named **Data Flow Task 1.** Click the **green arrow,** and then click the task named **Data Flow Task** to connect the two tasks. See Figure 9-26.

By connecting these two tasks, you have established a precedence constraint. Data Flow Task 1 must execute successfully before the Data Flow Task will execute.

10. You will now rename the data flow tasks so their function is clear. On the Control Flow tab, click **Data Flow Task 1.** In the Properties pane below Solution Explorer, scroll down, and double-click the **Name** text box. Type **ImportCountryData** in the Name text box. On the Control Flow tab, click **Data Flow Task.** In the Properties pane, scroll down and double-click the **Name** text box. Type **ExportCountryData** in the Name text box. Both data flow tasks have been renamed, as shown on the Control Flow tab. See Figure 9-27.

11. In this step, you'll add an Execute SQL task to delete existing records from the Country table before importing the data. In the SSIS Toolbox, click **Favorites,** and then click and drag the **Execute SQL Task** onto the Control Flow tab of the package designer. In the Properties pane, scroll down and double-click the **Name** text box.

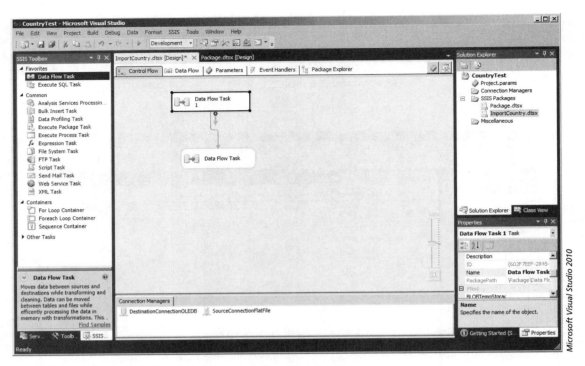

Figure 9-26 Add a new data flow task to the ImportCountry package

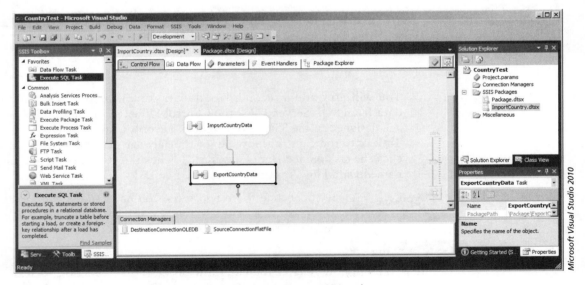

Figure 9-27 Rename the control flow tasks in the ImportCountry SSIS package

Type **DeleteExistingCountryRows** in the Name text box. On the Control Flow tab, click the task named **DeleteExistingCountryRows**. Click the **green arrow** below the DeleteExistingCountryRows task, and then click the task named **ImportCountryData** to establish a precedent constraint between the two tasks. See Figure 9-28.

12. You will now configure the DeleteExistingCountryRows Execute SQL task. On the Control Flow tab, double-click the **DeleteExistingCountryRows** task to display its properties. On the General page of the Execute SQL Task Editor dialog box, scroll

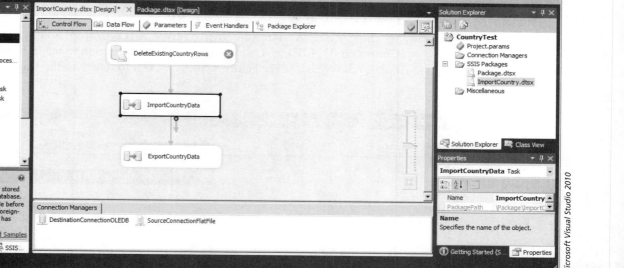

Figure 9-28 Add a new execute SQL task to the ImportCountry SSIS package control flow

down to the SQL Statement section and select **DestinationConnectionOLEDB** from the Connection drop-down list box. In the SQL Statement text box, type **DELETE FROM dbo.Country**. See Figure 9-29. Click **OK**.

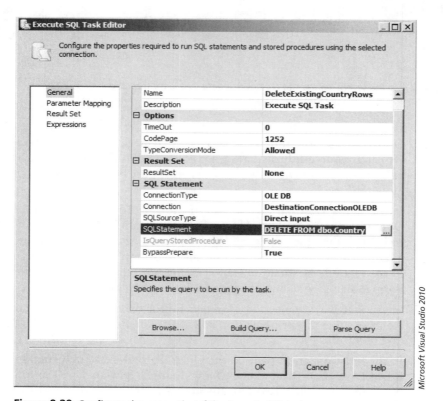

Figure 9-29 Configure the properties of the Execute SQL task

13. Next, you'll configure the ExportCountryData task to export data back out into a flat file. On the Control Flow tab, double-click the **ExportCountryData** task to open the Data Flow tab. In the Favorites section of the SSIS Toolbox, click and drag the **Source Assistant** onto the Data Flow tab.

14. In the Source Assistant – Add New Source dialog box, click **Destination-ConnectionOLEDB** to reuse the existing data connection to the ImportExport database on SQLSERVERUA. See Figure 9-30. Click **OK** to return to the Data Flow tab.

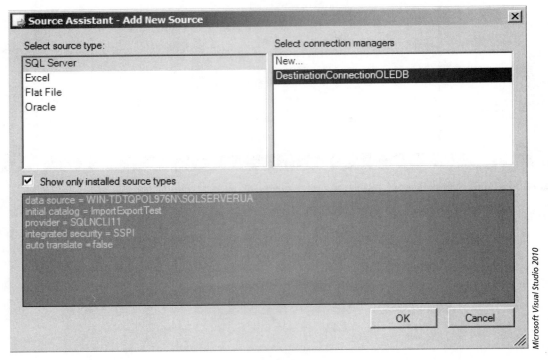

Figure 9-30 Use the source assistant to configure a data source for the ExportCountryData data flow task

15. On the Data Flow tab, double-click the task named **OLE DB Source** to open the OLE DB Source Editor dialog box. Select **[dbo].[Country]** from the Name of the table or the view drop-down list box. See Figure 9-31. Click **OK** to return to the Data Flow tab.

16. In the Other Destinations section of the SSIS Toolbox, click and drag the **Flat File Destination** onto the Data Flow tab. On the Data Flow tab, click the **OLE DB Source** task, click the **blue arrow**, and then click the **Flat File Destination** task to establish a data flow. Double-click the **Flat File Destination** task to configure its properties. In the Flat File Destination Editor dialog box, click the **New** button. In the Flat File Format dialog box, click the **Fixed Width** option button. Click **OK**.

17. In the Flat File Connection Manager Editor dialog box, type **CountryExport** in the Connection manager name text box. Click the **Browse** button next to the File name text box.

18. In the left navigation pane of the Open dialog box, click **Computer**, and then click **Local Disk (C:)**. Double-click **Downloads**. Right-click in the folder details. Click **New**, and then click **Text Document**. Name the text document **CountryExport**, and then click outside the filename. Click the **CountryExport** text document in the list of files. See Figure 9-32.

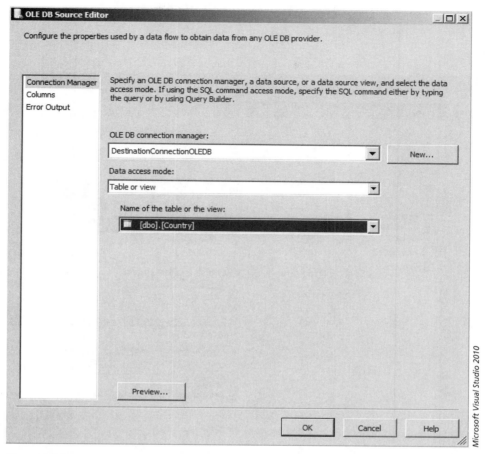

Figure 9-31 Select the table to use as the data source for the ExportCountryData data flow task

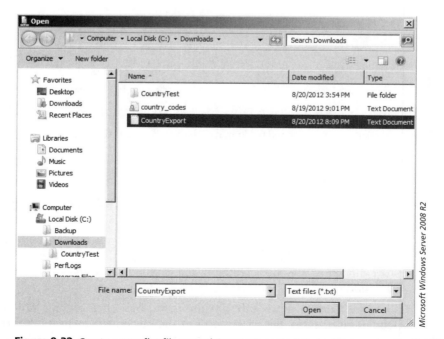

Figure 9-32 Create a new flat file named CountryExport.txt that will be used as the flat file connection

19. Click **Open**. See Figure 9-33. Click **OK** to launch the Flat File Destination Editor dialog box.

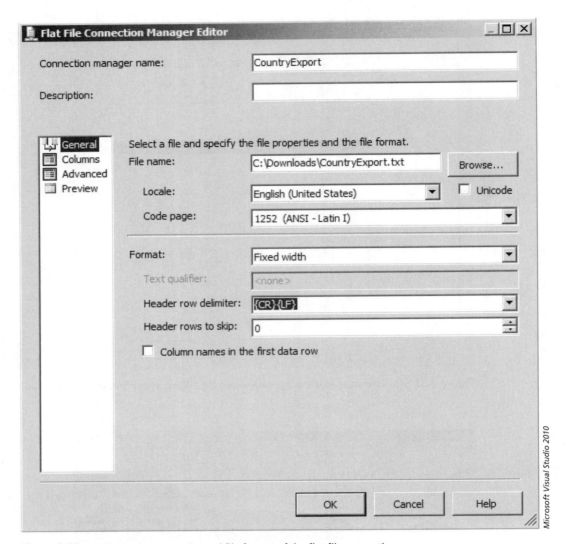

Figure 9-33 Configure the properties and file format of the flat file connection

20. In the Flat File Destination Editor dialog box, click **Mappings** in the left navigation list to review the mappings. See Figure 9-34. Click **OK**.

21. You have now completed configuration of the data flow to export data from the Country table to a flat file named CountryExport.txt. See Figure 9-35. Note that a new connection was also created in the Connection Managers pane at the bottom of the window.

22. Click the **Control Flow** tab. On the menu bar, click **Debug**, and then click **Start Debugging** or press the **F5** key to run the package. The tasks will run sequentially according to their precedence constraints. To recap, the series of steps was to delete existing data from the country table, load new data from the country_codes.txt source

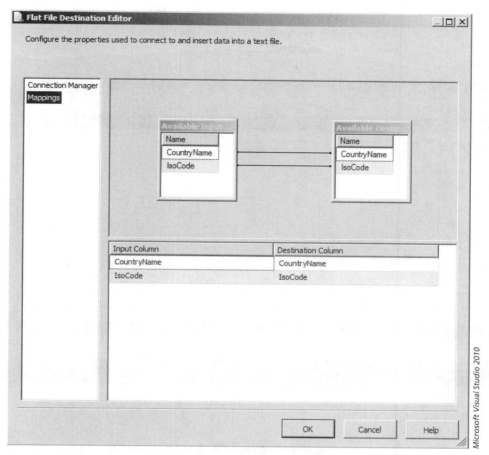

Figure 9-34 Configure the column mappings from the data source to the destination

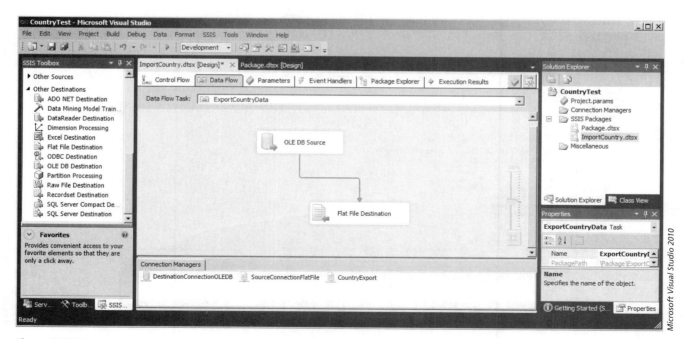

Figure 9-35 Design view of the completed ExportCountryData data flow

file, and then export the data into a fixed-width text file called CountryExport.txt. A green check mark should appear next to each task in the control flow that executed successfully. See Figure 9-36.

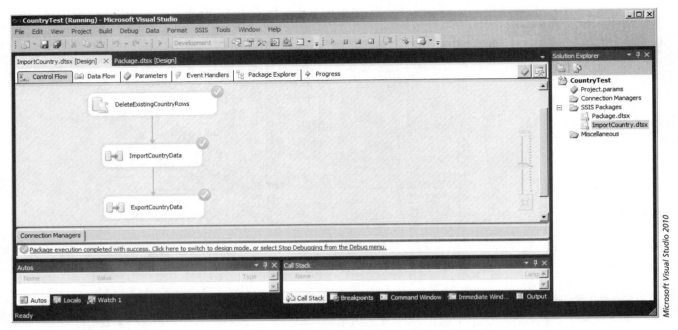

Figure 9-36 Control Flow tab showing that the ImportCountry SSIS package execution completed with success

23. Click the **Progress** tab to see the detailed results from each step along with any error messages that might be displayed. See Figure 9-37.

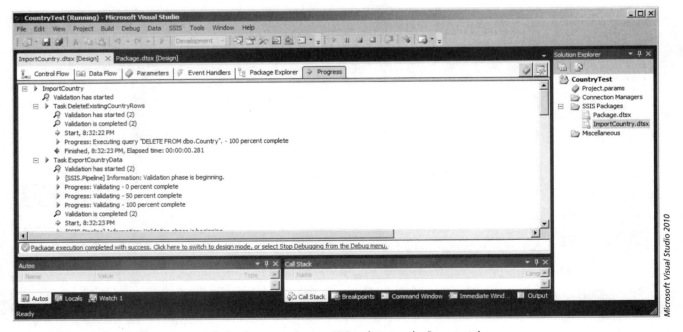

Figure 9-37 View detailed execution results for the ImportCountry SSIS package on the Progress tab

24. On the menu bar, click **Debug**, and then click **Stop Debugging**. Click **File**, and then click **Save All** to save your changes to the project.

25. Click the **Start** button, click **Computer**, double-click **Local Disk (C:)**, double-click **Downloads**, and then double-click **CountryExport**. The text file should be formatted as a fixed-width file with no delimiters separating the country name and code.

26. Next, you'll use the dtexec.exe utility to run an Integration Services package from a command prompt or a batch file. Click the **Start** button, type **cmd**, and then press the **Enter** key to launch a command prompt. Type the following command, and then press the **Enter** key to run the Integration Services package that you just created:

```
> dtexec /F
C:\Downloads\CountryTest\CountryTest\ImportCountry.dtsx
```

See Figure 9-38. Review the output at the command prompt and verify that the package successfully completed.

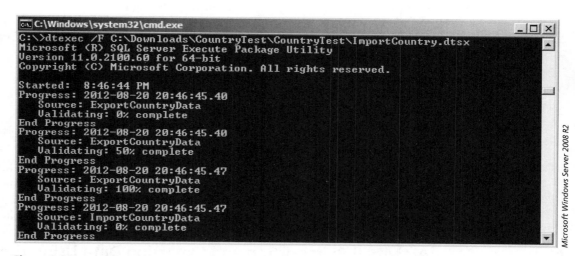

Figure 9-38 Use the dtexec.exe utility to execute the ImportCountry SSIS package from a command prompt

27. You have now completed this activity. Leave your Web browser and SQL Server Management Studio open for the next activity. You may close all other windows.

Bulk Copy Interface

An **application programming interface (API)** defines the communication protocol between two software applications that need to interact with each other. **Open Database Connectivity (ODBC)** is a platform-agnostic API that was designed to facilitate the interactions between a client application and a database management system. SQL Server provides support for ODBC through the **SQL Server Native Client (ODBC) driver**, which defines the functions available to a client application for accessing data on a SQL Server database. The SQL Server Native Client (ODBC) driver includes the SQL Server bulk copy functions, which allow a client application to efficiently add or copy rows from a table.

As a database administrator, you can leverage the bulk copy interface using one of three methods: by running the bcp utility, by using the BULK INSERT function, or by writing application code that interacts with the API directly. This section focuses on the bcp utility and the BULK INSERT function because they are widely used tools for moving large quantities of data between SQL Server and an external data source.

Tables in a SQL Server database may contain user-defined **triggers** that perform a secondary set of operations when data is inserted, deleted, or updated. By default, bulk operations do not fire triggers unless this action is explicitly requested. Inserting large quantities of data into a table when the recovery model is set to full will rapidly fill up the transaction log file and may cause the database size to grow. As you learned in Chapter 8, bulk copy operations are often used in conjunction with the bulk logged recovery model to minimally log operations and improve performance.

bcp Utility

The bcp utility (bcp.exe) is a Windows command-line application that uses the SQL Server Native Client (ODBC) driver to access the bulk copy API. The bcp utility allows a database administrator to move data between a SQL Server database and an external data file. The main advantages of the bcp utility are simplicity and performance. The syntax is straightforward to learn and does not require a detailed knowledge of the SQL language. Bulk copy is one of the fastest methods of transferring large quantities of data between a SQL Server database and an external data file. The main drawbacks of bulk copy are also in its simplicity. It lacks the capability to perform complex transformations to the data during transfer.

The bcp.exe application is installed as part of the SQL Server 2012 set of management tools. The default installation location is: C:\Program Files\Microsoft SQL Server\110\Tools\Binn\bcp.exe.

The following parameters must be supplied in the command:

- Database, schema, and table (or view)
- Path of the data file
- Type of operation, which includes copying data from a table to a file, importing data into a table from a file, and copying the output of a SQL query to a file

The bcp utility can also be run in conjunction with a format file that contains information such as data type, length, name, and order for each column. The format file allows you to import only certain columns, and it permits you to run the command noninteractively. There are a number of other arguments that can be supplied when running the bcp utility, as you'll see in Activity 9-3.

Activity 9-3: Importing and Exporting Data Using the bcp Utility

Time Required: 45 minutes
Objective: Move data between SQL Server and a data file using the bcp utility.

Description: In this activity, you'll review the Books Online for SQL Server 2012 topic "bcp Utility" to familiarize yourself with the syntax and arguments of the bcp utility. Then, you'll use the bcp utility to export data from a table to a data file. Finally, you will learn how to create a format file and copy data onto SQL Server using the bcp utility.

1. Return to your Web browser. Open the MSDN Library by typing http: // **msdn .microsoft.com/library** in the Address bar, and then pressing the **Enter** key. In the Search MSDN with Bing box, type **bcp utility** and then click the **Search** icon.

2. Click the top search result—**bcp Utility**—to open the "bcp Utility" topic. See Figure 9-39. Review the syntax, and then scroll down the page to read the input arguments and their descriptions.

3. Return to SQL Server Management Studio. Delete the text in the open Query Editor window, and then type the following SQL command:

```
DELETE FROM ImportExportTest.dbo.Country;
```

Press the **F5** key, or click the **Execute** button to run the query and delete all existing records in the Country table.

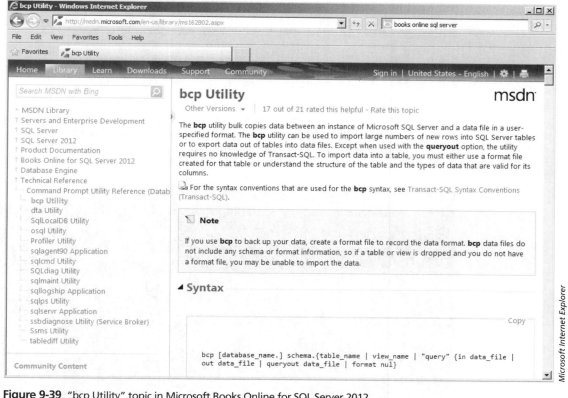

Figure 9-39 "bcp Utility" topic in Microsoft Books Online for SQL Server 2012

4. Click the **Start** button, type **cmd,** and then press the **Enter** key to launch a command prompt. Type the following command, and then press the **Enter** key:

```
> bcp ImportExportTest.dbo.Country in

c:\downloads\countryexport.txt

-Slocalhost\SQLSERVERUA -T
```

 The parameters are case sensitive. This command specifies that you want to import data (in parameter) into the Country table from the countryexport.txt file. The process should connect to the server (-S parameter) localhost\SQLSERVERUA using a trusted connection (-T parameter) with Windows integrated security.

5. As shown below, you are now prompted with a series of questions about the format of each field to import. Accept the default storage type by pressing the **Enter** key. Type **0** and press the **Enter** key for the prefix length of the field. This causes the utility to prompt you for the field length and field terminator. Accept the default field lengths by pressing the **Enter** key. Because the file is fixed length with no delimiters, accept the default field terminator of none by pressing the **Enter** key.

```
Enter the file storage type of field CountryName[char]:

Enter prefix-length of field CountryName[2]: 0

Enter length of field CountryName[100]:

Enter field terminator[none]:
```

```
Enter the file storage type of field IsoCode[char]:
Enter prefix-length of field IsoCode[2]: 0
Enter length of field IsoCode[2]:
Enter field terminator[none]:
```

6. You are asked if you want to save the information in a format file. Type **Y** and then press the **Enter** key. At the host filename prompt, type the following file location: **c:\downloads\countryexport.fmt**. Press the **Enter** key to save the format information and begin the copy. See Figure 9-40.

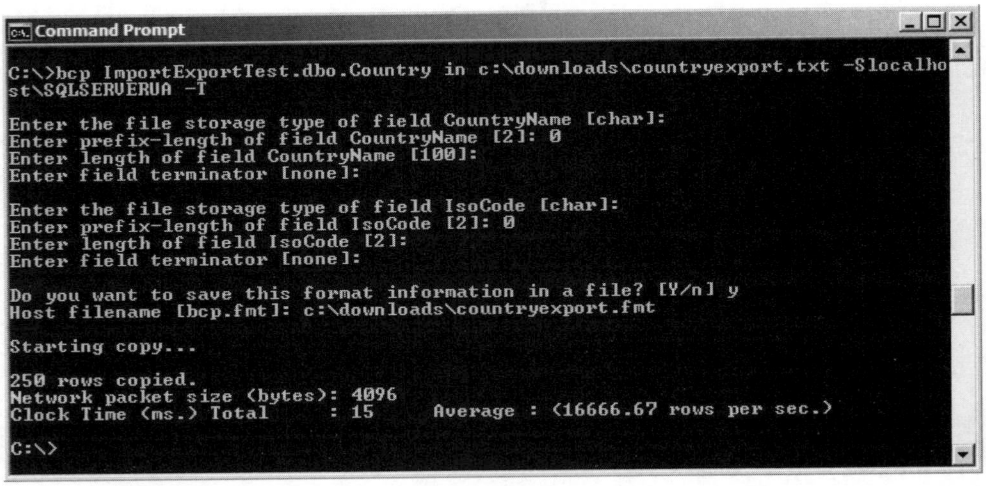

Microsoft Windows Server 2008 R2

Figure 9-40 Import data into SQL Server from a flat file using the bcp utility without a format file

7. Click the **Start** button, and then click **Computer** to open Windows File Explorer. Click **Local Disk (C:)**, double-click **Downloads**, and then double-click the **CountryExport.fmt** file. In the Windows dialog box, click the **Select a program from a list of installed programs** option button, and then click **OK**. Click **Notepad**, and then click **OK** to open the format file. See Figure 9-41.

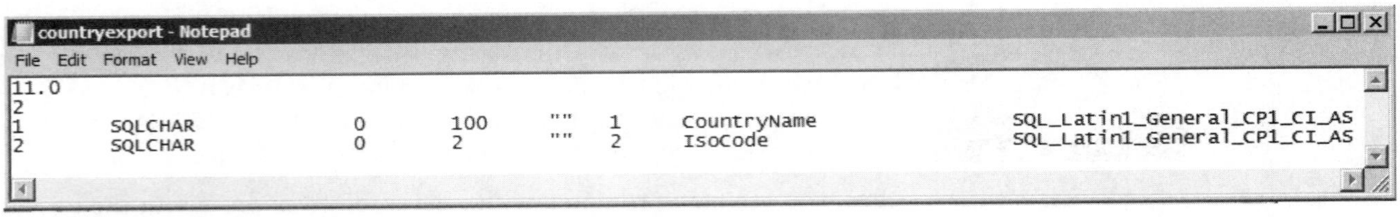

Figure 9-41 View the format file that was created using the bcp utility
Microsoft Windows Server 2008 R2

The first line of the format file is the version of SQL Server, in this case 11.0. The second line contains the number of columns in the source file, in this case 2. The remaining rows list the individual columns of data and specify the following information about the source and destination (from left to right):

- Field order (1, 2)
- Source file data type (SQLCHAR)
- Prefix length (0)

- Source file data length (100, 2)
- Source file field terminator ("")
- Destination table column order (1, 2)
- Destination table column name (CountryName, IsoCode)
- Destination table collation (SQL_Latin1_General_CP1_CI_AS)

8. Return to SQL Server Management Studio. Delete the text in the open Query Editor window, and then type the following SQL command:

```
SELECT * FROM ImportExportTest.dbo.Country;
```

Press the **F5** key, or click the **Execute** button to run the query and verify that the records have successfully been imported into the Country table.

9. Return to the open command prompt. Type the following command, and then press the **Enter** key:

```
> bcp ImportExportTest.dbo.Country out

c:\downloads\bcpexport.txt

-Slocalhost\SQLSERVERUA -T -c
```

The -c parameter specifies that the utility should use the character data format and therefore does not require the use of a format file. See Figure 9-42.

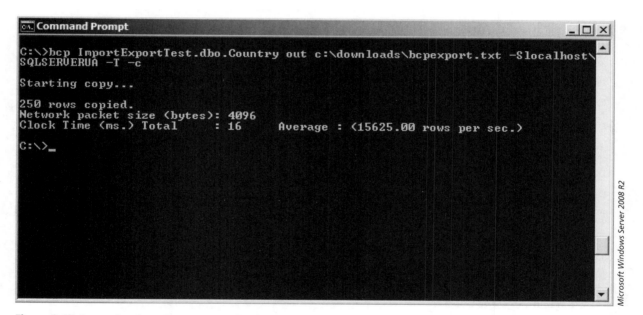

Figure 9-42 Export data from SQL Server to a flat file using the bcp utility

10. Return to the open Windows File Explorer and double-click **bcpexport.txt**. In the Notepad window, validate that the data was successfully copied from SQL Server in Step 9. See Figure 9-43.

11. You have now successfully completed this activity. Close the command prompt and Windows File Explorer, but leave the Web browser and SQL Server Management Studio open for the next activity.

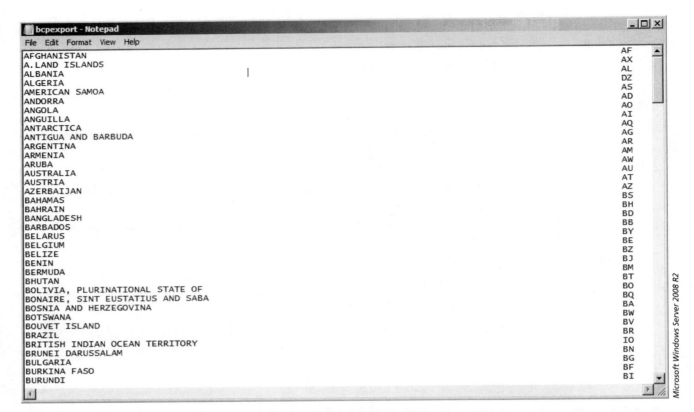

Figure 9-43 Review the data in the flat file that was exported from SQL Server using the bcp utility

BULK INSERT Statement

BULK INSERT is a SQL statement that uses the bulk copy interface. The BULK INSERT statement inserts records from an external data file source into a SQL Server table. The statement is executed directly from SQLCMD.exe or from Query Editor. Unlike the bcp utility, BULK INSERT can only be used to import data; it does not expose the bulk copy functions that permit data to be exported to a data file. To execute a BULK INSERT statement, the ADMINISTER BULK OPERATIONS permission must be assigned to the user in addition to the INSERT permission, which is required to add new records to a table. The basic syntax for a BULK INSERT command is as follows:

```
BULK INSERT <Database>.<Schema>.<Table>

FROM '<DataFilePath>'

WITH ( <Options> )
```

Similar to the bcp utility—although using the SQL language syntax—a number of arguments can be supplied in the WITH clause of the BULK INSERT statement to specify the behavior of the operation.

Activity 9-4: Inserting Data into a Table Using the BULK INSERT Statement

Time Required: 45 minutes
Objective: Move data between SQL Server and a data file using the BULK INSERT statement.

Description: In this activity, you'll review the Books Online for SQL Server 2012 topic "BULK INSERT (Transact-SQL)" to familiarize yourself with the syntax and arguments of the BULK INSERT statement. Then, you'll use the BULK INSERT statement to move data from a data file to a table using Query Editor.

1. Return to your Web browser. Open the MSDN Library by typing http: // **msdn .microsoft.com/library** in the Address bar and pressing the **Enter** key. In the Search MSDN with Bing box, type **BULK INSERT** and then click the **Search** icon.

2. Click the top search result—BULK INSERT (**Transact-SQL**)—to open the "BULK INSERT (Transact-SQL)" topic. See Figure 9-44. Read through this topic, noting that although the syntax differs from the bcp utility, many of the input arguments are similar.

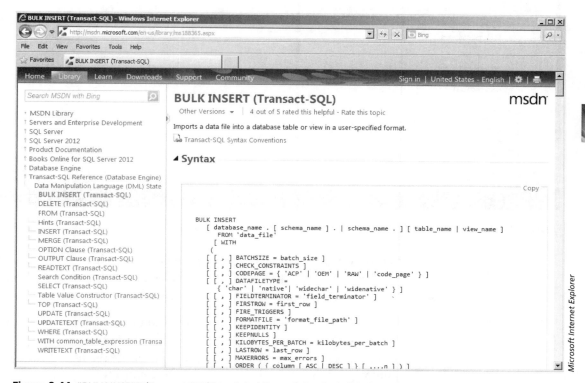

Figure 9-44 "BULK INSERT (Transact-SQL)" topic in Microsoft Books Online for SQL Server 2012

3. Return to SQL Server Management Studio. Delete the text in the open Query Editor window, and then type the following SQL command:

```
DELETE FROM ImportExportTest.dbo.Country;
```

Press the **F5** key, or click the **Execute** button to run the query and delete all existing records in the Country table.

4. In this step, you'll import data from the original country_codes.txt file. Delete the text in the open Query Editor window, and then type the following SQL command:

```
BULK INSERT ImportExportTest.dbo.Country

FROM 'C:\Downloads\country_codes.txt'

WITH

(DATAFILETYPE = 'char',
```

```
FIELDTERMINATOR = ';',

FIRSTROW = 2);
```

Press the **F5** key, or click the **Execute** button to run the query and insert records (excluding the header row) from the country_codes.txt file into the Country table. See Figure 9-45.

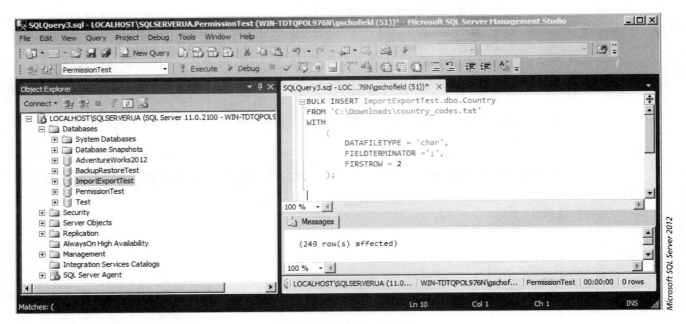

Figure 9-45 Use the BULK INSERT statement to insert data into a table from a flat file

5. Return to SQL Server Management Studio. Delete the text in the open Query Editor window, and then type the following SQL command:

```
SELECT * FROM ImportExportTest.dbo.Country;
```

Press the **F5** key, or click the **Execute** button to run the query and validate that the records were correctly imported into the Country table.

6. Return to SQL Server Management Studio. Delete the text in the open Query Editor window, and then type the following SQL command:

```
DELETE FROM ImportExportTest.dbo.Country;
```

Press the **F5** key, or click the **Execute** button to run the query and delete all existing records in the Country table.

7. In this step, you'll import data from the countryexport.txt file using the format file that you created during the previous activity. Delete the text in the open Query Editor window, and then type the following SQL command:

```
BULK INSERT ImportExportTest.dbo.Country

FROM 'C:\Downloads\countryexport.txt'

WITH

(

FORMATFILE = 'C:\Downloads\countryexport.fmt',

FIRSTROW = 2

);
```

Press the **F5** key, or click the **Execute** button to run the query and insert records (excluding the header row) from the country_codes.txt file into the Country table. See Figure 9-46.

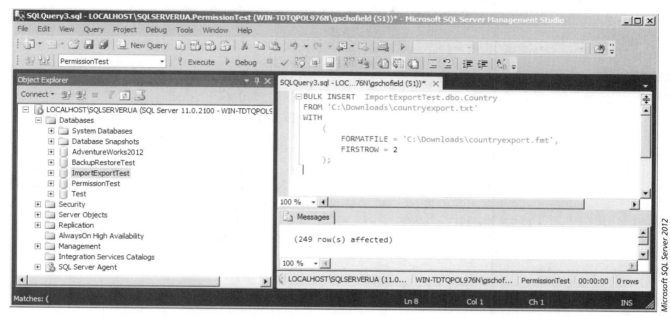

Figure 9-46 Use the BULK INSERT statement with a format file to insert data into a table from a flat file

8. You have now completed this activity. Close all windows by clicking the **X** in the upper-right corner of each application.

Chapter Summary

- The ability to integrate with other data sources is an important feature of a database management system. The process of data integration involves extracting, transforming, and loading (ETL) data. SQL Server offers several different management tools that can help to facilitate the process of extracting, transforming, and loading (ETL) data.

- When selecting the appropriate data integration tool for a given situation, a database administrator should consider a variety of factors, including performance, data source type, source file schema, and any logic that must be applied to transform the data as it is moved between the external source and the SQL Server database.

- SQL Server Integration Services (SSIS) is a component of SQL Server that can be used to integrate many different types of external data sources, while applying complex business rules and workflow logic during the integration process.

- The SQL Server Import and Export Wizard provides step-by-step instructions for designing an SSIS package that meets basic data integration needs and will move data between a source and a destination.

- SQL Server Data Tools is a comprehensive development environment that can be used to create a solution that caters to more complex data integration situations. SQL Server Data Tools use Visual Studio 2010 for developing database-oriented solutions for Analysis Services, Reporting Services, and Integration Services.

- The bulk copy interface enables a client application to efficiently perform bulk copy operations between a view or table on a SQL Server database and an external data file.

- An SSIS package groups together a set of one or more tasks as a series of logical steps into a single object that can be executed using the SQL Server Integration Services service. The order in which each task is executed within an SSIS package is known as the control flow.

- An integrated development environment (IDE) is an application that provides a developer with a comprehensive set of development tools to design, compile, and debug software within a single user interface.

- Integration Services has a runtime component that is installed as a Windows service—along with the Database Engine—to enable a package to be executed.

- An application programming interface (API) defines the communication protocol between two software applications that need to interact with each other.

- SQL Server provides support for ODBC through the SQL Server Native Client (ODBC) driver, which defines the functions that are available to a client application for accessing data on a SQL server. This API includes the SQL Server bulk copy functions.

- The bcp utility (bcp.exe) is a Windows command-line application that uses the SQL Server Native Client (ODBC) driver to access the bulk copy API. The bcp utility allows a database administrator to move data between a SQL Server database and an external data file.

- BULK INSERT is a SQL statement that uses the bulk copy interface and is executed directly from SQLCMD.exe or Query Editor to insert records from an external data file source into a SQL Server table.

Key Terms

Analysis Service tasks   Tasks that enable an SSIS package to interact with SQL Server Analysis Services to process data or perform a data mining operation.

application programming interface (API)   An interface that defines the communication protocol between two software applications that need to interact.

bcp utility   A stand-alone application that is run from a command prompt and that can be used for bidirectional data transfer.

bulk copy interface   An interface that enables a client application to efficiently perform bulk copy operations between a view or table on a SQL Server database and an external data file.

BULK INSERT   A SQL statement that can be executed to insert records from an external data file source into a SQL Server table.

connection manager   An object within an SSIS package that stores the configuration information necessary to connect to an individual data source.

control flow   The order in which each task in an SSIS package is executed.

data flow components   Steps within a data flow task that are connected together by the output of the previous component.

data flow tasks   Tasks that move data between a source and a destination; may include transformations that manipulate the data as it is moved between a source and destination.

data preparation tasks   Tasks that perform file or directory operations in an SSIS package.

Data Transformation Services (DTS)   A SQL Server legacy data integration tool with a graphical designer that had a limited range of functionality.

event handler   A software routine that specifies what should happen if a certain event occurs during execution of an SSIS package.

flat file   A text file that contains data; each row in a flat file represents a record. Individual fields within a record either occupy a fixed number of characters or are separated by a special character known as a delimiter.

integrated development environment (IDE)   An application that provides a developer with a comprehensive set of development tools to design, compile, and debug software within a single user interface.

maintenance tasks   Tasks that perform essential database maintenance functions.

Open Database Connectivity (ODBC) A platform-agnostic application programming interface (API) that was designed to facilitate the interactions between a client application and a database management system.

package configuration file A configuration file that will allow properties in an SSIS package to be overridden with the values in the configuration file during execution; has a .dtsconfig file extension.

scripting task A task that allows custom code to be executed to extend the functionality of the basic set of tasks in an SSIS package.

SQL Server Data Tools A comprehensive development environment that can be used to create a solution that caters to more complex data integration situations.

SQL Server Import and Export Wizard A wizard that provides step-by-step instructions for designing a solution that meets basic data integration needs.

SQL Server Integration Services (SSIS) A component of SQL Server that can be used to integrate many different types of external data sources, while applying complex business rules and workflow logic during the integration process.

SQL Server Native Client (ODBC) driver An application programming interface (API) that defines the functions available to a client application for accessing data on a SQL Server database.

SQL Server tasks Tasks that perform operations on schema objects and data on a SQL server.

SSIS package A collection of one or more tasks grouped together as a series of logical steps into a single object that can be executed using the SQL Server Integration Services service.

tasks The basic building blocks within an SSIS package; each task performs a specific activity or function.

transformation component A component within an SSIS package that manipulates data during the data flow as the data moves between the source and the destination during a data flow.

trigger A mechanism that performs a secondary set of operations when data is inserted, deleted, or updated.

user variable A storage unit within an SSIS package that can hold both static values or whose values can be set at run time.

Visual Studio An integrated development environment that includes a graphical designer, a code editor, and a debugger.

workflow tasks Tasks that permit an SSIS package to interact with other applications.

Review Questions

1. Which of the following data integration tools can *not* be used to export data from a SQL Server table?

   a. bcp utility

   b. BULK INSERT statement

   c. SQL Server Import and Export Wizard

   d. SQL Server Data Tools

2. Which of the following determines the execution order for the data flows within a data flow task in an SSIS package that contains multiple data flows?

   a. Package configuration file

   b. Control flow precedence constraints

   c. Data flow engine

   d. Event handlers

3.   What tool would be most appropriate for designing a data integration solution for a process that involves aggregating multiple sets of data?

   a.   BULK INSERT statement

   b.   bcp utility

   c.   SQL Server Data Tools

   d.   SQL Server Import and Export Wizard

4.   Which of the following is a characteristic of a format file?

   a.   It maps the fields within a flat file to the columns in a SQL Server table.

   b.   It can be used in conjunction with the bcp utility or BULK INSERT statement for loading a flat file data source into a SQL Server table.

   c.   It can be generated using the bcp utility.

   d.   All of the above

5.   What feature can be used to update the properties of an SSIS package at run time—for example, to differentiate between a production and development environment?

   a.   Event handlers

   b.   Package configuration file

   c.   Registry Editor

   d.   None of the above

6.   Which of the following is a consideration when using the bulk copy interface?

   a.   Bulk operations do not fire triggers by default.

   b.   Bulk operations may rapidly fill up the log file and grow the database size.

   c.   Bulk operations perform well but are limited in their functionality to manipulate data within the process.

   d.   All of the above

7.   Which of the following is most likely to improve the performance of a bulk copy operation?

   a.   Running the bcp utility locally on the SQL Server host to reduce network latency

   b.   Switching off transaction logging on SQL Server by using the bulk-logged recovery model

   c.   Using a format file

   d.   None of the above

8.   Which of the following is (are) the main advantage(s) of the bcp utility?

   a.   Ability to perform complex data transformations

   b.   Support of a wide variety of data source types

   c.   Simplicity and performance

   d.   Both options a and b

9.   Which of the following methods would be most appropriate for running an SSIS package on a routine basis?

   a.   The dtexec.exe utility

   b.   SQL Server Agent

   c.   The dtexecui.exe utility

   d.   Using SQL Server Data Tools and the Debug menu in Visual Studio

10. Which component within an SSIS package is primarily concerned with data integration?

   a. Data flow task

   b. Data preparation task

   c. Maintenance task

   d. Workflow task

Case Projects

Case Project 9-1: Market Research Firm

You work as a junior database administrator for a market research firm. Earlier today, you received a request from an analyst who needs a flat file extracted from a large table on a SQL Server database so he can load the file into his third-party analytical tool. He needs the comma-separated values file before the end of the day and has indicated that this is a one-time request. Complete the following:

- Compare and contrast the two best options for meeting his needs, given the scope of the request and any constraints that you have identified.
- Which solution would you choose and why?

A week later, the analyst informs you that the analysis he performed based on the extracted data was extremely valuable, and he has been asked to perform this analysis on a daily basis. That means you will need to set up a daily extract of the data. The analyst has also asked if you can implement a process to remove records from the flat file that have missing field values. He wondered if it would be possible for a list of these bad records to be sent to him in an email, or as a separate file output. Given the complexity of the process, you decide to develop an SSIS package using SQL Server Data Tools. Complete the following:

- Using Microsoft Books Online for SQL Server 2012, research and explain which control flow tasks and data flow components could be used to achieve this objective.
- Draw a design of the control flow and data flows that you propose to use.

Hands-On Projects

Hands-On Project 9-1: Using the Bulk Copy Interface

For this hands-on project, you will use the SQL Server named instance SQLSERVERHOA and the HandsOnOne database and tables that you created in previous chapters. The objective of this activity is to practice extracting and loading data using the bulk copy interface. Document your work by saving a copy of the files created in Steps 1, 2, and 4 and the screen shots taken in Steps 6 and 7.

1. Use the bcp utility to create a format file for the Customer table in the HandsOnOne database called Customer.fmt.

2. Use the bcp utility to extract all records in the Customer table into a flat file called Customer.txt.

3. Create a copy of the Customer.txt file called CustomerUpload.txt

4. Modify the contents of the CustomerUpload.txt file. Open the CustomerUpload.txt file in a text editor. Delete the existing customer records from the file and add a new customer record to the file with the following values:

- CustomerId = 5
- CustomerName = Bulk Insert Test
- CustomerAddressId = 1

Save the file, and then close the text editor.

5. Open SQL Server Management Studio and connect to the SQL Server named instance SQLSERVERHOA.

6. Open a Query Editor window, and use the BULK INSERT command in conjunction with the Customer.fmt format file to insert data from the CustomerUpload.txt file into the Customer table in the HandsOnOne database. Take a screen shot of the Query Editor window after successfully executing the query to document this step.

7. Construct and execute a query against the Customer table to verify that the new record was successfully inserted. Take a screen shot of the Query Editor window after successfully executing the query to document this step.

chapter 10

Monitoring SQL Server 2012

After reading this chapter and completing the exercises, you will be able to:

- Describe the daily monitoring tasks a database administrator should complete to evaluate the status of critical services and processes

- Use SQL Server Agent to configure automated alerts in response to system events and performance conditions

- Explain the importance of establishing a baseline set of values for use as a benchmark when monitoring system performance

- Assess the health of the system in real time using SQL Server Activity Monitor and the dynamic management views and functions

- Collect and analyze historical data using the data collector and the Management Data Warehouse repository

- Create and configure a SQL Server audit

To minimize the risk of unplanned service disruptions and ensure that agreed-upon service levels are met, a database administrator must monitor SQL Server 2012 on an ongoing basis. In the first section of this chapter, you'll learn about the main components of SQL Server that require frequent monitoring. Because these monitoring tasks should be automated wherever possible, you'll also learn how to configure SQL Server Agent to generate automatic alerts and notifications in response to system events and performance conditions.

The key to effective monitoring is being able to quickly distinguish the warning signs of a production issue from normal activity; a database administrator must, therefore, understand how the system is expected to perform under normal operating conditions. Although experience is useful, there is no substitute for quantitatively measuring and comparing system performance against a benchmark. The second section of the chapter covers real-time performance monitoring using SQL Server Activity Monitor and dynamic management views and functions.

Capturing performance data on a regular basis can be useful for analyzing a specific issue or for identifying trends over time. The third section of the chapter introduces the SQL Server Management Data Warehouse, which provides a comprehensive data capture, storage, and reporting solution for server and database-level statistics.

Many organizations store data that is highly confidential—such as personal customer information or intellectual property—that must be protected against unauthorized access. In these situations, it is necessary to keep an audit trail of database activity to monitor data access and demonstrate compliance both with internal controls and data protection or privacy policies that are required by law. During the final section of the chapter, you'll learn about auditing and how to configure a database audit.

Daily Monitoring Tasks and Configuring Automated Alerts

A database administrator must proactively monitor each SQL Server instance to minimize the risk of service disruption. After a discussion of the main components of the system that require monitoring, you'll learn how to automate these tasks using SQL Server Agent to generate automatic alerts.

Essential SQL Server Monitoring Tasks

The processes for monitoring the current state of each SQL Server instance should be undertaken consistently and on a daily basis at a minimum, although systems that must satisfy higher service levels may require more frequent monitoring. For a basic implementation, monitoring a SQL Server instance can be as simple as manually reviewing a checklist of items in order of priority each day. Table 10-1 lists a series of questions and corresponding required actions that

Table 10-1   Essential daily monitoring tasks—questions and required actions

Question	Required action
Are all SQL Server services running normally?	Check that all services are running in SQL Server Configuration Manager.
Are all databases online?	Use Object Explorer to check that no databases are offline.
Are remote users able to connect and execute a query?	Execute a query from SQLCMD or Query Editor, connected using the Named Pipes or TCP/IP protocol.
Have any system or resource errors occurred?	Check the events in the Windows application log and SQL Server log.
Have all scheduled jobs including maintenance plans completed successfully?	Check the SQL Server Agent error log and the Job Activity Monitor in Object Explorer.
Are there sufficient physical resources available to the SQL Server instance?	Check the physical disk drives that contain the data and log files for the SQL Server instance.
How is the SQL Server instance currently performing?	Use Activity Monitor to assess CPU and memory utilization and disk throughput, and monitor the system for resource contention and lock conflicts.

will help you identify the key areas of the system that must be monitored to determine if the SQL Server instance is functioning normally.

The first priority for a database administrator is to ensure that all services are running normally. Monitoring the status of services or stopping and starting a service should be done using the SQL Server Configuration Manager. The most critical services are the Database Engine Services, SQL Server Agent, and SQL Server Integration Services. Depending upon your specific implementation of SQL Server, you may also need to monitor other services (e.g., SQL Server Reporting Services). Once the state of each of the services has been verified, the databases hosted by the SQL Server instance should be checked using Object Explorer in SQL Server Management Studio to ensure they are online. Remote client/server connectivity should then be tested by connecting to the SQL server using the Named Pipes or TCP/IP protocol from a Query Editor or SQLCMD prompt and executing a simple SQL query. After completing those items in the checklist, you'll be able to determine if a SQL Server instance is running and if the databases are online and accessible to remote clients.

After establishing the current state of a SQL Server instance, databases, and network connections, the database administrator should check for recent errors and failure of scheduled jobs, focusing in particular on jobs that are responsible for taking and managing database backups. The **Windows application log** captures events generated by applications, such as a SQL Server instance, running on the Windows operating system. In parallel, the **SQL Server log** contains system events as well as certain user-defined events for a SQL Server instance. The **SQL Server Agent error log** records information, warning, and error events related to SQL Server Agent activity. For example, the events from a maintenance and backup plan scheduled using SQL Server Agent would be included in this log. These logs can either be viewed individually or together using the **Log File Viewer**, a feature within SQL Server Management Studio that aggregates events from different event logs.

Lastly, an administrator should check the performance of the physical system resources and determine how the SQL Server instance is currently performing. The physical disks that store the data and log files for each database must have adequate free space. Any disk with less than 15 percent free space remaining warrants further investigation. Later in the chapter, you'll learn how to use Activity Monitor to view the performance of the physical resources, such as CPU, memory, and disk throughput, and to identify poorly performing queries, resource contention, and blocking processes.

Activity 10-1: Performing Essential SQL Server Monitoring Tasks

Time Required: 45 minutes
Objective: Perform the essential SQL Server monitoring tasks using SQL Server and Windows management tools.

Description: In this activity, you'll use SQL Server Configuration Manager to check that the SQL Server instance and its related services are running correctly, confirm that all databases are online in SQL Server Management Studio, and ensure that the server is accepting remote client connections using the SQLCMD utility. Then, you'll check for errors in the Windows application log, SQL Server log, and SQL Server Agent error log and you will learn to read all these events together using the SQL Server Log File Viewer. Finally, you will ensure that the disk has adequate free space for the data and log files.

1. If necessary, start your computer and log on.

2. Click the **Start** button, point to **All Programs**, and then click **Microsoft SQL Server 2012**. Click **Configuration Tools**, and then click **SQL Server Configuration Manager**. Click **Continue** if prompted by the User Account Control dialog box.

3. In the left navigation pane of SQL Server Configuration Manager, click **SQL Server Services**. In the details pane, check that the following SQL Server services are running: SQL Server Database Engine Services named *SQL Server (SQLSERVERUA)*, SQL

Server Integration service named *SQL Server Integration Services 11.0*, and SQL Server Agent named *SQL Server Agent (SQLSERVERUA)*. See Figure 10-1.

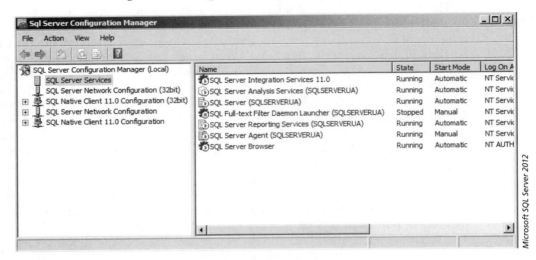

Figure 10-1 SQL Server Configuration Manager

If the state of one of the three services listed above is *Stopped*, right-click the service, and then click **Start**. Close the SQL Server Configuration Manager window after you have verified that all services are running normally.

4. Click the **Start** button, point to **All Programs**, click **Microsoft SQL Server 2012**, and then click **SQL Server Management Studio**. In the Connect to Server dialog box, enter **LOCALHOST\SQLSERVERUA**, and then click **Windows Authentication** from the authentication options. Click **Connect**.

5. In Object Explorer, click the **+** icon to the left of the Databases folder to view the folder contents. Check that all databases are online. Offline databases are indicated with the word *Offline* appearing in parentheses after the database name and a red downward pointing arrow on the database icon. Figure 10-2 shows that the AdventureWorks2012 database is currently offline.

Figure 10-2 Object Explorer with the AdventureWorks2012 database offline

6. To bring any offline databases online, right-click the database name, click **Tasks,** and then click **Bring Online.** A Bring database online dialog box opens, displaying the status of the operation. See Figure 10-3. Click **Close.**

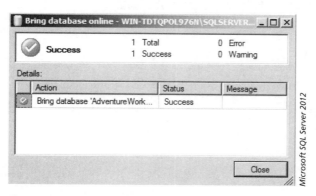

Figure 10-3 Bring database online status dialog box

7. Next, you'll check that you can establish a remote client connection to the SQL Server instance and execute a SQL query. To open a Command Prompt window, click the **Start** button, click **Run,** type **cmd** in the text box, and then click **OK.** Enter the following command, which will use a TCP/IP connection to connect to the named instance using the listener on TCP Port 4409 that you configured during Chapter 3. See Figure 10-4.

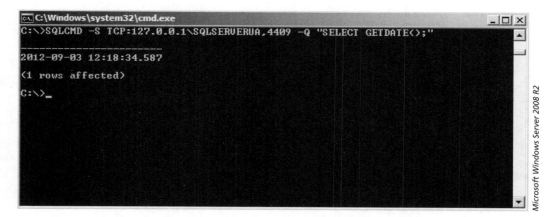

Figure 10-4 Verify client/server network connectivity using the SQLCMD utility

```
C:\> SQLCMD -S
    TCP:127.0.0.1\SQLSERVERUA,4409 -Q "SELECT GETDATE();"
```

The query should return the current date and time in the result set. Close the Command Prompt window after you have verified that the test was successful.

8. Now, you'll check the Windows application log for any recent error messages. Click the **Start** button, point to **Administrative Tools,** and then click **Event Viewer** to launch the Windows Event Viewer. In the left navigation pane, click the **+** icon to the left of Windows Logs to expand the folder. Click the **Application** log, and review the list of application events in the center pane. See Figure 10-5.

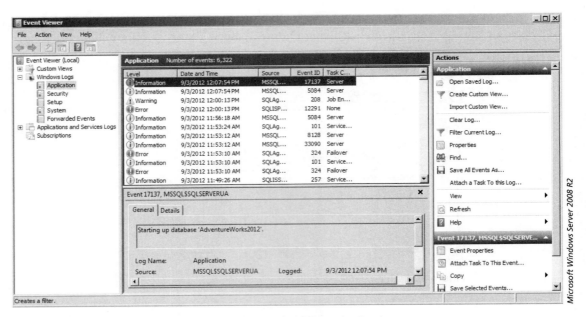

Figure 10-5 Windows Event Viewer displaying the Windows application log

9. The Windows application log contains several different types of events. By default, all event types are displayed. You should filter the view to display only Critical, Error, and Warning events. In the Actions pane on the right side of the window, click **Filter Current Log**. In the Filter Current Log dialog box, click the **Critical**, **Error**, and **Warning** check boxes in the Event level section. See Figure 10-6. Click **OK** to apply the filter and return to the Windows application log window.

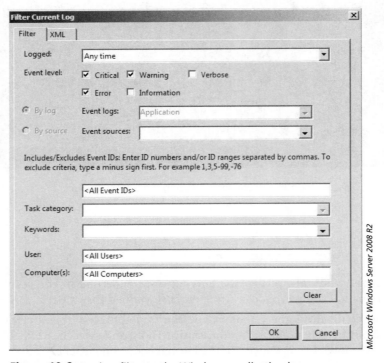

Figure 10-6 Apply a filter to the Windows application log

10. In the Windows application log window, review all Critical, Error, and Warning events by clicking each event and noting the event details on the General and Details tabs at the bottom of the application log window. Figure 10-7 shows the event details for an Error event that was generated due to failure of the BackupRestoreTest maintenance plan. In a production environment, any errors must be investigated and resolved.

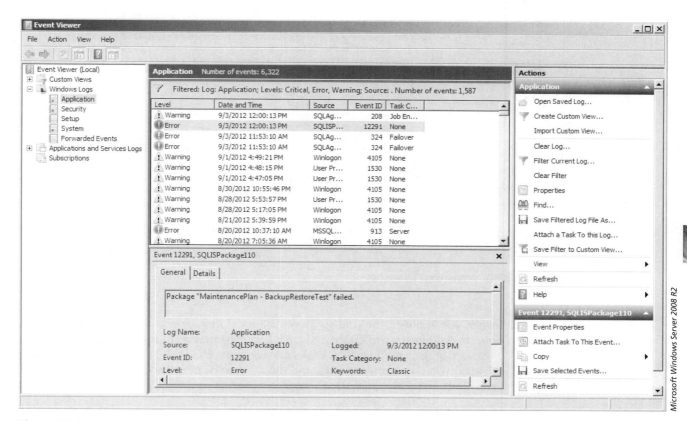

Figure 10-7 Filtered Windows application log

11. Close the Windows application log window and return to the SQL Server Management Studio window. In Object Explorer, click the **+** icon to the left of the Management folder to view the folder contents. Right-click the **SQL Server Logs** folder, point to **View**, and then click **SQL Server and Windows Log** to launch the Log File Viewer. See Figure 10-8.

The Log File Viewer is a flexible tool that allows you to aggregate and view all the logged events from the Windows operating system, Database Mail, SQL Server Agent, and the SQL Server database engine in a single list. In the Select logs pane on the left, you can click the check boxes of any log categories that you would like to include in the log file summary. Using the buttons on the toolbar, you can search, filter, or export the log file summary as a text file. Close the Log File Viewer.

The SQL Server Agent log is discussed in Activity 10-2.

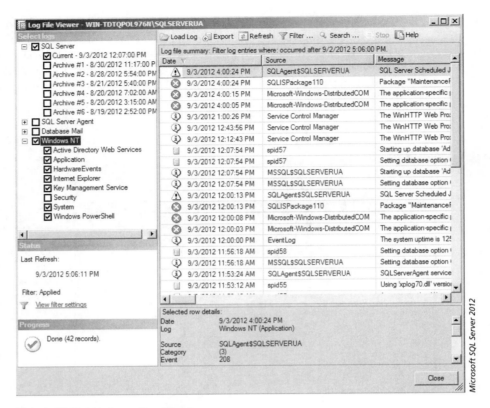

Figure 10-8 SQL Server Log File Viewer

12. Lastly, you'll check the free space on the local disk drives. Click the **Start** button, point to **Administrative Tools**, and click **Server Manager**. In the left navigation menu, expand **Storage**, and then click **Disk Management**. The Disk Management view shows the local volumes, their capacity, and the amount of free space (in terms of bytes and percentage). See Figure 10-9.

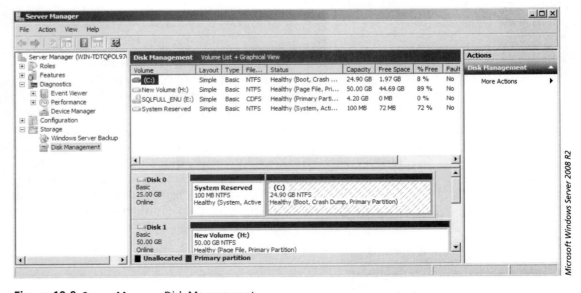

Figure 10-9 Server Manager Disk Management

13. You have now completed Activity 10-1. Close the Server Manager window but leave SQL Server Management Studio open for the next activity.

To quickly query the amount of free space on your local disk drives from within SQL Server Management Studio, open a Query Editor window and execute the following system procedure using a SQL command:

```
EXEC Master.sys.xp_fixeddrives
```

Automating Event Notification Using SQL Server Agent Alerts

Fortunately, it is possible to automate the majority of the monitoring tasks described in this section using SQL Server Agent, an important component of SQL Server that runs as a separate Windows service. In Chapters 7 and 8, you were introduced to SQL Server Agent as a framework for scheduling and executing database maintenance jobs. In this section, you'll learn how to configure SQL Server Agent to automatically send job status notifications and alerts.

Alerts are messages generated automatically in response to a system event or when a performance condition is met. A system event may be either a SQL Server event or a **Windows Management Instrumentation (WMI) event**, which is an event generated by the Microsoft Windows operating system. Each SQL Server error message is assigned a numerical **severity level** that describes the type of error and can be used to specify whether an alert should be generated. For example, a database administrator may want to receive only those alerts that relate to system or resource errors. The main ranges of severity levels and their function are as follows:

- *1–10*—Messages generated by a SQL Server instance for information purposes only; these are not genuine user or system errors.

- *11–16*—User-generated error messages that must be fixed by the user; for example, a syntax error in a SQL query would result in a user error being generated.

- *17–19*—System or resource-related warning messages that must be investigated further by the database administrator.

- *20–25*—Errors in this range are considered fatal, and may be caused by a serious system or resource failure that will result in service disruptions.

Each SQL Server Agent alert may only be configured for a single error level. Six separate alerts would be required to manage all errors with a severity level in the range of 20–25.

Performance conditions are rules defined by placing a threshold on the value of a specific performance counter monitored by SQL Server Agent. If the value of the performance counter exceeds the established threshold, an alert will be triggered. As an example, a performance condition might be used to monitor the percentage of free space on the disk and to raise an alert if it drops below 15 percent. A performance condition could also be used to raise an alert if the number of deadlocked processes is greater than or equal to one.

Job notifications and alerts can be sent to an email address or pager. **Database Mail** is the SQL Server component that is used to integrate with and send messages via an SMTP email server. To be able to send an alert or notification via email, the email address being used to send the message must have a profile configured using Database Mail. The recipient of an alert or notification must separately be configured in SQL Server Agent as an **operator**—an alias for an individual or group of people, with their email or pager information.

In general, for a production system, SQL Server Agent should be used to send notifications and alerts for the following events:

- SQL Server Agent job failure notifications

- SQL Server errors with a severity level of 17 and above

- Deadlocks

- Resource alerts that include high CPU or memory utilization and disk space shortage

Activity 10-2: Automating Alerts Using SQL Server Agent

Time Required: 60 minutes

Objective: Use SQL Server Agent to send automatic alerts in response to system events and performance conditions.

Description: In this activity, you will learn how to configure Database Mail, create a default mail profile, and add an operator. Then, you'll configure two types of alerts: a response to a SQL Server error message of a particular severity level and an alert that will trigger if a performance condition is met.

1. To be able to send automated alerts, you first need to configure Database Mail. Return to the SQL Server Management Studio window that you left open from the previous activity. In Object Explorer, click the + icon to the left of the Management folder to view the folder contents. Double-click **Database Mail** to launch the Database Mail Configuration Wizard. See Figure 10-10. Click **Next**.

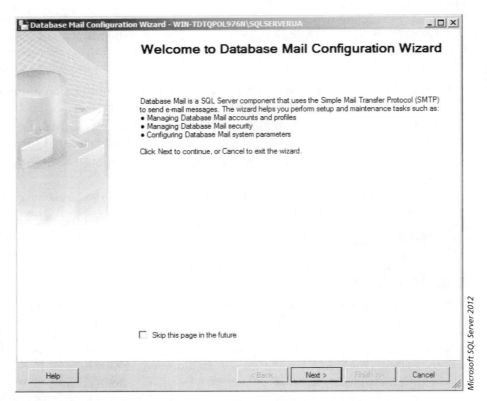

Figure 10-10 Database Mail Configuration Wizard welcome screen

2. In the Select Configuration Task window, ensure that the Set up Database Mail option button is selected. See Figure 10-11.

3. Click **Next**. If prompted by a Microsoft SQL Server Management Studio message box stating that the Database Mail feature is not available, click **Yes** to enable the feature.

4. In the New Profile window, type **SQLSERVERUA – Database Email** in the Profile name text box. See Figure 10-12. Click the **Add** button to set up a new SMTP account.

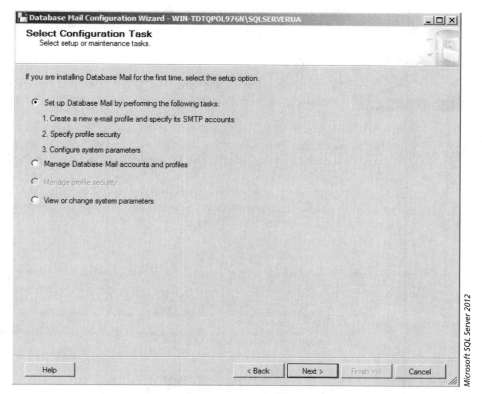

Figure 10-11 Database Mail Configuration Wizard—Select Configuration Task window

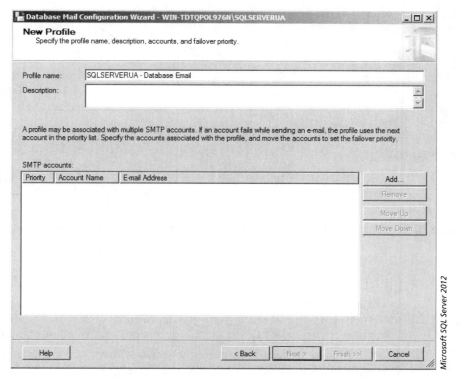

Figure 10-12 Database Mail Configuration Wizard—New Profile window

5. Before configuring a new Database Mail account, you'll need your email address, SMTP server address, port number, and authentication information.

NOTE   If you do not have access to an SMTP email address, you should enter dummy information in the Outgoing Mail Server (SMTP) and SMTP Authentication sections. You will still be able to complete the remaining steps in the activity, with the exception of sending email alerts.

In the New Database Mail Account dialog box, type **SQLSERVERUA Database Alerts** in the Account name text box. In the Description text box, type **SMTP account for sending SQL Server Agent alerts**. You should now enter your SMTP account details in the Outgoing Mail Server (SMTP) section, followed by your SMTP Authentication details in the SMTP Authentication section below. Figure 10-13 shows an account being set up with the gmail SMTP server on port 587 using SSL.

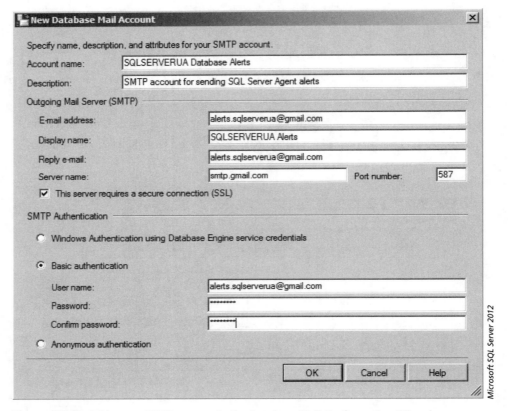

Figure 10-13 Add a new SMTP account in the Database Mail Configuration Wizard

6. Click **OK** to return to the Database Mail Configuration Wizard. Click **Next**.

7. In the Manage Profile Security window, click the **Public** check box. This allows any user to access the Database Mail profile. From the Default Profile drop-down list box, click **Yes** to make this the default public profile. See Figure 10-14. Click **Next**.

8. The Configure System Parameters window allows you to change several email settings—for example, the number of retry attempts, the maximum attachment size, blocked attachments file extensions, and logging options. Keep the default settings. See Figure 10-15. Click **Next**.

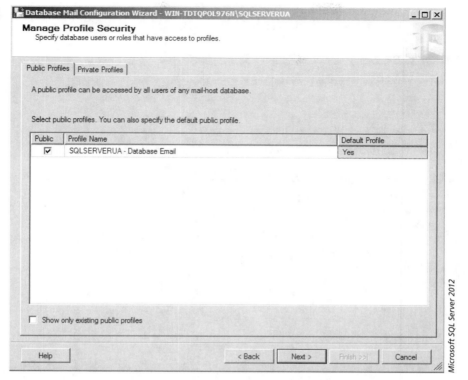

Figure 10-14 Database Mail Configuration Wizard—Manage Profile Security window

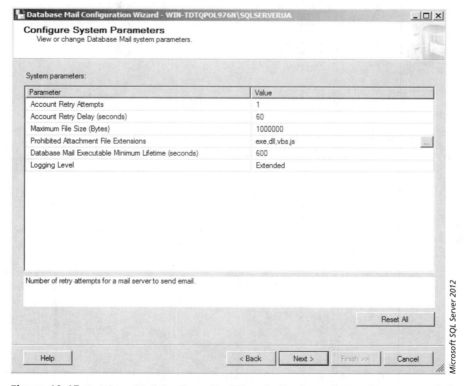

Figure 10-15 Database Mail Configuration Wizard—Configure System Parameters window

9. In the Complete the Wizard window, review the actions that will be performed. See Figure 10-16. Click **Finish**.

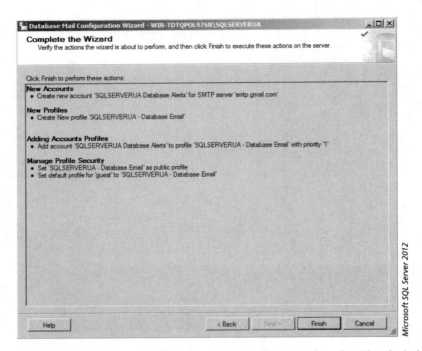

Figure 10-16 Database Mail Configuration Wizard—Complete the Wizard window

10. A status window opens and displays a "Success" message once the wizard completes the configuration changes. See Figure 10-17. Click **Close** to exit the wizard.

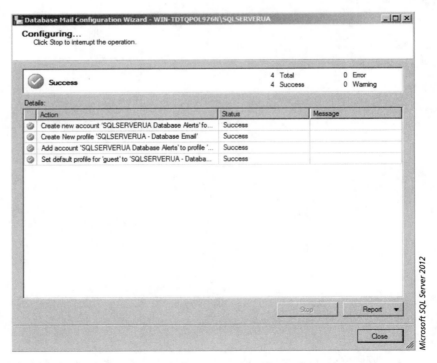

Figure 10-17 Database Mail Configuration Wizard—configuration status

11. Return to SQL Server Management Studio. In Object Explorer, right-click **Database Mail**, and then click **Send Test E-Mail**. In the Send Test E-Mail dialog box, type a valid email address in the To text box, and type **Database Mail Test** in the Subject text box. In the Body text box, type a short test message. See Figure 10-18. Click the **Send Test E-Mail** button.

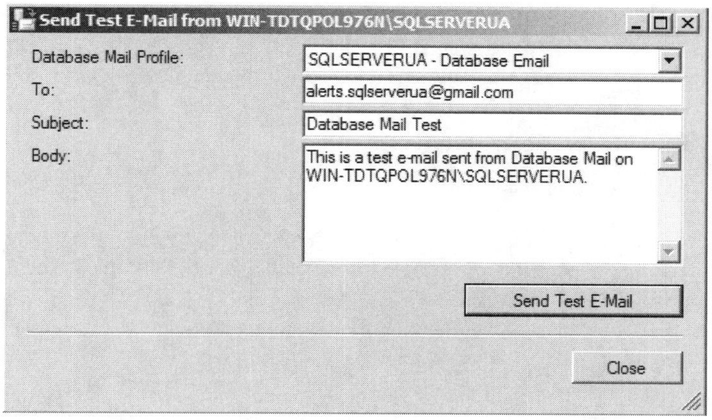

Figure 10-18 Send Test E-Mail dialog box

12. The email may take a few seconds to arrive depending upon the speed of your network connection. Figure 10-19 shows the Internet header of the email message that was created in Step 11. Note that the content is encoded in base64 but when decoded reads:

This is a test e-mail sent from Database Mail on WIN-TDTQPOL976N\ SQLSERVERUA.

```
Return-Path: <alerts.sqlserverua@gmail.com>
Received: from WIN-TDTQPOL976N (99-45-174-112.lightspeed.sntcca.sbcglobal.net. [99.45.174.112])
        by mx.google.com with ESMTPS id xm2sm3041415igb.3.2012.09.05.22.42.50
        (version=TLSv1/SSLv3 cipher=OTHER);
        Wed, 05 Sep 2012 22:42:51 -0700 (PDT)
Message-ID: <504837db.c2a0320a.0a96.5e4a@mx.google.com>
Sensitivity: Normal
Importance: Normal
MIME-Version: 1.0
From: "SQLSERVERUA Alerts" <alerts.sqlserverua@gmail.com>
To: alerts.sqlserverua@gmail.com
Reply-To: alerts.sqlserverua@gmail.com
Date: Wed, 05 Sep 2012 22:42:51 -0700 (PDT)
Subject: Database Mail Test
Content-Type: text/plain; charset=utf-8
Content-Transfer-Encoding: base64

VGhpcyBpcyBhIHRlc3QgZSltYWlsIHNlbnQgZnJvbSBEYXRhYmFzZSBNYWlsIG9uIFddJTilU
RFRRUE9MOTc2Tlx1TUUxTRVJWRVJVQS4=
```

Figure 10-19 Sample test email message from Database Mail

13. If you do not receive an email, you'll need to troubleshoot your configuration. (Even if you received the email successfully, you should still familiarize yourself with the processes described in Steps 13 and 14.) In Object Explorer, right-click **Database Mail**, and then click **View Database Mail Log**. Check the log file summary for errors. Figure 10-20 shows an example of an error event in the Database Mail Log that is due to an authentication problem with the mail server. Close the Database Mail Log.

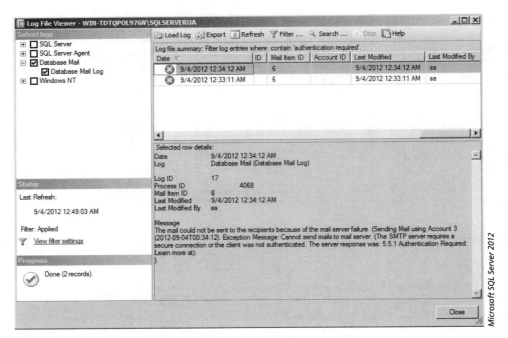

Figure 10-20 SQL Server Log File Viewer displaying the Database Mail Log

 You should obtain the SMTP server, port number, and SSL details from your email provider. If the test email fails, first check the Database Mail Log file. Double-check the account configuration settings. Finally, verify that you are able to reach the remote SMTP server through the firewall from the SQL Server host machine using the specified TCP port number. You can test the connection by adding Telnet as a feature in Server Manager and using it from a command prompt to connect to the SMTP server. As an example, to connect to the gmail SMTP server on TCP port 587, you would type the following command:

```
C:\> telnet smtp.gmail.com 587
```

14. To change the configuration, return to the Database Mail Configuration Wizard by double-clicking **Database Mail**. Click **Next**. Click the **Database Mail accounts and profiles** option, and then click **Next**. Click **View, change, or delete an existing account**, and then click **Next**. In the Manage Existing Account window, change the account configuration settings as necessary, then follow the instructions in the wizard to complete the configuration changes. Repeat Steps 11 through 13 to test the new settings.

15. Once you have successfully tested the database account and profile, you need to configure an operator. An operator contains the recipient information of the user who will receive the SQL Server Agent alert or notification via Database Mail. In Object Explorer, click the + icon to the left of SQL Server Agent, right-click the **Operators** folder, and then click **New Operator** to launch the New Operator dialog box.

16. On the General page of the New Operator dialog box, type **SQLSERVERUA Alerts** in the Name text box. Keep the Enable check box selected. In the E-mail name text box under Notification options, type a valid **email address** that you will send the alerts to. You can use the same email address that you used in Step 5 or use a different individual or group email address. See Figure 10-21. Click **OK** to create the new operator.

17. Now, you'll configure a new SQL Server event alert. In Object Explorer, right-click the **Alerts** folder in SQL Server Agent and then click **New Alert** to launch the New Alert dialog box.

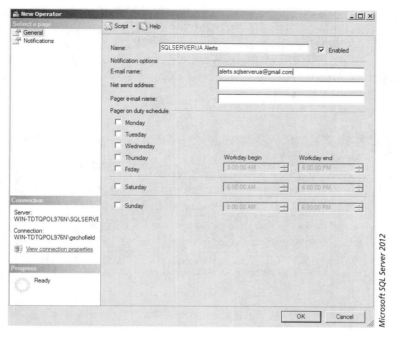

Figure 10-21 New Operator dialog box

18. On the General page of the New Alert dialog box, type **SQLSERVERUA Insufficient Resources** in the Name text box, and keep the Enable check box selected. Keep the SQL Server event alert Type option selected. In the Event alert definition section, keep the <all databases> Database name option selected, and then select **017 – Insufficient Resources** from the Severity drop-down list box. See Figure 10-22. Note that a separate alert must be configured for each event type.

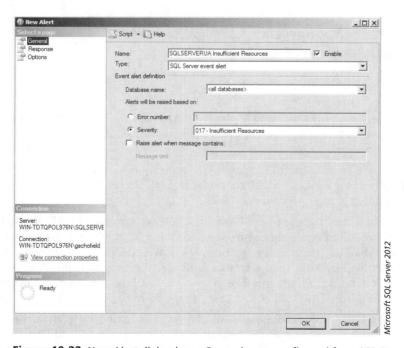

Figure 10-22 New Alert dialog box—General page configured for a SQL Server event alert

19. In the left pane of the New Alert dialog box, click **Response**. Click the **Notify operators** check box to select it. The SQLSERVERUA Alerts operator that you created in Step 16 should be listed in the operator list. Click the **E-mail** check box to the right of the SQLSERVERUA Alerts operator. See Figure 10-23. You can also add a new operator directly from this page by clicking the New Operator button.

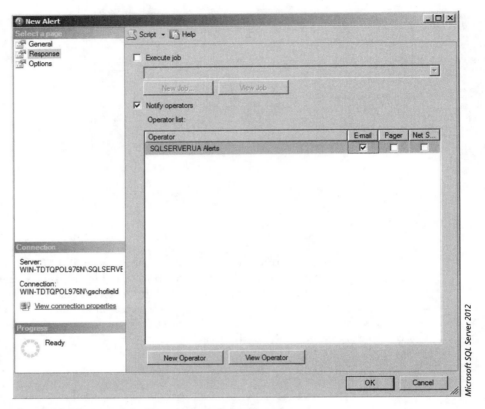

Figure 10-23 New Alert dialog box—Response page

20. In the left navigation pane of the New Alert dialog box, click **Options**. In the Include alert error text section, click the **E-mail** check box. See Figure 10-24. Click **OK** to create the alert.

21. You will now configure a new SQL Server performance condition alert. In Object Explorer, right-click the **Alerts** folder in SQL Server Agent, and then click **New Alert** to launch a New Alert dialog box.

22. On the General page of the New Alert dialog box, type **SQLSERVERUA CPU Usage** and keep the Enable check box selected. Select **SQL Server performance condition alert** from the Type drop-down list box. Select **Resource Pool Stats** from the Object drop-down list box, and then select **CPU usage %** from the Counter drop-down list box. Select **default** from the Instance drop-down list box. Select **rises above** from the Alert if counter drop-down list box, and then type **95** in the Value text box. See Figure 10-25.

23. In the left navigation pane of the New Alert dialog box, click the **Response** page. Click the **Notify operators** check box to select it. The SQLSERVERUA Alerts operator that you created in Step 16 should be listed in the operator list. Click the **E-mail** check box to the right of the SQLSERVERUA Alerts operator.

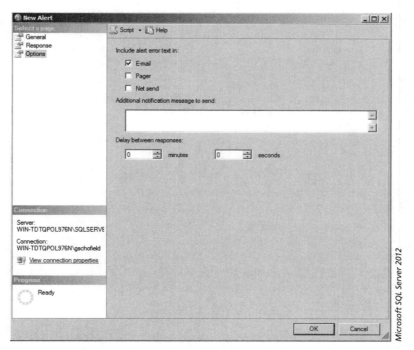

Figure 10-24 New Alert dialog box—Options page

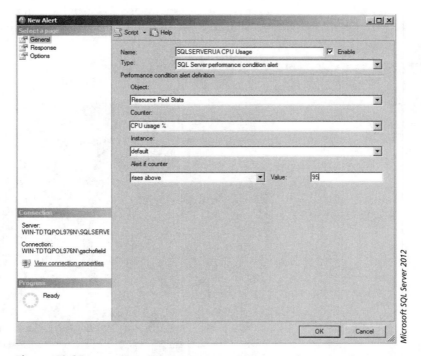

Figure 10-25 New Alert dialog box—General page configured with a SQL Server performance condition alert

24. In the left navigation pane of the New Alert dialog box, click **Options**. In the Include alert error text section, click the **E-mail** check box to select it. Type 5 in the Delay between responses text box. See Figure 10-26. Click **OK** to create the alert.

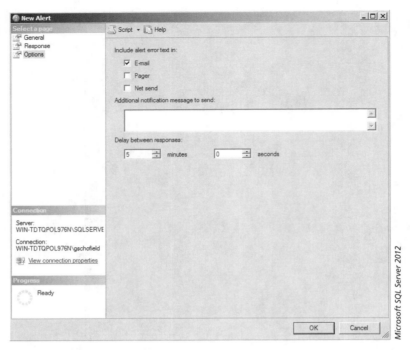

Figure 10-26 New Alert dialog box—Options page configured with a 5 minute delay between responses

25. You should see the two alerts that you created visible within Object Explorer in the Alerts folder of SQL Server Agent. See Figure 10-27. You have now completed this activity. Leave SQL Server Management Studio open for the next activity.

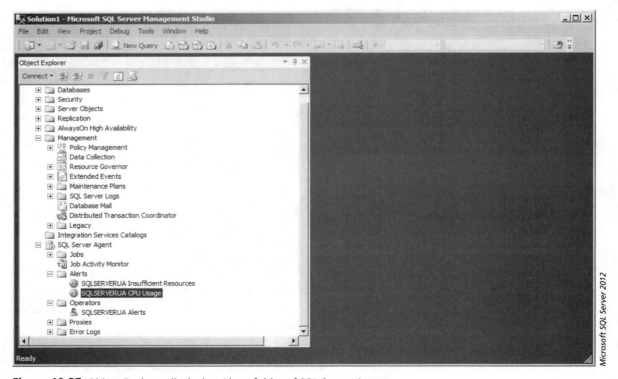

Figure 10-27 Object Explorer displaying Alerts folder of SQL Server Agent

Benchmarking and Real-Time Performance Monitoring

One of the most important roles of a database administrator is to monitor the performance of the SQL Server instances and their databases. This section introduces the SQL Server Activity Monitor user interface and its expansive range of dynamic management views and functions. To monitor a production system effectively, a database administrator must first understand how the system is expected to perform under normal operating scenarios with respect to CPU utilization, memory consumption, and disk throughput. It is always preferable to quantitatively measure performance rather than simply relying on the experience of an individual database administrator.

Benchmarking System Performance

To distinguish between normal and abnormal activity, the database administrator must understand how the system is expected to perform under normal operating loads. One way to measure system performance is to record a set of results—called a **baseline**—using specific configuration values and a particular set of database activities that can be used as future comparison points. The process to capture a set of baseline values consists of the following steps:

- Analyze and translate business requirements into a set of system requirements, for example, the number of users who will need to be connected to the system concurrently or the quantity of transactions that can be successfully processed within a certain time frame.

- Generate a workload to simulate the system activity using a SQL script or by recording and replaying a trace of actual activity using SQL Server Profiler.

- Capture and analyze the resulting performance of the system.

The baseline can be used to compare against the current system performance—a process known as **benchmarking**. Significant gaps that exist between current system performance and the baseline values should be investigated further using the knowledge you acquired during Chapter 7 for troubleshooting an individual performance problem.

SQL Server Activity Monitor

SQL Server Activity Monitor is a dashboard that allows you to monitor system activity through a simple graphical user interface. Activity Monitor is launched from SQL Server Management Studio; its interface is broken down into five sections, as described below:

- *Overview*—Displays graphs for four key system performance counters: % Processor Time, Waiting Tasks, Database I/O, and Batch Requests/sec. The % Processor Time graph measures how busy the CPU is. Waiting Tasks displays the total number of processes waiting for CPU, disk, or memory resources to become available; the number of waiting tasks may be indicative of bottlenecks and resource contention. Database I/O displays the throughput, measured as MB per seconds of data that is being transferred between memory and physical disk. Lastly, Batch Requests measures how quickly the database engine is servicing batch requests. The default refresh interval for all statistics is 10 seconds, but that can be changed to a set value that ranges from 1 second to 1 hour.

- *Processes*—Displays a list of currently connected active processes; the fields listed for each process are similar to the output of the sp_who2 system stored procedure. The Processes section also provides the capability to kill a process or launch a trace for an individual process.

- *Resource Waits*—Measures the length of time that a process has to wait for a particular resource on the system.

- *Data File I/O*—Displays the average speeds for read and write transfers of data to the physical disk along with the response time for each physical data and log file on the SQL Server instance.

- *Recent Expensive Queries*—Displays the top 10–15 most recent poorly performing queries; you can click on a query in this section to display the execution plan or to view the query details in a Query Editor window.

It is important to be aware that a number of the underlying queries used by the SQL Server Activity Monitor are performance intensive. Setting the refresh rate to poll the server at a frequency of less than 10 seconds or running Activity Monitor for long periods of time may result in a degraded overall system performance.

To view data in Activity Monitor, a user must either be a system administrator on the SQL Server instance or be granted the VIEW SERVER STATE server-level permission. If a user lacks permission, he or she will still be able to launch the tool but the text "No Data" will display in red in each section.

Dynamic Management Views and Functions

A **dynamic management view (DMV)** is a system view that enables information about the state of the underlying database management system to be queried in real time. **Dynamic management functions (DMF)** are system functions used in conjunction with dynamic management views. A dynamic management function offers similar capabilities to a view but with the additional ability to return a result set that is based on a set of input parameters supplied at the time of execution. Certain dynamic management views or functions operate at the level of the SQL Server instance and are known as **server-scoped**. Others allow information in an individual user database to be retrieved and are known as **database-scoped**. Dynamic management views and functions are an extremely powerful and flexible management feature.

To be able to query a dynamic management view or function, a user must be assigned the VIEW SERVER STATE or VIEW DATABASE STATE permission, depending upon the scope. Dynamic management views and functions are all assigned a dm_ prefix and belong to the sys schema. They can be found in the System Functions or System Views folder of the database. The server-scoped views and functions are stored in the master system database. Each user database contains a set of database-scoped views and functions.

Activity Monitor uses dynamic management views to retrieve several of its result sets. Unlike the **database console commands (DBCC)** that are a set of legacy (and often undocumented) procedures used to display system information and perform management tasks, a dynamic management view or function may be queried directly from Query Editor or SQLCMD using SQL syntax.

Activity 10-3: Monitoring SQL Server 2012 Using Activity Monitor and the Dynamic Management Views and Functions

Time Required: 45 minutes
Objective: Monitor SQL Server 2012 using Activity Monitor and the dynamic management views and functions.

Description: In this activity, you'll explore the different sections of Activity Monitor, and you'll learn about the functionality that can be used to monitor and troubleshoot SQL Server 2012 performance. You'll also learn about the dynamic management views and functions, which are powerful resources for monitoring the internal workings of the SQL Server instance and databases.

1. Return to the SQL Server Management Studio window that you left open from the previous activity. On the toolbar, click the **Activity Monitor** button or press the **Ctrl+Alt+A** keys to launch Activity Monitor. See Figure 10-28. Activity Monitor is divided into five sections: Overview, Processes, Resource Waits, Data File I/O, and Recent Expensive Queries.

2. Right-click in the **Overview** pane, point to **Refresh interval**, and then click **30 seconds** to change the refresh interval for the performance counters that are displayed in the four Overview graphs. Notice that you can also pause collection or manually refresh the performance counters from the same shortcut menu.

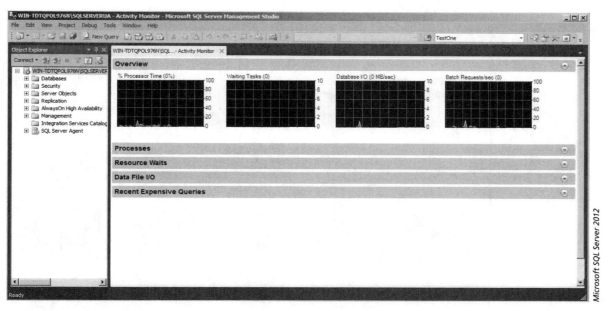

Figure 10-28 Activity Monitor—Overview

3. On the toolbar, click the **New Query** button to open a new Query Editor window, and then type the following SQL command:

```
USE AdventureWorks2012;

GO

SELECT * FROM Person.Person;

GO
```

Click the **Execute** button on the toolbar or press the **F5** key to run the query. See Figure 10-29.

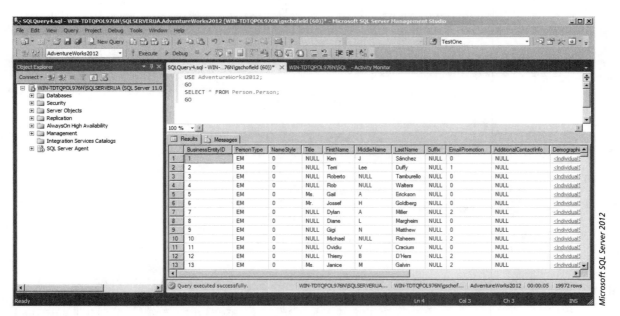

Figure 10-29 Open a new Query Editor window and execute a SELECT statement

4. Click the **Activity Monitor** tab to return to the open Activity Monitor window. Click the **Processes** bar to expand the Processes pane, which provides a view of sessions currently connected to the SQL Server instance. Use the scroll bar to locate the session you established in Step 3. See Figure 10-30. You can also use the column filters at the top of each column in the tabular display to filter the sessions. Review each column name to familiarize yourself with the statistics available for each session.

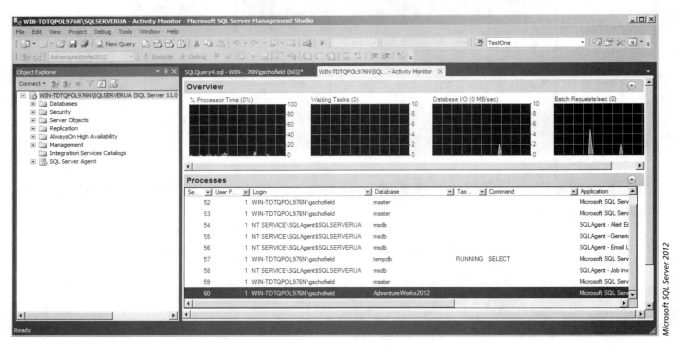

Figure 10-30 Activity Monitor—Processes

5. Right-click the row of the session that you created in Step 3, and then click **Details**. (Notice that you can also choose to kill the session or run a trace against the session from the shortcut menu.) A Session Details dialog box opens, displaying the last Transact-SQL command that was executed by the session. See Figure 10-31. Click the **Close** button to exit the dialog box.

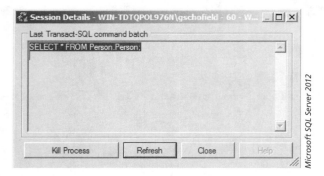

Figure 10-31 Activity Monitor—Session Details dialog box

6. Click the **Processes** bar again to collapse the Processes pane. Expand the Resource Waits pane by clicking the **Resource Waits** bar. See Figure 10-32. Each row in this pane displays the amount of time a process must wait to obtain access to a particular resource. High wait times may be indicative of a resource bottleneck.

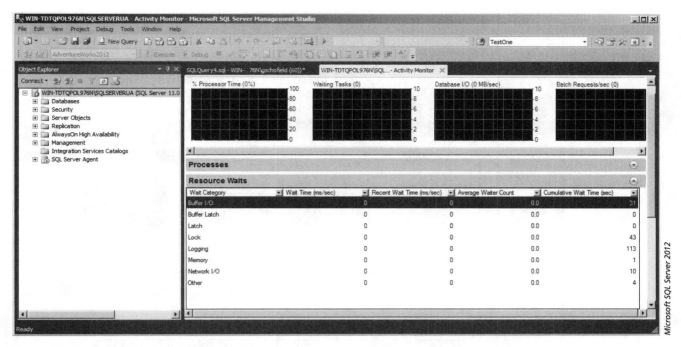

Figure 10-32 Activity Monitor—Resource Waits

7. Click the **Resource Waits** bar to collapse the Resource Waits pane. Expand the Data File I/O pane by clicking the **Data File I/O** bar. See Figure 10-33. Each row represents a physical data or log file, and the columns display the level of activity in terms of reading and writing data from the files along with the response time. Note that the information in this pane may take a few seconds to load.

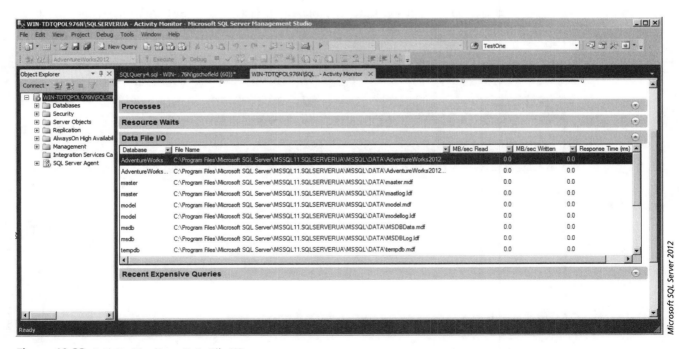

Figure 10-33 Activity Monitor—Data File I/O

8. Click the **Data File I/O** bar to collapse the Data File I/O pane. Expand the Recent Expensive Queries pane by clicking the **Recent Expensive Queries** bar. See Figure 10-34. This pane helps you identify poorly performing queries. However, because your SQLSERVERUA instance is not being heavily used, you are most likely to see the queries that are being run to retrieve the data for Activity Monitor.

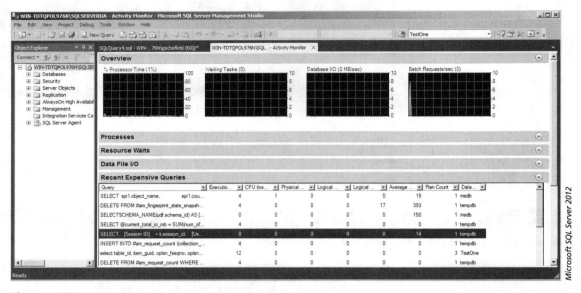

Figure 10-34 Activity Monitor—Recent Expensive Queries

9. In the Recent Expensive Queries pane, right-click one of the SELECT queries, and then click **Edit Query Text** to open the query in a new Query Editor window. This is a useful feature that enables you to see the SQL command that was executed. Return to the Recent Expensive Queries pane, right-click another SELECT query, and then click **Show Execution Plan** to view the query execution plan. See Figure 10-35.

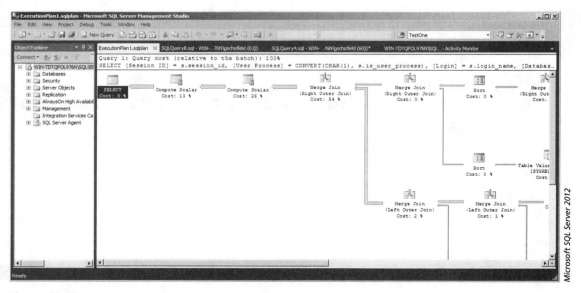

Figure 10-35 Activity Monitor—Show Execution Plan

10. Activity Monitor makes extensive use of dynamic management views and functions to return the underlying data sets. You'll now explore these in more detail. In SQL Server Management Studio, click **Help** on the menu bar, and then click **View Help** to launch Microsoft Books Online for SQL Server 2012 in a Web browser.

You can also use the keys **Ctrl+F1** to launch Microsoft Books Online for SQL Server 2012.

11. In the Search MSDN with Bing text box in the upper-left corner, type **Dynamic Management Views and Functions (Transact-SQL)** and then click the **Search** button. In the search results, click the top link **Dynamic Management Views and Functions (Transact-SQL)**, and then read the topic.

12. Notice that the dynamic management views and functions are organized by category under the "In This Section" heading. Click the **I/O Related Management Views and Functions** link. When the Web page opens, click the **sys.dm_io_virtual_file_stats (Transact-SQL)** link in the grid listing the different I/O-related dynamic management objects, and then read the topic. See Figure 10-36.

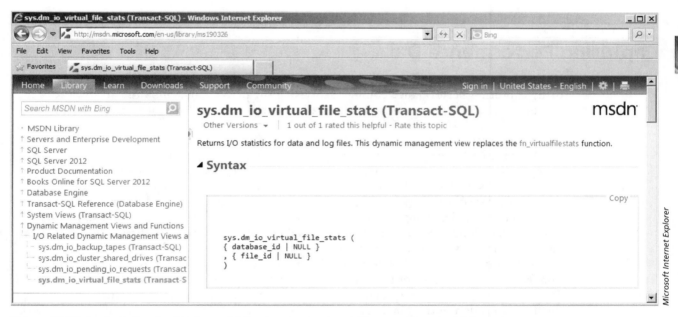

Figure 10-36 Books Online for SQL Server 2012—"sys.dm_io_virtual_file_stats (Transact-SQL)" topic

13. Return to SQL Server Management Studio, click the **New Query** button on the toolbar to open a new Query Editor window, and then type the following SQL command:

```
SELECT * FROM
    sys.dm_io_virtual_file_stats(NULL, NULL);

GO
```

Click the **Execute** button on the toolbar or press the **F5** key to run the query. See Figure 10-37. Note that the data set returned by the view is very similar to the Data File I/O pane of Activity Monitor, although the units are different.

14. You have now completed this activity. Close all open tabs in SQL Server Management Studio, but leave the application and the Web browser open for the next activity.

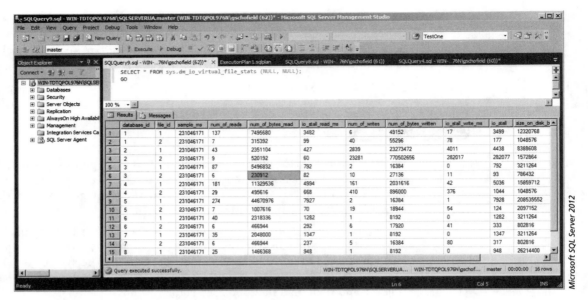

Figure 10-37 Query a dynamic management view

Capturing Performance Data

You can capture SQL Server performance data by using the SQL Server Profiler to record a trace or by capturing performance counter data using the performance monitor utility. Recall that a data collector set is a collection of statistics captured at predetermined time intervals. SQL Server traces and data collector sets are somewhat limited because they can only be used to capture a specific type of data.

The **data collector** is a feature of the SQL Server Management Data Warehouse that overcomes the limitations of traces and data collector sets as it can be used to capture several different types of data. A **data collection** is a specific instance of a data collector that specifies the method for collecting the data, the source of the data to collect, and the method for storing the collected data, including when to purge the data. A data collection may run continuously, on a schedule, or it may be run manually, as an ad hoc process. There are three predefined system data collection sets that collect data on disk usage, server activity, and query statistics.

A **collector type** is a method for collecting a specific type of data that is used by a data collection. Four standard collector types are installed with SQL Server: the Transact-SQL Query, SQL Trace, Performance Counters, and Query Activity. Each data collector type stores the results of the data collection in the **Management Data Warehouse (MDW)**, a centralized data repository installed on each SQL Server instance. You execute a data collection and manage the data inside the Management Data Warehouse by using a combination of SQL Server Integration Services and SQL Server Agent. The data that is stored in the Management Data Warehouse may be queried using SQL, and it can also be viewed using one of several predefined management reports.

Before using the data collector for the first time, you must install both SQL Server Integration Services and SQL Server Agent, as they are integral to the execution of a data collection set. You must also configure the Management Data Warehouse using a wizard that installs the relational database and the predefined data collection sets and maps users and logins to the database roles.

Activity 10-4: Configuring the Management Data Warehouse

Time Required: 60 minutes
Objective: Configure the Management Data Warehouse, execute a system data collection set, and view a summary of the data using the reports.

Description: In this activity, you'll use the Configure Management Data Warehouse Wizard to configure the Management Data Warehouse, install the predefined system data collection sets, and start a data collection. Then, you will use the standard Management Data Warehouse reports to view a summary of the data that is collected.

1. Return to the SQL Server Management Studio window that you left open from the previous activity. In Object Explorer, click the **+** icon to the left of the Management folder. Right-click **Data Collection**, and then click **Configure Management Data Warehouse** to launch the Configure Management Data Warehouse Wizard. See Figure 10-38. Click **Next**.

Figure 10-38 Configure Management Data Warehouse Wizard—Welcome window

2. In the Select configuration task window, keep the default Create or upgrade a management data warehouse option selected. See Figure 10-39. Click **Next**.

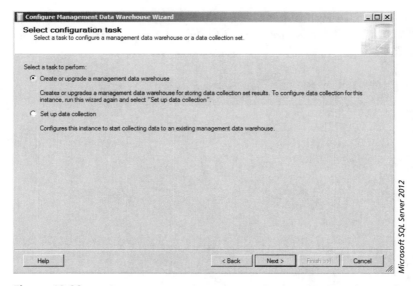

Figure 10-39 Configure Management Data Warehouse Wizard—Select configuration task window

3. The Configure Management Data Warehouse Storage window allows you to select an existing database or create a new database to store the data that will be collected. Click the **New** button to the right of the Database name drop-down list box. On the General page of the New Database dialog box, type **ManagementDataWarehouse** in the Database name text box. See Figure 10-40. Keep all other default settings, and click the **OK** button to create the database and return to the Configure Management Data Warehouse Storage window.

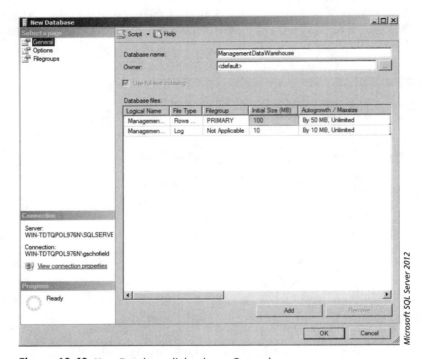

Figure 10-40 New Database dialog box—General page

4. The newly created ManagementDataWarehouse database should now be selected in the Database name drop-down list box in the Configure Management Data Warehouse Storage window. See Figure 10-41. Click **Next**.

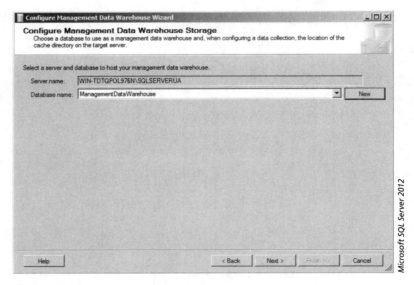

Figure 10-41 Configure Management Data Warehouse Storage

5. The Management Data Warehouse has three default system roles: mdw_admin, mdw_reader, and mdw_writer. The mdw_admin role enables a user to administer data collection jobs and manage the collected data. The mdw_reader role allows read-only access to the collected data. The mdw_writer role allows a user to read and write data into the warehouse. The Map Logins and Users window allows you to map existing logins and users to the Management Data Warehouse roles. The Administrator account that you are using to configure the Management Data Warehouse is a member of the sysadmin role, which by default has full administrative access, so it is not necessary for you to create additional mappings at this stage. See Figure 10-42. Click **Next**.

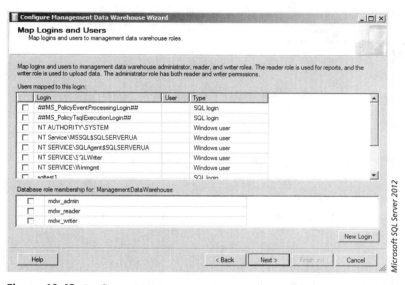

Figure 10-42 Configure Management Data Warehouse Wizard—Map Logins and Users window

6. The Complete the Wizard window displays the actions that will be performed to install and configure the Management Data Warehouse. See Figure 10-43. Click the **Finish** button to complete the wizard.

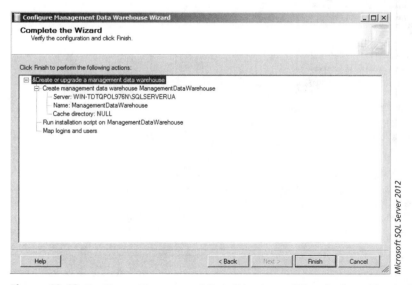

Figure 10-43 Configure Management Data Warehouse Wizard—Complete the Wizard window

7. The Configure Data Collection Wizard Progress window displays the progress of the installation and configuration steps. See Figure 10-44. After the wizard has successfully finished performing all steps, click the **Close** button to exit the wizard.

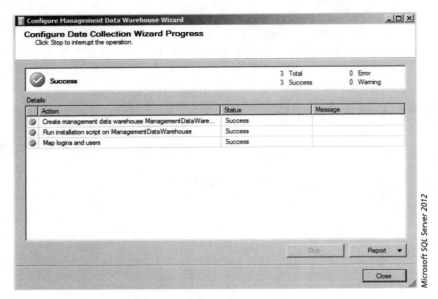

Figure 10-44 Configure Management Data Warehouse Wizard—Configure Data Collection Wizard Progress window

8. You are now ready to configure a data collection. In Object Explorer, right-click **Data Collection**, and then click **Configure Management Data Warehouse** to launch the Configure Management Data Warehouse Wizard. Click the **Next** button in the Welcome to the Configure Management Data Warehouse Wizard window. In the Select configuration task window, click the **Set up data collection** option button. See Figure 10-45. Click **Next**.

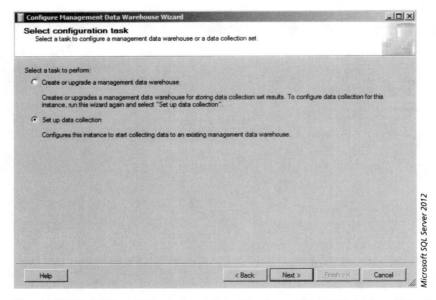

Figure 10-45 Configure Management Data Warehouse Wizard—Select configuration task window

9. In the Configure Management Data Warehouse Storage window, click the **...** button to the right of the Server name text box. The Connect to Server dialog box will be prepopulated with your machine name and the SQLSERVERUA instance. Click the **Connect** button. In the Configure Management Data Warehouse Storage window, click **ManagementDataWarehouse** in the Database name drop-down list box. Leave the Cache directory text box empty to use the TEMP directory of the data collector process. See Figure 10-46. Click **Next**.

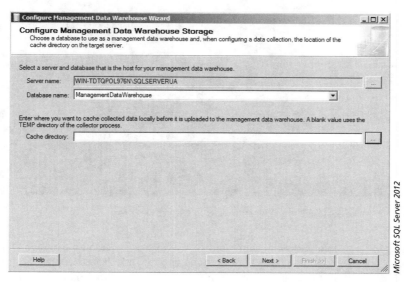

Figure 10-46 Configure Management Data Warehouse Wizard—Configure Management Data Warehouse Storage window

10. The Complete the Wizard window displays the actions that will be performed to configure and enable the data collection. See Figure 10-47. Click the **Finish** button to complete the wizard. After the Configure Data Collection Wizard Progress window shows that the configuration steps have successfully completed, click the **Close** button.

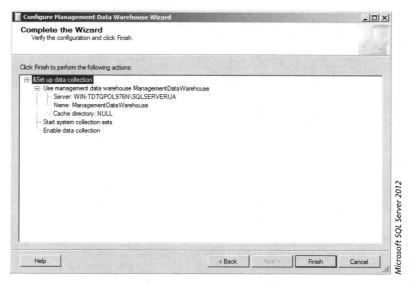

Figure 10-47 Configure Management Data Warehouse Wizard—Complete the Wizard window

11. In Object Explorer, click the **+** icon to the left of the Data Collection feature, and then click the **+** icon to the left of the System Data Collection Sets folder. See Figure 10-48.

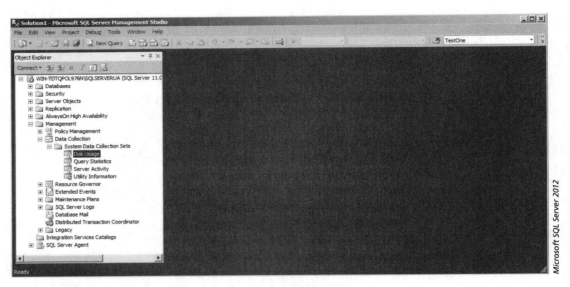

Figure 10-48 View the System Data Collection Sets in Object Explorer

 Four default system data collection sets are created when you initially set up a data collection using the wizard: Disk Usage, Query Statistics, Server Activity, and Utility Information. The first three data collection sets are scheduled to run every six hours. The Utility Information data collection set is an on-demand process.

12. Right-click the **Disk Usage** data collection set, and then click **Properties**. In the Data Collection Set Properties window, click **Description** in the left navigation pane. The Description page provides a description of the task. See Figure 10-49. The Disk Usage data collection set collects data about the disk and log usage for all databases.

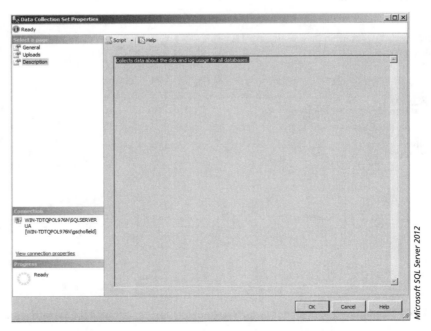

Figure 10-49 Data Collection Set Properties—Description page

13. In the Data Collection Set Properties window of the Disk Usage data collection set, click **Uploads** in the left navigation pane. The Uploads page provides details of the schedule to upload data into the Management Data Warehouse. See Figure 10-50. The Uploads page is grayed out because this particular set of data is configured in noncached mode, meaning that a single SQL Server Agent job manages both the collection and upload of data; hence, the ability to select a particular upload schedule is meaningless in this context.

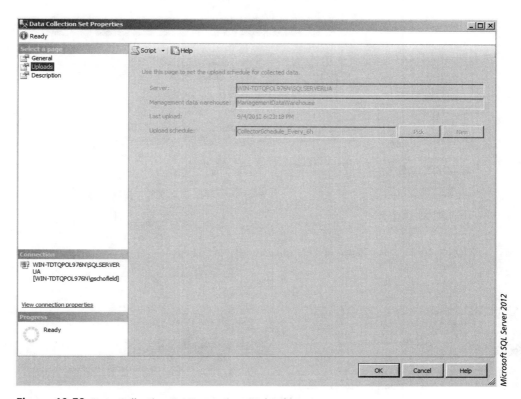

Figure 10-50 Data Collection Set Properties—Uploads page

14. In the Data Collection Set Properties window of the Disk Usage data collection set, click **General** in the left navigation pane. The General page provides configuration details of the data collection set, including the schedule, the selected data upload option, collection items, input parameters, the account to use for running the collection set, and the data retention period. In a production environment, you should use the cached data upload option if you want to upload data on a schedule that is independent to the data collection activity. Conversely, the non-cached data upload option is more appropriate for on-demand or infrequently gathered data collection sets. See Figure 10-51. Once you have finished reviewing the configuration details, click **Cancel** to exit the Properties window without saving any changes.

15. The data that is collected and stored in the Management Data Warehouse can be queried directly using a SQL query. The Data Collection feature also provides several preconfigured reports that leverage SQL Server Reporting Services to enable a database administrator to visualize and navigate the data over time. The preconfigured reports are Server Activity History, Disk Usage Summary, and Query Statistics History. Each report displays data collected by its respective system data collection set. In Object Explorer, right-click the **Data Collection** feature, point to **Reports**, point to **Management Data Warehouse**, and then click **Server Activity History**. The Server Activity History report opens as a tabbed window in the right pane of SQL Server Management Studio. See Figure 10-52.

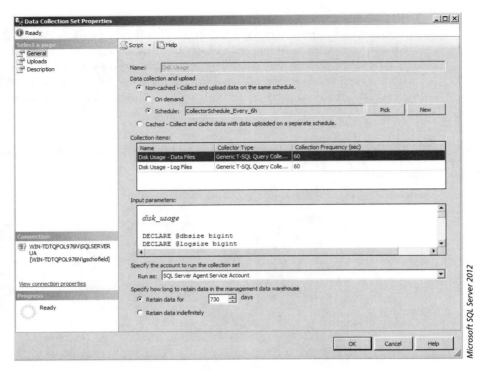

Figure 10-51 Data Collection Set Properties—General page

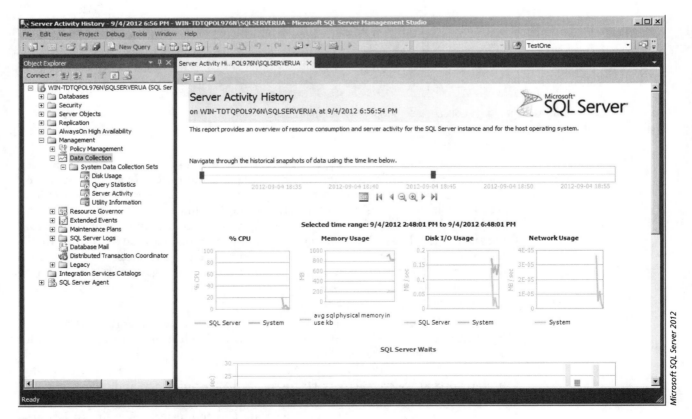

Figure 10-52 Server Activity History report—summary

16. The Server Activity History report displays a summary of data collected by the Server Activity system data collection set, including information on resource utilization and SQL Server activity. The top section of the report contains a timeline of historical snapshots of data and a set of navigation controls to modify the time range. Review the data within the report and experiment with the navigational controls to reduce, increase, or change the date range. The report also allows you to drill down to analyze data in more detail. Click the **Disk I/O Usage** graph below the navigation controls to see more detail. See Figure 10-53. Note that because the system data collection sets run only every six hours, you may not initially see any data on the report.

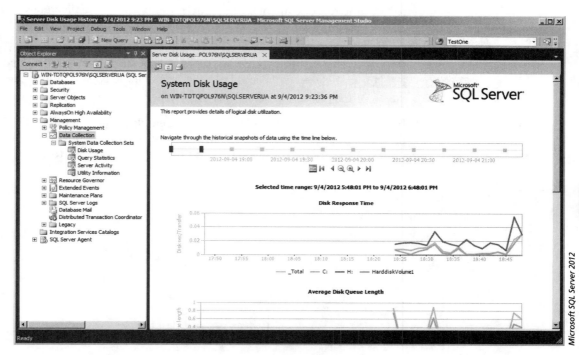

Figure 10-53 Server Activity History report – System Disk Usage detail

17. Repeat Step 15 to view the Disk Usage Summary and Query Statistics History. After you have finished reviewing the reports, close the open tabs in SQL Server Management Studio, but leave the application running for the next activity.

Database Audits

An organization may need to keep an audit trail of activities—such as capturing all user IDs and delete statements for a specific table—for monitoring and to demonstrate compliance with controls and policies. **SQL Server Audit** is a mechanism that enables certain server- or database-level events to be captured and written to a target that records the results of an audit. The target can be a file destination, the Windows application, or a security log. The following four steps are involved in creating an audit:

- Define an audit object.
- Create the server audit specification.
- Create the database audit specification.
- Enable the audit to begin capturing events.

Activity 10-5: Configuring an Audit

Time Required: 45 minutes

Objective: Configure an audit to capture login events.

Description: Use the Create Audit Wizard and the Create Server Audit Specification Wizard to configure an audit of successful and failed server login attempts. Enable the audit to capture the events and review the events in the audit log.

1. Return to the SQL Server Management Studio window that you left open from the previous activity. In Object Explorer, click the **+** icon to the left of the Security folder to view the folder contents. Right-click **Audits,** and then click **New Audit.**

The Create Audit Wizard allows you to create a new audit with a unique name and to specify the destination and file management options for the audit output. You can also use the wizard to define the actions that should be taken in the event of a log failure; those options include continuing, shutting down the server, and failing the individual operation.

2. In the Create Audit Wizard, keep all the default settings and type **C:\Trace** in the File path text box. See Figure 10-54. Make a note of the audit name, which, by default, is named Audit followed by a date and time stamp. Click **OK** to create the audit.

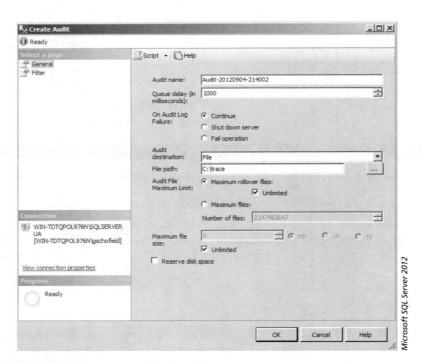

Figure 10-54 Create Audit Wizard

3. Next, you need to add a server or database audit specification to determine which security events to audit. For this activity, you will monitor server logins and add a server audit specification to the audit. Note that the process for adding a database audit specification is identical to the process for adding a server audit specification. In Object Explorer, right-click the **Server Audits Specifications** folder, and then click **New Server Audit Specification** to launch the Create Server Audit Specification Wizard.

4. From the Audit drop-down list box, select the audit name that you noted in Step 2. In the Actions grid, select **FAILED_LOGIN_GROUP** from the Audit Action Type drop-down list box in the first row. In the Actions grid, select **SUCCESSFUL_LOGIN_GROUP** from the Audit Action Type drop-down list box in the second row. See Figure 10-55. Click the **OK** button to create the Server Audit Specification and exit the wizard.

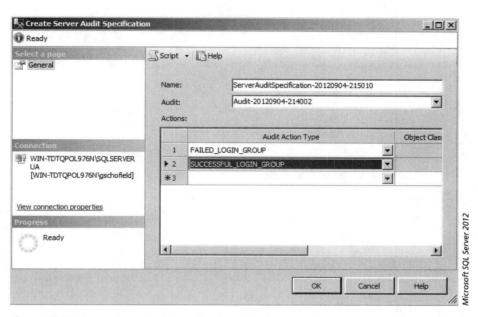

Figure 10-55 Create Server Audit Specification Wizard

5. In the Audits folder of Object Explorer, right-click the audit that you created in Step 2, and then click **Enable Audit**. Click the **Close** button on the Success dialog box. In the Server Audit Specifications folder of Object Explorer, right-click the server audit specification that you created in Step 3, and then click **Enable Server Audit Specification**. Click the **Close** button on the Success dialog box.

6. You will now attempt to connect to the SQLSERVERUA instance using an invalid password. On the toolbar in Object Explorer, click the **Connect** button, and then click **Database Engine**. In the Connect to Server dialog box, select **SQL Server Authentication** from the Authentication drop-down list box. Type **sa** in the Login text box, and then type **xyz** in the Password text box. Click the **Connect** button. An error message appears, indicating that the login failed for user 'sa.' See Figure 10-56. Click the **OK** button. Click the **Cancel** button on the Connect to Server dialog box.

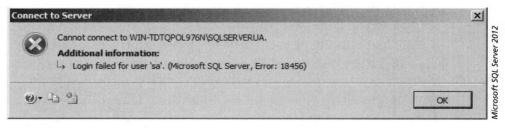

Figure 10-56 Login failed message box

7. Next, you'll confirm that this event was captured in your audit. In the Audits folder in Object Explorer, right-click the audit that you created in Step 2, and then click **View Audit Logs** to launch the Log File Viewer. In the list of events in the Log file summary section, click the event with the **LOGIN FAILED** Action ID. Read the selected row details in the lower pane. See Figure 10-57. Click the **Close** button.

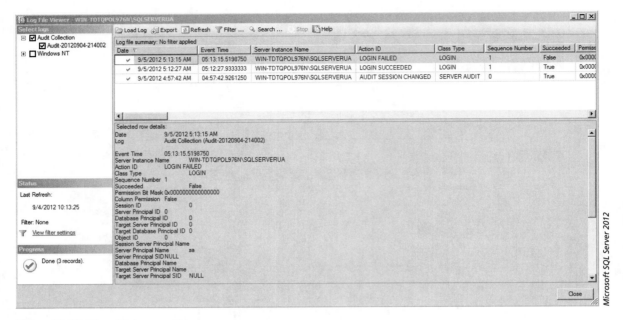

Figure 10-57 View database audit logs

8. You have now finished the activities in this chapter. Close all open applications.

Chapter Summary

- To minimize the risk of unplanned service disruptions and ensure that agreed-upon service levels are met, a database administrator must monitor SQL Server 2012 on an ongoing basis.

- After establishing the current state of a SQL Server instance, databases, and network connections, the database administrator should check for recent errors and failure of scheduled jobs, focusing in particular on jobs that are responsible for taking and managing database backups.

- SQL Server Agent can be configured to automatically send job status notifications and alerts.

- Alerts are messages generated automatically in response to a system event or when a predefined performance condition is met.

- To monitor a production system effectively, a database administrator must first understand how the system is expected to perform under normal operating scenarios with respect to CPU utilization, memory consumption, and disk throughput.

- A set of results called a baseline should be recorded using specific configuration values and a particular load scenario that can be used as future comparison points.

- SQL Server Activity Monitor is a dashboard that allows you to monitor system activity through a simple graphical user interface.

- Dynamic management views and functions enable information about the state of a SQL Server instance or the underlying database management system to be queried in real time.

- Capturing performance data on a regular basis can be useful for analyzing a specific issue and for identifying trends over time.

- The Management Data Warehouse provides a comprehensive data capture, storage, and reporting solution for several important types of data.

- A company may have tight controls or be subject to regulation that governs who can access a resource on a SQL server.

- SQL Server Audit is a mechanism that enables certain server-level or database-level events to be captured to demonstrate compliance with controls and procedures.

Key Terms

alert   A message generated automatically in response to a system event or when a performance condition is met.

baseline   A set of results recorded using a particular set of configuration values and a specific load scenario; can be used as future comparison points.

benchmarking   The process of using a baseline to compare against current system performance.

collector type   A method for collecting a specific type of data that is used by a data collection; four standard collector types are installed with SQL Server: Transact-SQL Query, SQL Trace, Performance Counters, and Query Activity.

database console commands (DBCC)   A set of legacy procedures used to display system information and perform management tasks.

Database Mail   The SQL Server component used to integrate with and send messages via an SMTP email server.

database-scoped   A dynamic management view or function that allows information in an individual user database to be retrieved.

data collection   A specific instance of a data collector that specifies the method for collecting the data, the source of the data to collect, and the method for storing the collected data, including when to purge the data.

data collector   A feature of the Management Data Warehouse on a SQL Server instance that is used to capture several different types of data.

dynamic management functions (DMF)   A system function often used in conjunction with dynamic management views; offers similar capabilities to a view but with the ability to return a result set that is based on a set of input parameters supplied at the time of execution.

dynamic management view (DMV)   A system view that enables information about the state of the underlying database management system to be queried in real time.

Log File Viewer   A feature within SQL Server Management Studio that aggregates events from different event logs.

Management Data Warehouse (MDW)   A centralized data repository installed on each SQL Server instance; used to capture the output of a data collection.

operator   An alias for an individual or group of people with their email or pager information.

performance conditions   Rules defined by placing a threshold on the value of a specific performance counter monitored by SQL Server Agent; if the value of the performance counter exceeds the established threshold, an alert will be triggered.

server-scoped   A dynamic management view or function that operates at the level of the SQL Server instance.

severity level   A numerical indicator that describes the type of SQL Server error; can be used to specify whether an alert should be generated.

10

SQL Server Agent error log   A log that records informational, warning, and error events related to SQL Server Agent activity.

SQL Server Audit   A mechanism that enables certain server-level or database-level events to be captured and written to a target that records the results of an audit.

SQL Server log   A log that contains system events as well as certain user-defined events for the SQL Server instance.

Windows application log   A log that captures events generated by applications running on the Microsoft Windows operating system.

Windows Management Instrumentation (WMI) event   An event generated by the Microsoft Windows operating system.

Review Questions

1. Which of the following actions would *not* be necessary to ensure that a remote client can connect to a SQL Server instance and execute a query against a database?

    a.   Use Object Explorer to check that all databases are online.

    b.   Check that all services are running in SQL Server Configuration Manager.

    c.   Check the physical disk drives that contain the data and log files for the SQL Server instance.

    d.   Execute a query from SQLCMD or Query Editor, connected using the Named Pipes or TCP/IP protocol.

2. Why would you *not* normally create an automated alert for SQL Server errors with a severity level of 1–10 or 11–16?

    a.   It is good practice to automate alerts for all severity levels.

    b.   Events with a severity level in the range 1–10 are for information only and do not warrant further investigation.

    c.   Events with a severity level in the range 11–16 are user errors and must be fixed by the user.

    d.   Both options b and c

3. What is the minimum number of alerts that would be required to capture all errors of severity level in the range 17–19?

    a.   1

    b.   3

    c.   6

    d.   Both options a and b, depending upon other factors

4. SQL Server Agent alerts should be used for which of the following scenarios?

    a.   SQL Server errors with a severity level of 17 and above

    b.   Resource alerts that include high CPU or memory utilization, disk space shortage, and deadlocks using performance conditions

    c.   SQL Server Agent job failure notification

    d.   All of the above

5. Why is establishing a baseline important for monitoring performance?

    a.   Baselines are not important because there is no substitute for experience.

    b.   A baseline can help a database administrator understand how the system is expected to behave under normal operating conditions.

    c.   Baselines are not relevant to performance monitoring.

    d.   Both options a and b

6. Which of the following actions may lead to degraded system performance when running Activity Monitor?

    a. Running Activity Monitor continuously for long periods of time

    b. Customizing the filter and sort order for each section

    c. Setting the refresh rate to 1 second

    d. Both options a and c

7. What is the difference between a dynamic management view and a dynamic management function?

    a. Dynamic management views may be queried using SQL.

    b. For complex queries, a set of input parameters may be supplied to a dynamic management function at the time of execution.

    c. Dynamic management functions may be queried using SQL.

    d. There is no difference; the term *function* and *view* are used interchangeably.

8. What permission must be granted to allow a user to query a database-scoped dynamic management view?

    a. VIEW SERVER STATE

    b. QUERY SERVER STATE

    c. VIEW DATABASE STATE

    d. QUERY DATABASE STATE

9. Which of the following is *not* true with respect to dynamic management views and functions?

    a. They belong to the sys schema.

    b. They are given the prefix dm_ in their name.

    c. Server-scoped dynamic management views and functions are stored in the master system database.

    d. Database-scoped dynamic management views and functions are stored in the msdb system database.

10. Which of the following is *not* a predefined system data collection set?

    a. % Processor Time

    b. Server Activity

    c. Query Statistics

    d. Disk Usage

11. What are the advantages of using the Management Data Warehouse and data collector versus other tools for collecting statistics?

    a. The Management Data Warehouse provides a standardized repository for storing and managing the data.

    b. The data collector can capture different types of data; the SQL Profiler and Windows Performance Monitor can only capture a single type.

    c. The data collector does not require further configuration after installation of a SQL Server instance.

    d. Both options a and b

12. Which of the following is *not* a step required to configure a database audit?

    a. Create a new audit object.

    b. Map the users and logins to the database roles.

    c. Create a database audit specification.

    d. Enable the audit.

Case Projects

CASE PROJECTS

Case Project 10-1: Vincent Tax Associates

You recently joined a small family-operated accounting business that specializes in preparing state and federal tax returns as well as providing tax advice for individuals and local small businesses. Although the business is well established, it is facing competitive pressure from on-line e-file firms, which offer a basic tax preparation and filing service at a low cost. The CEO of your firm recently approved the purchase of a new system for preparing and filing returns, and you have been hired to administer the SQL Server databases. The CEO is particularly concerned about the availability of the system during the peak tax season and has asked you to establish a formal process for monitoring their SQL Server databases. Complete the following:

- Construct a list of daily tasks and the priority in which they should be performed to monitor the service.
- Identify which tasks are good candidates for automation, and explain how you would automate these processes.
- Summarize the benefits of establishing a baseline to benchmark the current performance of the system.

Case Project 10-2: Granite Software Engineering, LLC

You work as a database administrator for a medium-sized software engineering firm that recently won a government contract to perform geospatial data analysis for the U.S. Navy. The contract stipulates that the company must implement stringent access controls to protect the security of the data, and it requires that the company demonstrate compliance with the controls. Complete the following:

- Explain the differences between the audit and data collection features of SQL Server 2012.
- Devise a plan that will enable you to demonstrate compliance with the access controls. Specifically, you must be able to report the time and user ID associated with any attempt to access or modify information in the database.

Case Project 10-3: Blue Water Insurance, LLC

Blue Water Insurance, LLC, specializes in underwriting marine insurance for containerized cargo ships. You work for the IT Department at Blue Water, and one of your responsibilities is to administer the company's SQL Server databases that support the company's proprietary quote management system. You have been asked to monitor the performance of the databases and identify trends that may necessitate upgrading the existing hardware infrastructure. Complete the following:

- What are the standard Microsoft tools at your disposal for monitoring SQL Server database performance?
- What SQL Server component could you use to capture a time series data set of performance statistics for analyzing trends in the performance of the database?
- Explain why establishing a baseline set of performance values would benefit your analysis.

Hands-On Projects

Hands-On Project 10-1: Configuring Alerts and Notifications for a Production Database

For this hands-on project, you will use the SQL Server named instance SQLSERVERHOA that you created in previous chapters. The objective of this activity is to configure a minimum set of alerts and notifications to effectively monitor a production system. Document Steps 3–5 by taking a screen shot showing the New Alert—General page or the SQL statement used to create the alert.

1. Using SQL Server Management Studio, configure Database Mail, create a default mail profile, and add an operator for the SQLSERVERHOA named instance.

2. Test your configuration from Step 1 by using Object Explorer to send a test email. Document this step by taking a screen shot of the email received in your email client, or copy and paste the Internet header of the email into a text document.

3. Configure an alert to monitor deadlocks, using the following settings:

   - Object: SQLServer: Locks
   - Counter: Number of Deadlocks/sec
   - Alert if counter rises above 0

4. Configure alerts for the following conditions:

   a. 017—Insufficient Resources

   b. 018—Nonfatal Internal Error Detected

   c. 019—Error in Resource

   d. 020—Fatal Error in Current Process Event

   e. 021—Fatal Error in Database (dbid) Processes

   f. 022—Fatal Error Table Integrity Suspect

   g. 023—Fatal Error: Database Integrity Suspect

   h. 024—Hardware Error

 Use Books Online for SQL Server 2012 to learn how to quickly create these alerts by executing a SQL script that can be reused for future configuration of a SQL Server instance.

5. Use your judgment to define appropriate thresholds for the following physical resources and configure alerts that will be triggered if a given resource exceeds those thresholds:

   a. CPU utilization

   b. Memory consumption

   c. Disk space shortage

3-key Triple DES A widely used symmetric encryption algorithm that applies the DES cipher three times to the data using three different 64-bit keys.

access token A user identifier from the Windows operating system that is created when the user initially logs on; applications that use Windows integrated authentication use access tokens to validate the user.

Active Directory Domain Service (AD DS) A directory service available in the Windows Server 2008 R2 operating system; uses a domain controller to store information about users, computers, and other devices on the network and to manage authentication. AD DS helps administrators securely manage this information and facilitates resource sharing and collaboration between users.

Active Directory Lightweight Directory Service (AD LDS) A lightweight implementation of AD DS that uses the same code base but does not require the creation of domains or domain controllers. Multiple instances of AD LDS may be run on a single server.

AES The successor to the DES algorithm; uses a 128-bit block cipher in conjunction with varying key sizes (128-bit, 192-bit, and 256-bit).

aggregate function A function used when grouping data to summarize data in a grouped column.

alert A message generated automatically in response to a system event or when a performance condition is met.

ALL A SQL keyword used to return all rows from a table or view.

ALTER A SQL statement used to change an existing object.

AlwaysOn A high-availability and disaster recovery solution offered in the Enterprise Edition of SQL Server 2012; requires additional servers and storage devices that are connected over a network.

Analysis Service tasks Tasks that enable an SSIS package to interact with SQL Server Analysis Services to process data or perform a data mining operation.

Analysis Services A data mining and analytical component of SQL Server 2012.

AND A logical operator that specifies that all conditions must be true.

application programming interface (API) An interface that defines the communication protocol between two software applications that need to interact.

AS A SQL keyword that can be used to create a column alias for an individual column, renaming the column returned in the result set.

ASC A SQL keyword used after a sort column name to indicate an ascending sort direction.

asymmetric keys A type of encryption key that uses a public key to encrypt data and a different, private key to decrypt data; also known as a public key. Anyone can use the public key to encrypt a message, but only the holder of the private key can decrypt that message.

attended installation An interactive installation of SQL Server 2012 completed using either the installation wizard or the command prompt.

authentication A process performed during logon when a user or application requests access to a system; the user provides credentials and the host system authenticates the identity of the user against an authentication database.

authenticator A column value that is unique to the row and is used in conjunction with the key to secure the data being encrypted; also known as a salt value.

Autogrowth A setting that specifies how much the database will increase the file size once it reaches a limit; can be stated in absolute or relative terms. The defaults are 1 MB for the data file and 10 percent for the log file. These settings should be sufficiently large to make file growth an infrequent event.

Availability Groups (AG) A compononent of AlwaysOn functionality; consists of a group of primary user databases with up to four replicas that will be used in the event the primary user database fails.

backup The process of taking a copy of a database file that can later be used to restore the database should a loss of data occur.

backup device A logical storage device that references a physical location where backup sets will be stored.

backup set The file that is the result of a backup operation.

baseline A set of results recorded using a particular set of configuration values and a specific load scenario; can be used as future comparison points.

bcp utility A stand-alone application that is run from a command prompt and that can be used for bidirectional data transfer.

benchmarking The process of using a baseline to compare against current system performance.

binary format A data format in which data is represented as a series of zeros and ones.

block cipher   A class of encryption algorithms that translates fixed-size blocks of unencrypted data into corresponding fixed-sized blocks of encrypted data.

blocking lock   A situation that is caused when a process must wait for locks to be released by other active processes before it is able to proceed.

bulk copy interface   An interface that enables a client application to efficiently perform bulk copy operations between a view or table on a SQL Server database and an external data file.

BULK INSERT   A SQL statement that can be executed to insert records from an external data file source into a SQL Server table.

bulk logged recovery model   A recovery model setting that selectively logs changes to the database; in particular, it excludes logging data related to bulk transactions.

bulk transaction   A large update to data, such as the insertion of data in a bulk copy operation.

Business Intelligence (BI)   A range of activities involved in analyzing raw data that enables an organization to extract knowledge used for making key business decisions.

camel case   A naming convention that concatenates (links together) words using uppercase for the first character of each word. Examples of this style are FirstName, LastName, and AdventureWorks2012. Camel case is easier to read than linking words together using underscores or other characters and should form the basic syntax for naming objects.

certificate authority   An external entity that issues and verifies digital certificates used for encrypting data.

CHECK   A constraint used to limit values of a column before a change is committed to the database—for example, a modified date may not be prior to the current date.

checksum   A unique variable that is computed based on the data contained in a page and used to verify the integrity of that data.

child object   An object that is contained within a parent object, for example a table is a child object of a database.

cipher   A cryptographic algorithm used in conjunction with a key to encrypt data.

CodePlex   Microsoft's open source project hosting site where you can find useful sample code for a wide range of Microsoft products.

collation   A database setting that specifies the character set, sort order behavior, and how characters are evaluated in comparison operations.

collector type   A method for collecting a specific type of data that is used by a data collection; four standard collector types are installed with SQL Server: Transact-SQL Query, SQL Trace, Performance Counters, and Query Activity.

column   A representation of an attribute of the object being modeled by a table; defined with a unique column name and data type.

command prompt   A command-line interpreter that provides a means of installing SQL Server 2012—by running setup.exe—and specifying SQL Server parameters on the command line, or by referencing a Configuration File (ConfigurationFile.ini).

comparison operator   A word in a SQL statement that is used to compare two values; returns a result of TRUE, FALSE, or UNKNOWN.

components   Core services bundled with a SQL Server edition, including the database engine, Master Data Services, Data Quality Services, Analysis Services, Integration Services, Reporting Services, and Replication.

composite index   An index on multiple columns; the most restrictive column should be placed first in a composite index because only the first column is used for building statistics.

compound conditions   A combination of conditions; can be created by combining multiple conditions in a WHERE or HAVING clause.

computed column   A column computed using arithmetic operators or string concatenation operators applied to values in existing columns.

concurrency control   An important feature of a multiuser relational database management system that protects the integrity of data by controlling access to logical resources.

configuration options   Settings that determine the behavior of a database. Before creating a new database, you should always take a full backup of the master system database, which stores the configuration settings.

connection manager   An object within an SSIS package that stores the configuration information necessary to connect to an individual data source.

constraint   A condition that imposes a limitation on a value or action; a column constraint specifies the allowable range of values that a column may contain, such as specific data types.

contention   A term used to describe a situation in which two processes compete for the same resource.

contiguous   A term used to describe records that are stored next to each other in sequence.

control flow The order in which each task in an SSIS package is executed.

core A physical unit within a processor that reads and executes program instructions. Traditionally, a processor was based on a single core, although multicore processors are now commonplace. *See also* multicore processor.

core-based licensing A SQL Server 2012 licensing option in which Microsoft measures the computing power of the host server by counting the number of processing cores; it replaces processor-based licensing in earlier versions of SQL Server.

cost-based algorithm A query optimization approach used to select the best execution plan by estimating the costs (e.g., number of I/O operations) for each alternative.

covering index A database object that physically stores all columns that are needed to query a single table; unlike a normal index, a covering index is able to return the required data directly to the query, thus eliminating the additional step of retrieving data from the underlying tables.

CREATE A SQL statement used to create an object.

crowd-sourcing The outsourcing of tasks to a distributed, undefined group of people.

DAEMON Tools Lite A third-party product that enables a disk image to be mounted as a virtual drive.

data collection A specific instance of a data collector that specifies the method for collecting the data, the source of the data to collect, and the method for storing the collected data, including when to purge the data.

data collector A feature of the Management Data Warehouse on a SQL Server instance that is used to capture several different types of data.

data collector set A collection of performance counters that is configured and scheduled on Performance Monitor to record time series data on a particular group of performance counters.

data control language (DCL) The component of the SQL language that allows you to configure the logical security in the database, such as by creating users and roles and by granting permissions to the various database objects.

data definition language (DDL) The component of the SQL language that provides the means to create and manage the schema of the logical objects in a database.

data file A file that stores database objects and their underlying data; these files are given a .mdf file extension. Data files are subdivided into physical units of storage called pages that are grouped together into extents for space management.

data flow components Steps within a data flow task that are connected together by the output of the previous component.

data flow tasks Tasks that move data between a source and a destination; may include transformations that manipulate the data as it is moved between a source and destination.

data manipulation language (DML) The most widely used component of the SQL language; provides the means to query and manipulate data.

data preparation tasks Tasks that perform file or directory operations in an SSIS package.

Data Transformation Services (DTS) A SQL Server legacy data integration tool with a graphical designer that had a limited range of functionality.

data type A column attribute that defines the type of data a column can store; acts as a constraint because it limits the type of values that can be stored. The main data types include unique identifiers, numbers of varying precision, dates and times, and text strings.

data warehouse A database designed for reporting and analytics.

database console commands (DBCC) A set of legacy procedures used to display system information and perform management tasks.

database context The database that is used by the database engine to resolve object names; unless otherwise specified, the database context is the default database.

database encryption key (DEK) A key used to encrypt the individual pages within the physical data and log files for Transparent Data Encryption.

database engine The core component within a database that controls data storage and access requests from client applications.

Database Engine Tuning Advisor A query-tuning wizard that uses the same optimization information as the query optimizer to provide a set of recommendations that may include additional indexes, indexed views, and partitions to improve query performance.

database index A logical database structure used to improve the speed and efficiency of data access. A database index is constructed based on a unique key, and it contains pointers to the underlying rows within the table.

Database Mail The SQL Server component used to integrate with and send messages via an SMTP email server.

database master key (DMK) A symmetric key used to protect asymmetric private keys and certificates that are stored in the database. In SQL Server 2012, the DMK uses the AES 256-bit algorithm.

database role   An object used to manage permissions on behalf of several database users without having to grant or revoke individual permissions for each user.

database trace file   A saved trace that can be replayed at a later point in time for analysis.

database transaction   A logical unit of work reading or writing from a database. Database transactions are important to maintain the integrity and consistency of the database. A logical unit of work reading or writing from a database; designed to roll back should the transaction fail.

database user   A database-level security principal; SQL Server logins are mapped to database users to access objects on an individual database.

database-scoped   A dynamic management view or function that allows information in an individual user database to be retrieved.

deadlock victim   The transaction that SQL Server chooses to cancel in order to deal with a deadlock situation.

deadlock   A situation in which two transactions each have a lock on a resource that the other transaction needs in order to complete.

declarative language   A programming language that uses a set of logical expressions to specify what to accomplish, rather than how to accomplish the results.

DEFAULT   A constraint that causes the value of a field to be autopopulated on insertion of a record if the value is not specified.

default instance   The instance of SQL Server 2012 to which a client who connects to the database will connect to if they don't specify a named instance; each database server may have one default instance of SQL Server 2012.

DELETE   A SQL statement used to delete rows from a table.

DESC   A SQL keyword used after a sort column name to indicate a descending sort direction.

differential database backup   A type of database backup in which copies are made only of pages that have changed since the last full database backup; less resource intensive than a full database backup.

dirty read   A database integrity problem that can occur when a transaction updating the database fails and the updated values are rolled back to their original state. If a concurrent process is reading the data at the same time, it may retrieve the values that were not ultimately committed to the database.

Display Estimated Execution Plan   A Query Editor option that displays the execution steps of a query based on the costs that the optimizer has estimated using database statistics.

DISTINCT   A SQL keyword used to remove duplicates from the result set and only return unique records.

domain controller   A server running a version of the Windows Server operating system, with Active Directory Doman Services (AD DS) installed.

DROP   A SQL statement used to delete an object.

dynamic management functions (DMF)   A system function often used in conjunction with dynamic management views; offers similar capabilities to a view but with the ability to return a result set that is based on a set of input parameters supplied at the time of execution.

dynamic management view (DMV)   A system view that enables information about the state of the underlying database management system to be queried in real time.

EncryptByKey   A SQL function that encrypts data using a key that has been registered with the database; provides the flexibility to choose an encryption algorithm.

EncryptByPassphrase   A SQL function that uses a passphrase to generate a key and uses the Triple DES algorithm to encrypt the data; does not require a key to be registered in advance with the database.

encryption   A reversible process involving the use of a key or passcode and an algorithm to convert data into an unreadable form.

encryption key management (EKM)   A feature that enables third-party key management solutions to be used in conjunction with SQL Server.

event   Any activity executed by the SQL Server database engine.

event handler   A software routine that specifies what should happen if a certain event occurs during execution of an SSIS package.

EXCEPT   An operator that returns rows from the first query that do not exist in the second query.

EXISTS   An operator used to compare a value of a column against the results of a subquery.

expiration date   A date assigned to a backup set; helps to ensure that existing backups on the media will not be overwritten until a specified time in the future.

extent   A physical storage unit that is a collection of eight pages, grouped together for space management.

external fragmentation   A type of fragmentation that occurs when the logical storage of data in pages and extents does not match the physical storage on disk, causing increased workload that the physical disk has to perform in order to retrieve the data.

Failover Cluster Instance (FCI) A set of redundant nodes that can be used to host the database instance should an error occur on the primary node; provides redundancy in the event of hardware or software failure on a SQL Server node.

file (or filegroup) backup A type of database backup in which a database backup is broken into smaller units (files or filegroups) for performance reasons.

filegroup A group of data files used for storage management. Each database must have a primary filegroup with at least one data file.

flat file A text file that contains data; each row in a flat file represents a record. Individual fields within a record either occupy a fixed number of characters or are separated by a special character known as a delimiter.

foreign key relationship A constraint that models the relationship that exists between two tables.

fragmentation A situation in which database records are stored out of order, causing a degradation in index performance.

FROM A SQL keyword used to specify a list of the names of tables or views that a query will use to retrieve data.

full database backup A type of database backup in which a copy of all nonempty pages in a data file is made; in a full database backup, the section of the transaction log for transactions that occurred during the backup is also copied.

FULL OUTER JOIN A type of join that returns all columns from both tables as well as rows that satisfy the join condition; where there is no matching row in one table, null values are returned for the columns in the other table.

full recovery model A recovery model setting that causes all changes to the database to be written to the transaction log.

fully qualified name An object that is referenced using all four identifiers.

GNU General Public License (GPL) A type of software license that is widely used for distributing free or open source software.

GRANT A SQL statement used to assign permissions directly to a database user or via a role.

GROUP BY A SQL keyword used in a SELECT statement to collect data across multiple records and then group the results by one or more columns. Grouping creates groups of rows that share common characteristics.

HAVING A SQL keyword used instead of the WHERE keyword to filter grouped data.

high availability (HA) A term used to describe a system that must be online and available for user access at most times; unplanned downtime of a high-availability system is likely to cause serious business disruption.

I/O performance A term used to describe the number of read and write operations that can be processed by the physical disk in a given time frame.

IN A logical operator used to compare a value of a column against multiple values.

Include Actual Execution Plan A Query Editor option that can be set prior to running a query in order to display the actual execution plan steps and costs once the query has completed.

incorrect summary A database integrity problem that occurs if a transaction attempts to read and summarize values while the data is in an inconsistent state due to a concurrent update process.

indexed view A database object that physically stores a copy of the data and performs as a virtual table. An indexed view is similar to a covering index but can be used to join and store data across several tables.

Initial Size A setting that defines the initial size of the data and log files; the defaults are 4 MB and 1 MB, respectively.

INNER JOIN A type of join that returns all columns from both tables but only those rows that satisfy the join condition.

INSERT A SQL statement used to insert a new row into a table.

installation wizard A Windows application that provides step-by-step guidance though the installation process; launched through the SQL Server Installation Center.

instance An occurrence or copy of an object.

integrated development environment (IDE) An application that provides a developer with a comprehensive set of development tools to design, compile, and debug software within a single user interface.

Integration Services A SQL Server 2012 component that provides extract, transform, and load (ETL) capabilities.

IntelliSense A text AutoComplete feature that helps with navigating the object hierarchy and SQL language.

internal fragmentation A type of fragmentation that occurs due to an accumulation of free space between records stored in the index page files, the fundamental logical storage unit used by SQL Server. Internal fragmentation results in growth of the index, and the unequal distribution of records leads to increased I/O and reduced performance.

Internet Protocol Security (IPSec)   A protocol that has been integrated with the Windows operating system to enable secure client/server connections on an Internet Protocol (IP)–based network.

INTERSECT   An operator that only combines rows that exist in both result sets.

IS NULL   A logical operator used to evaluate a column for the presence of a null value.

join conditions   A condition, included in the ON clause of a join statement, that specifies which columns from each table should be used as the matching key.

join   A database operation used for merging and retrieving data that is stored in more than one table or view.

Kerberos   A widely used network authentication protocol.

key   A parameter used in conjunction with a cryptographic algorithm to encrypt data.

layered security   A database security model (also known as defense-in-depth) that involves combining multiple security controls to prevent unauthorized access.

LEFT OUTER JOIN   A type of join that returns all rows from the left table and any matching rows from the right table; where there is no matching right table row, null values are returned for all right table columns.

length   The maximum number of characters that a string data type can store.

Lightweight Directory Access Protocol (LDAP)   A software protocol for enabling anyone to locate individuals, and other resources, such as files and devices, on a network—whether on the Internet or on a private network.

LIKE   A logical operator used to match a string based on a pattern.

linked server   A server that provides the capability to execute queries against a remote data source for running distributed queries. A linked server uses shared software components (called data providers) from the dynamic-link library (DLL) on the server to manage the interface between SQL Server and the external data source.

listener   A service that enables a client to connect to the SQL Server instance over a network.

lock modes   A type of database locking mechanism that governs when a process is eligible to gain concurrent access to a particular resource. The strictest form of lock mode, which does not allow concurrent access under any circumstances, is an exclusive lock.

lock-based concurrency control   A mechanism used by the SQL Server database engine to ensure that transactions that access the same resources are executed in a serial manner.

log file   A file that records the series of changes that occur to a database over time, and they enable a database to be restored to a specific point in time.

Log File Viewer   A feature within SQL Server Management Studio that aggregates events from different event logs.

logical fragmentation   A type of fragmentation that occurs if a page has insufficient space to store new data in sequential order (e.g., due to inserted records), and as a result, the page files become split.

logical operator   A word in a SQL statement that is used in conjunction with, or in place of, comparison operators to test column values.

logical structure   A way of organizing data, with defined rules for storing, manipulating, and retrieving the data; client applications interact with logical objects within a database rather than the physical files.

login   An authentication mechanism used to validate the identity of a user on a database server.

loopback address   An IP address that sends outbound packets of data directly back to the host computer to simulate a physical network.

lost update   A database integrity problem that can occur if two processes attempt to update the same record concurrently and the updates of one process are overwritten by the second process.

maintenance tasks   Tasks that perform essential database maintenance functions.

Management Data Warehouse (MDW)   A centralized data repository installed on each SQL Server instance; used to capture the output of a data collection.

management tools   A suite of tools and utilities for managing the SQL Server database.

Master Data Services   A SQL Server 2012 component that provides a centralized means to manage and validate data.

master database   A system database that stores the configuration settings that describe the structure and security of all the other databases.

Maxsize   A setting that allows you to specify a limit on the size of the database.

Microsoft Books Online   A comprehensive set of online technical product documentation that covers the features and tools for various Microsoft products; includes how-to guides and a language reference.

Microsoft Developer Network (MSDN) A Microsoft portal hosting online product documentation and tutorials; MSDN was originally designed for application administrators.

Microsoft Software Assurance (SA) An optional Microsoft maintenance program that provides ongoing access to Microsoft support and product updates for a fee.

model database A system database that is used as a template when creating a new user database.

multicore processor A processor with more than one core processing unit; able to execute multiple instruction sets in parallel with a consequent improvement in performance.

named instance A database instance on a server other than the default instance; each server can support up to 50 instances of SQL Server 2012.

Named Pipes An older interprocess communication mechanism that enables a client application to connect to a server process on the same or different hosts. Each SQL Server instance is able to listen on one named pipe.

normalization A step in the design process of physical relations that systematically splits relations that contain duplicate data in order to eliminate data redundancy and ensure data integrity.

NOT NULL A column-level constraint, added after the data type in the column definition, that specifies that the column may not accept a null value.

NOT A logical operator that reverses the truth of the original condition.

null value A column value that does not exist.

Object Explorer A component of SQL Server Management Studio that provides a tree view of the different database schema objects organized as a series of folders.

Online Transaction Processing (OLTP) A method of data processing that is geared toward transaction-oriented applications that have a substantial write component in their interaction with the database; an OLTP database is defined by a high volume of individual read and write transactions.

Open Database Connectivity (ODBC) A platform-agnostic application programming interface (API) that was designed to facilitate the interactions between a client application and a database management system.

operating system A platform that allows a computer system's hardware and software components to interface separately with multiple applications to perform requested functions and services.

operator An alias for an individual or group of people with their email or pager information.

OR A logical operator that specifies that any condition must be true.

Oracle VirtualBox A virtual machine software product from Oracle that allows you to install multiple virtual machines on a Linux, Mac OS X, Solaris, or Windows host operating system.

ORDER BY A SQL keyword used to sort a result set; should be added after the WHERE clause of the SELECT statement.

package configuration file A configuration file that will allow properties in an SSIS package to be overridden with the values in the configuration file during execution; has a .dtsconfig file extension.

page A physical storage unit in a data file.

partial backup A type of database backup in which only data in the primary filegroup and read-write filegroups are backed up by default.

performance conditions Rules defined by placing a threshold on the value of a specific performance counter monitored by SQL Server Agent; if the value of the performance counter exceeds the established threshold, an alert will be triggered.

performance counter A metric used by Performance Monitor to collect time series data on a particular performance characteristic of the operating system.

Performance Monitor A Windows management utility (perfmon.exe) that provides a view of different performance attributes on the host server by viewing data in real time or by replaying data from a log.

permission A right to perform an action against a database object.

precision The number of places after the decimal point in a numeric data type or the accuracy in the case of a date data type.

primary key The column or combination of columns that uniquely identify each record within a table.

procedure A precompiled block of code that enables frequently performed tasks for querying and/or manipulating data to be stored as objects within the database.

qualified name A combination of identifiers that uniquely defines the location of a database object.

Query Editor A component of SQL Server Management Studio that enables you to create SQL queries to be executed against a database.

query optimizer The component within the SQL Server database engine that builds a physical execution plan from the logical steps defined in a SQL query.

query tuning An optimization process to lower the duration of a query and overall costs by improving the design of the SQL code or by adding indexes.

rebuilding   An approach to defragmentation in which the index drops and re-creates the index from scratch and should be considered for indexes where the logical fragmentation is high.

recovery model   A type of configuration setting that specifies which type of database transactions should be recorded in the transaction log.

recovery point objective (RPO)   The maximum amount of data that may be lost, expressed as a time frame.

recovery time objective (RTO)   The amount of downtime that should be expected by the business before the system can be restored.

refactoring   The process of improving the design of code.

Registry Editor   A Windows management utility (regedit.exe) that allows you to view, alter, or delete Registry keys.

Registry key   A configuration value associated with a particular Windows software application.

reorganizing   An approach to defragmentation in which data is compacted in the page files to eliminate unused space and the logical order of the pages that occurred due to page splits is corrected.

Reporting Services   A set of tools and services in SQL Server 2012 that enable you to create, deploy, and manage reports.

reserved keyword   A word that also belongs to the SQL programming language and is restricted because its use may lead to ambiguity. If used as an object name, a reserved keyword must be surrounded by square bracket or double-quoted delimiters.

Resource Monitor   A Windows management utility (resmon.exe) for monitoring hardware resource utilization in real time using five individual tabs: Overview, CPU, Memory, Disk, and Network.

result set   The data returned by a SQL query.

REVOKE   A SQL statement used to remove permissions directly from a database user or from a role.

RIGHT OUTER JOIN   A type of join that returns all rows from the right table and any matching rows from the left table. Where there is no matching left table row, null values are returned for all left table columns.

risk assessment   A process undertaken to identify and objectively quantify all potential data loss scenarios.

role   A database object that groups together permissions on different database objects.

row   A logical instance of an object, commonly called a *record*, that is modeled by a table (e.g., an Employee); may contain several attributes that are defined as columns (e.g., first name, last name, Social Security number).

sa   The default system Administrator login when using SQL Server authentication.

scale   The maximum number of digits that a numeric data type can hold.

schema   A logical container that groups together collections of objects within a database and allows them to be managed as a group.

scripting task   A task that allows custom code to be executed to extend the functionality of the basic set of tasks in an SSIS package.

securables   The various objects in a database and a SQL Server instance that can be secured.

Secure Sockets Layer (SSL)   A protocol designed to encrypt data inside messages to secure client/server connections over the Internet.

security principal   An entity that can request access to a resource or securable; can be organized as single users or as groups.

SELECT   A statement used to retrieve data from a database object.

self join   A special case of a join in which a table joins onto itself.

Server and Client Access License (CAL) licensing   A user-centric licensing model in which a server license is required for each SQL Server 2012 installation and a CAL is required for each end user. Each user is able to access multiple servers with a single CAL.

Server Core   A stripped-down version of the Windows Server 2008 operating system that does not include the Windows Explorer Shell and that reduces potential security vulnerabilities and improves uptime.

Server Manager   A one-stop management interface introduced in Windows Server 2008 that provides quick access to tools for performing routine tasks, such as querying the server status and changing roles and features.

Server Process ID (SPID)   An identifier that is assigned to each connection or session on the SQL Server.

server-scoped   A dynamic management view or function that operates at the level of the SQL Server instance.

service master key (SMK)   A key that is created the first time a SQL Server instance is started; used to encrypt linked server credentials, login credentials, and the database master keys. The SMK uses the AES 256-bit algorithm.

SET   A parameter used in an UPDATE statement that specifies the name of the column to update along with the new column value.

severity level   A numerical indicator that describes the type of SQL Server error; can be used to specify whether an alert should be generated.

shared features A set of SQL Server features that are shared between multiple instances of SQL Server 2012 on a single host; includes many of the management tools, Integration Services, and Master Data Services.

shared memory A local procedure call that requires the client application to be running on the same host as the SQL Server instance. No configuration options are available with a shared memory connection.

simple recovery model A recovery model setting that causes the database engine not to record any events in the transaction log.

sp_configure A procedure that can be used to view and alter global configuration settings.

SQL Server Agent A service that allows routine management jobs to be created and scheduled for a SQL Server instance.

SQL Server Agent error log A log that records informational, warning, and error events related to SQL Server Agent activity.

SQL Server Audit A mechanism that enables certain server-level or database-level events to be captured and written to a target that records the results of an audit.

SQL Server Browser A service that performs instance lookup and name resolution for remote clients.

SQL Server Configuration Manager A tool for configuring SQL Server 2012 network protocols and managing component services.

SQL Server Data Tools A comprehensive development environment that can be used to create a solution that caters to more complex data integration situations.

SQL Server Features Discovery Report A report that displays the SQL Server 2012 instances, tools, and features currently installed on the server.

SQL Server Import and Export Wizard A wizard that provides step-by-step instructions for designing a solution that meets basic data integration needs.

SQL Server Installation Center A user interface that provides a single point of access to the various planning, installation, and maintenance wizards.

SQL Server Integration Services (SSIS) A component of SQL Server that can be used to integrate many different types of external data sources, while applying complex business rules and workflow logic during the integration process.

SQL Server log A log that contains system events as well as certain user-defined events for the SQL Server instance.

SQL Server login A login that operates at the level of the SQL Server instance and is a server-level security principal; may be granted permissions on server-level securables.

SQL Server Management Studio A management tool used to configure, manage, and administer the Database Engine Services, Analysis Services, Integration Services, and Reporting Services.

SQL Server Native Client (ODBC) driver An application programming interface (API) that defines the functions available to a client application for accessing data on a SQL Server database.

SQL Server Network Interface layer The network protocol layer that manages the handoff of TDS packets between the SQL Server and the operating system–supported network protocol at an endpoint.

SQL Server parameters Settings entered during the SQL Server 2012 installation process; used to specify the type of setup (install, uninstall, or upgrade), features to install, and other configuration settings. SQL Server parameters are specified manually for a command-line install or are generated automatically by the installation wizard to a ConfigurationFile.ini file.

SQL Server Profiler A management tool that enables a database administrator to capture events for the purpose of optimizing query performance, identifying and troubleshooting problematic queries, and monitoring workload.

SQL Server Resolution Protocol (SSRP) A protocol used by SQL Server Browser for performing instance lookup and name resolution for remote clients.

SQL Server tasks Tasks that perform operations on schema objects and data on a SQL server.

SQLCMD A utility that enables you to connect to the database from a command prompt and execute SQL commands and scripts.

SSIS package A collection of one or more tasks grouped together as a series of logical steps into a single object that can be executed using the SQL Server Integration Services service.

statement terminator A semicolon placed to mark the end of a SQL statement.

statistics Information about the distribution of values for a particular table or index (e.g., the number of rows or the size of the key) and used by the cost-based query optimizer.

string concatenation operator An operator that may be used to combine columns containing character strings.

Structured Query Language (SQL) A database programming language.

subquery A SQL query embedded within another SQL query.

support case A request for Microsoft product support.

surface area The number of potential security vulnerabilities that are exposed on an application due to the functionality that has been enabled.

symmetric keys A type of key that uses the same key to encrypt and decrypt data; also known as a secret key.

system database A database created during the SQL Server installation process for storing system configuration information.

table A collection of data stored in a database. In a relational database, tables are typically designed to model real-world objects and the relationships that exist between them. Tables are organized as a two-dimensional structure consisting of rows and columns.

table scan A scan of every record within a table, undertaken by a database engine in the absence of a suitable index for a query.

Tabular Data Stream (TDS) packet A message used by SQL Server for communication; when SQL Server is connected to a remote client, TDS packets must be encapsulated within a standard network protocol packet to enable the data to be sent over the network between the client and server.

tail The active transaction log that contains the database changes since the last transaction log backup.

tasks The basic building blocks within an SSIS package; each task performs a specific activity or function.

TCP/IP The most common protocol used for client/server connectivity.

TechNet A Microsoft portal hosting online product documentation, tutorials, and user forums; TechNet was originally designed for system administrators.

TOP A SQL keyword used to limit the result set to the number of rows defined by an expression in parentheses, which follows the keyword.

trace A log of events on the database management system that are captured using the SQL Server Profiler and commonly used for troubleshooting SQL Server performance issues.

transaction logs A database log that records changes that occur to the data in a database over time.

Transact-SQL A variant of the SQL language, developed by Microsoft and Sybase.

transformation component A component within an SSIS package that manipulates data during the data flow as the data moves between the source and the destination during a data flow.

Transparent Data Encryption (TDE) A type of encryption that uses a symmetric key called the database encryption key (DEK) to encrypt the individual pages within the physical data and log files.

trigger A procedural mechanism that can be configured to automatically fire an event when a row

is inserted, modified, or deleted; often used to satisfy compliance aspects of the business requirements by cascading details of a change into a related table or autopopulating metadata within a record.

truncation A process that occurs each time a database is backed up; causes space to be made available in the active transaction log for recording new activity.

trusted connection A connection established using Windows authentication.

unattended installation A noninteractive installation of SQL Server 2012 completed either by using the command prompt combined with a configuration file and the quiet parameter or by using the SysPrep utility to create an image file for virtual deployments.

UNION An operator that combines the rows from multiple SQL statements into a single result set.

UNIQUE A column-level constraint that enforces a unique value in the column.

UPDATE A SQL statement used to modify column values of an existing row in a table.

USE A SQL statement that changes the database context to a specified database.

User Account Control (UAC) A Windows Server security feature that ensures that any administrative changes to the configuration of the server—such as software installation—require explicit authorization.

user database A database that contains the data associated with a client application; each SQL Server instance may have one or more user databases.

user variable A storage unit within an SSIS package that can hold both static values or whose values can be set at run time.

view A virtual table that uses the result set of a saved query.

virtual account An auto-managed local service account, introduced in Windows 7 and Windows Server 2008 R2 to improve security and ease of management.

virtual CD/DVD drive emulator Software that emulates a physical drive and enables a disk image to be mounted; often used for installing software distributed as an ISO file. Windows does not provide native support for mounting disk images.

virtual machine An isolated guest operating system installed on top of a normal operating system.

virtualization The process of creating a virtual version of something—for example, a physical device, network resource, or operating system.

Visual Studio An integrated development environment that includes a graphical designer, a code editor, and a debugger.

VMware Workstation A virtual machine software product from VMware that enables multiple virtual machines to be installed on a host Windows operating system.

WHERE A SQL keyword used to filter the SELECT… FROM result set; operators are used within the WHERE clause to specify the filter criteria.

wildcard A character used in a SQL statement to match unknown characters within a string.

Windows application log A log that captures events generated by applications running on the Microsoft Windows operating system.

Windows Data Protection API (DPAPI) The key management system within the Windows operating system; SQL Server uses the DPAPI to encrypt the service master key.

Windows Management Instrumentation (WMI) event An event generated by the Microsoft Windows operating system.

workflow tasks Tasks that permit an SSIS package to interact with other applications.

workload A stand-alone query or a previously saved trace file that was generated using SQL Server Profiler; used for analysis by the Database Engine Tuning Advisor.

Index

A

access token, **199**, 232
Account folder, 144
Account Policies folder, 200
Account table, 137, 139, 141–143
Actions pane, 366
Active Directory Domain Service (AD DS), **10**, 23
Active Directory Lightweight Directory Service (AD LDS), **10**, 23
Activity Monitor. *See* SQL Server Activity Monitor
Add Copy of Existing Package dialog box, 337
Add Counters window, 242
Added counters pane, 244
Addition (+) arithmetic operator, 154, 155
Add Objects dialog box, 218
AD DS. *See* Active Directory Domain Service (AD DS)
ADD statement, 173
AD LDS. *See* Active Directory Lightweight Directory Service (AD LDS)
ADMINISTER BULK OPERATIONS permission, 352
administration tasks
  adding table with foreign key relationship, **137–145**
  altering database configuration settings, 132–136
  essential, 131–145
Administrators group
  adding members, 40
  adding user accounts, 40, 42
  SQL Server installation, 32
Administrators role, 10
Advanced Encryption Standard (AES) algorithm, **223**, 224, 232
AdventureWorks2012 database, 74, 150, 182, 216, 264, 364
  installing, 78–83
  managing and navigating, 83–88
  Online Transaction Processing (OLTP), 78–83
  physical files created for, 82
  Transparent Data Encryption (TDE), 228–229
AdventureWorks2012 folder, 84, 214, 218, 264
Adventure Works for SQL Server 2012 page, 78
AdventureWorks 2012 OLTP Script link, 79
AES. *See* Advanced Encryption Standard (AES) algorithm

AG. *See* Availability Groups (AG), 29
aggregate functions, **157**, 188
alerts, **369**
  configuring, 376–378
  emailing or sending to pager, 369
  error levels configuration, 369
  responding to error messages, 370–380
  triggered by performance condition, 370–380
Alerts folder, 376, 378, 380
ALL keyword, **154**, 165, 188
Allow Nulls attribute, 85, 139
ALTER ANY DATABASE permission, 199
ALTER INDEX REBUILD statement, 266
ALTER INDEX REORGANIZE statement, 266
ALTER ROLE statement, 199
alters, 401
ALTER statement, 132–133, 145, 173, 180
AlwaysOn feature, **29**, 67, 313
Amazon Web Services, 4
American National Standards Institute (ANSI), 150
Analysis Services, **29**, 40, 53, 67
Analysis Services Configuration window, 42
Analysis Service tasks, **321**, 356
analytical tools, 29
AND logical operator, 156, 188
ANSI. *See* American National Standards Institute (ANSI)
application programming interface (API), **347**, 356
Apply Recommendations dialog box, 264
arithmetic operators, 154
ASC keyword, **156**, 188
AS keyword, **154**, 160–161, 164, 188
asymmetric algorithms, 222–223
asymmetric keys, **222**, 232
attended installation, **31**, 67
Audit, 398
auditing databases, 398–400
  See also database audits
audit log, 398
Audits folder, 399–400
authentication, **10**, 23, 178, **198–199**, 232
  access token, **199**
  database servers, 120
  logins and, 120
  SQL Server authentication, 212
authentication modes, 178, 198–199
authenticator, **224**, 232

AUTHORIZATION clause, 179
AutoComplete feature, 153
Autogrowth, **120**, 145
automating
  backup plan, 303–313
  event notification, 369–380
Availability Groups (AG), **29**, 67
Available Bytes performance counter, 241
averages, 161
Avg. Disk Queue Length performance counter, 241
Avg. Disk sec/Read performance counter, 241
Avg. Disk sec/Write performance counter, 241
AVG aggregate function, 157, 161

B

backup and recovery plan
  automating backup plan, 303–313
  backup plans, 292–294
  implementing, 292–313
  restoring operations, 294–303
backup and recovery strategy, 76
  business requirements, 275–276
  differential database backups, **278**, 284–287
  file or filegroup backups, **278**
  full database backup, **277–283**, 285–287
  partial backups, **278**
  probability of occurrence, 274
BackUp Database dialog box, 277–278, 280–281, 284–285, 288–289, 291, 297
Backup Device dialog box, 280
backup devices, **277**, 280, 315
Backup Devices folder, 280, 285, 291, 297
Backup folder, 279, 282
backup plans
  automation, 303–313
  full database backup, 292
  full database backup plus differential database backup plus multiple transaction log backups, 294
  full database backup plus multiple transaction log backups, 293
  simple recovery model, 292
  single transaction log backup plus full database backup, 292
Backup Properties dialog box, 279
BackupRestoreTest_1 backup file, 280–282, 284, 289, 297

419

Backup Restore Test database, 288, 296, 301

BackupRestoreTest maintenance plan, 367

BackupRestoreTest MDF file, 297

Backup Restore Test_One Time.bak file, 287

backups, **274**, 315
  backup devices, **277**
  backup set, **277**
  database performance, 276
  destination, 299
  differential database backup, **278**, 284–287, 294
  expiration date, **277**
  file, 277, **278**
  filegroup, **278**
  frequency, 276
  full database backup, **277–283**, 285–287, 292–294
  large databases, 276
  media, 277
  multiple transaction log, 293
  off-site storage, 277
  online and offline, 277
  optimal time to schedule, 276
  partial, **278**
  physical location, 277
  production user databases, 59
  recovering database from, 294–303
  security, 30, 277
  simple recovery model, 292
  statistics, 286, 289
  tail, 297
  transaction logs, 277, 287–292
  types, 277–291

backup sets, **277**, 315
  appending differential database backup, 284–285
  backup devices, 280
  expiration date, **277**, 281
  folder to store, 278

Backup Timeline dialog box, 299

baseline, **381**, 401

Batch Requests/sec performance counter, 381

bcp.exe file, 348

bcpexport.txt file, 351

bcp utility, **320**, 347–351, 356

BEGIN TRANSACTION statement, 169

benchmarking, **381–388**, 401

BI. *See* Business Intelligence (BI)

Bikes table, 174, 176

binary format, **75**, 108

block cipher, **223**, 232

blocking locks, 250, 252, 267

Books Online for SQL Server 2012, 7, 12–17, 24, 29

"bcp Utility" topic, 348

"BULK INSERT (Transact-SQL)" topic, 353

(Ctrl+F1) shortcut keys, 387

"Database-Level Roles," 212

"Database Properties (Filegroups Page)", 126

"Data Type Conversion (Database Engine)" topic, 155

"Data Types (Transact-SQL)" topic, 155, 172

default database configuration settings, 117–119

"Dynamic Management Views and Functions" topic, 387

"Install SQL Server 2012 from the Command Prompt" topic, 55, 56

Bring Database Online status dialog box, 297

bulk copy functions, 347–351

bulk copy interface, **320**, 347–356

BULK INSERT statement, 81, **320**, 347, 352–355, 356

bulk logged recovery model, **287**, 315

bulk transactions, **287**, 315

Business Intelligence (BI), **2**, 23

Business Intelligence Edition, 2–4

business requirements, 275–276

C

CAL. *See* Server and Client Access License (CAL) licensing

Camel case, **122**, 145

capturing performance data, 388–397

CAST operator, 155, 162

certificate authority, **208**, 222, 232

certificates, 225
  backing up, 229–231
  keys and, 222
  self-signed, 208, 211

Certificate Store, 208, 210

Change Autogrowth for TestOne_log dialog box, 124

change password on next login password policy, 199

character data type, 122

character strings, 155

CHECK constraint, 173, 188

checksum, 315

child objects, **153**, 188

Choose a Data Source window, 325, 327

Choose a Destination window, 327

Choose Default Environment Settings dialog box, 335

Choose Name dialog box, 139

cipher, **222**, 232

client applications

enabled network protocols for, 51

functions available for accessing data, 347

interacting with database management system (DBMS), 347–355

remotely connecting to SQL Server instances, 74

user errors, 275

client network, 49

client/server connections
  Internet Protocol Security (IPSec), 208
  Secure Sockets Layer (SSL), 208–211

clustered indexes, 250

code
  comments (/* */), 226
  refactoring, **238**, 240

CodePlex, 78, 108

collation, 38, 67

collector types, **388**, 401

Column Filters window, 248

column-level encryption, 225–231

Column Mappings dialog box, 329

columns, 76, 108
  adding, 174
  aliases, 164
  altering, 173
  character strings, 155
  combining, 163
  compatible data types, 155
  constraints, 76
  data type attribute, 122
  data types, **76**, 173, 177
  dropping, 173–174
  filtering for trace, 248
  foreign keys, 175, 239
  naming, 122
  numeric and arithmetic operators, 154
  renaming, 176
  result sets, 154–155
  testing values, 156
  updating metadata, 77

combining data, 166–169
  joins, 163–164
  subqueries, **165**

command-line scripts, 55

command-line utilities, 74

command prompt, **28**, 67
  configuration file, 31
  dtexec.exe utility, 334
  dtexecui.exe utility, 334
  launching, 56
  parameters and settings as input parameters, 31
  quiet parameter, 31
  setup.exe file, 31
  SQL Server 2012 installation, 31, 54–59
  whoami command, 57

Command Prompt window, 94, 95, 365
comments (/* */), 226
COMMIT TRANSACTION
    statement, 169, 251
comparison operators, **155**, 188
    join conditions, 163
    WHERE clause, 155
Complete the Wizard window, 312,
    374, 393
Complete window, 66
components, **2**, 23, 28–29
composite indexes, **240**, 267
compound conditions, 188
computed columns, **154**, 188
concatenating strings, 155
concurrency control, **249**–250, 267
ConfigurationFile.ini file, 44, 46
configuration options, **116**–117, 146
Configure Data Collection Wizard
    Progress window, 392, 393
Configure Management Data Storage
    Wizard window, 393
Configure Management Data
    Warehouse Storage window, 390
Configure Management Data
    Warehouse Wizard, 389–397
Configure System Parameters window,
    372
Confirm Save As dialog box, 259
connection manager, **321**, 356
Connection Managers pane, 344
Connect to Server dialog box, 80, 83, 95,
    124, 132, 138, 140, 181, 203, 212,
    225, 247, 278, 325, 364, 393, 399
constraints, **76**, 108, 172–175, 239
Contact folder, 142, 144
Contact table, 137, 140–143
contention, **120**, 146
contiguously, **265**, 268
control flow, **321**, 356
CONVERT keyword, 155
Copy (Ctrl+C) shortcut keys, 130
core, **4**, 23
core-based licensing, 4, 23
cost-based algorithm, **255**, 268
cost-optimization algorithm, 263
COUNT aggregate function, 157
country_codes.txt file, 323–325, 339,
    344, 353–355
CountryExport.fmt file, 350
CountryExport.txt file, 342, 347
Country table, 348–349, 353–355
covering indexes, **240**, 268
CPU
    displaying usage, 53
    how busy it is, 381
    reviewing for anomalies, 53
    utilization, 241
Create Audit Wizard, 398–400
CREATE DATABASE permission, 213

CREATE DATABASE TestThree SQL
    query, 131
CREATE DATABASE (Transact-SQL)
    link, 119
CREATE INDEX statement, 173
CREATE LOGIN statement, 178
Create New Data Collector Set
    Wizard, 242–245
CREATE ROLE statement, 180
CREATE SCHEMA statement, 179
Create Server Audit Specification
    Wizard, 398–400
CREATE statement, **117**, 124, 146
CREATE TABLE statement, 137,
    172–173
CREATE USER statement, 178
CREATE VIEW statement, 173
crowd-sourcing, **12**, 23
CSV files, 81

D

DAEMON Tools Lite, **11**, 20, 23
daily monitoring tasks, 362–380
data
    binary format, **75**
    centralized management and
        validation, 29
    combining, 166–169
    encrypting and decrypting,
        221–231
    evaluating risk of loss, 274–275
    extracting, transforming, and
        loading (ETL), 29, 320
    importing and exporting, 323–333,
        335–347, 348–351
    joins, 163–164
    manipulating, 150–171
    merging, 165–169
    modifying, 169–171
    moving between source and
        destination, 321–333
    protecting integrity, 249–250
    querying, 150–171
    recording changes over time, 287
    restricting access, 198
    result sets, **153**, 239
    retrieving from database, 153
    speed of read and write transfers,
        77, 381, 385
    splitting across multiple tables, 239
    subqueries, **165**
    tables, 352–355
    value, 276
database administrator essential
    administration tasks, 131–145
database architecture
    logical database objects, 76–78
    physical database files, 75–76
    system databases, 74–75

database audits, 397–400
database console commands (DBCC),
    382, 401
database context, **153**, 188
database encryption key (DEK), **224**,
    232
database engine, **2**, 23, 367
    batch requests speed, 381
    instances copies of, 29
    locating records, 240
    network protocols supported,
        89–98
    query optimizer, 255
    SQL Server Network Interface
        layer, **89**
    system databases, **28**
    user databases, 28
Database Engine component, 53
Database Engine Configuration
    window, 40–42
Database Engine Services, 363
Database Engine Tuning Advisor, 240,
    258–265, 268
database index, **77**, 108
Database I/O performance counter,
    381
database-level permissions, 211
database-level security
    principal, 211
Database Mail, 367, **369**–370, 372,
    374–376, 401
Database Mail Configuration Wizard,
    370, 372, 374, 376
Database Mail Log file, 375–376
database management system
    (DBMS)
    information about state of, 382
    interacting with client applications,
        347–355
database master key (DMK),
    224–225, 232
database objects
    access control, 211–221
    covering index, **240**
    creation, 174–177
    deleting, 173
    fully qualified names, 239
    identifiers, 153
    managing, 174–177
    naming conventions, 122–123
    permissions, 211
    read-only access, 180
    SQL Server login, 211
Database Properties dialog box, 127,
    130–133, 288
database recovery model, 288–291
Database Role - New window,
    218–219
database roles, **179**–180,
    183, 188

databases
    altering configuration settings, 132–136
    Autogrowth setting, **120**
    availability, 276
    backup and recovery operations, 76
    backup types, 277–291
    binary format data, **75**
    bulk logged recovery model, **287**
    configuration options, **116–119**, 126
    consistency, 119
    creation, 123–131
    data access, 77
    database master key (DMK), 225
    data files, **75**, 119–120, 124
    data types, 122
    default settings, 117
    disk and log usage, 394
    dropping, 132
    encryption, 221–231
    essential administration tasks, 131–136
    filegroups, **119**, 126
    filestreams, 126
    foreign key relationships, **137–145**
    full recovery model, **287**
    graphical interface, 117
    implementation options, 116–119
    indexes, 173
    Initial Size setting, **120**
    integrity, 119, 239
    interdependencies, 276
    I/O performance, **119**
    keys registered with, 224
    limiting size, 120
    log files, **75–76**, 119–120, 124
    logical model, 239
    logical security, 150
    logical structure, **75**
    Maxsize setting, **120**
    monitoring, 363, 364–365
    naming, 117, 124
    object naming conventions, 122–123
    offline, 364–365
    Online Transaction Processing (OLTP), 78, 276
    ownership, 120–122
    performance, 276
    permissions, **120–122**, 212–221
    physical disk space, 120
    physical model, 239
    physical resources, 76
    planning, 116–131
    primary filegroup, 126
    rate of change, 276, 287
    read-only, 276
    recovering from backups, 294–303
    recovery model, **287**
    relationships, 239
    result set, **153**
    retrieving data from, 153
    schemas, **119**, 172–178
    security, 76
    simple recovery model, **287**
    sizes, 276
    storing unstructured data, 126
    tables, **76**
    template for, 75
    uncontrolled access to, 249
database-scoped, **382**, 401
Databases folder, 84, 124, 127, 130, 133–134, 136, 138, 214, 218, 280, 364
database trace file, **246**, 262, 268
database transactions, **119**, 146
database users, 178–179, **211–212**, 233
Datacenter Edition, 8
data collections, **388**, 391–393, 401
Data Collection Set Properties window, 394–395
data collector, **388**, 401
Data Collector Set folder, 260
data collector sets, **241**, 258, 268
    collector types, **388**
    configuration details, 395
    configuring, 241–245
    default system, 394
Data Collector Sets folder, 242
data control language (DCL), **150**, 178–188
data definition language (DDL), **150**, 172–178, 188
data files, **75**, 108, 119–120
    filegroups, **119**
    moving data into table, 353–355
    sizing, 120, 124
    storing, 120
data flow, 342
data flow components, **321–322**, 356
data flow tasks, **321–322**, 337, 339, 356
Data folder, 297
data integration tools and utilities, 320
Data Management Warehouse (DMW), 391
data manipulation language (DML), **150**, 188
    joins, 163–164
    merging data, 165
    modifying data, 169–171
    querying data, 157–163
    result sets, 154–157
    simple queries, 153
data mining tools, 29
data preparation tasks, **321**, 356
data providers, 98
data sources
    data flow task, 321
    integrating external, 320
    queries distributed across multiple, 99–102
Data Transformation Services (DTS), **321**, 356
Data Type attribute, 85
data types, **76**, 109, 122, 172
    compatible, 155
    explicit conversion, 155
    queries, 239
    selecting, 239
    tables, 139
data warehouses, **3**, 23
date data type, 122
dates, 94
DBCC. *See* database console commands (DBCC)
DBCC CHECKDB command, 296
dbcreator role, 199
db_datareader role, 180, 216
dbo.DatabaseLog table, 85–86
dbo user, 215
db_owner role, 121, 212, 215
deadlock, **250**, 268
deadlock victim, **250**, 268
declarative language, **150**, 188
DEFAULT constraint, 173, 188
default instance, **29**, 36, 67
defense-in-depth. *See* layered security
Define Back Up Database (Differential) Task window, 307, 308
Define Back Up Database (Full) Task window, 306, 307
Define Back Up Database (Transaction Log) Task window, 309
DEK. *See* database encryption key (DEK)
DeleteExistingCountryRows Execute SQL task, 340
Delete Object dialog box, 132, 136
DELETE permission, 219, 221
DELETE statement, **169–171**, 188
delete trigger, 77
DES. *See* 3-key Triple Data Encryption Standard (DES) algorithm
DESC keyword, **156**, 188
design, high-performance, 238–240
detecting locks, 250–255
Developer Edition, 2, 3
Developer Reference for SQL Server 2012, 12
diagnosing performance problems, 240–265
differential database backups, **278**, 284–287, 294–295, 315
directory-enabled application, 10
directory operations, 321

dirty read, **249**, 268
disk drives, monitoring free space, 368–369
Disk I/O Usage graph, 397
Disk Management view, 368
disks
    contiguously stored records, **265**
    measuring throughput, 241
    reviewing for anomalies, 53
    space requirements, 38
Disk Space Requirements window, 38, 39
Disk Usage data collector set, 394–395
Disk Usage Summary report, 395
Display Estimated Execution Plan option, **255**, 256–257, 268
DISTINCT clause, 240
DISTINCT keyword, **154**, 189
distributed query, 98
Distributed Replay Client window, 44
Distributed Replay Controller, 42–43
Division (/) arithmetic operator, 154
DMF. *See* dynamic management functions (DMF)
DMK. *See* database master key (DMK)
DML. *See* data manipulation language (DML)
dm_ prefix, 382
DMV. *See* dynamic management views (DMV)
documentation, 12–17
domain controllers, **10**, 24
Downloads folder, 323
DPAPI. *See* Windows Data Protection API (DPAPI)
DROP DATABASE script, 134
DROP LOGIN statement, 179
DROP statement, 132, 146, 173, 180, 189
DROP USER statement, 179
dtexec.exe utility, 334, 347
dtexecui.exe utility, 334
DTS. *See* Data Transformation Services (DTS)
.dtsconfig file extension, 334
.dtsx file extension, 321
dynamic-link library (DLL), 98
dynamic management functions (DMF), **382**–387, 401
dynamic management views (DMV), **382**, 382–387, 401

E

Edit, Find and Replace, Quick Replace command, 128
EKM. *See* encryption key management (EKM)

email address, **376**
Employees USER_TABLE table, 253
Employee table, 256
EncryptByKey() function, **224**, 233
EncryptByPassphrase() function, **224**, 233
encryption, **198**, 221–231, 233
    Advanced Encryption Standard (AES) algorithm, **223**, 224
    architecture, 224
    asymmetric keys, **222**
    block cipher, **223**
    cipher, **222**
    column-level, 225–231
    database encryption key (DEK), **224**
    database master key (DMK), **224**
    databases, 225–231
    encryption algorithms, 223
    encryption key management (EKM), **225**
    hierarchical approach to, 224
    keys, **222**
    log files, 224
    physical data, 224
    service master key (SMK), **224**
    symmetric keys, **222**
    third-party key management solutions, 225
    3-key Triple Data Encryption Standard (DES) algorithm, **223**, 224
    Transparent Data Encryption (TDE), **224**, 225
    Windows Data Protection API (DPAPI), **224**
encryption algorithms, 223
encryption key management (EKM), **225**, 233
enforce password expiration password policy, 199
enforce password policy of the local operating system password policy, 199
Enterprise Edition, 2–4, 8
environmental events, 275
Equal to (=) comparison operator, 155
error messages, 365, 369
Error Reporting window, 44, 45
Evaluation license, 34
event handlers, **321**, 356
events, **246**, 258, 268
    alerts, **369**
    automating notification, 369–380
    filters, 246
    instances, 248–249
    monitoring, 365–367
    result sets, 246
    trace, 247–248
    Windows operating system, 369

EXCEPT operator, **165**, 168, 189
exclusive lock, 249, 254
EXEC sp_configure command, 103
EXECUTE permission, 121, 211
Execute Query (F5) shortcut key, 128, 129, 131, 134, 141, 158
Execute SQL task, 339
Execute SQL Task Editor dialog box, 340–341
execution plans, 255–257
EXISTS operator, 189
expiration date, **277**, 315
explicit conversion, 155
ExportCountryData data flow task, 339, 342
exporting data, 323–333, 335–351
Express Edition, 2, 3–4
Express license, 34
extents, **75**, 109
external data sources, 320
external fragmentation, **265**–266, 268
extracting, transforming, and loading (ETL) data, 29, 320

F

FAILED_LOGIN_GROUP audit specification, 399
Failover Cluster Instance (FCI), **29**, 68
failover clusters, 29
FALSE result, 155
FCI. *See* Failover Cluster Instance (FCI)
features
    currently installed on local server, 46–49
    description, 36
    installation prerequisites, 36
    reviewing summary of, 44, 46
    selecting, 28–29
    shared features, **29**
Feature Selection window, 36–37
fields, autopopulating, 141
file backups, **278**, 315
File File Destination Editor dialog box, 344
filegroup backups, **278**, 315
filegroups, **119**, 126, 146
file operations, 321
files
    backing up, 277
    physical database files, 75–76
filestreams, 126
Filter Current Log dialog box, 366
filtering
    duplicated rows, 165
    grouped data, 157
    records in result set, 155–156
filters and capturing events, 246
Find and Replace dialog box, 128
firewalls, 198

fixed roles, 212, 216
FK_Contact_Account foreign key
    relationship, 143
Flat File Connection Manager Editor
    dialog box, 342
Flat File Destination Editor dialog
    box, 342
Flat File Destination task, 342
Flat File Format dialog box, 342
flat files, **322–333**, 356
flexible roles, 212
folders, storing backup sets, 278
FOREIGN KEY constraint, 173
foreign key constraints, 144
foreign key relationships, **137–146**
Foreign Key Relationships dialog box,
    143
foreign keys, 239–240
format files, 348, 350–351
fragmentation, **265–266**, 268
FROM clause, 153, 158, 164
FROM keyword, **153**, 189
full database backup plus differential
    database backup plus multiple
    transaction log backups, 294
full database backup plus multiple
    transaction log backups, 293
full database backups, **277–283**,
    285–287, 292–295, 315
FULL OUTER JOIN, **164**, 189
full recovery model, **287**, 288, 315
full table scans, 255
fully qualified names, 153, 189, 239

G

Gartner Research, 2
General page, 395
global configuration settings, 102–107
GNU General Public License (GPL),
    11, 24
GO keyword, 186
GPL. *See* GNU General Public License
    (GPL)
GRANT statement, **179**, 189
Greater than (>) comparison
    operator, 155
Greater than or equal to (>=)
    comparison operator, 155
GROUP BY clause, **157**, 240
GROUP BY keyword, 189
grouping records, 157
groups and security principals, 198

H

HA. *See* high availability (HA)
hardware, 29–30, 238
    failure, 275
    minimum requirements, 18–21

monitoring resource utilization, 49
    testing compatibility, 42
HAVING clause, **157**
HAVING keyword, 189
Help Viewer, 12
high availability (HA), **2**, 24
high-performance design, 238–240
HumanResources.Employee object,
    221
HumanResources.Employees table,
    226–228, 264

I

/IACCEPTSQLSERVER
    LICENSETERMS parameter, 57
IBM, 150
IDE. *See* integrated development
    environment (IDE)
identifiers, 122, 153
IMPLICIT_TRANSACTIONS, 251
ImportCountryData data flow task,
    339
ImportCountry.dtsx file, 337
ImportCountry.dtsx package, 339
importing data, 323–333, 335–351
Include Actual Execution Plan option,
    255–256, 259, 268
incorrect summary, **249**, 268
indexed views, **238**, 240, 268
indexes, 77
    adding or removing, 173, 240
    clustered, 250
    composite, **240**
    construction of, 238
    covering, **240**
    creation, 175
    defragmentation, 266
    foreign keys, 240
    fragmentation, **265–266**
    maintenance, 265–266
    primary keys, 240
    rebuilding, **266**
    reorganizing, **266**
    size, 266
Indexes folder, 264
/INDICATEPROGRESS
    parameter, 58
Initial Configuration Tasks Wizard, 8
Initial Size setting, **120**, 146
IN logical operator, 189
INNER JOIN, 163–**164**, 189
INSERT permission, 219, 352
INSERT statement, 144, **169–171**,
    189
Installation Complete window, 47
Installation Configuration Rules
    window, 44, 45
Installation for SQL Server 2012, 12
installation image file, 55

Installation Progress window, 47
Installation Rules window, 36, 37
installation wizard, 68
Instance Configuration window, 36,
    38
instances, **10**, 24
    client applications remotely
        connecting to, 74
    components specific to, 29
    database engine, 29
    default instance, **29**
    events, 248–249
    failing to start, 59
    global configuration settings,
        102–107
    hardware and number of, 30
    listing basic configuration settings,
        103
    minimizing footprint, 29
    monitoring, 238, 362–370
    named instances, **29**
    predefined fixed roles, 199
    Properties form, 106
    securables, **198**
    service master key (SMK), **224**
    sessions connected to, 384
    value in memory for, 103
instawdb.sql script, 81–82
integers, 122
integrated development environment
    (IDE), **333**, 356
Integration Services, **29**, 68
Integration Services Business
    Intelligence project, 333–335
IntelliSense, **153**, 189
internal fragmentation, **265–266**, 268
International Organization for
    Standardization (ISO), 150
Internet and secure transactions, 222
Internet Assigned Numbers Authority
    (IANA), 92
Internet Explorer, 55, 79, 323
Internet Protocol 4 and 6 (IP4 and
    IP6) network addresses, 92
Internet Protocol Security (IPSec),
    208, 233
INTERSECT operator, **165**, 189
I/O performance, **119**, 146
(Is Identity) property, 139
IS NULL logical operator, 155–156, 189
ISO. *See* International Organization
    for Standardization (ISO)
ISO/IEC 9075 standard, 150

J

jobs
    monitoring activity, 51
    notifications, 369
    scheduling, 51

Jobs folder, 313
JOIN clause, 166, 239
join conditions, **163**, 189
joins, **163**–164, 166–169, 189

K

Kerberos, **10**, 24, 89, 199
keys, **222**, 224–225, 233
Keys folder, 142

L

layered security, **198**, 233
LDAP. *See* Lightweight Directory
    Access Protocol (LDAP)
.ldf file extension, 76
LEFT OUTER JOIN, **164**, 189
length, **122**, 146
Less than (<) comparison operator,
    155
Less than or equal to (<=)
    comparison operator, 155
License Terms window, 35
Lightweight Directory Access Protocol
    (LDAP), **10**, 24
LIKE logical operator, 156, 189
linked server object, 99–102
linked servers, 74, **98**–102, 109
Linked Servers folder, 101
listener, 109
Local Security Policy window,
    200–202
local server, 46–49
lock-based concurrency control,
    249–250, 268
lock modes, **249**–250, 268
locks, detecting, 250–255
log files, **75**–76, 109, 119–120
    backups, 277
    database transactions, **119**
    encrypting pages, 224
    monitoring, 367
    restricting access, 198
    sizing, 124
Log File Viewer, **363**, 367, 400, 401
logical database objects, 76–78, 150
logical fragmentation, **265**, 268
logical operators, 155–**156**,
    161, 189
logical security, 30, 150
logical security objects, 178
logical structure, **75**, 109
LOGIN FAILED Action ID, 400
Login - New window, 204, 206
Login Properties - sa window, 208
Login Properties - sqltest1 window,
    214–216
Login Properties -sqltest1 window,
    215

logins, **178**, 189
    auditing successful and failed,
    398–400
    authentication, 120
    creation, 178, 181–182
    default role, 199
    managing, 200–208
    removing, 179
Logins folder, 204, 206, 207, 213
loopback adapter, 92
loopback address, 109
lost update, **249**, 269

M

maintenance functions, 321
Maintenance Plan -
    BackupRestoreTest, 304
maintenance plans, 266
Maintenance Plans folder, 303, 313
Maintenance Plan Wizard, 266,
    303–313
Maintenance Plan Wizard Progress
    window, 312
maintenance tasks, **321**, 356
Manage Existing Account window,
    376
management applications, 74
ManagementDataWarehouse
    database, 390
Management Data Warehouse
    (MDW), **388**, 401
    configuring, 388–397
    database to store data collected,
    390
    data collector, **388**
    default system roles, 391
    querying data, 395
    schedule to upload data, 395
Management folder, 303, 313, 367,
    370
management tools, **2**, 24, 29
Manage Profile Security window,
    372
Map Logins and User window, 391
master database, 103, 109
Master Data Services, **29**, 68
master key, 229–231
master service key (MSK), 229–231
master system database, 74–**75**, 266
MAX aggregate function, 157
Maxsize setting, **120**, 146
.mdf file extension, 75
mdw_admin role, 391
mdw_reader role, 391
mdw_writer role, 391
memory, 53, 241
merging data, 165–169
messages, 87, 89
Microsoft

online forums, 12
online technical documentation,
    13–17
    reporting errors to, 44
Microsoft CodePlex site, 78
Microsoft Developer Network
    (MSDN) Library, 6
Microsoft Developer Network
    (MSDN) Web site, **12**
Microsoft Developer Network site,
    117–119
Microsoft Enterprise Agreement, 4–5
Microsoft Evaluation Software
    License Terms, 34
Microsoft Management Console
    (MMC), 9
Microsoft Management Console
    (MMC) Local Security Policy
    window, 200
Microsoft Software Assurance (SA),
    5, 24
Microsoft SQL Server, 2
    See also SQL Server 2012
Microsoft Support, 12
Microsoft Windows. *See* Windows
    operating system
MIN aggregate function, 157
minimum hardware requirements,
    18–21
mission-critical system, 276
mixed authentication mode, 199–200
MMC. *See* Microsoft Management
    Console (MMC)
model system database, 74–**75**, 109,
    117
Modulo (%) arithmetic operator, 154
monitoring
    automating event notification,
    369–380
    benchmarking system performance,
    381–388
    capturing performance data, 388–397
    daily tasks, 362–380
    database audits, 397–400
    databases, 363, 364–365
    dynamic management functions
    (DMF), 382–387
    dynamic management views
    (DMV), **382**, 382–387
    error messages, 365
    events, 365–367
    free space on disk drives, 368–369
    instances, 362–370
    log files, 367
    physical resources, 363
    real-time performance, 381–388
    remote client/server connectivity,
    363, 365
    scheduled jobs, 363
    services status, 363, 364

SQL Server Activity Monitor, 382–387
SQL Server tasks, 362–370
msdb system database, 74–75
MSDN. *See* Microsoft Developer Network (MSDN)
MSDN Library, 55, 118, 353
MSDN sites, 13–17
multicore processor, **4**, 24
multiple-table updates, 250
multiple transaction log backups, 293, 294
Multiplication (*) arithmetic operator, 154

N

named instances, **29**, 36, 38, 68
    configuring TCP/IP for, 90–98
    TCP/IP listener, 74
    TCP ports, 89
Named Pipes, **89**, 109, 363
nesting subqueries, 170
NETSTAT command-line utility, 90, 95
network protocols, 74, 89
    for client applications, 51
    configuring, 90–98
networks, reviewing for anomalies, 53
network security appliance, 198
New Alert dialog box, 376–379
New Database command, 124
New Database dialog box, 123–126, 126, 390
New Database Mail Account dialog box, 372
New Folder folder, 247
New Group dialog box, 203
New Job Schedule dialog box, 307–309
New Linked Server Wizard, 99
New Operator dialog box, 376
New Profile window, 370
New Project dialog box, 335–336
New Query command, 158
New Query Editor window, 265
New User dialog box, 202, 203
normalization, **239**, 269
Notepad, 323, 350
Not equal to (<>) comparison operator, 155
NOT logical operator, 156, 189
NOT NULL constraint, 155, 172, 189
null values, **155**, 189
numeric data type, 122

O

Object Dependencies - Account dialog box, 144

Object Explorer, 74, 78, 109, 116–117, 123, 130, 132–134, 136–137, 144, 204, 206–207, 212–221, 277–278, 280, 284–285, 288–289, 291, 294, 296–297, 299, 303, 312–313, 325, 363–364, 367, 370, 375, 389, 394, 398–400
    automatically generating SQL queries, 87
    configuring linked server object, 99–102
    generating SQL CREATE DATABASE script, 128–129
    manually refreshing user interface, 127
    master database, 103
    navigating SQL Server Management Studio, 83–88
    Query Editor and, 87
    reopening, 85
    shortcut menu, 85
    table attributes, 86
    tree view of database schema objects, 84
Object Explorer (F8) shortcut key, 85
objects
    access control, 211–221
    deleting, 173
    fully qualified names, **153**, 239
    identifiers, 122
    naming conventions, 122–123
    properties, 85
    read-only access, 180
    shortcut menu, 85
Object types dialog box, 206
ODBC. *See* Open Database Connectivity (ODBC)
Ola Hallengren, 266
OLE DB Source Editor dialog box, 342
OLE DB Source task, 342
ON clause, 163
online forums, 12
Online Transaction Processing (OLTP), **78**, 109, 276
    Adventure Works 2010 database, 78–83
Open Database Connectivity (ODBC), **347**, 357
Open Database Connectivity (ODBC) provider, 98
Open dialog box, 323, 325, 342
Open File dialog box, 81, 260
operating systems, **8**, 24
operators, **369**, 401
    adding overhead to queries, 239
    configuring, 376–379
    performing operations on columns, 154–155

Operators folder, 376
optimizing queries, 240–265
Oracle, 11
Oracle provider, 98
Oracle VirtualBox, **11**, 24
ORDER BY clause, **156**–157, 240
ORDER BY keyword, 189
OR logical operator, 156, 189
outer joins, 163–164

P

package configuration file, **334**–335, 357
package designer, 339
Package.dtsx SSIS package, 334
pages, **75**, 109
Pages/sec performance counter, 241
parameters, **57**
parent object, 153
partial backups, **278**, 315
Password must meet complexity requirements Properties window, 201
password policies, 199–208
Password Policy folder, 200
performance
    capturing data, 388–397
    data collector sets, 388
    real-time monitoring, 381–388
    traces, 388
performance conditions, 369, 401
performance counters, **241**, 269, 381–382
Performance Counters collector type, 388
Performance Counters Limit dialog box, 261
Performance Monitor, **49**, 51–53, 68
performance optimization, 238
performance problems, diagnosing, 240–265
Performance Tools folder, 260, 262
permissions, **120**, 146
    database-level, 211
    database objects, 211
    databases, 120–122
    database users, 179
    data control language (DCL), 178
    full database backup, 279
    granting or revoking, 121, 178–179, 212
    grouping, 121
    managing, 212–221
    roles, **121**, 179–180, 212
    schemas, 122, 179–180, 211–212
    securables, 198
    security principals, 198
    server-level, 121
    SQL Server logins, 199

Permissions for Backup dialog box, 279
PermissionTest database, 215
Person table, 159
physical access controls, 198
physical database files, 75–76
physical data encryption, 224
physical disk, 241
physical files, 119
physical memory, 241
physical model, 239
physical resources, 76, 363
physical security, 30
planning
   SQL Server 2012 installation, 28–31
   user databases, 116–131
point-in-time recovery, 299
point-in-time restore, 287, 296
precedence constraints, 321
precision, **122**, 146
predefined data types, 122
predefined roles, 121
primary filegroup, 119, 126
PRIMARY KEY constraint, 173
primary keys, **77**, 85, 109, 137, 139, 141, 240
private key, backing up, 229–231
problem-solving strategies, 12
procedures, **77**, 109
processes, 381
   identifying causing locks, 250
   length of time waiting for resource, 384
   lost update, **249**
processor-based licensing, 4
Processor Queue Length performance counter, 241
processors, 241
% Processor Time performance counter, 241
% Process Time performance counter, 381
ProductCategory table, 158
production user databases backups, 59
Product Key window, 34
Product table, 159
Programs and Features window, 64
Properties command, 106
Properties pane, 339
Protocols for SQLSERVERUA Properties dialog box, 208, 210
public keys. *See* asymmetric keys
public role, 199, 204

Q

qualified names, **153**, 189
queries

automatically generating, 87
breaking into small transactions, 250
combining data, 166–169
data, 150–171
database context, **153**
database objects, 262–264
data sources, 99–102
data types, 239
design, 239
evolving, 238
execution statistics, 255
frequently run, 246
fully qualified names, 239
indexes, 240
locks, 251–252
long-running, 246
lowering duration, 238, 258–265
merging data, 166–169
modifying data, 169–171
most costly steps, 255
multiple locks and, 250
operators, 239
optimizing, 240–265
poorly performing, 252, 381, 386
remote data sources, 74
retrieving data from database, 153
separating logical specification from implementation, 150
simple, 153
text strings, 155
timeout settings, 105
troubleshooting performance, 258–265
well-formed, 238
Query Activity collector type, 388
query analyzer, 288
Query Editor, **78**, 109, 132–133, 250–255, 278, 302–303, 325, 348, 351–354, 383, 386
   color coding text, 150
   Display Estimated Execution Plan option, **255**, 256–257
   Include Actual Execution Plan option, **255**, 256
   IntelliSense, **153**
   Object Explorer and, 87
   SELECT statement, 87
Query Editor window, 117, 124, 128–129, 131, 134, 140, 158, 166–167, 174–177, 211, 213, 225–228
query optimizer, **150**, 189, 255, 263, 266
Query Statistics data collection set, 394
Query Statistics History report, 395
query tuning, **238**, 258–265, 269
Query window, 103, 105
quiet mode, 57–58
quiet parameter, 31

R

RDBMS (relational database management system), 2
read-only databases, 276
Ready to Install window, 44, 46
Ready to Remove window, 65, 66
Ready to Repair window, 60, 61
real-time performance monitoring, 381–388
rebuilding, **266**, 269
RECONFIGURE command, 105
records, 76
   contiguously, **265**
   result sets, 154–157
   sorting, 162
   table scan, **77**
   uniquely identifying, 77
recovery, 274
recovery model, 133, **287**, 288–291, 315
recovery objectives, 274–277
recovery point objective (RPO), 276, 315
recovery time objective (RTO), 276–277, 315
refactoring, **238**, 240, 269
Registry
   configuration values, 59
   reviewing changes, 49
   SQL Server Agent settings, 51
Registry Editor, **49**, 51, 68
Registry keys, **49**, 68
relational database management system. *See* RDBMS (relational database management system)
relational databases, 76
relationships, 239
remote client/server connectivity, 363, 365
remote connections to SQL Server 2012, 89
remote data source, querying, 98–102
removable storage devices, 56
Removal Rules window, 65
Rename command, 135
reorganizing, **266**, 269
repairing SQL Server 2012, 59–62
Repair Progress window, 62
Repair SQL Server 2012-Complete window, 63
reporting errors to Microsoft, 44
Reporting Services, **29**, 42, 53, 68
Reporting Services Configuration window, 43
reports, 29
reserved keywords, **122**–123, 146
Resource Monitor, **49**, 53, 68

resources
   backlogged requests for, 240
   level of activity, 240
   locking, 249–250
   monitoring performance, 240–241
   prioritizing allocation, 274
   processes waiting for, 381, 384
   utilization, 49
resource system database, 74–75
resource utilization, 240
Restore Database dialog box, 294,
   296, 299, 301
restore operations, 294–303
restoring
   point-in-time, 287
   transaction logs, 287
result sets, **153–155**, 168, 189
   combining rows, 165
   data needed in, 239
   events, **246**
   filtering records, 155–156
   grouping records, 157
   sorting, 156, 239
   summarizing records, 157
reviewing system changes, 49–54
REVOKE statement, 179, 189
RIGHT OUTER JOIN, **164**, 189
risk assessment, **274–275**, 315
roles, **121**, 146, 188
   adding or removing, 180, 199
   creation, 180, 183
   default, 199
   fixed, 199, 212, 216
   flexible, 212
   Management Data Warehouse
     (MDW), 391
   permissions, 179–180, 212
   public role, 199
   renaming, 180, 185
   schema permissions, 211
   server-level, 204
   user-defined, 199
Roles folder, 218
ROLLBACK TRANSACTION
   statement, 169
rows, **76**, 109
   combining in result sets, 165
   from first query not in second
     query, 165
   inserting and deleting, 169
   modifying, 170
RPO. *See* recovery point objective (RPO)
RTO. *See* recovery time objective (RTO)
Run dialog box, 200
run_value value, 103, 105

S

sa account, **199–200**
SalesOrderHeader table, 161

sa login, 207, 233
salt value. *See* authenticator
sa user, 208
Save and Run Package window, 331
Save As dialog box, 79, 247, 259
Save dialog box, 143
Save SSIS Package window, 331
Save Webpage dialog box, 323
scale, **122**, 146
scheduled jobs, 363
schema objects, 84, 87, 321
schemas, **119**, 146
   creation, 150, 179, 182
   database roles, 180
   defining, 172–178
   deleting, 180
   designing, 239
   evolving, 238
   managing, 150
   permissions, 122, 179–180,
     211–212
   planning, 238
   renaming, 180
scripting tasks, **321**, 357
scripts, 117
   custom code, 321
   DROP database, 132
secpol.msc file, 200
secret keys. *See* symmetric keys
securables, **198**, 233
secure Internet transactions, 222
Secure Sockets Layer (SSL), 233
security
   authentication, 198–199
   backups, 30, 277
   client/server connections, 208–211
   database object access control,
     211–221
   databases, 76
   encryption, **198**, 221–231
   firewalls, 198
   layered security, **198**
   linked server object, 101
   logical, 30
   minimizing footprint of instance, 29
   network security appliance, 198
   physical, 30
   physical access controls, 198
   restricting access to physical data
     and log files, 198
   SQL Server installation, 30–31
   SQL Server logins, **199**
   surface area, **198**
   virtual accounts, **31**
security admin role, 199
Security folder, 204, 213, 218, 398
security principals, **198–199**, 233
Select Backup Destination dialog box,
   281, 306–307, 309
SELECT clause, 169

Select Configuration Task window,
   370, 389
Select Database User or Role dialog
   box, 218
Select Features window, 65
SELECT...FROM query, 157–163
SELECT GETDATE() command, 94
Select Instance window, 61
Select Maintenance Task Order
   window, 305
Select Maintenance Tasks window,
   305
SELECT permission, 184, 186, 219
Select Plan Properties window,
   303–313
Select Report Options window, 311
Select Source Tables and Views
   window, 329
SELECT statement, 87, **153–157**,
   189
   result sets, 239
   subqueries, 165
Select User or Group dialog box, 204,
   206
Select User or Groups dialog box, 279
Select Users dialog box, 203
self join, **164**, 190
self-signed certificates, 208, 211
Send Test E-Mail dialog box, 375
Server Activity data collection set,
   394, 397
Server Activity History report, 395,
   397
Server and Client Access License
   (CAL) licensing, 4, 24
server audit specification, 398
Server Audits Specifications folder,
   398–399
Server Configuration window, 38, 39
Server Core, **8**, 24
server-level permissions, 121
server-level principals, 199, 211
server-level roles, 204
Server Manager, **8–9**, 24, 202–203
Server Objects folder, 280, 285, 291
Server Process ID (SPID), **211**, 233
Server Properties window, 106, 180,
   203
servers
   authentication, 120
   permissions, 212–221
   reviewing changes, 49
server-scoped, **382**, 401
service master key (SMK), **224**, 233
services
   assigning accounts, 38
   isolating, 30
   monitoring status, 50, 363, 364
Session Details dialog box, 384
sessions connected to instances, 384

SET parameter, 170, 190
SET STATISTICS TO command, 255
setup application, **32**
setup.exe file, 31, 57
Setup Role window, 36
Setup Support Rules window, 33–35, 60, 64
severity level, 401
shared features, **29**, 68
shared memory, **89**–90, 94, 109
shortcut menu, 85
simple recovery model, **287**–288, 292, 315
single transaction log backup plus full database backup, 292
SMK. *See* service master key (SMK)
SMTP accounts, 370
SMTP email address, 372
software
  installation requirements, 30
  interacting, 347
  redundancy, 29
  testing compatibility, 42
Solution Explorer, 334, 337
sorting result sets, 156, 162, 239
Source Assistant, 342
Source Assistant - Add New Source dialog box, 342
sp_configure procedure, 74, **102**–107, 109
sp_configure procedure (F5) shortcut key, 103
special characters, 122, 123
SPID. *See* Server Process ID (SPID)
sp_lock procedure, 250
sp_who2 procedure, 250
sp_who2 query, 211
SQL. *See* Structured Query Language (SQL)
SQLCMD.exe file, 94, 109, 352
SQLCMD utility, 97, 117, 363
SQL Configuration Manager, 90–98
SQL CREATE DATABASE script, 128–129
SQLFULL_ENU installation media, 32, 55, 60
SQLFULL_ENU ISO image, 20
SQLNLCI11 provider, 99
SQL parameters, **28**
SQL Profiler, 90, 98
SQL queries, 87, 123–124
SqlSamplesDatabasePath variable, 81
SqlSamplesSourceDataPath variable, 81
SQL Script Preview dialog box, 264
SQL scripts, 117, 123
SQL Server 2008, 2
SQL Server 2012, 2
  Business Intelligence Edition, 2–3
  components, **2**

configuration, 89–107
connecting to, 198–211
core-based licensing, 4
database engine, **2**, 28
Developer Edition, 2–3
directory-enabled application, 10
documentation, 12
downloading trial version, 18
editions, 2–4
encryption algorithms, 223
encryption architecture, 224
Enterprise Edition, 2–3, 8
evaluation edition license, 5
Express Edition, 2, 3–4
integration with Microsoft Windows, 8
licensing models, 4–5
management tools, **2**
minimum hardware requirements, 18–21
monitoring activity, 246
monitoring essential tasks, 362–370
parameters, 68
query optimizer, **150**
remote connections to, 89
researching editions, 5–7
Server and Client Access License (CAL) licensing, 4
services, 49–50
Standard Edition, 2–3
32-bit and 64-bit versions, 8, 11
uninstalling, 59, 62–66
upgrading versions, 30
version 10.0 (SQL Server 2008), 2
version 11.0 (SQL Server 2012), 2
version 10.5 (SQL Server 2008 R2), 2
Web Edition, 2, 4
SQL Server Activity Monitor, 381–387
  Data File I/O pane, 385
  Data File I/O section, 381
  dynamic management functions (DMF), 386
  dynamic management views (DMV), 382, 386
  Overview pane, 382
  Overview section, 381
  Processes pane, 98, 384
  Processes section, 381
  Recent Expensive Queries pane, 386
  Recent Expensive Queries section, 381
  Resource Waits pane, 384
  Resource Waits section, 381
  starting trace, 97
  viewing data, 382
SQL Server Activity Monitor (Ctrl+Alt+A) shortcut keys, 95, 382

SQL Server Agent, 51, **266**, 269, 363–364, 367, 376, 380, 388
  alerts, 369–380
  automating backup plan, 303–313
  notifications, 369
  operators, **369**
  performance conditions, **369**
SQL Server Agent error log, **363**, 402
SQL Server Agent job, 334
SQL Server Analysis Services, 321
SQL Server Audit, **397**, 402
SQL Server authentication, 120, 178, 180, 199, 212
SQL Server Browser, **89**, 109
SQL Server Configuration Manager, **49**–51, 68, 90–91, 93, 180, 208, 210, 363, 364
SQL Server 2012 database architecture, 74–88
SQL Server Database Engine component, 55
SQL Server Database Engine parameter, 57
SQL Server Data Tools, **320**, 333–335, 357
  importing and exporting data, 335–347
  predefined project templates, 334
SQL Server 2012 dialog box, 64
SQL Server error messages, 369
SQL Server Features Discovery Report, **31**, 46–49, 68
SQL Server Forums, 12
SQL Server Import and Export Wizard, **320**, 322–333, 357
SQL Server 2012 installation, 30–32
  authentication mode, 178
  business requirements detail, 28
  command prompt, 54–59
  components and features, 28–29
  directory structure, 53
  editions and license models, 28
  planning, 28–31
  process, 31–46
  repairing, 59–62
  reviewing system changes, 49–54
  SQL Server Features Discovery Report, 46–49
  SQL Server Installation Wizard, 31–46
  unattended installation, **31**
SQL Server Installation Center, **28**, 31–33, 46, 48, 59, 60, 68
SQL Server Installation Center-Maintenance window, 60
SQL Server Installation Center-Tools window, 48
SQL Server Installation Center window, 21

SQL Server Installation Wizard, 31–46, 59–62

SQL Server Integration Services (SSIS), **320**–347, 357, 363–364, 388
executing SSIS packages, 334–335
packages, 321–322
SQL Server Data Tools, 333–334
SQL Server Import and Export Wizard, 322–333

SQL Server log, **363**, 402

SQL Server login, 178–179, 181–182, 211, 233

SQL Server logins, **199**
changing password policy, 200–208
permissions, 199

SQL Server Management Studio, 77–78, 90, 99–103, 109, 116–117, 134, 137, 158, 178, 180–181, 200, 203–204, 206, 211, 225, 250–252, 255–257, 259, 262, 264, 277–278, 284, 288–289, 294, 297, 301–303, 312, 325, 333, 348, 351, 353, 354, 363, 367, 370, 375, 382, 387, 389, 398
Activity Monitor icon, 95
database creation, 123–131
launching, 79
Object Explorer navigation of, 83–88
opening files, 80
opening scripts, 81
Query Editor, 150
SQLCMD mode, 81

SQL Server management tools, 238, 240

SQL Server Native Client (ODBC) driver, **347**, 348, 357

SQL Server Network Interface layer, **89**, 109

SQL Server performance condition alert, 378

SQL Server Profiler, 241, **246**–249, 259–260, 269, 388

SQL Server Profiler window, 248–249

SQL Server Profile warning dialog box, 259

SQL Server 2008 R2, 2

SQL Server Reporting Services, 395

SQL Server Resolution Protocol (SSRP), **89**, 110

SQL Server 2012 Setup, 58, 64

SQL Server Setup Control component, 55

SQL Server Setup Control parameter, 57

SQL Server 2012 Setup Support Rules, 21

SQL Server 2012 Setup Wizard, 36–44

SQL Server tasks, **321**, 357

SQL Server 2012 Trial page, 18

SQLSERVERUA Alerts operator, 376–378

SQLSERVERUA data collector set, 245, 258, 260

SQLSERVERUA folder, 124, 133, 138, 278, 280, 325

SQLSERVERUA instance, 38, 40, 180, 203–204, 278, 393
configuring TCP/IP for, 90–98
invalid password, 399
linked server object, 99–102
listening for client connections, 93
new connection to, 213
restarting, 93
Secure Sockets Layer (SSL) encryption, 208–211
shared memory, 94
SQLCMD.exe utility, 94
viewing enabled protocols, 51

SQLSERVERUA2 instance, 54–60, 64

SQLSERVERUA root folder, 213

SQLSERVERUA -1.trc file, 260

SQL System Administrators group, 57

sqltest1 login, 206–207, 212–221

SQL Trace collector type, 388

SSIS. *See* SQL Server Integration Services (SSIS)

SSIS packages, **321**–322, 334–335, 357

SSIS Packages folder, 334, 337

SSIS Toolbox, 334, 337, 339, 342

SSL. *See* Secure Sockets Layer (SSL)

Standard Edition, 2–4, 8

Start Jobs dialog box, 313

statement terminator, 190

static TCP port, 92

statistics, **255**, 269
backups, 286, 289
updating, 266

STOPAT command, 296

string concatenation operator (+), **155**, 160, 190

strings, 122, 155

Structured Query Language (SQL), **2**, 24
See also Transact-SQL
backups, 277
data control language (DCL), **150**, 178–187
data definition language (DDL), **150**, 172–178
data manipulation language (DML), **150**–171
declarative language, **150**
naming conventions, 153
Transact-SQL, **150**
uppercase keywords, 153
variants, 150

subqueries, **165**, 166–170, 190, 239

Subtraction (−) arithmetic operator, 154

Success dialog box, 399

SUCCESSFUL_LOGIN_GROUP audit specification, 399

SUM aggregate function, 157

Summary log file, **65**

support case, **12**, 24

surface area, **198**, 233

symmetric algorithms, 222–223

symmetric keys, **222**, 228, 233

sysadmin group, 213, 215

sysadmin role, 121, 199, 200, 211

sys.dm_db_index_physical_stats dynamic management function, 266

SysPrep utility, 31

sys schema, 382

system
baseline, **381**
benchmarking performance, 381
configuration information, 28
downtime, 29
performance counters, 381
resources, 238, 240–241
reviewing changes, 49–54

system administrator, 382

system databases, **28**, 59, 68, 74–75

System Data Collection Set folder, 394

System Functions folder, 382

system-generated messages, 87

system software failures, 275

System Views folder, 382

T

Table Designer, 137, 138–139

tables, **76**, 85, 110
aliases, 164
attributes, 86
auditing, 77
cascading changes, 77
columns, **76**, 77, 122, 139, 153
constraints, 172–173
creation, 138–145, 172–173
data types, 139
default index, 77
deleting, 177
exclusive lock, 250–255
foreign key relationship, **137**–145
inserting data, 352–355
joins, 163
modifying, 173–174
moving data to flat file, 323–333
naming without character prefix, 122
primary key, **77**, 137, 139, 141
querying data, 157–163
renaming, 173
retrieving data from, 153

rows, **76**, 169–170, 258
  splitting data across multiple, 239
  table scan, 77
  triggers, **76–77**, **348**
  updating, 250–255
  value persisted in, 103
Tables, New Table command, 138
Tables and Columns dialog box, 143
table scan, **77**, 110
Tables folder, 85, 264
TABLOCK table hint, 251
Tabular Data Stream (TDS) packets, **89**, 110
tail, 288, 294, 297, 315
Take Database Offline status dialog box, 296
tasks, 321, 357
TCP dynamic ports, 92
TCP/IP, **89**, 90–98, 110, 363
TCP/IP listener, 74
TCP/IP Properties window, 92–93
TCP ports, 89
TDE. *See* Transparent Data Encryption (TDE)
TechNet, 13–17, 24
TechNet Evaluation Center Web site, 11
TechNet Web site, **12**
Telnet, 376
tempdb system database, 74–75
TEMP directory, 393
Test database, 135, 141
Test database folder, 138
TestDatabaseRole role, 218–219
test environment, 10–11
TestLogin login, 186
TestOne database, 124, 127–128, 133–135
TestOne dialog box, 124
TestRole role, 183–186
TestSchema schema, 182, 184, 186
TestTable table, 182, 186
TestThree database, 131, 134
TestTwo database, 128–130, 133, 136
TestUser user, 184–186
text strings, 155
third-party certificate authorities, 222
3-key Triple Data Encryption Standard (DES), 232
3-keytriple Data Encryption Standard (DES) algorithm, **223**, 224
throughput, 381
time, 94
time stamps, 77
TO DISK clause, 289
tools currently installed on local server, 46–49
TOP keyword, **154**, 162, 190
TO TAPE clause, 289
trace file, 258

Trace folder, 247
Trace Properties window, 247–248, 259
traces, 97, 110, **246**–249, 269, 388
transaction logs, **287**, 316
  backups, 277, 287–292
  multiple backups, 293, 294
  restore operations, 295
  single backup, 292
  tail, 288, 294, 297
  truncated, **287–288**
  type of transactions logged in, 133
transactions, 249–250
  Executing query status, 252
  executing without committing changes to database, 169
  type logged in transaction log, 133
Transact-SQL, **150**, 190
  See also Structured Query Language (SQL)
Transact-SQL Query collector type, 388
transformation component, 357
Transparent Data Encryption (TDE), **224**, 225, 228–229, 233
triggers, **76–77**, 110, **348**, 357
TRUE result, 155
truncated, **287–288**
truncation, 316
trusted connections, **199**, 233
tuning queries, 258–265
Tutorials for SQL Server 2012, 12

U

unattended installation, **31**, 68
uninstalling
  backing up production databases, 59
  multiple instances, 59
  SQL Server 2012, 59, 62–66
Uninstall or Change a Program feature, 59
Uninstall Program feature, 62–66
UNION operator, **165**, 166, 190
unions, 165–169
UNIQUE constraint, 173, 190
UNKNOWN result, 155
UPDATE permission, 218, 219
UPDATE statement, **170–171**, 190
UPDATE STATISTICS statement, 266
Uploads page, 395
User Access Control dialog box, 50
User Account Control dialog box, 20, 48, 51, 57, 60, 208, 313, 363
User Account Control (UAC), **10**, 24
User Account dialog box, 32, 180
user accounts, 38, 40, 42
user databases, 28, 68
  planning, 116–131
  replicas, 29

User Defined Data Collector Sets folder, 258, 260
user-defined data types, 122
user-defined filegroups, 119, 126
User Defined folder, 242
user-defined roles, 199
user-defined triggers, 348
user errors, 275
user-generated messages, 87
users
  authentication, **198–199**
  creation, 178
  database roles, **179–180**
  permissions, 179
  removing, 179
  roles, **121**
  schema permissions, 211
  security principals, 198
  validating, 199
user variables, **321**, 357
USE statement, **153**, 158, 190
Utility Information data collection set, 394

V

values, comparing, 155
VALUES clause, 169
variables, 81, 122
VeriSign, 222
View, Object Explorer command, 85
VIEW DATABASE STATE permission, 382
View Dependencies command, 144
views, 77, 110, **153**, 190
  creation, 172–173, 176
  deleting, 177
  indexed, 240
  modifying, 173–174
  renaming, 173
  retrieving data from, 153
VIEW SERVER STATE permission, 382
virtual accounts, **31**, 68
virtual CD/DVD drive emulator, **11**, 24
virtual DVD drive emulator, 20
virtualization, 24
virtualization software, **11**
virtual machines, **11**, 24, 32, 60
virtual service accounts, 38
Visual Studio 2010, **333–347**, 357
VMware, Inc., 11
VMware Workstation, **11**, 24

W

Waiting Tasks performance counter, 381
Web Edition, 2, 4
WHERE clause, 155–157, 159, 165, 167, 169–170, 239–240

WHERE keyword, **155**, 190
whoami command, 57
wildcards, 190
Windows accounts, changing
    password policy, 200–208
Windows application log, **363**,
    365–367, 402
Windows authentication, 120, 178,
    180, 199, 203–204, 225, 247,
    250, 278, 325, 329
Windows Data Protection API
    (DPAPI), **224**, 233
Windows dialog box, 350
Windows Event Viewer, 365
Windows Explorer, 56, 124
Windows File Explorer, 278–279, 282,
    287, 297, 350–351
Windows login, 40
Windows Management Instrumentation
    (WMI) event, **369**, 402

Windows operating system, 367
    Certificate Store, 208, 210
    events, 369
    integration with SQL Server 2012,
        2, 8
Windows Performance Monitor
    utility, 240–245
Windows Registry, 49
    See also Registry
Windows Server 2008 R2 operating
    system, 2, 8
    Control Panel, 59
    integrated security, 8–10
    management tools, 8–10
    Server Manager, **8–9**
    trial version, 11
    Uninstall or Change a Program
        feature, 59
    User Account Control (UAC), **10**
Windows services, 30

Windows Task Manager, 240
Windows users, 202–203
Windows utilities, 238, 240
WinTestGroup group, 203,
    206–207
wintest1 user, 202, 204
wintest2 user, 203
WITH clause, 251, 352
WITH FILE clause, 295
WITH GRANT OPTION clause,
    179
WITH RECOVERY option, 296
WMI. *See* Windows Management
    Instrumentation (WMI) event
workflow tasks, **321**, 357
workload, **258**, 269

X

XLOCK table hint, 251